To Mark
From Grandfather & Grandmother
Christmas 1970

CIVIL WAR BASEBALL

Union prisoners pass the time in a camp at Salisbury, North Carolina. This old print was made from a drawing by one of the prisoners, Major Otto Boetticher.

Photo courtesy American Heritage Publishing Company, Inc.

THE THIRD FIRESIDE BOOK OF BASEBALL

Edited by
CHARLES EINSTEIN

With an Introduction by
STAN MUSIAL

SIMON AND SCHUSTER · NEW YORK

PUBLISHED BY SIMON AND SCHUSTER
ROCKEFELLER CENTER, 630 FIFTH AVENUE
NEW YORK, NEW YORK 10020

FIRST PRINTING

LIBRARY OF CONGRESS CATALOG CARD NUMBER: 68-21308
MANUFACTURED IN THE UNITED STATES OF AMERICA

ACKNOWLEDGMENTS

The Editor wishes to express his gratitude to the following individuals and publishers for permission to include in this volume material from the following sources:

American Heritage Publishing Co., Inc., for "The Great American Game," by Bruce Catton, from *American Heritage*, © 1959.

Ashley Famous Agency, Inc., and King Features Syndicate for "This Was Baseball—or Was It?" by Jim Bishop.

A. S. Barnes & Company for "The Wansley Affair," from *The Hot Stove League* by Lee Allen, © 1955 by A. S. Barnes & Co., Inc.; "With Apologies to Henry Wadsworth Longfellow," by L. C. Davis, from *The Hot Stove League;* "A Kid Sees the Series," from *My Baseball Diary* by James T. Farrell, © 1957 by James T. Farrell; "The Flying Dutchman," from *Baseball's Greatest Teams* by Tom Meany, copyright 1949 by A. S. Barnes & Co., Inc.; "1917: Chicago White Six 8, New York Giants 5," from *My Greatest Day in Baseball*, copyright 1945 by A. S. Barnes & Co., Inc.

Les Biedermann and the *Pittsburgh Press* for "Pressure, Pressure."

Lloyd Biggle and Galaxy Publications for "Who's on First?" from *If* Magazine.

Boys' Life (published by the Boy Scouts of America) for "Strictly by Instinct," by D. S. Halacy, Jr.

Chicago Daily News for "1943: New York Yankees 2, St. Louis Cardinals 0," by Bill Dickey; "1934: St. Louis Cardinals 11, Detroit Tigers 0," by Frank Frisch; "1915: St. Louis Browns 2, Washington Senators 1," by George Sisler; 1917: Chicago White Sox 8, New York Giants 5," by Buck Weaver; "1904: Boston 3, Athletics 0," by Cy Young.

Myron Cope and *Sport* Magazine for "The Day I Batted Against Castro," by Don Hoak and Myron Cope, © 1964 by the Macfadden-Bartell Corporation.

Myron Cope and the *Saturday Evening Post* for "Dean Chance," © 1965 by the Curtis Publishing Company.

Doubleday & Company, Inc., for the selection from *A Pennant for the Kremlin* by Paul Molloy, © 1964 by Paul Molloy; "Brave and Honest Hutch," from *The Quality of Courage* by Mickey Mantle, © 1964 by Bedford F. Wynne; "A Great Pitcher Broods," from *A Pitcher's Story* by Juan Marichal, © 1967 by Juan Marichal and Charles Einstein.

E. P. Dutton & Company, Inc., for "The Great Debate: Mays or Mantle?" from *A Thinking Man's Guide to Baseball*, © 1967 by Leonard Koppett.

Jerry R. Erikson for "Alexander Cartwright, the Father of Baseball."

Bill Furlong and *Sport* Magazine for "Ernie Banks: The Evening of His Career," © 1967 by the Macfadden-Bartell Corporation.

Grosset & Dunlap, Inc., for "The Rube's Waterloo," from *The Redheaded Outfield* by Zane Grey, copyright 1920 by Grosset & Dunlap, 1948 by Lina Elise Grey.

Arnold Hano and *Sport* Magazine for "Orlando Cepeda: I Am Always Against the Wall," © 1966 by the Macfadden-Bartell Corporation.

Harper & Row for the selection from *Out of My League*, by George Plimpton, © 1961 by George Ames Plimpton; also for the selection from *The Long Season* by Jim Brosnan, © 1960 by James P. Brosnan.

W. C. Heinz for "One Throw," from *Collier's* Magazine, copyright 1950 by the Crowell-Collier Publishing Company.

Holt, Rinehart and Winston, Inc., for the selection from *Vaudeville*, by Joe Laurie, Jr., copyright 1953 by Joe Laurie, Jr.

Jerry Holtzman and the *Saturday Evening Post* for "Hitters in Waiting," © 1962 by the Curtis Publishing Company.

King Features Syndicate for "Leave Us Go Root for the Dodgers, Rogers," by Dan Parker.

Alfred A. Knopf, Inc., for "Baltic Cooperstown," from *Views of Sport*, by Red Smith, copyright 1952, 1954 by Red Smith; also "Hub Fans Bid Kid Adieu," from *Assorted Prose* by John Updike, © 1960 by John Updike (this selection first appeared in *The New Yorker*).

Barney Kremenko and *The Sporting News* for

"1964: San Francisco Giants 5–8; New York Mets 3–6."

Lawrence Lader and *True* Magazine for "Don't Trap Your Son in Little League Madness," by Joey Jay as told to Lawrence Lader, © 1965 by *True.*

Ann Landers for "We Can't Afford a Lawyer."

Ring Lardner, Jr., for "The Baseball Playboy, Past and Present," by John Lardner.

Bill Libby and *Sport* Magazine for "A Baseball 'Failure,'" © 1961 by the Macfadden-Bartell Corporation.

Ed Linn and *Sport* Magazine for "The Kid's Last Game," © 1961 by the Macfadden-Bartell Corporation.

J. P. Lippincott & Company for "Leroy Jeffcoat," from *Southern Fried Plus Six,* by William Price Fox, © 1962 by William Price Fox; the selection from *Baseball Has Done It* by Jackie Robinson, edited by Charles Dexter, © 1964 by Jackie Robinson and Charles Dexter; "Inside the Clubhouse," from *Baseball Is a Funny Game,"* by Joe Garagiola, © 1960 by Joe Garagiola and Martin Quigley; the selection from *Jocko,* by Jocko Conland and Robert Creamer, © 1967 by Time Inc.

Little, Brown and Company, for the selection from *It's Good to Be Alive,* by Roy Campanella, © 1959 by Roy Campanella.

Deane McGowen and *Sport* Magazine for "Baseball As It Used to Be," by Roscoe McGowen, © 1964 by the Macfadden-Bartell Corporation.

The Macmillan Company for the selections by Sam Crawford, Tommy Leach, Rube Marquard, Chief Meyers and Joe Wood, from *The Glory of Their Times,* © 1966 by Lawrence Ritter.

Marvin Josephson Associates for "My Son, the Outfielder," by Marvin Kitman.

Ogden Nash and the Curtis Brown Agency for "An Ump's Heart," from the *Saturday Evening Post,* © 1966 by the Curtis Publishing Company.

The New Yorker Magazine for "The Flowering and Subsequent Deflowering of New England," by Roger Angell, © 1967 by The New Yorker Magazine, Inc.

The *New York Daily News* for "1964: Philadelphia Phillies 6, New York Mets 0," by Dick Young.

The *New York Times* for "1935: Detroit Tigers 4, Chicago Cubs 3," by John Drebinger; copyright 1935 by the *New York Times;* "1924: Washington Senators 4, New York Giants 3," by James Harrison, copyright 1924 by the *New York Times;* "Hug" by John Kieran, copyright 1929 by the *New York Times.*

Jack Orr and *Sport* Magazine for "Busts of the Training Camps," copyright 1953 by the Macfadden-Bartell Corporation.

Frank O'Rourke and Harold Matson Company, Inc., for "Bonus Rookie," from the *Saturday Evening Post,* copyright 1950 by the Curtis Publishing Company.

Oxford University Press, Inc., for "The Great Player Revolt," from *Baseball: the Early Years,* © 1960 by Harold Seymour.

Harry Paxton and the *Saturday Evening Post* for "The American League Is Tougher," by Ralph Houk as told to Harry Paxton, © 1962 by the Curtis Publishing Company.

The *Philadelphia Bulletin* for "2500 Hits—and Every One Wrong," by Sandy Grady.

The *Philadelphia Daily News* for "Man With the Inhuman Arm," by Stan Hochman.

G. P. Putnam's Sons for "The Pinch-hitting Midget," from *Veeck—as in Wreck,* by Bill Veeck with Ed Linn, © 1962 by Mary Frances Veeck and Ed Linn; also for "Five O'Clock Lightning," from *The New York Yankees,* by Frank Graham, © 1958 by Frank Graham.

Random House, Inc., for the selection from *Papa Hemingway,* by A. E. Hotchner, © 1963 by A. E. Hotchner.

Jhan Robbins and *Sport* Magazine for "The Time He Hit One for Me," © 1963 by the Macfadden-Bartell Corp.

Harold Rosenthal for "Sunny Jim Bottomley."

Arthur Robinson and the *Sacramento Bee* for "Casey's Daughter at the Bat," © 1965 by the *Bee.*

The *San Francisco Chronicle* for "The 1959 All-Star Game," by Bob Stevens; "Group Therapy for Ballplayers," by Donovan Bess; "The Ones with All the Fingers Cost the Same," by Herb Caen; "The Sporting Way" by Stan Delaplane; "1968: Oakland A's 4, Minnesota Twins 0," by Dick Friendlich.

The *Saturday Evening* Post for "So You Think You Know Baseball," by Harry Simmons and Willard Mullin, © 1957 by the Curtis Publishing Company.

Charles Scribner's Sons for "A World's Serious," from *First and Last,* by Ring Lardner, copyright 1934 by Ellis A. Lardner, renewal copyright © 1962 by Ring Lardner, Jr.

Vince Scully and the Los Angeles Dodgers for the simultaneous broadcast of the 1965 Sandy Koufax perfect game.

Simon and Schuster for "Ban Johnson," from *The American Diamond,* by Branch Rickey and Robert Riger, © 1965 by Branch Rickey and Robert Riger.

Robert Smith for "Can You Spare a Dime?" from *Baseball,* copyright 1947 by Robert Smith.

The Sporting News for the selections by J. G. Taylor Spink.

Al Stump and *True* Magazine for "Ty Cobb's Wild, 10-Month Fight to Live," © 1961 by True.

Virginia Updike for "IOU" from *Score by Innings* by Charles Van Loan.

The Viking Press Inc. for "They're Afraid to Come Out," from *Can't Anybody Here Play This Game?* by Jimmy Breslin, © 1963 by Jimmy Breslin; and for the selections from *The High Hard One,* by Kirby Higbe and Martin Quigley, © 1967 by Kirby Higbe and Martin Quigley.

The World Publishing Company for the selection from *For 2¢ Plain* by Harry Golden, © 1959, 1958, 1957, 1956, 1955, 1952, 1948, 1945, 1943 by Harry Golden.

Archer W. Zamloch for the selection from *Where Are Baseball's .400 Hitters of the Dead Ball Era?* by Archer W. Zamloch, Sr., and Lefty O'Doul.

William Zinsser and the Sterling Lord Agency for "Ben Casey at the Bat," from the *Saturday Evening Post,* © 1966 by the Curtis Publishing Company.

Contents

List of Illustrations

Introduction

WHEN—AS GENERAL MANAGER *of the Cardinals—I attended baseball's winter meetings in Mexico City, following the 1967 season, half a dozen changes in the rules were proposed to speed up the game. In a way, I guess this* Third Fireside Book of Baseball *does the same thing. We can dip into it at any point—pick and choose—enjoy as little or as much as we like—with no unexpected time-outs.*

But what I have in mind goes beyond that, because this book shows that the idea of speeding up the game didn't originate in 1967. You'll find a reference to it here dating back to May 8, 1901.

And I think that's the point of it all. There's an old saying that the more things change, the more they remain the same, and if they do nothing else, the three books that make up the Fireside *library of baseball—the* Fireside Book of Baseball, *the* Second Fireside, *and now this* Third Fireside*—show how baseball, perhaps pre-eminent among American institutions, fulfills this simple truth.*

I like the fact that in this Third Fireside, *editor Charlie Einstein was generous in his use of the by-lines of baseball men themselves, over a range of seventy years or more. It's the players who make the game, and their contributions here—ranging from pure reminiscence to batting tips—have a particular (and, I guess, obvious) fascination for me.*

I know that's not all there is to baseball coverage, and Charlie Einstein, himself a veteran writer, knows it too. So here in this book, as in the two books that went before, we have the famous writers, the fiction, the photographs, the cartoons, the spot reports, the poetry of Grantland Rice and Ogden Nash—the whole great American world of baseball.

And a great American world it is!

STAN MUSIAL

Preface

WHEN he heard that this *Third Fireside Book of Baseball* was in the works, Russ Hodges, the famous Giant broadcaster, telephoned me in quixotic congratulation. "You are what they call the irregular anthologist," he said. "You publish your findings at intervals, like Smokey the Bear on fire prevention."

A tribute like that can cause introspection. They tell the story, after all, of Smokey the Bear returning home after a hard day's work at the ad agency, and he raps on the door of the cave. "Honey," he calls to his wife, "let me in." "Not till you take off that silly hat," she says.

The over-elaborate Editor's Preface is, I suppose, one sign of an anthologist's silly hat, so I will try to avoid it. It would probably be too late anyway. Together with the *Fireside Book of Baseball* and the *Second Fireside Book of Baseball,* this third volume brings the totals, in what can be called the *Fireside* baseball library, to more than three hundred text pieces, more than three hundred illustrations, and a grand sum overall of perhaps 1,500,000 words. There may be still a great deal left to say, but not by me.

Perhaps on account of the very size of these statistical totals for the three *Fireside* books, one point can be restated here in connection with a factor that made this third book just as absorbing and fascinating to put together as the first two, in some cases maybe even more so. I refer to the colorful and infinite variety that is so much the hallmark of baseball and its accompanying word and picture.

If anyone doubts this element of the unexpected, I can validate it, I think, in the form of the following AP story, which appeared in my morning newspaper (and, God knows, probably in yours), one early June date a few years ago:

CINCINNATI — National League President Warren C. Giles yesterday disallowed a protest filed by Philadelphia Manager Gene Mauch, who claimed that Pittsburgh pitcher ElRoy Face "was inside the Forbes Field scoreboard for six innings during the May 28 Phillies-Pirates game."

The Pirates said Face "went into the scoreboard after the fifth inning, and before the Philadelphia club came to bat in the top of the sixth inning" to use the rest-room facilities.

Giles said, "It has been common practice to use the ground-level lavatory facilities in the Pittsburgh scoreboard." He added:

"To allow a protest and order a game replayed, there must be conclusive evidence that the action which is the subject of the protest directly affected the final outcome of the game. I find no such evidence in this case."

Pittsburgh won the game, 6-5, in the ninth inning.

The key sentence there is of course the last one, since had Philadelphia won, Mauch would have canceled his protest and Giles therefore would have had no chance to deliver his ruling, and the more times I read that thing, the more . . .

Well. Let us get on with it. Great events have happened in the few years separating even the *Second Fireside* book from this *Third Fireside*, including the three perfect games, pitched four years apart, by Bunning in '64, Koufax in '65 and Hunter in '68. Three things that no one ever saw before have come true: a 100-to-1 shot winning the pennant (the Red Sox); an all-weather stadium (the Astrodome); and the Mets (the Mets). In franchise shifting and expansion, the effects of television and the 162-game season, the major leagues have undergone unusual upheaval within a strikingly short span of time.

If this third book reflects those things, that is only to be expected. Still and all, though, the great, the interesting, the colorful, occupy these pages with magnificent disregard for you, for me, or for the passage of the years. In the first *Fireside*, readers learned of an up-to-date wind-tunnel experiment to test whether a curve ball really curves. Here now in this *Third Fireside*, we find that a similar experiment—more primitive, but perhaps a shade more sensible too—took place in 1877. It is, I think, a superb definition of baseball itself that the old and the new can and do appear, in collections such as this one, with equal merit side by side.

In that respect, as in all others, such as format and purpose, this *Third Fireside Book of Baseball* is one and the same with the two books that went before; and, at the risk of sounding like Shirley Temple congratulating 20th Century Fox, I think a special word is in order in praise of Simon and Schuster, whose attractive production and careful attention to detail have had much to do with the success of this series. It seems the *Fireside* baseball books, whether singly or in sets, have been appealing gifts, and surely Yogi Berra could have used such a gift the night (as Joe Garagiola tells it) he spoke at a banquet and the committee couldn't think of something different to give him in thanks for his appearance. Finally, bereft of all other ideas, they settled on a grandfather clock; and as Yogi was trying to get the clock into his car in the parking lot after the dinner, a drunk staggered by and bumped into it.

"Why," Yogi said to him, "don't you watch where you're going?"

"Why," the drunk replied, "don't you get a wrist watch like everybody else?"

In addition to Peter Schwed and John Walsh of Simon and Schuster, I would like to thank Lurton Blassingame and the staff of his agency; Russ Hodges, Robert Begam, Chub Feeney, Mark Harris, John Taddeucci,

Red Patterson, Al Silverman, Frank Slocum, my own three sons (and my Uncle Abraham, too, for supplying the piece you'll find here that says Abner Doubleday didn't invent baseball), as well as dozens of contributors, for their help in bringing this *Third Fireside Book of Baseball* to life.

One such contributor deserves, in my judgment, particular notice: cartoonist John Gallagher. The first two *Fireside* baseball books were generous in their use of Gallagher cartoons, and this *Third Fireside* makes no departure from that pattern. In case you do not know why, the cartoons themselves will tell you.

Another contributor, Harry Golden, tells (in his book *Enjoy, Enjoy!*) of a time he made a speech in Kansas City:

I was sitting on the dais with the dignitaries when I noticed that a note was handed by an usher to a man in the last row. From hand to hand the note went, through forty rows of people, until it reached the chairman on the dais, who accepted it and solemnly read its contents. In fifteen minutes another note made its way from the usher over the forty rows up to the chairman. Again he read the note solemnly. After finishing it, he walked purposefully to the lectern and announced loudly: "End of the sixth inning: Kansas City Athletics 4, Washington Senators 0." I said to myself, What did they need me to make a speech for? They could sit here and pass these notes all night.

He's right. Enough with the silly hat. Let's start passing notes.

Scottsdale, Arizona, 1968

CHARLES EINSTEIN

READERS OF the first two *Fireside Books of Baseball* know Lee Allen, baseball's foremost historian, as an old friend by now. They also have read, in the pages of the preceding sister volumes, about the infamous Black Sox scandal of nearly half a century ago. Were there Black Sox before the Black Sox? There were, as Mr. Allen here makes evident.

The Wansley Affair

LEE ALLEN

THE BELIEF that big-league baseball is completely honest is not a myth; it is a fact. Anyone who has ever associated with professional players knows that they not only do not bet on games, they even avoid the company of persons who do. Although throughout the United States there is an enormous amount of money daily wagered on games, the players are disinterested. Their complete divorce from the gambling element cannot be traced to any superiority of character on their part, but is a tradition of the game, a heritage from the stern administration of Kenesaw Mountain Landis, who even barred for life an owner of the Phillies, Bill Cox, for betting on his own team.

Organized baseball has a phobia about gambling. The parks are policed to prevent it, the clubhouse bulletin boards have placards that shout in bold print the penalties meted out to players and club employees caught at it, and the most witless jockeys of the dugout know better than to joke about fixing games. Even when a player faced with a day off spends a harmless afternoon at the racetrack, he does it as quietly as possible and with the same sense of doing something naughty that a small child experiences when he raids the cookie jar.

Because of this fine record, the scandals that beset the game in its infancy become more piquant, racy reminders of an era when baseball belonged to the pool seller and the crook. It was the formation of the National League in 1876 and its subsequent firm dealing with dishonesty that made possible the reform, although there have been a few picturesque scandals since that time.

When the National League in 1877 expelled four Louisville players—George Hall, Al Nichols, Jim Devlin and Bill Craver—for selling games, newspapers hinted at an even earlier scandal, an episode mysteriously referred to as the "Wansley affair."

William Wansley was a catcher for the Mutuals, an early team in New York City, and the day of his downfall was Thursday, September 28, 1865. Baseball at that time was still an amateur endeavor in theory, although some players were accepting money for their services and had been for about five years, and there was considerable gambling at the Elysian Fields in Hoboken, New Jersey, where the Mutuals played their games against such opponents as the Atlantics, the Eckfords and the Excelsiors.

On the day in question the Mutuals were to meet the Eckfords, and on the night before Wansley had been given one hundred dollars by a gambler named Kane McLoughlin to make sure that the Eckfords won. According to the terms of the plot, which was hatched at the residence of one S. O'Donnell, Wansley was to bribe at least two other members of his team so that there could be no possible doubt about the result. He first asked the third baseman, Ed Duffy, to go along with him, and Duffy said he would only if the shortstop, Tom Devyr, would join them. Several hours before the players were to take the field, McLoughlin picked up Wansley, Duffy and Devyr in a wagon and drove them to the Hoboken ferry. Wansley gave Duffy and Devyr thirty dollars each, keeping forty for his share. All these deals were later freely confessed by Devyr.

The Mutuals took an early lead in the game,

but then collapsed, errors by Wansley being largely responsible. Here is the line score:

Mutuals	3	0	1	1	3	0	0	1	2—11
Eckfords	0	2	1	1	11	1	0	5	2—23

Wansley's histrionic abilities were apparently not subtle; in that horrible fifth inning his work as a catcher was so glaringly bad that he was forced to change positions with McMahon, the right fielder. But by that time the damage had been done. In five appearances at bat Wansley failed to reach first base, and his defensive contribution to the Mutual cause included six passed balls.

There was a crowd of thirty-five hundred at the game, and the fans, many of whom had a financial stake in the proceedings, quickly spread rumors of crooked work. In taking notice of the reports, Henry Chadwick, writing in the New York *Clipper,* said of Wansley: "The comments on his errors made him mad, and that is all there is to this talk of selling the game. Baseball has never yet been disgraced by any such thing, and never will, we hope."

But John Wildey, the president of the Mutuals, was highly suspicious, and bluntly accused Wansley of selling out. William H. Dongan, the club's secretary, then handed the player a note in which he was ordered to report to a committee of players at 8 P.M. on October 20 at the club's offices at 397 Hudson Street. Wansley appeared, made a full confession that implicated Devyr and Duffy, and the trio was expelled. But the episode was soon forgotten as the sport continued its rise to popularity.

Several years later Wildey was about to attend a game between the Atlantics and the Haymakers of Troy, New York. Seated in the park with James McKean, president of the Haymakers, he was astonished to hear that august official say that the result of the game was a foregone conclusion and that if he wanted to make a barrel of money to bet on the team from Troy.

It was this same McKean who in 1869 removed his Haymakers from the field after they had forged from behind to tie the score, 17 to 17, in a battle with the undefeated Red Stockings at Cincinnati. That action almost precipitated a riot among the twelve thousand customers, and at the Gibson House that night McKean had to have police protection for his players. The pretext on which McKean made his players leave the field was a silly controversy about a caught foul tip. The umpire, John R. Brockway, awarded the victory to the Red Stockings by forfeit, but the Haymakers claimed a tie. Later it was revealed that McKean and his friends had wagered sixty thousand dollars on Troy but, fearing defeat, he had avoided a payoff by stopping the game as soon as the score had been tied. The owner of the Haymakers was that fragrant politician, John Morrissey.

All through the five-year history of the National Association, the first professional league that began operations in 1871, contests were casually sold to the highest bidder, and frequently different players on the same team were betting on opposite sides. The result was almost complete chaos.

Even after the founding of the National League, which was formed to put an end to pool selling, fixed games and contract breaking, gamblers tried their best to influence the outcome of games. A New York pool seller, F. H. Seibert, apparently thought that the Mutuals, although by now a National League member, would be doing business at the same old stand, for in 1876 he offered that team's star pitcher, Bobby Mathews, two hundred dollars a game for every one he would sell.

Seibert gave Mathews in writing a code, as follows:

Mutuals—Anderson
St. Louis—Bertram
Cincinnati—Charlestown

If Mathews wanted Seibert to bet on St. Louis, he was to send a wire saying, "Buy Bertram," and so on, addressing all messages to George Howard at the New York Turf Exchange and signing them "Robert."

Mathews nodded that he understood the arrangement, pocketed the code, and at the first opportunity turned Seibert in to the organizer of the league, William A. Hulbert. That display of honesty by Mathews must have discouraged the betting gentry, but not greatly enough to prevent them from reaching the four Louisville players in the following year.

The credit for exposing the mess at Louisville should go to the team's vice president, Charles E. Chase, who first became suspicious when so many telegrams were being sent to Al Nichols, who was only a substitute third baseman. But recent research also reveals that John A. Haldeman of the Louisville *Courier-Journal,* a baseball writer who accompanied the team, played a large part in getting at the truth. Haldeman, suspecting the actions of the four, boldly confronted them and accused them of crooked work even before Chase was aware of what was going on, just as years later another courageous newspaperman, Hughie Fullerton, was to print the details of the Black Sox scandal despite threats from the gambler Arnold Rothstein. Hall, Nichols and Devlin all admitted their guilt, but the case against Craver was never actually proved. But the league's firm action in making their ineligibility permanent bolstered public confidence in the game.

The baseball world breathed more easily after the expulsion of the Louisville four. In an editorial, the 1881 *Spalding Guide* said:

> It is quite a mystery to us how any professional player possessed of common sense can ever be induced to enter any crooked-play conspiracy. Experience so plainly points out the policy of pursuing an honest course in his occupation, that it becomes a matter of surprise to see him adopt any other. Integrity of play is part of a professional's capital, as much so as his record for special skill at his home position. And yet, until within the past two or three years, occasional instances were known of men being led to risk reputation and character by the temptation of acquiring a few hundred dollars extra money. Here is an occupation which is healthy and recreative in its nature, involving nothing out of the way in the form of fatiguing labor, and for which the remuneration is five-, and in some cases tenfold, what the same individual would obtain in any ordinary business he is competent to engage in.

This was good advice, but it was not the whole story. It is true that the early players were in theory earning five or ten times what they might have made in some other occupation, but they were seldom paid on time and in some cases not at all. When Craver was asked by the Louisville directors if they could read his wires, he replied, "You can if you will pay me the two months' salary you owe me." The wires were not opened: Devlin, Nichols and Hall had not set such a condition on the reading of theirs.

The next episode of dishonesty to confront the game involved an umpire, Richard Higham. The year was 1882, the scene was Detroit, and the nature of his offense was to announce in advance the probable winners of games that he was to umpire.

It was William G. Thompson, president of the Detroit team, who first thought Higham's work was peculiar. In fact, he was sick and tired of watching his Wolverines lose games at which Higham officiated. For reasons of economy an umpire in those days stayed with a team for several weeks at a time. Of the first twenty-nine National League games played by Detroit, Higham called the decisions in twenty-six, and Thompson thought that was too much of a bad thing. Suspicious of the umpire's work, he hired detectives who succeeded in intercepting two letters that Higham had written and posted. One was completely innocent; the other is here printed verbatim:

> Friend Todd:
>
> I just got word we leave for the East on the 3 P.M. train, so I will not have a chance to see you. If you don't hear from me, play the Providence Tuesday, and if I want you to play the Detroits Wednesday I will telegraph you in this way, "Buy all the lumber you can." If you do not hear from me, don't play the Detroits but buy Providence sure, that is in the first game. I think this will do for the Eastern series. I will write you from Boston. You can write me any time in care of the Detroit BB Club. When you send me any money, you can send a check to me in care of the Detroit BB Club, and it will be all right. You will see by the book I gave you the other day what city I will be in.
>
> Yours truly,
>
> Dick

Armed with the two letters, Thompson summoned the other club owners to a special meeting of the league at the Russell House in Detroit on June 24. Higham readily admitted authorship of the innocent letter, but claimed he had never seen the other one. However, Thompson had the foresight to have in attendance a handwriting expert who gave his professional opinion that the letters had been written by the same person. Higham was then immediately blacklisted.

For a long time after his expulsion there were only occasional charges of dishonesty or suspicions that it existed. In 1886 a newspaper accused Tony Mullane, a prominent American Association pitcher, of throwing a game, but Mullane asked for an investigation and easily cleared himself. When the first World Series of this century was played between the Pirates and Red Sox in 1903, gamblers tried to reach Cy Young, the great Boston pitcher, through his catcher, Lou Criger. When Criger reported the bribe attempt to his league president, Ban Johnson, the plot was exposed. Because of his honest action, Criger for years was given a pension out of American League funds, long before the philosophy that all faithful employees should be pensioned became general. Ill of tuberculosis in Arizona, he put the money to good use.

Finally the Black Sox scandal came along to give the game its greatest challenge. The atmosphere of baseball at the time was murky. Prominent players had been mysteriously released; rumors were rife that a few players, operating on their own, had been selling games for years. Public confidence was shaken, and stern measures were called for. The dirty laundry that had accumulated in baseball's basement was finally brought out for airing and washing.

Although the eight Chicago players were acquitted in court of throwing the 1919 World Series to the Reds, they were permanently barred from the game, along with others who had knowledge of their scheming. The public exposure of their plot was, in the long run, a happy thing for baseball, because it helped bring about a revolution in operation and led to the establishment of a commissioner, Judge Landis.

In the first years of the Landis reign there were numerous rumors of scandal, but most of them involved games played before 1919. Although all such reports were carefully investigated, it finally became necessary to impose a statute of limitations, setting five years as the period after which charges against ballplayers would be void. Only in this way could an end be brought to the charges and countercharges that filled the air.

Since that time there has not been the slightest suspicion about a single major-league game and only a few instances of crookedness in the minors. In an editorial in the *Spalding Guide* for 1927 the veteran writer, John B. Foster, summed up the new spirit:

> The moral strength of this country is bound up in its sports. A nation that plays honestly deals honestly. The baseball player of today, instead of permitting himself to be warped by the whine and sophistry of the mercenary, should glorify himself by feeling that he is honored to be an exemplar to the best game in the world and one that holds a superlative brief for its existence in the splendid fact that it is honest to the core, and played by men who are as honest as their game, for *men* make the game, and crooks try to unmake it!

IT TOOK a superb World Series to top the wild four-way American League pennant race in 1967, for a wild race it was—but a superb Series too. Gibson, Brock & Co. *v.* Lonborg, Yastrzemski & Co. made for a brilliant Cardinal victory in seven games over the Red Sox, the 100-to-1 shot that won the A.L. pennant. The whole sweep of that memorable two weeks is contained in the following article by Mr. Angell—contained, in fact, in its very title.

1967: The Flowering and Subsequent Deflowering of New England

ROGER ANGELL

THE LAURELS all are cut, the year draws in the day, and we'll to the Fens no more. A great baseball season—the most intense and absorbing of our times—is over, the St. Louis Cardinals stand as champions of the world, and hundreds of thousands of New Englanders must winter sadly on a feast of memory. The autumn quiet that now afflicts so many of us has almost nothing to do with the Red Sox defeat in the last game of the World Series, for every Boston fan has grown up with that dour Indian-pudding taste in his mouth. New England's loss is not of a game or a Series but of the baseball summer just past—a season that will not come again, not ever quite the same. What will be remembered this winter, I think, is not so much a particular victory (Elston Howard blocking off the last White Sox base runner at the plate one night in Chicago, Carl Yastrzemski's eleventh-inning homer at Yankee Stadium) or a nearly insupportable loss (all those Baltimore games in September) as the shared joy and ridiculous hope of this summer's long adventure. I resisted at first, but it caught me up, and then I was sorry for anyone who was too old or too careful to care. Almost everyone on the seaboard was caught up in the end, it seemed. Forty-four New England radio stations poured out the news from the Fenway, and home-game telecasts by Ken Coleman, Mel Parnell, and Ned Martin made for late bedtimes from eastern Long Island to the Gaspé. Maine lobstermen pulling their traps off Saddleback Ledge called the news of the previous night's game from boat to boat through the foggy dawn air. The moderator of an August town meeting in Andover, Massachusetts, interrupted a hot budget debate to cry, "The Sox are leading, 2–1, in the sixth!" Three hikers descending the Brook Trail on Mount Chocorua, in New Hampshire, caught the afternoon score from a transistorized ascending climber. Sunday sailors off Manchester Harbor, on Boston's North Shore, hailed a winning rally with foghorns and salvos of cherry bombs, and then cheered when a power yacht broke out a large flag emblazoned "THINK PENNANT!" Late in August, a patient recovering from surgery stood at the window of his room in the New England Baptist Hospital night after night, watching the lights of Fenway Park across the city and hearing the sudden double roar of the crowd—first over his radio and then, in a deep echo, through the warm night air. The sense of belonging was best in the crowded streets near the ball park before game time. Up out of the subway on Commonwealth Avenue, up Brookline Avenue and over the expressway bridge, past the Pennant Grille, past the button hawkers ("GO SOX!") and the ice-cream wagons and the police horses;

carried along in a mass of children and parents, old ladies in straw porkpies, pretty girls with pennants, South Boston and Dorchester youths in high-school windbreakers, a party of nuns; then pushed and jammed, laughing at the crush, through the turnstiles and into the damp gloom under the stands; and out at last to that first electric glimpse of green outfield and white bases—this is the way baseball is remembered, and the way it truly was, for once, in the summer of the Red Sox.

Even a restrained backward look at this season and this Series must appear hyperbolic; already there is the odd temptation simply not to believe one's recollection or the record. The Cardinals, sixth-place finishers last year, lost their best pitcher for half the season and still won their pennant easily, entirely dominating the other powerful contenders that had given the National League its recent reputation for late-season violence. The Red Sox, who finished the 1966 season one-half game out of the cellar, captured the American League pennant on the last afternoon of the year by winning the second of two consecutive essential victories over the Twins and then waiting for the Tigers to lost their last game. The Baltimore Orioles, who won the 1966 World Series in four straight games, fell to sixth place this year, while the Red Sox, Twins, Tigers, and White Sox clawed and clung to each other like drowning swimmers at the surface of the American League for more than two months, in the closest pennant race in baseball history. The White Sox sank only two days before the end, at a moment when it appeared that they had the best chance to take the flag and the Red Sox the worst. Finally, the World Series, which promised only to be a numb, one-sided anticlimax, went the full seven games, producing some of the best baseball of the year, and was won at last by the better team.

An appreciation of the Cardinals must be postponed in this account until their appearance, in due course, in the World Series. An appreciation of the Red Sox must begin with a look at their prospects last April, which seemed inadequate even to sustain the wild vernal hopes that leap every year, jonquil-like, in the hearts of their followers. The Sox were a young team, probably a better one than their ninth-place finish indicated, but a review of the troops suggested only that hostilities should somehow be postponed. The up-the-middle strength, the traditional spine of a ball team, consisted of an earnest but light-hitting young catcher named Mike Ryan and two rookies—second baseman Mike Andrews and center fielder Reggie Smith. Third baseman Joe Foy and shortstop Rico Petrocelli could hit an occasional fly ball into the Fenway's short left-field screen, but both were subject to fatal spells of introspection when approaching ground balls. The large, slick-fielding George Scott was set at first, but last year, after making the All-Star team with his early slugging, he had apparently determined to hit every subsequent pitch out of the park, and wound up leading the league only in strikeouts. The two other outfielders—Tony Conigliaro in right and Yastrzemski in left—enjoyed star billing, but neither came close to .300 last year. Yaz, who had won the batting title in 1963, finished at .278, with sixteen home runs; he had never hit more than twenty homers in one season. There was, to be sure, a new manager—Dick Williams, up from two successful years with the Toronto farm—but a new manager in Boston has the same approximate hopes for tenure as a titled Balkan bridegroom in a Hollywood marriage. Any manager, however deep-browed, hates to do much thinking in the first two or three innings, and thus must own a pitching staff. The Red Sox had none, having failed in the winter to improve the corps that was the worst in the league last year. Their best starter, the youthful Jim Lonborg, could strike out batters but had proved too gentlemanly in the clutch ever to enjoy a winning season in the majors. There was one strong late reliever, John Wyatt, and some passable middle-innings men, but absolutely no other starters in sight.

Reasonable hope cannot be constructed out of such a sad pile of feathers, but the lifelong Red Sox fan is not a reasonable man. In him is the perpetual memory of a dozen seasons when the best of hopes went for nothing, so why is he not to believe that the worst of prospects may suddenly reward his fealty? If he is middle-aged, he remembers when, in the early nineteen-thirties, the team's owner, Tom Yawkey, acquired the Sox and almost bought a pennant within a few years, at an immense price, with a team built around such stalwarts as Jimmy Foxx, Joe Cronin, Lefty Grove, and a lanky young outfielder named Ted Williams. He remembers the home-grown squad of the mid-nineteen-forties, which included Williams, Dominic DiMaggio, Johnny Pesky, and Bobby Doerr. Those teams were wonderfully talented and exciting, but unfortunately they coexisted with two Yankee teams that were among the best in league history. There is one Boston pennant to treasure, in 1946, but that memory is accompanied by the awful vision of Enos Slaughter, of the Cardinals, racing all the way home from first on a double by Harry Walker and scoring the winning run of the Series while Johnny Pesky hesitated with the relay at short. There was a tie for first with the Indians in 1948, but the starting Red Sox pitcher for the one-game playoff was an aging journeyman named Denny Galehouse, who instantly unjustified the hunch. Since then, the Sox have been more at home in the second division than in the first. There are other interior daguerreotypes to sustain the New Englander—Ted Williams towering over the plate and grinding the bat between his fists before pulling an outside pitch into the bullpen, Dick Radatz fanning the side in relief—but these are matched by darker plates: Williams hitting .200 in that 1946 Series, Williams never hitting much against the Yankees, Walt Dropo and several other immobile croquet wickets letting grounders bounce between their legs at first, a dozen assorted infielders messing up a thousand double plays. I have studied the diehard Boston fan for many summers. I have seen the tiny, mineral-hard gleam of hope in his eye as he pumps gas under the blighted elms of a New Hampshire village or sells a pair of moccasins to a tourist in the balsam-smelling dimness of his Down East store, listening the while to the unceasing ribbon of bad news by radio from Fenway Park. Inside his head, I am sure, there is a perpetual accompanying broadcast of painful and maddening import—a lifetime's amalgam of ill-digested sports headlines, between-innings commercials, and Fenway Park bleacher cries:

"Hi, neighbor, have a Gansett! . . . DOUBLE-X 9 GAMES AHEAD OF BABE'S SWAT PACE. . . . Oh, God, *look*—Slaughter's going for home! C'mon, Pesky, throw the ball, throw the *ball!* . . . YAWKEY VOWS PENNANT. . . . but the lowly A's, rising for three runs in the eighth, nipped the Hose in the nightcap. . . . Hi, neigh-bor. . . . SPLINTER DEFIES SHIFT. . . . and now trail the Yankees by two in the all-important lost column. . . . *'He's better than his brother Joe—Domi-nic DiMaggio!'* . . . RADATZ IN NINETEENTH RELIEF STINT. . . . and if Pesky takes the ball over his *right* shoulder, Enos is dead, I'm telling you. . . . GOODMAN NEARS BAT CROWN. . . . Fenway scribes stated that Ted's refusal to doff his cap is nothing less than. . . . HIGGINS SEES PENNANT WITHIN TWO YEARS. . . . and Doc Cramer's shotgun arm *just* fails to cut down Averill at third. . . . DID NOT SPIT KID SWEARS. . . . the aging shortstop-manager, lately known in the press box as The Ancient Mariner ('who stoppeth one in three'). . . . ZARILLA TRADE STRENGTHENS O.F. . . . *'better than his brother Joe—Domi-nic DiMaggio!'* . . . HIGGINS, REHIRED, VOWS. . . . A bright spot in the Bosox seventh-place finish was Pete Runnels' consistent. . . . TED FIRST A.L. SLUGGER TO TOP .400 SINCE. . . . but Schilling dropped the ball. . . . delicious Narragansett Ale. So, *hi*, neigh-bor. . . . and Keller matched Gordon's awesome poke over the inviting left-field screen with. . . . MALZONE TRADE RUMORS DENIED. . . . and Slaughter, running all the way, beat the startled Pesky's hurried. . . . CRONIN, NEW MGR, VOWS. . . . the hotly fought junior-circuit gonfalon. . . . FOXX NEARS SWAT MARK. . . . as Slaughter crosses the plate. . . ."

By Memorial Day, the Red Sox were only a game above the .500 level, but Manager Williams and the front office had seen enough signs of life on the field to decide that their young enlistees would benefit from the assistance of some experienced noncoms. Successive deals in June brought Gary Bell, a strong right-handed starter, from the Indians and infielder Jerry Adair from the White Sox. Later in the summer, Elston Howard was bought from the Yankees to help behind the plate, and then Ken Harrelson, a brash, hot-dog outfielder with the Kansas City Athletics, signed aboard for a large bonus, after having so enranged the owner of the A's, Charles O. Finley, during a squabble that Finley threw him over the side.

Just before the All-Star game, in mid-July, Lonborg ended a five-game losing streak with a 3–0 shutout over the Tigers. Dick Williams said that this game marked Lonborg's arrival as a great pitcher, but it is likely that Lonborg's immense subsequent season was more the result of his decision in spring training to throw an occasional fast ball in the direction of the hitters' chins. "Keep count of how many batters I hit this year," Lonborg whispered to a sportswriter in April. Lonborg also kept count himself, recording the plunkees in ink on the back of his glove, like a fighter pilot pasting confirmed-kill decals on his plane's fuselage. The final bag came to nineteen, with several dozen near-misses, and the message got around the league that Lonborg was no longer a fine, friendly fellow to swing against. He finished the year with twenty-two wins, nine losses, and two hundred and forty-five strikeouts. Meanwhile, pitchers like Bell, Lee Stange, and José Santiago began showing signs of equal obduracy. Petrocelli, Conigliaro, and Yastrzemski were all off to fine seasons, the rookies Andrews and Smith proved to be quick and unflappable, and Dick Williams established his directorship once and for all by benching George Scott during three essential games because he was overweight. Late in July, the Sox won ten straight games, came home from a road trip in second place, and were met at Logan Airport by ten thousand true believers.

I refused to believe what was happening. Unpleasantly cool, I told Boston friends to keep their eyes on the other teams—the White Sox, who were clinging to first place on the strength of nothing but a fine pitching staff and some hilarious needling of the opposition by their manager, Eddie Stanky; the Twins, obviously the class of the league, who were just beginning their move; and the Tigers, who showed signs at last of wanting the pennant they had seemed capable of winning for the past two years. Then, too, I was waiting for the Red Sox bad break—the moment of ill fortune, the undeserved loss, that so often cracks the heart of a young team playing over its head. The break came on August 18th, and was infinitely worse than I had imagined. A fast ball thrown by the Angels' Jack Hamilton struck Tony Conigliaro on the cheekbone, finishing him for the season. In that instant, the Sox lost their right fielder, a bat that had already delivered twenty home runs and sixty-seven runs batted in, and the only man on the team who could fill the key fourth spot in the batting order. In a few days, I could see, the Red Sox would . . . In the next few days, the Red Sox overcame an 0–8 deficit in one game and won it, 9–8, jumped off on what proved to be a seven-game winning streak, and climbed from fourth place to within one game of the Twins and White Sox, at the top. I gave up; from that week on, I belonged.

Even to neutralists, the last weeks of the American League race must have seemed excessive. On any given evening late in August, knowing the leader often depended on which edition of the papers one happened to buy. In the first week of September, the four teams reshuffled themselves nervously, the Red Sox lost three games without giving up much ground, and on Labor Day at Yankee Stadium Eddie Stanky had to tackle one of his infielders, Pete Ward, to keep him from punching an umpire and thus being ruled off the turf for the rest of the way. On September 7th, there was a four-way tie for first. My baseball nerves had grown too raw to permit me to keep out of it, and a few days later I flew west to see the four top teams in action. When I arrived in Chicago on September 16th, the Twins, Red Sox, and Tigers were still even-up, and the White Sox, who had slipped a trifle, were making up lost ground brilliantly. Two days before, they had beaten the Indians with a tenth-inning grand-slam home run, and the previous night they had won the first of a three-game series with the Twins, which they had to sweep in order to stay alive. That night, even the half-empty bleachers in White Sox Park (racial troubles on Chicago's South Side cut heavily into the White Sox attendance this year) failed to diminish the wonderful baseball tension in the boxy old stadium. With two weeks to go, the season had narrowed down to the point where each pitched ball seemed heavy with omens, and spectators greeted the most routine enemy pop fly with nervous laughter and applause. The Twins' ace, Dean Chance, was seeking his nineteenth win, and after watching him jam the White Sox batters with his jumping fast balls and low curves I concluded that I was in on a mismatch. Looking confident and workmanlike, the Twins loaded the bases in the fifth on a hit batsman, a single, a sacrifice, and an intentional walk. The White Sox pitcher, Tommy John, then leaped anxiously after a hopper by Ted Uhlaender, managing only to deflect it, and threw the ball past first, as two runs scored. A third came in a moment later on a single, and a fourth in the next inning on a home run by Bob Allison, which the Chicago outfielders studied in flight like junior astronomers. In the bottom of the ninth, it was 4–1, Twins, and the crowd managed only a few imploring cheers for their dying banjo hitters. The first Chicago batter, McCraw, singled, and took third on Ron Hansen's single and Oliva's subsequent error in right. Colavito then hit a perfect double-play ball, which Manager Stanky or some other deity caused to bound suddenly over the third baseman's head, scoring a run. Josephson, the catcher, now dropped an unsurprising sacrifice bunt along the third-base line. Chance pounced on it eagerly, dropped it, cuffed it, scuffled with it, and finally merely glared at it as it lay between his feet like a kitten. The score was now 4–2, with none out and the bases full, and wild bird cries rose into the night. Manager Stanky dispatched his third pinch-runner of the inning to first, and Wayne Causey, batting in the pitcher's spot, came to the plate. Manager Cal Ermer of the Twins called in Jim Kaat, who threw a wild pitch, scoring a run and moving up the runners. Causey tied the game with a fly to right. More strategy ensued. Worthington came in to pitch. Smoky Burgess pinch-hit and was intentionally passed, giving way to another pinch-runner. Buford was also walked, to set up the force at all bases, and Pete Ward, the twelfth Chicago player to appear in this one-third of an inning, came to the plate. He had been hitless in his previous twenty-one times at bat, but he lined the 2–2 pitch smartly off Killebrew's glove and trotted to first, clapping his hands over his head all the way, as the scoreboard rocket display went off. Afterward, in the noisy Chicago clubhouse, I saw two Chicago coaches, Kerby Farrell and Marv Grissom, sitting silently side by side in front of their lockers. They had their pants and spikes off, their feet were propped up, and they were comfortably balancing paper cups of beer on their stomachs. Their seamed, down-home country faces were still alight with the game. As I passed, Farrell nodded his head once and said, "Hum-*dinger*."

The next day, a summery Sunday afternoon, Stanky got his sweep as Gary Peters shut out the Twins with four hits and won, 4–0. The cheerful, family crowd got as much pleasure from the scoreboard as from the game; it showed the Tigers losing to Washington, and the Red Sox in the process of dropping their third straight to Baltimore. The Tigers now led Chicago by half a game and the Twins and Red Sox by one, and I passed the time during my flight to Detroit that night trying to fathom the recently announced schedule for post-season playoffs that might be needed to determine a winner; it listed eleven different possibilities for the teams and sites involved in two-way, three-way, or four-way playoffs. The World Series might never come.

There was an enormous, noisy crowd the next night for the first of the Tigers' two-game series with Boston, and Tiger Stadium instantly justified its reputation as a hitters' park when the Red Sox jumped off to a three-run lead in the first. But no lead and no pitcher was safe for long on this particular evening; the hits flew through the night air like enraged deerflies, and the infielders seemed to be using their gloves mostly in self-defense. The Tigers tied it in the second with a cluster of hits, including a homer by Norm Cash, but the Red Sox instantly went one up, 4–3, after Yastrzemski's bulletlike single up the middle nearly nailed the second baseman on the ear. Cash's second homer retied it in the sixth, and then the rackety, exhausting contest seemed settled by Kaline's single and Northrup's double in the eighth, which put the home side in front for the first time. Just before that, though, in the Boston half of the eighth, there had been an extraordinary moment of baseball. With none out and Petrocelli at first and Dalton Jones on third, the Boston catcher, Russ Gibson, hit a sharp grounder to Dick McAuliffe at second. McAuliffe glanced once at third, freezing Jones there. Petrocelli, hoping for a rundown that would permit the run to score, stopped dead on the basepath, and McAuliffe, ball in hand, ran him back toward first, tagged him, and stepped on the bag in time to retire Gibson for an unassisted double play at first base. No one in the park—at least, none of the ballplayers and none of the sportswriters—had ever seen a play like it.

Yastrzemski came up in the ninth with one out and none on. He already had two hits for the night, and was in the homestretch of an extraordinary season at the plate and in the field, which had made him the favorite to win the Most Valuable Player award in his league. Boston sportswriters, however, are famously unimpressionable, especially when the Red Sox are behind. "Go on!" one of them shouted bitterly from the press box at this moment. "Prove you're the M.V.P.! Prove it to *me!* Hit a homer!" Yastrzemski hit a homer. In the tenth, Dalton Jones, a part-time infielder inserted in the Red Sox' lineup that night only because he hits mysteriously well in Tiger Stadium, won it, 6–5, with another homer. There were some seven hundred members of the Polish National Alliance staying at my hotel, and the delegates' celebrations in the lobby that night made it clear that Yaz's homer, his fortieth of the year, had been voted the finest Polish-American achievement since Cornel Wilde wrote the "Polonaise Militaire."

The next evening's game, mercifully, was a more languid affair, in which the Tigers kept putting men on base and allowing them to die there. In the third, they hit three successive singles without issue. The Sox had managed one scratchy run in the early going, but the Tigers' fine left-hander, Mickey Lolich, was striking out Boston batters in clusters, and he seemed sure of his seventh straight win after Jim Northrup hit a prodigious two-run homer onto the roof, ninety feet above the right-field wall. Detroit loaded the bases in the eighth with none out but again failed to score, and its lead was somehow only 2–1 when Jerry Adair led off the Boston ninth with a single. Lolich, working like a man opening a basket of cobras, walked Yastrzemski, and then George Scott, after botching up two tries at a sacrifice, singled up the middle to tie it. Earl Wilson, the ace of the Detroit staff, came on in relief for the first time in the year, and gave up a sacrifice to Reggie Smith and an intentional pass to Jones. He then threw a wild pitch, and Yastrzemski sailed in from third. Gibson's fly scored Scott, who slid under Kaline's peg in a cloud of dust and unbelieving silence. Boston won the game, 4–2, and I came home with my first solid conviction about the pennant race: The Tigers could not win it.

No one, it appeared, wanted that pennant in the end. The four teams fell toward the wire in a flurry of failures, in one stretch losing ten out of twelve games against weaker clubs. With three days to go, the White Sox needed only wins against the Athletics and Senators to make up their one-game deficit. Chicago, pitching its two aces, Gary Peters and Joel Horlen, lost both ends of a doubleheader to Kansas City on Wednesday, and then fell out of the race when it lost to the Senators two nights later. That coup de grâce administered by the A's, a last-place club that had lost both its franchise and its manager in recent weeks, was an act of defiant pride that everyone in baseball, with the possible exception of Eddie Stanky, could admire. Three teams, then, for the final weekend. Minnesota, a game up on Boston, could eliminate the Red Sox by winning either of its two games at Fenway Park. The Tigers, facing two doubleheaders at home against the Angels, would gain at least a tie and a playoff by sweeping the four games.

There was perhaps less expectancy than gratitude in the enormous crowd that threw itself into Fenway Park that sunny Saturday. The possibility of winning two games from the Twins while the Tigers lost two looked to be beyond even New England hopes, but there was the plain joy of being there and seeing the old, low-roofed, country-style grandstand and the humpbacked bleachers choked with that enormous sitting and standing assemblage of zealots, all there to shout for the team that had given them such a summer. There was a flurry of governors and dignitaries behind the home dugout, and a much more interesting swarm of kids balanced precariously on top of an immense Old Grand Dad billboard across the street behind the left-field fence. That pale-green, too close fence looked dangerous today —a target for the Twins' Harmon Killebrew, who was tied with Yastrzemski for the home-run lead, at forty-three each.

Then the game began, and all the Twins looked dangerous. They scored an instant run off Santiago in the top of the first, and only a line drive out to the third baseman saved further damage. Jim Kaat, the Twins' enormous left-hander, struck out four of the first nine Boston batters, looking as formidable as he did two years ago, when he beat Sandy Koufax in a World Series game. Kaat's last strikeout, however, was an immense misfortune for the Twins, because he pulled a tendon in his pitching arm and was forced to leave the game. The import of this blow, however, was not immediately visible. Kaat's replacement, Jim Perry, went on fanning the home side, while Santiago continued his anxious-making practice of pitching into and barely out of appalling jams.

It was still 1–0, Twins, when Reggie Smith led off the Boston fifth with a double to the left-field wall, and then Dalton Jones, pinch-hitting, was miraculously safe when his grounder to Carew suddenly leaped up and struck the second baseman in the face. Adair tied the game with a soft texas leaguer. Yastrzemski then sent a low shot that went past the diving Killebrew but was fielded by Carew in short right. Perry, perhaps still brooding about Boston luck, failed to cover first, leaving no one for Carew to throw to, and the Sox led, 2–1. The Twins tied it in the sixth, but Perry vanished, necessarily, for a pinch-hitter, and George Scott bombed reliever Ron Kline's first pitch into the center-field stands. Baseball luck creates intolerable pressure in a close game, and in the seventh the pressure of the luck and the tie destroyed the Twins. Mike Andrews was safe on a topped roller that trickled about twenty feet toward third, and a moment later shortstop Zoilo Versalles dropped Kline's peg in the middle of an easy double play, making all hands safe. All hands then came home on Yastrzemski's homer off Jim Merritt, which landed beyond the bullpen, and the Red Sox players, leading by 6–2, attempted to pound their hero into biscuit dough as he returned to the dugout. The ensuing Fenway din was diminished only faintly when Killebrew hit a two-run homer over the screen in the ninth off Gary Bell, tying Yaz for the title and bringing the game back to 6–4. It ended that way, but I had to wait until almost nine o'clock that night before my hunch about the Tigers was rejustified, via TV, as they lost their second game. Now there was one day left.

There was no reticence in Boston the next day. A woman calling the Ritz-Carlton that morning suddenly found herself in conversation with the hotel telephone operator, who exclaimed, "What if the bases had been loaded when Killebrew hit that ball? My heart can't *stand* it!" Bad nerves took me to Fenway Park early, and on the way I spotted an empty hearse with a fresh "GO, Sox!" sticker on the rear bumper. At the ball park, several hundred reporters could watch Ricky Williams, the manager's ten-year-old son, working out in uniform at first base during batting practice. I took this to be a last, brilliant managerial hunch by his father: Ricky had accompanied the squad during its all-winning road trip in July. "Look at him," Ken Harrelson said admiringly as the boy made a nifty, Gil Hodges pickup. "The kid has all the moves."

The big boys played the game, though—Chance against Lonborg—and the weight of it kept the crowd silent. The weight of it also seemed too much for the Red Sox. In the top of the first, Killebrew walked and Oliva doubled, and George Scott, relaying, threw the ball over the catcher's head for the first Minnesota run. In the third, there was another walk, and Yastrzemski let Killebrew's single into left field hop between his legs for another error and another run. The Red Sox managed a hit in each of the first four innings but could not advance the runners. Lonborg pitched on grimly, keeping the ball low. The immense crowd was so quiet that one could hear the snarling and baying of the Minnesota bench wolves between every pitch. The scoreboard reported Detroit ahead in its first game.

It was still 2–0 for the outlanders when Lonborg, leading off the sixth, laid down a sudden bunt on the first pitch and hoofed it out. Adair hit the next pitch through second. Dalton Jones fouled off his first attempt at a sacrifice bunt and then, seeing Killebrew and Tovar, the third baseman, charging in like cavalrymen, socked the next pitch past Tovar and into left, to load the bases for Yaz with none out. The screeching in the park was almost insupportable: *"Go! Go!* GO!" Yastrzemski tied the game with a single up the middle. When the count went to three and two on Harrelson, Yaz took off with the pitch, arriving at second just before Harrelson's high chopper got to Versalles behind the bag; utterly unstrung, Versalles threw home, far too late to get anybody. Dean Chance, unstrung, departed. Worthington, unstrung, came in and threw two wild pitches, letting in another run. The fifth scored when Reggie Smith's hot grounder bounced off the unstrung (or perhaps only unhappy) Killebrew's knee.

It was growing dark, but the dangerous season had one or two moments left. Jerry Adair collided with the oncoming Versalles on the basepath in the eighth, but held on to the ball and flipped out of the dust to first for a double play. The Twins, still fighting, followed with two singles. Allison then lined a hit to left; Yastrzemski charged the ball, hesitated only an instant at the sight of the runner racing for home, and then threw brilliantly to second to cut down the flying Allison. You could see it all happening in the same twilight instant—the ball coming in a deadly line, and Allison's deperate, skidding slide, and the tag, and the umpire's arm shooting up, and the game and the season saved. One more inning, and then there was nothing more to be saved except Lonborg, who had to be extricated—sans sweatshirt, buttons, and cap—from the hands of the local citizenry, who evidently wanted to mount him in the State House beside the sacred cod.

The Boston locker room presented a classic autumn scene—shouts, embraces, beer showers, shaving cream in the hair, television lights, statements to the press. ("Never," said Lonborg, "do I remember a more . . . ecstatic and . . . *vigorous* moment.") But then it all sagged and stopped, for this was still only a half triumph. Detroit had won its first game, and now we had to wait for the radio news of the second game to know whether this was the pennant or whether there would be a playoff with the Tigers the next afternoon.

During that long, painful interval in the clubhouse, there was time to look back on Yastrzemski's season. He had won the triple crown—a batting average of .326, a hundred and twenty-one runs batted in, forty-four homers—but this was not all. Other fine hitters, including Frank Robinson last season, had finished with comparable statistics. But no other player in memory had so clearly pushed a team to such a height in the final days of a difficult season. The Allison peg was typical of Yastrzemski's ardent outfield play. In the final two weeks at the plate, Yaz had hammered twenty-three hits in forty-four times at bat, including four doubles and five home runs, and had driven in sixteen runs. In those two games against the Twins, he went seven for eight and hit a game-winning homer. This sort of performance would be hard to countenance in a Ralph Henry Barbour novel, and I found it difficult to make the connection between the epic and the person of the pleasant, twenty-eight-year-old young man of unheroic dimensions who was now explaining to reporters, with articulate dispassion, that his great leap forward this year might have been the result of a small change in batting style—a blocking of the right hip and a slightly more open stance—which was urged on him in spring training by Ted Williams. There was something sad here—perhaps the thought that for Yastrzemski, more than for anyone else, this summer could not come again. He had become a famous star, with all the prizes and ugly burdens we force on the victims of celebrity, and from now on he would be set apart from us and his teammates and the easy time of his youth.

Detroit led for a while in its last game, and then the Angels caught up and went ahead, but the clubhouse maternity ward was an unhappy place. Players in bits and pieces of uniform pretended to play cards, pretended to sleep. Then, at last, it was the ninth inning, with the Angels leading, 8–5, and the Red Sox formed a silent circle all staring up at the radio on the wall. The Tigers put men on base, and I could see the strain of every pitch on the faces around me. Suddenly there was a double-play ball that might end it, and when the announcer said, ". . . over to first, *in* time for the out," every one of the Boston players came off the floor and straight up into the air together, like a ballet troupe. Players and coaches and reporters and relatives and owner Yawkey and manager Williams hugged and shook hands and hugged again, and I saw Ricky Williams trying to push through the mob to get at his father. He was crying. He reached him at last and jumped into his arms and kissed him again and again; he could not stop kissing him. The champagne arrived in a giant barrel of ice, and for an instant I was disappointed with Mr. Yawkey when I saw that it was Great Western. But I had forgotten what pennant champagne is for. In two minutes, the clubhouse looked like a Y.M.C.A. water-polo meet, and it was everybody into the pool.

A professional sport so constructed that four out of ten teams can still be in hot contention in the final three days of a hundred-and-sixty-two-game season would seem to be a paragon of aesthetic and commercial endeavor. It is possible that the only people in North America who do not hold this view of baseball at the moment are the big-league owners who are currently engaged in a scheme to dismantle their Parthenon. As matters now stand, it is almost certain that in 1917, when the current three-year television contracts expire, both leagues will be expanded from ten to twelve clubs and subdivided into six-team regional conferences; each team will continue to play all the other teams in its league (with the added possibility of a few inter-league contests, to whet midsummer appetites), but the standings will determine only conference champions. Two playoffs will then precede the World Series (or "Super Series," perhaps), with the excellent possibility that at least one pre-playoff playoff will be needed to settle one of the four conference races. The fact that the artificially constructed sub-leagues will almost surely produce some inferior champions is of no concern to these planners. What they see is more money and more prizes for all—the initial freshet of dollars that accompanies the appearance of each new, weak franchise team in an expanded league, and the guarantee of three autumn extravaganzas instead of one.

The magnet that is about to pull baseball into this tortured shape is television. The immense sports-television business has never been happy with baseball, which so far includes only two high-revenue packages—the All-Star game and the Series—each year. Moreover, the game does not produce tidy, two-hour segments of marketable time; a nationally televised midsummer Saturday game may creep along into the early evening, and it cannot be puffed up by advance billing, since the meaning of its outcome may not become apparent until late in September. This is almost intolerable to the young men in blazers who run sports TV; their dream is fifty weekends of world championships —in football, in baseball, in surfing, in Senior Women's Marbles, in anything—that are *not to be missed* by the weekend watcher. Every real fan senses, of course, that baseball's long, chancy season perfectly matches the slow, tension-building pace of the game on the field. He knows that baseball is so difficult a game that the worst team in any league is almost a match for the best, and thus a long schedule is necessary to determine a true champion. None of this appears to be of much import to the television industry or the baseball owners, who now propose to replace skill and courage by luck and promotion.

My objections, I am certain, will cut no ice with most baseball magnates, whose instant response to criticism of this nature is to smile and say, "Well, I'm in this for the money, of course." Of course. Baseball is a commercial venture, but it is one of such perfect equipoise that millions of us every year can still unembarrassedly surrender ourselves to its unique and absorbing joys. The ability to find beauty and involvement in artificial commercial constructions is essential to most of us in the modern world; it is the life-giving naïveté. But naïveté is not gullibility, and those who alter baseball for their quick and selfish purposes will find, I believe, that they are the owners of teams without a following and of a sport devoid of passion. They will find that they own only a business.

Cardinal fans who have managed to keep their seats through this interminable first feature will probably not be placated by my delayed compliments to their heroes. The Cardinals not only were the best ball club I saw this season but struck me as being in many ways the most admirable team I can remember in recent years. The new champions have considerable long-ball power, but they know the subtleties of opposite-field hitting, base running, and defense that are the delight of the game. Their quickness is stimulating, their batting strength is distributed menacingly throughout the lineup (they won the Series with almost no help from their No. 4 and No. 5 hitters, Cepeda and McCarver, while their seventh-place batter, Javier, batted .360), they are nearly impregnable in up-the-middle defense, and their pitching was strong enough to win them a pennant even though their ace, Bob Gibson, was lost for the second half of the season after his right leg was broken by a line drive. In retrospect, the wonder of the Series is that the Cards did not make it a runaway, as they so often seemed on the point of doing.

Fenway Park was a different kind of place on the first day of the Series. Ceremonies and bunting and boxfuls of professional Series-goers had displaced the anxious watchers of the weekend. Yastrzemski, staring behind the dugout before the game, said, "Where *is* everybody? These aren't the people who were here all summer." The game quickly produced its own anxieties, however, when Lou Brock, the Cardinals' lead-off man, singled in the first and stole second on the next pitch. Though we did not recognize it, this was only a first dose of what was to follow throughout the Series, for Brock was a tiny little time pill that kept going off at intervals during the entire week. He failed to score that time, but he led off the third with another single, zipped along to third on Flood's double, and scored on Maris's infield out. The Cardinals kept threatening to extinguish Santiago, the Red Sox starter, but bad St. Louis luck and good Boston fielding kept it close. Gibson, hardly taking a deep breath between pitches, was simply overpowering, throwing fast balls past the hitters with his sweeping right-handed delivery, which he finishes with a sudden lunge toward first base. He struck out six of the first ten batters to face him and seemed unaffronted when Santiago somehow got his bat in the path of one of his pitches and lofted the ball into the screen in left-center. It was a one-sided but still tied ball game when Brock led off the seventh (he was perpetually leading off, it seemed) with another single, stole second again, went to third on an infield out, and scored on Roger Maris's deep bouncer to second. That 2–1 lead was enough for Gibson, who blew the Boston batters down; he struck out Petrocelli three times, on ten pitches. The crowd walking out in the soft autumn sunshine seemed utterly undisappointed. They had seen their Sox in a Series game at last, and that was enough.

Five members of the Red Sox had signed up to write byline stories about the Series for the newspapers, and Jim Lonborg, not yet ready to pitch after his Sunday stint, kept notes for his column as he sat on the bench during the opener. He must have remembered to look at those earlier memoranda on his glove, however, for his first pitch of the second game flew rapidly in the suddenly vacated environs of Lou Brock's neck. It was Lonborg's only high pitch of the afternoon, and was fully as effective in its own way as the knee-high curves and sinking fast balls he threw the rest of the way. None of the Cardinals reached first until Flood walked in the seventh, and by that time Yastrzemski had stroked a curving drive into the seats just past the right-field foul pole for one run, and two walks and an error had brought in another for the Beantowners. There were marvelous fielding plays by both teams—Brock and Javier for the Cards, Petrocelli and Adair for the Sox—to keep the game taut, and then Yaz, who had taken extra batting practice right after the first game, hit another in the seventh: a three-run job, way, *way* up in the bleachers. After that, there was nothing to stay for except the excruciating business of Lonborg's possible no-hitter. He was within four outs of it when Javier doubled, solidly and irretrievably, in the eighth, to the accompaniment of a 35,188-man groan. (Lonborg said later that it felt exactly like being in an automobile wreck.) When Lonborg came in after that inning, the crowd stood and clapped for a long, respectful two-minutes, like the audience at a Horowitz recital.

Everyone in St. Louis was ready for the third game except the scoreboard-keeper, who initially had the Cardinals playing Detroit. More than fifty-four thousand partisans, the biggest sporting crowd in local history, arrived early at Busch Memorial Stadium, most of them bearing heraldic devices honoring "El Birdos"—a relentlessly publicized neologism supposedly coined by Orlando Cepeda. Home-town pride was also centered on El Ballparko, a steep, elegant gray concrete pile that forms part of the new downtown complex being built around the celebrated Saarinen archway. I admired everything about this open-face mine except its shape, which is circular and thus keeps all upper-deck patrons at a dismaying distance from the infielders within the right angles of the diamond. The game, like its predecessors, went off like a firecracker, with Lou Brock tripling on the first pitch of the home half. After two innings, Gary Bell, the Boston starter, was allowed to sit down, having given up five hits and three runs to the first nine Cardinal batters. That was the ball game, it turned out (the Cards won, 5–2), but there were some memorable diversions along the way. Nelson Briles, the Cards' starter, decked Yastrzemski in the first with a pitch that nailed him on the calf. Lou Brock, having led off the sixth with a single, got himself plunked in the back with a justifiably nervous pick-off throw by pitcher Lee Stange, and chugged along to third, from where he scored on a single by Maris. *L'affaire Yaz* was the subject of extended seminars with the press after the game. St. Louis manager Red Schoendienst stated that inside pitches were part of the game but that his little band of clean-living Americans did not know how to hit batters on purpose. Pitcher Briles stated that the sight of Yastrzemski caused him to squeeze the ball too hard and thus lose control of its direction. (He had improved afterward, not walking a man all day.) Manager Williams pointed out that a pitcher wishing to hit a batter, as against merely startling him, will throw not at his head but behind his knees, which was the address on Briles' special-delivery package. This seemed to close the debate locally, but that night the publisher of the Manchester, New Hampshire, *Union Leader* wrote an editorial demanding that the Cardinals be forced to forfeit the game, "as an indication that the great American sport of baseball will not allow itself to be besmirched by anyone who wants to play dirty ball."

The great American sport survived it all, but it almost expired during the next game, a 6–0 laugher played on a windy, gray winter afternoon. The Cardinals had all their runs after the first three innings, and the only man in the park who found a way to keep warm was Brock, who did it by running bases. He beat out a third-base tap in the first and went on to score, and subsequently doubled off the wall and stole another base. Gibson, the winner, was not as fast as he had been in the opener, but his shutout won even more admiration from the Red Sox batters, who had discovered that he was not merely a thrower but a pitcher.

The Red Sox, now one game away from extinction, looked doomed after that one, but Yastrzemski pointed out to me that most of his teammates, being in their early twenties, had the advantage of not recognizing the current odds against them. "Lonborg goes tomorrow," he said, "and then it's back to Boston, back to the lion's den." Lonborg went indeed, in a marvelously close and absorbing game that I watched mostly through Kleenex, having caught a pip of a cold in the winter exercises of the previous day. Two former Yankees settled it. In the Boston ninth, Elston Howard, who can no longer get his bat around on fast balls, looped a dying single to right to score two runs—a heartwarming and, it turned out, essential piece of luck, because Roger Maris hit a homer in the bottom half, to end Lonborg's string of seventeen scoreless innings. Maris, freed from his recent years of Yankee Stadium opprobrium, was having a brilliant Series.

Laid low by too much baseball and a National League virus, I was unable to make it back to the lion's den, and thus missed the noisiest and most exciting game of the Series. I saw it on television, between sneezes and commercials. This was the game, it will be recalled, in which the Red Sox led by 1–0, trailed by 2–1, rallied to 4–2, were tied at 4–4, and won finally, 8–4, burying the Cardinal relief pitchers with six hits and four runs in the seventh. Brock had a single, a stolen base, and a home run. Yastrzemski had two singles and a left-field homer. Reggie Smith hit a homer; Rico Petrocelli hit *two* homers. This was the first Series game since the Cardinal-Yankee encounters in 1964 in which any team rallied to recapture a lost lead, which may account for the rather stately nature of most of the recent fall classics. My admiration went out not only to the Red Sox, for evening the Series after being two games down, but to Dick Williams, for having the extraordinary foresight to start a young pitcher named Gary Waslewski, who had spent most of the season in the minors, had not started a Boston game since July 29th, and had never completed a game in the major leagues. Waslewski didn't finish this one, either, but he held the Cards off until the sixth, which was enough. Williams' choice, which would have exposed him to venomous second-guessing if it had backfired, is the kind of courageous, intelligent patchworking that held his young, lightly manned team together over such an immense distance. In the opinion of a good many baseball people, his managerial performance this year is the best since Leo Durocher's miracles with the Giants in the early nineteen-fifties.

Nothing could keep me away from the final game of the year, the obligatory scene in which Lonborg, on only two days' rest, would face Gibson at last. Fenway Park, packed to the rafters, seemed so quiet in the early innings that I at first attributed the silence to my stuffed-up ears. It was real, though—the silence of foreboding that descended on all of us when Lou Brock hit a long drive off Lonborg in the first, which Yastrzemski just managed to chase down. Lonborg, when he is strong and his fast ball is dipping, does not give up high-hit balls to enemy batters in the early going. After that, everyone sat there glumly and watched it happen. Maxvill, the unferocious Cardinal shortstop, banged a triple off the wall in the third and then scored, and another run ensued when Lonborg uncorked a wild pitch. In time, it grew merely sad, and almost the only sounds in the park were the cries and horns from Cardinal owner Gussie Busch's box, next to the St. Louis dugout. Lonborg, pushing the ball and trying so hard that at times his cap flew off, gave up a homer to Gibson in the fifth, and then Brock singled, stole second, stole third, and came in on a fly by Maris. A fire broke out in a boxcar parked on a railway siding beyond left field, and several dozen sportswriters, looking for their leads, scribbled the note, ". . . as Boston championship hopes went up in smoke." Manager Williams, out of pitchers and ideas, stayed too long with his exhausted hero, and Javier hit a three-run homer in the sixth to finish Lonborg and end the long summer's adventure. The final score was 7–2. Gibson, nearly worn out at the end, held on and finished, winning his fifth successive Series victory (counting two against the Yankees in 1964), and the Cardinals had the championship they deserved. I visited both clubhouses, but I had seen enough champagne and emotion for one year, and I left quickly. Just before I went out to hunt for a cab, though, I ducked up one of the runways for a last look around Fenway Park, and discovered several thousand fans still sitting in the sloping stands around me. They sat there quietly, staring out through the half darkness at the littered, empty field and the big wall and the bare flagpoles. They were mourning the Red Sox and the end of the great season.

PEANUTS
by
SCHULZ
LET'S HUSTLE A LITTLE MORE ON THOSE FLY-BALLS!
C'MON! MOVE IN ON THOSE GROUNDERS! THROW THE BALL! DON'T HANG ON TO IT!
ALL RIGHT! EVERYBODY OVER HERE ON THE DOUBLE! LET'S GO!
MANAGER
OKAY, TEAM, THIS IS THE START OF A NEW SEASON, AND I HAVE A FEW WORDS TO SAY..
3-27
Tm. Reg. U. S. Pat. Off.—All rights reserved
©1966 by United Feature Syndicate, Inc.

NOW, I THINK NO ONE WILL DENY THAT SPIRIT PLAYS AN IMPORTANT ROLE IN WINNING BALL GAMES..
MANAGER
SOME MIGHT SAY THAT IT PLAYS THE MOST IMPORTANT ROLE..
THE DESIRE TO WIN IS WHAT MAKES A TEAM GREAT..WINNING IS EVERYTHING!
THE ONLY THING THAT MATTERS IS TO COME IN FIRST PLACE!
WHAT I'M TRYING TO SAY IS THAT NO ONE EVER REMEMBERS WHO COMES IN SECOND PLACE!
MANAGER
I DO, CHARLIE BROWN... IN 1928, THE GIANTS AND PHILADELPHIA FINISHED SECOND.. IN 1929, IT WAS PITTSBURGH AND THE YANKEES.. IN 1930, IT WAS CHICAGO AND WASHINGTON.. IN 1931, IT WAS THE GIANTS AND THE YANKEES.. IN 1932, IT WAS PITTSBURGH AND...
AND ANOTHER GREAT SEASON GETS UNDERWAY!
SCHULZ
MANAGER

THIS STORY was datelined Gainesville, Fla., March 30, 1965.

The Remarkable Mr. Trammell

ASSOCIATED PRESS

IF YOU HIT a grand-slam home run and two doubles in a baseball game, you've done a hard day's work. But what about the guy who does all that in one inning?

Allen Trammell, a junior outfielder on the University of Florida baseball team, did all those things and more in a recent game against Kentucky.

Folks at Florida claim it's a feat without equal in the history of the game.

The first time Trammell came to bat in the sixth inning, Kentucky was leading 1 to 0. With men on first and second base, Trammell doubled 340 feet off the left center-field fence to knock in the tying run. He scored a minute later.

The next time up in the same inning, Trammell had three men on the bases and he clouted a fast ball 345 feet over the left center-field fence.

Even though it was getting to be monotonous, Trammell, a 5-foot-11, 185-pound halfback borrowed from the football team, doubled 360 feet off the deep center-field fence, scoring a man who was on first. As before, he too scored.

When Kentucky finally got the side out, Trammell had his grand-slam homer, the two doubles, six runs batted in and had scored three runs himself.

On the strength of Trammell's performance, Florida scored 18 runs in the sixth inning and went on to beat Kentucky 25 to 1.

Bill Kinard, football backfield coach at Florida, heard what Trammell was doing and made his way toward the youth, who was back at his spot in left field.

Yelling from the side of the field, Kinard said, "Trammell, you get one more hit and you'll be back in pads tomorrow."

He then muttered, as he headed back to his spring football chores, "Keep those scouts away from him."

Trammell, in Florida's 11 games to date, is batting .512 and has hit safely in 20 straight contests, including the last nine of last season. He batted .370 last year.

THE FOLLOWING appeared at the turn of the century—when McGraw and Robbie were on the same team, the deathless old Orioles.

Baltimore's Lament

BALTIMORE AMERICAN

When the team from Podunk Center comes to
play in Baltimore,
We will see the game presented as it was in
days of yore.
When the score was in the hundreds as the
coming shades of night
Called it at the seventh inning, and the players
had a fight;
When 'twas "out" if any fielder caught the ball
on its first bound,
And they "crossed the runner out" before he'd
traveled halfway round.
Oh, they'll give us old-time Base Ball, with the
old-time sort of score,
When the team from Podunk Center comes to
play in Baltimore.

The Orioles will hustle for the annual cham-
pionship
Of the Turnpike League; they'll try to beat the
team from Hutner's Slip,
And the nine from Perkin's Crossing must play
ball its very best,
While the Punkintown star pitcher's curves will
be knocked "galley west."
The club from Sleepy Hollow will agree that
Jerry Nops
Has a way of giving pitchers' fancy inshoots
knockout drops.
"Oh, kill him! Kill the umpire!" will the bleach-
ers loudly roar
If the team from Podunk Center tries to win
from Baltimore.

Our "Mugs" McGraw will do his best to play
Base Ball and win,
And he'll wear some zephyr coaxers on his
broad, determined chin;
And "Robby," too, will say "B'gosh" and chew
a wisp of hay
To conceal his strong emotion when a liner
gets away.
The Turnpike League will have a pennant
made of green goods bright,
And each team will play to win it with all their
strength and might,
So we'll see the game played this year as it was
in years before.
When the team from Podunk Center comes to
play in Baltimore.

SOMEWHERE IN the *Second Fireside Book of Baseball,* a psychoanalyst goes to a ball game. Move over, Doctor.

Group Therapy for Ballplayers

DONOVAN BESS

WHEN THE SCORE is tied in the tenth inning and the shortstop misses a routine line drive, the pitcher is likely to develop some mean feelings—especially if the error loses the game for him.

This type of baseball problem has won the fascinated attention of a University of California behavioral scientist who has made some research proposals which, he suggests, could turn a second-division ball club into a World Series winner.

His investigations are of extreme interest in this week of the on-and-off tense struggle for the National League pennant. Next spring, he may well be on the Giants' consulting staff—unless the Dodgers hire him first.

The case of the pitcher's mean feelings, when the shortstop goofs, is on the order of interpersonal problems that many corporations are trying to beat through a method called "sensitivity training."

Men who work together daily are brought into group sessions where, under a psychologist's tutelage, they develop better teamwork through exchanging their honest feelings about one another.

By the initiative of Dr. Richard Barthol, a UC industrial psychologist, the entire UCLA baseball team last spring enrolled in a fifteen-week "sensitivity group." They met for two hours every week, in two groups of ten. Each group was in the charge of two psychologists.

The main thing that happened to these twenty young men, said Professor Barthol, is that they stopped playing the "jock" game. (A "jock" is a man who feels he must clap a teammate hard on the shoulder, when greeting him, and must spout obscenity and in general be animalistic.)

Such he-man posturing cuts people off from one another and produces athletic inefficiency, Dr. Barthol said.

"In our culture, boys and men in general are raised to believe that soft feelings of affection, love and grief are not manly," the psychologist said. "For example, fathers and mothers will tell a five-year-old boy, 'Now stop crying—be a little man.'

"Many athletes believe they are supposed to have different kinds of feelings from the rest of us, and they call themselves 'jocks.'"

He said the sessions showed these young college men they were complex human beings with a need to share their real feelings, even in the locker room.

"The point is," said Dr. Barthol, "they cope better with reality. If they are angry in the game, they are less likely to use their athletic skills as well."

His research included putting a stopwatch on about fifty major-league ballplayers and observing their batting habits. All of the men (except one) watched the ball after hitting it, he said—and their median time of delay before running was .5 seconds.

That is a big hunk of time to lose when, according to his stopwatch, the major-league dash to first base tends to take about 4.2 seconds.

"The only player who consistently just ran, and didn't stop to watch the ball," the psychologist said, "was Willy Mays." (He said Mays sometimes watched when he hit home runs, apparently alerted somehow to the fact that the ball was going out of the park.)

Dr. Barthol said he could cure the ball-watching habit by applying "some very elementary psychological principles." He declined to detail his strategy.

The UCLA professor said there is much room for "empirical studies" of baseball by behavioral scientists. One fruitful study, he suggested, would be to test his theory that the use of diminutives by players encourages infantile (and inefficient) game play.

He cited an example—when the shortstop, acting as the team "take-charge man"—yells at the pitcher, "Humm, Jackie-baby!" This is a double diminutive: "baby" plus "little Jack."

(History is replete with examples. George Herman Ruth, a 220-pounder, was known as "the Babe" or "the Bambino." Young players bought at very high prices, for future use, are called "bonus babies.")

"This custom," said Professor Barthol, "implies the player is childlike, naïve, and small. The question I raise is: Would it be more effective to use active, strong masculine names?" One possibility, he said, would be for the take-charge men to shout something more like, "Come on, TIGER!"

The psychologist attacked the tendency of many managers to take out a good left-handed hitter when he's confronted with a left-handed pitcher in a game crisis.

"The managers say they're playing the percentages," he said. "I believe they are showing superstitious behavior."

Dr. Barthol said he also hoped research would be done into the meet-the-ball syndrome.

"Managers often tell the players all they have to do is just meet the ball, to hit well," he said. "But this causes confusion in the batter's mind because, meanwhile, he hears his teammates and the fans yelling at him, 'Murder the ball.' "

Overall, Dr. Barthol believes that big-league baseball players would play better ball after enriching their personalities—including developing intellectual interests. He believes field research would prove this.

THE VETERAN Les Biederman, sports editor of the Pittsburgh *Press*, assembles here some little-known facts surrounding one of baseball's best-known facts—the record-breaking 61 home runs hit by Roger Maris in 1961.

Pressure, Pressure

LES BIEDERMAN

SOME ATHLETES are made for the headlines and could live twenty-four hours a day in the white glare of the spotlight. This is their element. But then there are some who can't stand it.

One of those who couldn't care less for the spotlight and the publicity it brings is Roger Maris. He never was a person who wanted much attention, but his feats with the bat drew the spotlight to him.

Those who know Roger Maris say there are two sides to the man: He's cold, impersonal on the field but warm and friendly off the field.

Somebody once summed up Maris this way: His failure resulted from his success. He hit 61 home runs in 1961 as a Yankee and caught lightning in a bottle. Fame was thrust on him and he didn't know what to do with it.

"I never wanted all this notoriety," he told a friend. "I was content to be known as a good ballplayer. Maybe hit 25 to 35 home runs a year, drive in 100 runs and bat somewhere between .290 and .300. And I wanted to help win pennants."

Then came the deluge: the first man to beat the fabulous home-run record of Babe Ruth. And playing for a New York team at that.

Who wrote this script?

"It was a freak year in 1961," Maris, now a Cardinal, admits. "Everything broke perfectly for me. I missed just a game or so, was free of injuries.

"Every time I swung it seemed to be just right. If I had hit under the ball a fraction of an inch more, many of those homers would have been pop-ups. A fraction of an inch higher, they might have been infield outs."

Maris had quite a year in 1961: 61 home runs and 142 RBIs on a batting average of only .269. He had 159 hits and 61 were homers but 81 of his 159 hits were for extra bases.

Pressure, pressure: To sum up his career briefly, Maris never sought fame and never did enjoy it when it came.

Going down the stretch after Ruth's record, he had to face microphones every day. It was a mental strain and he even began to lose his hair.

Maris was not equipped by experience or temperament to handle the flood of publicity that accompanied his record-breaking home-run year and the season that followed in 1962.

His salary jumped from $37,000 to $72,000 and in the last two seasons with the Yankees (1965-66) he hit only 21 home runs. This averages out to about $6,800 a homer.

Injuries, injuries: Jim Ogle, who covers the Yankees for a Newark paper, knows Maris well and wrote a book about him after the 61-home-run season.

"He's essentially an introvert and became more of an introvert after the spotlight began to focus on him," Ogle says. "Even the Yankee front office hindered him.

"It was no secret when Mickey Mantle and Maris were running neck and neck after Ruth's record. Yankee brass rooted for Mickey. Roger had no ill feeling for Mickey, but it hurt him to think the front office would show a preference."

Injuries began to haunt Maris in 1965. Late in April he severely pulled a muscle making a catch and was out 26 games. Not long after he returned, he slid home and the little finger of his right hand came in contact with the umpire's foot and the finger was dislocated.

One day he heard something pop in his

hand. Instead of having X-rays immediately, the Yankees fumbled the ball. They discovered three months after the injury through X-rays the necessity for an operation.

Almost retired: Maris was disgusted and disillusioned last year with the Yankees. He had a bad season and so did the Yankees, finishing tenth.

He had injuries, disappointments and absences from his wife and six children.

"I made up my mind in the middle of the 1966 season this would be my last year;" he said. "When I returned to Yankee Stadium I told Ralph Houk what my decision was.

"But they traded me to the Cardinals and I still was considering retirement. But Stan Musial sent me the same contract and then left me alone to work out my problems.

"He was a player and he took the player's viewpoint. Then one day he called me and I was in the right mood and I said yes."

* * * *

During the winter meetings of 1959, the Pirates almost traded Dick Groat to Kansas City for Maris. The deal fell through and Maris went to the Yankees.

In 1960 both Groat and Maris became Most Valuable Players in their respective leagues. Suppose the Pirates and A's had made that deal in 1959—wouldn't the course of baseball history have been changed?

CHARLES O'GLASS

35
DRINK
BUY
20

35
DRINK
BUY
20
O'Glass

WHETHER YOU'RE a science-fiction fan or not, we'll wager that (a) you didn't expect to open up a baseball anthology and find something from a magazine called *If*, and (b) you'll find this novelette enjoyable indeed. Incidentally, this marks the only duplication of titles in the *Fireside* library. "Who's on First?" was the name of a piece in the first volume in this set too. That one, of course, was in fealty to Abbott and Costello.

Who's on First?

LLOYD BIGGLE, JR.

Priority Rating: Routine
From: Jard Killil, Minister of Juvenile Affairs
To: All Planetary Police Organizations
All Interplanetary Patrol Units
Subject: Juvenile detention escapee Muko Zilo
Enclosures: Character analysis, film strips, retinal patterns

All law enforcement agencies are hereby informed of the escape of Muko Zilo from the Juvenile Rehabilitation Center on Philoy, Raff III, Sector 1311. Escapee is presumed to have fled the planet in a stolen space yacht, Stellar Class II, range unlimited. His probable destination is unknown.

Escapee is not considered dangerous. He possesses low-grade intelligence and has no psi *ability higher than Class F.*

Kindly notify Philoy JRC immediately upon detention.

The major league baseball season of 1998 was only two weeks old, and Manager Pops Poppinger wished it was over and done with. Since opening day his Pirates had managed to lose fourteen games while winning none, and Pops had only the Baseball Managers' Tenure act of 1993 to thank for the fact that he was still gainfully employed. As a matter of fact, he had that same Act to thank for his regular paychecks during the 1996 and 1997 seasons.

"But it can't last," he muttered. "Congress will repeal the thing and cite me as the reason."

He strode through the locker room without a glance at his lounging ballplayers, entered his private office, and slammed the door. He did not want to talk to anyone, especially if that anyone happened to be wearing a Pirate uniform. He dropped an armful of newspapers onto his desk, tilted back in his chair until he could get his size-thirteen feet in a comfortable position, and opened the top paper to the sports pages. The headline made him wince. "WHEN IS A PIRATE?" it demanded. Pop stuck a cigar in his mouth as he read and forgot to light it.

"In the venerable days of yore," the article said, "when professional athletic organizations found it necessary to attach themselves to some unfortunate city in the mistaken belief that civic loyalty would induce the population to attend games in person and pay for the privilege, the fair city of Pittsburgh spawned two notable gangs of thieves, the baseball Pirates and the football Steelers. Both organizations had their days of glory. The record book says, if you care to believe it, that back in the seventies the Pirates won five consecutive world championships and the Steelers four.

"Those days of myth and fable are far behind us. If the Steelers stole anything during the football season just concluded, it escaped this writer's attention. The 1998 Pirates are so far removed from thievery that they will not take a game as a gift. They emphatically demonstrated their moral uprightness yesterday, when their opposition was stricken with that most tragic of baseball diseases, paralytic generosity. The Dodgers committed six errors and presented the Pirates with nine unearned runs. The Dodgers won, 27 to 9."

Pops carefully folded the paper and tossed

it over his shoulder. "Bah!" he said, striking a match. He puffed deeply. "Bah! Let 'em rave. It's for sure I ain't got any ballplayers, but I got lots of tenure."

The telephone rang, and he picked it up and growled a response.

"Who's pitching today, Pops?" a cheerful voice asked.

"I dunno," Pops said. "If you find some guy up there in the press box that ain't got a sore arm, send him down."

He slammed down the phone and reached for another paper. "PIRATES STILL IN REVERSE," a headline said. Pops tossed that one aside without reading it.

A knock rattled the door, and it opened wide enough to admit the large, grinning face of Dipsey Marlow, the Pirates' third-base coach.

"Scram!" Pops snapped.

"Some kid here to see you, Pops."

"Tell him I got a bat boy. I got a whole team of bat boys."

"He's older than that—I think. He's got a letter for you."

Pops straightened up and grinned. "From Congress?"

"It's from Pete Holloway."

"Send him in."

The kid shuffled in awkwardly. His dimensions looked to be about five feet five inches—in both directions. Oddly enough, he was not fat—in fact, there was an unhealthy thinness about his freckled face, and his overly large ears gave his features a whimsical grotesqueness—but he was shaped like a box, and he moved like one. He dragged to a stop in front of Pops's desk, fumbled through four pockets, and came up with a letter.

"Mr. Poppinger?"

The high, squeaky voice made Pops's ears ring. "I'm ashamed to admit it," Pops said, "but that's my name."

"Mr. Holloway told me to give this to you."

"The last I heard of Pete Holloway, he was lost in the woods up in Maine."

"He still is, sir. I mean, he's still in Maine."

"You came clear out here to California just to give me this?"

"Yes, sir."

Pops took the envelope and ripped it open.

"Dear Pops," he read. "This here kid Zilo is the most gawdawful ballplayer I ever see on two legs. He is also the luckiest man south of the North Pole. Put him in center with a rocking chair and a bottle of beer and every ball hit to the outfield will drop in his lap. He'll even catch some of them. Sign him, and you'll win the pennant. Yours, Pete. P.S. He is also lucky with the bat."

Pops scratched his head and squinted unbelievingly at Zilo. "What d'ya play?"

"Outfield," Zilo said. He quickly corrected himself. "Outfield, sir."

"Where in the outfield?"

"Anywhere, sir. Just so it's the outfield, sir."

Pops wasn't certain whether he should throw him out or go along with the gag. "I got three outfielders that get by. How about second or short? Between first and third I got nothing but grass."

"Oh, no, sir. Mr. Holloway had me play short, and I made nine errors in one inning. Then he moved me to the outfield."

"I'm surprised he didn't kill you," Pops said. "But you played ball for Pete?"

"Yes, sir. Last summer, sir. I went to see him a week ago to find out when I could start playing again, and he said he thought you could use me because your season started before his did."

"What'd you bat?"

"Six forty, sir."

Pops winced. "What'd you field?"

"A thousand, sir. In the outfield. It was—zero, in the infield."

Pops got up slowly. "Son, Pete Holloway is an old friend of mine, and he never gave me a bad tip yet. I'll give you a tryout."

"That's very kind of you, sir."

"The name is Pops. And it ain't kind of me after what happened yesterday."

Pops was standing in the corner of the dugout with Ed Schwartz, the club secretary, when the new Pirate walked out onto the field. Pops took one look, clapped his hand to his forehead, and gasped, "My God!"

"I told you I'd find him a uniform," Ed said. "I didn't guarantee to find him one that fit. He just isn't made the way our uniforms are made, and if I were you I'd make sure I wanted to keep him before I called the tailor. Otherwise, if you release him we'll have a set of uniforms on our hands that won't fit anyone or anything except maybe that oversized water cooler in the league offices."

Pops walked over to the third-base coaching box, where Dipsey Marlow was standing to watch batting practice. The Dodger dugout had just got its first incredulous look at Zilo, and Pops waited until the uproar subsided somewhat before he spoke.

"Think Pete is pulling my leg?" he asked.

"It wouldn't be like Pete, but it's possible."

"The way things is going, he ought to know better. I'll look him up when the season is over and shoot him."

Dipsey grinned happily. He was rather pleased with himself in spite of yesterday's loss. As third-base coach he'd been the loneliest man in the western hemisphere for seven straight days while the Pirates were being shut out without a man reaching third. Even if his team was losing, he liked to have some traffic to direct.

"You got nothing to lose but ball games," he said.

Zilo had taken his place in the batter's box. He cut on the first pitch, and the ball dribbled weakly out toward the pitcher's mound.

"He's a fly swatter," Dipsey said disgustedly.

Zilo poked two more lazy ground balls back at the pitcher and lifted a pop fly to the third baseman. Apparently satisfied, he borrowed a glove and wandered out to left field. He dropped a couple of balls that were hit right at him and stumbled over his own feet trying to reach one a few steps to his left.

"It's a joke," Pops said. "Pete must have seen him catch one. That's what he means by him being lucky."

Dipsey walked out to left field to talk with Zilo. He came back looking foolish. "The kid says it's all right—he's just testing the atmosphere, or something like that. It'll be different when the game starts."

"He says he hit six forty," Pops said dreamily.

"You going to use him?"

"Sure I'll use him. If I'm gonna shoot Pete, I gotta have a reason that'll stand up in court. As soon as we get ten runs behind, in he goes."

Pops headed back toward the dugout, and the tourists in the grandstand lifted a lusty chorus of boos. Pops scowled and ducked into the dugout out of sight. The dratted tourists were ruining the game. There had been a time when a manager could concentrate on what he was doing, but now he had to operate with a mob of howling spectators literally hanging over his shoulder and shouting advice and criticism into his ears. It got on the players' nerves, too. There was the Giants' Red Cowan, who'd been a good pitcher until they opened the game to tourists. The noise so rattled him that he had to retire.

"Why can't they stay home and see it on TV, like everybody else?" Pops growled.

"Because they pay money, that's why," Ed Schwartz said. "There's a novelty or something in seeing a ball game in the flesh, and it's getting so some of these tourists are planning their vacations so they can take in a few games. Bill Willard—you know, the L. A. *Times* man—he was saying that the National League is now California's number one tourist attraction. The American League is doing the same thing for Arizona."

"I don't mind their watching," Pops said, "if only they'd keep their mouths shut. When I started managing there wasn't anyone around during a game except the TV men, and they were too busy to be giving me advice. Even the sports writers watched on TV. Now they camp here the whole season, and you can't go out after the morning paper without finding one waiting for an interview."

"The tourists are here to stay, so you might as well get used to them. There's even some talk about putting up hotels for them, so they won't have to commute from Fresno to see the games."

Pops sat down and borrowed Ed's pen to make out his lineup. Ed looked over his shoulder and asked, "How come you're not using that new guy?"

"I'm saving him," Pops said, "until we get far enough behind."

"You mean until the second inning?" Ed said, and ducked as Pops fired a catcher's mask.

"That's the trouble with those tenure laws," Pops said. "They had to go and include the club secretaries."

The game started off in a way sadly familiar to Pops. The Dodgers scored three runs in the first inning and threatened to blast the Pirates right out of the league. Then, with the bases loaded and one out, the Pirate third baseman managed to hang onto a sizzling line drive and turn it into a double play. Pops's breathing spell lasted only until the next inning. Lefty Effinger, the Pirate pitcher, spent a long afternoon falling out of one hole into another. In nine innings he gave up a total of seventeen hits, but a miraculous sequence of picked-off runners, overrun bases and double plays kept the Dodgers shut out after those first three runs.

In the meantime, Dodger pitcher Rube Ruster was having one of his great days. He gave up a scratch single in the second and a walk in the fourth, and by the ninth inning he had fanned twelve, to the gratification of the hooting, jeering tourists.

The last of the ninth opened with Ruster striking out the first two Pirates on six pitches, and the Pirates in the dugout started sneaking off to the dressing room. Then first baseman

Sam Lyle ducked away from an inside pitch that hit his bat and blooped over the infield for a single. Pops called for the hit-and-run, and the next batter bounced the ball at the Dodger shortstop. The shortstop threw it into right field, and the runners reached second and third. Ruster, pacing angrily about the mound, walked the next batter on four pitches.

Pops jumped from the dugout and called time. "Hit six forty, did he?" he muttered, and yelled, "Zilo!"

The beaming Zilo jumped up from the far end of the bench. "Yes, sir?"

"Get out there and hit!"

"Yes, sir!"

He shuffled toward the plate, and the uproar sent up by the tourists rocked the grandstand. Dipsey Marlow called time again and hurried over to the dugout.

"You off your rocker? We got a chance to win this one."

"I know," Pops said.

"Then get that thing out of there and use a left-hander."

"Look," Pops said, "you know derned well the way Ruster is pitching we're lucky to get a loud foul off of him. That hit was luck, and the error was luck, and the base on balls happened only because Ruster got mad. He'll cool off now, and the only thing that keeps this going is luck. Pete says the kid's lucky, and I want some of it."

Marlow turned on his heel and stalked back to the coaching box.

Ruster coiled up and shot a bullet at home plate. Zilo swatted at it awkwardly—and popped it up.

The second baseman backed up three steps, waved the rest of the infield away, and got ready to end the game. The Pirate base runners, running furiously with two out, came down the stretch from third in a mournful procession. Zilo loped along the base path watching the Dodger second baseman and the ball.

The ball reached the top of its arc and suddenly seemed to carry. The second baseman backed confidently into position, changed his mind, and backed up again. Suddenly he whirled and raced toward center field with his eyes on the misbehaving ball. The center fielder was jogging toward the infield, and he picked up speed and came at a rush. The second baseman leaped for the ball. The center fielder dove for it. Neither man touched it, and they went down in a heap as the ball frolicked away.

The lumbering Zilo crossed home plate before the startled right fielder could retrieve the ball. The Pirates had won, four to three, and they hoisted Zilo to their shoulders and bore him off to the dressing room. The Dodgers quitted the field to an enthusiastic chorus of boos.

Pops went to the Dodger dugout to claim the ball. When he returned he found Dipsey Marlow still standing in his third-base coaching box staring vacantly toward the outfield.

"Luck," Pops said and gently led him away.

Rodney Wilks, the Pirates' brisk little president, flew over from L.A. that evening and threw a victory celebration in the ultramodern building that housed the National League offices. All of the players were there, and those who had families brought them. Women and children congregated in one room and the men in another. Champagne and milk flowed freely in both rooms.

National League President Edgar Rysdale looked in on the party briefly but approvingly. A team in a slump was bad for all the teams—bad for the league. When the race was a good one, fans frequently paid a double TV fee, watching two games at once or, if they had only one set, switching back and forth. If one team was floundering, National League fans would watch only one game. They might even patronize the American League. So the victory pleased the league president and also the other owners, who stopped by to sample the champagne and talk shop with Wilks.

Even Fred Carter, the Dodger manager, did not seem mournful, though Zilo's freak pop fly had ruined a nine-game winning streak for him. He backed Pops into a corner and said with a grin, "I been watching pop flies for thirty-five years, and I never saw one act like that. Did the kid magnetize his bat, or something?"

Pops shrugged. "I been watching baseball forty-five years, and I see something new seven times a week."

"Just the same, the next time that kid comes up I pass out the butterfly nets. He don't look like much of a hitter. Where'd you get him?"

"Pete Holloway sent him out."

Carter arched his eyebrows. "He must have something then."

"Pete says he ain't got a thing except luck."

"Isn't that enough? Think I'll go over and watch the Reds and Giants. Want to come?"

"Nope. Now that I finally won one, I'm gonna get some sleep tonight."

Pops saw Ed Schwartz talking with Zilo, and he went over to see what line the club secretary might be handing out. Ed was talking about the old days, and Zilo was listening intently, his dark eyes sparkling.

"Each team had its own city," Ed said, "and its own ball park. Think of the waste involved. There were twenty-four teams in each league, forty-eight parks, and even during the playing season they were in use only half the time, when the teams were playing at home. And the season only lasted six months. And there was all that traveling. We froze one day in Montreal and baked the next in New Orleans. Our hotel bill for the season used to look like the national debt, not to mention the plane fares. It was rough on the players in other ways. They only saw their families when they were playing at home, and just as they got settled somewhere they'd be traded and maybe have to move clear across the country—only to be traded again the next season or even the next week. Putting the entire league in one place solved everything. The climate is wonderful, and we almost never have a game postponed because of bad weather. We're down to eight teams in a league, which anyway is as many as the fans can keep track of. We have two fields, and they're used twice a day, for two afternoon and two night games. Each team has its own little community. Baseball, Cal., is growing, boy, and lots of players are settling here permanently and buying their own homes. You'll want to, too. It's a wonderful place."

"It's a soft place for club secretaries," Pops growled. "Ed used to have to worry about baggage, plane schedules, hotel reservations and a million and one other things. Now all he has to do is get the equipment moved a couple of hundred yards from one park to the other, now and then, and he gripes about it. Has he stopped talking long enough to get you settled?"

"Oh, yes, sir," Zilo said. "I'm rooming with Jerry Fargo."

"All right. Come out early tomorrow. You gotta learn to catch a fly ball without getting hit on the head."

Dipsey Marlow nudged Pops's arm and pulled him aside. "Going to play him tomorrow?"

"Might. We could use a little luck every day."

"I been listening to the big boys. Know what they're going to do? Put up a flock of temporary stands at World Series time. They think they might get fifteen thousand people out here for every game."

"That's their business," Pops said.

"Just tell me why anyone wants to take a trip and pay a stiff price to see a ball game when he can sit at home in his easy chair and see it for fifty cents?"

"People are funny," Pops said. "Sometimes they're almost as funny as ballplayers."

President Wilks came over and placed a full glass in Pops's hand. Pops sipped the champagne and grimaced. "It's all right, I guess, but it'll never take the place of beer."

"Finish in first division," Wilks said, "and I'll buy you enough beer to take you through the off season."

Pops grinned. "How about putting that in my contract?"

"I will," Wilks promised. "Do you want it in bottles or kegs?"

"Both."

"I'll take care of it first thing in the morning." He grinned and prodded Pops in the ribs, but behind the grin his expression was anxious. "Do you think we have a chance?"

"Too early to say. Sure, we only won one out of fifteen, but we're only ten games out of first. We been looking like a bunch of school kids, and if we keep that up we finish last. If we snap out of it—well, the season's got a long way to go."

"I hope you snap out of it," Wilks said. "Managers have tenure, but presidents haven't."

Pops found a bottle of beer to kill the taste of the champagne, and he made a quiet exit after instructing Marlow to get the players home to bed at a reasonable hour. The National League's two playing fields were a blaze of light, and the shouts of the two crowds intermingled. There seemed to be a lot of tourists in attendance—and tourists at night games made even less sense than tourists at afternoon games. It'd be nine or ten o'clock before some of them got back to their hotels. Pops walked slowly back to Pirateville, grumbling to himself. The large mansion designed for the manager Pops had turned over to Dipsey Marlow, who needed space for his eight kids. Pops lived in a small house a short distance down the street. His middle-aged daughter Marge kept house for him, and she was already in bed. She didn't like baseball.

Priority Rating: Routine
From: Jard Killil, Minister of Juvenile Affairs
To: All Planetary Police Organizations, Sectors 1247, 2162, 889, 1719
All Interplanetary Patrol Units, Sectors 1247, 2162, 889, 1719

Subject: Juvenile Detention Escapee Muko Zilo
Reference: Previous memorandum of 13B927D8 and enclosures

Information from several sources indicates that an unidentified ship, possibly that of Escapee Zilo, traveled on a course roughly parallel to Trade Route 79B, which would take it into or through your sectors. Because of the time elapsed since his escape, it is assumed that Zilo has found an effective planetary hiding place. Immediate investigation requested. Escapee is not—repeat not—dangerous.

Kindly notify Philoy JRC immediately upon detention.

Pops opened a three-game series against the Cubs with Zilo in left field. He figured the youngster would do the least damage there, since he was pitching Simp Simpson, his best right-hander, and the Cubs had seven left-handed batters in their lineup. At least that much of his strategy worked. In the first six innings only two balls were hit to left. One was a line drive single that Zilo bobbled for an error as the runner reached second. The other was a foul fly on which Zilo seemed about to make a miraculous catch until his feet got tangled and spilled him. At the plate he waved his bat futilely and struck out twice while the Cubs were taking a five-run lead.

In the last of the sixth the Pirates got men on first and second, and it was Zilo's turn to bat. Dipsey Marlow called time, and as the tourists hooted impatiently he strode back to the dugout. "Take him out," he said.

"Why?" Pops asked. "He's still batting .333. That's better than anyone else on this team."

"You gotta understand this luck thing. Yesterday it was luck to put him in. Today it's luck to take him out. I found a spider in my locker today, and that means . . ."

"Hit and run on the first pitch," Pops said.

Zilo fanned the air lustily and dribbled a grounder toward the first baseman. Suddenly it took an unaccountable eight-foot bounce over his head and rolled into the outfield, picking up speed. Zilo pulled up at first, breathing heavily, and the two runners scored.

Sam Lyle followed with a lazy fly ball to right. Zilo moved off first base and halted to watch the progress of the ball. The right fielder seemed to be having difficulties. He wandered about shading his eyes, backed up, finally lost the ball in the sun. The center fielder had come over fast, and he shouted the right fielder away, backed up slowly, and finally turned in disgust to watch the ball drop over the fence. Lyle trailed the floundering Zilo around the bases, and the score was 5 to 4.

Three fast outs later, Dipsey Marlow returned to the dugout and squeezed in beside Pops. "I take it all back," he said. "I won't argue with you again the rest of the season. But this spider of mine . . ."

Pops cupped his hands and shouted, "Let's HOLD 'em now. Let's WIN this one!"

". . . this spider of mine was in my sweat shirt, and my old mother always used to say spider in your clothes means money. Will the players get a cut of what those fifteen thousand tourists pay to watch a series game?"

"We got two hundred and twenty-four games to go," Pops said. "After this one. Get to work and pick us off a sign or two."

In the eighth inning Zilo got a rally started with a pop fly that three infielders chased futilely. He moved to second on a ground ball that took a bad hop and scored on a soft line drive that curved sharply and landed between the outfielders. The Pirates pushed over two more runs on hits that were equally implausible and took a two-run lead into the ninth.

The Cubs came back with a vengeance. The first two batters lashed out sizzling singles. Pops prodded his bullpen into action and went out to talk with Simpson. They stood looking down at the next Cub batter, the burly catcher Bugs Rice.

"Don't let him pull one," Pops said.

"He won't pull one," Simp said determinedly through clenched teeth.

Rice did not pull one. He didn't have to. He unloaded on the first pitch and drove it far, far away into left field, the opposite field. Pops sat down with the crack of the bat and covered his face with his hands.

"Now we gotta come from behind again," he moaned. "And we won't. I know we ain't *that* lucky."

Suddenly the men on the bench broke into excited cheers and a scattering of applause came from the tourists. Pops looked up, saw runners on second and third, saw the scoreboard registering one out.

"What happened?" he yelped.

"Zilo caught it," Dipsey Marlow said. "Didn't think he had it in him, but he backed up to the fence and made a clean catch. Took so much time getting the ball back to the infield that the runners had time to touch up and advance, but he caught it."

"He didn't. I know a homer when I see one, and that ball was gone. I can tell by the way it sounds and I can tell by the way it leaves the bat. I heard that one, and I saw it go. It should have cleared the fence by twenty feet."

"Your eyes aren't as young as they used to be. Zilo caught it against the fence."

Pops shook his head. He huddled down in a corner of the dugout while Simpson fanned one batter and got another on a tap to the infield and the Pirates had won two in a row.

That was the beginning. The Pirates pushed their winning streak to twelve, lost one, won eight more. They were twenty and fifteen and in fourth place. Zilo became something of a national sensation. Lucky Zilo Fan Clubs sprang up across the country, and he kept his batting average around the .450 mark and even got another home run when a solid fly ball to the outfield took crazy bounces in nineteen directions while Zilo lumbered around the bases. The rest of the team took courage and started playing baseball.

But not even a Lucky Zilo could lift the Pirates above fourth place. Pops's pitching staff was a haphazard assortment of aching, overage veterans and unpredictable, inexperienced youths. One day they would be unhittable, the next day they'd be massacred; and Pops found to his sorrow that luck was no answer to a nineteen-run deficit. Still, the season drifted along with the Pirates holding desperately to fourth, and Pops began to think they might even stay there.

Then Zilo sprained his ankle. The trainer outfitted him with crutches and applied every known remedy and a few unknown ones that Zilo suggested himself, but the ankle failed to respond.

"It beats me," the trainer said to Pops. "Things that should make it better seem to make it worse."

"How long will he be out?" Pops asked gloomily.

"I won't even guess. The way it's reacting, it could last him a lifetime."

Pops breathed a profane farewell to first division.

Zilo hobbled to every game on his crutches and watched with silent concentration from a box behind the dugout. Oddly enough, for a time the team's luck continued. Ground balls took freakish bounces, fly balls responded to unlikely air currents, and on some days opposition pitchers suffered such a loss of control that they would occasionally wander in and stare at home plate as though to assure themselves that it was still there. Ollie Richards, the Reds' ace and one of the best control pitchers in either league, walked seventeen men in three innings and left the game on the short end of a 6-to-3 score without having given up a hit.

Zilo's broad, good-natured face took on an unhealthy pallor. Wrinkles furrowed his brow, and his eyes held a tense, haunted look. As the team's luck began to fade, he grew increasingly irritable and despondent. On the day they slipped to fifth place, he met Pops after the game and asked, "Could I speak with you, sir?"

"Sure," Pops said. "Come along."

Pops held the door as Zilo swung through on his crutches. He got the youngster seated and settled back with his own feet propped up on his desk. "Ankle any better?"

"I'm afraid not, sir."

"Takes time, sometimes."

"Sir," Zilo said, "I know I'm not a good ballplayer. Like they say, I'm just lucky. Maybe this will be the only season I'll play."

"I wouldn't say that," Pops said. "You're young. Luck has took a lot of men a long way in baseball."

"Anyway, sir, I like to play, even if I'm not good. And I'd like to have us win the pennant and play in the World Series."

"Wouldn't mind having another winner myself before I retire."

"What I'd like to do, sir, is go home for a while. I think I could get my ankle fixed up there, and I'd like to bring back some friends who could help us."

Pops was amused. "Ballplayers?"

"I think they'd be better than I am, sir. Or luckier, maybe. Do you—would you give them a trial?"

"I'd give anyone a trial," Pops said seriously. "Mostly shortstops and second basemen and pitchers, but I'd have a look at anybody."

Zilo pushed himself erect on his crutches. "I'll get back as soon as I can."

"All right. But leave a little of that luck here, will you?"

Zilo turned and looked at Pops strangely. "I wish I could, sir. I really wish I could."

Ed Schwartz took Zilo to L.A. and put him on a plane for the east. For Maine. And at Baseball, Cal., the Pirates won two more games and went into a cataclysmic slump. They lost ten straight and slipped to sixth place. Pops put through a phone call to the Maine address Zilo had given him and was informed that there was no such place. Then he called Pete Holloway.

"I wondered what was happening to you," Pete said. "I haven't seen the kid. He dropped out of nowhere last summer and played a little sandlot ball for me. He never told me where he came from, but I don't think it was Maine. If he shows up again, I'll get in touch with you."

"Thanks," Pops said. He hung up slowly.

Ed Schwartz said thoughtfully, "I suppose I better get a detective on it."

"Detectives," Pops said and wearily headed for the field and another Pirate beating.

Two more weeks went by. The detectives traced Zilo to Maine, where he seemed to have vanished from the ken of mortal man. The Pirates were tottering on the brink of last place.

Then Pops received an airmail letter from Zilo—from Brazil.

"I got lost," he wrote plaintively. "We crashed in the jungle and they won't let us leave the country."

Pops called President Wilks into conference, and Wilks got on the phone to Washington. He knew enough of the right people to make the necessary arrangements and keep the matter out of the papers. Zilo was flown back on a chartered plane, and he brought four friends with him.

Ed Schwartz met them in L.A. and rushed them out to Baseball in President Wilks's own plane. They arrived during the fourth inning of another Pirate beating.

"How's the ankle?" Pops demanded.

Zilo beamed. "Just fine, sir."

"Get in there, then."

Zilo got his friends seated in the president's box and went out to loft a long fly ball over the fence for a home run. The Pirates came to life. Everyone hit, and a 10-to-0 drubbing was transformed like magic into a 25-to-12 victory.

After the game Zilo introduced his friends—as John Smith, Sam Jones, Robert White and William Anderson. Smith and Jones, Zilo said, were infielders. White and Anderson were pitchers.

Ed Schwartz took in their proportions with a groan and went to work on the uniform problem. Their builds were that of Zilo on a more lavish scale. They towered over Pops, answered his questions politely, and showed a childlike interest in all that went on about them.

Pops called one of his catchers over and introduced him to White and Anderson. "See what they got," he said.

He took Smith and Jones out for a little infield practice and watched goggle-eyed as they covered ground like jet-propelled gazelles and made breathtaking leaps to pull down line drives.

The catcher returned, drew Pops aside, and said awesomely, "They got curves that break three feet. They got sliders that do a little loop-the-loop and cross the plate twice. They got fast balls that I'm scared to catch. They got pitches that change speed four times between the mound and the plate. If you're figuring on pitching those guys, you can get yourself another catcher."

Pops turned the ceremony of signing them over to Ed Schwartz, handed releases to four players who weren't worth the space they were taking up on the bench, and went home to his first good night's sleep in more than a month.

Priority Rating: Urgent
From: Jard Killil, Minister of Juvenile Affairs
To: All Planetary Police Orzanizations
All Interplanetary Patrol Units
Subject: Juvenile detention escapees
Enclosures: Character Analyses, film strips, retinal patterns

All law enforcement agencies are hereby informed of the escape of four inmates of the Juvenile Rehabilitation Center on Philoy, Raff III, Sector 1311. Escapees have high psi *ratings and may use them dangerously. Kindly give this matter top priority attention and notify Philoy JRC immediately upon detention.*

The next day Pops started Anderson against the Braves. The Pirates bounced forty hits over and through and around the infield and scored thirty-five runs. Anderson pitched a no-hit game and struck out twenty-seven. White duplicated the performance the following day. Thereafter Pops pitched them in his regular rotation. He wasn't sure whether they hypnotized everyone on the field or just the ball, but as Dipsey Marlow put it, they made the ball do everything but stop and back up.

Pops's other pitchers suddenly began to look like champions with Smith and Jones playing behind them. In spite of their boxlike builds, they ranged about the infield with all the agility of jack rabbits. No one ever measured how high they went up after line drives, but one sports writer claimed they were a hazard to air traffic and should be licensed as aircraft. They sped far into the outfield after fly balls. Jones made more catches in right field than the right fielder, and it was not an unusual sight to see Jones and Smith far out in center centesting the right to a descending ball while the center fielder beat a hasty retreat. And both men swung murderous bats.

The Pirates had won fifty-seven games in a row and rewritten the record book when Zilo timidly knocked on the door of Pops's office. He was carrying a newspaper, and he looked disturbed.

"Sir," he said anxiously, "it says here that we're ruining baseball."

Pops chuckled. "They always say that when one team starts to pull away."

"But—is it true?"

"Well, now. If we kept on winning the way we are now, we wouldn't do the game any good. People like to see a close race, and if one team wins too much, or loses too much, a lot of people stop watching the games. And that ain't good. But don't let it worry you—we'll do our best to go on winning, but we'll drop a few, one of these days, and things will be back to normal. Your friends been playing over their heads and we've been luckier than usual. That can't last forever."

"I see," Zilo said thoughtfully.

That evening Pops ruefully wished he'd kept his big mouth shut. Talking about a slump when you're winning . . .

Anderson got knocked out in the first inning and lost his first game. White failed the next day, and the Pirates dropped five straight. Then they got off on another winning streak, but the talk about their ruining the game had quieted down. Pops never bothered to remind Zilo how right he'd been. He wasn't going to jinx the team again.

"Those baseball players of yours," his daughter said to him one evening. "You know—the funny-looking ones."

"Sure, I know," Pops said. "What about 'em?"

"They're supposed to be pretty good, aren't they?"

Pops grinned wickedly. "Pretty fair." It would have been a waste of time referring Marge to the record book—or what was left of it now.

"I was over at the bowling alley with Ruth Wavel, and they were there bowling. They had everybody excited."

"How'd they do?"

"I guess they must be pretty good at that, too. They knocked all the pins over."

Pops grinned again. Marge's idea of a sport was crossword puzzles, and she could go through an entire season without seeing a single game. "Nothing unusual about that," he said. "Happens all the time."

She seemed surprised. "Does it? The people there thought it was something special."

"Someone was pulling your leg. How many strikes did they get?"

"How many what?"

"How many times did they knock all the pins down?"

"I didn't count them. They knocked all of them down every time. All evening. It was the first time they'd ever bowled, too."

"Natural athletic ability," Pops muttered. He was thinking that they'd never played baseball before, either, except that Zilo told him he'd been coaching them. The more he thought about it, the odder it seemed, but he was not one to argue with no-hit games and home runs and sensational fielding plays. No manager would argue with those.

To all ships of the Space Navy Sectors 2161, 2162, 2163 General Alert Five escapees Juvenile Rehabilitation Center Philoy Raff III Piloting stolen space yacht Stellar Class II range unlimited have been traced through Sector 2162 destination unsurveyed quadrant C97 Contact base headquarters Sector 2162 for patrol assignments Acknowledge Zan First Admiral.

The season leveled into a five-team race for first place. The Pirates stayed in first or second, playing either with unbelievable brilliance or with incredible ineptitude. Pops took the race stoically and shrugged off the tourist hysteria that enveloped Baseball, Cal. He was doing so much better than he had thought possible in his wildest moments of pre-season optimism that it really didn't matter where he finished. He was a cinch to be Manager of the Year. He might add a pennant and a World Series, or he might not. It didn't matter.

Another season might see him in last place again, and a smart manager quit when he was ahead—especially when he was well along in his sixties. Pops called a news conference and announced his retirement at the end of the season.

"Before or after the World Series?" a reporter asked.

"No comment," Pops said.

The club owners erected their World Series stands early and the tourists jammed them—fifteen thousand for every game. Pops wondered where they came from. National League President Rysdale wandered about smiling fondly over the daily television receipts, and President Wilks sent Pops a load of beer that filled his basement.

Over in Baseball, Arizona, the American League officials were glum. The Yankees, who were mainly distinguished for having finished last more frequently than any other team in major league history, had suddenly and inexplicably opened up a twenty-game lead, and nobody cared any longer what happened in the American League.

"Three weeks to go," Pops told his team. "What d'ya say we wrap this thing up?"

"Right!" Zilo said happily.

"Right!" Smith, Jones, Anderson and White chorused.

The Pirates started on another winning streak.

To all ships of the Space Navy patroling unsurveyed quadrant C97 Prepare landing parties for planetary search This message your authorization to investigate any planet with civilization at level 10 or below Contact with civilizations higher than level 10 forbidden Space intelligence agents will be furnished each ship to handle high-civilization planets Acknowledge Zan First Admiral

The last week of the season opened with the Pirates in first place, five games ahead of the Dodgers. A provident schedule put the Dodgers and Pirates in a three-game series. The league hastily erected more stands, and with twenty-two thousand howling tourists in attendance and half of Earth's population watching on TV, White and Anderson put together no-hit games and the Pirate batters demolished the Dodger pitching staff. The Pirates took all three games.

Pops felt enormously tired, and relieved that it was finished. He had won his pennant and he didn't see how he could lose the World Series. But he had never felt so old.

President Wilks threw another champagne party, and the sports writers backed Pops into a corner and fired questions.

"How about that retirement, Pops? Still going through with it?"

"I've gone through with it."

"Is it true that Dipsey Marlow will take your place?"

"That's up to the front office. They ain't asked my opinion."

"What if they did ask your opinion?"

"I'd faint."

"Who'll start the series? Anderson or White?"

"I'll flip a coin," Pops said. "It don't matter. Either of them could pitch all thirteen games and not feel it."

"Does that mean you'll go all the way with just Anderson and White?"

"I'll use four starters, like I have most of the season."

"Going to give the Yankees a sporting chance, eh?"

"No comment," Pops said.

President Wilks and League President Rysdale rescued him from the reporters and took him to Rysdale's private office.

"We have a proposal from the American League," Rysdale said. "We'd like to know what you think of it, and what you think the players would think of it. They want to split up the series and play part of the games here and part of them in Arizona. They think it would stir up more local interest."

"I wouldn't like it," Pops said. "What's wrong with the way it is now? Here one year, there the next year, it's fair to both sides. What do they want to do—travel back and forth between games?"

"We'd start out with four games here, and then play five in Arizona and the last four back here. Next year we'd start out with four in Arizona. It used to be done that way years ago."

"I know," Pops said. "But I like it better the way it is. One ball park is just like another, so why change around?"

"They think we would draw more tourists that way. As far as we're concerned, we're drawing capacity crowds now. It might make a difference in Arizona, because there are fewer population centers there."

"They just thought of it because it's in California this year," Pops said. "Next year they'd want to change back."

"That's a thought," Rysdale said. "I think I'll tell them it's too late to change, but we might consider it for next year. That'll give us time to figure all the angles."

"Good," Pops said. "Next year you can play in Brazil, for all I care."

In the hallway Pops encountered half a dozen of his players crowding around infielder Jones. "What's up?" he asked Dipsey Marlow.

"Just some horsing around. They were practicing high jumps, and Jones cleared nine feet."

"So?"

"That's a world record by six inches. I looked it up."

To Jard Killil, Minister of Juvenile Affairs Space ship presumed that of JRC escapees found down in jungle unsurveyed quadrant C97 Planet has type 17D civilization Intelligence agents call situation critical Am taking no action pending receipt of further instructions Requesting Ministry take charge and assume responsibility Zan First Admiral

Pops retired early the night before the Series opened, having ordered his players to do the same. Marge was out somewhere, but Pops left the night light on and went to bed. He didn't sleep, but he was relaxing comfortably when she came in an hour later.

She marched straight through the house and into his bedroom. "Those ball players of yours —the funny-looking ones—they were at the bowling alley."

Pops took a deep breath. "They were?"

"They'd been drinking!"

Pops sat up and reached for his shoes. "You don't say."

"And they were bowling, only—they weren't bowling. They'd pretend to throw the ball but they wouldn't throw it, and the pins would fall down anyway. The manager was mad."

"No doubt," Pops said, pulling on his trousers.

"They wouldn't tell anyone how they did it, but every time they waved the ball all the pins would fall down. They'd been drinking."

"Maybe that's how they did it," Pops said, slipping into his shirt.

"How?"

"By drinking."

He headed for the bowling alley on a dead run. The place was crowded with players from other teams, American and National League, and quite a few sports writers were around. The writers headed for Pops, and he shoved them aside and found the manager. "Who was it?" he demanded.

"Those four squares of yours. Jones, Smith, Anderson, White."

"Zilo?"

"No. Zilo wasn't here."

"Did they make trouble?"

"Not the way you mean. They didn't get rough, though I had a time getting them away from the alleys. They left maybe ten minutes ago."

"Thanks," Pops said.

"When you find them, ask them how they pulled that gag with the pins. They were too drunk to tell me."

"I got some other things to ask them," Pops said.

He pushed through to a phone booth and called Ed Schwartz.

"I'll take care of it," Ed said. "Don't worry about a thing."

"Sure. I won't worry about a thing."

"They may be back at their rooms by now, but we won't take any chances. I'll handle it."

"I'll meet you there," Pops said.

He slipped out a side door and headed for Bachelor's Paradise, the house where the unmarried Pirates lived with a couple of solicitous houseboys to look after them. All the players were in bed—except Smith, Jones, Anderson, White and Zilo. The others knew nothing except that Zilo had been concerned about his friends' absence and had gone looking for them.

"You go home," Ed said. "I'll find them."

Pops paced grimly back and forth, taking an occasional kick at the furniture. "You find them," he said, "and I'll fine them."

He went home to bed, but he did not sleep. Twice during the night he called Ed Schwartz, and Ed was out. Pops finally reached him at breakfast time, and Ed said, trying to be cheerful, "No news is supposed to be good news, and that's what I have. No news. I couldn't find a trace of them."

The reporters had picked up the story, of course, and their headlines mocked Pops over his coffee: PIRATE STARS MISSING!

Ed Schwartz had notified both President Wilks and President Rysdale, and the league president had called in the FBI. By ten o'clock police in every city in the country and a number of cities in other countries were keeping their eyes open for missing Pirates. And they remained missing.

When Pops reached the field for a late-morning workout there was still no word. He banned newsmen from the field and dressing room, told Lefty Effinger he might have to start, and went around trying to cheer up his players. The players remembered only too well their fourteen-game losing streak at the beginning of the season and the collapse that followed Zilo's departure. The gloom hung so thickly in the dugout that if Pops could have thought of a market for it he'd have bottled and sold it.

An hour before game time, Pops was called to the telephone. It was Ed Schwartz, calling from L.A. "I found them," he said. "They're on their way back. They'll be there in plenty of time."

"Good," Pops said.

"Bad. They're still pretty high—all except Zilo. I don't know if you can use them, but that's your problem."

Pops slammed down the phone.

"Did they find 'em" Dipsey Marlow asked.

"Found 'em dead drunk."

Marlow rubbed his hands together. "Just let me at 'em. Ten minutes, and I'll have 'em dead sober. I've had experience."

"I dunno," Pops said. "These guys may not react like you'd expect."

The delinquent players were delivered with time to spare, and Marlow went to work enthusiastically. He started by shoving them into a cold shower, fully dressed. Zilo stood looking on anxiously.

"I'm sorry," he said to Pops. "I'd have

stopped them, but they went off without me. And they never had any of that alcohol before and they didn't know what it would do to them."

"That's all right," Pops said. "It wasn't your fault."

Zilo had tears in his eyes. "Do you think they can play?"

"Leave 'em to me," Marlow said. "I'm just getting started." But when he emerged later he looked both confused and frustrated. "I just don't know," he said. "They tell me they're all right, and they look all right, but I think they're still drunk."

"Can they play?" Pops asked anxiously.

"They can walk a straight line. I won't say how long a straight line. I suppose you got nothing to lose by playing them."

"There ain't much else I can do," Pops said. "I could start Effinger, but what would I use for infielders?"

There is something about a World Series. Even Pops, who had seen every one for forty-five years as player, manager or spectator, felt a momentary thrill and a clutching emptiness in his stomach as he moved to the top step of the dugout and looked out across the sunlit field. Along both foul lines the temporary stands were jammed with tourists. Beyond them areas were roped off for standees, and the Standing Room Only signs had been taken down hours before. There was no space left of any kind.

Ed Schwartz stood at Pops's elbow looking at the crowd. "What is it that's different about a hot dog when you buy it at a ball park?" he asked.

"Ptomaine," Pops growled.

Clutching his lineup, he strode toward home plate to meet the umpires and Yankee manager Bert Basom.

Basom grinned maliciously. "Your men well rested? I hear they keep late hours."

"They're rested well enough," Pops said.

A few minutes later, with the national anthem played and flag raised, Pops watched critically as Anderson took his last warm-up pitches. He threw lazily, as he always did, and if he was feeling any aftereffects it wasn't evident to Pops.

But Anderson got off to a shaky start. The Yankees' lead-off man clouted a tremendous drive to left, but Zilo made one of his sensational lumbering catches. The second batter drove one through the box. Jones started after it, got his feet tangled, and fell headlong. Smith flashed over with unbelievable speed, gloved the ball, and threw to first—too late. Anderson settled down then and struck out the next two batters.

Zilo opened the Pirates' half of the first with one of his lucky hits, and Smith followed him with a lazy fly ball that cleared the fence. The Pirates led, 2 to 0.

The first pitch to Jones was a called strike. Jones whirled on the umpire, his big face livid with rage. His voice carried over the noise of the crowd. "You wouldn't know a strike zone if I measured it out for you!"

Pops started for home plate, and Jones saw him coming and meekly took his place in the box. Pops called time and went over to talk to Dipsey Marlow.

"Darned if I don't think he's still tight. Think I should lift him?"

"Let him bat," Marlow said. "Maybe he'll connect."

The pitcher wasted one and followed it with a curve that cut the outside corner. "Strike two!" the umpire called.

Jones's outraged bellow rattled the center-field fence. "What?" he shrieked. He stepped around the catcher and stood towering over the umpire. "Where's the strike zone? Where was the pitch?"

The umpire gestured patiently to show where the ball had crossed the plate. Pops started out of the dugout again. The umpire said brusquely, "Play ball!"

Still fuming, Jones moved back to the batter's box. His high-pitched voice carried clearly. "You don't even know where the strike zone is!"

The pitcher wound up again, and as the ball sped plateward Jones suddenly leaped into the air—and stayed there. He hovered six feet above the ground. The ball crossed the plate far below his dangling legs, was missed completely by the startled catcher, and bounced to the screen.

The umpire did not call the pitch. He took two steps forward and stood looking up at Jones. The crowd came to its feet and players from both teams edged from their dugouts. A sudden paralyzed hush gripped the field.

"Come down here," the umpire called weakly.

"What'd you call that pitch? Strike, I suppose. Over the plate between my knees and armpits, wasn't it?"

"Come down here!"

"You can't make me."

"Come down here!"

"You show me where it says in the rules that I have to bat with both feet on the ground."

The umpire moved down the third base line and summoned his colleagues for a conference. Pops walked out to home plate, and Zilo followed him.

"Jones," Zilo said pleadingly.

"Go to hell," Jones said. "I know I'm right. I'm still in the batter's box."

"Please," Zilo pleaded. "You'll spoil everything. You've already spoiled everything."

"So what? It's about time we showed them how this game should be played."

"I'm taking you out, Jones," Pops said. "I'm putting in a pinch hitter. Get back to the dugout."

Jones shot up another four feet. "You can't make me."

The umpire returned. "I'm putting you out of the game," he said. "Leave the field immediately."

"I've already left the field."

Pops, Zilo and the umpire stood glaring up at Jones, who glared down at them. At that critical moment Smith took charge. He walked slowly to home plate, soared over the heads of those on the ground, and clouted Jones on the jaw. Jones descended heavily. Smith landed nearby, calmly drying his hands on his trousers.

Effective as his performance was, nobody noticed it. All eyes were on the sky, where a glistening tower of metal was dropping slowly toward the outfield. It came ponderously to rest on the outfield grass while the outfielders fled in panic. The crowd remained silent.

A port opened in the side of the looming tower, and a landing ramp came down. The solitary figure that emerged did not use the ramp. He stepped out into midair and drifted slowly toward the congregation at home plate. There he landed, a tremendous figure, square like Zilo and his friends but a startling eight feet tall, trimly uniformed in a lustrous brown with ribbons and braid in abundance.

Zilo, Jones and Smith stood with downcast eyes while the others stared. Anderson and White moved from the dugout and walked forward haltingly. The stranger spoke one crisp sentence that nobody understood—nobody, that is, except Zilo, Jones, Smith, Anderson and White.

Smith and Jones lifted slowly and floated out to the ship, where they disappeared through the port. Anderson and White turned obediently and trudged to the outfield to mount the ramp. Only Zilo lingered.

A few policemen moved nervously from the stands and surrounded the ship. The hush continued as the tourists stared and half of Earth's population watched on TV.

Pops looked from the ship to the lofty stranger to Zilo. Tears streaked Zilo's face.

"I'm sorry, Pops," Zilo said. "I hoped we could finish it off for you. I really wanted to win this World Series. But I'm afraid we'll have to go."

"Go where?" Pops asked absently.

"Where we came from. It's another world."

"I see. Then—then that's how come you guys played so well."

Zilo wiped his eyes and blubbered miserably. His big, good-natured face was in the throes of torment. "The others did," he sobbed. "I'm only a Class F telekinetic myself, and that isn't much where I come from. I guess you'd call me a moron. I did the best I could, but it was a terrible strain keeping the balls I hit away from the fielders and stopping balls from going over the fence and holding balls up until I could catch them. When I hurt my ankle I tried to help out from the bench, and it worked for a while. Sometimes I could even control the ball enough to spoil a pitcher's control, but usually when the ball was thrown fast or hit hard I couldn't do anything with it unless I was in the outfield and it had a long way to go. So I went back where I could get my ankle fixed, and I brought back the others. They're really good—all of them Class A. Anderson and White—those are just names I had them use—they could control the ball so well they made it look like they were pitching. And no matter how hard the ball was hit they could control it, even when they were sitting on the bench."

Pops scratched his head and said dazedly, "Made it *look* like they were pitching?"

"They just pretended to throw, and then they controlled the ball—well, mentally. Any good telekinetic could do it. They could have pitched just as well sitting on the bench as they did on the pitcher's mound, and they could help out when one of our other pitchers was pitching. And Smith and Jones are levitators. They could cover the ground real fast and go up as high as they wanted to. I had a terrible time keeping them from going too high and spoiling everything. I was going to bring a telepath, too, to steal signs and things, but the four were the only ones who'd come. But we did pretty good anyway. When we hit the ball Anderson and White could make it go anywhere they wanted, and they could control the balls the other team hit, and nothing could get past Smith and Jones unless we wanted it to. We could have won every game, but the papers said we were spoiling baseball, so we talked it over and decided to lose part of the time. We did the best we could. We won the pennant, and I hoped we would win this World Series, but they had to go and drink some of that alcohol, and I guess Jones would have spoiled everything even if we hadn't been caught."

The stranger spoke another crisp sentence, and Zilo wiped the tears from his face and shook Pops's hand. "Goodby, Pops," he said. "It was lots of fun. I really like this baseball."

He walked slowly out to the ship, passing the police without a glance, and climbed the ramp.

Reporters were edging out onto the field, and the stranger waved them back and spoke English in a booming voice. "You shall have a complete explanation at the proper time. It is now my most unpleasant duty to call upon your president to deliver the apologies of my government. Muko Zilo says he did the best he could. He did entirely too much."

He floated back to the ship. The ramp lifted, and the police scattered as the ship swished upward. The unpire-in-chief shrugged his shoulders and gestured with his mask. "Play ball!"

Pops beckoned to a pinch hitter, got a pitcher warming up to replace Anderson, and strode back to the dugout. "They been calling me a genius," he muttered to himself. "Manager of the Year they been calling me. And how could I lose?"

A sportswriter leaned down from the stands. "How about a statement, Pops?"

Pops spoke firmly. "You can say that the best decision I made this year was to resign."

An official statement was handed out in Washington before the game was over. That the Yankees won the game, 23 to 2, was irrelevant. No one cared, least of all the ballplayers.

Priority Rating: Routine
From: Jard Killil, Minister of Juvenile Affairs
To: Milz Woon, Minister of Justice
Subject: Escapees from the Juvenile Rehabilitation Center, Philoy, Raff III, Sector 1311

A full report on the activity of these escapees has no doubt reached your desk. The consequences of their offense are so serious they have not yet been fully evaluated. Not only have these escapees forced us into premature contact with a Type 17D civilization for which neither we nor they were prepared, but our best estimate is that the escapees have destroyed a notable cultural institution of that civilization. I believe that their ages should not be used to mitigate their punishment. They are all juveniles, but they are nevertheless old enough to know right from wrong, and their only motive seems to be that they were enjoying themselves. I favor a maximum penalty.

Baseball, as students of the game never tired of pointing out, was essentially a game of records and statistics. The records were there for all to see—incredible records, with Jones and Smith tied with a hundred and forty-two home runs and batting above .500, with Anderson and White each hurling two dozen no-hit games, and with the strikeouts, and the extra-base hits, and the double plays, and the games won, and the total bases, and the runs batted in, and the multitudinous individual and team records that the Pirates had marked up during the season. The record book was permanently maimed.

It was not the beginning of the end. It was the end.

Who had done all this? Four kids, four rather naughty kids, who, according to the strange man from outer space, were not especially bright. Four kids from another world, who had entered into a game requiring the ultimate in skill and intelligence and training and practice, entered into it without ever playing it before, and made the best adult ballplayers the planet Earth could offer look like a bunch of inept Little Leaguers.

The records could be thrown out, but they could not be forgotten. And it could not be forgotten that the four kids had made those records when they weren't half trying—because they didn't want to make Earth's ballplayers look too bad.

Supposing—just supposing—the people from outer space were to send a team made up of intelligent adults? No one cared to contemplate that possibility.

So it was the end. The Yankees took the World Series in seven straight games, and no one cared. The stands were empty, and so few people paid to see the games on TV that the series ended as a financial catastrophe. A committee met to decide what to do about the aliens' records and reached no decision. Again, no one cared. The various awards for the most valuable players and managers of the year and the various individual championships were never made. The oversight was not protested. People had other things on their minds.

And when a dozen TV comedy teams simultaneously resurrected an ancient, half-legendary, half-forgotten comedy sketch, they got no laughs whatsoever. The sketch was called "Who's on First?"

This Was Baseball—or Was It?

JIM BISHOP

IT WAS a picture day. The sun was warm, the clouds high and white, sailing like slow caravels across Ebbets Field. Uncle Wilbert Robinson, the fat manager of the Dodgers, walked out to home plate and presented the lineup card to an umpire.

The Dodgers and the Pirates were about to play ball. About 8,000 fans sat watching, some on the high rim of the park. A taxi driver yelled, "How many on base?"

A fan yelled back, "Dodgers have three on." The cab driver was surprised. "Yeah?" he said. "Which base?"

It was Dazzy Vance's turn to pitch, but he had wounded a knuckle on a batted ball. So Robinson sent a raw recruit out to the mound.

This was his first tryout in the majors and he was proud and scared. He would face the Waners today—Paul and Lloyd—and he got the galloping tremors every time he thought of it. Behind the kid was an old and wise infield, and a young and stupid outfield.

In the outfield, the three men could run like deer. They also caught fly balls like deer. The right fielder, whom we will call Barney, had lumps from catching fly balls on his forehead.

The kid went out, tossed his warm-up pitches, and then threw a straight ball to the lead-off man. The 8,000 fans paused in mid-peanut to watch the pill arc up into the sunlight, head for right field, and bounce off the wall. The right fielder played the carom wrong, and the center fielder tossed to third.

It was a double. The kid studied the next batter, and threw a slow roundhouse. The batter smacked it on a line drive to the wall. One run was in and the man was on second with a standup double. The third man waited for two pitches, then repeated the dose. Two runs in, a man on second.

Uncle Wilbur waddled out to the mound. "Okay, kid," he said "that'll be all for today." The boy clutched the ball. "I'm not leaving," he said grimly. Uncle Wilbur stopped chewing his gum. "You're not what?" The kid said, "Not leaving. You let me take it, now let me finish it."

Uncle Wilbur was properly horrified. "Kid," he said, "get off this mound before I call the park cops."

The pitcher began to plead. The plate umpire asked Uncle Wilbur to please make up his mind. Robinson began to talk to the kid under his breath. "Do you realize," he said, "that this could mean your career, you idiot?" The kid hung his head and thought it over. Now the manager began to plead. "You'll have other days, kid," he said.

The pitcher saw that there was no hope. He would like to have lasted an inning. Now he'd like to have lasted for one out, because he had a great pick-off play he wanted to display.

At last, in disgust, he turned toward the outfield and heaved the ball as hard as he could. The ball hit the fence and caromed off. Barney, dozing, decided that the shelling had commenced again. He peeled the cap back, jumped to his feet, fielded the carom perfectly, and tossed to second.

Uncle Wilbur watched on his way to the dugout. He shook his head. "Best throw he made all season," he muttered.

JOHN GALLAGHER

Courtesy *Sport* Magazine ©

"Today's probable pitchers . . ."

JOHN GALLAGHER

Courtesy *Sport* Magazine ©

THERE WAS the temptation to label this one science fiction too, on account of its being a chapter from Jimmy Breslin's astonishing book *Can't Anybody Here Play This Game?* Incredible to relate, though, every word of it is true. The subject, it goes without saying, is the New York Mets in their first year under Casey Stengel.

"They're Afraid to Come Out"

JIMMY BRESLIN

THE SECOND HALF of the season for New York Mets was, generally speaking, a catastrophe. The second half of the season consisted of the months of July, August, and September, although some of the more responsible players on the team insisted it never really happened. Whatever it was, it left an indelible impression on many of those connected with the club.

In Rochester, New York, during the winter, Casey Stengel sat in the lobby of the Sheraton Hotel, and, in the middle of one of his highly specialized lobby seminars, he stopped and shook his head.

"Everybody here keeps saying how good I'm looking," he said. "Well, maybe I do. But they should see me inside. I look terrible inside."

And in Tilden, Nebraska, one afternoon, Richie Ashburn called a Philadelphia advertising agency to tell them that he would certainly like to retire from baseball and take their offer to announce the Philadelphia Phillies games.

"Weren't you making more with the Mets?" he was asked.

"Yes, quite a bit more."

"Why did you quit, then?"

"Well," he said.

He meant he was taking a big cut in pay for the privilege of not having to go through another year with the Mets.

From a non-Met viewpoint, however, the last part of the 1962 season was something else. It was not rough. It was, instead, the finest thing to happen to the sport of baseball since Abe Attell helped save the game by deciding that, seeing as long as it made people so mad, he was not going to become involved with anyone who was trying to fix World Series games.

You see, in the last fifteen years baseball has needed help. This is becoming a tired, predictable game. It is overexposed on television. It is played too slowly to maintain a hold on this fast-moving era. And, probably worst of all, it has become so commercialized, and the people in it loaded with so many gimmicks, that it all reminds you of the front window of a cheap department store. For money, a baseball player will go to the end of the world to embarrass himself. One word from Madison Avenue, the world center for poor taste, and a ballplayer will rub some hog-suet compound into his hair and say it isn't greaseless. Or he will make a toy-company commercial that should be jammed by the FCC. Or, most sickening of all, for a check of $500 or so he will show up at any dinner of any organization this side of the Murder, Inc., Old-Timers Association and sign autographs for the kids, mutter some sort of speech, then disappear out the side door with the waitress from the cocktail lounge. All of it is demeaning at best, and in the long run harmful to the game. Other athletes from other sports go in for this too, and they have the same quick-buck air about them, but since baseball is the biggest sport it is the one in which this sort of thing is most prevalent. And most sickening. The idea of a ballplayer taking money to go out and promote his own business is, at best, disgraceful.

And, in the playing of the game itself, baseball acts as if we are still in a depression and nobody has any place to go. There is the manager's strategy. With nominal maneuvering, a major-league manager can halt a game for ten minutes while changing pitchers. Baseball still thinks this is 1934. Only this is 1963 and people are working and have money and move around and spend it. The entire character of leisure time has changed drastically. Since 1945 everything has changed with it except baseball, and that is baseball's trouble right now.

But last season the New York Mets came to the rescue. Dressed in their striped uniforms, with blue lettering and orange piping, they put fun into life. It was hell to play for them, but for anybody who watched them it was great. This was what you wanted out of life. This was Bert Lahr in *The Wizard of Oz* or the Marx Brothers in *Room Service*. The Mets tried to play baseball, and the players trying to do it were serious. But the whole thing came out as great comedy, and it was the tonic the sport needed. People did not follow the Mets. They loved the Mets.

Absolutely anything the Mets did last season, from a viewer's position, was great. They were great during the season. And even in the long winter layoff they didn't let anybody down. In January, for example, the Mets called up their three best pitchers from the minor leagues. They were Larry Bearnath, who won 2 and lost 13 at Syracuse; Tom Belcher, 1 and 12 at Syracuse; and Grover Powell, who was 4 and 12 between Syracuse and the Auburn, New York, club. The three had a combined record of thirty-seven losses and only seven wins.

"I saw all their old pitchers," cab driver Martin Goldstein, hack license 437-265, assured us one afternoon. "But I can't wait to see Stengel bring one of these new ones out of the bullpen."

It will be hard to top the final half of last season, however. All of it went along the lines of the night game the Mets played against the Reds at Crosley Field on August 10, although dates are of no consequence here because things were substantially the same each day or night the team took the field.

In the third inning of this particular contest, Frank Robinson of the Reds led off with a double down the left-field line off Al Jackson, the Mets' pitcher. Wally Post then grounded out, Robinson holding second. Robinson then stole third. The batter, Don Pavletich, walked. There was now one out, men on first and third. The Mets' infield came up a step or so. The hope was for a sharply hit ground ball which could be converted into a double play or a play at home plate to prevent the run from scoring.

Jackson pitched to Hank Foiles, the Reds' catcher. Pitched beautifully, too. Al's curve was coming in low, the kind of pitch that winds up being hit on the ground. Which is exactly what Foiles did. He hit a sharp one-hopper toward first. Throneberry made a great stop. Then he straightened up and looked around. He found that the ball had been hit so sharply that it gave him all the time he needed to make an inning-ending double play any way he wanted.

Here was Pavletich running toward second. He wasn't halfway there. Throneberry could throw to second for one out, then take the return throw and get the batter. That would be easy. Foiles was still scrambling away from the batter's box. There was another play Marv could make too. He could step on first and then throw to second. Only then they would have to tag Pavletich out at second. That could be dangerous, for Robinson might score in the meantime. But you still had plenty of time. When you have time you rarely make errors. Marvin stood alongside first base, the ball firmly held in his glove, and thought it out. Then he made his decision.

He threw to the plate. His throw arrived just after Robinson slid across with a run.

There were now runners on first and second with one out. Pitcher Jackson seemed to sway a little on the mound. Then he threw four balls to Vada Pinson, and that loaded the bases.

Don Blasingame stepped in to hit. By now, Jackson had talked himself into trying again. He stretched, then came in with that good low curve once more. Blasingame slapped a hard ground ball straight at Rod Kanehl at second base. It was a certain double-play ball. Kanehl, in his exuberance, neglected to field the ball. It kicked off his leg, and another run scored. The bases were still loaded.

Jackson now has forced the Reds to hit into two certain double plays. For his efforts, he has two runs against him on the scoreboard, still only one man out, the bases loaded, and a wonderful little touch of Southern vernacular dripping from his lips.

Jim Maloney, the Cincinnati pitcher, stepped in. The count ran to three and two on him. Then, for some reason, the Cincinnati base runners broke with the pitch. With two out, this is normal. But there was only one out here, and there is a slight suspicion somebody on the Reds was so mixed up by now he thought there were two out and he had the runners going. At any rate, Jackson came right back with that low curve, and Maloney went for it and here came another grounder straight at

Kanehl. This time Rod wasn't going to make any mistakes. He kept his head down, scooped up the ball, and flipped it to second with the same motion. It was a fine move for starting a double play. Except Blasingame, running from first with the pitch, was now standing on second. He was safe. So was everybody else. During the maneuvering, the third Red run of the inning came across.

Jackson held out his glove for the ball, scuffed the dirt, then looked down for the sign so he could pitch to the next hitter. Don't ever say Al Jackson is not a well-trained pitcher. People come out of West Point and go on to become big generals and they don't have this kind of discipline. And when Leo Cardenas got in to hit, Jackson came right back with that curve ball and he got Cardenas to go for it and hit into the dirt.

The ball went right at Charley Neal at shortstop. The temptation was to go for the inning-ending double play, short-to-second-to-first. It looked easy. But you were not going to get Charley Neal into a sucker game like this. No, sir. Charley straightened up and fired the ball to first base to get one out. The fourth run of the inning came across.

When this happened, Richie Ashburn, out in right field, turned around and looked up at one of the light towers. In his time Ashburn had seen many things. Granny Hamner in a clutch: he always moved the runner up a base. Joe DiMaggio going after a fly ball: he covered half an outfield and never seemed to do anything hard enough to work up a sweat. Jackie Robinson bothering a pitcher: he would brazen the guy into a mistake. He had, Richie felt, seen just about everything. Except this.

"I don't know what's going on, but I know I've never seen it before," Ashburn mumbled.

Then he turned around and watched as Jackson finally got the third out and headed for the bench with the all-time record for making batters hit into consecutive double plays that did not work. As he got to the dugout, Stengel thought kind things about him.

"If I let this man go out there again, he may never be the same," Casey said. He ordered Ray Daviault to come in and pitch the fourth inning. This he neglected to tell Jackson. So when the Mets made their third out, Al picked up his glove and went out to the mound. He was in the middle of a warm-up pitch when the public-address announcer proclaimed, "Now pitching for New York, Number 35, Ray Daviault."

Jackson stopped dead.

"Everybody here crazy," he announced.

It went pretty much like this from the first day of July until the last day of the season, in September. Only a true hero could win a game for the Mets. Jackson, who was to wind up losing twenty, began to trust nobody. When he won a game, he won it by pitching a shutout. Even then, he was never too sure until he was back in the dressing room.

There was a night game in St. Louis that showed this. Jackson had a 1–0 lead as the ninth inning began. Ken Boyer was the first Cardinal hitter. Boyer hit sharply down the third-base line. Felix Mantilla went the wrong way for the ball, and it went through into left field. The Met's left fielder was Joe Christopher. Casey Stengel had put him into the game for defensive purposes. Christopher advanced on the ball, then touched it several times before finally holding on to it. Boyer had pulled up at second by the time Christopher was able to make the throw.

With one pitch the Mets had not only allowed the first man up to reach base, but they also had allowed him to advance into scoring position. Jackson, however, did not fold. He bent his back a little more and got the next two hitters. Then Red Schoendienst came up to pinch-hit. He is old, this Schoendienst, and maybe he has never been the same since being hit with tuberculosis a couple of years ago. But he is still Red Schoendienst, and in a spot like this he is dangerous. Jackson worked carefully on him. He got Red to go for an outside curve. Red hit a high pop foul alongside first. It was an easy third out. The fans started moving toward the exits. The Mets' outfielders started to come in for their showers. The bullpen crews reached for their gloves. Everybody moved but Jackson. He had been around too long. He was staying where he was until the result was official.

Throneberry circled under the pop fly. First, he moved in a little circle. Then he began to move in a bigger circle. With a great last-moment stab, Marvelous Marv got his glove on the ball. The ball hit the thumb part of Marv's glove and bounded away. Jackson then walked Schoendienst.

The next hitter was Bob Whitfield. He slammed a pitch right back at the mound. Now pitchers are not out there to make heroes of themselves. In self-defense they'll stop a batted ball. But only for that reason. Generally they like it much better if the ball goes past them and is handled by an infielder. That's what infielders are for. But this case was different.

Jackson knew all about his infielders. He knew all about his outfielders too. He caught one glimpse of the ball as it buzzed toward his shoetops. Then Al Jackson went down for it. The thing could have hopped up and broken his jaw just as easily as not. It didn't matter to Jackson. He knew the only way he could win was to risk his life. With a loud slap, Jackson stopped the ball. Then he came up and threw to Throneberry at first. Marvin held on to the throw. The game, for a wonder, was over.

It was things like this that made an indelible impression upon a nineteen-year-old boy from Stockton, California, named Robert Garibaldi. Last July, Garibaldi, a sophomore at Santa Clara, was the most sought-after pitching prospect to come along in many years. He was a left-hander, and the bidding was up to $125,000 for his signature on a contract.

The Mets had sent Red Ruffing, the old Yankee pitching ace, to look over the kid for them. Ruffing's report was short and impressive: "Has big-league speed. Has big-league control. Ready right now."

On July 3 the Mets were in San Francisco. By the end of the fourth inning they were trailing by a tidy 10–1. Out of the dugout came Stengel. He ran up the right-field line and disappeared through a door leading to the clubhouse. Many people were speculating that Casey had decided he couldn't take any more. They were wrong. Stengel most certainly could take more. In fact, Casey Stengel at this point thought he could do anything. He had just heard that the Giants were going to sign Garibaldi the next day. So he had made a hurried date with George Weiss to drive to Stockton, sixty miles away, and try to charm Garibaldi into going for a Mets contract.

Charm the lad he did.

"He was wonderful," Garibaldi says. "It was great meeting him. I'd read about him all my life."

Stengel and Weiss sat down in the boy's living room and talked for two hours with him. They got down to money. The Giants reportedly had offered $130,000. The Mets certainly would top that, Weiss assured the boy. The boy said thank you, but there was no money in the world that could make it worth his while to pitch for the Mets. He signed with the Giants the next day.

This statement seemed borne out a week or so later when the Mets were in Milwaukee. The ace of their bullpen, Craig Anderson, who was in the midst of losing sixteen games in a row, needed a rest. For a relief pitcher Stengel called upon Wilmer (Vinegar Bend) Mizell. This one came on to walk the first three batters to face him in the seventh. Then he decided to effect pinpoint control and he served up a pitch that Joe Adcock hit six miles for a grand-slam home run. Out came Vinegar Bend. Stengel waved to the bullpen for somebody else. Nobody came.

"They're afraid to come out," everybody said.

For a Mets pitcher there were only two possibilities every time he took the mound. Either he was going to be hit for some of the longest home runs in baseball history, or he was going to have to stand around and watch his teammates make those astonishing plays.

Sometimes it was a combination of everything. There was one bright Sunday in July in Cincinnati when the Mets lost two games. Not easily, either. It all began the day before, when Roger Craig, with the class of a real professional, had walked over to Stengel and volunteered for relief pitching in the doubleheader. Stengel nodded. It touches an old guy like this when a pitcher volunteers to work between starts. So in the ninth inning of the first game, with the score tied 3–3, Casey took Craig up on his offer. Roger came in from the bullpen, and immediately Cincinnati sent up Marty Keogh as a pinch hitter. Craig threw him one pitch. Keogh did not swing. Craig threw another pitch. Keogh swung. He hit the ball eight miles and the Reds won, 4–3.

"They get beat on favors now," everybody said.

Craig, however, was only part of the day's show. During the course of the eighteen innings the Mets managed to set some sort of an all-time record by getting four runners thrown out at home plate. In the first game Choo Choo Coleman was out trying to score from second on a single to left. In the second game Stengel jauntily ordered a double steal in the second inning. Cannizzaro was on first and Kanehl on third. Cannizzaro broke for second and drew a throw. Kanehl raced for the plate. The Cincinnati shortstop, Cardenas, cut off the throw, fired home, and that took care of Kanehl. In the fourth inning Elio Chacon, on first, put his head down and tried to go all the way around when Jerry Lynch, the Reds' left fielder, messed up a single. Chacon never saw Vada Pinson, the fine center fielder, come over for the ball. He should have, because Pinson, as he demonstrated here, throws quite well. He cut down Chacon at home by six yards. Finally, in the fifth inning, with Jim Hickman on third and breaking for the plate with the swing, Kanehl hit the ball hard. And squarely at third. Hickman was out by a mile at the plate.

In pitching for the Mets, then, it was best to take no chances. Don't volunteer, don't rely on getting any runs, no matter how many teammates get on base. The password was: beware. And the one who seemed to know this better than anyone was Ralph Branca. He had nothing to do with the team officially. His job was talking on a pre- and post-game program for a radio station. But by being around the Mets he understood that anything could happen. So on July 14, when the Mets held an Old Timers' Day and Branca was out in the bullpen, he did not merely sit on a bench and look at the crowd. He stayed loose. He also stayed determined.

The moment Bobby Thomson came up to bat, here was showman Leo Durocher waving to the bullpen for Branca to come in and pitch. Ralph walked in, just as he had come in that day in 1951. Thomson greeted him with a smile. Everybody else out on the field lolled around and made jokes about the situation.

Branca did not say any jokes. And a small thought crossed his mind: Stick the first pitch right in his ear. He dismissed it.

He then wound up and nearly broke his arm off throwing his best curve at Thomson. He threw a couple more of them, and Bobby, fooled by one, barely lifted an easy fly to center field.

Following this, the Mets took the field to play the Dodgers. In the stands to watch them were such as Zack Wheat and Carl Hubbell and Frank Frisch. At the end of five and a half innings the Mets were slightly behind. They were behind by 17–0, and that night Frankie Frisch sat in his house in New Rochelle and he told the neighbors, "I don't have to go out of this house again as long as I live. I've seen everything."

This view was being echoed on 52nd Street in New York, where the man named Toots Shor runs his restaurant and bar. He is generally considered to be the town's number-one sports fan, and around his circular bar he is known, simply, as The Best Customer.

"I have a son," Toots announced over brandy, "and I make him watch the Mets. I want him to know life. You watch the Mets, you think of being busted out with the guy from the Morris Plan calling up every ten minutes. It's a history lesson. He'll understand the depression when they teach it to him in school."

He shook his head. "That Frank Thomas is one helluva guy, you know. But he makes a throw against the Cardinals. He's on third base and he makes a throw to first. He makes the wildest wild throw in baseball history. It goes 125 feet over the first baseman's head. Nobody ever done a thing like that. Well, what the hell, there never was a club like this."

Anderson is a case in point here. His sixteenth loss was memorable. It left him two short of the all-time National League record, and only a step or two short of asking to be farmed out to an institution. The date was September 8, and the Mets were in Houston for a day-night doubleheader. They were leading, 3–2, in the ninth inning of the day game when Bob Lillis of Houston singled. Johnny Temple bunted down the first-base line. Marvin Throneberry approached the ball thoughtfully. Marvelous Marv's estimate was that the ball would roll foul. He was wrong. He then picked it up and threw to first, too late to get the runner. Stengel waved to the bullpen for help. Here came Anderson. Craig was in great form. He worked on Joe Amalfitano and got him to hit into a double play. Then he walked Norman Larker. This brought up Bob Aspromonte. He hit a sinking liner to left field. Frank Thomas broke for the ball. Then he charged the ball. Then he dove for the ball. He did not make the catch. Temple rounded third and scored the tying run. Larker, the runner from first, rounded second and began to go for third. Thomas grabbed the ball, stood up, and looked at Larker. It was going to be a close play at third. But Thomas was taking no chances. He was not going to let anybody reach second base. So he fired to second. There was nobody there. Aspromonte, the hitter, had remained at first. Kanehl and Neal, the Met's keystone combination, as the announcers call it, were widely scattered over the area. Thomas's throw roared past second untouched by human hands. Larker reached third, made the turn, and headed for home.

Throneberry made a remarkable save on the throw. He knew exactly what was going on. Larker was heading home with the winning run. A good throw would cut Larker down. Throneberry wanted to make that good throw. So he aimed at the plate. He took aim as if his life depended on this throw. He also took so much time aiming his throw that Larker simply slid across the plate with the winning run.

Jay Hook was another pitcher who found the Mets trying. On August 6, a hot Monday night at Los Angeles, Jay allowed the Dodgers five hits. He did not walk a man. But in the sixth inning of a 1–1 game Maury Wills of the

Dodgers dragged a bunt past the mound and beat it out. He then stole second. This infuriated Chris Cannizzaro, who was catching Hook. Chris crouched down and looked out at second. Willis was taking his usual long lead off the base. Chris planted his feet and got ready to make a comeback. He was going to pick Willis off. On the first pitch, Chris threw to second. Threw hard. If there is one thing he can do, it is throw a baseball hard. He threw this one so hard that the only reason Wills had to hold at third and not score was that Jim Hickman, the Mets center fielder, caught the ball on the fly. Willie Davis then hit a ground ball, and Wills came across with what was to be the winning run.

Hook also had the privilege of pitching when the Mets lost their hundredth game of the year. This was late in August at Philadelphia. Jay went ten innings before losing to the Phillies, 3–2. He lost the game primarily on a ground ball to Charley Neal at short. Don Demeter hit the ball. Neal picked it up and made a bad throw to first. It pulled Throneberry off the bag. Marv had to come up the line and into foul territory to stay with the throw. He grabbed it. Then he went to tag Demeter. His feet slipped and he fell on his face.

This was Throneberry's best kind of play. And because of this, people sitting behind first base at the Polo Grounds soon began to show up with T-shirts which read VRAM (MARV spelled backwards) on them. And they took up a great chant: "Cranberry, strawberry, we love Throneberry."

This was the Marvin Throneberry Fan Club. At the peak of the season over a hundred letters a day were arriving at Marvin's locker at the Polo Grounds.

"The hell of it all is, I'm really a good fielder," Throneberry kept insisting.

This was something Ralph Houk gladly backed up one evening during the summer, in Washington. Houk, who manages the Yankees, sat in the bus taking his team to the ball park and he chewed on a cigar and talked about Marvelous Marv.

"I can't understand what's happening to that Throneberry," he said. "I had him three years at Denver. He's not that bad a ballplayer at all. Why, he opened the season with the Yankees one year there [1958]. Skowron was hurt, I guess. Marv never made plays like they say he makes now. I guarantee you he never did. If he ever played that way for me, I'd of killed him with my bare hands."

The year Marvelous Marv had in 1962 just happened, then. Nobody had any indication he knew how to play baseball this way. He just arrived from Baltimore one day in May and replaced an ailing Gil Hodges at first. After that, things began to happen. They kept happening too, and by August 18 he was an institution.

On that night the Mets' management held a special day in honor of Stan Musial. But the fans, proudly wearing their VRAM T-shirts and shouting their cheer, showed much more affection for Throneberry. Musial? He was fine. Great guy, magnificent baseball player. A perfectionist. Only who the hell needed him? The mob yelled for Marvelous Marv.

"I hated to take the play away from Stan on his big day here," Marv apologized after the game.

Throneberry is a balding, likable fellow who has been known to buy a writer a drink, something unheard of in a ballplayer. He is anything but a clown. He simply came into the 1962 season accident-prone, and he barely got out alive. Nothing went right at any time. There was even one night, late in the season, when there was supposed to be some sort of a small party in his honor at a little Italian restaurant called the Grotto on the West Side. Somebody mixed things up, and 125 people showed up instead of an expected 30. The lone chef, hired to work this small party on a usually dead Sunday night, took one look at the mob and pulled off his hat.

"Small-a party, huh?" he said. "Well, you take this small-a party to the Automat. 'Cause that's where I'm going to have my dinner on the way home."

The place got so jammed that there was no room for Marvelous Marv when he arrived. After trying to get in, he finally gave up and went across the street from his party and had dinner in another place.

The strange thing about the Mets is that, for all their great comedy on the field, they had no real characters off the field. This was a team of twenty-five nice young men who came to the big leagues to play baseball. The fact they played it rather strangely was, obviously, out of their control. The only player on the club who might be counted as unusual is Frank Thomas. His only quirk is that he wants to be an airline hostess. Yet here again you are dealing with a basically serious matter, because Thomas is a damn good airline stewardess.

"He's awful neat," Miss Barbara Mueller of United Airlines noted one day. "He does everything the way the regulations say you should. Outside of this girl Jane, who handles first class on our New York to San Francisco champagne flight, I think that Frank Thomas is the best stewardess on United Airlines."

Once the Mets are airborne, going to or from a game, Thomas jumps out of his seat, strides up the aisle to the kitchenette, and takes over the running of the plane. Trays slide in and out, coffee is poured, and he starts moving rapidly up and down the aisle, serving meals. He is very particular about it too. One night, en route to Houston by plane, Thomas started serving the back of the plane first. He thrust a tray under the nose of Barney Kremenko, the sportswriter, and a couple of partners he had gotten into a pinochle game. The partners were not good at pinochle. Thus Mr. Kremenko preferred to have nothing break up his game.

"We're not ready now," Barney said. "We'll eat later."

"All right," Thomas announced. "But that means you eat last, and I don't want to hear any squawks about it."

Offended, Thomas stormed off. Any housewife can understand how he felt. Here he had a whole meal prepared, and it was being turned down.

Presently Kremenko's game broke up. He hailed the regular stewardess and asked her to bring a tray, which she did. Thomas found out about this some minutes later. His eyes flashed.

"You cheated," he told Kremenko. "I told you to wait your turn, and you cheated. That's the last time you're going to pull that."

Otherwise, to travel or live with this club was to be with a normal group of young men in the major leagues. In fact, as Ashburn observes, the Mets were the only losing club he can recall on which there was no dissension.

"Any losing team I've ever been on," Richie says, "had several things going on. One, the players gave up. Or they hated the manager. Or they had no team spirit. Or the fans turned into wolves. But there was none of this with the Mets. Nobody stopped trying. The manager was absolutely great, nobody grumbled about being with the club, and the fans we had, well, there haven't been fans like this in baseball history. So we lose 120 games and there isn't a gripe on the club. It was remarkable. You know, I can remember guys being mad even on a big winner."

By this he meant a rather famous episode in more recent baseball history. On the last day of the 1950 season Ashburn's Phillies held a one-game lead over the Brooklyn Dodgers. At Ebbets Field, in the ninth inning, the score was tied, 1–1, with none out and Dodgers on first and second. The highly dangerous Duke Snider was at bat against Robin Roberts of the Phillies. Ashburn was in center field. If anything happened and the runner on second, Cal Abrams, scored, the Dodgers would tie for the pennant and go into a playoff heavily favored.

At shortstop for the Phillies was Granny Hamner. When they played it with money on the table, Hamner was one of the real big ones. It has been a while since he has been around, and maybe some people forget him, but when they talk about big men in the clutch Granny Hamner should always be mentioned. On this afternoon, with Abrams edging off second, Hamner flashed the pick-off sign to Stan Lopata, the Phillies' catcher. With Snider, a left-handed batter, up, Hamner was playing over toward second. For the pick-off throw, he would duck in behind Abrams and take the throw. Oh, they wouldn't get Abrams. That would be too much to ask for. The idea was to keep him as close to the bag as possible. If Snider bunted, they could try for Abrams at third. If he hit away and the ball went into the outfield, there still would be a chance to get Abrams at the plate.

Lopata called for a pitch-out. In center, Ashburn moved in. He would back up second in case of a bad throw. Hamner began to edge toward second. Abrams had not picked up the action yet. On the mound, Roberts nodded he had the sign. He started to go into his stretch. Then he threw. He threw a fast ball right down the pipe. Hamner's mouth fell open. Snider rapped it on a line up the middle, over second, and into center field. Abrams started running. Dirt flew from his spikes as he tore around third. From the stands came one great roar: "*Abie, you should run fast.*"

But in the middle of this huge mistake, here was Ashburn. He had raced in to back up second base. And as he came in, the ball landed right at his feet. By now, Richie was only a short distance on the outfield grass behind second. He picked up the ball and threw to the plate. And suddenly all of Brooklyn realized what was happening. Halfway down the line, Abrams was beaten. A wail rang out over Brooklyn as Lopata tagged out Abrams. Roberts, whose bacon had been saved, proceeded to get out of the inning unscathed.

In the tenth inning Dick Sisler hit a home run into the left-field seats and the Phillies won the pennant. But after the game Hamner didn't want to talk to anybody. Particularly Roberts. He wanted to kill Roberts.

"I need a drink," he kept saying. "Alone."

The Mets never had even a faint tinge of this. This was a nice, placid, thoughtful team. There was one Sunday night, coming back to New York from Chicago, when Solly Hemus, the coach, and a couple of the players sat in the lounge part of the plane, and the talk was the same as you would hear anyplace around the major leagues. Except they soon got to talking about throwing knockdown pitches at Willie Mays.

"The pitch right after you throw at him, that's the time to watch him," Joe Pignatano, one of the catchers, said. "He's ready then. He's mad."

"Knock him down twice in a row, then," a tall kid said.

"Do you mean knockdown pitches bother Mays?" they were asked.

"Bother him?" one of the players said. "He's scared to death. If he wasn't so scared of being hit with a ball, he'd hit .600."

"You go up to him before the game," one of them said, "and you tell him, 'Willie, sometime today. Sometime today I'm going to stick it right in your ear.' He'll be standing around the batting cage and he gives you this: 'Go ahead, man, throw at me all you want. It don't bother me, man.' But that's talk. I know it bothers him."

They sat and discussed handling Mays with these pitches. It was excellent talk, and it would have made a great impression on the listener except for one thing. It was a red-covered scorebook, and a flip through the pages showed little items like this:

May 26: Mays hits two home runs against the Mets. *May 27:* Willie gets four hits against the Mets. *June 1:* A home run. *June 2:* Another homer. *June 3:* Still another homer. *July 4:* Willie hits two homers and has seven runs batted in.

I closed the book. "You're right," I told one of the players. "Mays is a yellow dog."

Why a discussion of this type should come up at all is a question. If there is one matter which irked Stengel over the season, it was the refusal of his pitchers to throw tight pitches and move the batter back. Against the Mets, all hitters practically stepped on the plate and remained there until they had either hit the ball out of sight or reached base through an error.

Stengel, in one of the finest talks on baseball anybody has ever heard, made much of this one night.

"All these pitchers we have," he said, "I see them with their lovely wives and their lovely children. Oh, grand children. So they go out there to pitch, and here is the batter. Ohhh, he digs right in there and he swings that bat and he has a wonderful toehold. And our pitchers, they say they won't throw at him. They say you have to think of the lovely wife and children the batter has. Well, some of these pitchers of mine ought to think about their own children. That batter up there doesn't care about them. He's in there to take the food right off the table from the pitcher's children. These fellows of mine, they better start thinking of their own lovely children and move that batter back off of the plate a little."

It was excellent thinking. However, every time you bring it up, you also think of the game against the Reds on August 12, and it shows, as well as anything, the way the Mets, advice or no advice, played baseball all year.

Before the game a home-run-hitting contest was held. Wally Post of the Reds had five pitches thrown to him. He pulled four of them over the left-field wall to win the contest. Now in a contest such as this the batter tells the man pitching to him just where to put the ball. Then it is thrown at three-quarter speed. In Post's case he wanted it a little bit over belt high and a little bit on the outside.

As each contestant comes up, opposing pitchers normally watch closely from the dugout. Whatever pitch the home-run hitter calls for is the one never to give him in a game.

Later in the day, in the eighth inning with two on and the Reds ahead, 5–4, Post was sent up as a pinch-hitter. On the mound for the Mets was Kenneth MacKenzie, who is a graduate of Yale University. Don't ever let anybody tell you that a guy can get into Yale just because he has money behind him. It takes more than that. Those kids that go to Yale have to be very good spellers. So MacKenzie is no dunce. This is a bright boy.

He threw a pitch a little bit over belt high and a little bit outside to Post. Wally hit it exactly three miles over the left-field fence.

Courtesy *The New Yorker* Magazine, Inc. ©

"Poor guy. He's been traded to the Yankees."

J. MIRACHI

Courtesy *The New Yorker* Magazine, Inc. ©

"Look, son, when you yell at me, slam your cap on the ground and jump on it. The crowd loves *that bit."*

SOME PEOPLE object to the fact that stories by-lined by baseball figures frequently are composed, or at least put into finished form, by professional writers. This makes me a little sore. A lawyer I know, who jeers at ghost-writing in baseball, has his briefs ghosted by another lawyer. He sees nothing wrong in that, even though he himself is in business to be articulate, while ballplayers aren't.

And that's the end of that speech, except that it fits in especially well right here, because Jim Brosnan, the pitcher, never needed a ghost. I should say Jim Brosnan, the former pitcher, because what was for him an effective career in the majors is now ended, foreshortened, we can only suppose, by the fact that he wrote as well as he did, wrote the truth, and—*J'Accuse!*—wrote his own stuff.

Here are some excerpts from his first book, a diary of the 1959 season.

From *The Long Season*

JIM BROSNAN

February 19—St. Petersburg, Fla.

The day we arrived in St. Petersburg, the sportswriters were gleefully describing the number of "holdouts" on the Cardinal club. Each major-league baseball team has its share of stubbornly discontented ballplayers in the spring. (Most of them sign, but some of them stubbornly insist on a measure of content.) The practice of printing the salary of each signed player causes a great deal of depression among the less fortunate who have not yet signed. Although it is seldom true that the amount printed is, in fact, the amount to be received by the player, the press establishes a caste system within the club by asserting that certain players make, or should make, more or less than the other players.

Vinegar Bend Mizell's reaction to contract discussions was that of any shrewd, hard-nosed Alabama farmer who always got plenty of peanuts for his peanuts and why shouldn't the subsidy remain the same? If the farmer has a bad year on the farm nowadays, the Government still supports him in the style to which he has become accustomed. "It's a matter of principle," cried Wilmer, according to the paper.

"We're still pretty far apart," said Devine.

"Go get 'em, Will," I thought. "I'm with you."

"You can't win," said Larry Jackson, as he signed just one day before we opened.

"Vinegar probably wants to be traded," went the rumor in the clubhouse. "Left-handers think they got the world by the tail."

March 20—St. Petersburg, Fla.

Five consecutive days of rain! Let's go back to Arizona.

No one can work out. Gloom has saddened the sweet natures of the coaching staff. They can't even run the pitchers in the outfield. The water soaks right into the ground, though. If the rain would let up for a few hours we could throw a little, anyway. This whole state is like a sieve; pretty soon that water will be sloshing back up out of the sand. Can't be much more room to run off.

The best thing about rain during the season is the bridge game that helps kill time. Only three bridge players on the club this year, however: Cimoli, Jackson and I. Pollet could give us a fourth, but he won't play. When he and I trained together with the Cubs, he played every night. Guess coaches and players aren't allowed to mix socially. All we're after is a nice, sociable game! (Jackson and I played for five yen a point in Japan. Lost twenty thousand in a three-hour train ride. Rained there, too.)

Finally scared up a foursome. Had to play on the table in the press room. Only dry surface in Al Lang Field. Hemus gave interviews to New York sportswriters while we played. "We're going to score more runs this season." (Christ, we looked as bad now as we did all last year. What's he call "more runs"—three a game?) "Blaylock and Broglio ought to win twelve to fifteen games apiece." (He's out of his mind, and the bell hasn't rung yet.) "Jackson and Mizell have looked good. Brosnan's been excellent." (Sweet guy, that Solly.)

"Better make this the last hand, boys," Pollet interrupted. "We're going to fly to Cuba."

"Yes, we are," said Cimoli disdainfully. "Two no-trump."

Jackson passed.

"The Reds tried to fly to Havana yesterday," said Gino. "They sat on the runway for an hour and a half. Then they went home. It's too wet to fly, or anything else. What do you bid, partner?"

Pollet circled the table, looking at all four hands. "Gino, if Bing can find us a ball park down there, we're going. Cincinnati took off an hour ago. They're playing the Dodgers tonight."

"Bet it rains in Havana," said Nunn. "Three no-trump."

April 9—St. Louis

"The night before" is one of those peculiarly personal phrases that frequently repeat themselves in a man's memory. It can refer to a wild time, or to a sad moment, or to the traditional misty haze of dim reckoning. For the professional ballplayer, the night before Opening Day is full of extreme nervous tension. All of winter's fond hopes and daydreams, all of the spring-training trials and successes, all of the promise-filled publicity, focuses eyes, in the baseball world, on the players. There's no more time to think and dream, to plot and scheme, for this is it . . . the championship game. Only the first of 154, perhaps, but to eight teams it's the only chance to be as good as any other team in the league for one whole day. You may have won every game in spring training, hit 1.000, or pitched perfect ball, but you're no better than the next guy when the first pitch of the season starts on its way.

It usually rains, it seems to me, the night before we open the season. It did in '54, I recall, and again in '57, and '58. It's raining now, which is another good reason to go to bed at ten o'clock, to try to sleep, and then to read, and then to write a letter. Perhaps it would be better to talk it out, letting the sound of words soothe the nerves. If I was simply worried, and nervous about how badly I might bungle the job tomorrow, I would prefer to talk it out. But I feel only a mysterious concern for the security that my successful spring has given me. Perhaps the Law of Averages *will* punish my pride the next time out. In this game you have to do it over and over again . . . the better you do, the more you are expected to do. Pride's price, and it is sometimes cruelly exacted by that insidious Law.

It's better to write about it. Let the sight of words console my nerves. (One reason I married my wife was to have someone to console me. She was three hundred miles away, but I could write it as easily as I could talk about it. I took out my pen.)

Dearest Wife, and Lover, etc.,

With the spring training season ended, and my ambitious efforts rewarded as handsomely as possible, I would not have surprised my ego had I grown peacock feathers as we flew in from Florida. Hemus, noting that I hadn't given up a run in three weeks, and only three all spring, has made me No. 1—publicly hailed, or branded, me as such. Long Man, indeed!

No peacock I, though. Truthfully I'm slim-hipped, loose-armed, flat-bellied . . . and featherless. Certainly I've had a successful spring. Surely, the bell rings tomorrow, and we start from scratch. If I start to give up runs now, I'm a bum again. Success breeds a maggoty fortune that needs constant replenishment and refurbishing.

Still, there's the sun, just eight hours away. And here I am, and here's nervous bowels, and here's the issue—win, or lose everything. The prestige of my position must be upheld by the act of triumph; and every pitch must be impressive. And then, there's the next game. Success breeds also a feeling of insecurity. Where can you find a comfortable spot to relax, at the top? It's a definite problem of balance, for there's no handhold above, and damn little support to lean on. Besides, when you climb to the top of the ladder, the Achilles tendon is exposed, almost indefensibly. Eight other guys want this job. If the knives start to jab, they may hit this heel if it's left carelessly unprotected. I'm trying to remember, here in the rain, if I made obeisance to the proper gods. Will my unguarded rear go unscathed? Let's face it, I can be had. The black forces of despair have made it with me before!

It's another year. You'll have your sorrowful, pining days as before, waiting behind, never any more sure than I am that I can do it. It's harder to sit, hopefully, on the bench than to play the game. But this man's ready to start a new season, and we're the team that can take it all. . . . You and I. Not the Cardinals, probably. Hemus is optimistic about *his* chances; but I'm confident about ours. So let's round those bases, and have fun, and love, for the long season ahead.

I Love You, etc.,
MEAT

Rereading, folding, sealing, and stamping the letter took just as much energy as I had left for the night. I turned out the light and slept.

May 10—St. Louis

It was past nine o'clock by the time I returned from the ball park. I had left the hotel at ten A.M. full of bacon and eggs and premature fatigue; for we had another doubleheader. The flagpole quivered in the brisk wind at Busch Stadium. The flag flapped audibly above the center-field wall. Like the finger-snapping of a sardonic giant, the noise greeted me as I walked up into the Cardinal dugout. One look at the flag pointing straight out over the scoreboard and I collapsed on the bench to rest. It looked like a long and windy day.

No pitcher in his right mind volunteers to pitch on such a day, unless he's a masochist, or wants to go home early. His least mistake is often turned into a fly ball that swiftly becomes a home run. Baseballs became Ping-pong balls in the whipping wind. By the grace of a benevolent commissioner a new rule shall someday be adopted by the National League: When the wind velocity exceeds twenty miles per hour, the pitcher may throw basketballs instead of baseballs.

Naturally, I was the first man to relieve in the first game. Disgustingly I threw a gopher ball to Thomson (a belt-high fast ball right over the outside corner. Now, Bobby shouldn't hit that ball out of the park!). Morbidly, I cursed my luck. Hungrily, I ate two cups of Bauman's chicken soup. (Doc plays chef on doubleheader days so that his boys don't lose weight from not having lunch.)

Nervously, I returned to the bench as we tied the score and went into extra innings. Angrily, I helped protest an umpire's decision that ruined our chance to score in the tenth. (Noren was on third when B. G. Smith grounded to Dark. With nobody out Noren headed home and was caught in a rundown. Averill, the Cub catcher, chased Noren back toward third and threw the ball to Dark. Noren suddenly stopped, turned, and ran into Averill who was still moving down the base line. As soon as he hit Averill Noren stopped, cried "Foul!" and was tagged out by Dark. Noren's play, clever as it was, didn't impress Burkhart, the umpire. Noren had deliberately run into a defensive man who didn't have the baseball. Therefore, Averill couldn't make a play on Noren. Moreover, he had no business being in Noren's way. Averill had been right behind Noren, and couldn't stop in time to avoid contact, so that his intention to obstruct—as the rules put it—was hardly premeditated. Bad intentions or not, Averill might legally have been judged guilty and the run allowed. The umpire sympathized with Averill, however. Hemus took it as a personal insult, and announced that he would protest to the highest magistrate.)

Sadly, I watched as Averill, in the eleventh, hit a fly ball that blew into the first row of seats in left field, to win the game for Chicago, 10–9. Singleton was the winning pitcher for the Cubs; McDaniel lost it. Singleton, McDaniel, and I, plus four other pitchers, got into the second game, also. McDaniel won this one and Singleton lost it. For seven hours we played to a virtual draw. It's an ill wind that blows straight out from home plate.

June 3—Pittsburgh

"What's an introvert, Prof?"

Cunningham and I stood in the outfield at Forbes Field, in Pittsburgh, as the Cardinal batting practice began.

"An introvert, Joey, is a guy who stands in right field during batting practice, saying nothing to anyone, and catching only those baseballs hit right at him that might be dangerous."

"You're an introvert, then, huh?" Cunningham said. "You might be surprised but I'm interested in things like that. You read a lot of books. Where can I learn more about introverts and extroverts? I want to know what I am."

"If I don't get to pitch pretty soon," I said, "you can learn something from me. I'm going to become an extrovert and blow my top."

"Yeah," Joe said, "you haven't pitched since that time you won in Chi. It's funny."

"Hilarious," I agreed. "Where you playing, today, Joe? Did he tell you?"

"As of right now, this minute, I'm starting in right field. But there's an hour left before game time, so don't mark me down in your score card yet."

"It's about time he let you play every day, Joe."

Cunningham shook his head. "I don't know

about this right field, though. Tell me, Prof, you think I'm improving out here?"

"Stand around here with me and you'll improve yourself right back onto the bench," I said.

"You're kinda bitter, aren't ya, Jim? In Japan, you were full of laughs all the time. Everybody was beginning to think you were really a nice guy, after all."

I smiled a bitter smile. "That's when I was going good, Joe."

"You weren't pitching though, remember."

"In Japan, Joey, you didn't have to pitch to go good."

"Whaddya tryin' to say, Professor?" He laughed and ran back to the dugout to take his hitting practice.

Pollet sneaked up on me as I dozed. "James, wake up. You're startin' the second game in Philadelphia on Sunday."

What a way to be jolted from a lazy reverie!

"Did you say 'startin' Sunday,' Howard?" I asked. "What's going on?"

"Don't you want to start?" Pollet asked.

I shrugged my shoulders. My nerves had been conditioned all spring for the tensions of a relief pitcher. "Sure, why not?" I said.

But this is so sudden, Solly. There must be something fishy going on. Not having pitched in a week, I should be strong, though. I'll go ask Bauman if he's got any of those nine-inning pills. Imagine! Starting a game!

June 7—Philadelphia

Riding on the train back from New York to Philly, I figured it out. Hemus had decided to trade me. Philadelphia needed a relief pitcher; and I was a relief pitcher. To avoid the chance that I might not get into a game at Philly, Hemus decided to start me. After June 15 there could be no trades between teams. June 15 was only one week away; just time enough to set up a showcase. There was no other sensible reason. I had pitched poorly against Philly three times within the last six weeks. But we had lost ten games already on the road trip; another would be hardly noticed. If I pitched well, Philly might give up somebody of value. Hemus had played for Philly in 1958 and must know the players he wanted on his club. Hemus didn't like me. I didn't like Hemus. I didn't like Philadelphia either. It's too far from New York. Why couldn't he have started me against San Francisco? That's a good town.

By the time I reached Connie Mack Stadium, I had talked myself into a depressing cynicism. Warming up before the game, I didn't feel right. Just hot under the collar.

Ashburn led off for Philly. "I'll curve him," I thought. Ashburn looked at four curve balls and walked.

Bouchee hit second. "I'll jam him with sliders," I thought. Bouchee popped up.

Freese hit third. "I got to keep the ball down," I thought. Freese hit a high slider into the upper deck of the left-field stands. The Philly fans started to laugh, again. (Those miserable fans.)

Philley hit fourth. "I'll be careful with him," I thought. "Last time I overpowered him with fast balls. Wind's blowing out to right. I'll make him hit to left." Philley pulled a sinker ball into right field for a single. I could see action in the bullpen down the right-field line.

Harry Anderson hit fifth. I had played semi-pro ball with Harry when I was in the Army. "He can't hit the ball up and in," I thought. Anderson ripped a slider up and away from him off the scoreboard for a triple. Hemus ran to the dugout phone.

Sawatski was sixth. "Keep the ball up on him," I thought. I felt helpless. My directions weren't getting through to my arm. Sawatski lined a 3–2 pitch into right field. "At least I didn't walk him," I thought.

"Just like batting practice!" yelled a miserable fan.

George Anderson hit seventh. "Here, Sparky," I said to myself. "Hit it." George Anderson lined a single to center. Out of the dugout came Hemus.

How do you like that for a start?

September 27—Pittsburgh

The last day of every season comes, eventually.

The last time to pack the duffel bag with gloves and shoes, jockstraps and jackets, souvenirs and clippings that litter each locker.

The last hours of a Team. (For a new season must mold a new team.)

The last moment to say, "Good-bye" . . . to say, "Good luck!"

But it's also the time to say, "See you in the spring, buddy!" Every ballplayer thinks he can come back again, to play another year. On the last day of the season baseball is a game that professionals really do *play;* it no longer seems like work to them. It is virtually impossible for a ballplayer to convince himself that he will never play the game again. On the last day of the season baseball, truly, is in his blood.

I stuffed my glove into a duffel bag, and picked up the last shirt from my locker. The empty locker symbolizes the cold, blue sadness of the last day of the season. There is something poignant and depressing about clearing out, for good; abandoning your own place in the clubhouse. They even take the nameplate down, and who's to know what player dressed in which locker?

We won both games during the final weekend, ending the season on a positive note, and almost bringing a smile to Hutchinson's face. Four nights earlier, Philadelphia had beaten us in a doubleheader, forever quenching the aftertaste of our fourth-place ambitions. Actually, we needed no such reminder that we didn't deserve to finish in the first division, but the Phillies kicked us anyway.

To add to the insult, the bus driver, hired to drive us to the airport for our flight to Cincinnati, lost his way. Aimlessly he drove through the midnight-quiet streets of the city, finally reaching a dead end in the railroad yards. His tired, subdued passengers, at first annoyed, became increasingly hilarious at this final, farcical coincidence. When we had a bad day, we had ourselves a mess!

A railroad watchman asked, in a bewildered voice, "How in the world did you ever get that big thing in here?" as if the driver had accomplished an impossible feat. A voice from the back of the bus asked, "Any of you bums want to take the train?" as a freight rumbled down the tracks behind us. And a cab suddenly appeared, the driver grinning as he inquired if he could guide us back to the highway. Hutchinson hired him immediately.

As the bus bumped onto the main road headed toward the airport, Frank Robinson yelled to the driver, "What's the matter, Bussy, you ashamed to be seen with us?" The nearly possible truth of this question convulsed everyone, including the bus driver, who almost drove off the road.

We had nothing to be ashamed of. Or, rather, we would prefer to think of those days which we could be proud of. Every baseball season is just long enough for each player to do something to which he can look back with satisfaction. On the last day of the season those are the moments you want to remember, and probably those are the memories that make you a little sad.

That final look at the empty locker brings no smile to a ballplayer's face. No matter how successful his season, he must feel sad at the sight of his locker, finally swept bare of tangible remembrances of the long season. No more sweaty, dirty uniforms to hang there; no more fan letters, newspaper clippings, baseballs and other souvenirs to clutter the locker with his own personality. A ballplayer can stuff the shirts, the glove, and the souvenirs into a bag and take them home for the winter, but they lose some of their appeal when they're removed from the locker. It's their natural setting. They belong there.

On the last day there really is not much tangible evidence of the sweat, the tears, the applauding cheers of the season passed by, that a ballplayer can take with him. A bagful of gloves, shoes and jockstraps; a fistful of clippings and fan mail; a line of statistics following his name in the record book. Of these, only the record will remain, permanently a part of him. Something he can never change, or replace. Something he can use that will never wear out. (Or, if he's had a bad season, something that can be used against him.) I'd already used my line in the book: "Brosnan, James Patrick, Cincinnati, Won 8, Lost 3, ERA –3.36." (There are some figures for my months with St. Louis, too, but I slough over them. My record with the Reds is what they were interested in.)*

Gabe Paul had said, "We liked what you did for us this year. We expect you to do better next season. We're happy to have you with us." Then he offered me the contract that I was after and I signed it. I wanted no more baseball problems till February 1960.

Shoving two World Series tickets into my jacket pocket next to the copy of my 1960 contract, I made the rounds of the room, saying my *au revoirs*. Hutchinson was last in my tour of the clubhouse. He looked up from the trunk into which he had packed his equipment, shoved a huge bear paw at me, and said, "Good luck. You did a good job for me. Have a good winter." And he almost smiled.

I thanked him and went home.

* In mid-season of 1959, Brosnan was traded from St. Louis to Cincinnati, where he was to become the main right-handed reliever for the Redleg pennant winners of 1961.—Ed.

HERB CAEN, the famous, jaded big-city columnist? Read this one.

"The Ones with All the Fingers Cost the Same"

HERB CAEN

KID," said Buddy Ryan, "you run like you got a safe on your back."

Buddy Ryan was the red-faced, white-haired manager of the Sacramento Solons (or Senators) of the Pacific Coast League. The kid, lumbering down to first base after rapping a sharp dribbler just short of the pitcher's mound, was me. The year was 1933—and Mr. Ryan's words, shimmering in the dust and sweat of Moreing Field, were the death blow to my dreams of becoming a professional baseball player.

Head bowed, tears trickling down my cheeks (I was allergic to hay fever in those days), I shambled back to the clubhouse and took off my uniform. My meteoric career on the sandlots of Sacramento, which had won me this desultory tryout with the Senators, was over, and at the ripe old age of seventeen it was already time to hang up my spikes.

"Caen, 1b," would never be seen in the box scores of America. Suicide seemed too easy a way out, so I got a job on a newspaper.

Baseball, which was to rule my life completely for ten glorious years to the exclusion of Mozart (my mother wanted me to be a pianist) and girls (what did they know about baseball anyway?), was thrust upon me by my father in one innocent gesture.

He came home from work one day with a gift: a first baseman's mitt and a white baseball cap. From then on, the die was cast. I became passionately interested in all first basemen who wore white caps—and fortunately, George Sisler, the greatest first baseman of them all, filled the bill perfectly. The St. Louis Browns, for whom he performed, wore white caps, and most of the other teams, especially the hated Yankees, wore black ones. I was probably the only St. Louis Browns fan west *or* east of the Mississippi.

Years later, I asked my father, who cared nothing for baseball, how he happened to buy a first baseman's mitt.

"Well," he said with Alsatian simplicity, "the ones with all the fingers cost the same and don't look like as much."

Thus does Fate, coaching from the sidelines, send us to our positions.

We played our first game in a vacant, rocky lot at the corner of 26th and Q Streets. The terrain was more suited to a Civil War battle than baseball, but we chopped down the weeds, carted off the boulders, and sprinkled the dusty infield with watering cans. Home plate was an old enameled roasting pan sunk upside down in the dirt, and the bases were burlap sacks filled with straw and kept in place with railroad spikes (we were a block from the tracks) that made each slide a bloody adventure.

We were luckier than most kids for we had a real left-field fence which was in itself a handicap. The fence marked the boundary of Old Man Rentschler's property—and although Old Man Rentschler was undoubtedly a splendid citizen, all we knew was that if we hit the ball over the fence into his garden, he'd refuse to throw it back. The idea was never to hit a home run over the left-field wall unless Mr. Rentschler was away.

Right field was no better. It was dominated by a pair of flats with long rows of windows, but therein, oddly enough, lay our fortune. One day Bob Vance, a left-handed hitter of considerable power for a man of nine, hammered a line drive through one of the windows—and we stood there, panic-stricken, waiting for the irate tenant to descend on us.

Descend on us he did, but he wasn't irate. A portly, smiling, round-faced man, he tossed the ball back to us and said, "Don't worry about it, kids, I'll take care of it. And here's another ball —yours got kinda cut up."

He was, oh heavenly day, Jack Downey, trainer for the Sacramento club, and a more delightful neighbor for a mob of baseball-crazy kids would be hard to imagine. From then on, he threw us a veritable fortune in used baseballs and cracked bats—and we became center-field hitters exclusively.

Watch out for Old Man Rentschler in left. And watch out for Mr. Downey's windows in right.

One day we all walked over to Payne's Pharmacy on Y Street and asked Mr. Payne if he'd sponsor us in the Winter League. He did, and bought us each a black cap with a white "P" on it. From then on I was interested exclusively in teams with black caps and white "P's," and that, naturally, would be the Pittsburgh Pirates. I imagine I knew more about Pie Traynor, George Grantham, Spec Meadows, Kiki Cuyler and the Waner boys than they knew about themselves. The old white cap went in the trash can, and Gussie Suhr replaced George Sisler in my affections.

Then my father, again innocently, complicated my life by buying me a uniform—a beautiful white flannel uniform with garish orange-and-black socks. This made me the only kid in the neighborhood with a uniform, and the results were classically predictable and inevitable.

The first time I came to bat in my creamy white splendor, a tough kid from 27th Street named Giddings said, "Caen, if you strike out we're gonna take that uniform offa you and throw it in the river."

Thus unnerved, I struck out on three straight, dropped the bat and streaked up Q Street. My teammates, whooping and hollering and led by the unspeakable Giddings, nailed me in the park a block away, stripped me down to my BVDs, tied the uniform in a dozen knots and threw it into a palm tree.

Life had left its first ugly welt on my psyche. If you can't trust the men you play ball with, what is there left?

And so the long, hot summer years rolled by, all of us talking, eating and dreaming baseball. (I used to fall out of bed in the middle of the night, hollering "Get him at the plate!" and my father would ask me at breakfast, "Well, who won?")

I graduated finally from the neighborhood to the Sacramento Cubs, a well-uniformed team run with professional discipline by a National Guard sergeant major named Jack Tracey, who taught us the lore of signals, the magic of the hit-and-run and the importance of looking like ballplayers at all times—steely of eye, grandly aloof to the hecklers in the bleachers, our jaws rhythmically chewing huge wads of gum. When we spat on our hands and glanced at the third-base coach while knocking the dirt from our spikes, you could see that we were no longer kids. We were men, facing the problems of men with heroic calm.

The Cubs were a good ball club. Our catcher, Bill Salkeld, went on to the Boston Braves. Some of the others, like Cliff Perry and Punky Madden, moved up to the fastest semi-pro teams. And since Sacramento at that time was producing strings of fine players—Stan Hack, Myril Hoag, Alex Kampouris, Joe Marty, Bill Svilich, Boo Coyle—it was only a matter of time before I, too, had delusions, all of them swept away in that one sentence from Buddy Ryan: "Kid, you run like you got a safe on your back."

Long after all these memorable events, I said to Jack Tracey, "How come you kept me on the Cubs so long? When you think about it, I wasn't half as good a ballplayer as the other guys on the team."

"No, you weren't," agreed Jack, looking at me quizzically, "but you were the only one who could write up our games so the sports pages would print 'em."

At long last, the truth—and, even twenty years later, it hurt.

THE SIMPLE FOREWORD to Roy Campanella's book says: "This book was written during a period of convalescence, at a time when I was fighting to get well. I needed a helping hand in its preparation. I was fortunate in that I had two—Joe Reichler of the Associated Press and Dave Camerer of the Columbia Broadcasting System. To them, my sincere thanks."

Here are the first two chapters from that book.

From *It's Good to Be Alive*

ROY CAMPANELLA

MY MIND is so full of thoughts as I sit in my wheelchair and get ready to dictate the story of my life . . . a life that has been so eventful, so exciting, so wonderful . . . a life that was almost taken away from me but which God spared . . . a life such as few people have been fortunate enough to live.

Where shall I start? How do I begin? There is so much to tell. Shall I begin with the automobile accident? When I recovered consciousness in the car and discovered I was paralyzed? Shall I start with the time I came out of the anesthesia after they cut a hole in my windpipe to allow me to breathe?

Shall I open with the time I presented a baseball to a little boy in the hospital with me; and, after I had apologized for not being physically able to autograph it for him, he said simply, "That's all right, Mr. Campanella, I can't see."?

Then there was the World Series day in Yankee Stadium when I slumped in my wheelchair and cried unashamedly as the huge crowd stood on its feet and cheered me for five full minutes.

Baseball has been my life ever since I was old enough to throw one, so perhaps I should start from the day I played my first professional game; or when I joined the Brooklyn Dodgers organization; or when I hit the first of my 242 major-league home runs; or when I won the first of my three Most Valuable Player awards.

Perhaps the proper beginning would be the day I left Rusk Institute to begin a new life, my life in a wheelchair as a quadriplegic? There are so many starting points, so many new phases, so many milestones, it's hard to decide just where to begin.

What stands out most in my mind of all that has happened since the fateful morning of January 28, 1958, when the world turned upside down for me, was something that happened at Holman Stadium in Vero Beach, Florida, nearly fourteen months after my accident.

From where I was sitting in my wheelchair, I could see this little crippled old lady struggling up the steep ramp. She wore steel braces on both legs. Slowly she made her way up with the aid of a wooden crutch under her right arm. Her left arm hung loosely at her side, paralyzed. Her snow-white head was tilted slightly to the left.

Her attendant, a middle-aged man, walked slowly alongside, ever on the alert to grab her should she stumble or fall. Once or twice he tried to assist her, but she shrugged him off. She finally made the top of the ramp where I was sitting. She was gasping and out of breath. She opened her mouth to speak; but no words came. She stood there looking at me in the chair. Her eyes, sorrowed by years of suffering, looked down on my paralyzed body. She slowly lifted them to my face. Reaching out an old, thinned right arm, she took my limp hand in hers.

"Mr. Campanella," she finally managed to say, "I came a long, long way to see you. More than a thousand miles. I just had to see you and thank you, for you gave me the courage and the will to go on when everything seemed hopeless." Her voice trailed off. She was all spent from the excitement, the long trip, the steep climb, the deep emotion. She was very old, and she must have weighed all of eighty-five or ninety pounds. Who was she? Why had she made this long trip? Had she really come just to see me? I wanted to say something to her as she stood there looking down at me, barely able to stand up and refusing to support herself on the arm of her attendant. Then I saw she was ready to speak again.

"Oh, I'm so glad I came," she said earnestly. "You see, I was a patient in the same hospital with you in New York. At the same time. I had a stroke and my entire left side became paralyzed. I couldn't even talk. They didn't give me much hope. As for me, I didn't care whether I made it or not. Then you were brought in. The people at the hospital said you had no chance to live. Crushed vertebrae. A broken neck.

"But you did live. The doctors marveled at your courage. They were thrilled with your faith. They set you up as the example, the inspiration. You became a symbol.

"I don't know exactly when I stopped giving up. All I know is that one day I decided that I just didn't want to stop yet. I was determined to get back on my feet. It was you who gave me the courage, the will to live."

I sat there without saying a word. I just couldn't find any. I've never been accused of being the quiet, shy type. I'm a firm believer in free speech. But that was one time when my tongue was stuck in my mouth. It was most embarrassing. I wanted to thank her. I wanted to ask her name; find out where she was from; learn whether she had any children. But all I could think of was that this wonderful little crippled old lady had come down the length of the United States just to say hello to me—me, Roy Campanella, a Negro ballplayer who happened to have an accident that ended his career and maybe put him for the rest of his life in a wheelchair.

I thought about that a long time after she left. I thought about this little old lady. I thought about the hundreds, no, thousands of people, strangers, who had come to see me since I arrived at this Dodgers spring-training camp. Men and women who had come to shake my hand, to encourage me and wish me well; boys and girls who had come just to look at me and ask for my autograph and who turned away, some disappointed, some embarrassed, when I apologized for not being able to hold a pen or pencil. I thought of the hundreds of thousands of letters and telegrams I had received while in the hospital, from people in all walks of life, from people all over the world—from President Eisenhower down.

The Dodgers and Reds were playing an exhibition game. As a rule no one watches a game with more interest and more concentration than I do. But at this moment the game could have been miles away. I was sitting in back of the last row of the grandstand, behind home plate. My two attendants, Jimmy Williamson and Danny Mackey, were standing on each side of me, to protect me from foul balls. I had been flown down from my home in Glen Cove, Long Island, only a week before to begin my duties as special coach of all the pitchers and catchers in the Dodgers organization.

Being there with my old buddies, with Pee Wee and Duke and Gil and Carl and Clem and my protégé Johnny Roseboro, and being back with the game I love so much was a wonderful thing for me both physically and mentally. Only a year before, when I was lying flat on my back in Glen Cove Community Hospital, fighting for my life, I didn't dare dream that I would ever be back on a baseball field where I had made my living for twenty years, where I had grown from a scared boy into a confident man, where I had learned that on a ball field it doesn't matter who you are or what you are, but how you're fielding, or hitting, or pitching. It's what you do on that baseball diamond that counts. Nothing else.

I'm a lucky guy. I've got so much to be thankful for. Don't feel sorry for me. Please. I'm on my way back, and I'm going to make it.

Some people may think the Lord turned His back on me because of the accident. That's not so. I consider myself very lucky that I was able to play ball for twenty years, half of them in the big leagues. And even when I had the accident I was lucky. How many people have similar accidents and are killed? I could have burned up in that automobile, and I could have died in the hospital after I got pneumonia. The car turned over on me and the engine was running for I don't know how long. The gasoline could easily have leaked out and caught fire, and I couldn't have done anything about it. I tried to turn off the ignition with my left hand. I couldn't move my arm. I couldn't move anything. That's when I knew my whole body was paralyzed.

I have made a great deal of progress. I'm going to make more. There was a time when I couldn't move my arms or my head, when I couldn't sit up. For many months after the accident I couldn't use my hands at all. I couldn't eat or drink by myself. Now I can do all those things. Each day I feel stronger and every day I try something new.

It doesn't take too much fight if you have the courage and the faith. All of us want to live and I'm one of them. And I hope to continue to live and maybe to help some others in the same condition who may have given up just a little.

My last year as a ballplayer was 1957. That was the year Walter O'Malley, owner of the Dodgers, decided to move them out of Brooklyn to Los Angeles. I first began hearing rumors of the switch in February of that year when spring training began at Vero Beach. I remember it was on the eve of Washington's Birthday. The Dodgers' pitchers and catchers had been down early and working out before the others arrived. And it was that evening that Mr. O'Malley made a startling announcement. Ever since baseball has been played there have been player swaps and deals. But this was no player deal. This was a franchise deal! Mr. O'Malley and Phil Wrigley, Jr., owner of the Chicago Cubs, had exchanged minor-league clubs. The Cubs got the Dodgers' Fort Worth club in the Texas League in exchange for Chicago's Los Angeles club of the Pacific Coast League. The deal included the ball parks. That meant that the Dodgers now had Wrigley Field in Los Angeles and a foothold on the Coast if and when.

I should have figured it out right then. Why would Mr. O'Malley make such a deal unless he intended to move? Looking back, it's so obvious. But somehow I didn't see it then. Maybe because I didn't want to see it. I had spent nine of my happiest years in Brooklyn. That's where I wanted to finish my playing career. I got my wish all right, but in a much different way.

Not everybody was as innocent as me, though. The people on the West Coast got the idea pretty quick. The newsprint was hardly dry on those Los Angeles papers when the politicians came swarming in on us at Vero Beach. They arrived in camp like conquerors, looking us over the way a guy does a piece of property knowing he's about to own it. Always looking for an angle, the photographers rigged up a Dodger cap with the letters *L A* on it and asked me to pose with the Los Angeles mayor, Norris Poulson, wearing the cap. I went along with it but to me it was a big joke. The Dodgers leave Ebbets Field? Maybe. But the Dodgers leave Brooklyn? Never.

After we shook hands, Mayor Poulson put one arm around me and said, "Campy, next year you'll no longer be a Brooklyn Bum; you'll be a Los Angeles Bum."

"That'll sure be the day," I grinned.

At the time I wasn't thinking about where I'd be playing "next year." I was more concerned with this year. I was coming off a bad season and was looking to make a good comeback. In '56 I'd played the entire season with two bad hands. The left one had been operated on in '54. Some people thought that after '56 I'd had it.

One big reason why I was looking to a good year was because the pain had left my hands. The numbness was still there but the pain had gone, and I could grip a bat again and had been strengthening my hands by swinging a loaded bat in the cellar of my store. And finally, this was the odd year. This was '57, and I had won the National League's Most Valuable Player award three times, all in odd years—1951, 1953, and 1955. If ballplayers are superstitious, this at least was a happy hunch.

For ballplayers, spring training is a time for tuning up, getting set for the season ahead. Each man has to prepare himself, and of course I was thinking most about my hands and my ability to play as well as I had in my good years. Pee Wee Reese was worried about his legs and his back, being the oldest player on the team. Carl Erskine was trying to come back from arm trouble. Duke Snider had a bad knee and was hoping he could get through the season without undergoing surgery. Don Newcombe had his usual sore arm in the spring. Each of us, especially the veterans, had a personal problem.

But we had a mutual concern: the possibility of this being our last year as the Brooklyn Dodgers. As time wore on, we began to think more and more about moving to Los Angeles, and we talked about it almost every day in the clubhouse and on the bench. Some were for it; some didn't care much either way; and others, like myself, didn't like it. We all had personal reasons for the way we felt.

Gil Hodges was like me. He wanted no part of the West Coast. "I just don't want to move," he said. Gil had lived in Indiana until he got to the big leagues. "I live in Brooklyn," he said. "I'm not just a Dodger ballplayer. Brooklyn is my home. I don't want to have to sell my house, take my kids out of school, leave old friends and all that."

Snider felt the opposite. "I guess it's better for me if we shift. I got an avocado ranch up there in the valley not too far from L. A.," he said.

Reese didn't want to go. He wanted to finish his career in Brooklyn. I guess he played there longer than any other player in history. And nobody was more popular in Brooklyn than Pee Wee. He asked me how I felt about moving.

"Man," I said, "I don't like it nohow. I got my business in New York. I got my home in Glen Cove. Yes, and my youngsters are in good schools. Then there's my boat. Jersey City is as far west as I wanna go."

The Dodgers had played eight games in Jersey City the year before, in '56, because Mr. O'Malley was trying to prove his point to New York City officials that the Dodgers were too big for Ebbets Field. We had simply outgrown the old park. We needed a much bigger field, with bigger and better parking areas. Now, we had another eight games scheduled for Jersey City in '57. I kinda looked forward to those games. Not because I loved hitting in that prairie-sized park. Heck, no. It's just that I would take my boat from the dock near my home in the morning and have an enjoyable cruise down Long Island Sound, into the East River and then on into the Hudson River, and tie up at Jersey City. All our games there were played at night, and so it gave me a day on the water. Oh, how I enjoyed those trips.

The rumored shift to California was only a minor annoyance compared to what was really worrying me. My hands. They weren't right. I knew it in spring training just as soon as I began to bear down. The old breaks and the old and new operations all started hurting at once. At thirty-five, plus, my hands felt more like eighty-five. I wore a kid glove on my mitt hand to help ease the impact on catching a fast ball. Foul tips hurt the bare hand.

As that '57 season wore on, the daily pounding made the hands worse. Occasionally I hit the ball hard, but I knew I wasn't myself at the plate. Manager Walter Alston knew it too. He had to bench me. I was really hurtin'. I didn't like to ride the bench, but the rest did help some. That season I managed to catch a hundred games for the ninth consecutive year. I hit only .242, and the thirteen homers were a very little bit for old Campy. My spirits hit a new low in August, and to make it worse, it was in that month that I found out for sure that we were going to Los Angeles. The only thing that could save us was a miracle—like New York giving us a new ball park, strictly a thousand-to-one shot.

Even though most of us older players were having a bad year, our young pitchers such as Johnny Podres and Don Drysdale were very strong. We managed to stay in the pennant race until August as part of a five-team dog-fight. It was strictly dog-eat-dog and the fans loved it. Then everybody but Milwaukee started losing all at once—St. Louis, Cincinnati, Philadelphia and Brooklyn. Just like that, the race cracked wide-open. The Braves won the flag in a breeze and the Cardinals beat us out for second place. Milwaukee clinched on September 23, and we just played out the schedule for those last half-dozen games.

The Giants had announced early in August that they were quitting New York for San Francisco, so we felt pretty sure, that last week of the season, that we were locking up Ebbets Field. Mr. O'Malley hadn't announced our move officially, but the rumors were too strong. When I went behind the bat in the windup game in Ebbets Field, I knew it was goodbye to that cozy park. It was Thursday, September 28, 1957, and the few fans on hand for the wake waved goodbye after the final out.

We finished the season that weekend in Philadelphia. I drove down and took Roy, Jr., then eight, with me. Tony, two years younger, was slated to go too, but at the last minute he stayed home with his mother. Whenever we played in Philadelphia in all my years in the National League, I stayed with my parents rather than with the team at the Warwick Hotel.

With nothing at stake, I ordinarily would not have had to catch any of those last three games. But I needed one more to give me a league record of catching a hundred games nine years in a row. Ballplayers don't usually watch such things too closely. But I was proud of it. The reporters with the club reminded me of it. They told Alston, too.

So the manager had me catch the first game of the Sunday doubleheader. I knew it was my last game as a Brooklyn player, but had no idea it would be my last game ever. I caught three innings and that completed exactly twenty years in organized professional baseball, ten years in Negro ball and ten in the National League. And my son Roy, Jr., sitting in a box seat behind home plate, saw me catch my last game of baseball.

I drove to New York after the game. I didn't return to my parents' house because Roy had to get back home and into bed so as to be fresh for school the next morning.

I saw every game of the World Series at

Yankee Stadium. The Braves and Yankees had a day off for travel from Milwaukee to New York after the fifth game. On that day, when there was no game, O'Malley announced he was transferring the club from Brooklyn to Los Angeles. It was finally official. Here it was, the move I kept hoping and hoping wouldn't ever happen to us.

It meant that we now had to decide on the things we had talked about in spring training: whether to move our families west and pull out of New York altogether or to just rent in California and remain Eastern people.

My wife Ruthe and I had talked it over at times during the summer hoping we never would be forced to decide, but being sensible enough to realize it might be forced on us. I had to decide whether to sell the business, the house, real estate I own in Harlem, and the boat.

We were very happy in the house, a large, rambling ranch house on Long Island Sound with our own dock. It was wonderful for the children. We knew what we had here. We didn't know what we would get there. And we didn't feel it was right to uproot the children.

My liquor store was doing well, and I saw no sense in selling it. It was the best investment I ever made. I remember when I first mentioned the liquor business, Branch Rickey was dead set against it. Mr. Rickey is a very religious man. He preaches from the pulpit and is a nondrinker. His only vice is smoking expensive cigars. He didn't think that liquor and baseball were a good mix and felt that people might get the wrong idea if a ballplayer sold whiskey.

"Campy," he said, "why don't you invest your money in a sporting goods store or something else where there will be no taint?"

I told him, "Mr. Rickey, you're a white man. Maybe you don't understand the problem a colored man has going into business. How many businesses do you think are open to colored men, outside of entertainment? My people drink. They'll make better customers for whiskey than for sporting goods."

I convinced Mr. Rickey. It was the only time I ever outtalked him. I had no trouble with Mr. O'Malley. He was all for it, and he loaned me the money to get started. So, like I say, I decided to hold onto the store; but the boat was something else.

"I sure hate to sell the *Princess*, Campy," Ruthe said. "But think of the problems it would create. There's no sense shipping it to California. We don't even know where we're going to live. We'd have no place to keep it there and no chance to use it."

I knew she was right.

I decided to get my last licks in enjoying the boat on a one-week fishing cruise in the Atlantic in the nice weather in October.

In many ways that was the most interesting vacation I ever had. I hired a captain and crew of two plus a guide to smell out the fish and bait up the rods. We were after tuna, sail, and marlin.

We picked up the professionals at Montauk, way down at the tip of Long Island. "We" included some fellas—old friends of mine, who didn't get seasick, liked to fish, eat, laugh, and enjoyed drinking beer and tossing the cans in the Atlantic. Once we pulled the hook at Montauk we didn't stop until we were nearly fifty miles out to sea.

As self-appointed cook, I was in charge of the galley. I'd remembered to bring along some frozen meat—pork chops, steaks, and two pheasants. These provisions were brought along just in case. Actually, we expected to eat fish practically every meal. Fish that we caught and boated.

But as things turned out, it's a good thing I brought along that meat. If we'd had to depend on what we caught, we'd have starved. During those first two days out to sea, we never even raised a tuna or sail, much less a marlin. But we did tie into two blue sharks. Each weighed close to 400 pounds. The one I caught took me nearly one and one-half hours to boat. Man, rasslin' with that fish straightened me up! I thought I was in good shape following a full season and all. But that old shark really dragged me out! When I boated him he snapped at me and just missed my toe. We kicked him overboard and cut the other one loose.

On the third and fourth day, we didn't see even a fin. About sundown, I called our home in Glen Cove on the ship-to-shore phone.

"Ruthe," I said, "we're not too lucky out here. We're comin' home."

And that's what we did. I knew that was about the last time I'd be aboard the *Princess*. She would be put up for sale that winter.

It costs cash to maintain a yacht, plenty of it. But for the pleasure she gave my family and me, it was worth it. Some of the nicest times I've ever known have been aboard that boat. One day maybe, when I'm able to do more and get around even better than now, I'll get another boat. There will probably be a lot less of her, but she'll be all boat and something that maybe I can pilot again.

I didn't sell the boat right away. It wasn't until the following June, while I was still in the hospital, that it was sold at auction for $20,000, which was just enough to pay off the notes. I had paid $36,000 for it in 1955 and must have put in about $12,000 in improvements, so I took a pretty good bath.

I got my first look at L.A. in November of 1957. The city threw a welcoming luncheon to celebrate coming into the major leagues. Reese, Snider, Hodges and I were invited. Hodges and I caught a plane from New York together. Reese flew in from Louisville, Kentucky, and Duke drove up from his ranch. While we were there I spent a few days looking for a house to lease but couldn't find what I wanted.

I didn't run into racial or social problems. It was just that it wasn't easy to find the right place for a large family with small children.

After enjoying Christmas at home, I returned to the Coast in January to resume house-hunting and also to appear on a TV spectacular in a salute to Miss Ethel Barrymore. Bing Crosby, Frank Sinatra, Laraine Day, Lauren Bacall, Orson Welles, Joseph Cotten, Hoagy Carmichael were among the theater people on it. Leo Durocher, Braves manager Fred Haney, and Casey Stengel were there too. I presented Miss Barrymore with a season pass for the Dodgers home games, and to her nephew I presented an autographed ball, signed by the whole team. I had to rehearse for a week and spent the free time looking for a place to live.

I was fortunate to find a family in L.A. who would lease me their home all furnished. It was a lovely place in Lincoln Park. I told them that I had young children, and Mrs. Wood said that was all right as she was sure they wouldn't break anything. I phoned Ruthe in Glen Cove, and she was pleased. But I wanted her to actually see it herself. I wouldn't sign the lease until she saw it, so I arranged to come back with her the first Sunday in February.

I'm glad that I didn't know then what would happen to me before Ruthe and I could keep that date.

I'll never forget January 28, 1958. That was the date the world turned around for me.

On Sunday night, the 26th, I attended the Baseball Writers Dinner at the Waldorf-Astoria in New York. I usually go to this affair, which includes a show that kids people and events in baseball. I was sitting at one of the Dodgers tables, with Gil Hodges, Don Drysdale, and Sandy Koufax, when I was interrupted by Harry Wismer, the radio man.

Harry had a TV show on Monday night after the television of the fights at St. Nicholas Arena. He said the Harlem Branch of the YMCA had told him to call me. They had a fund-raising drive on and felt I could help them by appearing on TV. He asked me to appear the next night.

I had been close to the kids at the "Y" working with them in the winters in the gym, and wanted to help. I told Harry I'd go on with him, and we set up the date.

The show was to go on around 10:45 P.M., depending on the length of the fight. I told Wismer to call me at the store before four in the afternoon to make the final arrangements.

Monday was a raw, wintry day. When I walked out of the house to my car around 9:30 in the morning, the wind was howling off the Sound. I got into my 1958 Chevrolet station wagon after waving goodbye to Ruthe and the kids and telling them to watch me on TV that night.

It had snowed a few days before and the roads were icy and treacherous, particularly Eastland Drive and Dosoris Lane, near where I live. Dosoris Lane leads into Glen Cove Road, which in turn leads to Northern State Parkway and on into New York.

When I got into the city, I didn't go straight to my store, which is at Seventh Avenue and 134th Street. Instead, I headed for the Curry Chevrolet service department at 136th and Broadway, a couple of blocks from the store.

The wagon wasn't running right. The motor needed adjustment and the radio was out of whack. These were minor things, but I figured I might as well take it in early in the week and get them fixed. They were busy and said I couldn't get the car back that day. "I want to do a good job for you, Campy," the service manager said. "No sense rushing it. We couldn't get it done in one day and have it the way I'd like it."

I agreed to leave it and rented a 1957 Chevy sedan so I could get around during the day and get home that night. I got to the store around 11 A.M. Cynthia Mason, my secretary, had been away on a two-week vacation; and there were many points to go over, as I had been filling in for her.

Wismer called me before noon and said everything was all set and that I should be at the studios on 67th Street off Central Park West at 10 P.M. I agreed. I told him I'd go out to dinner and be there afterwards. But at nine o'clock after I returned from dinner, Harry called back.

"Campy," he said, "why don't we call off this thing tonight and do it next Monday? That will give me a chance to publicize your appearance, and we should get a larger audience next week. It will mean more money for the 'Y.' "

"Okay, Harry," I said.

Louis Johnson, my clerk, was alone at the time; so I stayed there with him. I usually left the store at four in the afternoon to beat the traffic leaving the city at night, but I had been delayed so long by now that I stayed on.

Johnson and I shifted some stock, and it got so late that I decided to stay until closing and check out the cash register ribbons. We closed the store at midnight, but there was still work to be done. We set up the burglar traps and cleaned up the store.

I counted the receipts and closed the safe, and by the time we had finished, it was about 1:30 in the morning of January 28th. I always have been careful to clean up the store—no empty boxes, no trash on the floor—and to put the plastic covers on the cash registers. I left before two and walked to the car.

How does a man know when he is taking the last steps of his life? I haven't taken one since.

I was tired and it was cold and late. But I drove carefully, as I usually do. I've always been a careful driver and never have been a fast driver. I had never had an accident. The roads in the city had been cleared up from the snowstorms but those in the suburban areas had not been cleaned fully, and they had slippery patches of ice and snow.

I managed the main highways without any trouble and made a left turn into Dosoris Lane, passing the school my children go to. I went down Dosoris Lane and came to this S curve which is a couple miles from my home.

There were big ice patches on the road. They looked like white spots. I could see them clearly. I wasn't going fast, I don't think more than 30 or 35 miles an hour, though I wasn't looking at the speedometer. I followed the road around the bend in the S and was headed for the right side of the road as I came out of the bend. Then I suddenly lost control. The car wouldn't behave. I tried to steer it away from the side of the road. The brakes didn't hold. The surface was sandy and icy. I fought the wheel. The brakes were useless.

I tried furiously to swerve and felt a chill in my spine when I saw I couldn't. I saw this telephone pole right where I was heading. If this had been my own station wagon, which is three hundred pounds heavier and had snow tires, I might have gotten it out of the skid. I managed to turn it away from hitting the pole dead center, but not enough to miss it altogether.

I just did hit it, the right front fender crashing against it. The car bounced off and turned completely over, landing on its right side. I felt the car turning over and the force of it tore my hands from the wheel. The collision knocked me forward and down onto the floor on the passenger's side of the front seat.

I guess my neck hit the dashboard as I plunged. Anyway, my body jackknifed, and I was wedged in under the dash and on the floor. I never thought I was that small to fit into such a small space.

I've gone through the accident a hundred times in my mind. I can still see that pole. You know, it was just about a year later that we went over the same road when Ruthe was driving and I saw patches of ice in exactly the same place. A shudder shot through me at the memory of that night.

"Please, Ruthe," I cautioned her, "take it easy here. This is where it happened."

I guess I never really blacked out for a while, because I remember thinking that the car might catch fire. I was pinned down there under the dashboard with the car overturned. I could feel no pain. In fact, I couldn't feel a thing. But I knew the motor was running. I tried to reach up to turn off the ignition, but I couldn't reach the key. I couldn't move my arms.

That's when the terrible thought came to me: "I'm paralyzed."

I was terrified. I cried out, "O Lord, have mercy on me."

I couldn't move anything.

I don't know how long I lay there, but it seemed long to me. The next thing I knew, a light was shining through the window of the car.

"Why, it's Campy," the fellow with the searchlight said.

"Yes, it's me," I groaned. "Please help me. Help me, somebody. I can't move."

The man with the light was a police officer. Patrolman Frank Poepplein. I recognized his voice. He used to wave to me in town at times and stop and talk. "Okay, Campy," he said. "Just take it easy. We'll get you out."

"Turn off the ignition," I pleaded. "The car will catch fire."

Moments later I must have blacked out for

good. I found out later that the sound of the crash woke up people in houses along the road. I've read since that a doctor crawled into the car and gave me a shot with a needle. But I don't remember that at all. As a matter of fact, I don't even remember being taken out of the car. Ruthe told me later that Poepplein had worked his way into the car and held me rigid while a wrecker got it back on its wheels. It took twenty minutes to free me. They had to use crowbars to get me loose. They laid me face down and rushed me to Glen Cove Community Hospital in a Nassau County police ambulance.

In the meantime, Patrolman Poepplein went to my home. Ruthe was waked up by the bell. It was now nearly four o'clock.

"I hate to come with bad news like this, Mrs. Campanella," he said, nervously. "But your husband has had an auto accident and is on the way to the hospital. I'll be glad to take you there."

They arrived at the hospital about 4:30 A.M. By that time, I already had been wheeled into the X-ray room. There were two doctors there: Dr. Gilbert Taylor and Dr. Charles W. Hayden. Dr. Taylor was holding my head.

"I don't want to alarm you, Mrs. Campanella," Dr. Taylor said. "But your husband is in a state of shock. I'm afraid he's paralyzed. He can't move his legs."

Dr. Robert Sengstaken, chief of neurosurgery at the hospital, had already been called. When he arrived, he examined the X-ray pictures. Interns on duty had read the wet plates which indicated damage to the upper part of my spine. He confirmed this. The X-rays showed that two vertebrae had slipped and overlapped each other.

"He has a fracture and dislocation of vertebrae five and six," Dr. Sengstaken said. "He's paralyzed from just below the shoulders to the toes. He can't push his arms out or grasp, but he can pull his arms in if they're held out for him."

"We've got to operate immediately. We haven't a moment to lose. The quicker it's done, the better. The pressure on his spinal cord must be relieved quickly."

Dr. Sengstaken said he had to have Ruthe's permission before he could operate. She said she was willing to go along with whatever the doctors thought best.

"Perhaps it would be a good idea to call the ball club," Dr. Hayden suggested.

Ruthe thought that Mr. O'Malley was on his way from his home in Amityville, Long Island, to Los Angeles, so she called Buzzy Bavasi, the Dodgers' vice president, at his home in Scarsdale. It turned out that it was Bavasi who had left for Los Angeles, but Mrs. Bavasi gave Ruthe the number for Bavasi in L.A., and Dr. Hayden got on the phone and explained the situation to him.

It was close to seven o'clock when Dr. Sengstaken gathered his operating team of three doctors and six nurses. They took me up to the operating room on the elevator. Ruthe walked along beside me. I was on my stomach, face down, but I knew she was there.

When we reached the door of the operating room, Dr. Sengstaken drew her aside.

"Mrs. Campanella, please go home. There's nothing you can do here now. I assure you that you can help your husband more by getting a few hours' sleep. Your children need you, too. We'll keep in touch with you. I promise that we'll call you as soon as the operation is over."

Ruthe didn't want to leave but she realized the doctor was right. As she turned to go, I said, "Honey, it hurts."

THIS FOND APPRECIATION appeared in *American Heritage,* the distinguished journal of our national history, as written by its editor, the eminent Pulitzer Prize-winning historian, Bruce Catton.

The Great American Game

BRUCE CATTON

BY THE CAREFULLY REPEATED definition of men who stand to make money out of its acceptance, baseball is the Great American Game. The expression was invented long ago and it has been rammed home by talented press agents ever since, even in times when most Americans seemed to be interested very largely in something else. But what has given the phrase its sticking power is not the fact that a big industry has kept plugging it, or the allied fact that unceasing repetition has dinned it into an unreflecting public's ears for generations, but simply the fact that in its underlying essence it is perfectly true.

Baseball is the American game, great or otherwise, because it reflects so perfectly certain aspects of the American character that no other sport quite portrays.

It has few of the elements of pure sportsmanship, as that dubious word is commonly accepted, and it is not notably a game for gentlemen. But it does embody certain native-born fundamentals, including above all others the notion that the big thing about any contest is to win. It also is built upon the idea that anything you can get away with is permissible, and it is the only sport (at least the only one since the Roman populace sat in the thumbs-down section at the gladiatorial games) that puts an invitation to homicide in one of its enduring sayings: "Kill the umpire!" (The thing has actually been attempted, too, more than once.) It is pre-eminently the sport for the professional rather than for the amateur, the sport in which the well-intentioned duffer neither is given nor especially wants a part.

Almost everyone in the country has played it at one time or another, but almost nobody except the professional dreams of going on playing it once full manhood has come. It is a spectator sport in which each spectator has had just enough personal experience to count himself an expert, and it is the only pastime on earth that leans heavily on the accumulation of page upon page of inherently dry statistics. It is also an unchanging pageant and a ritualized drama, as completely formalized as the Spanish bullfight, and although it is wholly urbanized it still speaks of the small town and the simple, rural era that lived before the automobile came in to blight the landscape. One reason for this is that in a land of unending change, baseball changes very little. There has been no important modification of its rules for well over half a century. The ball in use now will go farther when properly hit, and the gloves worn on defense are designed to do automatically what personal skill once had to do, but aside from these things the game is as it was in the early 1900s. Even the advent of night baseball, which seemed like pure sacrilege when it was introduced two decades ago, has made little difference; the pictorial aspect of the game—which is one of its most important features—has perhaps even gained thereby. The neat green field looks greener and cleaner under the lights, the moving players are silhouetted more sharply, and the enduring visual fascination of the game—the immobile pattern of nine men, grouped according to ancient formula and then, suddenly, to the sound of a wooden bat whacking a round ball, breaking into swift ritualized movement, movement so standardized that even the tyro in the bleachers can tell when someone goes off in the wrong direction—this is as it was in the old days. A gaffer from the era of William McKinley, abruptly brought back to the second half of the twentieth century, would find very little in modern life that would not seem new, strange, and rather bewildering, but put in a good grandstand seat back of first base he would see nothing that was not completely familiar.

But that is only the surface part of it. Baseball, highly organized, professionalized within an inch of its life, and conducted by men who like dollars better than they like sport, still speaks for the old days when nine young men in an open park somehow expressed the hot competitive instincts of everybody and spoke for home-town pride.

And perhaps the central part of all of this is the fact that in its essence baseball is still faintly disreputable and rowdy. Its players chew tobacco, or at least look as if they were chewing it; many of them do not shave every day; and they argue bitterly with each other, with their opponents, and with the umpires just as they did when John McGraw and Ed Delahanty were popular idols. They have borrowed nothing from the "sportsmanship" of more sedate countries; they believe that when you get into a fight you had better win, and the method by which you win does not matter very much. Anything goes; victory is what counts.

This John McGraw, for example. When he was playing third base and there was a runner there, and someone hit a fly to the outfield, McGraw would unobtrusively hook his fingers in the player's belt so that the takeoff for the plate, once the ball was caught, would be delayed by half a second or so. He got away with it, too, and no one thought the worse of him, until one day a base runner unbuckled his belt in this situation and, legging it for home, left the belt dangling in McGraw's hand, tangible evidence of crime. Note, also, that baseball knows about the bean ball—the ball thrown at the batter's head to drive him away from the plate and hamper his hitting process. A big leaguer was once killed by such a pitch; it has been condemned by everybody ever since then, and it is still a regular feature of the game.

In its essentials, then, baseball is plebeian, down-to-earth, and robustious. Even half a century ago it was dwindling to the rank of secondary sport in the colleges. Professors who have adjusted themselves to the presence on the campus of *soi-disant* students who are paid to attend college so that they may play football have a way of considering the football player one cut above the baseball player. The former may be a hulking behemoth of pure muscle, wholly incapable of differentiating between Virgil's *Eclogues* and Boyle's law, but he does not seem quite as uncouth as the baseball player—who, in his own turn, may also be on the campus as a paid hand, the difference being that he is being paid by some major-league team that wants to see his athletic skills developed, while the football player gets his from ardent alumni who want to see the college team beat State on Homecoming Day next fall. There has never been any social cachet attached to skill on the diamond.

The reason, obviously, is that baseball came up from the sandlots—the small town, the city slum, and the like. It had a rowdy air because rowdies played it. One of the stock tableaux in American sports history is the aggrieved baseball player jawing with the umpire. In all our games, this tableau is unique; it belongs to baseball, from the earliest days it has been an integral part of the game, and even in the carefully policed major leagues today it remains unchanged. Baseball never developed any of the social niceties.

In the old days, when (as we suppose, anyway) most of us lived in small towns, or at least in fairly small cities, the local baseball team represented civic pride, to say nothing of representing at the same time the dreams of a great many young men who wished to be much more athletic than they actually were. In very small towns, its games were usually held in Farmer Jones's pasture, where the difficulty, in a hot moment of split-second play, of distinguishing between third base and some natural cow-pasture obstacle sometimes led to odd happenings; and in slightly larger places the county fairground or a recreational park at the end of the streetcar line provided the arena. In any case, muscular young men, wearing the singularly unbecoming uniforms that were standardized 75 years ago, presently took their positions on the grass, and the game was on.

It was, and still is, hotly competitive, and within reasonable limits anything goes. If the umpire (there was just one, in the old days) could be suborned to give all vital judgments in favor of the home side, all well and good; no one ever blushed to accept a victory that derived from an umpire's bias. If he could be intimidated, so that close decisions would go as the spectators wanted them to do, that also was good. This often happened; an umpire who decided a crucial play against the home team was quite likely to be mobbed, and few pictures from the old-time sports album are more authentic or more enduring than the vision of an umpire frantically legging it for the train, pursued by irate citizens who wished to do him great bodily harm. It took physical courage to render impartial judgments in old-time small-town baseball, and not all umpires were quite up to it.

If the umpire could be deceived while the game was on, that also was good. A man running from first to third on a base hit would cut twenty feet short of second base if he thought he could get away with it, and no one dreamed of censuring him for it. If an opposing player could be intimidated, so that he shirked his task, that was good, too. Not for nothing was the greatest baseball player who ever lived, Ty Cobb, famous for sitting on the bench just before the game sharpening his spikes with a file. An infielder, witnessing this, and knowing that Cobb was practically certain to ram those spikes into his calf or thigh in a close play, was apt to flinch just a little at the moment of contact, and out of that split second of withdrawal Cobb would gain the hair's edge of advantage that he needed. It was considered fair, too, to denounce an opponent verbally, with any sort of profane, personal objurgation that came to mind, on the off chance that he might become unsettled and do less than his best. (This still goes on, like practically all of the other traditional things in baseball, and the "bench jockey"—the man who will say anything at all if he thinks it will upset an enemy's poise—can be a prized member of a big-league team even now.)

Baseball is conservative. What was good enough in Cap Anson's day is good enough now, and a populace that could stand unmoved while the Federal Constitution was amended would protest with vehemence at any tampering with the formalities of baseball. It looks as it used to look; the batter still grabs a handful of dust between swings, the catcher still slams the ball over to third base after a strikeout, and the umpire still jerks thumb over right shoulder to indicate a put-out. (Dismayingly enough, some umpires now grossly exaggerate this gesture, using an elaborate full-arm swing, but possibly the point is a minor one.)

An inning begins; the pitcher takes his warm-up tosses, now as in the days half a century ago, and after three, four, or five of these he steps aside and the catcher whips the ball down to second base. The second baseman tosses it to the shortstop, two yards away, and the shortstop throws it to the third baseman, who is standing halfway between his own base and the pitcher's box; the third baseman, in turn, tosses it over to the pitcher, and the inning can get started. To vary this formula is unthinkable; from the Little Leaguers up to Yankee Stadium, it is as one with the laws of the Medes and the Persians.

Then action: players shifting about, pounding their gloves, uttering cries of encouragement (which, like all the rest, are verbatim out of the script of 1900); and the batter approaches the plate, swinging two bats (another ironclad requirement), tossing one aside, planting his feet in the batter's box, and then swinging his single bat in determined menace. The fielders slowly freeze into fixed positions; for a moment no one anywhere moves, except that the pitcher goes into his stretch, takes a last look around, and then delivers—and then the frozen pattern breaks, the ball streaks off, men move deftly from here to there, and the quick moments of action are on.

In all of this there is unending fascination, coupled with the knowledge that wholly fantastic athletic feats may at any moment be displayed by any one of the players. Even an easy fly ball to the outfield or a simple grounder to short can call forth a nonchalant, effortless expertness that a man from another land would find quite incredible. (I once took an Englishman to see his first baseball game, and he was dumfounded by the simplest plays, marveling at what all the rest of us took for automatic outs.) In no contest can the split second be so important. A routine double play can make both outs with no more than half a second to spare, and if the half second is lost anywhere, the player who lost it will be derided for a clumsy oaf.

Primarily a team game, baseball is also the game for the individualist. The team play is essential, and when you watch closely you can see it, but the focus is usually on one man. A base runner streaks for second with the pitch, falls away while in full stride, and slides in in a cloud of dust, baseman stabbing at him with gloved hand, umpire bending to peer through the murk and call the play; an outfielder runs deep and far, arching ball coming down—apparently—just out of his reach, trajectories of fielder and baseball coming miraculously together at the last, gloved hand going out incredibly to pick the ball out of the air; a pitcher who has been getting his lumps looks about at filled bases, glowers at the batter, and then sends one in that is struck and missed . . . always, some individual is trying for an astounding feat of athletic prowess and, now and then, actually accomplishing it.

Hence baseball celebrates the vicarious

triumph. The spectator can identify himself completely with the player, and the epochal feat becomes, somehow, an achievement of his own. Babe Ruth, mocking the Chicago Cubs, pointing to the distant bleachers and then calmly hitting the ball into those bleachers, took a host of Walter Mittys with him when he jogged around the bases. (There is some dispute about this, to be sure; he was jawing with the Cubs, but purists say he did not actually call his shot. This makes no difference whatever.) It was the same when old Grover Cleveland Alexander, the all-but-washed-up veteran of many baseball wars, came into the seventh inning of a decisive World Series game, found the bases filled with Yankees, and struck out Tony Lazzeri, going on to win game and Series; and this was after a wearing night on the tiles, Alexander having supposed that his work was over until next spring. Many an aging fan shared in Old Alex's triumph.

These things are part of baseball's legend, for the game never forgets its gallery of immortals. That it actually has a tangible Hall of Fame, with bronze plaques to commemorate the greatest, is only part of the story; the noble deeds of the super-players are handed down in bar-side stories, year after year, losing nothing in the telling. Some of the heroes have been supermen, in a way, at that. There was, for instance, Shoeless Joe Jackson, barred from baseball in mid-career because he let himself be bribed to help lose a World Series. (He did not do very well at losing; even under a bribe, he batted .375 in that Series—a natural hitter who just couldn't make himself miss even when paid to do so.) A sandlot pitcher tells of a day, a whole generation later, when, pitching for a textile-mill team in the Carolinas, he found on the opposing team none other than Jackson —a pathetic, fat, doddering wreck in his late fifties, with a monstrous belly like some disreputable Santa Claus, still picking up a few odd bucks playing semipro ball under an assumed name. The young pitcher figured Jackson would be easy; a low inside curve, coming in close to the overhang of that prodigious paunch, was obviously the thing to throw. He threw, Jackson swung, and swung as he used to thirty years earlier, and the ball went far out of the park, one of the most authoritative home runs the young pitcher ever witnessed. Old Jackson lumbered heavily around the bases, and halfway between third and home he turned to accost the young pitcher. "Son," he said, "I always could hit them low inside curves."

There were others cast in similar molds. . . . Rube Waddell, the wholly legendary character who, when cold sober, which was not often, may have been the greatest pitcher of them all: the man who now and then, on a whim, would gesture the entire outfield off the premises and then retire the side without visible means of support; Walter Johnson, who once pitched fifty-odd consecutive scoreless innings, and who to the end of his days had nothing much in his repertoire except an unhittable fast ball; Tris Speaker, who played such a short center field that he often threw a batter out at first on what ought to have been a legitimate down-the-middle base hit; and lean Satchel Paige, who in his great days in the Negro leagues had a way of pointing to the shortstop and then throwing something which the batter must hit to short, and who then would go on around the infield in the same way, compelling the opposition to hit precisely where he wanted it to hit. The legends are, in some ways, the most enduring part of the game. Baseball has even more of them than the Civil War, and its fans prize them highly.

Under the surface, baseball is always played to a subdued but inescapable tension, because at any second one of these utterly fabulous events may take place. The game may be distressingly one-sided, and the home team may come up in the ninth inning five runs behind, and in a clock game like football or basketball the margin would be physically unbeatable; but in baseball anything can happen, and the tiniest fluke can change everything. (Remember the World Series game the Yankees won when a Brooklyn catcher dropped a third strike with two men out in the ninth?) A commonplace game can turn into a hair-raiser at any moment, and things do not actually need to happen to create the suspense. A free-hitting, high-scoring game may be most eventful, but few strains are greater than the strain of watching a pitcher protect a 1–0 lead in the late innings of a routine game. Nothing, perhaps, actually happens—but every time the ball is thrown the game may turn upside down, and nobody ever forgets it.

All of this is built in, for the spectator. Built in, as well, is the close attention to records and statistics. Batting averages and pitchers' records are all-important; to know that a Rogers Hornsby, for instance, could bat more than .400 in three different years—that is, could average getting two hits for every five times he came to the plate, 154 games a year, for three years—is important. It has been suggested, now and then, that big-league playing schedules be reduced from 154 games to some smaller figure, and the suggestion has always been howled down: it would upset all the averages. Unthinkable; how do you compare today's pitcher with Walter Johnson or Lefty Grove if today's pitcher plays in fewer games every year?

The circumstances under which baseball is played nowadays have changed greatly, to be sure. Less than half a century ago, every town that amounted to anything at all was represented in some league of professional players, and these leagues—the minor leagues, of hallowed memory—have been dissolving and vanishing, as more and more spectators get their games by television or by radio and ignore the local ball park. The Little Leagues have come up, and semi-subsidized sandlot leagues, and even college baseball is here and there enjoying a new lease on life—after all, the new players in the big leagues have to come from somewhere, and besides, young Americans still like to play baseball; but the old pattern is gone, and even the major leagues themselves have undergone profound changes and, to a purist from the old days, are all but unrecognizable. Where are the St. Louis Browns, or the Philadelphia Athletics, or the Boston Braves—or, for the matter of that, even the magnificent New York Giants, and the Brooklyn Dodgers? Gone forever, to be sure, with new cities taking over, and with a few old-timers muttering that the last days are at hand.

Actually, the last days are probably a long, long way off, for baseball even in its modern guise has not changed in its essentials. It is a rough, tough game, encased by rules that were to be broken if the breaking can be accomplished smoothly enough, a game that never quite became entirely respectable, a game in which nobody wants to do anything but win. It will undoubtedly be around for a good time to come, and it will continue, in spite of its own press agents, to be in truth the great American game.

Or so, at least, believes one old-time fan.

WIDE WORLD

THE POWER...

Carl Yastrzemski

WIDE WORLD

THE UMP IS UP...

Imperturbable umpire Bill Valentine keeps his eye on the play from an unaccustomed position. The runner was out.

HOENIX GAZETTE

THE UMP IS...THE UMPS ARE...ER...UH...

Safe or out? This classic picture was taken by youthful photographer Brian Lankar, who at the time was in his first week on the job.

ROBERT RIGER

. . . AND THE GLORY

Stan Musial

WE DO NOT know of any source which traces the basic modern version of baseball so far back in time as this one.

A Letter to the Erie *Tribune*

ANDREW H. CAUGHEY

Erie, Pa., April 8, 1910

To the Editor of *The Tribune:*

Sir: I find this morning in *The Tribune* an article on the "Origin of Base Ball" quoted from another periodical. In this article it is said that Base Ball probably grew out of the English game of "rounders."

I am in my eighty-third year, and I know that seventy years ago, as a boy at school in a country school district in Erie County, Pa., I played Base Ball with my schoolmates; and I know it was a common game long before my time. It had just the same form as the Base Ball of today, and the rules of the game were nearly the same as they are now.

One bad feature of the old game, I am glad to say, is not now permitted. The catchers, both the one behind the batter and those on the field, could throw the ball and hit the runner between the bases with all the swiftness he could put into it—"burn him," it was called. That cruel part of the game has been abolished; the ball is now thrown to the base before the runner reaches it, if possible, and this puts him out.

I never heard of the game called "rounders." "One old cat" or "two old cat" was played then as now; but it was nothing like the Base Ball of my boyhood days. Real Base Ball, with some slight variation of the rules, as it has come down to the present day must be at least a hundred years old; it may be a thousand. Perhaps it has come down to us from the old times of the Greeks and Romans, as many games and other good things have done.

ANDREW H. CAUGHEY

The most colorful umpire of the postwar period was—hands down—Jocko Conlan. And the most colorful piece of umpire reminiscence belongs—hands down—to Jocko Conlan.

From *Jocko!*

JOCKO CONLAN *and* ROBERT CREAMER

I never wanted to be an umpire in the first place. When I was a ballplayer the thought never entered my mind. I wanted to play ball and then I wanted to become a manager. But in 1935, when I was with the Chicago White Sox, I was fooling around with Ted Lyons in the dressing room one day and I broke my thumb. I didn't bother to tell Jimmie Dykes, who was the White Sox manager then. I was getting toward the end of my career, and I hadn't been playing much anyway.

So, of course, the next day Dykes said, "Jocko, you're playing center today."

I said, "I don't think I can, Jim. I hurt my thumb and I can't grip the bat."

"How did you do that?"

"I dove for a ball in practice," I told him. "My thumb hit the ground, and I think it's sprained."

I don't know whether he believed me, but he said, "All right. I'll put somebody else in."

This was in St. Louis. We were playing the Browns a doubleheader in Sportsman's Park, and it was 114° that day. You could see the heat coming up out of the ground. It was terrible, like a brickyard. There were only two umpires assigned to the doubleheader, Harry Geisel and Red Ormsby, and during the first game the heat got to Ormsby and he passed out. They had to carry him off the field. Geisel went behind the plate, but he needed somebody to umpire the bases, and I spoke up. I don't know why; I had never umpired before. But I said, "I'll umpire. I can't play anyway."

Dykes, who could be pretty sarcastic said, "That's for sure." I said, "Yeah? Well, never mind. I'll umpire."

And I did. I went out and umpired the bases in my Chicago White Sox uniform. I had a couple of close decisions but no real trouble. The only argument I had was when Luke Appling of the White Sox hit what looked like a triple. Luke wasn't too fast and I was always very fast, so I ran along with him as he went around the base paths. I yelled, "Come on! Let's go! Get the trunk off your back." He was my teammate, and I was rooting for him to get the triple. Luke had an old country-boy accent and he was yelping, "I'm doin' the best I kin." He slid into third base, but they had him.

"You're out!" I said.

Dykes was coaching at third, and he screamed.

"What do you mean, he's out? He's not out! He's safe!"

"He's *out*," I said.

Dykes yelled, "The man was safe."

Old Appling was still lying there in the dirt, and he looked up at Jimmie.

"No, Papa Dykes," he said. "He's right. He had me. He just got me."

"He *missed* you," Dykes shouted.

"He didn't miss him," I said. "I called him out, and he's out."

Dykes drew himself up, very dignified—gee, he was funny; it was great playing for Jim—and he put this hurt look on his face. "You're a fine guy to have on a ball club," he said, and he walked away.

I worked both games of that doubleheader and finished the series because Ormsby was still feeling pretty weak. That was all I did, but after the season was over Harry Grabiner, the general manager of the White Sox, called me into his office and asked me if I'd like to become an umpire.

"You're pretty near the end as a player, Jock," Grabiner said. "I'd give it a try if I were you."

I thought about it for a while, and then I

said, "All right. O.K." Grabiner sent me around to talk to Will Harridge, president of the American League, and Harridge said, "We had good reports on the job you did in St. Louis. We can always use good umpires. I thought if you were interested we'd help you along. We'd see to it that you got a job."

"In the American League?" I said. "I'll take it."

"No, sir," said Harridge. "We won't take an umpire on unless he has experience. You'll have to go to the minor leagues for that, Jocko."

So I went to the minor leagues. Harridge got me a job in the New York-Pennsylvania League, and I went there in 1936. I earned $300 a month for a season that ran not quite five months. I was thirty-six years old, I was married, I had two children and I was starting a minor league job at the magnificent salary of $1,500 a year. Well, they say an umpire has to have a lot of nerve.

I umpired in the minors for five years, and the most I earned in one year was $3,000. Even when I got to the big leagues my salary was terrible. I have always been grateful to Ford Frick, who was president of the National League then, for giving me a chance to umpire in the major leagues. But the money was awful. I was paid $3,600 my first year, plus $7 a day for expenses. That didn't include travel between cities, which was handled separately, but with the $7 you had to pay for your hotel room, three meals, laundry, cleaning and pressing, and getting yourself to and from the ball park. When I look back at it now I wonder how we made it.

Considering their responsibility and their importance to the game, umpires have always been poorly paid. It's no wonder we went on strike that time in 1964—or almost went on strike. What is a wonder is that we waited so long.

I was raised $900 my second year, but then World War II came in and after the 1942 season they sent me a contract with—imagine this —a $250 raise. This was the major leagues! I argued and I got $500, but that seemed to be the standard for an umpire's raise. I can't say that I was well paid under Ford Frick. The first few years under him I made less money than I had as a minor league ballplayer in Rochester, New York, fifteen years before.

After Warren Giles came in as league president, when Frick moved up to be Commissioner of Baseball in 1951, things became a lot better. Giles is the best friend the umpires ever had. He saw to it that we got better pay, that young fellows got decent salaries to start out with and that umpires who had been in the league a long time, and who had started at much lower salaries than the newer fellows, got bigger raises to even things out. I don't say Giles overraised us, but he did raise us real good, and today the National League umpires get more money per man than American League umpires. Top salary in the American League is about $15,000 now, but it's closer to $20,000 in the National. Rookie umpires start at $9,500. (I was a big-league umpire nearly ten years before I got $9,500.) Warren Giles made umpiring a decent job, and every umpire owes him a vote of thanks.

He was really so much better than Frick. Frick was a nice man, but he never did anything. He didn't seem to have much interest. You very seldom saw him at a ball game, except at the World Series or opening day or at an All-Star game. Giles is at ball games all the time, in whatever city he may be in at the moment. Frick to me was just a guy who got his pay. What did he ever do? Whenever a problem came up when he was commissioner he'd say, "That's a league matter." And he always seemed worried about spending money, even on little things. For instance, they give the players and the umpires in a World Series a little memento—a ring or a cigarette case, something like that. Nice, but nothing extravagant. One year—it was 1957—Frick met with the umpires and he asked each one what he wanted, and he didn't ask me. I said, "What about me?" He said, "There isn't any for you this year." I said, "Why not?" He said, "You've been in enough World Series. You don't need any memento this time." I said, "If all these guys are entitled to a memento, I am, too." But he wouldn't give in, and I never got one that year.

And then in 1961 I was in the Series again and we had the same meeting, and this time he asked me what I wanted. I said, "Well, I don't know. You turned me down the last time I worked a Series. How can I ask you for something now?" He said, "Do you want a ring?" I said, "No. I don't want a ring. I got a ring." He said, "I'll send you a pin then." I said, "I'll take it." He sent it to me, and it's a beauty, I'll say that. But I still don't understand why he wouldn't give me anything that other time.

Frick did another thing to me in the 1957 Series. He fined me $100, and I still think he had no right to. I was in the washroom in the umpires' quarters in Yankee Stadium before the first game of the Series when Beans Reardon and Larry Goetz came busting in. Reardon and Goetz had both retired from umpiring by then, but they were still close to the game.

"We want to get a couple of baseballs for Hal Stevens," Reardon said. The umpires always had a few extra baseballs, and old Hal Stevens of the Stevens concession family was one of the grandest men anyone could ever want to meet. A fine, warm man, and he loved the umpires. It was a natural thing for Reardon and Goetz to get a couple of baseballs for him.

"Help yourself," I said, "but you're not supposed to be in here, you know." Frick had issued orders that no one was to be allowed in the dressing rooms before the game. I guess the idea was that they didn't want anybody talking to the umpires—hoodlums looking for information that could help them with bets or setting odds or anything like that. It was a good order. Reardon and Goetz took the baseballs and left.

The next day I was to work behind the plate, and ten minutes before the game began Charlie Segar came in. He was Frick's assistant.

"The boss wants to see you," Charlie said.

"*Now?*" I said.

"Yes, now." I went out on the field and walked over to Frick's box. The first thing he said was "I'm fining you $100."

"For *what?*"

"You let two umpires in your dressing room, and I told you the order was nobody allowed in the dressing room."

"I know that," I said, "but I didn't let them in. They came in. All they wanted was a couple of baseballs for Hal Stevens, and then they left."

"Well, that's it."

I said, "You mean you'll take $100 off me for that?"

"Who were the umpires?" he said.

"If you know I let two umpires in, you must know who they were."

"Reardon and Goetz," he said.

"I want to tell you something, Mr. Frick," I said. "I broke in with Reardon and Goetz. I never knew two more honorable guys in all my life. They served you and baseball well for more than twenty years. If I can't give them a baseball, as decent and loyal as they are, then I don't care. You can have the $100. Keep it."

And then I had to go up and umpire behind the plate. A World Series game, and I had to go through that ten minutes before it began. That was the game I turned the lights on—early, at 2 o'clock in the afternoon. Nobody had ever turned the lights on that early before in a World Series game, but it was just too dark around the plate and I went over and had them turned on. The next day Frick complimented me. They were telecasting the game in color, and the TV people were having trouble with their pictures before the lights went on. Frick said the TV people had called him to thank him, and he passed the compliment on to me. But he never gave me back my $100.

Umpires don't get paid enough for working a World Series, anyway. Even before expansion you'd get to work in a Series only about once every four or five years, and now it's once every six or seven. It used to be that the four regular umpires got $2,500 apiece for a Series, and the two alternates $1,000. Now it's $4,000, and all six umpires get that. I felt—and I argued for it back in 1945—that they should pool one winning share and one losing share for each two umpires and split it evenly between them. The presidents of the two leagues, Frick and Harridge, voted against it. They said it was the players' money and the umpires couldn't touch it. I said, "Players' money? It's the people's money. It's supposed to go to the participants. Umpires are participants just as much as the players are." But they said no.

They used the same argument when they put the Player Pension Plan in after World War II. One of the great injustices in baseball was leaving the umpires out of that plan. I always felt that if Ford Frick, as president of the National League, had insisted that the umpires be included back when they were drawing up the plan, there never would have been any question about it.

In the 1950s and 1960s we tried several times to get the player representatives to suggest that we be brought into the plan. We talked to different fellows—Ted Williams and Stan Musial and Gil Hodges and others—and they came out openly and said they thought it was only right. Robin Roberts was the head of the National League player representatives at the time. Somebody told me once that Bob Carpenter, the owner of the Phillies, said that Roberts ought to end up with a million dollars, he was such a tough negotiator about money. "He's as cold as ice," Carpenter said. I believe it. I collared Roberts after a players' meeting one year.

"Did you fellows decide anything about the umpires?" I asked him.

He looked right through me with those blue eyes of his.

"What?" he said.

"I hear you talked about the pension plan," I said.

"Why, yes, we did," he said.

"Did you decide anything about the umpires?"

He gave me one of the most disgusted looks I ever saw in my life.

"We didn't even discuss you fellows."

"Isn't that nice," I said. "Great guys like Williams and Musial and Hodges say the umpires belong in the plan as much as they do, but you don't even discuss it."

There had been a pension plan in force for the umpires—it had been in force when I went to umpiring in 1936—but it wasn't too impressive. You got $100-a-year pension for each year you umpired; in other words, if you umpired eighteen years you retired on $1,800 a year. That wasn't bad in the middle of the 1930s, when a guy would get married on $35 a week, but by 1950 it wasn't the same thing, not by a long shot. But it was never changed until Warren Giles succeeded Frick as president of the National League.

Giles raised the pension the first year he was in office. He upped the basic rate from $100 a year to $150 and then later to $200, and he made the increase retroactive for umpires who were still in the league. We contributed 5 percent of our salaries to the pension, but it was worth it because the pension was doubled.

Even so, it still didn't compare to what the ballplayers were getting. And there were other things we wanted—insurance and hospitalization and things like that. We had Blue Cross, but we paid for it. So we organized an umpires' association in the National League. It was really started by Augie Donatelli and myself in 1963. We planned a meeting in Chicago on an off day because Chicago was the easiest place for umpires traveling east and west to new assignments to get together. We elected five directors: Tom Gorman, Al Barlick, Shag Crawford, Augie Donatelli and myself. We had decided that we wanted a lawyer, and because the meeting was to be held in Chicago, where I had lived for so long, they asked me to suggest one. I know a lot of lawyers in Chicago, and we settled on John J. Reynolds, a young fellow I knew, a very intelligent man. I got in touch with Reynolds, and he was interested, so he came to the meeting and sat down and talked to us. He listened to what we had to say, and he explained some things to us. He told us what he thought he could do, and he told us what his fee would be.

We talked it over, and we decided to retain him. The following winter the major-league meetings were to be held in Los Angeles. We agreed to have a meeting of our own there, because Reynolds thought it would be good for us to be in Los Angeles then. We would be there more or less like a lobby, working for our interests and trying to get the owners to do something for us.

I think we made a mistake in not telling Giles in the first place that we were hiring a lawyer, because anything we got would have come through Giles anyway. But after we retained Reynolds he went down to Cincinnati and met Giles, and he made a good impression. Giles agreed to let him talk to the league's executive board in Los Angeles. Buzzie Bavasi of the Dodgers was on that board, and John Holland of the Cubs and Bill DeWitt of the Reds.

Reynolds spoke to the board and requested that certain things be done for the umpires. He asked for hospitalization, life insurance, increased pension benefits and things like that, very similar to what the ballplayers were getting. The main thing was the pension. We wanted it raised to $300 for each year of service. We figured that a man who had umpired twenty years deserved a $6,000 pension. We thought that was fair.

When Reynolds was through talking, the executive board recommended that he be given the opportunity to present his case to the pension board. I believe Bavasi made the motion, and Holland seconded it. The pension board had John Galbraith of Pittsburgh as chairman, and men like Don Grant of the Mets and Walter O'Malley of the Dodgers were on it, and a few others. Giles arranged for Reynolds to talk to the pension board, and he seemed to be pretty well received. It was encouraging. They said they'd take his proposals under advisement.

When nothing happened, the umpires got restless. We had another meeting in May of 1964. About the same times Giles got the pension base raised from $200 to $250. He didn't know about the May meeting; he just did that on his own.

But the umpires wanted the $300 base, and they wanted the other benefits. They felt the owners were giving them the runaround. We met in May at the Union League Club in Chicago and took a vote and decided to go out on strike on July 4. I was against the strike. I thought it was a mistake, and I said so.

They said, "We're going out on strike."

I said, "Look, whatever you decide to do, I'll go along with it, because I'm an umpire and I'm all for the umpire getting everything that's coming to him. But you're doing it the wrong way. You're trying to bulldoze them. Why don't we send the lawyer down to talk to Giles again and explain our position. That's what we hired the lawyer for."

I didn't get anyplace with them. If you have ever been in a meeting with twenty umpires you know *nobody* gets anyplace. There are twenty different motions and twenty different seconds. It's the damnedest conglomeration you ever heard in your life. That was the reason we hired the lawyer in the first place, to get something done. One man can talk for twenty, and that's the proper way to do it. I didn't get anyplace with them.

"We're going out on strike," they said. "We're going on strike the Fourth of July."

"What a day," I said. "One of the biggest days of the year in baseball. You're really going to defy them."

About a month later I was working a ball game in Los Angeles. It was in June, getting close to July. Buzzie Bavasi came to me, and he said, "I want to ask you a question about something that's just beginning to dawn on us. Are the umpires really going out on strike?"

I said, "Yes, they are."

"Are *you* going out on strike?" he said.

Buzzie was always a big help to the umpires and a good friend to me. But I said, "Buzzie, I'm an umpire. I have to go along with them. It's the only thing I can do. I don't like it. I think we should have gone to Giles again. But that's the way it is."

Buzzie said, "Gee. Everybody is beginning to think about this. It's a bad thing. It's pretty serious."

I said, "I know how to stop it."

"You know how to stop the strike?" he said. "How?"

"I *think* I know," I said. "At least, I have an idea."

The All-Star break that year was the 6th, 7th and 8th of July and the strike was set for the 4th. All major-league clubs are represented at the All-Star game, and they usually have a meeting.

I said, "If you can give our lawyer, Reynolds, representation at the All-Star game—so he can present our case to *all* the owners there—I think the strike would be postponed."

"That's all?" he said. "It's that simple? You think that would do it?"

The thought had just come to me, but I said, "If he can talk to them I think we'd vote to put it off."

Bavasi phoned Giles, and Giles promised that Reynolds could speak to the owners. When the umpires heard that, the strike was called off. The fact that the owners would hear Reynolds was very important, because that was the only chance we had of getting our case before all of them. And they came to an agreement with us. We didn't get everything we wanted, but we did get the big thing. The pension was raised to $300 for each year of service up to the age of fifty-five (you can work past fifty-five but your pension doesn't get any bigger). There were other details. Instead of paying 5 percent of our salaries into the pension fund, we paid a flat $350. Each umpire was insured for $20,000 ($50,000 for accidental death). Hospitalization is still being argued about.

But the main thing was, the strike was off. The umpires' demands, which were reasonable, were recognized.

Maybe the owners recognized, too, that baseball without umpires is nothing. They can't play without us. They should remember that.

JOHN GALLAGHER

Courtesy *Sport* Magazine ©

JOHN GALLAGHER

Courtesy *Sport* Magazine ©

At the time this article appeared, in *The Saturday Evening Post* of April 10, 1965, Dean Chance was with the Los Angeles Angels, and so, appropriately, Myron Cope entitled his piece "The Angel Who Doesn't Fear to Tread." Subsequently Mr. Chance was traded, making him an ex-Angel. Somebody said that if he was swapped to the Cardinals, that would make him an arch-Angel, on account of the Gateway . . . ah, never mind. Important thing is, he still don't fear to tread.

Dean Chance

MYRON COPE

Wilmer Dean Chance, farmer, baseball pitcher and *enfant terrible* of the sporting scene, sat folded into the right front seat, his bony knees almost to his chin, as the car sped north through the winter night toward Cleveland. To the journalist chauffeuring him, he declared, "You could call your story *The Most Exciting Pitcher Since Bobby Feller*. You ever heard of a year like I had? I led the league in wins, with twenty. I had the lowest earned-run average in both leagues—1.65—the lowest since 1943, and which by the way is only one one-hundredth from being the lowest since 1919." Actually, it was 16/100 from the 1919 record held by Walter Johnson, but the difference seemed hardly worth an interruption. "My God, you could go back further and call your story *The Most Exciting Pitcher Since Dizzy Dean*. Holy cow, I shut out the Yankees three times and another time shut them out for fourteen innings before I got pulled for a pinch hitter. No pitcher in history ever did that. No man alive ever pitched like that. The Yankees *averaged* .089 batting against me. Talk about pressure, I'm *greatest* under pressure. When I was a rookie, the largest crowd that seen me was 55,000 at Yankee Stadium, and I went the hell out there with the bases loaded and none out and blew down Howard, Skowron and Lopez on eleven fast balls. Fifty thousand seen me at the All-Star game last year, and I was the best damn pitcher out there. You could call the story *From Rags to Riches*. Or how's this? *The Greatest Year Ever!*"

Farmer Chance's words rang with happy defiance. His gray-green eyes, set in a baby-white face, focused straight ahead, as if the highway over which he rolled were Fred Haney, the Los Angeles general manager whom he has trampled in salary battles. In Wayne County, Ohio, he now owned 83 prime acres, 60 head of Angus and Hereford and 100 hogs, and he was getting 140 bushels to the acre on his corn yield. Pitching baseball for the Los Angeles Angels, he had seen the bright lights and been up late enough to watch them go out. Grandly, he now patted down his black hair, which had been styled in gorgeous waves by a Hollywood hairdresser recommended to him by his former teammate and fellow *bon vivant*, Bo Belinsky.

"Listen," he tore on, "I led the league in innings pitched—278. I gave up only seven home runs in the whole 278, which is phenomenal, and I wouldn't be surprised that it's got to be a record, but no records are kept. I won five games by 1–0, which tied an all-time record held by Johnson and Hubbell. I pitched eleven shutouts, the most since 1920. I had a lot of two-hitters and three-hitters—you can call Kaze, the publicity guy, and check that out. My earned-run average in home games was 1.00," Chance specified, converting the truth—1.08—into round figures. "Man, you ever heard statistics like mine? You can call the story *The Farm Boy Makes Good*."

Baseball season was coming on, but Chance was hell-bent to clean up the last of the banquet-circuit money; on this swing he would go from Cleveland to New York to Philadelphia to Harrisburg. He wore his favorite ensemble—

black overcoat, black suit, white shirt, black tie, black socks, black shoes. "He looks like a divinity student," a man had remarked at a banquet to Dick McCann, curator of the National Professional Football Hall of Fame. "You mean," McCann had replied, "he looks like an altar boy who just stole the sacramental wine." Sartorially unpredictable, Chance at Christmastime had appeared at his lawyer's office in a powder-blue coat and burgundy necktie, demanding, "Isn't this good-looking?" The lawyer had answered, "We ought to sue the guy who sold it to you."

The Angels climbed from ninth place to fifth last year, and no small part of the reason was that the fashion plate, just turning 23, pitched better than anyone else in baseball. He became the youngest player ever to win the Cy Young award, a plaque that goes each year to baseball's most valuable pitcher.

Now, still reciting his deeds, Chance sang out: "In my last 57 innings against the Yankees, I gave 'em one run. One lousy run. I told Vic Power, 'Vic, I'm gonna strike out Mantle this time'—and bang, Mantle hits one out of the park, the only stinking run they got all year off me. I should have won thirty games and had fifteen shutouts, but I got no hitting behind me. I don't know if it will get better this year, but it sure as hell can't get worse. Three games of mine they blew in the field. In one of them the little guy"—presumably five-foot-five outfielder Albie Pearson, though Chance in a burst of diplomacy wouldn't say—"louses one up in the ninth. Nobody's perfect, you can't blame them, but there's three games. So I won twenty, and my God, I had a blister on my finger early in the season. I need one more big season, and I'll go to Japan and pitch three exhibitions for twenty-five grand apiece. I don't even want to think about winning thirty. Thirty! Gosh, I'd break my tail for thirty. I'd pitch every day the last two weeks and go home every night and soak my arm in a bucket of hot water. You gonna use my picture on the cover? You could put on the cover *The Amazing Rise of Dean Chance. From Farm Boy to Great Money Pitcher*. You put this story on the cover, and there ain't nobody who's not gonna read it. For crying out loud, I mean *nobody*. They pass it up, they're a mental case."

The car pulled into a hotel near Cleveland-Hopkins Airport, and Chance went to bed, though not directly to sleep. After a thousand or so words, spoken in the darkness, he sighed, "Some of these ballplayers that go broke are such nice guys, it's a crying shame to see them end up busted. I want that security." So saying, he forthwith began to snore.

The encomiums that Dean Chance showers upon himself cannot properly be classified as bragging. Being the son of a Midwestern dirt farmer, he is a tough horse trader, and he knows that one does not get the best price by calling attention to the animal's spavined joints and loose teeth. Already he has reduced to shambles baseball's traditional rule that high salaries are arrived at by gradual accumulation of seniority. This year Fred Haney offered him $40,000. Chance countered with a demand for $50,000, and sideline observers unanimously surmised the two men would compromise at $45,000. Chance, however, made a point of defeating the sideline observers, making Haney cough up "just a pinch more" than $45,000. His salary probably is the highest ever paid a 23-year-old baseball player.

The fact is, Haney has found that negotiating with his rural *Wunderkind* is like talking to a Missouri mule. Getting the money due him, explains Chance, is no different "than knowing the price of corn." When he does not get it, he lays siege to Haney, blasting him in the newspapers till Haney wilts. Does the general manager resent such abuse? "Not really," says Haney, "because each time it happens he phones me and says he was misquoted."

In the end, Haney dares not tell his persecutor to spend the summer slopping hogs, for the young man is irreplaceable. Last season, only his third in big-league ball, he blossomed into a powerful pitching machine. All arms and legs, six feet three and 200 pounds, he winds up in a series of jerks, kicks and spasms, turns in the direction of center field, and without bothering to look at the batter till the last instant, whiplashes the ball at a speed that curls a batter's hair. "It's a god-awful delivery," says Rocky Bridges, a former Angel coach. "He throws a lot of things at you and then the ball."

Most of all, Chance's pitching style is characterized by his pugnacity, by the sheer joy he derives from the battle. Against Washington, in a late-season performance last year, he somehow gave the Senators the impression he was trying to break their skulls. Accordingly, when Chance himself strode to bat, Washington pitcher Bennie Daniels fired two pitches close to his head.

"Everyone on the Washington team congratulated Daniels," says Chance, proceeding with delight to the epilogue. "So he come up, and I lowered the boom on him. I threw the ball a foot out of the batter's box and still missed him by half a foot, that's how fast he was running. I guess I put the point across to Mr. Daniels."

American League batters fume that Chance throws illegal spitballs, secretly moistening the baseball while going through his strange windup. Baltimore slugger Brooks Robinson suggests, in fact, that Chance does so merely to satisfy a compulsive urge for mischief. "He doesn't really need a spitter, because he's got such good stuff," says Robinson. On the basis of the accused's retort, it is difficult to determine if he throws any spitters or not. "I didn't even throw two or three spitters last year," he begins. "I didn't throw one, not one. It's just that my fast ball sinks, so they think it's a spitter. I throw fewer spitters than anyone in the league."

Whatever his transgressions, practically every game that Chance wins is a suspense-packed race—a race in which he works with frantic speed to complete the game before one of his teammates blows it. Last season his supporting cast finished seventh in fielding and eighth in batting. "Those guys," says Sir Walter Burke, a traveling Boston Irishman who is one of many Runyonesque characters Chance has collected around the circuit, "could be standing on Pier Four and all they could catch is a cold." When Angel infielders successfully field a grounder, Burke goes on, they sometimes are so astonished that by the time they have thrown to first base the runner is safe. "You can hear Chance swearing on Coney Island," adds Burke.

Chance, on the advice of friends, tries to accept his teammates' errors as graciously as he can. The truth is, however, that he thoroughly enjoys the occasional sparks that his presence in the big leagues creates. "Nuts to the charts," he says of the laboriously prepared reports that track the strengths and weaknesses of opposing players. "The charts don't mean a thing. If I'm gonna get beat, there's one man who's gonna beat me," he goes on, thumbing himself emphatically in the chest, "and he's right here."

Pregame clubhouse meetings, he contends, are largely a waste of time. "Who tells you how to pitch the opposing hitters?" Chance demands. "Your hitters do. It's a joke. If I don't know more about pitching than those hitters do, I don't deserve to pitch." In the end, says Chance, the ability to win boils down to one quality. "There's a word for it, and the word is gutsiness. I got gutsiness."

Roy Bates agrees that Chance does. Bates coached him at Northwestern High, a red-brick country schoolhouse in the northwestern part of Wayne County. When Chance first reported for the baseball team, Bates asked him, "What can you throw?"

"I got eight different pitches," piped Chance, "including a snake ball and a super-snake ball." Having no time to wash out the freshman's mouth with soap, Bates made him tuck in his shirttail, straighten his cap, and run 100 laps around the field.

In succeeding years, Bates watched the evolution of Dean Chance with both amusement and awe. The first time the farm boy went on a road trip, a waitress asked him how he wanted his steak prepared. "Medium rare, well done," he replied. Later, when asked if he cared for dessert, he answered, "No, ma'am, but I'll have another steak if it's all right." As a pitcher, Chance began mowing down everybody in sight. He was so invincible that one day, when he gave up two solid hits in a row, Coach Bates rushed to the mound, alarmed at what seemed a collapse.

"I put on the wrong shoes," explained Chance. "They're two sizes too small." Bates went to work with a knife, giving Chance's toes air, and then settled back to watch him pitch a shutout.

On at least one occasion Bates arrived late for batting practice and found Chance practicing knockdown pitches on his teammates. "He wanted to throw at anybody," recalls Bates. "I wouldn't let him throw at people, but one day a shortstop from Shreve called us a bunch of so-and-so farmers, so I said, 'Dean, next time that guy bats I want him down.' Dean's first pitch to the kid was a little high, but his second pitch I'll never forget as long as I live. That kid sat down so fast that he left his helmet sitting in midair. The ball passed between his helmet and his noggin. He was so scared he committed six errors in the next two innings."

After having accumulated a high-school record of 18 no-hitters, 51 victories and only one defeat, Dean Chance commanded a $30,000 bonus from the Baltimore Orioles and set off on a bus to the Orioles' Class D farm in Bluefield, West Virginia. His spirits were high, for the Orioles had sent him $34 for travel, and the bus ticket had cost only $12. To his great astonishment, however, Appalachian League hitters, a notch better than Ohio schoolboys, promptly teed off on his most precious home-brewed pitch—a creation he had heralded as "my one-pronged fork ball."

Reduced to his fast ball, snake ball, and

super-snake ball, Chance nevertheless won 10 games and lost only three, all the while deporting himself outrageously. To amuse himself, Chance knocked on a teammate's door and hurled a bucket of water in the respondent's face. He paid another teammate to walk through a crowded restaurant clad in nothing but undershorts. ("What makes this story good," Chance laughs today, "is that here is a ballplayer who signed for $75,000 parading around in his shorts for twenty-five bucks.")

Moving on to a winter instructional league in Florida, Chance poured a pitcher of beer on a teammate, was socked in the jaw, shook off the blow, and cheerfully pronounced it just repayment. At Appleton, Wisconsin, his next stop, he reported four days late, advising the club's business manager, "If you want to win a game for a change, pitch me." While in Appleton he helped win one game hours in advance by luring the opposing pitcher into an all-night poker game. He also married a Wisconsin farm girl, Judy Larson, and after being sold to Los Angeles for $75,000, proceeded to the Angels' Dallas-Fort Worth farm club, where he won only nine games and lost twelve during the season.

"Who says I had a lousy record?" Chance demands. "I had twenty-eight saves in relief! Nine wins and twenty-eight ball games saved —that's a phenomenal record."

Stepping into the big leagues in 1962, Chance immediately achieved notice by falling into the fast company of Bo Belinsky, a city slicker in suède shoes, whose skill with a pool cue and zest for life fascinated the farm boy. "Nobody except my mother has done more for me than Bo," Chance has testified, drawing a comparison that is interesting inasmuch as his mother is a country-church Sunday-school teacher. In the trunk of his car he now carried a $50 pool cue, complete with soft-grain leather case. Early in the season Fred Haney picked up the morning newspaper and read that Belinsky had heaved an incompatible lady friend out of his Cadillac at 5:30 A.M. Because tagalong Chance had been at the scene, he—like Belinsky—was fined $250, the first cruel blow that filled him with resolve to separate the club from large sums of its money.

As it happened, Chance was then on his way to an admirable 14–10 pitching record and the Angels were winning with astonishing frequency, so he braced the front office for a type of benefit that he has since popularized—the mid-season raise. He demanded, and got, a boost from $6,000 to $11,000. "We were in third place," he says, getting swiftly to the root of Haney's capitulation, "and everybody was out of their minds."

Haney granted him $18,000 the next season but promptly took back $500 when Chance arrived late for a spring-training exhibition game. "I'd pitched seven innings the day before and didn't give up one lousy run," Chance fumes.

"Haney said, 'Next time it's a thousand.' All this stuff builds up inside you. You get tired of getting it stuck to you."

Meanwhile, Chance introduced a new twist to intrasquad games, rejecting the time-honored proposition that pitchers are supposed to lob the ball so hitters can unlimber their muscles. It hurt him to see the hitters enjoying themselves. "So I struck out six of 'em in a row," Chance recalls, delighted by the memory. "Wagner, Thomas, a whole string of them. Oh, Lord, were they moaning."

Fortified by his salary raise and new fame, the ascending Angel had invested $5,000 in a sporting-goods shop, which now folded. He recouped $4,000 peddling inventory to Los Angeles stores, each of which demanded he make a personal appearance. "I had to sign a lot of autographs to get rid of all those sweat socks," sighs the boy pitcher. To make matters worse, he was well on his way to losing 18 games, for the Angels had rediscovered their natural impulse to overrun easy fly balls and stomp grounders.

Chance viewed their errors less than kindly. After striking out 12 in one game, he proclaimed, "I *had* to strike 'em out. I didn't dare let 'em hit the ball to anyone."

Teammates retaliated by filling his locker with garbage and posting a sign above it that read, I'M NOT NATURALLY STUPID, I'M JUST PRACTICING. Still, Chance continued to denounce ineptitude wherever he saw it. Demanding a substantial raise for 1964, he called Haney's attention to the fact that in his 18 defeats the Angels had supplied him with only 28 runs. Nevertheless, Haney refused to raise his $18,000 salary a nickel, arguing that Chance had begun the previous season in poor physical condition, because he had refused to allow spring training to interfere with his pool game. "I'm not going to give you a raise till you prove you're willing and ready to make baseball your number-one objective," Haney declared, adding that he would give him a raise in mid-season if his performance merited one.

Chance, noting that one cannot deposit

promises in the bank, signed his contract under protest and immediately mounted a fierce attack on Haney in the newspapers, spicing it with trade rumors that he whispered to sportswriters—Chance for Minnesota's Bob Allison, Chance for San Francisco's Orlando Cepeda. "Hell, yes," he says. "I put Haney on the spot." No sooner had he recorded his second victory than he demanded Haney pay up. Recalling that Haney refused, Chance says, "I told him, 'Then you'll get $18,000 worth of pitching and no more.' Around and around we went, and I said, 'I'm not wasting any more of my valuable time here.' He just sat there. What could he say? He thought I was crazy."

Undaunted, Chance took his case to club president Bob Reynolds. "Dean didn't exactly go over Haney's head," wrote Jim Murray in the Los Angeles *Times*. "He went right through it." Soon after, Haney caved in, hiking Chance's pay to $25,000. By now the intrepid farmer had wrung mid-season raises from management in two years out of three, a pattern that normally might touch off a run on the front office. The Angels, however, created no such problem for Haney. "For crying out loud," says Chance, pinpointing the reason, "they weren't doing nothing."

Meanwhile, on a July afternoon Chance proved to himself that he was worth every penny he was getting. Pitching three innings for the American League All-Stars, he shut out the National League on two hits, which was quite a feat because, he says, "I went to bed a quarter past four." As the season wore on, Chance won nine straight games and narrowly escaped involvement in a hotel-room brawl in which his roommate, Belinsky, scored a quick knockout over an elderly Los Angeles sportswriter, Braven Dyer. The Angels suspended Belinsky but accepted Chance's solemn oath that, far from participating in the fisticuffs, he had been in the bathroom showering. "I guess that proves he's clean-living," observes Rocky Bridges.

Back in Wayne County, meanwhile, a country lawyer named Hank Critchfield measured the full import of the local boy's success and decided it was time to touch up his public image. Critchfield, a stolid, ruddy-faced man with a shock of iron-gray hair and a small-brimmed fedora that sits atop his head like a loosened bottle cap, is Chance's longtime friend and counselor. He was chiefly concerned that Wayne County had acquired the wrong impression of its native son, who by now was the father of a two-year-old son and had expressed the intention of becoming a substantial landholder. ("I'm gonna own so much land, it'll be phenomenal," was the way he put it.) Though Chance does not smoke and scarcely ever drinks, his much-publicized friendship with night-owl Belinsky had made him seem a bad boy to many in the community. "Around here," says one Wayne County man, "if you get caught with a case of beer in your icebox, it's as serious as getting caught crawling in someone's bedroom window."

Upon Dean's return home at season's end, lawyer Critchfield coached him meticulously for a forthcoming speech before a Wooster service club. "The only thing I didn't cover," says Critchfield, "was gambling. So he ends his speech by saying he loses all his money at poker and gin rummy."

Notwithstanding his furious campaign for money and security, Chance grabs his share of restaurant checks, and then some. Actually, Chance's friends suspect that money itself gives him little more pleasure than the challenge he experiences in foxing it out of someone's pocket.

On the go all winter, he flew one day to Madison, Wisconsin—a $69 flight with a change of planes in Chicago—for lunch. "I got a guy there who's got nothing but cash," he said. "He wants to put me on network TV. I should make a hundred G's out of it." He would star, he said, in a marionette show, to be called *Dean Chance and His Funny Friends.* In Madison, tossing a few ideas off the top of his head, Madison Avenue style, Chance told the cash man, a metals tycoon named Marion LaMarr Roberts:

"We can have a guy showing a puppet how to hit a ball, and then I can say, 'Hey, that's not the way to hit. I've got a guy here who can show you.' And then I'll bring in Mickey Mantle. Don't that sound great, Marion?"

The tycoon winced. No money changed hands at lunch, but Chance left Madison richer by one title: executive vice president of the *Funny Friends* production company.

The TV executive's travels next took him to New York. He had come to the big city to say a few words at a Friday luncheon held by a shirt company, but he stayed the weekend. He treated his hotel-room telephone and TV set as if they were new inventions. For a solid stretch of two hours he phoned friends around the country to say hello. "Haney's really a good kid," he remarked, and promptly phoned Los Angeles to tell Haney hello. The good kid, unfortunately, was not in. Tiring of the phone,

Chance watched a 1948 movie, sitting on the edge of a chair no more than 18 inches from the TV.

From New York, the Wayne County traveler proceeded to Philadelphia. "I'm being honored there," he explained, relishing the sports-page cliché. There was no stopping him. He had money, fame and an expense account from any city where he might choose to speak. He was growing tired from travel, and his face was becoming slightly sallow, but Lord, he had never had such fun. Stretching out on a hotel bed one afternoon shortly before reporting for spring training, the *enfant terrible* contemplated his future.

"I could be washed up tomorrow," he said, "and they'll send me to Siberia." On the other hand, he could become baseball's first $100,000 pitcher. "That," he purred, "is a nice round figure." The mere thought of $100,000 sent his mind surging back to the day he rode a bus to Bluefield, West Virginia, in the Appalachian League. "That was the first time I'd ever left home alone." And he was moved to add:

"If it'll help you any, you can write in the story that I was wearing overalls and work shoes. Hell, you gotta make a living too."

JEFF KEATE

Courtesy Publishers-Hall Syndicate

"Attaboy, Slugger! First time in weeks you've got some wood on the ball."

The Glory of Their Times, one of the most fascinating baseball books to come along in years, is the work of Lawrence S. Ritter, Ph.D., chairman of the Department of Finance at the Graduate School of Business Administration of New York University. Tape recorder in hand, Mr. Ritter traveled thousands of miles to record the reminiscences of old-time baseball greats, and we are privileged to include several of these now in the *Fireside* baseball library. Leading off: the legendary "Wahoo Sam" Crawford.

"We Were Considered Pretty Crude"

SAM CRAWFORD

I DON'T KNOW how you found me, but since you're here you might as well come in and sit down. I don't have much time, though. Got a lot of things to do. But it's a hot day, so come in and rest a while.

Yeah, I'm sort of hard to find. Still bounce around a lot, you know. Always on the move. Probably a hangover from all those years in baseball—Boston today, Detroit tomorrow, never long in one place. I do have a house down in Hollywood, but I can't take that town. Too much smog. Too many cars, all fouling up the air. Can hardly breathe down there. Too many people too. Have to stand in line everywhere you go. Can't even get a loaf of bread without standing in line. Pretty soon they'll be standing in line to get into the john! That's not for me.

No, I don't have a telephone. If I had a lot of money, I wouldn't have one. I *never* was for telephones. Just don't like them, that's all. Anybody wants to talk to you, they can come to see you. I do have a television over there—it was a gift—but I never turn it on. I'd rather read a book. Don't even watch the ball games. Heck, I don't even buy a newspaper. Nothing but trouble in it. Just spoils your day. That's the way I look at it, anyway. Maybe I'm wrong, I don't know.

So you're doing a book about baseball in the old days. Why does a young fellow like you want to spend his time on something like that? Do you remember what Robert Ingersoll used to say? "Let the dead past bury its dead." That's what he used to say. Robert Ingersoll, remember him? A great man. I always admired him. He was a very famous lecturer in the late 1800s. Very famous and very controversial. He was supposed to be an atheist, but he wasn't really. More a skeptic, more an agnostic, than an atheist. Anyway, those days are all back in the past. We're going to spend the rest of our lives in the future, not in the past: "Let the dead past bury its dead." On the other hand, Santayana said, "Those who forget the past are condemned to repeat it." So maybe there are two sides to this matter. But I don't think we'll ever repeat the old days in baseball. They'll never come back. Everything has changed too much.

You know, there were a lot of characters in baseball back then. Real individualists. Not conformists, like most ballplayers—and most people—are today. Rube Waddell, for instance. Boy, there was one of a kind. They never made another like him. I played on the same team with Rube back in 1899, the Grand Rapids club in the old Western League. We were both just starting out, but it wasn't hard to see even then that Rube was going to really be something.

"Listen," he'd say, "I've got so much speed today, I'll burn up the catcher's glove if I don't let up a bit."

And he'd go over to the water barrel—we had a barrel filled with ice water in the dugout—and dip the dipper in and pour ice water all over his left arm and shoulder.

"That's to slow me down a little," he'd say. And then he'd go out there and more likely than not he'd strike out the side.

Rube was just a big kid, you know. He'd pitch one day, and we wouldn't see him for three or four days after. He'd just disappear, go fishing or something, or be off playing ball with a bunch of twelve-year-olds in an empty lot somewhere. You couldn't control him 'cause he was just a big kid himself. Baseball was just a game to Rube.

We'd have a big game scheduled for a Sunday, with posters all over Grand Rapids that the great Rube Waddell was going to pitch that day. Even then he was a big drawing card. Sunday would come, and the little park would be packed way before game time, everybody wanting to see Rube pitch. But half the time there'd be no Rube. Nowhere to be found. The manager would be having a fit. And then just a few minutes before the game was supposed to begin, there'd be a commotion in the grandstand, and you'd hear people laughing and yelling, "Here comes Rube, here comes Rube."

And there he'd come, right through the stands. He'd jump down onto the field, cut across the infield to the clubhouse, taking off his shirt as he went. In about three minutes—he never wore any underwear—he'd run back out on the field in uniform all ready to pitch and yell, "All right, let's get 'em!"

By the end of that season—1899—we were both in the big leagues, Rube with Louisville and me with Cincinnati. I should say big *league,* because there was only one major league then, the National League. The American League didn't start until a couple of years later.

By 1903, though, we were both in the American League. I went to the Detroit Tigers and Rube went with Connie Mack's Philadelphia Athletics. Rube was at his peak those years he was with Connie. He was amazing. Way over twenty wins almost every season, and always leading the league in strikeouts. How good he'd have been if he'd taken baseball seriously is hard to imagine. Like I say, it was always just a game with Rube. He played 'cause he had fun playing, but as far as he was concerned it was all the same whether he was playing in the big leagues or with a bunch of kids on a sandlot.

The main thing you had to watch out for was not to get him mad. If things were going smoothly, and everyone was happy, Rube would be happy too, and he'd just go along, sort of half pitching. Just fooling around, lackadaisical, you know. But if you got him mad somehow, he'd really bear down, and then you wouldn't have a chance. Not a chance.

Hughie Jennings, our manager at Detroit, used to go to the dime store and buy little toys, like rubber snakes or a jack-in-the-box. He'd get in the first-base coach's box and set them down in the grass and yell, "Hey, Rube, look." Rube would look over at the jack-in-the-box popping up and down and kind of grin, real slow-like, you know. Yeah, we'd do everything to get him in a good mood, and to distract him from his pitching.

When you think about people like Rube Waddell, and crowds standing in the outfield during a crucial big-league game, you start to get some idea of how different it all used to be. Baseball players weren't too much accepted in those days, either, you know. We were considered pretty crude. Couldn't get into the best hotels and all that. And when we did get into a good hotel, they wouldn't boast about having us. Like, if we went into the hotel dining room—in a good hotel, that is—they'd quick shove us way down in the corner at the very end of the dining room so we wouldn't be too conspicuous. "Here come the ballplayers!" you know, and down in the corner we'd go.

I remember once—I think it was in 1903—I was with the Detroit club, and we all went into the dining room in this hotel, I believe in St. Louis. Well, this dining room had a tile floor, made out of little square tiles. We sat there—way down at the end, as usual—for about twenty minutes and couldn't get any waiters. They wouldn't pay any attention to us at all. Remember Kid Elberfeld? He was playing shortstop for us then, a tough little guy. Anyway, Kid Elberfeld says, "I'll get you some waiters, fellows."

Darned if he didn't take one of the plates and sail it way up in the air, and when it came down on that tile floor it smashed into a million pieces. In that quiet, refined dining room it sounded like the Charge of the Light Brigade. Sure enough, we had four or five waiters running around there in no time.

You know, there were a lot of little guys in baseball then. McGraw was a fine ballplayer, and he couldn't have been over five feet six or seven. And Tommy Leach, with Pittsburgh—he was only five feet six, and he couldn't have weighed over 140. Dummy Hoy was even smaller, about five-five. You remember him, don't you? He died in Cincinnati only a few years ago, at the age of ninety-nine. Quite a ballplayer. In my opinion Dummy Hoy and Tommy Leach should both be in the Hall of Fame.

Do you know how many bases Dummy Hoy

stole in his major-league career? Over 600! That *alone* should be enough to put him in the Hall of Fame. We played alongside each other in the outfield with the Cincinnati club in 1902. He started in the big leagues way back in the 1880s, you know, so he was on his way out then, and I had been up just a few years, but even that late in his career he was a fine outfielder. A *great* one.

Did you know that he was the one responsible for the umpire giving hand signals for a ball or a strike? Raising his right hand for a strike, you know, and stuff like that. He'd be up at bat, and he couldn't hear, and he couldn't talk, so he'd look around at the umpire to see what the pitch was, a ball or a strike. That's where the hand signs for the umpire's calling balls and strikes began. That's a fact. Very few people know that.

It's funny how little things like that come back to you, after all these years. That was over sixty years ago when we played together. He was a little fellow, like I said, only five feet five. But he had real large strong hands. He used to wear a diamond ring—we all did in those days—but his knuckles were so big that he had a ring with a hinge on it. A real hinge. He couldn't get a ring that would go over his big knuckles and still fit right, so he had one made with a hinge so that he could put it on and then close it and it would lock in place. Did you know that he once threw three men out at home plate in one game? From the outfield, I mean. That was in 1889. And still the baseball writers don't give him a tumble for the Hall of Fame. It's not right.

Of course the greatest pitcher in those days was Walter Johnson. Boy, what a pitcher Walter was! He was the best I ever faced, without a doubt. Did you know that I was playing with Detroit the day Walter Johnson pitched his first major-league game? His very first. In fact, I beat him. I hit a home run off him and we beat him—I believe the score was 3–2.

I think that was late in 1907. We were after the pennant that year, our first pennant, and we needed that game badly. Big Joe Cantillon was managing Washington at the time. He was a nice guy, Joe was, always kidding. Anyway, before the game, Joe came over to the Detroit bench and said, "Well, boys, I've got a great big apple-knocker I'm going to pitch against you guys today. Better watch out, he's plenty fast. He's got a swift."

He told us that, you know. And here comes Walter, just a string of a kid, only about eighteen or nineteen years old. Tall, lanky, from Idaho or somewhere. Didn't even have a curve. Just that fast ball. That's all he pitched, just fast balls. He didn't *need* any curve. We had a terrible time beating him. Late in the game I hit one—I can remember it as though it were yesterday—it went zooming out over the shortstop's head, and before they could get the ball back in I'd legged it all the way around.

I must say, though, that the greatest all-around ballplayer I ever saw was over in the National League. I played against him for four years, from 1899 through 1902, when I was with Cincinnati, and he was first with Louisville and then with Pittsburgh. People always ask me about Ty Cobb, you know: "You played in the outfield next to Cobb for all those years. Don't you agree that he was the greatest player who ever lived?"

Cobb was great, there's no doubt about that; *one* of the greatest. But not *the* greatest. In my opinion, *the* greatest all-around player who ever lived was Honus Wagner.

Cobb could only play the outfield, and even there his arm wasn't anything extra special. But Honus Wagner could play any position. He could do everything. In fact, when I first played against him he was an outfielder, and then he became a third baseman, and later the greatest shortstop of them all. Honus could play any position except pitcher and be easily the best in the league at it. He was a wonderful fielder, you know, terrific arm, very quick, all over the place grabbing sure hits and turning them into outs. And, of course, you know he led the league in batting eight times.

You'd never think it to look at him, of course. He looked so awkward, bowlegged, barrel-chested, about 200 pounds, a big man. And yet he could run like a scared rabbit. He had enormous hands, and when he scooped up the ball at shortstop, he'd grab half the infield with it. But boy, Honus made those plays! He looked awkward doing it, not graceful like Larry Lajoie, but he could make every play Lajoie could make and more. Talk about speed. That bowlegged guy stole over 700 bases in the twenty-one years he played in the big leagues. A good team man, too, and the sweetest disposition in the world. The greatest ballplayer who ever lived, in my book.

Cobb and Wagner met head on in the 1909 World Series, you know, Detroit against Pittsburgh. We lost in seven games, the first time the series went the full seven games. Wagner stole six bases in that series, as many as our whole team, and Cobb stole only two. Honus was one of those natural ballplayers, you know what I mean? Like Babe Ruth and Willie Mays. Those fellows do everything by pure instinct. Mays is one of the few modern players who are just as good as the best of the old-timers.

Don't get me wrong. I'm not running Cobb down. He was terrific, no doubt about it. After all, he stole almost 900 bases and had a batting average of .367 over twenty-four years in the big leagues. You can't knock a record like that. I remember one year I hit .378—in 1911, I think it was—and I didn't come anywhere close to leading the league: Joe Jackson hit .408 and Cobb hit .420. I mean, that's mighty rugged competition!

They always talk about Cobb playing dirty, trying to spike guys and all. Cobb never tried to spike anybody. The base line belongs to the runner. If the infielders get in the way, that's their lookout. Infielders are supposed to watch out and take care of themselves. In those days, if they got in the way and got nicked, they'd never say anything. They'd just take a chew of tobacco out of their mouth, slap it on the spike wound, wrap a handkerchief around it, and go right on playing. Never thought any more about it.

We had a trainer, but all he ever did was give you a rubdown with something we called "Go Fast." He'd take a jar of Vaseline and a bottle of Tabasco sauce—you know how hot that is—mix them together, and rub you down with that. Boy, it made you feel like you were on fire! That would *really* start you sweating. Now they have medical doctors and whirlpool baths and who knows what else.

But Ty was dynamite on the base paths. He really was. Talk about strategy and playing with your head, that was Cobb all the way. It wasn't that he was so fast on his feet, although he was fast enough. There were others who were faster, though, like Clyde Milan, for instance. It was that Cobb was so fast in his *thinking*. He didn't outhit the opposition, and he didn't outrun them. He outthought them!

A lot of times Cobb would be on third base, and I'd draw a base on balls and as I started to go down to first, I'd sort of half glance at Cobb at third. He'd make a slight move that told me he wanted me to keep going—not to stop at first, but to keep on going to second. Well, I'd trot two-thirds of the way to first and then suddenly, without warning, I'd speed up and go across first as fast as I could and tear out for second. He's on third, see. They're watching him, and suddenly there I go, and they don't know what the devil to do.

If they try to stop me, Cobb'll take off for home. Sometimes they'd catch him, and sometimes they'd catch me, and sometimes they wouldn't get either of us. But most of the time they were too paralyzed to do anything, and I'd wind up at second on a base on balls. Boy, did that ever create excitement. For the crowd, you know; the fans were always wondering what was going to happen next.

Cobb was a great ballplayer, no doubt about it. But he sure wasn't easy to get along with. Every rookie gets a little hazing, but most of them just take it and laugh. Cobb took it the wrong way. He came up with an antagonistic attitude, which in his mind turned any little razzing into a life-or-death struggle. He always figured everybody was ganging up against him. He came up from the South, you know, and he was still fighting the Civil War. As far as he was concerned, we were all damn Yankees before he even met us. Well, who knows, maybe if he hadn't had that persecution complex he never would have been the great ballplayer he was. He was always trying to prove he was the best, on the field and off. And maybe he was, at that.

One thing that really used to get Ty's goat was when I'd have a good day and he didn't. Oh, would he ever moan then. Walter Johnson and I were very good friends, and once in a while Walter would sort of "give" me a hit or two, just for old times' sake. But when Ty came up there, Walter always bore down all the harder. There was nothing he enjoyed more than fanning Ty Cobb.

You see, Walter always liked my model bat. Somehow he got the idea that my bats were lucky for him. So very often when the Senators came to Detroit, Walter would come into our clubhouse and quietly ask me if I could spare a bat for him.

"Sure, Walter," I'd say, "go take any one you want."

He'd go over to my locker, look them over, pick one out and quietly leave. Well, whenever the occasion arose when it wouldn't affect a game, Walter would let up a bit on me, and I'd have a picnic at the plate—like, if Washington had a good lead and it was late in the game. I'd come up to bat and Gabby Street, Walter's catcher, would whisper, "Walter likes you today, Sam."

That was the cue that the next pitch would be a nice half-speed fast ball. So I'd dig in and belt it. Of course if it was a close game all that was out the window. The friendship deal was off then. Cobb never did figure out why I did so well against Walter, while he couldn't hit him with a 10-foot pole.

Well, this is more than I've talked in years, and it's good. I don't see many people, and even when I do I don't talk about baseball too much. I read a lot. My favorite writer is Balzac. A wonderful writer. But I rarely talk about baseball. There are very few people around, you know, who remember those old days.

It's like when I got elected to the Hall of Fame, back in 1957. I was living in a little cabin at the edge of the Mojave Desert, near a little town called Pearblossom. Nobody around there even knew I'd been a ballplayer. I never talked about it. So there I was, sitting there in that cabin, with snow all around—it was February—and all of a sudden the place is surrounded with photographers and newspapermen and radio-TV reporters and all. I didn't know what in the world was going on.

"You've just been elected to the Hall of Fame," one of them said to me.

The people living around there—what few of them there were—were all excited. They couldn't figure out what was happening. And when they found out what it was all about, they couldn't believe it. "Gee, you mean old Sam? He used to be a ballplayer? We didn't even know it. Gee!"

From then on, of course, I've gotten thousands of letters. I still get a lot. Mostly from kids, wanting autographs. Sometimes they send a stamped envelope, and sometimes they don't. But I've answered every one by hand. In 1957, when I was elected to the Hall, I also went back to Detroit. It was the 50th anniversary of all the players who were still alive who had been on that 1907 pennant-winning team. I enjoyed that, but I wouldn't put on a uniform. I went out in civilian clothes and waved to the fans, but I refused to put on a uniform. I want to be remembered the way I used to be. When they think of Sam Crawford in a Detroit uniform, I want them to think of me the way I was way back then, and no other way.

This is a period piece, which Lee Allen dates back to 1923. At that time, baseball's club owners not only refused to put numbers on their players' backs, but scorned doubly such futuristic amenities as the recording of hits and errors on the scoreboard.

With Apologies to Henry Wadsworth Longfellow

L. C. DAVIS

Tell me not in mournful numbers
On the baseball player's back
Who that bimbo is that lumbers
To the plate the pill to crack.

While the pastime is progressing
And improving every day,
We must keep the rooters guessing
While they pay and pay and pay.

Likewise, showing hits and errors
On the board, the magnate fears
Would abet the silk shirt wearers
Also known as gamboliers.

Let us then be up and doing
On the old established plan,
Still achieving, still pursuing
The elusive iron man.

TWO INIMITABLES: the gentle, genial Stan Delaplane and a hot dog at the ball park. How come it took till now to get the both of them into the *Fireside?*

The Sporting Way

STANTON DELAPLANE

WE DON'T GET much sports in this department. I can't get in the depths of despair when outfielder McTootsieroll pulls a muscle.

I have a neck myself that baffles medical science. But nobody writes about it. I just put on a felt collar and take an aspirin.

Even so, it seems to be baseball season. So, to press.

The most important thing about baseball is the hot dog. There are several stories about its origin. You can't tell the players without a program; and you can't tell the true story of hot dogs without a lie detector.

One story goes like this:

"Charles Feltman brought the frankfurter from his native Bavaria in 1871 and featured it at his famous Coney Island restaurant, introducing the hot dog to the U.S."

Here's another:

"It was at the St. Louis Louisiana Exposition in 1904. A concessionaire loaned white gloves to his patrons so they could hold the piping-hot wieners.

"He found many people didn't return the gloves. So he turned to his brother, a baker, and had a bun made to fit the sausage. Thus inventing the hot dog."

This should add to your enjoyment of the national pastime invented by Abner Doubleday.

A little history spread on the chin along with the mustard.

I used to get background on the hot dog from Mr. Irving Hoffman, the New York historian.

Mr. Hoffman was press agent for Coney Island hot dogs. His stationery carried the message: "When a man bites a dog, that's news."

Once the King of England visited the U.S. President Franklin D. Roosevelt gave him a hot dog. Shown in all the photos.

The President announced that it was "a genuine Coney Island red hot."

The King and the hot dog (he said it was excellent) became famous. Down in Trinidad, a calypso singer wrote a song about it:

The King take de hot dog in his hahnd
Ahnd he face hot dog, mahn to mahn.

People talked about it all over the U.S. For it showed that English royalty was not stiff as a stick. Just give them a good old American hot dog, and they were just like you and me.

Hoffman retired shortly after. For you cannot go on topping yourself on work like that.

I don't know where the story of St. Louis and the white gloves comes from.

The story that Feltman brought the hot dog to Coney Island comes from the archives of the august *National Geographic.* (Though I wonder if this wasn't planted by Hoffman, too.)

I favor this version. When I was a baseball fan, hanging on the exploits of "Shoeless Joe" Jackson and worrying about "Red" Faber's arm, hot dogs were sold as "Coney Island red hots."

They contained mustard AND chopped pickle—which is the mark of the genuine article, beloved of the King of England.

That is my contact with the sporting world —the hot dog. Oh, once I tried to be a sportswriter. I wrote, "Snively hit a home run."

The sports editor was aghast. He said, "He wafted the spheroid over the pickets! Can't you write English?"

I had to admit I couldn't. Not sports English. So they put me back on pistol-packing mamas, talking dogs and club luncheons. I made a living out of it.

UNDER ITS FINE sports editor, John P. Carmichael, the Chicago *Daily News* issued during World War II a series of reminiscences entitled *My Greatest Day in Baseball,* primarily for the entertainment of servicemen. The series fast became a winner for baseball fans everywhere, and was republished at least twice in varying book forms. A number of its entries are to be found now in the *Fireside* library. Here's one.

1943: New York Yankees 2, St. Louis Cardinals 0

BILL DICKEY
***as told to* JOHN P. CARMICHAEL**

MY BIGGEST DAY? Well, I used to think it was the afternoon in 1932 when Babe Ruth didn't hit me right on the chin. I put a raw egg in one of his spikes before a game and you can imagine what happened when he set that big dog of his down inside. He really was "red" when he pulled the foot out, with egg drippin' all over and he looked around the clubhouse and yelled; "I can whip the man that did that."

Well, nobody answered and the Babe got madder 'n' madder and growled around and finally I said, "I did it, Babe," and he glared at me and took a couple of steps toward my locker and suddenly started to laugh and said, "Aw, to hell with it" and changed socks and shoes. He'd a been a pretty big guy to tangle with.

A day I remember for the laugh we all got was in '30 when Bob Shawkey had the club and Lefty Grove was pitchin' against us. To me he was the fastest man I ever saw and he was having a field day against the Yanks. Red Ruffing was sittin' on the bench and just for fun he kept telling everybody; "I can't understand how you guys don't hit him. He's just nice and fast . . . boy, I like to hit those kind of pitchers. Sure wish I was in there today."

Finally we got the bags loaded in the eighth with two out, and Shawkey looked down the line and motioned to Ruffing. "I know you want to take a crack at Grove," said Bob, "so pick up a bat and go up there." We all gave Red a big hand when he walked to the plate. Then we sat and watched. Grove threw three times. Ruffing hardly got a good look at any of 'em. He was back in a minute without ever getting the bat off his shoulder . . . three strikes and out!

That World Series of '38 with the Cubs was a honey . . . especially the day that Hack and Jurges collided going after a ground ball and Lou Gehrig scored from first base. I can still see Diz Dean chasin' the ball back on the grass while your left fielder (Carl Reynolds) stood around and watched. But I guess when you come down to it, this last World Series . . . the last game when I hit a home run . . . is the biggest day of all.

One of the newspapermen in the clubhouse afterwards hollered at Joe McCarthy; "Hey, Joe, how about ol' Bill Dickey there," and Joe reached over and slapped me on the back and said, "Bill and I have come a long way . . . we practically started together on the Yanks." That's about right, too . . . it was the eighth series for both of us and we won out seven times. Joe and I were the old-timers of them all.

You know the Yanks are supposed to beat everybody, all the time. Nobody thinks it strange or remarkable when we win; they take it for granted. If we lose, they figure it was accidental and something must be wrong. I rather thought the Cards had a better team, during the season, than we did, although I thought we could beat them in the Series. But they had a great pitcher in Mort Cooper, one of the sharpest, most consistent hitters I ever saw in Stan Musial and a regular floating ghost at short. That skinny Marion is a wonder. Phil Rizzuto, who was with us in '42, was the only shortstop I ever saw as good on slow-hit balls.

The '43 Series was a tough one and some of those games could have changed scores very easily. Take that second one in which Cooper beat us 4—3. We had one run home in the ninth, a man on third and nobody out when I came to bat. I hit the hardest ball, for me, of the whole Series. Caught it good . . . but it was a line drive right into the hands of Klein. Five feet either side and I'd a been on first with another run home and still no outs.

Then there was the ninth inning of the fourth game, with Russo leading 2—1. There was one gone when Marion doubled and the tying run was on second. They sent up that third-string catcher . . . oh, wait a minute, Sam Narron . . . to hit and we got two strikes on him in a hurry. Then I decided to waste one and called for a high, outside fast ball. I didn't expect him to hit at it . . . didn't want him to, in fact, because I was only setting him up for another curve. But for some reason I caught Crosetti's eye just after giving Russo the sign and motioned Frank over toward second a few steps.

It was a good thing I did, because Narron hit that outside pitch . . . pretty smart down toward second base and if Frank hadn't been over there, it'd been a hit and we'd a never got Marion at home. Even as it was Crosetti had to make a quick stop and throw. That was a hard hit ball and it was good strategy to send a fellow like Narron up because we didn't know anything about him or what he couldn't hit. Hell, he'd hardly played all season.

I think even if we'd lost next day, the fifth game, we still would have won the Series, but maybe it's just as well it didn't go any longer. You remember Cooper striking out five of us in a row at the start, including me, and he was fast. You could see he'd made up his mind to throw everything he had into that last effort and we got some good breaks along the way. That play Crosetti made on Klein to start the fourth or fifth inning. . . . I don't see how he ever got to the ball, but he did and it got their leadoff man out of the way and gave us a margin to operate on.

Then the next frame Kurowski led off and bunted safely toward third on the first pitch. I was a little afraid of Spud Chandler losing his control, because I didn't think he was as sharp in either Series game as in most of his season starts, and sure enough he got wild and walked Ray Sanders on four pitches. There were two men on, nobody out, and no score in the game. Up came Johnny Hopp, a left-handed hitter to boot, and Chandler threw three straight balls to him.

McCarthy wigwagged me to go out to the mound and see what happened. Spud said he wasn't tired or anything; he just didn't want to give Hopp a clean shot. But I told him to "come on and get the ball over" and called for a sinker. It was good for strike one, just around the knees, and, naturally, Hopp didn't swing. After all, Chandler had thrown seven straight balls. I took a chance he wouldn't even cut at the 3—1 pitch and asked for a curve. It was called strike two, so it was 3—2 and the next pitch was "for the money."

It was . . . but for our money. I signaled for a fast ball and Chandler threw one at least a foot off the plate, outside. The bases should have been loaded with nobody gone. I don't know why Hopp swung at the ball, but he did . . . and fanned. There was one of the two big breaks of the whole Series in our favor; that one and the day in New York when Lindell knocked the ball out of Kurowski's hands. Anyway, with Hopp gone, we got the next two easily.

There were two out in the sixth when Keller bounced the ball between first and second for a hit and I came up. I wasn't trying to outguess Cooper. I wasn't trying to hit the ball out of the park either. I wanted a fast ball and I only wanted to meet it squarely, just so it would go safe. Well, I got it . . . and hit it good, but not hard. At least I didn't think so, but when I was running to first, I saw the ball heading for the roof and Earl Combs (Yank coach) yelled at me, "You got one, Bill." But the only thing I thought was "We'll get a run, anyway, for Spud, and maybe it'll be enough." Then I saw Art Fletcher (at third) wavin' his cap and I knew it was a home run and we had two runs.

It didn't mean so much at the time; it wasn't until that night, when I was in bed, that I began to realize I'd won the game and the Series with one blow and we were champions again and I'd had a pretty darn good season for an old man who'd been playing up there sixteen years.

DEFEATED BY the Gas House Gang in the 1934 World Series, the Detroit Tigers stormed back to take it all the following year. What a team they were—Cochrane, Bridges, Gehringer, Greenberg, Rowe—and the Goose!

1935: Detroit Tigers 4, Chicago Cubs 3

JOHN DREBINGER

THE GOOSE HANGS HIGH once more in the world of baseball, and tonight all Detroit is madly dancing through the streets and rending the air with a mighty chant: "Yea, Goose! Yea, Goose! Yea, Goose!"

For in the last half of the ninth inning of as dramatic a diamond conflict as was ever played, Leon Allen Goslin, who as a mere gosling ten and eleven years ago smashed six home runs that made history in these October classics, cracked a modest single over second base and into center field.

It scored Mickey Cochrane, and as the indomitable leader of the Tigers crunched his spikes into the white rubber plate, Detroit's hopes and prayers for a world baseball championship, for which it has patiently been waiting ever since the inception of the American League in 1901, finally were realized.

For that shot off the bat of Goslin the Goose brought the World Series of 1935 to a close at Navin Field. It snuffed out the Chicago Cubs in the sixth game by a score of 4 to 3, and gave to the Tigers the lion's share of the prize money by a margin of four games to two.

Detroit, waiting for this moment for thirty-four years and repulsed in four previous pennant-winning campaigns, at last was sitting astride the baseball universe, and when this became an actuality on the wings of Goslin's hit, pandemonium broke loose.

The fans, numbering in paid attendance 48,420, the largest crowd ever to see a ball game in this city, stormed on the field and made for the Tiger bench. Frantically the police strove to keep those in front from being toppled down the steps of the dugout and getting seriously crushed in the wildly jubilant throng.

A self-appointed cheerleader leaped on the roof of the dugout and the triumphant cry of victory began. The thousands still in the stands swung in tune, and soon the very rafters and steel girders of Navin Field trembled to the vibrations of "Yea, Goose! Yea, Goose! Yea, Goose!"

For more than an hour thousands still remained on the field, and as each member of the triumphant Tigers ventured forth there was a wild rush. Details of police struggled to get their charges safely out of the stadium and into waiting cabs.

Outside in the streets of the downtown sections bedlam prevailed. Streamers, ticker tape and papers of every description were showered from windows while sirens and horns from a million automobiles set up an almost terrifying din.

The climax on this comparatively warm and sunshiny afternoon came as suddenly as it did dramatically. For eight innings of this battle, a titanic pitching duel between the slim, trim Tommy Bridges and the husky and left-handed Larry French, fortunes veered from one side to the other.

There was a Tiger run in the opening round. It was matched by the grimly fighting Chicagoans in the third. In the fourth the American Leaguers forged ahead with a tally, but in the fifth Billy Herman, brilliant second baseman, belted a home run into the left-field bleachers with a comrade aboard the bases, to put the Cubs in front, 3 to 2.

In the sixth, however, Marvin Owen lined a perfect single to left. It was Marvin's first blow since the great struggle had started last Wednesday. It scored Billy Rogell, who previously had doubled, and the battle was deadlocked again at 3-all.

In the ninth Stanley Hack led off Chicago's last-ditch stand. He smashed a great three-bagger into the extreme center-field corner of the playing area. The Cubs for the third in this series had a man on third base at a crucial moment where only a fly ball was needed to turn the tide the other way.

But Bridges, who spun the Detroiters to their first triumph in this Series would not permit this straining Chicagoan to advance another step toward home. He struck out Billy Jurges. The next batter was French himself. But he could not hit the ball farther than Bridges, who tossed out his pitching adversary at first.

Finally the long fly came. It was struck by little Augie Galan, but Goslin camped himself under the ball and held it fast for the third out.

The battle, still deadlocked, raged into the last of the ninth. French, undismayed, struck out Herman Clifton, called the Flea. But Cochrane, with two singles already to his credit, opened fire with his third.

Next came Charlie Gehringer, the silent man of the Tigers—the only silent man on the premises at this tense, nerve-racking moment. Charlie drove the ball viciously on a low line squarely into the hands of Phil Cavaretta, the youthful Cub first baseman.

Had Phil been able to freeze to this ball and thereby complete a double play, the Cubs perhaps might yet be carrying on. But the drive was entirely too hot for the Italian youngster to hold, and though he recovered the ball in time to retire Gehringer at first, his hurried throw to second arrived too late to head off the flying Cochrane.

Now came the Goose. Two days after Cochrane had been appointed manager of the Tigers on Dec. 12, 1933, he swung a deal with the Washington Senators that had brought Goslin to the Tigers. Since then there have been days when the Goose, a hero in the World Series of 1924 and 1925, seemed about ready to be cooked and served. But Mickey stuck to the Goose, and at this throbbing moment the patience of the man in the iron mask was rewarded.

Swinging from the left side of the plate, the Goose sent a screaming foul line into the lower stand where the fans were imploring him to do something better than that. On the next pitch he did. He did not swing very hard on the ball but met it squarely and it soared in a low arch over second base. Herman made a despairing reach for it. Frank Demaree tore in from center field. He picked up the ball on the first bounce, but his throw to the plate proved nothing more than a last defiant gesture. For Cochrane, off at the crack of the bat, had rounded third almost before the ball had struck the ground and as he streaked across the plate the battle was over.

With the receipts totaling $147,551 today, it marked the close of the seventh million-dollar Series. The grand total of money taken in reached $1,173,794, including $100,000 obtained for the radio rights.

Cochrane, generalissimo of the Tiger forces, made a slight last-minute shift in his battlefront for today's game. Still forced to carry on without his heaviest siege gun, Hank Greenberg, out of action with a damaged wrist after the second game of the Series, Iron Mike put the right-handed-hitting Gerald Walker in center field, in place of the left-swinging Jo-Jo White, and Clifton, who had been plugging the gap so superbly at third base, was heading the Detroit batting order.

Bridges retired the first three Chicagoans without exacting anything unusual from his helpers behind him. Then the Tigers went to work wrenching their first run away from French in this same opening round.

Clifton went out on an infield grounder, but Cochrane singled to left and the Tigers were off. Gehringer banged a single into right, his boss was on second base and the crowd was on its feet. Goslin lifted an easy pop fly to Jurges, but Pete the Fox followed with a whistling bounder down the third-base line.

Hack dived for the ball. It eluded his grasp and bounded into left field for a two-bagger. Cochrane raced home and Gehringer pulled up at third. French passed Walker intentionally to fill the bases. Rogell topped the ball in front of the plate, French tore in to scoop it up and his short toss to Gabby Hartnett forced Gehringer at home for the third out.

Two innings later the Cubs swung into action. Jurges opened the third with a single to center, and after French had struck out, Galan rifled a single into right. That put Jurges on third, and on the next play Billy was over the plate, tying the score at 1-all, as Herman poked another one-base thump into right field. Galan tried to make third on the hit only to get nailed by a perfect throw on the part of Fox. Klein wafted a high fly to Fox in right for the third out.

The two teams remained on even terms until the fourth when the Tigers launched another offensive. Walker opened with a single to left. Rogell followed with a blow to right. Owen then forced Rogell at second and Walker moved around to third on the play. The Cubs' infield swung back in the hope of executing a double play on Bridges. But though Tommy did dump a grounder into the infield, Hack, Herman and Cavaretta, striving for the double killing, just missed getting Bridges at first. It was simply a force play at second base for the second out and Walker had scored during the play. The Tigers were in front once more, 2 to 1.

But the joy of the fans was short-lived. In the fifth, with one down, French himself singled to right and after Galan had taken a third strike, Herman pulled a high fly toward left. It soared over the twenty-foot screening and fell among the spectators.

Now the Cubs were leading, 3 to 2, and French held the advantage until two had been retired in the sixth inning. Then came the first of the afternoon's really dramatic events. Rogell dropped a double into the extreme left-hand corner of the field. Owen came up. French breezed one down the middle. The next instant the ball sailed into left for a single, and amid an incredible din Rogell dashed home, tying the count at 3-all.

Now the fighting became the sort to grip players and spectators alike. In the eighth the Tigers launched a threat when Fox singled and Walker pushed him on to second with a sacrifice. But French fanned Rogell, passed Owen intentionally and wound up this inning by striking out Bridges.

Swiftly the events of the ninth closed down on the battle. There was the Hack triple, which might have prolonged the struggle even into another game had someone behind him come up with at least a fly ball before it was too late. Then came the two shots by Cochrane and Goslin, and tonight they are gaily parading through the streets roaring and bellowing, "Yea Goose!"

Detroit at last has come into its own at the top of the baseball heap. The American League, too, is on top once more and for the first time since 1932 when the Yankees crushed another Cub team in four straight games. But this Cub team had not been crushed. It already had made baseball history this year by sweeping into the National League pennant on the crest of an amazing 21-game winning streak.

The Detroiters had been struggling courageously ever since the second game with their heaviest clouter, Greenberg, out of action. They had been forced to fight on with a makeshift infield. But when the crucial moment arrived for the final killing, they had a Goslin to do it, and the goose hangs high tonight.

THIS LITTLE ESSAY on self-destruction brings to mind the time half a dozen years ago when manager Alvin Dark, enraged after a loss, threw a stool in the clubhouse and amputated his own finger in the process. Ed Bailey, who was playing for Dark then but had formerly played under Fred Hutchinson at Cincinnati, was not impressed. "Dark throws stools," Bailey said. "Hutch throws rooms."

Trip No. 7,091

MELVIN DURSLAG

IN HIS 15 YEARS in professional baseball, all in the major leagues, Al Kaline had come to bat officially 7,090 times.

A .305 lifetime hitter, he had gone out 4,827 times, meaning that this experience, by 1967, was scarcely novel.

It remains unaccountable what strange seizure gripped Al following his 7,091st trip to the plate the other day. Striking out—he had done this some 650 times, including 66 times last season—he returned to the. dugout, and, with a thrust that shook the world, slammed his bat into the rack with such force that he broke his finger.

The upshot is as follows: Whereas Willie Mays was voted out of the All-Star game's starting lineup this year, Kaline, who was voted in, had put himself out.

Of even more significance, this superb batsman, who was hitting .328 this year, immobilized himself for three or four weeks during a time his team was very much in the pennant race.

As athletes go, Kaline is no temper case. He has no reputation as a locker-puncher, a cooler-kicker, or a uniform-ripper. And heaven knows he has never upset the buffet table in the clubhouse.

But the bat rack is no place for a guy to get frisky with his emotions. Two years ago Mickey Mantle struck out in a game against Boston. In his estimation, it was a craven act.

Walking to the dugout, he placed the bat tidily in the rack—and then tried to break off the handle with his hand. Mickey is stronger than the ordinary man, but not even he could destroy Louisville's most famous product. Instead, he pulled a muscle in his neck, causing him to sit the next several days with his head cocked at a slight angle.

This posture, of course, is all right if you are inspecting girls walking down a staircase, but it isn't recommended for hitting a baseball.

Self-destruction has been a lingering problem in sports, many discovering, regrettably, that man is not tougher than the implements he creates.

Frank Howard once had the strongest throwing arm in baseball. He hurled some colossal shots from the deepest extremities of the field to home plate. Gradually, the Dodgers, for whom he used to play, noticed deficiencies in his throws.

Launching an investigation, they found that when Frank struck out, he comported himself admirably on the field. He walked to the dugout, placed his helmet delicately on the bench and put the bat gingerly in the rack.

All he did was sit down and smash his elbow into the wall behind him. For a guy who struck out as often as Frank, it was a dangerous practice, and some feel his arm hasn't been the same since.

Now we examine the sad case of Bob Lee, the Cincinnati relief pitcher, who used to work for the California Angels. Throwing in the bullpen at Boston's Fenway Park, Lee was taunted by a sailor who grew so persistent in his defacement of the pitcher that only one course of action remained. Bob threw a punch. He must have taken a little something off it, because the sailor was able to duck. The fist hit an iron railing and Lee missed the balance of the season with a broken hand.

Repeatedly, managers lecture their players on bottling emotions. Casey Stengel one day scolded the Yankees for throwing bats when they struck out. "I want you to laugh it off," said Casey.

Billy Martin fanned. He walked to the dugout, fell to the floor and convulsed himself in mock laughter. Then looking up at Mantle, he said, "You were supposed to do this, too."

"I tried," said Mickey, "but when I strike out, I can't laugh."

Those who defend temper eruptions in sports ascribe them unfailingly to man's frailties. "You're dealing with humans," they say.

However, if I own a pennant contender and my .328 hitter busts his finger on the bat rack, or any manager gets thrown out for using language he knows positively will get him the boot, I say nuts to humans. Give the game to hyenas.

They know how to laugh.

JOHN GALLAGHER

Courtesy *Sport* Magazine ©

". . . . And that's going to be all for Pearson."

Subtitled "A Freemason Was the Father of Baseball," the following article appeared in the Fall 1962 issue of the *Royal Arch Mason* magazine. Alexander Cartwright is celebrated in baseball's Hall of Fame as the "father of modern baseball," but quite evidently Mr. Erikson's research leads him to conclude the word "modern" should be eliminated.

Alexander Joy Cartwright

JERRY R. ERIKSON

The National Baseball Hall of Fame was established in Cooperstown, New York, and dedicated on June 12, 1939 as a shrine to honor the greats of the national pastime. It also honored Abner Doubleday, who supposedly originated the game of baseball there in 1839 as claimed in a story published in 1907. This report was written by A. G. Mills, who was chairman of a committee appointed to determine just when, where and how baseball originated and who was responsible. He pictured Doubleday in Cooperstown in 1839, as a schoolboy who made a diagram and drew up rules for baseball. The facts are that Doubleday in 1839 had been a student at West Point for two years and was twenty years old. In those days any male aged twenty was a man and not a schoolboy. After retiring from the Army in 1873, Doubleday took up writing articles for many magazines, choosing his own subjects. This was during the period when baseball leagues were being established on a firm footing and it is reasonable to suppose that if Doubleday had anything to do with the beginnings of baseball he would have written something about it. He never wrote a line about baseball, and with the exception of the Mills report there has never been any mention that he ever played baseball, let alone his having originated the game. No copy of his supposed diagram or rules exists anywhere, and up until 1907 no one in Cooperstown was aware that Doubleday had ever played baseball on the village green some seventy years before.

In 1938, in the midst of the preparations for the baseball centennial a year later, the committee was surprised to hear from Bruce Cartwright of Honolulu, a grandson of Alexander Cartwright. He had old clippings, the diary of his grandfather and much else to prove that Cartwright, and not Doubleday, was the real founder of modern-day baseball. This bombshell did not phase the baseball folks, however, for they had gone too far and spent too much money to change the program to conform to the facts placed at their disposal by Bruce Cartwright. They did condescend to have an "Alexander Cartwright Day" during the festival —an event which was honoring the wrong man, the wrong town and the wrong date.

Alexander Joy Cartwright was born in New York City on April 17, 1820, and as a boy played rounders, one old cat and all the other games then in vogue which involved bases and a ball. By 1842 he was one of a group of young men of the professional, financial and social set who would lay their waistcoats neatly aside and enjoy a few rounds of the newfangled game of baseball. Some of the first games were played on a vacant lot on 27th Street, where Madison Square Garden was to be built later, and then as the city began to crowd them out, moved to a larger field at what is now Lexington Avenue and 34th Street. Cartwright, a natural athlete and adept at any position, was one of the leaders of this group of young men who enjoyed these Sunday ball games and were always trying to make them more exciting.

On September 23, 1845, after three years of

informal games, they organized a social and baseball club known as the "Knickerbockers." Clubs of an earlier era had been formed for sport and recreation, but these usually played cricket. Even though most of the Knickerbockers were cricket players, this was the first baseball club ever formed. Having decided that baseball was to be the sport, they did not want to play the haphazard and disorganized kind of game then common. They wanted standard, set rules, and Cartwright, who was a draftsman and surveyor, was selected to head the committee to formulate definite rules of play.

During the winter of 1845–46 they worked out the details for a regulation game, drawing on *Carver's Book of Sports* and discarding or revamping the rules for rounders and town ball then in use. Early in 1846 Cartwright was ready with his diagram for a new type of baseball, which, with few exceptions as regards the positions of the players, is the baseball diamond of today.

His fourteen rules provided for foul lines; nine men per team, with unalterable batting order; three outs per side and twenty-one aces, or runs, to determine the winner. This was later changed to nine innings per game. One of the most important changes made in the game was the injunction that "in no instance is a ball to be thrown at him" (the base runner). This "plugging" the runner with a thrown ball to make a put-out was used in the game of rounders and often caused serious injury.

The club roughed out the new "diamond-square" and practiced for several Sundays before announcing that they were ready for "play at baseball" and were willing to meet any club under the "Knickerbockers Rules of Baseball." The challenge was accepted by another club called the New York Team. However, when they learned that under the new rules a team was limited to nine men, they changed the name to the New York Nine.

As the time neared to select a field for play, none on Manhattan Island was found suitable, so a committee went looking for a new site. They took the ferry across the Hudson River and their search ended at an old cricket ground at Elysian Fields, a summer resort in Hoboken, New Jersey, which was found to be ideal for the new baseball diamond. An error was made in laying out the pitching distance, 45 feet instead of 46 as outlined by Cartwright. There was no disagreement over the one foot, so 45 feet became the standard pitching distance until a change was made to 50 feet in 1881 and later changed to the present 60 feet, 6 inches.

On June 19, 1846 the Knickerbockers took the field against the New York Nine in the first baseball game played under standard rules. Cartwright, who was one of the best players on the club, chose instead to umpire this historic first game. An odd note of the contest was that the umpire fined Davis, pitcher for the New York Nine, six cents for swearing and the fine was paid on the spot. Tangling with the umpire was another first in this first game of baseball.

The Knickerbockers were defeated 23 to 1 in four innings, and the unexpected defeat somewhat depressed them and there were no more games with other clubs until 1851. They continued to play practice games by choosing sides among themselves. For a practice game in April 1849 the regular Knickerbocker team appeared in what were the first baseball uniforms —long woolen trousers of blue, white flannel shirts and straw hats. Mohair hats were substituted in 1855. Since this regalia was almost identical with the cricket uniforms used elsewhere, it is believed that these baseball uniforms were simply those which the Knickerbockers had used in earlier cricket matches.

The new game of baseball was slow in catching on. Finally, by May 1857, there were so many clubs in the field that the Knickerbockers called a convention in New York and their complete set of rules was adopted, with the one important exception that nine innings, not twenty-one runs, constituted a game. On March 10, 1858, three delegates from each of twenty-five clubs met in convention to form the game's first league, the National Association of Baseball Players. Their rules gained nationwide prestige and the game of baseball was on its way to becoming the national pastime.

The first story about baseball appeared in a newspaper in April 1853. It mentioned an impending game between the Knickerbockers and Gothams and was written by State Senator William Cauldwell for the New York *Sunday Mercury*, of which he was editor and owner for fifty years. Frequently thereafter he contributed articles about baseball. Senator Cauldwell was the first supervisor of the town of Morrisania, New York, and at his death in 1907, at the age of eighty-three, was said to be the oldest active newspaperman in New York City. He was made a Mason in Lily Lodge No. 342, Bronx, New York, receiving the degrees in

February and May of 1858 and was a Mason for nearly fifty years.

Gold had been discovered in California, and on March 1, 1849, Alex Cartwright and a dozen friends set out for the Pacific coast. Under the leadership of President D'Arcy of the Camden and Amboy Railroad, they traveled by train to Pittsburgh, where they purchased a covered wagon and all the supplies they felt would be needed for the trip across the Western plains. The wagon and camping outfit were shipped ahead to St. Louis, where the group arrived after 42 days of travel, during which time they managed to work in a little baseball at various stopovers. In Independence, Missouri, 47 days out of Pittsburgh, Cartwright and company changed leaders, joining up with a veteran frontiersman and former army officer named Russell. Riding horseback part of the time and traveling the balance on foot, the New Yorkers reached the frontier town of Boundary, where they waited for a wagon train to be made up.

Alex and his friends played baseball with the Indians and frontiersmen of the community and had many laughs as they watched the converts to the New York game attempt to imitate their own grace with the ball and bat, such as catching the ball with the hands cupped and allowing the hands to "give" with the throw. He left a diary dealing with his trip across the country, and one entry reads: "April 23, 1849. During the past week we have passed the time fixing wagon covers, stowing property, etc., varied by hunting, fishing and playing baseball. It is comical to see the mountain men and Indians playing the new game. I have the ball with me we used back home."

When the wagon train left Boundary at last, Cartwright and his friends were part of a train that included 32 wagons and 119 men. The first day Alex covered the entire 28 miles on foot and each day marched 15 to 20 miles, occasionally mounting a horse. Like many greenhorns, he grew sick from the steady diet of buffalo meat, which was the bread and butter of the Santa Fe Trail. Only once were they attacked by hostile Indians, who were driven off without any harm being done to the travelers.

Cartwright was twenty-nine at the time, standing six feet two, weighed about 225 pounds, was enormously muscled, with swarthy complexion, dark brows and deep-set eyes. With his thick black beard he made the perfect picture of a forty-niner, and his giant stature must have won him respect on all sides.

Cartwright reached San Francisco in July and there met his brother Alfred who had come to California by ship around Cape Horn. At the end of five weeks, tired of the gold rush, they decided to return to the East. They booked passage on the Peruvian bark *Pacifico,* which was bound for the East coast by way of China. Alex became ill between San Francisco and the Sandwich Islands, as Hawaii was then known, and he was put ashore at Honolulu, August 28, 1849. While recovering he fell in love with the islands and determined to make his home in Honolulu. In 1851 his family arrived, a wife and three children.

He was a prominent and respected citizen and merchant of Honolulu until his death in 1892. He organized the Honolulu fire department and was its chief engineer; president of the Chamber of Commerce and of the stock board; consul for Peru at Honolulu for many years and administrator of the estates of Queen Emma and of King Kalakaua. He was a baseball pioneer until the end and was never too busy to discuss it with any who were interested. A familiar figure, with white hair and flowing beard, he often visited the schools throughout the territory and with chalk and blackboard would explain baseball to the native youngsters as well as to the sons of the white planters.

Cartwright also had a long and distinguished Masonic career in Honolulu. On December 19, 1849 he petitioned Lodge *Le Progrès de l'Océanie* and was raised March 1, 1850. This lodge was founded by Captain M. Le Tellier April 8, 1843, under dispensation of the Supreme Council of France, and the first few meetings were held on his barque *Ajax,* which was lying in Honolulu harbor. In 1905 Lodge *Le Progrès* affiliated with the Grand Lodge of California as Oceanic Lodge No. 371. Lodge *Le Progrès* being dormant in 1851, Cartwright and a dozen other Master Masons met in Honolulu to consider forming a new lodge. As a result of this and later meetings, Hawaiian Lodge U.D. was granted a dispensation on January 12, 1852 by the Grand Lodge of California. The first regular meeting of the new lodge was held February 19, 1852 and Cartwright was elected secretary. A year later at the first annual election of officers of Hawaiian Lodge No. 21 he was elected senior deacon and progressed through the chairs, skipping senior warden, and was elected master for two terms, 1855 and 1856.

On June 17, 1860, members of the two lodges, *Le Progrès* and Hawaiian No. 21, acted together for the first time to assist in laying the cornerstone of the new Queen's Hospital, with King Kamehameha IV, past master of Lodge *Le Progrès,* acting as grand master and Cartwright as junior grand warden. This was the first public Masonic ceremony in the islands.

At the request of King Kamehameha V, a dimitted member of Hawaiian Lodge, the cornerstone of the new Government Building was laid with Masonic ceremonies on Monday, February 18, 1872, with Cartwright officiating as acting grand master. On Saturday, January 4, 1879, the cornerstone of the first Masonic Hall in the islands was laid. Cartwright, who was the lone survivor among those who were on the original roll of the lodge in 1852, again officiated as acting grand master, and when the hall was dedicated the following September, he again performed these duties. Brother Cartwright died in Honolulu, July 12, 1892 and was buried in Nuuanu Cemetery with Masonic services by the lodge he had served so faithfully for forty years.

Thus we have the story of Cartwright's contribution to the game of baseball, which has never been truly recognized. He drew the baseball diagram and worked on the fundamental rules, both of which are the foundation of the game as we know it today. He had a hand in the organization of the first baseball club, which formed the first team; he helped to select the first baseball uniforms, and umpired the first game played under set rules. In 1938 he was elected to the Baseball Hall of Fame at Cooperstown, where real baseball was not played until long after Cartwright had played it. It is ironical that organized baseball in his adopted land of Hawaii did not honor his connection with the game until the spurious Doubleday Centennial in 1939. In June of that year a delegation of players from the Kauai League gathered at his grave to revere his memory. And the chances are if you asked any one of these young players where baseball was first played, he would have answered: "In Hoboken, New Jersey, in 1846." Because that is what his father would have taught him and like as not, his father had it straight from Alexander Cartwright, who invented the game and, like Johnny Appleseed before him, scattered the seeds of baseball across the country.

From James T. Farrell's book *My Baseball Diary,* here is the first game of the 1917 World Series—as seen from high up in the right-center-field bleachers. For the climactic game of the Series, as seen from third base, *cf.* Buck Weaver's story at the end of this book.

1917: Chicago White Sox 2, New York Giants 1

JAMES T. FARRELL

I had heard the World Series talked of before I understood anything about baseball. In fact, I had grown up on the feats of the 1906 Chicago White Sox, known as the Hitless Wonders. My uncles, my brother Earl, and my father had spoken of how this team had beaten the famous Chicago Cubs, managed by Frank Chance. The names of White Sox players of that year had acquired an almost legendary significance—Jiggs Donohue, George Davis, Fielder Jones, Nick Altrock, and the substitute infielder, George Rohe, who had smashed out a triple and become the Series hero. And there were Pat Dougherty, Lee Tannehill, Ed Walsh, Billy Sullivan and Doc White, all of whom I had seen play.

My first opportunity to see a World Series game was in 1917 when my team, the White Sox, and the New York Giants, managed by Muggsy McGraw, were to play. My Uncle Tom was on the road selling, but he sent me a money order for five dollars so that Earl and I could see a couple of games. The opening game was on a Saturday morning. Earl slept with me at my grandmother's the night before, and we arose at about 4 A.M. I had read newspaper stories of how lines of fans waited all night to buy bleacher seats. I wanted to do this. I was thirteen that year. Like many fans, I saw baseball as a historic sport. I hoped to see a historic World Series. I could talk of this in the years to come, just as I had heard my father and my uncles, and other men, talk of the 1906 Series. And since 1911 I had waited for the White Sox to win a pennant. Now it had happened. I was inwardly excited, and filled with a sense of the dramatic.

Outside it was dark. There had been some rain the night before and I was anxious about the weather. We were very quiet in the kitchen, which was off my grandmother's bedroom in the flat on South Park Avenue where we lived. She had prepared sandwiches for us to take along to the game, but we made our own breakfast. During all my boyhood years coffee and sweet rolls never tasted better than they did on that October morning of 1917.

And there, against the radiator, was my shaggy Airedale dog, Gerry. I loved her. My uncle had found her on a street in Boston and had shipped her home to us. With her black tip of a nose, she stared at us mutely pleading for food. We gave her breakfast. We tried to get her to drink coffee, but she wouldn't touch it.

Finally, and well before 5 A.M., we were off, leaving by the back door, going down the back stairs, and along the alley to Fifty-eighth Street in the chilly pre-dawn. We took the elevated train to Thirty-fifth Street, the Thirty-Fifth Street trolley to Wentworth Avenue, and found the lineup of men waiting before the bleacher ticket office. It was still dark when we took our places in this line. There were about three hundred men ahead of us in one of the waiting lines. My anxiety disappeared. I had feared that there might be thousands waiting when I arrived. I had attributed to others, and to grown men, my own feelings about baseball. I was a boy still in short pants. The men about us in line greeted our coming with friendliness. They liked seeing such a young and devoted fan waiting as they were.

It was a bit raw, and here and there men had built fires. Vendors were out with hot coffee and we bought and drank quite a quantity of it. About every hour, we ate. I felt important and I was very happy. All the cares I had in my mind were those of my own impatience for time to pass, so that I would get inside of the ball park—so that it would be time for the players to come out on the field for practice—so that it would be time for the game to begin. And of course, there was the greater care or worry—would the White Sox win? I had impatiently looked forward to all of this. I was flattered and pleased with myself when one of the men in line said he thought I was a brave little fellow, to come out so early to see the game. And there was much baseball talk. I spoke up with the authority of an old-time fan. Earl and I talked of how many games we'd seen together—of Babe Ruth pitching, Smoky Joe Wood in the box, Tris Speaker, Ed Walsh's no-hit game in 1911, Rabbit Maranville and his singular way of suddenly jerking out his hands at the level of his belt line to catch pop-ups. And we discussed the White Sox and Giant players. Now, we would have more to talk about.

The dawn came, gray and still chilly. My sense of excitement grew. This long wait was an adventure rather than a boring experience. These strange men standing in line, sitting on boxes, squatting by a fire, playing poker, chatting intermittently about baseball, showing the same concerns as I did about the weather, shivering a bit as I did—they and I were bound together by a common passion. And those around me were kind and friendly. I felt secure and unafraid and I was like them. And then, too, I was here in line and would actually see something which I believed that almost all of the men and boys in America were interested in and wished they could see. Then also, I was a boy. Someday I would grow to be a man, and—I hoped—a big-league star who would play in a World Series game . . . while other men and boys would stand in line to see me as I was standing in line to see Eddie Collins, Joe Jackson, Ray Schalk and all of the other players who would be out on the diamond of Comiskey Park.

The hours passed. Behind us, the line swelled rapidly. Looking behind me, the men stretched out of sight, and I was told that the line was over two blocks long. A cold sun was coming up. Twice men approached Earl and me and offered us money for our place. The men about us told us to let these men in and for us to stay in line. We made about a dollar that way, but the third time we were asked, the men behind us said that was enough. We held our places this time rather than sell them.

At ten o'clock, the line began to move. The gates were open. We got inside and took seats high up in the right-center-field bleachers. Fans poured in after us and the gates were quickly closed. The big bleachers at Comiskey Park were jammed with fans.

I controlled my impatience as best I could, waiting through the morning, looking out at the large empty playing field, and at the empty grandstand and box seats. The crowd kept pouring into the bleachers, and into the pavilion.

There was the diversion of a band. And Earl and I ate more than we should. And there was the constant sense of expectancy. Finally, after the slow wait, there was a cheer. The White Sox were coming out. Far away in their dugout, a few players could now be seen. Then more, and the players appeared on the field to engage in warm-up catching practice. And then, very soon, the White Sox engaged in their batting practice.

The White Sox wore new red, white and blue uniforms instead of their regular season all-white uniforms. These latter were white with a black S on the left side of the shirt. The stockings were pure white. The new World Series uniforms, occasioned by the War, were trimmed with red and blue. The S on the shirt was red and blue against a white background and the white stockings were banded with blue and red stripes. I liked these new uniforms very much and hoped they would be worn in the 1918 season. They weren't.

We sat through the long practice session, alternately interested, impatient and bored. The air of tension, expectancy and excitement slowly grew through the periods of fielding and batting practice. The grandstand and box seats began to fill up. There were sporadic cheers for players, as one or another hit a long ball in the batting practice. There were the Giants to watch when they took their turn at batting practice. Two of the Giant players in whom Earl and I were most interested were Benny Kauff, the center fielder, and Heinie Zimmerman, the third baseman. Heinie Zimmerman, several years earlier, had been one of Earl's favorites. He had then played on the Cubs and in 1912 he had led the National League in hitting. During the 1913 and 1914 seasons in particular, Zimmerman had received much publicity because of his run-ins with umpires. He had acquired the reputation of being hotheaded, had been put out of some games, and had almost become engaged in a serious fight with Rabbit Maranville and one or two other players of the Boston Braves. He was a natural hitter, and I feared that he would be dangerous to the White Sox. Benny Kauff had led the Federal League in batting and had been heralded as a new Ty Cobb. When the Federal League had broken up, Kauff had been one of the most sought-after of the players. McGraw had gotten him for the Giants. He hadn't fulfilled the expectations, but in 1917 he had hit over .300. Kauff batted and threw left-handed, and we took him at the value which sportswriters had placed on him. Still, I insisted and believed that Happy Felsch, the White Sox center fielder, was a much better player. We'd both read that Kauff was a very fancy dresser and that he was supposed to carry twenty-six suits around with him, and we talked of this, watching him catch flies during the fielding practice.

Finally the practice and the opening ceremonies were over with, and the White Sox ran out onto the field, full of pep, and hailed by cheers. I was confident. For there was Eddie Cicotte in the box. When he was right, he was almost unbeatable. McGraw had been expected to pitch his ace, Schupp, but he pulled a surprise and sent in Slim Sallee.

On the fifth pitch, George Burns, the New York left fielder, stung a single over second base. A bad beginning. But the game was young. Earl said that now Buck Herzog, the Giant second baseman, would try to sacrifice. Instead Herzog hit an easy fly to Joe Jackson in left field. McGraw was going to keep trying to cross up the White Sox. Well, this time it hadn't worked. Then Benny Kauff hit an easy fly to Joe Jackson. And on the second ball pitched to Heinie Zimmerman, Burns went down to second. There was a tense moment. Schalk would get him. But Burns slid around Eddie Collins for a stolen base. It was Cicotte versus Heinie. But Zimmerman flew out to Happy Felsch in center field. I always enjoyed watching Felsch snag fly balls and considered him to be the equal of Tris Speaker as a fielder.

One Giant inning was safely gone. Now if the White Sox would go out and give Cicotte a lead, he would hold it. And the White Sox leadoff man and right fielder, Shano Collins, lined a one-base hit to right field. Then McMullin, the third baseman, sacrificed Collins to second. It looked good and there was drama in the very first inning. With a man on second and one out, the two White Sox stars, Eddie Collins and Joe Jackson, were coming up. And Eddie Collins was a good money player. But the Giant shortstop, Art Fletcher, threw Eddie Collins out at first by a step, and Buck Herzog killed our hopes when he went back at top speed and snagged a low fly off Joe Jackson's bat. Sallee looked as though he would be hard to beat.

The game turned into a pitcher's battle. The play was almost airtight. But in those days, a pitcher's battle was as interesting as a slugging match is today. In the second inning, the Giant first baseman, Holke, got an infield hit, but Cicotte neatly picked him off first base. In the third inning, the Giants put two men on base, but Benny Kauff ended the inning by fouling out to Chick Gandil off of first base.

The White Sox scored in the third inning. Heinie Zimmerman was booed because Cicotte handcuffed him at the plate, and the fans liked to razz Zim. But he made a fine play at third base in the third inning, robbing Ray Schalk of a hit. Then Eddie Cicotte, a switch hitter, and a good batsman, lined a single to center. A moment later, the crowd was yelling when John Shano Collins shot a line single to right field. Cicotte was running the bases as pitchers do not in the modern game. Robertson, the Giant right fielder, recovered the ball fast. He had a powerful left arm. I watched him throw, eager but confident. Far away in the infield there was the slide and the play, and then disappointment and disgruntlement. Cicotte was out. What was the matter with Pants Rowland, the White Sox manager, and Kid Gleason, the coach? All around me, they were condemned. I sat back glum. A chance to score had been killed. However, Collins had gone to second on the play. Fred McMullin was at bat. He hit the ball on a line to center field. Benny Kauff played one of the roles for which he, like Heinie Zimmerman, was destined. He played the goat. Kauff dashed in for the ball, took a foolish dive, trying to make a shoestring catch. He failed. John Collins scored. McMullin was on second base. My hero, Eddie Collins, was at bat and I was happy. Eddie Collins popped out to Art Fletcher. But our White Sox were winning one to nothing, and with Cicotte in top form, this might be all that was needed.

Heinie Zimmerman opened the fourth inning by delighting many of the fans. He walked up on a pitch and lunged. Ray Schalk, the catcher, caught the foul ball which he hit. In the White Sox half of the fourth inning, Happy Felsch became a World Series hero. He swung. The ball traveled. The crowd shouted. It knew what had happened. So did George Burns over in left field. He started to run and then he stopped to watch Felsch's powerful drive sail through the sunny afternoon. The ball landed in the bleachers. Home Run Baker in his heyday couldn't have done better. Happy Felsch trotted around the bases. In those days, such home runs were achievements.

In four innings, the White Sox had given me in the right-center-field bleachers and Eddie Cicotte on the mound all that we needed—two runs.

But in the fifth some of my smug confidence was cracked like smashed china. Lew McCarty, the New York catcher, insulted Eddie Cicotte. Babe Ruth never was able to hit a home run off him. McCarty would have done this if he didn't have to run on a game leg which had been broken earlier in the season. McCarty unleashed a tremendous drive to right-center field. Because of his bad leg he was slow in turning this into a triple. Then Slim Sallee sent McCarty home with a single and the Sox only led two to one.

In the sixth inning Benny Kauff did as well at bat as he'd done in the field on McMullin's low liner. He fanned on three pitched balls. In the Giant seventh, Shoeless Joe Jackson took the same kind of a dive as had Benny Kauff. But where Benny became a goat, Joe flung himself into the role of hero. With Holke on first base, Lew McCarty smashed a low liner to left. Jackson came in and went for the ball head first. He caught the ball inches off the ground in one of the most spectacular catches I have ever seen. The umpires rushed out to left field as Jackson lay sprawled with the ball safe in his hands and thumbed an out signal amid many cheers. Then Slim Sallee ended the inning with an easy fly to Happy Felsch.

In the eighth inning, Benny Kauff didn't fan. He hit a slow easy roller to Buck Weaver, who made a wild throw for the only White Sox error of the day. With Zimmerman at bat, Kauff took a lead off first. This was a mistake. Cicotte threw quickly to Chick Gandil. Kauff was trapped and thrown out on a relay to second. The Ty Cobb of the Federal League was no Ty Cobb against the White Sox, and the fans liked this.

Heinie Zimmerman was first up in the Giant ninth. Zim had made no hits all day, but he had offended the South Side of Chicago by making two fine fielding plays. Now what would he do? He tapped to Cicotte in the pitcher's box and didn't even run. Art Fletcher and Davy Robertson were also easy outs, and Cicotte walked off the field after pitching one of his masterpieces in his first World Series game. In 1919, it was different.

THE NAME of William Price Fox is important among present-day writers of fiction, and this baseball story is a reason why.

Leroy Jeffcoat

WILLIAM PRICE FOX

ON LEROY JEFFCOAT'S forty-first birthday he fell off a scaffold while painting a big stucco rooming house over on Sycamore Street. Leroy was in shock for about twenty minutes but when the doctor brought him around he seemed all right.

Leroy went home and rolled his trousers and shoes into a bundle with his Sherwin-Williams Company cap and jacket. He tied the bundle with string to keep the dogs from dragging it off and put it in the gutter in front of his house. He poured gasoline over the bundle and set it on fire. That was the last day Leroy Jeffcoat painted a house.

He went uptown to the Sports Center on Kenilworth Street and bought two white baseball uniforms with green edging, two pairs of baseball shoes, a Spalding second baseman's glove, eight baseballs and two bats. Leroy had been painting houses at union scale since he got out of high school, and since he never gambled nor married he had a pretty good savings account at the South Carolina National Bank.

We had a bush-league team that year called the Columbia Green Wave. The name must have come from the fact that most of us got drunk on Friday nights and the games were always played on Saturdays. Anyhow the season was half over when Leroy came down and wanted to try out for second base.

Leroy looked more like a ballplayer than any man I've ever known. He had that little ass-pinched strut when he was mincing around second base. He also had a beautiful squint into or out of the sun, could chew through a whole plug of Brown Mule tobacco in four innings, and could worry a pitcher to death with his chatter. On and on and on . . . we would be ahead ten runs in the ninth and Leroy wouldn't let up.

But Leroy couldn't play. He looked fine. At times he looked great. But he knew too much to play well. He'd read every baseball book and guide and every Topp's Chewing Gum Baseball Card ever printed. He could show you how Stan Musial batted, how Williams swung, how DiMaggio dug in. He went to all the movies and copied all the stances and mannerisms. You could say, "Let's see how Rizzuto digs one out, Leroy." He'd toss you a ball and lope out about forty feet.

"All right, throw it at my feet, right in the dirt." And you would and then you'd see the "Old Scooter" movement—low and quick with the big wrist over to first.

Leroy could copy anybody. He was great until he got in an actual game. Then he got too nervous. He'd try to bat like Williams, Musial, and DiMaggio all at once and by the time he'd make up his mind he'd have looked at three strikes. And at second base it was the same story. He fidgeted too much and never got himself set in time.

Leroy played his best ball from the bench. He liked it there. He'd pound his ball into his glove and chatter and grumble and cuss and spit tobacco juice. He'd be the first one to congratulate the home-run hitters and the first one up and screaming on a close play.

We got him into the Leesboro game for four innings and against Gaffney for three. He played the entire game at second base against the State Insane Asylum . . . but that's another story.

When the games ended, Leroy showered, dried, used plenty of talcum powder and then spent about twenty minutes in front of the mirror combing his flat black hair straight back.

Most of the team had maybe a cap and a jacket with a number on it and a pair of shoes.

Leroy had two complete uniform changes. After every game he'd change his dirty one for a clean one and then take the dirty one to the one-day dry cleaner. That way Leroy was never out of uniform. Morning, noon, and night Leroy was ready. On rainy days, on days it sleeted, and even during the hurricane season, Leroy was ready. For his was the long season. Seven days a week, three hundred and sixty-five days a year, Leroy was in uniform. Bat in hand, glove fastened to belt, balls in back pocket, and cut plug going. And he never took off his spikes. He would wear a set out every two weeks. You could see him coming two blocks away in his clean white uniform. And at night when you couldn't see him you could hear the spikes and see the sparks on the sidewalk.

The Green Wave worked out on Tuesday and Thursday in the evening and we played on Saturday. Leroy worked out every day and every night. He'd come up to Doc Daniels' drugstore with his bat and ball and talk someone into hitting him fly balls out over the telegraph wires on Mulberry Avenue. It could be noon in August and the sun wouldn't be any higher than a high foul ball, but it wouldn't worry Leroy Jeffcoat. He'd catch the balls or run them down in the gutter until the batter tired.

Then Leroy would buy himself and the batter a couple of Atlantic ales. Doc Daniels had wooden floors and Leroy wouldn't take his baseball shoes off, so he had to drink the ale outside.

Doc would shout out, "Leroy, damn your hide anyway. If you come in here with those spikes on I'm going to work you over with this ice-cream scoop. Now you hear?"

Leroy would spin the ball into the glove, fold it and put it in his back pocket.

"Okay, Doc."

"Why can't you take those damn spikes off and sit down in a booth and rest? You're geting too old to be out in that sun all day."

Leroy was in great shape. As a rule, house painters have good arms and hands and bad feet.

He would laugh and take his Atlantic ale outside in the sun or maybe sit down in the little bit of shade from the mailbox.

Later on, he would find someone to throw him grounders.

"Come on, toss me a few. Don't spare the steam."

He'd crowd in on you and wouldn't be any more than thirty feet out there.

"Come on, skin it along the ground."

You'd be scared to throw it hard but he'd insist.

"Come on, now, a little of the old pepper. In the dirt."

Next thing you'd be really winging them in there and he'd be picking them off like cherries or digging them out of the dust and whipping them back to you. He'd wear you out and burn your hands up in ten minutes. Then he'd find somebody else.

Leroy would go home for supper and then he'd be back. After dark he'd go out to the streetlamp and throw the ball up near the light and catch it. The June bugs, flying ants and bats would be flitting around everywhere but he'd keep on. The June bugs and flying ants would be all over his head and shoulders and even in his glove. He might stop for a while for another Atlantic ale, and if the crowd was talking baseball he'd join it. If it wasn't and the bugs were too bad, he'd stand out in the dark and pound his ball in his glove or work out in the mirror of Doc Daniels' front window. In front of the window he became a pitcher. He worked a little like Preacher Roe but he had more class. He did a lot of rubbing the resin bag and checking signs from the catcher and shaking them off. When he'd agree with a sign he'd nod his head slow . . . exactly like Roe. Then he'd get in position, toss the resin aside, and glare in mean and hard at the batter. He took a big reach and stopped and then the slow and perhaps the most classic look toward second base I've ever seen—absolutely Alexandrian. Then he'd stretch, wind, and whip it through. He put his hands on his knees . . . wait. It had to be a strike. It was. And he'd smile.

And read a sports page? Nobody this side of Cooperstown ever read a page the way Leroy Jeffcoat did. He would crouch down over that sheet for two hours running. He'd read every word and every figure. He went at it like he was following the puzzle maze in *Grit* trying to find the pony or the seventeen rabbits. He had a pencil about as long as your little finger and he'd make notes along the margin. When he finished he'd transfer the notes to a little black book he carried in his back pocket. Leroy would even check the earned run average and the batting and fielding average. I don't mean just *look* at them . . . he'd *study* them. And if he didn't like them he'd divide and do the multiplication and check them over. And if they were wrong he'd be on the telephone to the *Columbia Record* or else he'd write a letter.

Leroy was always writing letters to the sportswriters. Like he'd read an article about how Joe DiMaggio was getting old and slipping and he'd get mad. He'd take off his shoes and go inside Doc Daniels', buy a tablet and an envelope, get in the back booth and write. Like: "What do you mean Joe DiMaggio is too old and he's through. Why you rotten son of a bitch, you just wait and watch him tomorrow."

Next day old Joe would pick up two for four and Leroy would take off his spikes and get back in that back booth again. "What did I tell you. Next time, you watch out who you're saying is through. Also, you print an apology this week or I am going to personally come up there and kick your fat ass. (Signed) Leroy Jeffcoat, taxpayer and second baseman, Doc Daniels' Drugstore, Columbia, S. C."

This would be a much better story if I could tell you that Leroy's game improved and he went on and played and became famous throughout the Sally League. But he didn't.

He got a little better and then he leveled off. But we kept him around because we liked him (number one), that white uniform edged in green looked good (number two), and then, too, we used him as an auxiliary man. A lot of the boys couldn't make it through some of those August games. When you start fanning yourself with a catcher's mitt, it's hot. All that beer and corn whiskey would start coming out and in most games we would wind up with Leroy playing.

One game, Kirk Turner, our right fielder, passed out right in his position in the short weeds. We had to drag him into the shade and Leroy ran out to right field and began chirping. He caught a couple and dropped a couple. At bat he decided he was Ted Williams and kept waiting for that perfect ball that Ted described in *The Saturday Evening Post*. The perfect ball never came and Leroy struck out twice. In the seventh he walked. It was his first time on base in weeks and he began dancing and giving the pitcher so much lip the umpire had to settle him down.

Our last game of the year and the game we hated to play was with the South Carolina State Penitentiary down the hill.

First of all, *no one* beats "The Pen." Oh, you might give them a bad time for a couple of innings but that's about all. It's not that they're a rough bunch so much as it's that they play to win. And I mean they really play to win.

Anyhow we went down and the game started at one-thirty. The high walls kept the breeze out and it was like playing in a furnace. Sweat was dripping off my fingertips and running down my nose.

Billy Joe Jasper pitched the first inning and they hit him for seven runs before Kirk Turner caught two long ones out by the center-field wall.

We came to bat and Al Curry, our catcher, led off. Their pitcher's name was Strunk and he was in jail for murder. The first pitch was right at Al's head. He hit the dirt. The crowd cheered. The next pitch the same thing; Al Curry was as white as a sheet. The next pitch went for his head but broke out and over the inside of the plate. Al was too scared to swing and they called him out on the next two pitches.

Jeff Harper struck out next in the same manner. When he complained to the umpire, who was a trusty, he went out and talked to Strunk. It didn't do any good.

I batted third. It was terrifying. Strunk glared at me and mouthed dirty words. He was so tall and his arms were so long I thought he was going to grab me by the throat before he turned the ball loose. I kept getting out of the box and checking to see if he was pitching from the mound. He seemed to be awfully close.

I got back in the box. I didn't dig in too deep. I wanted to be ready to duck. He reached up about nine feet and it came right at my left eye. I hit the dirt.

"Ball one."

From the ground: "How about that dusting?"

"You entering a complaint?"

"Yes."

"I'll speak to him."

The umpire went out to see Strunk and the catcher followed. They talked a while and every few seconds one of them would look back at me. They began laughing.

Back on the mound. One more beanball and once more in the dirt. And then three in a row that looked like beaners that broke over the plate. Three up. Three down.

At the end of five innings we didn't have a scratch hit. The Pen had fourteen runs and the pitcher Strunk had three doubles and a home run.

We didn't care what the score was. All we wanted to do was get the game over and get out of that prison yard. The crowd cheered everything their ball team did and every move we made brought only boos and catcalls.

At the end of seven we were still without a hit.

Leroy kept watching Strunk. "Listen I can hit that son of a bitch."

I said, "No, Leroy, he's too dangerous."

"The hell he is. Let me at him."

Kirk Turner said, "Leroy, that bastard will kill you. Let's just ride him out and get out of here. This crowd makes me nervous."

But Leroy kept insisting. Finally George Haggard said, "Okay, Leroy. Take my place." So Leroy replaced George at first.

Strunk came to bat in the eighth and Leroy started shouting. "Let him hit! Let him hit, Billy Joe! I want to see that son of a bitch over here."

He pounded his fist in George's first baseman's glove and started jumping up and down like a chimpanzee.

"Send that bastard down here. I want him. I'll fix his ass."

The crowd cheered Leroy and he tipped his hat like Stan Musial.

The crowd cheered again.

Strunk bellowed, "Shut that nut up, ump."

The umpire raised his hands, "All right, over there, simmer down or I'll throw you out."

The crowd booed the umpire.

Leroy wouldn't stop. "Don't let him hit, Billy! Walk him. Walk that beanball bastard. He might get a double; I want him over here."

Billy Joe looked at Al Curry. Al gave him the walk sign.

Two balls . . . three balls. . . .

"You getting scared, you bastard? Won't be long now."

The crowd laughed and cheered.

Again the Musial touch with his cap.

Strunk shouted, "Listen, you runt, you keep quiet while I'm hitting or I'll shove that glove down your throat."

Leroy laughed, "Sure you will. Come on down. I'll help you."

Four balls. . . .

Strunk laid the bat down carefully and slowly walked toward first. Strunk got close. The crowd was silent. Leroy stepped off the bag and Strunk stepped on. Leroy backed up. Strunk followed. Everybody watched. No noise. Leroy stopped and took his glove off. He handed it to Strunk. Strunk took the glove in both hands.

Leroy hit him with the fastest right I've ever seen.

Strunk was stunned but he was big. He lashed the glove into Leroy's face and swung at him.

Leroy took it on the top of his head and crowded in so fast Strunk didn't know what to do. Leroy got him off balance and kept him that way while he pumped in four lefts and six rights.

Strunk went down with Leroy on top banging away. Two of us grabbed Leroy and three got a hold of Strunk. They led Strunk back to the dugout bleeding. He turned to say something and spat out two teeth. "I ain't through with you yet."

The crowd went wild.

Someone shouted, "What's his name? What's his name?"

"Jeffcoat . . . Leroy Jeffcoat."

They cheered again. And shouted, "Leroy Jeffcoat is our boy." And then, "Leroy Jeffcoat is red-hot."

Leroy tipped his hat Musial-style, picked up George Haggard's glove and said, "Okay, let's play ball."

Another cheer and the game started.

The Pen scored two more times that inning before we got them out. We came to bat in the ninth behind 21 to 0. Strunk fanned me and then hit Coley Simms on the shoulder. He found out that Leroy was batting fifth so he walked the next two, loading the bases so he could get a shot at him.

So Leroy came up with the bases loaded and the prison crowd shouting "Leroy Jeffcoat is our boy."

He pulled his cap down like Musial and dug into the box like DiMaggio. The crowd cheered and he got out of the box and tipped his cap.

Strunk was getting madder and madder and he flung the resin down and kicked the rubber. "Let's go, in there."

Leroy got in the box, whipped the bat through like Ted Williams and hollered, "Okay, Strunk, let's have it."

Zip. Right at his head.

Leroy flicked his head back like a snake but didn't move his feet.

The crowd booed Strunk and the umpire went out to the mound. We could hear the argument. As the umpire turned away, Strunk told him to go to hell.

The second pitch was the same as the first. Leroy didn't move and the ball hit his cap bill.

The umpire wanted to put him on base.

Leroy shouted, "No, he didn't hit me. He's yellow. Let him pitch."

The crowd cheered Leroy again. Strunk delivered another duster and the ball went between Leroy's cap bill and his eyes. This time he didn't even flick his head.

Three balls . . . no strikes.

Two convicts dropped out of the stands and trotted across the infield to the mound. They meant business. When they talked, Strunk listened and nodded his head. A signal passed around the infield.

The fourth pitch was right across Leroy's chest. It was Williams' ideal ball and it was the ball Leroy had been waiting for all season. He hit it clean and finished the Williams swing.

It was a clean single but the right fielder bobbled it and Leroy made the wide turn toward second. The throw into second was blocked and bobbled again and Leroy kept going. He ran in spurts, each spurt faster than the last. The throw to third got past the baseman and Leroy streaked for home, shouting.

He began sliding from twenty feet out. He slid so long he stopped short. He had to get up and lunge for home plate with his hand. He made it as the ball whacked into the catcher's mitt and the crowd started coming out of the stands.

The guards tried to hold the crowd back and a warning siren sounded. But the convicts got to him and paraded around the field with Leroy on their backs. The game was called at this point and the reserve guards and trusties came out with billy clubs.

Later Coley and I learned from the Pen's manager that the committee had told Strunk they wanted Leroy to hit a home run. We never told the rest of the team or anybody else about that.

After we showered at The Pen we all went back to Doc Daniels' drugstore. Everyone told everyone about it and when Doc Daniels heard it he came outside and personally led Leroy into the store with his spikes on.

"Leroy, from now on I want you to feel free to walk right in here anytime you feel like it."

Leroy smiled, and put his bat and his uniform bag up on the soda fountain. Doc bought Atlantic ales for everyone. Later, I bought a round and Coley bought a round.

And just as we were settling down in the booths with sandwiches, potato chips, and the jukebox going, Leroy picked up his glove and started spinning his ball off the ends of his fingers and said, "I'm getting a little stiff. Anyone feel like throwing me a few fast ones?"

A BREED OF CAT not specifically celebrated by the *Fireside* library heretofore is discussed here—the player-manager. And the breed of cat is probably Cheshire, because it seems to be disappearing completely. There've been some great ones in the past, who were brilliant not only as players but simultaneously as managers too—Frank Chance, Tris Speaker, Frank Frisch, Mickey Cochrane. But only one combined a world championship as a manager in the same season as his own election as his league's Most Valuable Player. The year was 1948—in the summer of which this magazine article appeared.

They're Just Wild About Boudreau

STANLEY FRANK

IN THE VAST excitement created in Cleveland this summer by the purposeful pass the Indians are making at their first pennant since 1920, a more arresting development has been overlooked. This is the year the garbled voice of public opinion is winning more ball games than the base hit ringing clear. Baseball has always been a community project in Cleveland, and for once the fans' masterminding of events on the field is justified.

It is impossible to envision the Indians as contenders for the pennant without Lou Boudreau, the only playing manager in the major leagues and the best shortstop in baseball. If it were not for the fans, Mr. B. might be performing his miracles elsewhere and the Indians long ago would have set up light housekeeping in fourth place, where they were consigned in preseason polls. Cleveland has had a fair share of great ballplayers—Speaker, Young, Lajoie, Burkett, Joss, Jackson, Covelski, Ferrell and Feller—but nobody has ever begun to approach Boudreau's astonishing popularity. The citizens have tolerated raids on the municipal treasury and skulduggery in City Hall, but the incident that was closest to provoking a public uprising was the report last October that Boudreau was to be traded to the St. Louis Browns.

Boudreau is a thoroughly unremarkable young man of thirty-one who, as a player and a personality, presents a bat-bagful of contradictions. He is easily the slowest ballplayer since Ernie Lombardi was thrown out at first base trying to stretch a double into a single. His right ankle has been broken three times, he has flat feet and an alderman's bay window, yet he is the acknowledged master at a position that demands agility. His stance at the plate is a burlesque of stylish form, but he won the American League batting championship in 1944 and at mid-season this year he was outhitting everyone in sight except the redoubtable Ted Williams. Boudreau was the youngest major-league manager in history when he was given his job at the age of twenty-four, and he still makes mistakes that once were marked off to inexperience. He is the only man in the game who is booed and cheered by the same fans on general principles. The customers swoon when he hitches up his pants before hitting or fielding a ball, but they shudder when the same gesture is interpreted as a piece of masterminding.

Obviously Boudreau is an extra-special curve ball in the dizzy baseball business, as Bill Veeck has discovered. Veeck, who may be described as an affable Larry MacPhail, is the young (thirty-four) president of the Cleveland ball club with a well-advertised aversion for neckties, losing teams and Boudreau's managerial talents. When he took control of the team in June, 1946, Veeck immediately set out to promote new interest in the Indians—and a new manager.

Veeck was confronted by a situation that could prevail only in baseball. In the free-enterprise system, new owners of a private business are conceded the right to shake up the executive staff inherited from the old management and install their own men. Although baseball is eminently a private business, the game also belongs to the fans, and is a quasi-public institution. No one understands this unique status better than Veeck. He was well aware of Boudreau's popularity and the resentment that would be aroused if he, a newcomer, bounced the people's choice. His first step was to convince the fans that every move he made was for the improvement of the team.

Sportswriters familiar with Veeck's methods knew he wanted a more personable front man than Boudreau, who generates magnetism in inverse ratio to his distance from the fans. Candidates for the job mentioned most prominently were Charley Grimm, who had been associated with Veeck in a highly successful operation at Milwaukee, and Jimmie Dykes, who had been fired by the White Sox a month previously. Veeck studiously refrained from denying the rumors. Instead, he dropped two-ton hints all over Cleveland that he considered Boudreau something less than a genius of strategy. Whenever three or more people held still long enough, Veeck swung into a pat speech: "Boudreau is the greatest ball player, bar none, I've ever seen and"—a pregnant pause—"one of the best managers in the league."

Having planted these time bombs, Veeck proceeded to put on so many circuses in his ball yard that the sixth-place Indians set an attendance record by playing to more than 1,000,000 admissions at home in 1946. When 1,521,978 customers paid their way last season to watch the team finish a distant fourth, Veeck decided he was established solidly enough to drop Boudreau overboard.

During the World Series in New York, Veeck confidentially told no more than two dozen reporters he had a deal on the fire. It involved Boudreau, outfielder George Metkovich and pitchers Red Embree and Bryan Stephens. They were to be sent to the Browns in exchange for shortstop Vernon Stephens, outfielder Paul Lehner and pitchers Jack Kramer and Bob Muncrief. That was on October third, the day the Yankees' Bill Bevens was one out away from pitching the first no-hitter in World Series history. The most dramatic ball game ever played went unnoticed in Cleveland. The populace was too busy looking for a rope, a tree and Veeck's neck.

Newspapers carrying the story hit the street at five o'clock in the afternoon. At 5:20 Veeck began to receive long-distance phone calls at his New York hotel from strangers. An hour later telegrams poured in. The first, from a clergyman, read: "Don't come back to Cleveland if you trade Boudreau." Associates left holding the fort at home urged Veeck to return before barricades were erected in front of his office.

Veeck flew back to Cleveland after the game the next day. Arriving at midnight, he immediately set off on crutches—he lost his right foot in the South Pacific with the Marines—to conduct a one-man poll in the downtown section. At every street corner, crowds gathered and held up traffic to protest Boudreau's departure.

"The people weren't abusive," Veeck says. "They just told me I was crazy."

During the next ten days Veeck personally answered some 15,000 letters addressed to him. Approximately 7,000 more anonymous postcards and poison-pen notes advised him to drop dead—or, at least, take a dry dive off the fifty-two-story Terminal Tower. Eighty per cent of the letters threatened a boycott of the team if Boudreau left. The Cleveland *News* printed a ballot asking readers to express their opinion of the trade. Of 7,000 ballots mailed in, 90 percent from men fans were against it. Women were opposed, 99 to 1. Boudreau is a dark, handsome bloke who looks like Tyrone Power—if you don't look too closely—he has three small children and he is a good provider, a parlay which has never failed to captivate the feminine vote.

Veeck knew when he was licked. St. Louis took him off the hook by ending negotiations abruptly. But he still goes through the motions of defending the deal on a straight baseball basis.

"Changes had to be made in the team," he contends. "Boudreau, apart from Feller, was my only trade bait. I needed a center fielder and two good pitchers. The Browns had the men to fill those weak spots. Sure, giving up Boudreau would've hurt us at shortstop. But in Stephens I was getting the next best man in the league at the position. Besides, St. Louis had just released Muddy Ruel and needed a manager. Nothing definite was said, but I spoke with the Browns in anticipation that Boudreau would get the job. I couldn't send him to a team where he'd be just another player. The grandstand wolves really would've skinned me alive if I made a deal that cost Boudreau money and prestige."

Friends insist Veeck would have gone through with the trade, despite the outraged screams, if St. Louis had not called all bets off. They offer this as evidence that the trade must have been advantageous to Cleveland. Insiders say Veeck knew that the Browns, who were in serious financial difficulties, had already closed a deal with the Boston Red Sox—announced six weeks later—in which they received $400,000 for ten players. According to the story, Veeck concocted a dummy trade as a trial balloon to test Mr. B.'s standing with the public as Boss Man. It is significant that Veeck made no attempt to pin down Clark Griffith, owner of the Washington Senators, who said he would be very happy to have Boudreau as his playing manager.

Throughout the uproar, Boudreau let his admirers do all the talking for him. He was quoted as having said he would be willing to stay with the Indians as a player, but he now refuses to confirm or deny the statement.

Veeck never considered retaining Boudreau without portfolio. "You couldn't expose him to that embarrassment and set up an intolerable situation for the man who succeeded him," he snaps. "It would destroy his dignity." After getting full publicity mileage out of the situation, Veeck gave Boudreau a two-year contract at an increase in salary. With bonus clauses pegged to attendance, he will earn close to $50,000 this year. Veeck has repeatedly said he is opposed to holdover commitments. But he signed Boudreau through the 1949 season to placate the fans.

Experts on the curious behavior of Cleveland baseball nuts suspect the staggering crowds the Indians have been pulling this year are as much a vote of confidence in Boudreau as an expression of faith in the team's chance to cop its first pennant since 1920. None of the ten major-league cities has gone longer without a winner than Cleveland—none roots for a team more fervently. On August first, the Indians had played to an unprecedented total of 1,444,925 cash customers in forty-six of their seventy-seven home games. Barring a total collapse on the field, the Indians are certain to break the all-time attendance record of 2,265,512 in one season made by the Yankees in 1946. Never before has a ball club promised to draw double the population of a metropolitan area.

The Cleveland fan has been disappointed so often by the Indians that in his moments of wildest exultation he seems to be waiting apprehensively for the roof to fall in. His worst suspicions are generally confirmed, yet he will blow his top, given the flimsiest encouragement for same. When the team jumped away to an imposing lead in mid-June, an extra operator had to be put on the telephone switchboard to inform callers that World Series reservations would not be accepted until September, if ever. Upon returning home the team promptly went into a tailspin that brought it down from the clouds with a sickening jolt.

To complicate matters, Bob Feller was in the worst slump of his career. On June nineteenth, Feller announced he was giving up all outside activities to concentrate on his pitching and help the Indians win the pennant. Maybe it was sheer coincidence, but the next day, 82,781 spectators, the largest crowd ever to see a major-league ball game, jammed Municipal Stadium.

Boudreau is out there every day, playing shortstop as though he invented it and getting the hits that promise to touch off a rally. Baseball fans are creatures of habit. They have been rooting for Boudreau, the boy manager, so long they resent being reminded that he is, in point of continuous service with one team, the most established manager in the American League except Connie Mack—who antedates everyone in baseball but Abner Doubleday, the founding father. The fans admit Boudreau has limitations as a strategist. But they argue that he wins more games as a player than he loses as a manager—and they may be right.

The strangest part of Cleveland's love affair with Boudreau is his casual acceptance of it as his divine right. Boudreau has a deep conviction that he was anointed to be a leader. Only a youth extremely sure of himself would have had the brass to apply for the manager's job with only two full seasons in the big leagues behind him.

"The job never scared me. Why should it?" he demands. "I was elected captain of my high-school and college basketball teams in my sophomore year. When I was fifteen, coaches were talking things over with me. Say, I even was elected president of Phi Sigma Kappa, my fraternity, when I was a sophomore. I expected some of the older guys on the team would be jealous of me, but I knew I could handle them."

This spiel sounds just as naïve now as it did seven years ago. But Cleveland sportswriters, none of whom considers Boudreau a favorite dreamboat, no longer shrug it off with a sardonic laugh. The ceased to regard him as an innocent youngster when, in his first press conference, he suggested that all newspaper stories be submitted to him for approval before appearing in print. The immodest proposal greatly stimulated the reporters' capacity for criticism, but they agree unanimously that the fellow has a genuine gift for leadership.

"He showed it in the first big-league game he played nine years ago," Gordon Cobbledick, of the Cleveland *Plain Dealer*, relates. "You had to be there to believe it. Halfway through the first inning, this kid from the bush was running the team—and everybody on the field and in the stands knew it. Damnedest thing I ever saw."

As manager, M. B. never permits anyone to forget that he is the absolute boss. All other managers send a coach to the umpires with the batting order before a game. Boudreau does the chore himself. Last year when the Indians were going poorly, Boudreau, from his position at shortstop, gave the signals for the pitches called by the catcher. He confides in no one and is suspicious of any insignificant gesture that bypasses his authority. Although he always has had experienced, high-priced assistants, he seldom asks for advice. One of his coaches is Bill McKechnie, who won four pennants in the National League as a manager. McKechnie, once an affable source of information for newspapermen, has been impersonating a clam since his arrival in Cleveland two years ago. Boudreau wants all questions put to him directly.

"I like having a finger in everything that happens on the ball club," he says. "Keeps me more interested in my own job."

Boudreau has been hardly tactful in his relationships with his teammates. The problem of establishing proper accord with the players, which gives managers more sleepless nights than wild rookie pitchers, is doubly difficult for an active athlete who must exercise discipline over men performing on the field with him. If he remains one of the boys, he will be accused of ratting on his own kind when it becomes necessary to crack the whip. If he holds himself aloof from the troops, they will say he has gone high-hat, and team morale will suffer. The wretch can't win.

Like all playing managers before him, Boudreau took the convenient way out. He gave his colleagues the absent treatment. As we have said, any course would have left him open to criticism. But Boudreau got a particularly large dose because he was the youngest regular on the team and it was felt that he needed the leavening touches of clubhouse horseplay. Ray Mack, his inseparable buddy and double-play partner who had come up through the minors with him, had to get a new roommate when Louie, his old pal, mounted the high horse he still rides.

Boudreau has few contacts with the players off the field. He and his wife rarely associate with the help in Cleveland. On the road, he eats, travels and goes to the movies with his coaches and he sits in on poker games or bull sessions only with club officials and newspapermen. The Indians are not a closely knit crew, yet morale was never better on a team notorious for international dissension before Boudreau took charge. He has had trouble with only two players, both chronic malcontents. Jim Bagby was fined $100 for loafing in 1945 and sold to Boston. Boudreau put up with Jeff Heath's brooding for four years before unloading him.

Although fond of putting on the big, brisk executive routine, Boudreau is strictly a ballplayer in habits and attitudes. His intellectual interests include movies, prizefights and the best restaurant in town. Pound for pound, he is the most spectacular man with a knife and fork in baseball and, perhaps, the whole wide world. Anything in the food line is fine with him as long as it is a double order. Like most of his co-workers, he is a pinball artist and perfects his technique during the off season by practicing at home on an elaborate contraption that does everything but spout soda pop and play "The Stars and Stripes Forever" when the jackpot is hit.

Cleveland fans, always articulate second-guessers, are kept in splendid voice by Boudreau's managerial tactics. The chief gripe against him is that he plays dull, unimaginative baseball relieved by wild hunches which generally backfire. Boudreau follows the book in going for one run at a time in a league that traditionally shoots for big innings. They say Veeck had to be restrained from leaping out of the press box last year when, in a close game with the Red Sox, a squeeze play was called with runners on first and third, none out, and L. Boudreau, the team's leading hitter, at bat. The signal was missed. The Red Sox converted Boudreau's bunt into a double play and the Indians lost the game.

A young fellow himself, Boudreau is impatient with rookies and keeps them on the anxious seat with his constant lineup shifts. Players shuttle in and out of Boudreau's doghouse for reasons that make no sense. Last year Dale Mitchell topped the team in hitting with .316, but this season he kept steady company with a splinter on the bench until mid-June.

Mel Harder, the old curve-ball specialist who is now a coach, almost gave himself laryngitis in spring training last year urging the boss to take a good look at a kid relegated to the bull-pen corps. Boudreau didn't listen until July thirty-first, when he finally gave Harder's boy a chance to start a game. He won it and added nine more during the last two months of the season. The kid happened to be Bob Lemon, author of this season's first no-hit, no-run game and the team's most dependable pitcher.

The one contribution Boudreau has made to the great American game of baseball was more a product of pique than pure strategy. On July 14, 1946, Boudreau hit a home run and four doubles in the first half of a doubleheader with the Red Sox—marking the first time since 1889 that a player got five extra-base hits in one game. The achievement went for Mr. Sweeney. The Red Sox won the game, 11–10, on Ted Williams' three homers.

"I was so damn mad at seeing my hits wasted," Boudreau admits, "that I came up with that cockeyed Williams shift on the spur of the moment. I knew he could pop short flies to left for doubles all day long, but I was willing to take that chance as long as somebody else had to drive him in. Massing the team toward right field worked swell for a long time and everybody copied the shift, but we don't use it any more. Williams has smartened up—the bum murders us by hitting to left if we switch on him."

All Boudreau's shortcomings as a manager are canceled by his sheer brillance as a player. He is unquestionably the greatest infielder in the game today and perhaps its best competitor. Stripped of his bat and glove, he would have trouble holding a job. He is a prize exhibit of leadership by example. That is Boudreau's only recommendation as a manager. It is one that has never been a drug on the market.

When the St. Louis Cardinals were winning three straight pennants during the war, the label of "Mr. Shortstop" was pasted on Marty Marion. Today Boudreau's superiority over Marion is so clear that National League partisans no longer dispute it. Since 1940, which also marked Marion's first full season in the majors, Boudreau has handled more chances, made fewer errors and participated in more double plays. Last year Boudreau established the all-time record for shortstops with a fielding average of .982. In 1944 he set another mark by figuring in 134 double plays.

For a bloke who has a trick ankle and never could run fast, Boudreau covers a lot of territory, some of it in highly unorthodox fashion. In recent years he has been hurling himself headlong at sharp grounders, blocking the ball with his body and, in appropriate situations, shoveling the ball to second base for force plays while lying prone. Only a spoilsport will rise to point out that another shortstop would not have to resort to such heroics to reach the same ball. A superb sense of anticipation—which he credits to his basketball training—compensates for Boudreau's dreadful lack of speed. He has slowed up so much in the last two seasons that he is already talking of shifting to third base, which can be played on a handful of dimes.

Where Boudreau runs away and hides from all other shortstops is in the hitting department. That he is able to hit at all, to make no mention of the .375 he was flirting with at midseason, is a constant source of wonder to purists. At the plate, Boudreau resembles a man leaning over a fence to read a neighbor's paper while in the act of beating a carpet. His southern exposure sticks out at right angles to his head and legs. He cocks the bat stiffly abaft his right ear in a manner that is ludicrous to everyone but the pitcher.

"There are a dozen better hitters in the league, but nobody is tougher in the clutch than Boudreau," Bucky Harris, the Yankee manager, says. "He's to the Indians what DiMaggio is to us, what Williams is to the Red Sox, what Musial is to the Cardinals."

It is interesting to speculate on the depths the Indians would be plumbing today if not for two former semipros who had sons. Like Papa Feller, Boudreau's father was a frustrated ballplayer who dreamed of the day he would see his boy in the big leagues. He died of a brain tumor before his wish was fulfilled.

Lou Boudreau, Sr., was born at St. Anne, Illinois, in a small colony of French immigrants, a circumstance which prompted pressbox romanticists to call young Lou "The Flying Frenchman" when he went up to Cleveland. The nickname failed to stick for obvious reasons. Boudreau never could fly and he is no more French than domestic champagne. There is, in fact, as much German as French blood on both sides of his family, and his maternal grandmother was Jewish.

When Louie was eight years old his informal baseball education began under the tutelage of his father, a machinist at the Buda Company in Harvey, Illinois, where the family still lives. Every day after the plant closed, Lou junior and senior went to the Whittier Elementary School field for a practice session until nightfall. The boy wanted to be a catcher like his older brother Al, but his father groomed him for third base, the position he had played. When the time and money could be spared, the two Lous traveled twenty-two miles to Chicago to see Sunday games.

Louie presently was the best baseball player at Thornton High, but he was more outstanding on the basketball court. The first youth ever picked on the All-State quintet three successive years, he had no difficulty getting, in 1936, a scholarship to the University of Illinois from a state senator. That took care of tuition. To make expenses, he was a waiter and dishwasher at his fraternity house and earned fifty cents an hour as a clerk in the Illinois A. A. through the National Youth Administration—a New Deal gimmick which put more athletes through college than all the well-heeled alumni extant.

One summer he also assembled gas ranges when he wasn't engaged with the company softball team that went to the quarter-finals of the so-called world championships at Chicago.

In 1937 Boudreau found an easier way to make the money which was needed at home after the separation of his parents. Several major-league clubs were interested in the kid who had been the leading scorer of the Illinois basketball team that tied Minnesota for the Big Ten title and the chief run-producer of the baseball team that won the championship outright. The late Harold Irelan, a Cleveland scout, was the only envoy with the presence of mind, however, to put a little something on the line. Boudreau agreed to report to Cleveland after graduation in consideration for $100 a month which was to be paid to his mother as long as he remained in school, a bonus of $1,000 for signing the contract, and the promise of another $2,500 when he played in sixty games with the Indians.

The contract ended financial problems at home—and Boudreau's varsity career. In February 1938 the Western Conference declared him ineligible as a professional but hinted that the ban would be lifted if he canceled the contract with Cleveland. Boudreau turned down a score of offers from professional basketball teams and piously rejected a chance to make a fast touch in Hollywood by appearing in a quickie with Stanford's Hank Luisetti. Four months later he learned his case would not be reopened. Miffed, Boudreau joined the Indians' farm team at Cedar Rapids in the Three-I League.

Once Boudreau decided baseball was his business, he wasted little time making it pay off. In 1939 he was sent to Buffalo, where he was hitting .331 when the Indians recalled him and Ray Mack in August to improve their uneasy position in fifth place. The Indians proceeded to win thirty-six of their last fifty-six games, and finished third.

What should have been a spectacular season for Boudreau was spoiled on the last bounce in 1940. He topped the shortstops in fielding and drove in 101 runs. But the Indians, clearly the best team in the American League, blew the pennant in September with the "Crybaby" rebellion against Manager Oscar Vitt. Boudreau may be stretching the truth when he says he "didn't know what the hell was going on," but he took no part in the rumpus. The older players told him to keep his nose clean, a sterling piece of advice.

Missing out on the World Series was perhaps the best break Boudreau could have gotten. Only Mack, his roomie, knew he played through the last two weeks of the season with an inflamed appendix. Peritonitis had already set in when he entered the hospital after the final game. Dr. Edward Castle later told him he would surely have been a goner had he delayed the operation for such nonsense as a World Series.

When Roger Peckinpaugh, who had succeeded Vitt as manager, voluntarily bowed out in 1941, virtually every unemployed baseball man was mentioned as a candidate for the job. Boudreau's application was a big laugh to everyone but the late George Martin, a paint manufacturer who was a stockholder in the Indians. Martin, intrigued by the thought of a twenty-four-year-old manager, suggested to President Alva Bradley that Boudreau, the All-American-boy type, would take the heat off the club by enlisting the sympathy of the fans.

For ten days the Cleveland clients were in a towering tizzy, recalling that Bucky Harris and Joe Cronin had won pennants in their first years as boy managers. Pearl Harbor and Feller's immediate enlistment in the Navy disabused the fans of such foolish notions. Nothing was expected of the Indians with Feller gone, and Boudreau surprised no one. Third place in 1943 was the highest the team finished. In the meantime Boudreau, a very green pea, was learning his job.

Veeck is reconciled to having Boudreau on his payroll indefinitely and appears reasonably satisfied. He should be. Wherever the Indians finish, Boudreau's popularity should be able to pack in the fans until 1952, when Veeck estimates his expanded farm system will begin to show results.

"Frankly, we'll be living on our wits for the next three years," Veeck says, "but I'm not looking ahead that far. All I'm worrying about now is today's game. Boudreau is a good enough manager to win the pennant, but I don't think he will. He hasn't the team for it. We've got a two-man pitching staff, Feller and Lemon. Feller must regain his old touch and finish like a four-alarm fire if we're going to have a look-in for the World Series."

While on the subject, how would Cleveland look if Boudreau had been traded last year?

"Sometimes," Veeck says with a grin, "the best deals are the ones you don't make."

PHIL INTERLANDI

Courtesy *Look* Magazine ©

"Martha, do you have anything you want to say before the baseball season starts?"

Dick Friendlich is known as the author of a series of boys' fiction books on baseball. To my knowledge, he never had his hero pitch a perfect game. That would have been too much. So, on the night of May 8, 1968, Friendlich found himself assigned to cover an event that wasn't fiction at all.

1968: Oakland A's 4, Minnesota Twins 0

DICK FRIENDLICH

The Athletics' Jim "Catfish" Hunter last night became the first American Leaguer in 46 years to pitch a regular season perfect game.

The 22-year-old right-hander retired 27 Minnesota Twins batters in order in hurling the A's to a 4–0 triumph before a small but howling crowd of 6928 at the Oakland Coliseum.

Hunter also was his team's leading batter, driving in three runs.

When the 6-foot native of North Carolina blazed a fast ball past pinch hitter Rich Reese for a swinging third strike to nail down his history-making performance his teammates—some of them with tears of happiness in their eyes—rushed to the mound, hoisted him to their shoulders and carried him to the dugout.

Hunter threw 107 pitches and went to a three ball count on only six hitters.

No American League pitcher had thrown a perfect game during the league season since Charlie Robertson of the Chicago White Sox against Detroit in 1922, 24 years before Hunter was born.

The only other perfect game pitched by an American Leaguer came in the World Series of 1956, when the New York Yankees' Don Larsen set down Brooklyn without permitting a Dodger to reach first base.

In recent years there have been two perfects by National League hurlers. Jim Bunning of the Phillies had one against the New York Mets in 1964 and Sandy Koufax of the Los Angeles Dodgers did it against the Cubs in 1965.

However, Hunter's no-hitter is the second in the American League so far this season. Baltimore's Tom Phoebus hurled one against Boston 10 days ago.

Immediately after the game, Athletics' owner Charles O. Finley telephoned their dressing room from his home in La Porte, Ind., and told Hunter he would receive a $5,000 bonus.

Relying principally on his fast ball and slider, Hunter struck out 11 Twins. Only three balls were hit hard enough to give him any trepidation.

Two went to left fielder Joe Rudi, called up from Vancouver only today and playing his first game in the big park. Both were sinking line drives, one by Cesar Tovar in the fourth and another by Rod Carew in the seventh. The other real tough chance was a hard hit high bounder by Bob Allison in the fifth, but third baseman Sal Bando judged the odd hop perfectly and threw out Allison.

The ninth inning found everybody in the park, except Hunter apparently, tighter than a G-string on a violin.

There was, as the Catfish's catcher Jim Pagliaroni remarked, an uneasy quiet in the A's dugout from the fifth inning on. But nobody said anything. Everybody, Hunter included, knew what was going on.

John Roseboro, the former Dodger, batted for shortstop Jack Hernandez and grounded out in routine fashion to John Donaldson at second base. Catcher Bruce Look struck out for his third straight time, this one on a called strike and Reese, a .154 hitter, came up to swing for relief pitcher Ron Perranoski.

Hunter went to one strike and two balls on Reese, who then fouled the next four pitches into the stands as you could hear the gasps and loud exhaling of the fans.

Hunter then fired a fast ball that was a little high and a little inside but not so much so it could not have been a strike. Pagliaroni started for the mound, but plate umpire Jerry Neudecker called it ball three and the crowd booed.

They might have been saved their breath because Hunter's next pitch was on the inside corner and Reese didn't come close to it.

In the dressing room, Reese said that the ball three call was correct.

"There was no chance that I was going to take a pitch that was even close," he said. "If it was anywhere near the strike zone I was going to swing and I did."

For six innings, it looked as though all Hunter could get, even if he did pitch a perfect game was a draw. Twins right-hander Dave Boswell, who had some trouble with his control, was pitching from a stretch in each of the first five innings, but with the aid of his own determination and a couple of timely double plays, escaped without a run being scored against him until the seventh.

In that inning, his own wildness and Hunter's application of a do-it-yourself program gave Oakland a 1–0 lead.

Rick Monday opened with a sinking line drive to center that Ted Uhlaender got his glove on but could not hold. It went for a double and after Rudi strick out, Boswell wild pitched Monday to third. Hunter shoved a bunt down the first base line which Boswell fielded but with no chance for a play at the plate. He also had no play at first base because Harmon Killebrew was charging the bunt too, and there was no one covering the bag so Hunter charged across for the unmolested single.

The A's added three runs in the eighth in a weird inning that saw Floyd Robinson come to bat against Boswell as a pinch hitter for Rudi with the bases loaded and two outs. Boswell went 2–0 on Robinson at which point Twins manager Cal Ermer called in Perranoski from the bullpen.

Oakland manager Bob Kennedy countered by sending Danny Cater up to the plate to finish Robinson's turn at bat and Perranoski completed the walk on two pitches, forcing in Ramon Webster, who had singled earlier in the inning. Hunter then slashed a single to right to drive in Pagliaroni and Monday for some insurance runs, which as it turned out he could have saved for his next start.

THERE'VE BEEN some wide margins in the scores of World Series games. But nobody ever clinched a Series, before or after, by a final-game score like this one.

1934: St. Louis Cardinals 11, Detroit Tigers 0

FRANKIE F. FRISCH
***as told to* KEN SMITH**

I FINALLY got to sleep on the night of October 8, 1934, in my hotel in Detroit. The next day was the most important day of my whole baseball career so far, and I knew it.

When I had been a fresh kid, with John J. McGraw's Giants in the 1921, '22, '23 and '24 World Series, I never fretted about anything. Slept like a baby and played with an abandon I wish I had had in the three Series during the '30s. McGraw and the older men like Dave Bancroft, Heinie Groh and Casey Stengel did the worrying in the old days. A young squirt isn't afraid of anything. Life's a breeze and every day is a lark.

But in the 1930, '31 and '34 Series, the responsibility was terrific. This stuff you hear about old codgers mellowing and losing the competitive urge is the bunk. It grows stronger with age, especially when you are playing second base and managing the Gashouse Gang.

Well, we were even-Stephen at three games apiece, in the 1934 Series—the Cardinals against the Tigers. You can imagine how I would feel if we blew this, of all Series, after such a donnybrook as we had been through in the first six games. I lay there in the sheets, figuring pitches for Mickey Cochrane, Charley Gehringer, Goose Goslin and Hank Greenberg, knowing that here was the one big game of my life whether I played a personal part in the playing end, or not. I don't have to thumb back and say, "Let's see, now, which *was* my biggest day?"

You can imagine what was on my mind lying there before the seventh and deciding game. Dizzy Dean had won the first for us in Detroit, 8–3. Schoolboy Rowe, who had a tremendous year with the Tigers, had beaten us the second game, 3–2, the Schoolboy retiring 22 batters in a row starting with the fourth inning. Paul Dean had won the third battle, but the Tigers had taken the fourth and fifth, and the city of Detroit was beginning to lay the red carpet for a championship celebration.

Then Paul came back and won the sixth game with a single, 4–3. I'll never forget old Dizzy hugging Paul in the dressing room after the game, wrestling him and yelping, "You're the greatest pitcher the Dean family ever had," and then Diz would pound everybody else on the back and brag about his kid brother. Diz had announced at the start of the year "me and Paul will win 50 games," and they'd darn near done it, Diz winning 30 and Paul 19. Diz had said they'd murder the Tigers in the Series, too, and now they had between them won three games—the only ones we had taken.

I remember John Carmichael coming up to me in the confusion of that dressing room after the sixth game and asking, "Dean tomorrow—the other Dean?" and me sitting there, all in from the strain, and answering, "If I last till tomorrow, maybe. It'll be Dean or Wild Bill Hallahan."

Carmichael took one look at Diz charging around the room with a white pith helmet—the kind Englishmen wear on tiger hunts—and hollering how he'd take the seventh game tomorrow. Carmichael said, "Wild horses can't keep Dean off that mound tomorrow, Frank."

I looked. Dizzy had a rubber tiger, a Detroit souvenir, by the tail and was whacking Bill DeLancey over the head with it and then throwing it into the showers at Pepper Martin. I knew inside me Diz would pitch it. He had a terrible head cold and only two days before had been knocked out running the bases, but there'd be no use fighting against it—he was the boy and the chips were sure down.

Incidentally the wolves had been on me for putting in Dizzy to run for big, slow Virgil Davis in that fourth game—the time Diz went into second so high and hard that Charley Gehringer, trying for a force-out, hit Diz in the head. But I didn't mind the criticism. We were out to win. We were the Gashouse Gang and I knew Diz would give 'em something to worry about running bases as well as pitching.

Well, morning came for the big game and then at the park Diz took the ball and warmed up with what looked like 50,000 Tiger fans hooting at him, and him grinning and yelling at each of us Cards who passed, "I'll shut 'em out. Get me a couple of runs: that's all. I'll blank the blank-blank blankety-blanks."

Dizzy said he'd shut 'em out and he did. And with the score 0–0 to start the third he singled and stretched it to get to second.

Pepper Martin, the Wild Horse, was up next and he hit a slow hopper to Greenberg and went down so fast he beat the throw. Three years before, Pepper had driven Mickey Cochrane crazy running bases in the Series between the Athletics and the Cards and now he did it again.

Then Auker walked Rothrock and the bases were full. And I was up. I couldn't let the rest of them make an old man out of the playing-manager, so I doubled and all three of 'em came in.

That was all for Auker and in came Schoolboy Rowe. Our bench stood up and gave him the "How'm-I-doin'-Edna?" chant. He had asked that during a radio interview, throwing in a little message to his girl, and he papers had been riding him about it. Rip Collins welcomed Rowe with a double and I scored. Then DeLancey doubled and Rip scored—and away went Schoolboy with a lot of others besides us asking Edna how he was doin'.

We kept on hitting, and Cochrane, who was fit to be asylumed by this time, kept bringing in more pitchers. Dizzy got his second hit of the inning by racing like Pepper to first on a slow grounder, bringing DeLancey in. By the time the inning was over we had seven runs and I figured maybe Dizzy would be winded by all that hitting and base running he'd done in the inning, but, heck, no. He beat the rest of the team out to position and could hardly take time to make his warm-up throws.

The Tigers were sore with that score standing against them and Dizzy holding them helpless. They called us plenty of names, but we had the fanciest name-callers in the game and poured it right back and, I suppose, more so.

It was like playing ball at the foot of Vesuvius. And in the sixth came the eruption. Pepper started by singling and, seeing Goslin in left juggle the throw momentarily, he went on to second. Rothrock and I went out, but Medwick lammed the ball against the screen for a double and kept on to third, sliding in hard. Marv Owen on third got the ball and stepped on Medwick's leg. Joe kicked up from his position on his back and hit Owen in the chest. They started to fight, and both teams boiled out. The panic was on, but nothing to what happened after the umpires had quieted everybody down and got the inning played out.

As Medwick went out to left field, the Tiger fans met him with cushions, bottles, lemons, and some of them took off their shoes and tried to bean him. They tried to climb the 18-foot wire fence to murder him. For 15 minutes the game was stopped and finally Commissioner Landis told Cochrane and me to bring Owen and Medwick up to his box. He asked Medwick, "Did you kick him?" and Joe said, "You're darn right, I did!" They wouldn't shake hands and the noise got worse. Cochrane would run out and beg the bleachers to be good, but they would have none of his advice. So Landis put both Medwick and Owen out of the game and we went on to finish it.

So it ended 11–0. Dizzy had done what he said he'd do and we'd done more than he asked us.

IN THE EVENING of a great career, Ernie Banks was in there, pushing the amazing Cubs toward their amazing first-division finish in the 1967 National League pennant race.

Ernie Banks

BILL FURLONG

THE SUN WARMED the small of his back between the shoulder blades. The ageless sun. It had shone this way on that afternoon in September 1953, when Ernie Banks first reported to the Chicago Cubs. He didn't have a glove of his own: Eddie Miksis, a Cub infielder, loaned him one. Ray Blades, a Cub coach, was even more helpful: he gave him a book called *How to Play Baseball.* That was almost fourteen years and more than 400 home runs ago.

"The Brooklyn Dodgers!" said Ernie Banks. "We were playing the Brooklyn Dodgers!" Banks talks in a booming *bonhomie* that denies failure and defies defeat. The Cubs lost that day to the Brooklyn Dodgers. They were to lose the next day and many, many days after that. They were to set records for losing: no team ever finished in the second division more regularly than the Cubs. No team ever lost more games than did the Cubs in Ernie Banks's time. Yet Banks twice won the Most Valuable Player award. No player had ever won it with a team that played so poorly and finished so low. More, Banks won it two years in a row, something no other National League player has ever been able to do. "Without Ernie Banks," Jimmy Dykes, manager of several major-league teams, once said, "the Cubs would finish in Albuquerque."

Now he was thirty-six and in the evening of his career and the Cubs were winning. On this day they were in fourth place, only four and a half games out of first place. And the reason—or much of the reason—was Ernie Banks. He was batting .311, he was leading the club in homers and in runs batted in and he was tied in total bases. Now he sat in the dugout and smelled the fresh grass on the field and listened to the loudspeaker booming popular songs and watched the chromoscope of pregame activity around him.

"I *told* you we were gonna win the pennant," he said to a ball-park guard who sauntered by.

"Yeah," said the guard with exaggerated cynicism. "If you'd only start hitting, maybe this ball club could do something."

Banks flashed a big happy smile; his teeth are white and even and his smile comes on like a beacon of new hope.

Hope. It is Ernie Banks's watchword. He is a positive thinker of the most virulent kind. "He's a sweetheart," says a newspaperman. "He doesn't know how to be mean or malicious." Once Banks visited a friend in a white neighborhood in strife-torn Chicago and emerged from the house to find all the air let out of his tires. It was a puerile trick played by a puerile person—one more worried about a man's skin color than his accomplishments. But Banks had no word of complaint or anger. He merely asked where he could find a garage so he could get his tires pumped up.

Nor did he complain in the early 1960s as people began to suggest more and more that Ernie had passed his peak. He was getting old now—into his early thirties. His long looping stride was covering as much ground as ever, but not as quickly. His homer production had fallen off and so had his batting average: in 1963 it had dipped to .227 and in the three years following he'd batted .264 or so, getting up only to .272 last year.

When the 1967 season opened, he was named player and coach; it seemed like a discreet way to set him on the road to retirement. Manager Leo Durocher announced that he was going to put John Boccabella on first base and let him play his way onto the team. He played his way off first base in a few days in spring training, and Ernie Banks took over. Then early in the season, Clarence Jones was put on first base with the chance to prove he belonged there. In a few days, he'd played himself back into the minor leagues and Ernie Banks took over again. And through it all, he'd never uttered a word of complaint. He had a program for success.

He had started before the season began. He decided to work his way down to 180 pounds. When he first came up to the Cubs—after playing in the Negro baseball leagues—he weighed 168 to 175 pounds, "depending on how hot it is." Over the years his weight crept upward and in 1966 it had reached 185 pounds. "I thought it would help me in my stamina—that I'd have a little more left in the season," he says. He leaned against a bat propped up on the sod and watched the Cincinnati Reds straggle out of the dugout and line up for pregame calisthenics. ("Rack the Reds! Rack the Reds!" he called out.) He turned back to the matter of batting. "But I found that just those few extra pounds really cut down on your timing, your rhythm," he says. Between seasons, he decided to play at 180 pounds or lower in 1967. He went on a diet, played handball three times a week to sharpen his timing and endurance while taking off the weight.

When spring training started, Banks was lighter than he'd been in years, and sure enough, his reflexes were quicker. Also the Cubs had moved back to Arizona for spring training and Banks found that he could get much more batting practice at the new site. In 1966 the Cubs had trained at Long Beach, California, and it seemed that the team spent its batting-practice time in buses going from one field or one city to another for exhibition games. As a result, the whole team had a miserable first half of the season. The Cubs didn't win their nineteenth game of '66 until June 19. In 1967 they weren't about to duplicate the mistakes of '66: they got plenty of practice and plenty of conditioning and they started out playing first-division ball.

Banks, in particular, made the most of his batting time. During the off season he had devoted many evenings in his home watching movies of his batting in 1966. "I was pulling off the ball," he says. He showed how he was pulling so that he was getting body movement —his shoulders and torso—instead of wrist movement into his swing. "You've got to feel the wrists moving," he says. "It's the hands and wrist movement that's important, not the body movement." He also found that he was tending to swing too hard, as if he were *trying* to hit the ball hard. His old fluent, natural rhythm was gone in his efforts to get a lot of power into his swing.

He decided to use a heavier bat that would force him to slow down his swing and just meet the ball. "I tried it late last season and it felt right. It felt good," he says. The bat—a Vern Stephens model—weighed 36 ounces and was 35 inches long. Banks had long used a much lighter bat—31 ounces—and he was loath to change. "But I watched Roberto Clemente and I noticed he used several different bats, depending on who was pitching." Banks decided that if Clemente could change a bat every game or so, he—Banks—could change it once or twice in a lifetime.

Standing in the sun of Wrigley Field now, Banks was unaware of the long, hard, studied look being given him by Sammy Ellis, the young Cincinnati pitcher. The day before, Banks had dropped a couple of soft hits into left field against Ellis, and Sammy was considering him as if Banks were a new and disturbing mystery. Later he was to pass by him and say, "Hey, Banks, whatsa matter? Softstroke. Old soft-stroke." He waved his arms in a mock batting swing that was short and easy. If Banks was a mystery to Sammy, he was a mystery to other pitchers in the league. For his change back to a heavier bat was as astonishing as Napoleon giving up Europe, as startling as Beethoven writing rock-'n'-roll. In his time Banks had not merely played the game of baseball—he had revolutionized it. He was the first great slugger of the "Era of the Lively Bat" and he had introduced the era by going to a lighter, snappier bat.

The result: he became the hardest-hitting shortstop in the history of the major leagues. In one six-season span—1955–60—he hit more home runs than any other player in the majors. (He hit 248 homers in that period. Mickey Mantle hit 236; Willie Mays hit 214.)

But more than that, the entire style of slugging changed. All over major-league baseball, the batters began following Banks's precedent. The light-but-lively bat became the style for sluggers in the big leagues.

As it happened, the lively-bat era that Banks introduced was ideally tailored to his own physical dimensions. He looks as burly as a broomstick and his weight is as carefully disguised as a CIA agent. "I carry it in my toes," he says wryly. "I've got very muscular toes." He is a small-boned man with delicate features.

In his batting helmet, he looks a trifle like "little boy lost." But he has powerful wrists and forearms—"you grip them and they feel like steel," Bob Scheffing once said when he was manager of the Cubs. He got his power into the swing by the snapping of the wrists, not by a big powerful sweep of his arms. In effect, he lashed his bat at the ball, a little like snapping a whip. The effect had the beauty and brevity of great art. "Ernie Banks swings a bat the way Joe Louis used to punch: short and sweet," said Clyde McCullough, long a major-league catcher. The result is that the ball leaps off the bat. "Ernie hits line drives, not fly balls," said Scheffing. "And they get off his bat so fast and hit the wall so fast that he frequently gets only singles instead of doubles."

It was difficult now—in the glorious sunshine of the time of Ernie Banks's resurgence—to remember him as a shortstop—or the long years the Cubs devoted to finding a man who could play the position as well as Ernie Banks. "Smalley . . . Miksis . . . Eldon White . . . Jerry Kindall . . . Morgan—was it Bobby Morgan—of the old Dodgers?" Banks says, running down the roster of potential Cub shortstops like a priest reciting the litany. He has a remarkable memory. He can recall without effort each of the eleven men who have served as Cub manager or head coach (in the years when president Phil Wrigley of the Cubs was indulging this aberration) since he came up to the Cubs. He can remember all the hotels that he stayed in during his six-nation swing through Europe last winter (that included a private audience with Pope Paul) and the characteristics and street address of each ("Those big rooms in the Hotel Stockholm in Paris—oh how I love those big rooms and high ceilings and big bathtubs! Elegance! Style! History! The feeling of a great age! Antiquity! The 18th century and all its elegance!").

He can also remember the adjustments he had to make when, joining the Cubs in '53, he found himself a major-league shortstop. He and Gene Baker came in together, the first Negroes to play for the Cubs. Baker was 5½ years older than Banks and he'd played shortstop in the minors, and he'd played it ably. But when the two men reached the Cubs—Ernie's only experience being with the Negro-league Kansas City Monarchs—Baker shifted to second and Banks was sent in at shortstop. "They felt that Gene had more experience and could make the change more easily than I could," says Ernie. Gene Baker finished his major-league career and retired many years ago. "Gene Baker!" says Banks. "Works for John Deere company in Davenport, I-owa! Foreman or something! A wonderful man! Doing very well, that Gene Baker!"

Ernie Banks did very well at shortstop. He was never a truly great fielder because he had only an average throwing arm. But he was good enough. In 1959 he handled more chances than any other shortstop in baseball—and he set a record for fielding by shortstops that still stands: .9850 in 154 games.

But then he injured a leg and that made it more difficult to cover ground at shortstop. In 1961 the Cubs shifted him to left field, but that was not the ideal position for a man with a bad leg and a throwing arm that was never powerful. So the next year, the Cubs moved him to first base—and there he has performed ably and occasionally brilliantly. Last year, for instance, only one first baseman in the National League committed fewer errors than Banks—Bill White of Philadelphia, who had nine errors to ten by Banks. And only one first baseman in the National League handled more chances than Banks—White again, who appeared in 28 games more than Banks.

It wasn't as easy as magic. Banks had to learn when to charge the ball on a bunt and when to play back. He had to learn when to run for the bag on a grounder to first and when to flip the ball to the pitcher coming over to cover the base. He had to learn, most of all, not to chase every ball hit to his right—as he'd been doing for years as a shortstop—but instead to move to the bag and let the second baseman handle the ball. "Instinctively I'd move to the ball instead of to the bag," he says. He brought to all this a great asset: wonderful, relaxed hands that can hold anything they reach. And to that asset he brought his temperament: positive thinking and great determination.

He always had the determination; the positive thinking developed in all the years of frustration (for his team, not himself). It took determination—and a superb, if muffled, talent—to make it to the big leagues. Ernie grew up in the shadow of the Depression. Born on January 31, 1931, Ernie was the second of twelve children sired by Eddie Banks, a onetime semi-pro catcher who later became a wholesale grocer in Dallas, Texas. Young Ernie played football and basketball and softball and ran track—but never baseball. "My dad, he bought me a glove for about $2.98 when I was a kid but he had to bribe me with nickels and dimes to play catch," Ernie has said.

But his natural athletic talent was so obvious

that it had to lead to the big leagues. The route was devious: he played softball so well that when he was seventeen, he got a chance to play with a semipro team, the Amarillo Colts, that barnstormed the South and the Middle West. That, in turn, led to a summer swing with the Kansas City Monarchs baseball team. He spent two years in the Army, then returned to the Monarchs to bat .386 and hit 20 home runs. It was an active life but hardly an affluent one: "Five, ten, maybe 15,000 miles a year and our biggest payday was in Lincoln, Nebraska—$20 for the night." But the Cubs bought him from the Monarchs in 1953—and that led him to affluence.

Today Ernie Banks lives on the quiet, tree-lined street in an upper-middle-class section of Chicago's South Side. Forty years ago, this neighborhood was the "elite" section for Chicago's "upwardly mobile" Irish; today the Irish have moved out and the more affluent Negroes have moved in. Ernie and his family—he has three children—live in a dark brick two-story home with a front balcony and a gabled attic. It's on a corner lot and though Ernie says it has only three bedrooms it has a sense of spaciousness and size that more modern homes lack. There is an occasional touch of the modern in the neighborhood: on the fence of Banks's back yard are scribbled some graffiti—"Napoleon most powerful on 83rd St." But for the most part, the quiet sidewalks and middle-of-the-street parkways lie in the quiet sun with the majesty and serenity of the 1920s.

On a recent day, Ernie Banks arose at seven o'clock to help his wife Aloyce get his children off to school. He's an early riser, an "A.M. person," as he says. This is ideal for the baseball-in-the-sun played in Wrigley Field. Every night he can be in bed before ten o'clock—"I try to stay awake for the ten o'clock news but sometimes it's quite a struggle," he says.

On this morning, about 9:15, Ernie sat down to a breakfast of oatmeal, a poached egg and coffee. He isn't on a special diet now to hold down his weight. "I just cut out the sweets and eating between meals," he says. He was wearing a tailored fatigue suit, a one-piece coverall that was as stylish as Brooks Brothers, as utilitarian as a napkin. After breakfast, he would go upstairs to change into brown slacks, a yellow turtleneck shirt and a green, "mod" two-button sweater.

In sunglasses Ernie looks like any of the young modish men of the affluent South Side. At thirty-six, his skin is free of wrinkles, his easy movement unmarred by the strain on his muscles. It is the reward of a graceful approach to life: as he approached a cross-street in his Cadillac de Ville—equipped with stereo speakers—a Mustang darted out in front of him and the driver turned to give him a dirty look and outrageous cry. "Easy, brother," murmured Ernie, "it's too nice a day to get all worked up."

He maneuvered through the maze of one-way streets and turned into the parking lot of the Seaway National Bank just as the weather-time sign flashed 9:47. The bank, all glass and metal and natural wood, is a model of the new structure of finance: it serves Negro and white customers with all banking services—including that most difficult of help for Negroes, mortgage financing—and it has Negro and white help working side by side. Ernie works here winters in the New Accounts division. He hopes to make finance a career once he leaves baseball. He's taking a correspondence course in banking from a banking institute right now, though he tends to concentrate more on it while he's on the road. But now he just wanted to cash a check and stop to chat with friends. At a desk was another bank officer whose brother had stopped by Ernie's house to sell him an encyclopedia.

"My boys are working out in the Little League now—over at the YMCA," he told the man. Ernie has twin sons, Joey and Jerry, who are going on eight years old. "They're gonna be ballplayers" he said—then he added that he'd bought the encyclopedia. "They're gonna be *smart* ballplayers!"

At 10:02 A.M., he eased the car out of its parking place and again began threading the maze of one-way streets. "I told Billy Williams I'd pick him up on the way to the ball park," he said. Williams was waiting on the sidewalk outside his home. He was dressed in a business suit; after the game he was going to the far northern suburb to fulfill a speaking date. Banks swung the car onto Jeffrey Boulevard and into Jackson Park. The street winds among the greens and fairways of a golf course here, and Ernie and Williams gossiped about the difficulties of getting a par on the hole nearest the traffic. "See those two traps—that's where I spend my time," Ernie said. He is a desultory golfer. He enjoys the game but does not approach it with the fervor of an ultimate destiny. "There has to be some fun in life," he told me. "Everything is competition—the ball game is competition, even the guy trying to beat you away from the traffic light is competition." For all his apparent ease, there are deep tides of tension running in Ernie Banks: his fingers ripple nervously on the bat handle in ball games, his fingernails are bitten down near the quick.

He was cruising down the Outer Drive now with the incomparable vistas of the lakefront of Chicago—its magnificent deceit, for it is no more reflective of the turmoil of the city than a cymbal is of a symphony. "This is my favorite view," said Banks. He slowed the car slightly at 47th Street and pointed to the sweep of the city, with its skyscrapers looming silvery into the sky. "It's even better at night—a clear night when you see all the lights of the city."

It usually takes Banks 30 minutes, perhaps 35 minutes, to drive to the ball park. On this day he pulled into the parking lot well before 11 o'clock. At the gate the guards and youngsters waiting for autographs greeted Ernie like the familiar deity he is to them. He was easy and gregarious; he holds back nothing of himself in talking to Cub followers. To everybody he reiterates that he'd always said the Cubs would be up there—"The Cubs will be heaven-ly in 'Sixty-seven-ly" is the slogan he'd conceived a long time ago.

In the locker room, Banks changed clothes leisurely. He sat on his chair, keeping his bare feet carefully on his sandals; he did not move unshod about the locker room. The only sign of his age appeared from that perspective: there are a few barely perceptible thinning spots in his hair. ("That's okay—my father was completely bald by the time he was 35.") The side walls of the clubhouse are pale yellow, the ends walls gray. The cubicles are gray metal screening. This was home—the complete environment of Ernie Banks, ballplayer. Here he can ponder the game's subtleties. The first 13 times he'd come up with runners in scoring position this year, he got only one hit—a scratch single to the infield. Now he was hitting in the clutch, getting the decisive hit, the game-winning hit, and he was closing in on the league leaders in runs batted in. Today he would be facing Jim Maloney, the marvelously talented Cincinnati pitcher. A fast-ball pitcher—his fast ball above the waist tends to rise, his fast ball below the waist tends to drop. "A challenging pitcher," says Banks. "He gets to the 3-and-2 and he's going to come at you with his best pitch."

It was two and a half hours until game time. On the blackboard at the end of the clubhouse, the names of the Cub players were chalked in a batting-practice schedule in varying colors. Banks was scheduled for 11 A.M., but there were four others who would bat before him. He selected some bats in a stack just inside the door. He'd take his turn—first five swings, then four, then three, then two—and he'd sing along with the loudspeaker system and he'd cheer the Reds on in their calisthenics and he'd indulge himself in the luxury of the sun. ". . . in the bee-yoo-ti-ful confines of Wrigley Field," he'd say time and time again. Then once, perhaps twice, he'd be back in the clubhouse before the game began. He'd have a cup of hot soup—that would be his entire lunch. He'd pick up his well-worked glove and put aside the new glove he was testing. He'd search for a few sticks of Wrigley's gum to chew during the game. And then he'd be ready to play ball.

The game started at 1:30—before some of the players in night games were out of bed. It ended 2:56 later. The Cubs won 5–4 on Ron Santo's hit with the bases loaded in the ninth. Banks got a single in four times at bat and scored one of the runs.

After the game, he was immersed in the well-being of team success. The Cubs had taken two of three from the league leaders, had stayed even with them into the ninth inning and pulled the game out.

Thirty minutes later Banks was in street clothes and ready to leave the ball park. The portable radio in the clubhouse was still playing, but now nobody noticed it. Banks likes to be surrounded by music. ("That's my favorite song." he said when the theme from *Dr. Zhivago* came over the radio.) So when he got into his de Ville, he switched on the stereo. Music flooded out and filled the car. He was on his way home.

It would be another two and a half hours before he ate—ten and a half hours in which he'd had nothing but a paper cupful of soup and a few chews of Wrigley's spearmint. After dinner he would be a few minutes with his children. Then their bedtime, and his bedtime.

And the next day he would be back in the soaring embrace of Wrigley Field in the daytime. In the sun that warmed and caressed the small of the back. The agelesss sun. The sun that had passed the zenith and yet held its warmth and hope and strength-giving vitality even now for Ernie Banks in the evening of his career.

THE ADROIT HAND of Martin Quigley, who also helped Kirby Higbe in the memoirs reproduced a few pages hence, is acknowledged by Joe Garagiola for having helped to produce in finished form his book *Baseball Is a Funny Game,* which was (and deservedly so) a best seller when it first came out at the turn of the 1960s. All that having been said, Garagiola's still Garagiola.

Inside the Clubhouse

JOE GARAGIOLA

I HAVE WALKED through many a clubhouse door and have modeled quite a few different uniforms. In the minor leagues it was with Springfield, Missouri, in the Western Association, and with Columbus in the American Association. In the big leagues with the St. Louis Cardinals, Pittsburgh Pirates, Chicago Cubs and New York Giants. Those were the home clubhouses I got to know. Of course, I also did time in the visitors' clubhouses in all those leagues.

A clubhouse isn't fancy but the walls hear, the stools see and the boards talk. They all differ, but basically they are all the same . . . a row of lockers . . . a manager's office . . . a training room. Depending on how the team and you are going, the clubhouse can be Heartbreak Ridge or the Street of Dreams.

The Cardinal home-team clubhouse now has to rank as the best I have ever been in. It has big lockers and a lounge with telephone, record player and easy chairs. The washrooms are spacious with plenty of washbasins and mirrors.

The visitors' clubhouse at Busch Stadium has been improved considerably, but it is not as plush as the Cardinals': no easy chairs or record player, but there now is the luxury of a locker. What is now the trainer's room used to be the entire dressing room. The comics used to say about the old visitors' clubhouse, "They'll have to paint this before they can condemn it." Lefty Gomez, star Yankee pitcher, once said the showers were so high and he was so small that by the time the hot water got to him, it was cold.

As far as visiting-team clubhouses in the big leagues go, I would rank them all fairly even, with the edge to the Milwaukee and Pittsburgh clubhouses. The Dodger clubhouse at Ebbets Field was always an experience because the walk to it involved going past those fans that made "Ya bum, ya" famous. Yes, Virginia, it is different out in Los Angeles.

A big advantage to being the home team, besides the fact you get the last time at bat, is the home-team locker room. A team spends most of the season there, and everything is done to make it comfortable.

The Pittsburgh clubhouse is a roomy one, but in my time it was also the busiest. At times it looked like a Sears, Roebuck sale was going on with power mowers actually on display. Visitors are usually kept out of the clubhouse, but at Pittsburgh when you started talking to someone, you didn't know if he was the new third baseman or a salesman for the Encyclopaedia Britannica.

The Giant clubhouse at the Polo Grounds was a contemporary-style split-level. Walk down a flight of stairs and you were on the level with the card tables, and off to the side was the manager's office.

Down another flight and you were in the locker room. From there steps led up to the shower room, on still a third level. Card playing was a big thing with the Giants in 1954 when we won the pennant. Gin rummy and hearts were the favorites. "It relaxes while keeping 'em on their toes" was the defense used whenever card playing was questioned.

The Chicago Cub clubhouse is the most crowded. Your locker is sometimes a nail in the wall. To get to the clubhouse from the field you have to use a long ramp. This ramp or catwalk leading to the clubhouse can make you feel like a Hall of Famer or the condemned man on the long walk to the guillotine, because the rabid Cub fans stand underneath and let you have it, one way or the other. Over seventy-seven games it is really an experience.

The Cardinal clubhouse is a great one for music, with the emphasis on hillbilly records. Max Lanier, a pitcher, was the big hillbilly fan when I was there, and Stan Musial was a great man to beat out the rhythm on coat hangers. Now the Cardinals have their own songwriter in catcher Hal Smith. He is the author of such songs as "Sittin', Spittin' and a-Whittlin'," "Churn Full O' Chitlings (and a Belly Full of You)" and "Purt Near but Not Plumb."

Reading material is a big part of the clubhouse. *The Sporting News* is the big favorite, because you can check on what the guy who had the locker next to you is doing with his new club. Comic books rank high. If Yogi Berra can sharpen his eyes on them, they can't be too bad for you. Most players can tell you how Dick Tracy will come out and nobody really cares if Little Orphan Annie is forty-six years old. The Pittsburgh clubhouse has changed, though, and the lockers are now loaded with college magazines and the *Wall Street Journal.* Max Surkont, a pitcher, used to call the locker section where Dick Groat, Jack Shepherd, the O'Brien twins and Laurin Pepper (all college and bonus boys) had their lockers the Gold Coast, while he refers to his row, which at the time included Sid Gordon and Dick Littlefield, much-traveled veterans, as the Bowery.

Routines, moods, and action change with every clubhouse. Bill Klem, most famous of all umpires, once said there are 154 games in a season and you can find 154 reasons why your team should have won every one of them. Blame luck, the wind, a rock-headed play or the umpire. To this you might add the clubhouse boy who is blamed for almost anything.

Yosh Kawano, Butch Yatkeman, Eddie Logan, Byron Jorgensen . . . *What's My Line* would have a hard time figuring out what they do. Japanese rice tycoon the first one? No! Middleweight fighter the second one? No! Irish tenor the next? No! Swedish ski instructor the last one? No! These are clubhouse boys, combination valet, equipment expert, loan company, buffer and the personification of the three famous monkeys.

The truest statement regarding these see-no-evil, hear-no-evil and speak-no-evil boys was made by Mort Cooper, then a star pitcher with the St. Louis Cardinals. One of the cocky rookies was really getting on Butch Yatkeman, letting him know that Butch was the clubhouse boy and he a player. After a while Mort snapped, "Butch was here before you came, and Butch will be here after you're gone."

The clubhouse boys get salaries, but depend heavily on tips, so it's easy to see why the stars are given extra attention, although I have never seen a raw rookie abused. Yosh Kawano, Cub clubhouse boy, made no bones about it. Ralph Kiner was traded to the Cubs on Yosh's birthday in 1953, and Yosh always said that this was the best birthday present he ever received. When big Kiner was traded to Cleveland, Yosh said, "This is the first time a clubhouse boy ever had to take a cut."

Solly Hemus, an infielder, was one to take real advantage of the star treatment. Of course, if there was one ballplayer who could take advantage of the breaks, it would be Hemus.

Solly, dressing next to Stan Musial during spring training, noticed that every day all of Musial's shoes were shined. So Hemus slipped his shoes into Musial's locker and got them shined every day, courtesy of Stan Musial.

The clubhouse boy has to please twenty-five guys at the same time and is a very important part of the baseball picture. He has to live by the sign that was hung in the Milwaukee visitors' clubhouse by clubhouse boy Tommy Ferguson: WHAT YOU HEAR HERE, WHAT YOU SEE HERE, AND WHAT YOU SAY HERE MUST STAY HERE.

The trainer's room is usually away from the lockers—except in the Cub clubhouse, where if you're not careful Doc Sheuneman might be rubbing you down when all you want to do is get a sweat shirt from your locker. Everybody collects in the trainer's room or on the table to tell him their troubles.

Sometimes a ballplayer will come up with his own cure, and the trainer might go along with it if only for the psychology involved. The most famous of these home-brew cures was the secret snake oil that the ageless Satchel Paige came up with while a member of the St. Louis Browns.

The former trainer of the Cubs, the late Andy Lotshaw, had a favorite story about secret cures. It involved Guy Bush, the Cubs's star pitcher, when he complained about a sore arm. Into his kit Andy went for his sure cure. He rubbed the arm and finally pronounced

Bush fit, and he went out and won. After that, it was ritual for Andy to rub the arm with the secret ointment. It was only after Guy Bush was finished as an active pitcher that Andy revealed his secret. On that first day Andy had run out of liniment and grabbed the first bottle of liquid he could get his hands on, which happened to be a bottle of Coca-Cola.

Like most trainers, Andy Lotshaw was great on tales about his ability as an athlete. He claimed that as a hitter his eyes were so sharp that he could hit the spitball on the dry side.

Doc Weaver, late trainer of the Cardinals, was a great guy for working on the feet, and he developed the famous Dr. Weaver's Wonder Walkers, inner soles that many of the ballplayers still use. Pepper Martin, the Wild Horse of the Osage, was one of his first customers. How Doc's eyes would light up when he would tell about the great experiment with John Leonard, as Doc called Pepper. He had worked on those inner soles until he knew they were perfect. Before a Sunday doubleheader he gave them to Pepper, who wore them during batting and infield practice. The first time up Pepper topped the ball and was an easy out. The second time up he tapped one right back to the pitcher, easy out. The third time up, in the seventh inning with the bases loaded, he topped the ball again and was thrown out by the pitcher. When he got back to the bench, Pepper took the inner soles out and threw them against the wall hollering, "They make me too high, and I'm hitting over the ball."

Trainers do many things that you would have to call the "extra" that pays off. Doc Weaver would always make sure that a Cardinal victory was more than just another win for the pitcher. Doc would get the last-out ball and paint the line score on it with little figures depicting the highlights of the game. It made the victory more than just another win. Games aren't won on muscle alone.

The trainer is always watching over his boys because he knows you don't have to cure an ailment you can prevent.

"You shouldn't work out in a short-sleeved sweat shirt, Tom. You ought to wear a long-sleeved shirt so you can keep that body heat. When you're sweating, you're heated. Let the cool air hit you, and the chill will tighten those muscles." Said to one, but five guys nonchalantly walk to their lockers for long-sleeved sweatshirts.

"Let me trim those eyelashes, Stan, it will let you see the ball better." (Never heard that one before, thinks the rookie, but it sounds logical.) "The loose lashes won't be irritating your eyes." (That sounds good, thinks another.) "See better, bound to hit better and you won't be rubbing around there during the game." (I never had that done before, but I'll ask him to trim mine when he's through.)

"Don't just stand there, Hal, sit down. It might be a long night. You know what they always say—Why stand when you can sit, why sit when you can lie down? Know what I do when I go back to the hotel after a long day and lie down to rest? I elevate my feet. Really stirs up the circulation down there and it makes you feel good. Give it a try."

"That's it, keep those nails trimmed. You'll never have an ingrown nail if you keep them trimmed like that. Better yet, you won't have it ripped off by a ball." (This one looks long, and I'm catching tonight, better trim it.)

"Giving those flying feet a grease job, eh, Ken? That's the way to use foot cream. Vaseline is good too. Get between those toes and you'll never have a blister or a soft corn. Got to keep those wheels spinning."

That is the run of the conversation that you'll hear in the trainer's room, as he looks out for his boys.

What the trainer can't do for you, the team physician can. Treating an athlete is different, because the main thing going for a ballplayer is that he has to play. Every day he doesn't play is gone, and it's a short career at best. The last thing a player wants to hear is that he has to rest his injury. You can appreciate how ticklish the team doctor's job can be.

The late Surgeon General of Baseball, Dr. Robert F. Hyland, was a pro among the pros. It was he, more than anybody else, that brought home the importance of "getting 'em back in the lineup." To him ballplayers' hurts were his hurts; they were deep hurts and sometimes diathermy couldn't get to them nor could surgery. It's a great team in the Hall of Fame, and I'll bet Dr. Hyland is still the first one in the clubhouse when there's an injury.

Practical jokers are a part of every clubhouse. They always have been and always will be. Walker Cooper has to be right up on top of the modern players' list. If you ever walked into your locker and felt all "knotted up," look for big Coop. That's his favorite, and he can get twenty-five knots into one sweat shirt.

Del Rice, when catching with the Cardinals, got even with Cooper by tying all Coop's clothes into knots. Coop came back at him. When Del went to put his shoes on, they wouldn't budge. Cooper had nailed down every pair with a spike that could have held two giant redwoods together.

The late Mel Ott, when managing the New York Giants, went out one night to the preliminary meeting with the umpires and the rival manager, his lineup cards in his right-hand pocket. Up at the plate he reaches into his pocket, but no lineup card comes out. From the stands it looks like manager Ott is really nervous, leaning forward and then backward, now almost on his knees. While the meeting at home plate was still in session, he strode to the dugout. "Cooper," manager Ott screamed, "you're fined $50 for cutting the bottom out of my pocket."

Ralph Kiner, the great slugger, belongs on the all-time practical jokers' nine. In St. Louis one night he nailed down trainer Doc Jorgensen's shoes and cut his tie in half. Doc couldn't leave for a while, but the next day he had a new pair of shoes and tie courtesy of Ralph Kiner. Doc probably still doesn't know who took all his bottles and equipment out of his kit and stuffed it with sandwiches. What a surprise it was when one of the players got spiked and Doc ran out on the field, opened his bag, reached for the Merthiolate and came out with a braunschweiger sandwich.

Once when the Pirates were having a rough time winning a game, Frankie Frisch, the manager, started a get-tough policy and was slapping fines on everybody.

Elbie Fletcher, the first baseman, got the first prize, a $500 fine. As most ballplayers do when this happens, he headed for the trainer's room to moan.

"What have you got worth $500?" he asked Doc Jorgensen.

"That's about what the diathermy machine would cost," Doc said. Fletcher lugged it out of the trainer's room and put it in his locker.

In came Jeep Handley. "What you got for $250, Doc?"

"That cabinet with the medicine in it should be worth that," answered Doc. Into Handley's locker the cabinet went. This went on until Al Gerheauser came in: "I just got hit with a $50 dandy, so what's left that's worth fifty bucks, Doc?"

"All that's left is the sun lamp, Al." And to his locker the sun lamp went.

Frisch got the last laugh, though, when he collected the fines.

Did you ever try to look through a pair of sunglasses that were coated with zinc oxide? How about putting a thin tissue paper between the ham and cheese so as to give the sandwich more body? Ever smoke a cigar that had cotton soaked in alcohol packed into it?

If Don Gutteridge, later a White Sox coach, never does believe a trainer again, you can't blame him. Worried about a condition in his mouth, he sought out trainer Bob Bauman when both were with the Browns (and on that club you had to make your own excitement). Bauman knew it wasn't serious, but he diagnosed it as a bad case of trench mouth and prescribed a harmless, foul-tasting medicine for two weeks.

Once Johnny Mize had taken an extra-hard workout and came into the Giant clubhouse drenched with perspiration. He took off his sweat shirt and went to get a drink of water. Trainer Frank Bowman soaked the sweat shirt with alcohol. When Mize came back, Doc asked him how he felt. "Tired but good," said Mize.

"Better stay away from that hard stuff, though, John. That's what really knocks you," Bowman said in a kindly voice.

"What are you talking about? I was in early last night and only had a couple of beers."

"Oh yeah? It's okay with me but don't kid me, I'll prove it to you."

With that he dropped a match and the sweat shirt was aflame.

"That's alcohol that you sweated out, John!"

The embarrassed Mize grabbed the shirt and put out the fire.

"Don't say anything about this to anyone, Doc," he pleaded.

Ever wonder what's going on out on the field when the trainer runs out? Well, first he sizes up the injury and minimizes it to the player. If it's serious, he makes the decision and there is no byplay. If it's a minor injury, though, look for something funny. Like once in a game with the Phillies, when Solly Hemus was playing with the Cardinals, Solly went down to field a ground ball and it took a bad hop. Down he went in a heap. Out came Doc Weaver, and the rest of the team collected around the little scrapper. As he came to his feet, there were smiles that could easily be seen from the stands. I'm sure fans were wondering what's so funny about a guy getting hurt. Here's what happened. Hemus had said, "Doc, use a lot of that red Merthiolate, this game might be televised in color."

The clubhouse bulletin board can be a combination of train schedules, court orders and vital statistics. On it you can find anything from what time the train leaves to who was fined for what and thanks for the baby's gift. Somebody has to add something all the time.

On the Cardinal bulletin board, when the notice for the team-picture time was posted, someone added, "Better wait until June 15" (trade date deadline), and the way general manager Frank Lane was then moving the players, it didn't sound like a bad idea.

There are some serious directives that get on the bulletin board, but these are the least read—too official-looking. The player representative usually reads them, and he is forever answering questions about them.

Ever wonder if somebody painted "fighting phrases" on the walls of a clubhouse? In baseball that is rare. I have seen newspaper clippings put on the bulletin board to stir up a team. These are usually statements made about a particular player or the team spirit. The only sign I have ever seen is the one on the wall in the Pittsburgh clubhouse: YOU CAN'T MAKE THE CLUB IN THE TUB.

A lot of conversation in the clubhouse begins and ends with the "swindle sheets" used by the clubhouse boys. These are the lists used to keep track of charges for soft drinks, gum, tobacco, etc. Get involved in a few Coke games and have somebody charge a few to you, and you begin to scream.

A Coke game is the bunting game that the players get into before the regular game. Instead of getting an error when he misses the ball, a player is charged with a Coke. I remember a variation of this game that could be expensive. It was the year that the Detroit Tigers signed catcher Frank "Pig" House to a bonus contract. In addition to a bundle of cash, House was given two automobiles. Joe Ginsberg, then with the Tigers, was in a Coke game during spring training with House. I hollered to Ginsberg, "Pretty fast Coke game with that House in it." He came back with, "Cokes? We play House for automobiles."

Gussie Busch, the owner of the Cardinals, got the same type of jockeying while in a pepper game that had Stan Musial as the hitter. It was a custom of Busch and two or three of his associates to work out a bit during spring training. During a Coke game, one of the jockeys hollered to Musial, "Hey, Stan! What do you play Gussie for, breweries?"

The most important thing, in winning or losing a game, that happens in the clubhouse is the pregame meeting. There are a lot of different thoughts regarding this meeting. Eddie Dyer would have a meeting every day. It was mostly strategy and was held right before the game to be played that day. Marty Marion would have a meeting before every series. Phil Cavaretta, Stan Hack, Fred Haney and Bill Meyer were all about the same—a meeting before the series with the pitcher and catcher holding forth and the rest of the club listening. Leo Durocher had his meeting with the pitcher and the catcher, and was the most dramatic. His enthusiasm was contagious.

In 1954 while the Giants were on their way to a pennant, the Milwaukee Braves began to close in. Leo held a meeting and all he kept saying was "We're in first place, they got to worry. We pick up ground when we get rained out. We're in first place, why worry? Let them worry." It certainly wasn't like Knute Rockne, but when the boys left the clubhouse, they knew they were in first place. They finished there, and a lot of the credit has to go to the pep talk by Durocher.

The main purpose in the clubhouse meeting is to discuss the hitters. Eddie Dyer would have the pitchers take up the hitters and tell the rest of the club how he wanted them to be played. The secret book on the different clubs doesn't vary, it's the execution that varies. You realize how true this last statement is when you go from a pennant contender, the Cardinals, to a second-division club, the Pirates, which happened to me in 1951.

Rogers Hornsby, the Hall of Famer, has an observation that bears thinking about. About our 1952 Pirate team the Rajah said, "You guys have a fifty-fifty team. You get 'em out in the clubhouse but lose on the field." Very rarely is there a big difference on how to pitch a hitter, and very rarely does it end up any other way when a pitcher is stuck than to say, "Crowd him with the fast ball and make him hit the curve ball that is low and away." The magic words, if you want to sound like the expert: high and tight and low and away. A strategy meeting could very well at times be called a meeting of the Society for Advancement of the High and Tight and Low and Away.

It works like this. You are the home club and you have just finished taking batting practice. The whole club is off the field, and the manager hands the starting pitcher the scorecard. Let's say it's the first game against the Braves. Vinegar Bend Mizell is your pitcher.

Vinegar takes the scorecard and begins with the lineup that will start against him. "The first hitter is Schoendienst. He will be batting right-handed against me and is a better high-ball hitter batting right-handed. He's a good fast-ball hitter. I will try to keep him from hitting the fast ball. I will try to get him out by throwing him change-ups and making him chase the bad high fast ball. Play him straight away and not too deep. He likes to hit and run once in a while. Doesn't try to bunt too much for a base hit while batting right-handed. He doesn't try to steal too much any more but I know he can run and I'll be watching him.

"Johnny Logan. This guy is really a streak hitter and he has been hitting good his last five games. I think he is a better fast-ball hitter. He's a first-ball hitter. I'll try to make him chase the bad curve ball and make him hit my slow stuff. If I have to throw him the fast ball I'll crowd him with the ball. Play him to pull the ball with nobody on base, but with somebody on first base he will try to go to right field. He will hit and run and will bunt. He doesn't run too much.

"Eddie Mathews. He will chase the bad low ball but can hit the low strike ball a mile. I try to keep the low fast ball out of the strike zone. I can throw him slow curve balls and will try to make him hit my curve ball. If I have to throw my fast ball it will be inside and I'll be throwing for his belt buckle up. He will bunt me especially if they need a base runner. He doesn't steal much but can run. Play him strictly to pull and deep.

"Hank Aaron. I'll be moving the ball around and try to get a strike on him by throwing breaking balls away from him. He likes the ball out away from him and if I have to throw my fast ball it will be in real tight. I can change up on him. I think he is a better low-ball hitter. He's a bad-ball swinger and can hit the bad ball. My out pitch will be something besides the fast ball. If I have a good change-up today, that's what it will be. Play him deep and not too far over. He won't pull right down the line. He won't bunt nor does he try to steal too much.

"Joe Adcock. This guy really tries to guess me. A real guess hitter. I like to move the ball around on him and I can change up on him. I can throw my fast ball in on his fist because he comes right into the ball. He likes the ball out over the plate. Play him deep and to pull. He has good power in right center. Doesn't bunt nor does he try to hit and run.

"Andy Pafko. He'll probably play against me. He's a spray hitter to all fields with good power. He's a first-ball hitter and a fast-ball hitter. He will chase the bad curve ball especially when he has two strikes on him. I will try to crowd him with the fast ball and change up on him. With two strikes I'll throw bad curve balls. He won't pull me right down the lines so guard both slots, right center and left center. He bunts for a hit once in a while, so be alive.

"Wes Covington. He's a low-ball hitter and likes the ball out over the plate. I will try to get him with curve balls and I think I can change speeds on him. He won't bunt and doesn't hit and run. Play him deep and to pull. Protect the hole in left-center field.

"Del Crandall. Likes to hit the fast ball and will pull everything. I think I can change up on him. When I throw the fast ball it will be in on him. I will try to pitch him right on his belt buckle. He will bunt if he catches the third baseman back. Will try to hit and run at times. Play strictly to pull.

"That's the starting lineup. Watch the hit and run from Logan. Mathews might bunt if they need a base runner."

After this the pitcher will run down the roster to take up the pinch hitters that are likely to see action against him.

The meeting is usually rounded off by the manager taking charge and reminding his starting lineup about signals and any injuries on the other club. If the pitcher is a weak fielder or might be lax on holding men on base, this is discussed. Anything about the other club that might fall into the category of trick plays is discussed, such as "Be careful now of the delayed steal, they like to try it. Watch the second baseman on the bunt situation, they like to try the pick-off play. Be careful when they get a man on second base, see that they don't steal the signs."

I think sometimes that the opposition is discussed too much. You keep pointing out their strong points and trying to find out their weaknesses and you end up making everybody wonder "If he's that good or that tough to pitch to, how come he's only hitting .220?" You might also wonder if a meeting can work to build up tension. We really battled the Brooklyn Dodgers during 1947, 1948 and 1949, and after a series with them, there was a strong emphasis on no letup against the Phillies. "Don't let up, don't let up, be careful, don't hold this guy cheap, and so on." The end result, whatever ground was made up against Brooklyn, the Cardinals dropped it to the Phillies.

Another danger is in the so-called "out" pitch discussed in detail by the pitchers. What is a good "out" pitch for one pitcher may be a home-run pitch for the other. It is not rare to have a pitcher call a catcher out to the mound and say, "This guy is wearing me out. Bill said he gets him out with a change-up, I think I'll try it." You can realize the danger; here the whole game is riding on this time at bat and your pitcher wants to begin experimenting.

I would say that Howard Pollet, a star National League pitcher and now pitching coach with his first team, the St. Louis Cardinals, held the ideal meeting. He never would say what particular pitch he would throw for the out but would set up his defense and tell where he would throw.

Pollet talking of Pee Wee Reese: "He'll hit me straight away. I want the left fielder over a bit toward left center, the center fielder shade him a bit toward right . . . the right fielder over toward right center . . . third baseman give him the line except with two outs and be alive for the bunt . . . I want the shortstop over near the bag—with a man on at first, the second baseman will have to protect the hole between first and second. I'll be pitching my fast ball down and I will change up on him."

There never was any of that "I'm going to curve him and keep it here" or "I'm going to fast-ball him there." The reason I liked this meeting so much is that the defense knew where they should be playing and yet Pollet wasn't putting thoughts into another pitcher's head. As I said earlier, I have battled right out on the mound with pitchers who want to try and get him out like So-and-so is getting him out because he is just wearing me out. Each individual pitcher has to find out for himself. It might end up that he does get the hitter out the way they say, but just because a Pollet got a Jackie Robinson out on a change of pace doesn't mean that Robinson couldn't hit the change that another pitcher would throw.

When the meeting gets muddled and the wheels really begin to spin, somebody always tries to dazzle the club with grammar. When this happens you can look for somebody to break it up with a crack. It was in a meeting of the Pittsburgh Pirates. They had discussed just about everybody on the Chicago Cub team except traveling secretary Bob Lewis. At this point the player to strategize was Jim Davis, a pitcher. (Jim by reputation was a very weak hitter; a foul ball by him called for a tape measure.) "How's about this Jim Davis, he's a switch-hitter, how we gonna pitch him?"

"He ain't no switch-hitter," came the answer, "he hits three ways, right-handed, left-handed, and seldom."

It was during one of the meetings that Howard Pollet was conducting in Chicago when the Phillies' catcher came up. Howard had covered the two regular catchers, Andy Seminick and Stan Lopata, but he didn't know too much about Gus Niarhos (hitting .190 at the time).

"I've never pitched against Niarhos before, how should we play him?"

"Easy," came the answer. "Just throw him fast balls and bunch him around the mound."

When a manager asks if there are any questions during one of these meetings, you can expect the unexpected. Pepper Martin once broke up a meeting that Ray Blades was having when both were with the St. Louis Cardinals. During spring training the Cardinals were working out twice a day while the Yankees across town were working out only once a day. When Ray asked for suggestions, Pepper got up and said he had been noticing that the Yankees were holding only one workout a day and that they had been winning pennants and world championships, so he was wondering if it wouldn't be wise to follow the Yankees and only have one workout a day.

Blades replied, "No. It's two workouts a day, and the Yankee record should be an incentive for us. You should want to be like the Yankees and work twice as hard on the mistakes and two workouts will do it. . . . That's it. . . . Anything further, Pepper?"

"Yeah," said Pepper, "I got a jackass back in Oklahoma, and you can work him from sunup till sundown, and he ain't never going to win the Kentucky Derby."

In another meeting before a crucial series, with Frankie Frisch the manager, it was Pepper again who broke the tension. Frisch was handling the scorecard and ran down the roster of the other team from owner to bat boy. All the trick plays were brought up. Watch the wind, be careful of the stands, the grass had just been cut, and on and on to even how many times to use the resin bag. It was a complete coverage from Frankie and one of his longest meetings. Finally to make sure, Frisch asked, "Does anybody have any questions?"

Pepper said, "Yeah, Frank, I do."

"What's on your mind, Pepper?"

"Well, Frank, I just don't know what to do. Should I paint the body of my midget racer black and the wheels red, or the wheels black and the body red?"

Dizzy Dean would often take up his own team's lineup and remind his teammates what the great Jerome Herman would do if he worked against them.

Terry Moore, the Cardinal great, says that

Bill DeLancey, the Cashouse Gang catcher, fractured Frisch with an answer during a meeting. At a meeting after Cub catcher Gabby Hartnett had won the game for the Cubs with a home run, Frisch said to DeLancey, "Dee, what was the pitch Hartnett hit?"

"How do I know?" DeLancey fired back. "I haven't caught that pitch yet."

In these meetings the pitcher or pitchers who worked the day before are often asked for opinions, especially if a certain hitter on the opposing club is going "red hot." It was on one of these situations that Don Newcombe eased some of the World Series tension for the Brooklyn Dodgers. Newk, if you remember, opened the 1952 series for the Brooks and lost a heart-breaker 1 to 0 when Tommy Henrich hit a home run. From the bench it looked like a change of pace. Nobody was sure, but it was certain that it wasn't his fast ball. In the meeting the next day when the Dodgers got to Henrich, they asked Newcombe, "What did Henrich hit for the homer?"

Newk looked up and said, "A change of space."

Yogi Berra is regarded as the man with the answers because of his knack of cataloging the hitters. During the All-Star game of 1949, it was his humor that came to the front, instead of his memory. The meeting had almost developed into a filibuster as everybody was chipping in on how to get Stan Musial out. After listening for about ten minutes, Yogi simply stated, "You guys are trying to stop Musial in fifteen minutes while the National League ain't stopped him in fifteen years."

The keeper of the clubhouse is each player. He spends more time here than in his own home during baseball season. It's where twenty-five guys battle every day but have to live like one. It's a continually changing scene, the clubhouse, because trades are such an important part of baseball. It is in the clubhouse that trade announcements are usually made.

The big Ralph Kiner trade between the Pirates and Cubs was finally announced in the clubhouse. I was with the Pirates and had reported for the day's game as usual (and in 1953 that took courage) but had a feeling that something unusual was going to happen. We had been hearing rumors, but what really made us feel that something was going to happen was the presence of newspapermen in the press box. It was only 11:30 and they were in the press box already. On a normal day most of the writers wouldn't get there until the sixth inning because nothing was going to happen before then anyhow. The Pirates took batting practice at the usual time, and the Cubs would start their batting practice at 12:30. At 12:30 both managers called their teams off the field. I remember the time so well because I remember turning to George Metkovich and saying, "George, remember the time and date, 12:20 on June 14, 1953 . . . this is history. We will see the biggest deal in baseball; with both teams going off the field, it must be twenty-five Cubs for twenty-four Pirates plus cash."

Fred Haney was the manager of the Pirates then, and when the whole team was seated in the clubhouse, he said, "We have just made a trade." (This was the biggest understatement since Stan Musial said he thought he could hit.) Sitting on a trunk, I never dreamed I was in on it. I thought I was set for a couple of reasons. I had a good year in 1952, hitting .272, twenty-two points higher than I had ever hit; I had played in 112 games and had showed up for 154 (and when you lose 112 like we did, showing up was worth something); I had made a lot of luncheons, and I had done the extra things like catching batting practice.

The first player Haney told was Ralph Kiner. "I hate to see you go, but you are the man they wanted. I think it will be better for all concerned. Thanks for everything." Kiner admitted that the deal didn't surprise him too much. The next player was Howard Pollet. Howard knew about it because he was to have pitched the night before but was bypassed because of the pending deal. George Metkovich, an outfielder, was next. The Catfish knew it because Haney had mentioned the possibility of the deal to him.

I'm sitting back wondering how many are involved. Is it really a twenty-five-for-twenty-four deal? What are we getting? After all, I knew I had that good year in 1952, and a couple days before I had a meeting with Mr. Rickey to back up my confidence. Mr. Rickey, a very dramatic speaker, had grabbed those bushy eyebrows, looked up to the sky, and said, "By Judas Priest, Joe, we're turning the corner. We're coming out of the wilderness, and you, my boy, figure in my plans."

I could see Haney deliberate and think hard what he was going to say next. A lump came to his throat as he spoke softly the next three words, "*Where's the Dago?*" (They hardly ever use your name in the clubhouse.)

I thought he meant Pete Castiglione, the infielder, so I hollered, "Which one, me or Castiglione?" (thinking I knew all the time).

Haney said, "You! You're the one."

"Me, you must be kidding! I figure in the Pirate plans, and, besides, my wife did the home-stand shopping yesterday."

"No, it's you, Dago. I couldn't tell you anything because I didn't know until this morning. Got anything you want to say?"

"Yeah, if anybody wants to get off this club, rent my apartment. Bill Howerton and Bill McDonald had it before me." (Gene Hermanski, a Cub who was in the deal, took it and lasted about two years.) With that we loaded our stuff, walked through one door and through another, and we were Chicago Cubs. That's a typical day—a Pirate in the morning, a Cub in the afternoon. Confusing? Well, follow it through. Here I was with the Chicago Cubs in Pittsburgh leaving for New York that night, and my family was in Pittsburgh heading back for home in St. Louis until I find a house for them in Chicago. You never know what's going to happen behind those clubhouse doors.

Behind these doors the moods can go from New Year's Eve to a dead-on-arrival morgue scene in a matter of minutes.

They're all clubhouses, from the Cardinal clubhouse that saw and heard the shouts when Slaughter scored the winning run in the 1946 World Series to the clubhouse in Dallas that saw a tough competitor like Phil Cavaretta break down and cry when he was let out as manager of the Chicago Cubs. His only crime—he wanted to win. Go good, and each board seems to sing when it's only squeaking; go bad, and they won't even squeak. They might be the most uncomfortable lockers when you're going good and change to the most comfortable when you're leaving. Get the pink slip and each clothes hook seems to say, "Hang it there, you'll be back." It doesn't take much time to put your equipment in a big-league locker, but it's a lifetime taking it out. You get a round-trip ticket, and every player someday has to give up his locker. Be it the square cage with four clothes hooks or a nail in the "donkey's room," it's the big leagues. You have walked through the clubhouse doors to the dugout.

From *For 2c Plain*

HARRY GOLDEN

THE BASIC SUPERSTITION of the East Side centered around the fear that something would break the spell when everything was going all right. Too much praise was the greatest danger, because it would call attention to the evil spirits, who, out of jealousy, would harm a handsome child, a prosperous business, or a happy home. No one really knows the origin of this. We do know that the superstition is universal, including, of course, the habit of knocking on wood when you hear good news. Take an example in America where the same superstition exists. It is almost a crime to call attention to the baseball game while a pitcher is heading toward a no-hit performance. No member of the team will utter a word, or even look at the pitcher. They must talk of other matters. This is all to distract the attention of the evil spirits. Inning after inning the pitcher will go back to the players' dugout and no one will say a word. So here we have Anglo-Saxon ballplayers from Texas, Georgia, and the Carolinas steeped in the folklore which we thought was singularly an Eastern European tradition. It is interesting to note that the fear of the evil eye is automatically transferred to the spectators in the stands. No one yells while a man is pitching a no-hit game. Instinctively they try not to look at the pitcher. They talk nervously about things completely unrelated to the ball game.

* * *

Ty Cobb, the Georgia Peach, was the greatest ballplayer who ever lived. He began where all other ballplayers left off. He had a special place in my heart, along with Enrico Caruso, Franklin D. Roosevelt, Winston Churchill, Irving Berlin, Al Jolson, and John Barrymore.

I once heard a Columbia University professor deliver a lecture on Ty Cobb. He said that if Cobb had entered banking, he would have been the leading banker in America; if he had gone into politics, he would have become President; he was a born leader, a man who would always win; he would have been in the number-one spot of whatever field of endeavor he chose.

As far as teams were concerned, of course, I was always a New York Giants' man.

On warm spring days we walked from the East Side to the New York World Building on Park Row to watch the baseball game on the electrically operated board. I also saw many a game during the summer vacations. I found that I could see the game at the Polo Grounds and get back in time to sell newspapers to the home-going factory workers. On the Bowery at Houston Street was a large bakery which sold pretzels to the Polo Grounds concessionaire, Mr. Harry Stevens. We kids in the neighborhood alternated in delivering those pretzels, and I got the job as often as any of them. The pay was twenty-five cents for the errand and ten cents carfare, plus the privilege of seeing the game. The pretzels had to be delivered by twelve o'clock, with the game not scheduled to start until around three P.M.; but the only chance you had of seeing the game, without paying, was to stay inside the park. However, I did not sit in the stands for three hours just twiddling my thumbs like a dope. I moseyed around, got to know the players, ran their errands and made myself useful in many other ways around the clubhouse, and once I even helped the groundkeepers put the tarpaulin down over the infield during a sudden shower before game time. I became friends with the Giants' Captain, Larry Doyle, and players George Wiltse, Al Demaree, Leon Ames, Otis Crandall, George Burns, Buck Herzog, and Jeff Tesreau, and received many a smile from the aloof but kindly Christy Mathewson himself.

There was a billboard behind the center-field bleachers advertising flypaper: "Last year George Burns caught 198 flys, but Ajax Flypaper caught 19 billion, 865 million, etc., flies." A good advertisement. I also recall a lady with a very large black picture hat sitting in the front row of the center-field bleachers, and often on weekdays she was all alone out yonder, and just as the Giants took the field, you could hear her battle cry in every corner of the Polo Grounds—"Come on, Artie"—and the shortstop Arthur Fletcher would wave his glove at her, everybody would applaud, and then the first visiting batter stepped up to the plate. Probably Mr. Fletcher's wife or sister. There was a big player by the name of Heinie Zimmerman playing third base and the fans behind him rode him unmercifully. Once Zimmerman ran up to the stands in New York and socked a guy for calling him names. That personal touch in baseball is gone. It is more of a business today.

The Giants represented the New York of the brass cuspidor—that old New York which was still a man's world before the advent of the League of Women Voters; the days of swinging doors, of sawdust on the barroom floor, and of rushing the growler.

The Yanks also played in the Polo Grounds in those days and the star attraction was the famous Hal Chase, who played first base for a while. Later he got into trouble with gamblers, but that was in the National League. Among the Yankee players I knew in those days was a picther by the name of Ray Caldwell, who was nuts about Jewish food, and I took him down to the East Side several times so he could eat knishes.

But when the Detroit Tigers came to New York, I did not go near the clubhouse if I could help it. I didn't want to speak to or meet Ty Cobb.

I wanted it left as it was—just sitting in the grandstand, watching every move of that great and wonderful man.

WIDE WORLD

Did you ever want to be in Julian Javier's shoes? This harrowing picture might change your mind. That's Orlando Cepeda on the left, Roger Maris on the right, and You-know-who in between.

475 FT.

475 FT.

475 FT.

475 FT.

ROBERT RIGER

This unusual sequence shows the great Warren Spahn doing two things that he did probably better than any of his contemporaries: *top to bottom*, throwing to the batter; *left to right*, throwing to first base. The key photo, of course, is the second one down. Can you tell whether he's going to throw to the plate or to first? No? Rest easy. Neither could the guy leading off first.

N. Y. DAILY NEWS

SWINGING FRIAR

The Reverend Capistran Ferrito, of New York, and admirers.

THE RISING young star in the East, among sportswriters over the past decade, has been, pretty much by common consent, Sandy Grady of the Philadelphia *Bulletin*. The subject matter, in the following sample, is pretty good too.

2,500 Hits—and Every One Wrong

SANDY GRADY

IT MAY NOT thrill you to hear that Henry Aaron recently popped his 2,500th base hit, and that someone will preserve the baseball as a priceless artifact. When the bartender at your local taproom pulls his 25,000,000th draft beer, no mobs cheer to see the glass bronzed, autographed and enshrined.

It was shocking, though, to hear Henry confess that he'd been doing it all wrong for 2,500 base hits and 13 years. You know, like Douglas Corrigan landing in Ireland and exclaiming, "What, this isn't California?" That's poor Henry Aaron, too—doing it backwards all these years with nobody in baseball having the heart to tell him.

Certainly Henry can't depend on the Braves. They won't even count his base hits for him.

"Mean anything, getting 2,500 hits, Henry?"

Aaron sipped his beer pensively. He stared at the questioner, as though asked how he would react if suddenly made general of the Israeli Army.

"How would I know?" said Henry. "I don't even know how many I got."

He was too wide-eyed to be kidding. Much had been made in the press box of Henry's statistical mountain, but nobody had tipped off Henry. A guy pulled out some scrawled notes. He showed Henry that only 41 guys since the Ice Age had 2,500 hits. And only eight—Cobb, Musial, Speaker, Wagner, Collins, Lajoie, Waner and Anson—have 3,000. Aaron looked at the names and said, "Wow," softly.

"You're a cinch to make the 3,000 list, especially since you'll play as long as Mays," said the man.

Aaron giggled, as if he were being needled. "If I don't get hurt, maybe. But play as long as Willie? I'm not figuring on that. Willie's 40, isn't he? I'm 33 now. Few more years, and that's it. Especially if I get caught on a rebuilding team and I'm just hanging around in the shuffle. That's good-bye."

"Ever think you'd like to teach hitting to young players, the way Musial and Williams and DiMaggio do?"

"Like it very much," said Aaron, suddenly interested. "But I wouldn't teach 'em to do it my way. I've done it the wrong way."

Now it was the questioner's moment to stare at Henry. He thought of other statistics he'd seen in the Braves' brochure—ten years over .300, five times 40 or more homers, the swarm of awards and trophies . . .

"Yeah, I've got a hitch in my swing," said Aaron. "And I hit off the front foot. Now I wouldn't teach those things. I'd try to help a young player with his own style, not mine. The big thing is bat control."

Not that Henry was apologetic about these, er, stylistic faults. "Most of the good hitters have a hitch in their swings, a sort of delayed bat cock," said Aaron. "Rich Allen has it, Musial had a big one, Mays does, too. When a kid goes wrong, he drops his hands when he makes that hitch. Then he's in trouble on inside stuff. Now about hitting off the front foot —Musial was way out front, too. Remember? But he kept the bat back until the last split-second. You can commit your body, not that bat. There's your leverage."

"Don't you help young hitters in the spring?"

Aaron grinned. "Be glad to, but they never ask," he said. "I guess they watch, but they never say anything. It's different now. When I came up in 1954, a rookie felt his way along.

Now they're here two days and they take over the clubhouse."

"Are you the same hitter you were, say, five years ago?"

He cocked his head, pondered. "Maybe not as quick at times. Take the other day against the Mets. Young fellow [Tom] Seaver, real fast, struck me out. Threw it past me. I thought, uh-huh, he'll try that again. Seventh inning, he did. But he'd slowed a bit. I hit it in the seats and we won. So I may not be so quick, but you get wiser to make up for it."

He seemed pleased by the benefits of age. Aaron has changed, though, since the move from Milwaukee. He seems noticeably lustful for a pulled ball over the left-field fence, less interested in hits to all fields. He nodded at this.

"Maybe it's subconscious, wanting to please the new fans in Atlanta," he said. "Maybe it's getting older and stronger. I don't know of anything that pleases more than a ball out of the park."

"Or anything that puts more hitters in Cadillacs," said the man.

"Not me," said Aaron, grinning. "Just a li'l ol' Riviera."

There is pride beneath the languor. Irritated recently by what he considered unflattering comparisons between himself and Roberto Clemente on an Atlanta broadcast, Henry nearly decapitated the Pirates. One wondered which honors excited Henry the most at summer's end.

"Leading in homers and runs batted across," said Aaron, then with a show of teeth: "But wining the MVP thing, well, that means you had one great year."

Especially doing it all wrong, Henry Aaron's way.

HERE THEY ARE: the fabled 1927 Yankees.

Five O'Clock Lightning

FRANK GRAHAM

THE DEFEAT in the 1926 World Series was a dark interlude between the Yankees' unexpected triumph in the pennant race that year and their rise in 1927 to a peak which many believe they never have surpassed. This, they say, was the team. Greater than any that had gone before, greater than any that has followed.

The training season was uneventful, because there was little for Huggins to do. Born of their eagerness to redeem themselves for the loss of the Series, a new spirit burned brightly in the players. New bonds had been forged in the crises they had met. Huggins had no need to demand their loyalty. It was his completely.

With few changes, the makeup of the team was the same as 1926: Ruth, Combs and Meusel in the outfield; Gehrig, Lazzeri, Koenig, and Dugan in the infield. Johnny Grabowski, a good journeyman catcher, had been purchased from the White Sox to work with Bengough and Collins. Cedric Durst and Benny Paschal were the extra outfielders. For protection in the infield, there were Gazella, Roy Morehart, and Julian Wera. The brunt of the pitching would be borne by Hoyt, Pennock, Shocker, and Pipgras, who had been brought back from St. Paul, where he had finished his schooling for the majors. To help out there were Ruether, Thomas, Braxton, Shawkey, and Joe Giard. And to the staff had been added one of the most amazing players ever to wear a Yankee uniform.

His name was Wilcy Moore, and he was a dirt farmer from Hollis, Oklahoma. Nobody knew exactly how old he was. He said he was twenty-eight, but nobody believed him. The chances are he was at least thirty. He was big, broad-shouldered, slow-moving, good-natured, and a great favorite with the other players. For six years he had toiled in the minor leagues with no thought or hope of getting to the majors. He had good years and bad ones. When he picked up a little money, he went home and put it in the bank or bought new tools for his farm.

So far as he was concerned, the 1926 season had been just about the same as other good ones he had had. Pitching for Greenville in the South Atlantic League, he had won thirty games and lost only four. When it ended, he packed his stuff and said good-bye to the other players. Good-bye forever, he thought to himself, for he had about made up his mind that the time had come for him to quit trouping around the country and stay in his fields. And then, the night before he was to leave, he learned that he had been sold to the Yankees.

"I didn't know anybody from the Yankees had looked at me," he said later. "I didn't know they'd ever heard of me. And nobody in our front office ever had said anything to me about me being sold. Maybe it just happened—or maybe they were keeping it as a surprise for me. Anyway, I thought I'd come up and see what it was like up here."

His equipment for pitching in the major leagues was limited but sound. It consisted of a sinker—a low, fast ball that broke sharply downward as it reached the plate—almost flawless control, and nerves of steel—or no nerves at all. He also had, or thought he had, a curve ball, and he used to beg Huggins to let him throw it once in a while, but Hug always shook him off.

"Your curve ball," Hug said, "wouldn't go around a button on my vest."

He was used almost exclusively as a relief pitcher. By common consent of those who played with him or against him, he was the best they ever saw.

The other players, admiring him for his pitching, laughed at him as a hitter. And with reason. He had the perfect stance at the plate and the perfect swing. The only trouble was that he always swung in the same spot, no matter where the ball was, so that if he hit it, it was by accident. Ruth, after one look at him in batting practice at the training camp, bet him $300 to $100 that he wouldn't make three hits all season. He made five. When he got home he wrote the Babe a letter.

"The $300 come in handy," it said. "I used it to buy a fine pair of mules. I named one Babe and the other Ruth."

Once the season opened, there never was any doubt that the Yankees would win the pennant. Ruth, Meusel, Gehrig, and Lazzeri daily terrorized the opposing pitchers; and there wasn't a man in the batting order, down to the pitcher's spot, who couldn't break up a ball game by hitting one out of the park. Hoyt's arm, which had bothered him the year before, was strong again. Pennock was—well, Pennock. Shocker, with proper rest, was a hard man to beat, although by now he was pitching mostly with his head. Huggins picked assignments carefully for Pipgras, and the youngster won regularly. Braxton, Thomas, and the others filled in effectively. When any of the pitchers faltered, there was always Moore. The power of the team blinded the onlookers to the skill and smoothness of its fielding.

Enemy teams cracked and broke wide-open before their assaults. When one of them did strike back and put a Yankee pitcher to rout, Moore ambled in from the bullpen, and the struggle was over. There was an incident one night in Detroit when Mike Gazella said something that indicated how the rest of the Yankees felt about Moore. The players were watching a big fire in an office building near their hotel. Flames roared and dense black smoke poured from the stricken building as the constantly augmented ranks of firemen poured water on it from every angle. At last the flames died down and thin white smoke rose from the seared walls.

"We can go home now," Mike said. "They got Wilcy Moore in."

The race was virtually decided as early as the Fourth of July. The Senators, in a June spurt, had moved up on them, and the holiday doubleheader between the teams packed the Stadium. But when the games were over, the departing crowd knew that never again would the Senators be dangerous. The Senators knew it, too; for the Yankees had won the first game 12 to 1 and the second 21 to 1.

Ruth, with his genius for rising to every occasion, was having his greatest season. When he had hit fifty-nine home runs in 1921, it had seemed that no one, himself included, ever would approach that mark. Now he was slamming the ball out of every park on the circuit, and his total was mounting. Gehrig wasn't far behind him. They were the Home Run Twins. Babe and Lou. The greatest combination of power hitters the game had ever known.

The team struck so often in the late innings that Combs called this delayed attack "five o'clock lightning." The phrase caught on, spread through the league and seeped into the consciousness of opposing pitchers. They began to dread the approach of five o'clock and the eighth inning.

Always in demand for exhibition games in the minor-league towns during the season since Ruth had been a member of the team, the Yankees were in even greater demand now, so that they scarcely had a day off. Open dates found them in St. Paul, Dayton, Buffalo, Indianapolis. Even Cincinnati and Pittsburgh, having no American League teams, booked them.

Sometimes the players grumbled about this, but actually they enjoyed it. And no one enjoyed it more than the Babe. He snarled traffic and jammed the parks wherever he went. His progress through the countryside was like that of a President or a king. Even in the smallest towns, no matter how late the hour, there would be crowds at the station hoping to catch a glimpse of him. And the Babe never failed them. He would leave his dinner or a card game, even get up out of bed, to go out on the platform and greet his admirers and shake the hands stretched up to him.

"How did you know he was coming through?" a reporter asked a grinning section hand at one crossroads village where, for some reason, the train had stopped one night.

"The station agent told us," he said. "Every station along the line knows he's coming."

One of the secrets of the Babe's greatness was that he never lost any of his enthusiasm for playing ball, and especially for hitting home runs. To him a homer was a homer, whether he hit it in a regular game, a World Series game, or an exhibition game. The crack of his bat, the sight of the ball soaring against the sky—these thrilled him as much as they did the fans.

In Indianapolis one day—this was when the ball park was down by the railroad tracks—he went to bat three times without hitting a ball out of the infield, and the overflow crowd was having a fine time razzing him. But on his fourth trip, he really got hold of one. He hit it high and far over the right-field fence where, as those in the press box on the roof of the grandstand could see, it went bouncing and rolling among the boxcars in the freight yard. The crowd howled. They had seen many a home run, but never one like that. And the Babe? He was as happy as though the world championship had hung on that drive.

"I guess I didn't show those people something!" he said, on his return to the dugout. "Make fun of me, will they?"

In Toronto—the Babe usually played first base, with Gehrig in right field in these games—a crowd of small boys piled down out of the bleachers in the eighth inning, crowded around the big guy, and refused to be driven back by the umpires or even the police. Seeing the situation was hopeless, the umpires called the game, whereupon the kids leaped on the Babe joyfully and bore him to the ground.

"I had the presence of mind," the Babe said, "to put my cap between my teeth and hold onto it like a dog. Otherwise, one of those little suckers would have stole it for a souvenir."

Once the Yankees went to Sing Sing to play the prison team. The Babe hit one over the right-field wall in batting practice, then hit one over in center, where the yard is deepest. The prisoners roared.

"Well," one of them yelled, "there's something goes out of here, anyway!" And another: "Oh, boy! I'd like to be riding on that one!"

The Babe had a great time. When a convict umpire called one of the prison players safe in a close play at the plate, he boomed, "Robber!"

When the Yankees, clowning, permitted a prison player to steal a base, Ruth wanted to know if there weren't any cops in the joint. Turning to the first-base bleachers, he asked what time it was, and when a half dozen inmates eagerly told him, he roared, "What difference does it make to you guys? You ain't going anyplace."

The prisoners thought that was wonderful, although if someone else had said it they might have felt differently.

But those were diversions. The serious business of clinching the pennant remained—although it must be said for them that the Yankees attacked that with as much relish as they put into the fun-making. The decisive game took place in Boston on Labor Day. Up to that time they had, for the most part, strictly adhered to the training rules. But that night the lid was off. All Huggins asked them to do was to show up at the Back Bay station in time to get the 1 A.M. train for New York, and they all made it.

There were some passengers on the train who will never forget that they rode with the Yankees that night. The three cars for the players were at the head end of the train, which was unusual. The players clambered aboard near the rear end and marched through. Two of the cars through which they had to pass were compartment cars, and the shoes of the occupant had been placed in front of each closed door for the porter to shine. Someone kicked one of the shoes. The others thought it was a great idea. When the Yankees had passed, there in the forward end of each car was a pile of shoes that must have taken hours to sort the next morning.

Having clinched the pennant, the Yanks kept right on hammering. They wanted to win—and did—every game they possibly could. They set an American League record by winning 110 games and losing 44. They won the pennant by seventeen games. Ruth smashed his own record for home runs by hitting sixty and had a batting average of .356. Gehrig hit .373 and made forty-seven homers. Hoyt, with twenty-two victories, was the league's leading pitcher in games won and lost. Moore, with an average of 2.28, was the best in the matter of earned runs allowed.

In the National League the Pittsburgh Pirates, under Donie Bush, had won the pennant after a terrific struggle with the Cardinals. This was a good team, with Clyde Barnhart and the Waner brothers, Lloyd and Paul, in the outfield, Joe Harris at first base, George Grantham at second, Glenn Wright at shortstop, the great Pie Traynor at third base, Earl Smith and Johnny Gooch to divide the catching, and such pitchers as Ray Kremer, Vic Aldridge, Lee Meadows, Carmen Hill, and Johnny Miljus.

The Series opened in Pittsburgh. Hotel accommodations were inadequate for the crowds that poured into the town. For a while, nobody seemed to know where the Yankees could be housed. Just in time Barrow received word that a new hotel, the Roosevelt, had been completed and would throw open its doors to the Yankees as its first guests. On the bulletin board in the clubhouse at the Stadium the day the team left New York was a notice:

"The Yankees will open the Hotel Roosevelt in Pittsburgh."

And under it a player wrote, in pencil:

"And how!"

All was confusion in the hotel when they arrived early in the morning of the day before the first game. The lobby was packed with fans eager for a close-up of Ruth, Gehrig, Lazzeri, Pennock, and the other famous players—so packed that Huggins, his short-stemmed pipe in his mouth and his dinky traveling bag in one hand—was almost trampled in the rush as the players made their way to the desk.

Arrangements had been made for the Pirates to work out about ten o'clock that morning and then withdraw, leaving the field to the Yankees. By the time the Yankees appeared, the Pirates had dressed and were in the stands. Also in the stands or hovering back of the plate were the newspapermen and photographers sent from all over the country to cover the Series.

"You're starting tomorrow, Waite," Huggins said to Hoyt. "Go out there and take about ten minutes of batting practice. Just lay the ball in there."

Straight as a string, Hoyt laid the ball up to the plate. Combs, Koenig, Ruth, Gehrig, Meusel, Lazzeri, Dugan, Collins, Grabowski, walked up and hit it. Up against the stands. Into the stands. Over the fences. It was a terrifying demonstration of power hitting.

In the stands the Waner brothers, great ballplayers in their own right but little men, stood talking with Ken Smith, New York *Mirror* reporter, as the Yankees slugged the ball. Ruth hit one over the fence in center field, Gehrig hit one high in the seats in right field, Meusel hit one over the fence in left field. Lloyd turned to Paul.

"Jesus," he said fervently. "They're big guys!"

Paul shook his head. The Waners walked out. Most of their teammates followed them. They had seen enough. It is undoubtedly true that right there the Yankees won the Series. Before a ball had been pitched in actual competition, they had convinced the Pirates that theirs was a losing cause.

The Yankees won the first game, 5 to 4, with Hoyt taking a decision over Kremer. Hoyt failed to finish the game, however. He got in trouble in the eighth inning and was hauled out, whereupon Moore stalked in from the bullpen to turn the Pirates back and sew up the game.

Pipgras hooked up with Aldridge in the second game, and the Yankees romped in, 6 to 2. There were some who thought Huggins was taking a long chance in starting Pipgras, but the youngster vindicated his manager's judgment by yielding only seven hits scattered over as many innings.

Now the Series moved to New York. As the Yankees were riding down to the station that night, a newspaperman in a cab with Lazzeri and three other players said, "If you fellows don't wind this Series up in these next two games, I'll shoot you."

And Lazzeri said, "If we don't beat these bums four in a row, you can shoot me first."

The other players nodded. That's the way everybody on the ball club felt.

Huggins called on Pennock in the opening game in New York, defying the dope that no left-hander could beat the Pirates. For seven innings, pitching against Meadows, Pennock did not allow a hit, and, the way he was going, it looked as though he would be the first pitcher in World Series history to hang up a no-hit game. Ironically, he was stalled by his own teammates, for in the eighth inning the Yankees, runless since the first, when they had scored twice, set upon Meadows savagely, drove him from the box, and scored six runs, one of which was a homer by Ruth. Sitting on the bench through that long half-inning, Pennock cooled out. He got rid of Wright, the first man to face him in the eighth, but Traynor singled and Barnhart doubled, Traynor scoring. In the ninth Lloyd Waner singled to left. Pennock had missed a no-hit game and a shutout as well. But his three-hit performance, the score of which was 8 to 1, still stands as one of the finest ever seen in a World Series.

Later, in the clubhouse, the taciturn Meusel was moved to ask, "Who said a left-hander couldn't beat the Pirates?"

And a reporter, to whom the question was addressed, said, "Plenty of guys. But they meant the left-handers in the National League. They haven't any like Pennock in that league."

The outcome of the Series was not assured. The Yankees not only would win but would win in four games, as they had promised themselves. They did it, too. But not without a few chills and shakes along the way. The Pirates, probably reckoning that all was lost anyway, were free of the tension which had gripped them through the three preceding games and put up a stubborn struggle against Moore, who was allowed to pitch a game of his own as a reward for his great relief work during the season. Ruth, who had driven in the Yankees' first run in the first inning, made his second homer of the Series off Hill in the fifth with Combs on base. But the Pirates, who also had made a run in the first, made two in the seventh, and the game went into the last half of the ninth still tied.

Hill had been removed for a pinch hitter in the seventh, and Miljus was pitching for the Pirates. He walked Combs, leading off, and Koenig, intending only to sacrifice, beat out the bunt he had rolled toward third base. With Ruth up, Miljus let go with a wild pitch and the runners moved up. Miljus then purposely passed the Babe and the bases were filled. With Gehrig and Meusel coming up, Miljus really was in a jam; but, pitching desperately, he fanned both. There still was Lazzeri. In his eagerness to get rid of Tony, Miljus turned on too much stuff. A fast ball, sailing, whizzed over Gooch's head as the catcher tried frantically to knock it down, and Combs crossed the plate with the winning run.

Ruppert, trembling in his box next to the dugout as the struggle went on, was almost incoherent with joy as he saw Combs racing home and realized that once more his team was the best in the world. The disappointment of the previous October had been forgotten.

JOHN GALLAGHER

Courtesy *Sport* Magazine ©

THIS IS the third of the Zane Grey baseball stories to adorn the *Fireside* baseball library, and it introduces his most famous fictional ballplayer—Whitaker Hurtle, known more familiarly as the Rube.

The Rube's Waterloo

ZANE GREY

IT WAS about the sixth inning that I suspected the Rube of weakening. For that matter he had not pitched anything resembling his usual brand of baseball. But the Rube had developed into such a wonder in the box that it took time for his letdown to dawn upon me. Also it took a tip from Raddy, who sat with me on the bench.

"Con, the Rube isn't himself today," said Radbourne. "His mind's not on the game. He seems hurried and flustered, too. If he doesn't explode presently, I'm a dub at callin' the turn."

Raddy was the best judge of a pitcher's condition, physical or mental, in the Eastern League. It was a Saturday and we were on the road and finishing up a series with the Rochesters. Each team had won and lost a game, and, as I was climbing close to the leaders in the pennant race, I wanted the third and deciding game of that Rochester series. The usual big Saturday crowd was in attendance, noisy, demonstrative and exacting.

In this sixth inning the first man up for Rochester had flied to McCall. Then had come the two plays significant of Rube's weakening. He had hit one batter and walked another. This was sufficient, considering the score was three to one in our favor, to bring the audience to its feet with a howling, stamping demand for runs.

"Spears is wise all right," said Raddy.

I watched the foxy old captain walk over to the Rube and talk to him while he rested, a reassuring hand on the pitcher's shoulder. The crowd yelled its disapproval and umpire Bates called out sharply, "Spears, get back to the bag!"

"Now, Mr. Umpire, ain't I hurrin' all I can?" queried Spears as he leisurely ambled back to first.

The Rube tossed a long, damp welt of hair back from his big brow and nervously toed the rubber. I noted that he seemed to forget the runners on bases and delivered the ball without glancing at either bag. Of course this resulted in a double steal. The ball went wild—almost a wild pitch.

"Steady up, old man," called Gregg between the yells of the bleachers. He held his mitt square over the plate for the Rube to pitch to. Again the long twirler took his swing, and again the ball went wild. Clancy had the Rube in the hole now and the situation began to grow serious. The Rube did not take half his usual deliberation, and of the next two pitches one of them was a ball and the other a strike by grace of the umpire's generosity. Clancy rapped the next one, an absurdly slow pitch for the Rube to use, and both runners scored to the shrill tune of the happy bleachers.

I saw Spears shake his head and look toward the bench. It was plain what that meant.

"Raddy, I ought to take the Rube out," I said, "but whom can I put in? You worked yesterday—Cairns' arm is sore. It's got to be nursed. And Henderson, that ladies' man I just signed, is not in uniform."

"I'll go in," replied Raddy, instantly.

"Not on your life." I had as hard a time keeping Radbourne from overworking as I had in getting enough work out of some other players. "I guess I'll let the Rube take his medicine. I hate to lose this game, but if we have to, we can stand it. I'm curious, anyway, to see what's the matter with the Rube. Maybe he'll settle down presently."

I made no sign that I had noticed Spears's appeal to the bench. And my aggressive players, no doubt seeing the situation as I saw it, sang out their various calls of cheer to the Rube and of defiance to their antagonists. Clancy stole off first base so far that the Rube, catching somebody's warning too late, made a balk and the umpire sent the runner on to second. The Rube now plainly showed painful evidences of being rattled.

He could not locate the plate without slowing up and when he did that a Rochester player walloped the ball. Pretty soon he pitched as if he did not care, and but for the fast fielding of the team behind him the Rochesters would have scored more than the eight runs it got. When the Rube came in to the bench I asked him if he was sick and at first he said he was and then that he was not. So I let him pitch the remaining innings, as the game was lost anyhow, and we walked off the field a badly beaten team.

That night we had to hurry from the hotel to catch a train for Worcester and we had dinner in the dining car. Several of my players' wives had come over from Worcester to meet us, and were in the dining car when I entered. I observed a pretty girl sitting at one of the tables with my new pitcher, Henderson.

"Say, Mac," I said to McCall, who was with me, "is Henderson married?"

"Naw, but he looks like he wanted to be. He was in the grandstand today with that girl."

"Who is she? Oh! a little peach!"

A second glance at Henderson's companion brought this compliment from me involuntarily.

"Con, you'll get it as bad as the rest of this mushy bunch of ballplayers. We're all stuck on that kid. But since Henderson came she's been a frost to all of us. An' it's put the Rube in the dumps."

"Who's the girl?"

"That's Nan Brown. She lives in Worcester an' is the craziest girl fan I ever seen. Flirt! Well, she's got them all beat. Somebody introduced the Rube to her. He has been moony ever since."

That was enough to whet my curiosity, and I favored Miss Brown with more than one glance during dinner. When we returned to the parlor car I took advantage of the opportunity and remarked to Henderson that he might introduce his manager. He complied, but not with amiable grace.

So I chatted with Nan Brown, and studied her. She was a pretty, laughing coquettish little minx and quite baseball-mad. I had met many girl fans, but none so enthusiastic as Nan. But she was wholesome and sincere, and I liked her.

Before turning in I sat down beside the Rube. He was very quiet and his face did not encourage company. But that did not stop me.

"Hello, Whit; have a smoke before you go to bed?" I asked cheerfully.

He scarcely heard me and made no move to take the proffered cigar. All at once it struck me that the rustic simplicity which had characterized him had vanished.

"Whit, old fellow, what was wrong today?" I asked, quietly, with my hand on his arm.

"Mr. Connelly, I want my release, I want to go back to Rickettsville," he replied hurriedly.

For the space of a few seconds I did some tall thinking. The situation suddenly became grave. I saw the pennant for the Worcesters fading, dimming.

"You want to go home?" I began slowly. "Why, Whit, I can't keep you. I wouldn't try if you didn't want to stay. But I'll tell you confidentially, if you leave me at this stage I'm ruined."

"How's that?" he inquired, keenly looking at me.

"Well, I can't win the pennant without you. If I do win it there's a big bonus for me. I can buy the house I want and get married this fall if I capture the flag. You've met Milly. You can imagine what your pitching means to me this year. That's all."

He averted his face and looked out of the window. His big jaw quivered.

"If it's that—why, I'll stay, I reckon," he said huskily.

That moment bound Whit Hurtle and Frank Connelly into a far closer relation than the one between player and manager. I sat silent for a while, listening to the drowsy talk of the other players and the rush and roar of the train as it sped on into the night.

"Thank you, old chap," I replied. "It wouldn't have been like you to throw me down at this stage. Whit, you're in trouble?"

"Yes."

"Can I help you—in any way?"

"I reckon not."

"Don't be too sure of that. I'm a pretty wise guy, if I do say it myself. I might be able to do as much for you as you're going to do for me."

The sight of his face convinced me that I had taken a wrong tack. It also showed me how deep Whit's trouble really was. I bade him good night and went to my berth, where sleep did not soon visit me. A saucy, sparkling-eyed woman barred Whit Hurtle's baseball career at its threshold.

Women are just as fatal to ballplayers as to

men in any other walk of life. I had seen a strong athlete grow palsied just at a scornful slight. It's a great world, and the women run it. So I lay awake racking my brains to outwit a pretty disorganizer; and I plotted for her sake. Married, she would be out of mischief. For Whit's sake, for Milly's sake, for mine, all of which collectively meant for the sake of the pennant, this would be the solution of the problem.

I decided to take Milly into my confidence, and finally on the strength of that I got to sleep. In the morning I went to my hotel, had breakfast, attended to my mail, and then boarded a car to go out to Milly's house. She was waiting for me on the porch, dressed as I liked to see her, in blue and white, and she wore violets that matched the color of her eyes.

"Hello, Connie. I haven't seen a morning paper, but I know from your face that you lost the Rochester series," said Milly, with a gay laugh.

"I guess yes. The Rube blew up, and if we don't play a pretty smooth game, young lady, he'll never come down."

Then I told her.

"Why, Connie, I knew long ago. Haven't you seen the change in him before this?"

"What change?" I asked blankly.

"You are a man. Well, he was a gawky, slouchy, shy farmer boy when he came to us. Of course the city life and popularity began to influence him. Then he met Nan. She made the Rube a worshiper. I first noticed a change in his clothes. He blossomed out in a new suit, white negligee, neat tie and a stylish straw hat. Then it was evident he was making heroic struggles to overcome his awkwardness. It was plain he was studying and copying the other boys. He's wonderfully improved, but still shy. He'll always be shy. Connie, Whit's a fine fellow, too good for Nan Brown."

"But, Milly," I interrupted, "the Rube's hard hit. Why is he too good for her?"

"Nan is a natural-born flirt," Milly replied. "She can't help it. I'm afraid Whit has a slim chance. Nan may not see deep enough to learn his fine qualities. I fancy Nan tired quickly of him, though the one time I saw them together she appeared to like him very well. This new pitcher of yours, Henderson, is a handsome fellow and smooth. Whit is losing to him. Nan likes flash, flattery, excitement."

"McCall told me the Rube had been down in the mouth ever since Henderson joined the team. Milly, I don't like Henderson a whole lot. He's not in the Rube's class as pitcher. What am I going to do? Lose the pennant and a big slice of purse money just for a pretty little flirt?"

"Oh, Connie, it's not so bad as that. Whit will come around all right."

"He won't unless we can pull some wires. I've got to help him win Nan Brown. What do you think of that for a manager's job? I guess maybe winning pennants doesn't call for diplomatic genius and cunning! But I'll hand them a few tricks before I lose. My first move will be to give Henderson his release."

I left Milly, as always, once more able to make light of discouragements and difficulties.

Monday I gave Henderson his unconditional release. He celebrated the occasion by verifying certain rumors I had heard from other managers. He got drunk. But he did not leave town, and I heard that he was negotiating with Providence for a place on that team.

Radbourne pitched one of his gilt-edged games that afternoon against Hartford and we won. And Milly sat in the grandstand, having contrived by cleverness to get a seat next to Nan Brown. Milly and I were playing a vastly deeper game than baseball—a game with hearts. But we were playing it with honest motive, for the good of all concerned, we believed, and on the square. I sneaked a look now and then up into the grandstand. Milly and Nan appeared to be getting on famously. It was certain that Nan was flushed and excited, no doubt consciously proud of being seen with my affianced. After the game I chanced to meet them on their way out. Milly winked at me, which was her sign that all was working beautifully.

I hunted up the Rube and bundled him off to the hotel to take dinner with me. At first he was glum, but after a while he brightened up somewhat to my persistent cheer and friendliness. Then we went out on the hotel balcony to smoke, and there I made my play.

"Whit, I'm pulling a stroke for you. Now listen and don't be offended. I know what's put you off your feed, because I was the same way when Milly had me guessing. You've lost your head over Nan Brown. That's not so terrible, though I daresay you think it's a catastrophe. Because you've quit. You've shown a yellow streak. You've lain down.

"My boy, that isn't the way to win a girl. You've got to scrap. Milly told me yesterday how she had watched your love affair with Nan, and how she thought you had given up just when things might have come your way. Nan is a little flirt, but she's all right. What's more, she was getting fond of you. Nan is meanest to the man she likes best. The way to handle her, Whit, is to master her. Play high and mighty. Get tragical. Then grab her up in your arms. I tell you, Whit, it'll all come your way if you only keep your nerve. I'm your friend and so is Milly. We're going out to her house presently—and Nan will be there."

The Rube drew a long, deep breath and held out his hand. I sensed another stage in the evolution of Whit Hurtle.

"I reckon I've taken baseball coachin'," he said presently, "an' I don't see why I can't take some other kind. I'm only a rube, an' things come hard for me, but I'm a-learnin'."

It was about dark when we arrived at the house.

"Hello, Connie. You're late. Good evening, Mr. Hurtle. Come right in. You've met Miss Nan Brown? Oh, of course; how stupid of me!"

It was a trying moment for Milly and me. A little pallor showed under the Rube's tan, but he was more composed than I had expected. Nan got up from the piano. She was all in white and deliciously pretty. She gave a quick, glad start of surprise. What a relief that was to my troubled mind! Everything had depended upon a real honest liking for Whit, and she had it.

More than once I had been proud of Milly's cleverness, but this night as hostess and an accomplice she won my everlasting admiration. She contrived to give the impression that Whit was a frequent visitor at her home and very welcome. She brought out his best points, and in her skillful hands he lost embarrassment and awkwardness. Before the evening was over Nan regarded Whit with different eyes, and she never dreamed that everything had not come about naturally. Then Milly somehow got me out on the porch, leaving Nan and Whit together.

"Milly, you're a marvel, the best and sweetest ever," I whispered. "We're going to win. It's a cinch."

"Well, Connie, not that—exactly," she whispered back demurely. "But it looks hopeful."

I could not help hearing what was said in the parlor.

"Now I can roast you," Nan was saying, archly. She had switched back to her favorite baseball vernacular. "You pitched a swell game last Saturday in Rochester, didn't you? Not! You had no steam, no control, and you couldn't have curved a saucer."

"Nan, what could you expect?" was the cool reply. "You sat up in the stand with your handsome friend. I reckon I couldn't pitch. I just gave the game away."

"Whit!—Whit!—"

Then I whispered to Milly that it might be discreet for us to move a little way from the vicinity.

It was on the second day afterward that I got a chance to talk to Nan. She reached the grounds early, before Milly arrived, and I found her in the grandstand. The Rube was down on the card to pitch and when he started to warm up Nan said confidently that he would shut out Hartford that afternoon.

"I'm sorry, Nan, but you're way off. We'd do well to win at all, let alone get a shutout."

"You're a fine manager!" she retorted, hotly. "Why won't we win?"

"Well, the Rube's not in good form. The Rube—"

"Stop calling him that horrid name."

"Whit's not in shape. He's not right. He's ill or something is wrong. I'm worried sick about him."

"Why—Mr. Connelly!" exclaimed Nan. She turned quickly toward me.

I crowded on full canvas of gloom to my already long face.

"I'm serious, Nan. The lad's off, somehow. He's in magnificent physical trim, but he can't keep his mind on the game. He has lost his head. I've talked with him, reasoned with him, all to no good. He only goes down deeper in the dumps. Something is terribly wrong with him, and if he doesn't brace, I'll have to release—"

Miss Nan Brown suddenly lost a little of her rich bloom. "Oh! you wouldn't—you couldn't release him!"

"I'll have to if he doesn't brace. It means a lot to me, Nan, for of course I can't win the pennant this year without Whit being in shape. But I believe I wouldn't mind the loss of that any more than to see him fall down. The boy is a magnificent pitcher. If he can only be brought around he'll go to the big league next year and develop into one of the greatest pitchers the game has ever produced. But somehow or other he has lost heart. He's quit. And I've done my best for him. He's beyond me now. What a shame it is! For he's the making of such a splendid man outside of baseball. Milly thinks the world of him. Well, well; there are disappointments—we can't help them. There goes the gong. I must leave you. Nan, I'll bet you a box of candy Whit loses today. Is it a go?"

"It is," replied Nan, with fire in her eyes.

"You go to Whit Hurtle and tell him I said if he wins today's game I'll kiss him!"

I nearly broke my neck over benches and bats getting to Whit with that message. He gulped once.

Then he tightened his belt and shut out Hartford with two scratch singles. It was a great exhibition of pitching. I had no means to tell whether or not the Rube got his reward that night, but I was so happy that I hugged Milly within an inch of her life.

But it turned out that I had been a little premature in my elation. In two days the Rube went down into the depths again, this time clear to China, and Nan was sitting in the grandstand with Henderson. The Rube lost his next game, pitching like a schoolboy scared out of his wits. Henderson followed Nan like a shadow, so that I had no chance to talk to her. The Rube lost his next game and then another. We were pushed out of second place.

If we kept up that losing streak a little longer, our hopes for the pennant were gone. I had begun to despair of the Rube. For some occult reason he scarcely spoke to me. Nan flirted worse than ever. It seemed to me she flaunted her conquest of Henderson in poor Whit's face.

The Providence ball team came to town and promptly signed Henderson and announced him for Saturday's game. Cairns won the first of the series and Radbourne lost the second. It was Rube's turn to pitch the Saturday game and I resolved to make one more effort to put the lovesick swain in something like his old fettle. So I called upon Nan.

She was surprised to see me, but received me graciously. I fancied her face was not quite so glowing as usual. I came bluntly out with my mission. She tried to freeze me but I would not freeze. I was out to win or lose and not to be lightly laughed aside or coldly denied. I played to make her angry, knowing the real truth of her feelings would show under stress.

For once in my life I became a knocker and said some unpleasant things—albeit they were true—about Henderson. She championed Henderson royally, and when, as a last card, I compared Whit's fine record with Henderson's, not only as a ballplayer, but as a man, particularly in his reverence for women, she flashed at me:

"What do you know about it? Mr. Henderson asked me to marry him. Can a man do more to show his respect? Your friend never so much as hinted such honorable intentions. What's more—he insulted me!" The blaze in Nan's black eyes softened with a film of tears. She looked hurt. Her pride had encountered a fall.

"Oh, no, Nan, Whit couldn't insult a lady," I protested.

"Couldn't he? That's all you know about him. You know I—I promised to kiss him if he beat Hartford that day. So when he came I—I did. Then the big savage began to rave and he grabbed me up in his arms. He smothered me; almost crushed the life out of me. He frightened me terribly. When I got away from him—the monster stood there and coolly said I belonged to him. I ran out of the room and wouldn't see him any more. At first I might have forgiven him if he had apologized—said he was sorry, but never a word. Now I never will forgive him."

I had to make a strenuous effort to conceal my agitation. The Rube had most carefully taken my fool advice in the matter of wooing a woman.

When I had got a hold upon myself, I turned to Nan white-hot with eloquence. Now I was talking not wholly for myself or the pennant, but for this boy and girl who were at odds in that strangest game of life—love.

What I said I never knew, but Nan lost her resentment, and then her scorn and indifference. Slowly she thawed and warmed to my reason, praise, whatever it was, and when I stopped she was again the radiant bewildering Nan of old.

"Take another message to Whit for me," she said, audaciously. "Tell him I adore ballplayers, especially pitchers. Tell him I'm going to the game today to choose the best one. If he loses the game—"

She left the sentence unfinished. In my state of mind I doubted not in the least that she meant to marry the pitcher who won the game, and so I told the Rube. He made one wild upheaval of his arms and shoulders, like an erupting volcano, which proved to me that he believed it, too.

When I got to the bench that afternoon I was tired. There was a big crowd to see the game; the weather was perfect; Milly sat up in the box and waved her scorecard at me; Raddy and Spears declared we had the game; the Rube stalked to and fro like an implacable Indian chief—but I was not happy in mind. Calamity breathed in the very air.

The game began. McCall beat out a bunt; Ashwell sacrificed and Stringer laced one of his beautiful triples against the fence. Then he scored on a high fly. Two runs! Worcester trotted out into the field. The Rube was white with determination; he had the speed of a bullet and perfect control of his jump ball and drop. But Providence hit and had the luck. Ashwell fumbled, Gregg threw wild. Providence tied the score.

The game progressed, growing more and more of a nightmare to me. It was not Worcester's day. The umpire could not see straight; the boys grumbled and fought among themselves; Spears roasted the umpire and was sent to the bench; Bogart tripped, hurting his sore ankle, and had to be taken out. Henderson's slow, easy ball baffled my players, and when he used speed they lined it straight at a Providence fielder.

In the sixth, after a desperate rally, we crowded the bases with only one out. Then Mullaney's hard rap to left, seemingly good for three bases, was pulled down by Stone with one hand. It was a wonderful catch and he doubled up a runner at second. Again in the seventh we had a chance to score, only to fail on another double play, this time by the infield.

When the Providence players were at bat their luck not only held good but trebled and quadrupled. The little texas-league hits dropped safely just out of reach of the infielders. My boys had an off day in fielding. What horror that of all days in a season this should be the one for them to make errors!

But they were game, and the Rube was the gamest of all. He did not seem to know what hard luck was, or discouragement, or poor support. He kept everlastingly hammering the ball at those lucky Providence hitters. What speed he had! The ball streaked in, and somebody would shut his eyes and make a safety. But the Rube pitched on, tireless, irresistibly, hopeful, not forgetting to call a word of cheer to his fielders.

It was one of those strange games that could not be bettered by any labor or daring or skill. I saw it was lost from the second inning, yet so deeply was I concerned, so tantalizingly did the plays reel themselves off, that I groveled there on the bench unable to abide by my baseball sense.

The ninth inning proved beyond a shadow of doubt how baseball fate, in common with other fates, loved to balance the chances, to lift up one, then the other, to lend a deceitful hope only to dash it away.

Providence had almost three times enough to win. The team let up in that inning or grew overconfident or careless, and before we knew what had happened some scratch hits, and bases on balls, and errors, gave us three runs and left two runners on bases. The disgusted bleachers came out of their gloom and began to whistle and thump. The Rube hit safely, sending another run over the plate. McCall worked his old trick, beating out a slow bunt.

Bases full, three runs to tie! With Ashwell up and one out, the noise in the bleachers mounted to a high-pitched, shrill, continuous sound. I got up and yelled with all my might and could not hear my voice. Ashwell was a dangerous man in a pinch. The game was not lost yet. A hit, anything to get Ash to first—and then Stringer!

Ash laughed at Henderson, taunted him, shook his bat at him and dared him to put one over. Henderson did not stand under fire. The ball he pitched had no steam. Ash cracked it—square on the line into the shortstop's hands. The bleachers ceased yelling.

Then Stringer strode grimly to the plate. It was a hundred to one, in that instance, that he would lose the ball. The bleachers let out one deafening roar, then hushed. I would rather have had Stringer at the bat than any other player in the world, and I thought of the Rube and Nan and Milly—and hope would not die.

Stringer swung mightily on the first pitch and struck the ball with a sharp, solid bing! It shot toward center, low, level, exceedingly swift, and like a dark streak went straight into the fielder's hands. A rod to right or left would have made it a home run. The crowd strangled a victorious yell. I came out of my trance, for the game was over and lost. It was the Rube's Waterloo.

I hurried him into the dressing room and kept close to him. He looked like a man who had lost the one thing worth while in his life. I turned a deaf ear to my players, to everybody, and hustled the Rube out and to the hotel. I wanted to be near him that night.

To my amaze we met Milly and Nan as we entered the lobby. Milly wore a sweet, sympathetic smile. Nan shone more radiant than ever. I simply stared. It was Milly who got us all through the corridor into the parlor. I heard Nan talking.

"Whit, you pitched a bad game but"—there was the old teasing, arch, coquettishness—"but you are the best pitcher!"

"Nan!"

"Yes!"

THE PASSAGE of the years does not dim the wacky, marvelous place of the 1960 World Series in the annals of baseball. Pittsburgh won the first game 6–4, the fourth game 3–2, the fifth game 5–2. The Yankees won the second game 16–3, the third game 10–0, the sixth game 12–0. Thus, going into the final seventh game at Pittsburgh, New York had scored 46 runs to 17 for the Pirates, yet the Series was even in games at three victories apiece!

The line score of that last game read:

New York	000 014 022–9
Pittsburgh	220 000 051–10

And how did the Pirates score the winning run? Ah. Read here. And see elsewhere in this book for a photograph commemorating the event.

1960: "Dad Would Have Loved It"

WILL GRIMSLEY

DAD WOULD have loved it—I only wish he could have been here today."

The tears in Bill Mazeroski's eyes were half from joy and half from sad memories as he sought to resurrect the drama of the ninth-inning home run which smashed the New York Yankees, 10 to 9, and brought Pittsburgh its first World Series victory in 35 years.

"Dad always wanted to play big-league baseball himself," Mazeroski reminisced. "He was considered a great prospect. Once he was ready to sign with the Cleveland Indians and then he had a foot cut off in a mine accident.

"From then on, all his hopes and ambitions were wrapped up in me, because I was an only son.

"Dad had to work hard in the mines, but whenever he could he always would try to catch me in a ball game or two. Then a year and a half ago he died of lung cancer."

Mazeroski, who hit the first and last home run of this wild Series, said he remembers tossing a baseball around and swinging a bat ever since he was big enough to walk.

"I was born in Wheeling, West Virginia," he said, "but the family moved to Adena, Ohio. It was a pretty hard life. But Dad was determined that I become a major-league ballplayer and he used to play with me by the hour."

As for the hit itself which won the seventh and climactic game of the Series—a prodigious blow over the 406-foot brick wall in left field—Mazeroski said he never once doubted that it would go all the way.

"I came to bat intending to go for the long ball," he said.

"The first pitch by Ralph Terry was a slider, a ball. The second was a high, fast one.

"I caught it on the fat of my bat. I knew immediately it was a well-hit ball. I watched it sail over the fence as I rounded the bases.

"I touched every base. As I rounded second, I saw people coming out to meet me, but I kept going.

"What did I think? I was too excited and too thrilled to think. It was the greatest moment of my life."

The Pittsburgh second baseman, who homered in the fourth inning of the opening game, said the Pirates never once despaired in the long, up-and-down game which at one stage saw the Yankees lead by 7–4.

"We kept telling each other we could do it. All year we've been a fighting, come-from-behind ball club. We always felt we could pull it out—even after the Yankees tied it up in the ninth—but I didn't think I'd be the guy to do it."

Mazeroski, 24, a slender six-footer, was a right-handed pitcher in high school but his coach converted him into an infielder to take advantage of his hitting.

JOHN GALLAGHER

Courtesy *The Saturday Evening Post*

"Now there's a good cut!"

CONSIDERING THE PROP being used here, would you call this a case of a manager using his head?

Strictly by Instinct

D. S. HALACY, JR.

SMILEY SHAKES his head and eases his toothpick over to a corner of his mouth.

"Where did you get him?" he asks, keeping his eyes glued on the kid as he takes the long windup.

I watch Hick Thomas burn that fast one over the plate and see Smiley cringe as the ball slams into the mitt.

'I'd hate to catch that boy!" he says, whistling softly.

"Try batting him once," I suggest. Glancing at the big sign swinging in the grandstand, I grin. Yeah, I can grin now, but once . . .

DON'T THROW CUSHIONS ON THE PLAYING FIELD, the letters spell out, and it always reminds me that a seat cushion is why Hick is pitching such hot ball for me now.

It was in February the new crop came dragging in, and it didn't look too promising. The bonehead who does our scouting must spend all his time at a pinball machine as the stuff we get is all off the bottom of the barrel.

We shook the straw out of them and got them herded together into the park, where I gave them the old hoo-raw about this and that. How maybe we aren't the top, but we're no soft touch, and they can cut the mustard or get back to shucking corn. Then I remembered something that bum of a scout may have forgotten to mention.

Namely, I don't want any left-handed hurlers, and if there are any, it's all a mistake and to pick up train fare in the office and leave me alone as of now.

We happened to be long on southpaws at the moment, having three, and only two right-handers—a condition I don't go for at all. The three lefties were a sorry bunch, one a near-sighted gink who kept squinting and asking for the sign again, and a barrel-shaped number who couldn't make first on a clean triple. Not that he'd ever even hit a single.

I figured the trio to win maybe one game among them. My right-handed twirlers were okay, and I was thanking my lucky stars they were both strong as mules. They would have to be, from the looks of things.

After my lecture, I look the rookies over and finally come to this scraggly beanpole of a guy, with a big Adam's apple and nothing but freckles.

"Let me guess," I say. "You must be Thomas, my new pitcher." With a shape like that he can't be anything else, unless it's maybe for selling popcorn in the upper bleachers.

"Yes, sir," he gulps, that Adam's apple going like a turkey gobbler. "That's me all right." His face gets a shade redder, and he fidgets from one foot to the other.

"Relax, kid," I tell him. "It's just a game. Let's see you throw a couple." A simple enough request, but a couple minutes later I wish heartily that I hadn't asked. I've seen all kinds of ball playing in my day, but this takes the fur-lined jockey cap.

The first pitch clears the backstop by about twenty feet, but I don't say a word. Charley Mantz, my old standby catcher, grumbles a little as he retrieves the ball and tosses it back to the kid. He points carefully to his mitt and the new pitcher tries again, sweat popping out all over him. I holler and shut my eyes as the horsehide sails at a guy bunting easy ones off to one side. The ball bounces off his head with a hollow click, and I rush over to see if anything is left of Pete Nichols, my one and only home-run hitter.

Pete is walking around in small circles with

his eyes crossed and his tongue out, and it looks bad for a while. Fortunately, he snaps out of it in a couple of minutes.

I corner this so-called pitcher and give him the works. But he gives me straight answers. He knows the game, he is definitely on the roster, and he says he is a pitcher. I scratch my head. I can't let him bean any more of the boys, and he is getting paid. Finally I put a bat in his hands and give him a ball to hit to some boys out in the field.

Well, I will say he kept them on their toes. Nobody had the faintest idea where the fungoes would land, least of all this Thomas specimen. He was even hitting fouls. What I mean is, he was keeping everybody busy.

You know how it is at the start of the season, you gotta keep moving around, checking on all of them; so I didn't pay too much attention to Hick Thomas the next few days. Just stuck him out there batting flies and what have you for the fielders. I did notice he was getting a little more control. Like being able to hit the ball ahead of him instead of behind.

One afternoon I catch him pitching very easy to a rookie catcher, like he is learning how to pitch. An idea hits me, and I go over to him.

"Son," I ask, "did you by chance fall off the train coming out here?" Amnesia maybe, you know. But he says he didn't, so I have to let it go at that.

By the time the season starts, I am ready to write my brother in Jersey and take him up on that furniture-store deal. If we win ten games the whole season, it will be because the all-girl nine is added to the league.

After a month the other teams get up a petition to drop us from the league, and it looks bad. Of course they can't do it, but comes the end of the season and look out, yours truly. Hick Thomas I have used exactly once as a runner for the pitcher with the bum eyes, who gets himself hit by a pitched ball and heads for the mound, instead of first base.

I still haven't been able to get in touch with my scout who signed Thomas, and as yet I haven't figured the freckled stringbean out. He still insists he is a pitcher, but he can't hit the backstop yet, much less the plate.

Well, it is all very boring, as you can guess. We are playing the Bobcats one Sunday, having lost the first game by a score I will not mention, though you could look it up in Ripley. Well on the way to repeating in the second fracas, I realize I am getting short of players. There is an epidemic of mumps in town, and about the only spare I have is Thomas, patiently warming the bench as usual.

In the fifth, Stinky Reiss, my shortstop, gets in the way of a pitched ball. It is a noble gesture, but gets him knocked sillier than a fifth-generation moron. I send in Hick Thomas, wondering if I'll have to get out there myself or just forfeit the game.

Hicks dies at third and takes up his spot between second and third. He is a third baseman like I am a cello player, but I am past caring by now. I settle back for laughs. They are not long coming.

The first batter lines one at Hick, and he fumbles it around like a hot potato and finally boots it into center field. The runner goes clear to third, and I can see Hick's face, red as a beacon as the fans boo him. The thing that amazes me is the local yokels still show up for these games.

The number-two man dribbles an easy grounder between second and third and Hick pounces on it this time and actually hangs on! The runner on third has beat it for home, thinking Hick will repeat the last play. Instead the lanky kid heaves the horsehide for the plate. Only it goes wide—way wide. I let out a yell as the ball heads for my big fat pitcher, who just stands there and takes it on the chin.

The ground shakes as he hits, and I look up to see Hick running toward the sleeping pitcher. That's when the cushions come sailing out of the stands. One of them catches Hick alongside the head and he goes ankles over elbows into the dirt.

When he picks himself up, I can see the murderous gleam in his eyes. But before I can make a move, he stoops and grabs up the cushion that hit him and sails it back into the stands. My mouth drops open. Wide-open. There is a blood-curdling scream as the cushion finds its mark and bedlam breaks loose. I join my fleeing ballplayers, and as I pass Hick I tell him to see me first thing in the morning at the park, if it is still there.

Next morning he shows up with a knot the size of a cue ball on his head, and a scared look in his eyes.

"Okay, kid," I say to him. "I'm giving you one more chance to pitch." I heave him a glove and he looks at it in surprise and gulps. Charley Mantz, the catcher, hollers a protest, but I make him squat down back of the plate. Then I fold my arms and watch Hick wind up.

He lets the ball go, and it streaks into Charley's mitt. He is so surprised he drops the ball.

My suspicions are correct. My ivory-skulled scout had signed me a left-hander in spite of everything!

I am about to give Hick his fare home, when Charley finds his voice and yells at the gawky pitcher, who is flexing that long, left arm.

"Do that again," Charley says, holding up the mitt. I watch and the ball burns in there so hard Charley whistles. And Charley has been up to the majors and back. Suddenly I get interested.

"That's a pretty nice fast one," I say to Hick. "How's your control?"

"Shucks," the skinny lefty says, "that ain't my fast ball!" He is blushing all over, but I figure he is kidding. I pick up a bat myself and step into the box.

"All right," I tell him, "let's see your fast one, then."

Hick grins and winds up all over the mound. I swing hard, but I never see the ball. Then I hear Charley pound his fists into the mitt.

"How 'bout that!" Charley says, and I turn around. The ball is in his mitt. I don't know how it got there, but I do know I have me a pitcher.

"And that's the whole story," I tell Smiley as we watch Hick retire the third batter. He has pitched ten balls and looks a little ashamed as it seldom takes him over nine.

"Yeah," Smiley says, pulling out the toothpick. "But how did you know the kid was a southpaw? That's what gets me."

I look at Smiley in disgust. "You miss the whole point," I tell him. "All the time he'd been pitching right-handed. But when he picked up that cushion, mad as he was, he forgot his act. Forgot I didn't want no southpaws, and let fly with his left! Strictly by instinct, see?"

THIS WAS WRITTEN shortly following the celebrated 1966 trade that sent Orlando Cepeda from the Giants to the Cardinals. The following year, in leading the league in runs batted in and pacing the world-champion St. Louis team, Cepeda became the first unanimous choice for Most Valuable Player in National League history.

Orlando Cepeda

ARNOLD HANO

LAST SEASON in Houston, after San Francisco had won a ball game, the Giants climbed into the bus that would shortly take them to their hotel. A fan leaped aboard, to ask for autographs.

Orlando Cepeda said, "Sir, this bus is for players only."

The fan eyed Cepeda. "I knew it," he snarled. "They said you're a hothead and a so-and-so. They're right. You are."

The fan got off and hurled abuse from the safety of the sidewalk, or until Cepeda shut the window.

"The fans," says Orlando Cepeda today, explaining the moral of the little incident, "believe what they read. They read, 'Cepeda has a hot head. He is a so-and-so. He has no guts. He does not hustle. His knee doesn't hurt; he is just faking.' They hear all this and they believe it."

And then Cepeda adds, "Why? Why do people say these things about me? Why do they believe these things? Why? Why? Why?"

Orlando Cepeda limped into the 1966 baseball season carrying a bag of questions on his back. He is a man tormented by what has happened to him, is happening to him. He is tormented because he doesn't know why.

He has become a man who plays under the gun, a man at bay. He says it differently. "I am always against the wall," he says. He does not mean in the outfield, of course. He means it metaphorically. He has become a target. When Cepeda broke in with the Giants in 1959, a big rawboned, happy-go-lucky, 20-year-old kid, the fans loved him. He could do no wrong. He could hit, he could field, he could run. He played the game with great zest. Just before the season started, in a training game, manager Bill Rigney said, "All right, the regulars take the field." Cepeda hung back. Rigney said, "C'mon, Orlando, that means you." Cepeda says, "It made me feel great. I was a regular!"

He hit a home run his first day in the majors. He played with such zest you could almost smell it. Sometimes he overplayed and in his eagerness he'd overslide a base or two. It made everybody love him that much more. When the rookie season was over, Giant fans, in a San Francisco newspaper poll, selected him solidly over Willie Mays as the most valuable Giant. He hit .312 with 25 home runs and 96 RBIs; he led the league in two-base hits with 38. The world was his.

The years have slid by. The world has turned around. Now he hears more than an occasional boo. More and more the image of the zestful 20-year-old rookie has faded. In its place is a very different image. It is a very neat image. It fits our prejudices, both national and racial. He is a Latin; therefore he is temperamental, explosive, lazy. He is Negro; therefore he is sullen, he has no guts, he is not mentally alert. After the ugly Marichal-Roseboro incident of last August 22, Los Angeles manager Walt Alston was quoted in the press as saying, "Cepeda irritates me even more than the other guy. Orlando is a muscle man, a big tough guy. And what does he do when trouble starts? He comes out with a bat."

Alston—if he said it—was not the only one. John Kennedy, Dodger utilityman, was quoted as saying it was the third time Cepeda had grabbed a bat when trouble started on the diamond. To which Cepeda snorted a few days later, "I guess when you hit .198 you got to say something." But Cepeda could not answer them all. The Associated Press put it on the wires, *Newsweek* ran it; so did many newspapers. Orlando Cepeda had brandished a bat during the melee. You could write the rest yourself. Only a coward goes for a bat in a brawl.

Only one thing was wrong with the story. It happens not to be true. Cepeda had no bat that day.

Nor has Cepeda ever gone for a bat in a major-league skirmish.

"How does Kennedy know it was the 'third' time?" Orlando asked rhetorically last summer when he talked about the incident. "Was he there in 1958?"

In 1958, in Forbes Field, pitcher Ruben Gomez, Cepeda's friend, teammate and fellow Puerto Rican, began parting the hair of Pittsburgh batters. Danny Murtaugh finally led a charge of Pirates at Gomez. Cepeda came bounding out of the Giant dugout. Willie Mays tackled him, and that was that. But the story had it (and I, among others, have repeated it in print): Cepeda had taken a bat with him, and he was out to get Murtaugh. Even this bothers Cepeda, and it bothers him today, eight years later. "How did they know I was out to get Murtaugh? Did they read my mind? Maybe I was out to get the bat boy." The main point is: Cepeda had no bat that day either.

Why, then, didn't he deny the story?

"Nobody asked me."

Until 1965, nobody had asked the man most involved.

Why ask? He's neatly tagged. We've got him boxed. The man with the hot head, the man who grabs a bat in tight spots, the man who irritates us polite white men who respect the rules of the game and demand others respect them too, but when they do, we look for rules they haven't broken and we clobber them with those.

There is a convention in American baseball that says a man must show his anguish if he loses. It proves he cares. Kick a few lockers, down a quick beer or three, singe the air with curses. It makes for a great competitor. Latin ballplayers, by and large, do not respect the convention. They play; they lose; it is over. They whistle in the clubhouse; they dress quickly and go to the Jazz Workshop on North Beach, and they enjoy their evenings. Tomorrow is another day, another game.

It annoyed Alvin Dark no end. After a loss, he couldn't stand Cepeda and the Alous and Marichal and the rest jabbering excitedly in a language Dark did not understand, instead of grieving in simmering black silence. One day he said to Cepeda, "Speak English in the clubhouse." Cepeda refused. Dark writhed. But then Alvin Dark always wanted his players to be made in his own image. It drove Dark to suggest things he should have kept to himself; it drove him, in fact, from San Francisco to Kansas City, which is one of the longest drives in the world.

It even brought out the funnyman in Orlando Cepeda. "Now Alvin is in Kansas City marking his pluses and minuses on a piece of paper. He will need lots of paper, to make all those minuses." It is a reference to Dark's exotic way of grading his ballplayers. On Dark's Giants, Willie Mays was a big plus, but Orlando Cepeda, after hitting 35 home runs in 1962, driving in 114 runs, and batting .306, was a definite minus, so big a minus the Giants tried to cut his salary. But Orlando Cepeda does not hold grudges. He says, now, "I hate to complain. I'm lucky to be alive. I don't hate anyone. Even Alvin Dark. From my heart, I say hello to Alvin Dark."

He says he hates to complain, but he is honest enough to complain. Three days before the 1966 season opened, he said in all seriousness, "I have to learn to have two faces." Orlando Cepeda, like many Latin players, thinks in one-faced ways. Things are going great, or they are going terrible, but they seldom are going great-and-terrible. He knows black or white, but not gray. He has not adjusted to the so-so world, where you take the good with a grain of salt, because you know you'll go 0-for-5 the next day.

"How do they know I am not sad when we lose?" he asks. "Just because I do not put on the sad face, how do they know what is in my heart?"

Well, they don't know, and Orlando Cepeda knows they don't know, so he says he must wear two faces, one that is true to himself, and the other that adjusts to the outside world. (He won't be able to, of course, because he is just not that way. But at least he has started to take the notion seriously.)

So this is Orlando Cepeda, who carried a bum knee into 1966 and a worse reputation.

You read to him what a ghost-writer for Stan Musial said recently of Cepeda: "Defensively, either at first base or in the outfield, he hasn't had nearly as much interest as he has had with a bat in his hands."

And Cepeda howls, "Why does he say that? It kills me. Why? Why? I think I'm a good first baseman. If I was a good first baseman when I came up, why wouldn't I be better now, when I know so much more?" Then he answers his own question. "They say I am bad, so they put a tag on me, and nobody questions it."

It kills him.

But nothing really touches Cepeda so much as the charge that he—and other Latins—are gutless. This is a direct arrow into his manhood, his courage, and he is more than baffled by the accusation. He is sickened by it.

"We have enough guts just to come here," he says, his lips thinned. "We have enough guts to face the people here."

Which is perhaps the proper place to begin this story, now that I have belabored you with my introduction.

Orlando Cepeda came to the United States from Puerto Rico in March of 1955. He was a 17-year-old high-school senior at the time. Had he stayed he would have graduated in May. But he had a chance to play big-league ball, and he wanted to try it. He came to the States without a contract. All the Giants were risking was a round-trip fare between Puerto Rico and Melbourne, Florida, where the then New York Giants trained their minor-league prospects. Cepeda looked good enough to be signed to a contract and was assigned to Salem, Virginia, at $225 a month.

Cepeda spoke no English. No Salem player spoke Spanish. Try that one for size. It's a great life, if you're a Trappist monk. In recent years Cepeda has been told how lucky he was and is. "If I was back in Puerto Rico, they keep telling me, I'd be cutting cane. They don't even know Puerto Ricans are American citizens. They think of us as some kind of animal. People are surprised when they learn I have a brother who is an accountant. Cutting cane, that is all they think we are good for."

The month he spent in Salem wasn't even as good as cutting cane. The first day the players got on a bus to drive through the South from Melbourne to Virginia, they stopped at a restaurant. Everybody got out, except Cepeda. "I was told to stay on the bus. I had to eat on the bus. I wasn't allowed in a restaurant. I wasn't ready for that. Nobody had told me. You don't think that takes guts, to adjust to that?"

Obviously he didn't quite adjust. He hit poorly and, playing third base, fielded worse. His manager could not get through to him, what with the language barrier and the Giants' idiocy in not bringing along a second player who spoke Spanish and English both. In a doubleheader one day, while Cepeda struck out six times and made a costly error at third, his manager took to muttering, "Sonofabitch," whenever Cepeda showed himself.

It meant nothing to Cepeda, but a month later, when the Giants finally did send a Cuban player, George Gonzalez, to Salem, Cepeda asked Gonzalez what this word was he was being called. Gonzalez told him.

To this day, it astonishes Cepeda. "In this country, everybody says we are hot-tempered and fight so much. Well, here, everybody fights with his mouth. They say hateful things. In the Latin countries, if a man insults your mother, he would get killed."

Cepeda sat down and painfully wrote a letter to the Giant front office. "I cannot play for my manager. He has insulted my mother." The Giants looked at his stats—.247 average, with one home run in 26 games—and agreed he could use a change of scenery.

So they sent him up north to Kokomo, and all Cepeda did was lead the league with .393. He led the Northern League, at St. Cloud, the next year, under Charley Fox, in batting, home runs, runs batted in and games played, and after an equally fine year at Minneapolis in the American Association in 1957, the Giants called him up and one day Bill Rigney said he was a regular.

But even as a major leaguer there have been embarrassments. In 1959 he and Felipe Alou went to a downtown Pittsburgh restaurant after a game, and the headwaiter looked at the two strapping handsome young men, dressed conservatively and expensively, and refused to believe what he saw.

"We've got no jobs open," he said.

They explained they had a job. What they wanted was a meal.

"Sorry," the headwaiter said. "We don't serve you here."

In 1962, in Houston, on the day of a ball game, Orlando Cepeda tried to take in an afternoon movie. They refused to let him in. (Ironically, the movie was *West Side Story*, with its feud between Puerto Ricans and Anglos.)

These things take their toll. "When I am in

Houston," Orlando Cepeda says—in 1966—"I do not go anywhere."

What does he do?

"I sit in my hotel room and play records. Music does not let me down."

Cepeda insists if you are to judge his courage, you judge it with these incidents in mind. But he says, "It does no good to explain. They put blanks on their faces."

He uses his knee as an arguing point. It is his right knee, and in December of 1964 Cepeda underwent surgery in a New York hospital.

The surgeon stared at the knee and then back at Cepeda when the big ballplayer checked in.

"How the devil," the doctor asked, "did you play with that thing for two years?" The cartilage had been chewed to pulp, the bone rested on bone, not unlike the condition in Mickey Mantle's legs. A nerve had been pinched in the process, and the whole thing was as much fun as chewing ground glass.

He played with it—Cepeda explains today—because nobody believed it was hurting him. "If I said it hurt, they thought I was faking. I could hardly get my uniform on and off, it hurt so much, it was so swollen. They would see how swollen it was. They put on a blank face."

So Cepeda played with the deteriorating knee in 1963 and 1964—hitting .316 and .304—wrapping the knee before each game. Finally he couldn't stand it any longer and he dragged the knee to a hospital.

Recuperation has been slow. At Mayo Clinic one day last year doctors were so concerned they warned Cepeda his knee might never be better, and that his career might be over. He was shocked for a few minutes; then he decided it wasn't so. The next day the doctors decided they'd been wrong and his knee was getting better. But it's been getting better very slowly.

Cepeda went on the disabled list on May 7, 1965, and did not come off until August 18, 1965, which did the Giants no good at all. Cepeda appeared in just 33 games last season, nearly all of them pinch-hitting turns, batting 34 times, and hitting one home run, which won a game in the final days of the season when the Dodgers and Giants were locked in their spectacular stretch war. When you realize the Giants lost by two games, without Cepeda's usual 30 home runs, you can see what the knee cost the club.

The year 1965 was a ghastly one. "Herman Franks would ask me, 'Does it hurt?' I was afraid to say it hurt. Yet I couldn't run. You could see it swell after a workout, and they'd ask me if it hurt. They said I was faking. Last year I should not even have gone to the ball park. But then they say, 'He doesn't care. He doesn't go to the ball park.' They don't know how hard it is for me to come to the park and sit on the bench. I am no use sitting on the bench."

Not playing, Cepeda ballooned to 230 pounds, which did his knee no good whatsoever, carrying 20 pounds of blubber. So in the winter of 1965–66, he began a serious regimen to get both his knee and the rest of him back into top shape. He worked out at Santurce, back in Puerto Rico, where he and his wife—and now their baby son, who checked in at ten-plus pounds—live in the off season. He ran on the beach or in a gym. During the winter league, Cepeda ran in the ball park and threw a ball back and forth. He lifted weights with his sore right leg until he could hoist a hundred pounds up to 75 times just by straightening his right knee. In his positive-thinking way, he says, "It is not that the right knee is so weak, but that the left knee got so much stronger. Now I have to make my right knee as strong as my left."

He arrived in Arizona in early 1966 in superb physical condition, except for the question-mark knee. But another problem plagued him. Once he had been the Giant first baseman, and, some thought, one of the better in the league. In his freshman year, he led the league in assists. But with Willie McCovey coming up in 1959 and unable to play any other position, Cepeda shifted to third base, for two days of butchery, and then to the outfield. This spring he said to Herman Franks, "Will I get a chance to play first base?"

To Cepeda's dismay (he worshiped Franks up until that moment, and still thinks highly of him, but it is no longer worship), Franks said, "No."

"How about when I am strong and confident?" Cepeda pursued.

"No," Franks said flatly.

"At first I was sore," Cepeda says today. "But then I thought about it. The next day it was finished. I decided I would be the best left fielder there is. Now I do not want to play first base."

He says he does not resent Willie McCovey. "Willie McCovey is one of my best friends in the United States. In the world. It is not his fault. I do not have any resentment for him. I am happy for him. It is his living. He is doing a helluva job. I just want to play baseball and show everybody I can play."

But it has been a struggle to show them. In spring training Cepeda limped badly at first. To make matters more perplexing to those who do not understand such injuries, there would be moments he seemed to run as well as ever, going from first to third on a single, racing in the outfield for a long drive. In a game against the Dodgers, near the end of the exhibition grind, Cepeda limped going down to first on a routine ground ball. Later, with Lou Johnson on first and John Roseboro at bat, and Cepeda playing deep in left center, Roseboro sliced a dinky fly ball down the left-field line. Cepeda charged the ball—running very well—made a lunging catch, and then fired a strike to first base that nearly nipped a stunned Lou Johnson, retreating to first. It was a fine play, but more important it showed how well Cepeda could run. Why, then, did he limp so much?

"It is a habit," he says. "When I have to go hard, I forget about it and I go all out, without a limp. But when I think about it, I limp. It is getting less all the time. But it is a habit, and I will have to shake it."

The Giants were not sure he could. Cepeda's salary had been cut after 1965. "It was not a big cut," he says, "not as much as it could have been. Chub Feeney promised to give me my money back if I played 150 games this year."

So Cepeda, with his single-faced confidence, readied himself for 150 or more games. He said, on April 9, as the Giants prepared to play California's Angels in a two-game set that would open Anaheim Stadium, "I feel I can play every game. It will be easy to play 150 games."

But he sat on the bench in Anaheim, as Len Gabrielson played left field, and the idea of 150 games began to fade once the season started. Gabrielson was the Giant starting left fielder. In the first five games, Cepeda got to bat just once—and on that occasion he was hit by a pitched ball. In the sixth game, Cepeda started against right-handed Barry Latman, but he went 0-for-3. The next day he started at Wrigley Field and hit his first 1966 home run.

As Willie McCovey went into a slump, Franks relented and did play Cepeda a bit at first base. On Saturday night, May 7, the Giants were playing the St. Louis Cardinals. In the third inning, the Giants scored 13 runs. The highlight was a bases-loaded home run by Cepeda.

The Cardinals must have been impressed. The next afternoon, Cepeda again played first base and got two more hits. But the Giants were impressed, too—by Willie McCovey. He pinch-hit a three-run homer.

That did it. Following the game Cepeda and Cardinal pitcher Ray Sadecki exchanged uniforms. Orlando Cepeda would now play first base regular for the Cardinals. "Orlando is a great hitter," Franks said, "but we had a duplication of ability with McCovey, also a first baseman, and I know Cepeda was a little unhappy not playing every day."

Cepeda may have been a little unhappy leaving the team he had been with all his major-league life, but he is a man with his own resources.

Music certainly is one of them. No matter where he is, he has his music. In his hotel room, you'll talk to him while Jimmy Smith and his funky organ roll through the room, or the Ramsey Lewis trio, or Miles Davis. When a game is over, and he is on the road, he searches out a jazz spot and he relaxes. When he is at home, Orlando turns on the player. He plays it until one or 1:30 in the morning, and then he goes to sleep, and when he awakens, around 11, he automatically flips on the player.

He has other resources. His mother, back in Puerto Rico, is a source of strength. Cepeda bought his mother a home early in his big-league career, and now regularly sends her $350 a month. Cepeda's wife Annie, and their baby son Orlando Xavier, are other sustaining forces. He says Annie is "a shy girl, very soft." He says nobody really knows him, except his mother and his wife. But he also says, "Nobody really knows anybody else."

He says he takes the game "cool" now, mainly because his mother keeps reminding him how "hard" his father took the game. Cepeda's father died, a young man, on April 27, 1955. The next day Orlando played his first professional game, for Salem. "My father, when his team lost, wanted to fight everybody. He took it all too hard. Everything he took hard. He argued all the way to the hospital that he wasn't sick. Then he fell into a coma and was dead in a week. He had a malarial infection of the liver. My mother put his picture in front of me. My mother said, 'Look at your father. Look what happened to him.' So I take it easy."

Or at least he says he does, or at least he tries to take it easy. He has his records in his room, but right next to his bed is a bottle of sleeping pills. He says he never has felt discouraged in his life, and he does not feel discouraged now; he says his mental attitude "is great," but he has his problems and they crop out of nearly every sentence. He says he loves jazz so much "because it is like life. The more you listen to it, the more you understand and appreciate it." But in the next breath: "Life is hard. When you have everything, a good job, money, fame, you think it is going to be easy. But it is not. It is harder."

And he tells of a middle-aged fan who follows the Giants around, one of those ball fans nearly every team seems to attract, a man with nothing better to do, apparently, than to follow a wish-fulfilling dream, a man who attaches himself to athletes to enhance his own unheroic life.

"One day this man told me he knew my father. He is an unshaven man, with shabby clothes. He and I got to talking. I found I liked him. The players look at me. 'You talk to that bum?' they say. I give him a ride to the game or to his hotel. I give him money once in a while. It does not matter what he looks like. It is what is inside that counts. If a man needs help badly, nobody gives. If a man is a millionaire, everybody loves him, and will give him anything. It is not fair."

What is fair is important to Orlando Cepeda. He wants people to treat him as he is, not as they think he is. But he does not know how to go about showing them how he is. He said, just before the 1966 season started, "I wish one day Gaylord Perry or Tom Haller would invite me over to their place one evening, as friends."

But, then, he never invited Gaylord Perry or Tom Haller to his house one evening, as friends. He says, "I don't try to please people. You never will please yourself if you try to please others." But maybe it will be different in St. Louis, maybe it will be truly different for Orlando Cepeda. Maybe the green grass and chalked lines that became a battleground for Cepeda will once more become a playing field. Maybe now he can walk away from that wall.

QUICK, NOW, what was the count when Bobby Thomson hit the home run, and how many were out? Who made the final out in Don Larsen's perfect game, and how? Perhaps the memory blurs, and—great though those moments were—they remain great on account of a single individual.

By contrast, take this game nearly half a century ago. A note in the first *Fireside Book of Baseball* says this may have been the greatest game of all time, and my research since then goes only to confirm this even more. For sustained excitement over twelve innings' time, and for cast of characters—and for the clarity with which its details are still remembered today—I think this has got to be it.

1924: Washington Senators 4, New York Giants 3

JAMES R. HARRISON

IN THE GAME of all games the Senators won. In twelve innings of baseball that tried men's souls and tortured their nerves, the Senators won. They beat the Giants before the President today, 4 to 3, and the championship came to the capital.

Fate and chance and the breaks of the game brought victory in the twelfth. Hank Gowdy, the New York catcher, tripped over his mask and dropped a foul fly. Travis Jackson fumbled an easy roller. After the muff Ruel hit a two-bagger, and after the fumble Earl McNeely hit another. As the ball leaped over Lindstrom's head and rolled into left field, the little Napoleon met his Waterloo.

After all, the baseball drama had a happy ending. The people's team won. Youth and courage triumphed over the mechanical power of a great baseball machine that was slowly grinding out another victory. In the last act Walter Johnson was not a tired old man. As the curtain went down before 35,000 people he was the great Kansas giant again, the Coffeyville Cyclone who breezed a ball so fast that other men couldn't see it.

In the greatest game of championship baseball ever played in this country history repeated itself. If Walter Johnson went back to 1912, so did John J. McGraw. Tonight he must be thinking of that other Series, when in the tenth inning a fielder dropped a fly and another failed to catch a foul, and the Red Sox went on to win. It was McGraw's turn in the twelfth inning today, but for the second time in twelve years the fortunes of the game went against him.

Here was a game that hung on the roll of a ball or the twist of a wrist. In years to come they will call Gowdy's failure the $50,000 muff and Jackson's misplay the $50,000 fumble. But it was not Gowdy nor Jackson who decided the game. It was not McNeely nor Ruel, nor Harris who won it. Not the Senators but the luck of the play beat the Giants.

Washington, a city gone mad tonight, will talk of this game for years to come. They will tell you of that great twelfth inning when Muddy Ruel doubled and McNeely doubled and the winning run came over. They will narrate the great story of Bucky Harris' home run in the fourth which gave the Senators a one-run lead. They will mention with a glow the single of Bucky Harris that tied the score in the eighth. Also they will tell you of Walter Johnson, who came to the mound in the ninth and held the Giants at bay for four thrilling innings.

They will tell you how Johnson, after waiting eighteen years for a World Series and failing twice, came through in the third great test. They will boast of Ruel and Mogridge and McNeely and Sam Rice, and nobody will overlook Roger Peckinpaugh, who was on the sidelines during the bitter battle.

But tonight Washington is too full for utterance. Thousands are tramping the streets in the wildest celebration ever seen in baseball. From the White House to the Capitol the clamor rises. The streets are full of jostling, joy-crazed citizens, blowing horns, manipulating rattlers, firing pistols and making a din that can be heard for miles. On the banks of the Potomac there is bedlam and madness tonight.

All the pent-up enthusiasm of a baseball-crazy city is being loosened. With the tension off, the world serene and peaceful again, all the capital is giving itself over to a delirium of thankfulness.

The President has issued a statement on behalf of a grateful nation, and there is some prospect that the House and Senate will go into special session and pass a resolution naming Walter Johnson and Bucky Harris as the great heroes of the hour.

Scenes indescribable took place at the park after Muddy Ruel dented the plate with his spikes and left a mark that posterity will cherish reverently. As the game ended the crowd poured like a great flood on the field. From bleachers and grandstand thousands streamed to the diamond. Caught in a vortex of the whirlpool, the Washington players had to be rescued by the police. McNeely, whose hit had won the game, was surrounded before he was six feet away from first base and hoisted to the shoulders of the fans. He was thumped and pummeled and hugged and reached the bench a very crushed young man.

On the grass near the bleachers fans turned handsprings for joy. Other staid citizens danced and skipped around the field, throwing their hats into the air, caring not where they fell. In front of the Washington dugout fully 5,000 persons pushed and elbowed. The air was full of flying cushions and torn programs. Pieces of newspapers floated down like snow from the upper tier. Hats and canes and overcoats departed abruptly from their owners as the massed thousands stood and cheered in a paroxysm of ecstasy.

You may talk of your college celebrations, but there has been none to compare with this demonstration. New Haven, after a Yale football triumph, was a deserted village compared to Washington. Cambridge and Princeton never saw the riotous enthusiasm that the capital is seeing tonight.

The story of this game will be told and retold for days and weeks and years. In the main it is the story of two evenly matched teams staking on the fortunes of one contest the highest honors in baseball. Into three hours of the best baseball ever played were compressed the hopes and aims of a whole season. Six months of preparation and hard play hung in the balance in a single afternoon. A misplay here, an error there and a championship would be decided.

It was a game that either team might have won. All the ifs and buts of this contest, if piled end on end, would make a mass higher than the Washington Monument. The Giants may mourn because of the errors of Gowdy and Jackson, but on the other hand two Washington mistakes in the sixth sent the Giants into a two-run lead that looked impregnable.

In the end it was the breaks of the game that told. Twice a ball rolled toward Lindstrom, struck hard ground and bounced freakishly over the third baseman's head. On the last occasion the sun, streaming through the rear of the stand, struck Lindstrom's eyes and blinded him just as he was set for McNeely's ground drive. If either ball down the third-base line had bounded truly, if the sun had been higher or lower, the Giants would have won.

Harris' home run in the fourth, which scored the first run of the game, was also a vagary of fate. When the coin was tossed to determine where the deciding game would be played, Clark Griffith called the toss and won. If the game had been played at the Polo Grounds, Harris' drive would have been caught. On the flip of a coin, as much as on anything else, the 1924 championship was decided. That was the kind of series it was.

In the sixth the Giants, playing with the precision of a machine, scored three runs and seemed to have the game won. Mogridge, then pitching for Washington, gave Young a base on balls and got into a hole with George Kelly. At the count of 3 and 1 Young was away for second and Kelly swung. The ball went to center for a single and Young raced to third.

At this point McGraw sent Irish Meusel to hit for Bill Terry because a left-hander was in the box, but Harris could be just as strategical himself. He met the move by withdrawing Mogridge and calling Fred Marberry from the bullpen. Meusel immediately drove a long fly to

Rice, and Young scored after the catch with the tying run.

But the Senators weren't out of the woods yet. Wilson bounded a single over the pitcher's head to center, and Kelly, by daring base running, made third. Here were runners on first and third, with only one out, yet the Giants wouldn't have scored another run but for the same thing that beat them later—the breaks of the game. For when Jackson rolled an easy grounder to Judge, the first baseman fumbled. Even worse than that, when he got the ball he stood with it in his hand while Kelly sprinted to the plate and Jackson ran past Judge to first.

There was one unearned run, and another developed when Gowdy cracked a grounder to Bluege. An easy double play was in sight, but Bluege let the ball roll through him to short left, and Wilson hurried in from second.

The next act in the great drama took place in the eighth. Virgil Barnes, pitching with marvelous skill and superb confidence, had allowed only three hits up to that time.

When Bluege, the first batter in the eighth, lifted a foul which Gowdy caught, the crowd groaned in deep misery. Nemo Liebold, short and squatty, appeared at the plate to bat for Taylor, and it was Liebold who started Washington to a tie score. He caught one of Barnes's fast ones squarely on the end of his bat and slapped a two-bagger which grazed third base as it passed.

Even now there wasn't much hope in the situation. Ruel was at bat, and Muddy hadn't made a hit in the series. But the slim little catcher could deliver this time. He punched a swift grounder toward right, and Kelly was lucky to break it down. On the hit Liebold went to third, and Tate was sent to the front to bat for Marberry.

Barnes's control deserted him in this crisis and he walked Tate, filling the bases. But when McNeely lined squarely into Meusel's hands, the Giants breathed easier. There were two out, and Harris, who was at bat, had made two hits already. Still the New York camp was somewhat worried. Gowdy stopped the game while he ran over to the bench and talked with McGraw. Whatever the Little Napoleon said might have been wise, but it couldn't cope with the workings of fate. Harris didn't hit the ball hard, but just as his grounder hit in front of Lindstrom the pellet took a sudden leap, cleared the fielder's head by a foot and rolled on out to left field.

Miller and Ruel, of course, scored easily, and the winning run was on second base with Rice up. In this critical situation McGraw again turned to Nehf, the little southpaw, who yesterday had been beaten by the Senators. Rice sent a grounder spinning to Kelly and was out easily at first.

Walter Johnson walked to the mound as the ninth inning started, and from that moment on the Giants were a beaten team. Hit him they did on Wednesday, and hit him they did in four innings today. But here was a different Johnson, a Johnson something like the great pitcher who this season had contributed twenty-three victories to Washington's pennant effort. Here was a Johnson cooler and fitter than he had been at any time in the series, with a curve ball better controlled and a fast ball that twice struck out Kelly when a hit would have spelled victory.

After all, there was still something in Johnson's good right arm. His baseball epitaph was not written after Wednesday's game. He had failed twice, but the glorious moment came when he tried and won in the supreme crisis of the Series.

True, he wasn't the Johnson of old. The Giants got a man on base in every inning against him. Walter probably would have given ten years of his life to have turned the clock back ten years. The Johnson of 1913, the Kansas Cyclone and the Speed King, would have mowed the batters down as fast as they came up. But with what he had in this hour and day, 37 years old and a veteran of eighteen years' service, Johnson performed one of the heroic achievements of his career.

Frisch tripled to deep center in the ninth, a mighty blow, and again it looked as if the Giants would win. However, Johnson, calling on strategy, passed Young intentionally, fanned Kelly on three pitched balls and made Meusel go out on a grounder to Miller.

The Washington half of the same inning throbbed with action. It was a dark and somber crisis for the Giants. Following Frisch's pretty falling stop on Goslin's grounder, Judge singled to center. Bluege hit to Kelly, who threw too quickly to second, which was uncovered because of Jackson's slowness in covering. When he got the fling in his glove Jackson dropped it, and the pill rolled several feet behind him, with Judge scurrying to third and Bluege safe at first.

A long fly meant the game, and so McGraw again switched pitchers, yanking Nehf out and ordering Hugh McQuillan to the little hill. The crowd was in a frenzied uproar now. Nerves were stretched to the breaking point. But the

Giants were still cool, an emotionless baseball machine, and they stopped the rally as quickly as it had started. Jackson pounced on Miller's sharp grounder, threw to Frisch, and the latter flung to Kelly for a double play.

What a game this was!

Into the tenth inning it went, with audience and actors strained to the point of agony. The crowd was as silent as death itself when Johnson walked Wilson, the first batter to face him, but the old master was not to be rushed off his feet. He fanned Jackson, then made a beautiful stop of Gowdy's grounder for a double play at second and first.

The Senators were easy for McQuillan in the tenth. At the start of the eleventh Heinie Groh batted for McQuillan and singled to right. Southworth ran for the crippled third sacker and raced to second on Lindstrom's sacrificial bunt. Again the winning run was on second, but Frisch fanned, again Walter walked Young purposely, and again Kelly struck out.

In the eleventh it was Bentley pitching for New York. When two were out, Goslin doubled to right center and Judge walked, yet the Senators could not break through.

And then came the twelfth, the greatest inning played in baseball since 1912. For the Giants Meusel opened by hitting the first ball to right for a base, but Wilson fanned, Jackson forced Meusel, and Gowdy flied softly to left.

Frisch was in front of Miller's grounder as the Washington half began. Ruel raised a high fly not ten feet from the plate. Gowdy hardly had to move from his tracks, but he misjudged badly. The Giant catcher stepped this way and that, circling around. At the last minute he made a furious lunge to his right but stumbled over his mask, nearly fell to one knee and dropped the ball.

Fate was working in some mysterious way against the Giants. Given another chance, Ruel slammed a vicious drive inside third for two bases and the crowd roared gleefully. When Johnson grounded to Jackson, the youthful shortstop fumbled and lost his man, Ruel staying at second.

The stage was set now for the big climax. The round, ashen bat of Earl McNeely supplied it. Down the third-base line, straight for Lindstrom, scurried the ball, bouncing viciously. As Lindstrom crouched the sun blinded him. He threw out his hands but the ball hopped like a thing possessed, shot up and over his head and never stopped.

Meusel came up cleanly with the ball but a throw to the plate would have been useless. There was no catching Ruel, who ran as he had never run before in his life. While Meusel walked in with the ball, Ruel crossed the plate.

After all Mr. McNeely was worth the $50,000 they paid for him. In future years they can speak of this as the $50,000 hit, for $50,000 was the difference between the winners' and losers' share. In glory and distinction there is no difference. The better team didn't win, nor did the better team lose. In this Series there was no better team.

So ended the greatest game of ball ever played—not only the greatest but the most critical. It was a game fit to set before a President. Calvin Coolidge, on October 10, 1924, saw the best and finest that the national game can produce.

For the second time in twelve years McGraw has had a world title snatched from him because of errors. When Snodgrass muffed a fly in Boston in 1912 and Merkle and Meyers let a foul drop between them, McGraw thought that his cup was full. But today it ran over.

This has been the most remarkable Series ever played. Before the first ball was thrown there was the sensational episode of the suspension of two New York players. For the first time a pennant winner went into a World Series under the charge that they were tainted from top to bottom.

Ban Johnson, president of the American League, refused to attend because of the scandal. There was a demand that the Series be called off, which would have been the unwisest possible move. For the Series, with its ultimate result, the quality of the playing and the appearance of the President at three games, has been a tremendous benefit to baseball. The game fight and remarkable playing McGraw's men have turned many people back to them. Even Washington, frenzied and wild, was willing to admit tonight that a team like the Giants doesn't have to buy pennants.

Still, the country will rejoice in New York's defeat. There never will be a more popular victory than this. Bucky Harris and Walter Johnson and their mates had caught the public imagination as no team before had caught it. The Senators represented the sentiment and romance in baseball, and millions of people will think it a pretty good world after all when Washington's right can prevail over New York's might.

Washington thinks so, anyhow. The whistles are still blowing and the horns blowing and the red fire burning. The bells are ringing in the new champions and ringing out the old.

MR. HAVEMANN, in the following article, puts his finger on the most-repeated fan complaint of the postwar era. The title says it all.

So Throw the Ball!

ERNEST HAVEMANN

ONE DAY when my wife turned on our television set to a Yankee-White Sox game, I noticed something that intrigued me. I happened to have the *The New York Times* on my lap, and when the catcher threw the ball back to Jim Brosnan, the Sox pitcher, I found that I could safely look away from the television screen, read a couple of paragraphs in the *Times* and still get my eyes back in time for the pitch.

Since then I have been timing baseball games with a stopwatch, and I can only conclude that the modern pitcher *hates* to pitch. He cannot bear the thought of throwing the ball to the plate. His ingenuity at postponing the fateful moment is uncanny. In the fastest game I have seen recently, the pitchers on the two teams held the ball for a total of one hour, eight minutes and 30 seconds!

My research into this baffling phenomenon has shown that, as modern pitchers go, Brosnan is fairly fast. He was serving up the ball on an average of every 17½ seconds. There are dozens of big-league pitchers, I soon discovered, who take much longer than that.

Brosnan *looks* slow. To watch him you would think he was taking forever. But this is because he has not developed an elaborate camouflage to conceal his procrastination. Once he has the ball, he just stands there until he throws it back. A man who stands motionless for 17½ seconds is bound to be conspicuous.

Most pitchers look fast but are really slow. Take Philadelphia's Jim Bunning. After Bunning gets the ball, he spends ten seconds busily adjusting his cap. You can't blame him for that, can you? But he does it *every time!* His cap doesn't need adjusting that often any more than his right ear.

After he has finished with the cap, Bunning bends slowly forward, like a man with a bad sacroiliac, rests both hands solidly on his knees and peers in for the catcher's sign. Students of the game assure me that Bunning has only three basic pitches—a fast ball, a curve and a slider. The catcher's sign can mean only one of three things. Yet Bunning studies it as if it were the Rosetta stone and he a nearsighted archeologist.

The techniques are endless. A good, determined time killer can waste ten seconds just taking off his cap and mopping his brow. He can pound the ball into his glove for ten more seconds, then take off the glove and rub the ball a while. Dave Morehead of the Red Sox likes to turn around and stare toward center field and simultaneously rub the ball, as if he considered it impolite to do so in view of the batter.

Scraping the dirt around the mound with the side of the shoe is another useful device. Roger Craig of the Cardinals and Tracy Stallard of the Mets scrape the dirt so long and painstakingly that they almost seem to be writing love letters in the sand. Stan Williams of the Yankees, who is a sort of decathlon man among the time wasters, is adept at all these techniques and sometimes uses every one of them before a pitch, topping off his repertoire with his unique habit of flapping his arms across his chest like an Eskimo trying to get his circulation going. He does this even when the temperature is 100 in the shade.

For the slowest of all pitchers, day in and day out, my records point clearly to Lew Burdette of the Cardinals. Burdette is an itchy fellow who never throws the ball until he has thoroughly scratched his scalp, forehead, nose, lips and chin, and often his elbows, shoulders, chest and small of the back as well. His ex-manager Fred Haney once said, "Burdette would make coffee nervous."

One evening Burdette was coasting along in the ninth with a 6–0 lead over the Mets, no threat going, the game in the bag; yet he stood fidgeting for 53 seconds before throwing a pitch to Duke Snider. For a rough idea of how interminable 53 seconds can be, ask a friend to call you on the telephone and let it ring for 53 seconds.

My notes show that the record for a single pitch, however, is held by Carl Willey of the Mets. Carl gave up two hits at the start of a game, then did something that is almost incredible, even in this era of slow-motion pitchers. Facing the third batter, Dick Groat, he held the ball for 45 seconds, started his pitching motion, then thought better of it and stopped. Poor fellow, he was not yet ready; he had been trying to rush matters. Naturally the umpire called a balk. After the runners had moved up a base, Willey held the ball for 50 more seconds before he could finally bring himself to let go of it. Total elapsed time between pitches: one minute, 35 seconds, not counting the delay caused by the balk call.

Willey also set another record. He was knocked out after pitching two-thirds of an inning, at which point he had already held the ball a total of 12 minutes, 29 seconds. If you project this figure to a full nine innings, and add the time it takes for the teams to change sides, you come up with a ball game that takes exactly six hours just for the time when nothing is happening. The way our pitchers are going, they might make it someday.

THIS EXERCISE in the difficult form of the short-short story has distinguished credentials. First printed in *Collier's* in 1950, it was selected for inclusion also in the collection *Best Short Shorts* which included such all-time classics as W. F. Harvey's "August Heat" and Saki's "The Open Window."

One Throw

W. C. HEINZ

I CHECKED INTO A HOTEL called the Olympia, which is right on the main street and the only hotel in the town. After lunch I was hanging around the lobby, and I got to talking to the guy at the desk. I asked him if this wasn't the town where that kid named Maneri played ball.

"That's right," the guy said. "He's a pretty good ballplayer."

"He should be," I said. "I read that he was the new Phil Rizzuto."

"That's what they said," the guy said.

"What's the matter with him?" I said. "I mean—if he's such a good ballplayer, what's he doing in this league?"

"I don't know," the guy said. "I guess the Yankees know what they're doing."

"He lives here in this hotel?"

"That's right," the guy said. "Most of the older ballplayers stay in rooming houses, but Pete and a couple other kids live here."

He was leaning on the desk, talking to me and looking across the little lobby. He nodded his head. "Here he comes now."

The kid had come through the door from the street. I could see why, when he showed up with the Yankees in spring training, he made them all think of Rizzuto. He isn't any bigger than Rizzuto, and he looks just like him.

"Hello, Nick," he said to the guy at the desk.

"Hello, Pete," the guy at the desk said. "How goes it today?"

"All right," the kid said, but you could see that he was exaggerating.

"I'm sorry, Pete," the guy at the desk said, "but no mail today."

"That's all right, Nick," the kid said. "I'm used to it."

"Excuse me," I said, "but you're Pete Maneri?"

"That's right," the kid said, turning and looking at me.

"Excuse me," the guy at the desk said, introducing us. "Pete, this is Mr. Franklin."

"Harry Franklin," I said.

"I'm glad to know you," the kid said, shaking my hand.

"I recognize you from your pictures," I said.

"Pete's a good ballplayer," the guy at the desk said.

"Not very," the kid said.

"Don't take his word for it, Mr. Franklin," the guy said.

"I'm a great ball fan," I said to the kid. "Do you people play tonight?"

"We play two games," the kid said.

"That first game's at six o'clock," the guy at the desk said. "They play pretty good ball."

"I'll be there," I said. "I used to play a little ball myself."

"You did?" the kid said.

"With Columbus," I said. "That was twenty years ago."

"Is that right?" the kid said. . . .

That's the way I got to talking with the kid. They had one of those pine-paneled grillrooms in the basement of the hotel, and we went down there. I had a cup of coffee and the kid had a Coke, and I told him a few stories and he turned out to be a real good listener.

"But what do you do now, Mr. Franklin?" he said after a while.

"I sell hardware," I said. "I can think of some things I'd like better, but I was going to ask you how you like playing in this league."

"Well," the kid said, "I guess I've got no kick coming."

"Oh, I don't know," I said. "I understand you're too good for this league. What are they trying to do to you?"

"I don't know," the kid said. "I can't understand it."

"What's the trouble?"

"Well," the kid said, "there's nothing wrong with my playing. I'm hitting .365 right now. I lead the league in stolen bases. There's nobody can field with me, but who cares?"

"Who manages this ball club?"

"Al Dall," the kid said. "You remember, he played in the outfield for the Yankees for about four years."

"I remember."

"Maybe he's all right," the kid said, "but I don't get along with him. He's on my neck all the time."

"Well," I said, "that's the way they are in the minors sometimes. You have to remember the guy is looking out for himself and his ball club first."

"I know that," the kid said. "If I get the big hit or make the play, he never says anything. The other night I tried to take second on a loose ball and I got caught in the rundown. He bawled me out in front of everybody. There's nothing I can do."

"Oh, I don't know," I said. "This is probably a guy who knows he's got a good thing in you, and he's trying to keep you around. You people lead the league, and that makes him look good. He doesn't want to lose you to Kansas City or the Yankees."

"That's what I mean," the kid said. "When the Yankees sent me down here they said, 'Don't worry. We'll keep an eye on you.' So Dall never sends back a good report on me. Nobody ever comes down to look me over. What chance is there for a guy like Eddie Brown to see me in this town?"

"You have to remember that Eddie Brown's the big shot," I said, "the great Yankee scout."

"Sure," the kid said, "and I'll never see him in this place. I have an idea that if they ever ask Dall about me, he keeps knocking me down."

"Why don't you go after Dall?" I said. "I had trouble like that once myself, but I figured out a way to get attention."

"You did?" the kid said.

"I threw a couple of balls over the first baseman's head," I said. "I threw a couple of games away, and that really made the manager sore. So what does he do? He blows the whistle on me, and what happens? That gets the top brass curious, and they send down to see what's wrong."

"Is that so?" the kid said. "What happened?"

"Two weeks later," I said, "I was up with Columbus."

"Is that right?" the kid said.

"Sure," I said, egging him on. "What have you got to lose?"

"Nothing," the kid said. "I haven't got anything to lose."

"I'd try it," I said.

"I might," the kid said. "I might try it tonight if the spot comes up."

I could see from the way he said it that he was madder than he'd said. Maybe you think this is mean to steam a kid up like this, but I do some strange things.

"Take over," I said. "Don't let this guy ruin your career."

"I'll try it," the kid said. "Are you coming out to the park tonight?"

"I wouldn't miss it," I said. "This will be better than making out route sheets and taking orders."

It's not much of a ball park in this town—old wooden bleachers and an old wooden fence and about four hundred people in the stands. The first game wasn't much of a game either, with the home club winning something like 8 to 1.

The kid didn't have any hard chances, but I could see he was a ballplayer, with a double and a couple of walks and a lot of speed.

The second game was different, though. The other club got a couple of runs and then the home club picked up three runs in one. In the top of the ninth the home club had a 3–2 lead and two outs when the pitching began to fall apart and the other club loaded the bases.

I was trying to wish the ball down to the kid, just to see what he'd do with it, when the batter drove one on one bounce to the kid's right.

The kid was off for it when the ball started. He made a backhand stab and grabbed it. He was deep now, and he turned in the air and fired. If it goes over the first baseman's head it's two runs in and a panic—but it's the prettiest throw you'd want to see. It's right on a line, and the runner is out by a step, and it's the ball game.

I walked back to the hotel, thinking about the kid. I sat around the lobby until I saw him come in, and then I walked toward the elevator as if I were going to my room but so I'd meet him. I could see he didn't want to talk.

"How about a Coke?" I said.

"No," he said. "Thanks, but I'm going to bed."

"Look," I said. "Forget it. You did the right thing. Have a Coke."

We were sitting in the grillroom again. The kid wasn't saying anything.

"Why didn't you throw that ball away?" I said.

"I don't know," the kid said. "I had the idea in my mind before he hit it, but I couldn't."

"Why?"

"I don't know why."

"I know why," I said.

The kid didn't say anything. He just sat there, looking down.

"Do you know why you couldn't throw that ball away?" I said.

"No," the kid said.

"You couldn't throw that ball away," I said, "because you're going to be a major-league ballplayer someday."

The kid just looked at me. He had that same sore expression.

"Do you know why you're going to be a major-league ballplayer?" I said.

The kid was just looking down again, shaking his head. I never got more of a kick out of anything in my life.

"You're going to be a major-league ballplayer," I said, "because you couldn't throw that ball away, and because I'm not Harry Franklin."

"What do you mean?" the kid said.

"I mean," I explained to him, "that I tried to needle you into throwing that ball away because I'm Eddie Brown."

THE FRANKEST and (most times unintentionally) funniest baseball autobiography in current print is Kirby Higbe's *The High Hard One*. Higbe came to greatness under Leo Durocher (as who didn't?) on the Brooklyn Dodger pennant team of 1941. Before then, though, he pitched for the Cubs and then the Phillies (as who didn't?)—and those Phillies were the famous Futile Phillies. Mr. Higbe, front and center.

From *The High Hard One*

KIRBY HIGBE *with* MARTIN QUIGLEY

I PITCHED good relief ball for the Cubs the early part of that season and was given three raises in five weeks. Then Gabby, who was now manager, called me into his office and said, "Hig, I hate to tell you this, but you have been traded to the Phillies for Claude Passeau. We tried to give them somebody else, but Doc Prothro wouldn't take anybody but you." The Cubs also got Ray Harrell, a pitcher, and Joe Marty, an outfielder, because Claude was an established star.

Doc was a fine manager who drank about twenty Cokes a day and was as nervous as a cat in a room full of rocking chairs. Managing that club would have made anybody nervous.

After driving two days from Chicago, I got to the ball park about 4 P.M., and Doc asked me if I could pitch that night. I said, "That's what I'm here for."

We were playing Pittsburgh, which had some power with the Waner brothers, Arky Vaughan, and Bob Elliott. I saw that night how things were going to be. I gave up five hits and got beat 1–0.

They called us the Futile Phillies. We won 44 games in 1939, but did better in 1940, when we won 45.

About the middle of the first season, old Hughie Mulcahy had won 10 and lost 9, and the sportswriters were saying he could be the first pitcher to win 20 for the Phils since Grover Cleveland Alexander. He pitched great ball but ended up something like 11 and 22. I ended up 12 and 15.

One game, when Boom Boom Beck was pitching for us against Bucky Walters and the Reds, the infield booted in two runs in the first inning. Then Boom Boom didn't give them a chance to boot the game away until the thirteenth inning. After the game, he told Doc to lock the clubhouse doors, and he really gave those ballplayers hell. He said his wife could play infield better with an apron on than any of them. He said he was going to buy them all aprons and tell them when to drop the aprons to stop a ball.

How much good his talking did showed up the next day, when I went out and got beat by Paul Derringer 2–1 in twelve innings. I gave up two hits, and both runs were unearned.

We took a nine-game losing streak into the Polo Grounds for a four-day series. The Giants beat us the first two games. I pitched the first game of the Sunday doubleheader and got beat in the eleventh inning 1–0 when Harry Danning broke his bat and hit a Chinese home run that just made it down that short right-field line. That was our twelfth loss in a row. We went into the bottom of the tenth in the second game tied 2–2. They got us out in the eleventh, and Doc said, "Hig, they are going to call the game on account of darkness after this inning. For God's sake, go in there and get us a tie."

The first man up hit a ball to our shortstop, who picked it up beautifully and nearly killed a spectator in a box behind first base with his throw. With the runner on second, I walked the next man intentionally, and they bunted the runners up. With runners on second and third and one out, I loaded the bases with another intentional walk. The next hitter lifted a short fly to our center fielders. The runner on third didn't even make a feint as if he was going to try to score after tagging up, but our center fielder threw anyway—all the way to the top of the screen behind home plate. That made it thirteen in a row for us and two losses for old Hig in one day.

In the clubhouse, old Doc said, "I want the whole club to go out tonight and get drunk, loosen up." I don't know what he meant, because that club was never anything but loose. Doc was waiting on me when I got in about 7 A.M. "Hig, what in the world did you go out and get loaded for? I don't want you associating with that bunch of bums."

There were games when I could have whipped everybody in the stands by myself. But one Friday night Mulcahy beat Cincinnati, and the next day I beat them. Our winning streak drew the biggest crowd I ever saw in Philly, about twelve thousand fans. Doc said, "Hig, you may have to relieve in both games. We don't want to look bad in front of all these people." But we were down six runs in the first game before I could get to the bullpen, and we lost the second game 11–1. We didn't draw that many people the whole rest of the year.

The man who owned the ball club, a Mr. Baker, had died and left the club to his secretary, but he didn't leave any money to run it with. So Gerry Nugent, the husband of the secretary, sold promising players every year to stay in business. With the players he sold, you would have had one of the best All-Star teams of those years. Among them were Passeau, Bucky Walters, Dolf Camilli, Chuck Klein, Curt Davis, and Dick Bartell.

When a good ballplayer went to the Phillies, he would hustle and bear down in the hope he would be sold to a good ball club. It was hard to pitch for that club, but I kept thinking I would be with a good club if I kept on trying.

Some of the ballplayers gave up trying, and then they weren't even good enough for the Phillies to unload. Some of the players had been big stars in their time. If we could have taken seven or eight years off them, we would really have had a big-league club. They had plenty of heart, but the old legs just wouldn't go.

One of the outfielders was about as strong and smart as an ox. He would go up to the plate, especially with men on base, and take three mighty swings and come back to the bench with the runners still on base. "They didn't cheat me out of my swings," he would say. One day I told him, "Anybody can go up there and knock the air out of the park. I want to see somebody go up there and hit the ball and drive in a few runs." He got real mad and wanted to fight.

We had a little catcher named Walter Millies, a good receiver but not much of a hitter. Little Walter came up to bat in the last of the ninth in a 3–3 game against St. Louis, a man on third and one out. The Cardinal outfield came in on him so it looked like seven infielders. Walter hit a tremendous clout for him, a short fly to right, but Slaughter was playing him so close it went over his head. The runner scored and won the game, but Walter sprinted to second base. The official scorer gave him credit for a double because it was the first extra-base hit of his career, and I bet he never did get another.

That was the first full year in the majors for both Mort Cooper of the Cardinals and me, and we both made the rookie team. I was pitching against him in St. Louis, going into the eighth tied 1–1, and I got the first two men out. Then Slaughter hit a line drive right at our center fielder. All he had to do was raise his glove, but he charged in under it. When we got the ball back, Slaughter was sitting in the dugout. Old Hig had lost another one, and Mort had another win.

After one like that, the players would pat me on the back: "Tough luck, Hig." I got tired of that tough-luck stuff.

The victories were so far between that we pitchers figured we were entitled to a night out to celebrate every time we won one. We had two pitchers that had so few chances to celebrate they went the other way and drowned their sorrows when they lost.

You have to have one run before you go out to the ball park. With the Phillies you needed four or five, because on a good day our club would give away two or three. We had some pitchers that really bore down all the way, and it was heartbreaking to see them pitch really fine games and get beat because we didn't get any runs or booted the games away.

After the season I went home for a month and then back to Philly to talk contract with Mr. Nugent. My hotel and food cost me more while I was there negotiating than the raise I got. But he did promise me a bonus of $1,000 if I won 15 games the next year. I had won 12, and he said we were going to have a much better club in 1940 so I ought to win 15 easy.

We went to Miami for spring training, and the rooms in our hotel were so small you had to go out in the hall to change your mind. When you shaved you dusted the mirror with your eyelashes. You had to leave a window open or you couldn't get the key in the keyhole. It was nothing like Catalina and being with a first-place club. We rode bicycles from the hotel to the ball park.

We had a good spring exhibition season for us. We won four games. When we opened in New York, I pitched against Carl Hubbell. We were 1—1 in the seventh. Babe Young hit a ground ball to Gus Suhr at first base. When I ran over to cover the base, he said, "Hig, hold them until I come to bat again, and I'll hit a home run off old Carl and win this one for you." Damn if he didn't. We won it 3—1, but even this great event didn't get too much attention. That was the day Bob Feller pitched a no-hitter opening game against the White Sox.

It rained the next three days, and we went back for the opener in Philly. Doc said, "You pitch the opener here too, Hig. Maybe you can win them all this year if it rains enough."

Harry Gumbert of the Giants and I had a 0—0 duel going into the eighth. I had the bases loaded, with Mel Ott the hitter. I went to 3 and 2 on him and tried to get him with a curve. It went a little low and forced in the run. They beat me 1—0. I told Doc that I didn't believe I would take him up on his offer to pitch them all.

After the game my wife asked me why I didn't throw Ott a fast ball. "You might have got it over the plate." I was mad about losing anyway, and by the time I got through telling her why I threw the curve ball, she just did the cooking and didn't come out to see me pitch a game for a month.

She decided to go when I was pitching against the Dodgers. The first five men got hits off me. When she walked into the park I was already in the showers. She said to the fellow sitting next to her, "I thought Higbe was going to pitch today." He said, "The bum started and has departed." I told her next time she wanted to see me pitch, come to the park early.

I started the last game of that series against the Dodgers. Whitlow Wyatt and I were having a real good 1—1 game. Joe Medwick came up for them in the seventh and hit one out of town and laughed all the way around the bases. I didn't see anything funny about it. When he crossed home plate, I hollered, "You'll be up there again, and we'll see who gets the next laugh." He came up in the ninth, and I let him have one in the ribs. He started out after me. But Benny Warren threw the ball back to me, and I told Joe I would let him have another in the ribs. He trotted down to first. But they beat me 2—1.

In the clubhouse I really gave the ball club hell for not getting me any runs. They promised me plenty of runs next time I pitched. It was against Paul Dean and the Giants, and damn if we didn't win 19—2. They said, "See, Hig, all you gotta do is ask."

Once, after losing eight in a row, we went into New York and Mulcahy beat them 3—0. We decided we were going to celebrate the victory. One of the players started throwing soft-drink bottles out of the window of his room in the Governor Clinton Hotel. One went through the top of a taxi, and he had close misses with a dozen others before the police figured out where the bombs were coming from. They were going to lock him up until they found out he played for the Phillies. One of the cops said, "Let them have their fun. They don't have much chance to celebrate."

We lost the next seven in a row before I beat Cincinnati 3—2 in eleven innings.

When we played Boston, it was something to see each team trying to give the game back to the other. We were fighting for last place, and Boston was fighting to take it away from us. We beat them out both years.

We had one pitcher who could really throw that seed for six or seven innings; then they would start knocking him around. After pitching seven and two-thirds no-hit innings against the Cubs, he told Doc, "I really pitched a good game out there for seven innings."

"Son," Doc said, "you are in the big leagues now, and all the games up here go nine innings."

"After pitching on this club for a couple of months," the boy said, "I'm not sure whether I'm in the big leagues or not."

"Don't ever think you are not in the big leagues, son," Doc told him. "We may not be a big-league club, but we are playing against big-league clubs."

Old Doc was a fine manager, and he really wanted to win, but you have got to have the horses to win, and he didn't have them. I bet he walked ten thousand miles in the third-base coaching box that season.

As we came to the last game of the season, I had won 14 and lost 19. The last game was my chance to win 15 and earn the $1,000 bonus Mr. Nugent had promised me. It was raining at Ebbets Field, but the Dodgers wanted to get the game in to keep from giving refunds, and I wanted my chance at number

15. We waited and finally got started. We made five errors and got beat 2–1. Neither run was earned. I told Mr. Nugent I thought I deserved the bonus. He said, "You didn't win fifteen." I didn't get it.

In November I went back to Philly to talk contract. I talked for three days, trying to get up to $10,000. He showed me every contract on the club, and the highest was for $7,500. He said, "Hig, I will give you eighty-five hundred, and you will be the highest-paid man on the ball club."

If he was going to trade me or sell me to another club, I decided I would wait and bargain with the new club. So I asked him. He said, "Not a chance." I believed him and signed. I left Philly that cold night and drove home. At midnight I turned on the radio for the news and heard that I was sold to the Brooklyn Dodgers for $100,000 and three players (pitchers Vito Tamulis and Bill Crouch and catcher Mickey Livingston). I was shocked but deliriously happy. When I got home I called Mr. Nugent and asked him to pay my bonus out of the $100,000 he got for me. He said the money was all spent. But Mr. Larry MacPhail, the Dodgers' president, raised my salary to $10,000. I spent the winter hardly able to wait to go to spring training with the Dodgers.

JEFF KEATE

Courtesy Publishers-Hall Syndicate

"Cleverest guy in the league at rattling a pitcher!"

The Day I Batted Against Castro

DON HOAK *with* MYRON COPE

CUBA WAS AN American baseball player's paradise when I played there in the winter of 1950–51. Later, as a major-league third baseman, I became one of the better-paid ballplayers, but I was just an $800-a-month minor leaguer when I went to Cuba.

There the Cienfuegos club paid me $1,000 a month plus $350 a month for expenses. I had a cottage apartment at the elegant Club Nautico on the beach near Havana. The rent, thanks to a reduced rate obtained by the owner of our team, was $150. The $150 included:

(a) A spacious living room with floor-to-ceiling windows; two bedrooms; two baths; a screened patio in the rear; a dazzling flower garden out front.

(b) A fine old Cuban lady named Eeta, who did my housekeeping and cooking. (I had to pay her bus fare.)

(c) A guard to watch over my apartment.

Late at night, after the baseball games were over, I fished off the coral reefs for yellowtails and eels. By day, I went scuba diving for lobster or napped on the beach or walked across the road to the golf course to shoot a round. Cuba was the best place in the world to play baseball.

But even in those days, the students at the University of Havana were politically restless. At the Havana ball park they'd frequently interrupt our games by staging demonstrations on the field.

They would pour down from the stands and parade across the field carrying banners. They would set off firecrackers and blow horns and shout slogans for ten or fifteen minutes and then go back to their seats. The dictator, Fulgencio Batista, tolerated them, perhaps because he did not consider them a serious threat to his power. His police allowed them to spend their energies. As a matter of fact, Batista himself sometimes witnessed the demonstrations, for he attended many games. Surrounded by bodyguards, he would sit through the commotion with arms folded across his chest and just a trace of a smile at the corner of his lips.

Another regular customer at the park was Fidel Castro. He had just received his law degree from the university, but he remained a well-known and flamboyant leader of the students. As a baseball fan, he belonged in the nut category.

I knew Castro's face well and I suspected he was something of a wild man because of the company he kept. He often came to the park with a man named Pedro Formanthael, who played right field for the Marianao club. Pedro was about forty but an excellent ballplayer. He stood no more than five feet ten but was built very solidly and could hit with power. He wore a great mustache and had a temper that was just as black. He always carried a pistol a foot long, and I wondered how he fit it into his jacket. Anyhow, he and Castro were great pals.

Our Cienfuegos club was playing Pedro Formanthael's team in the Havana park the night I came face to face with Castro.

It was approximately the fifth inning, as I recall, when the firecrackers went off. Up went the banners. The horns blared, and down from the stands came the students—perhaps 300 of them. As fate would have it, I had just stepped into the batter's box when all hell broke loose. "Here we go again," I thought as I stepped out of the box to await order.

But on this night the demonstration took an unexpected turn.

Castro marched straight out to the mound and seized a glove and ball from the Marianao pitcher, a tall Cuban whose name I can't recall. The pitcher shrugged and walked off the field.

Castro then toed the rubber, and as he did so his appearance on the mound was so ridiculous that I cannot forget a single detail of it. He wore no glasses then, but he did have a beard —a funny little beard at the point of his chin that he obviously had taken great care to groom. He was tall and rather skinny.

He wore a long-sleeved white shirt—a type of shirt many Cubans favored. It had pleats like a formal dress shirt and a square bottom which was worn outside the trousers. Castro also wore tight black slacks and black suede shoes with pointed toes. His footwear was almost dandy, and as I see pictures of today's Castro in army fatigues and combat boots I am amused by the contrast. However, I don't suppose a guy in black suede shoes would stand very well at the head of a people's revolution.

Anyhow, Castro put on the glove and ordered the Marianao catcher—a Cuban veteran named Mike Guerra, who had played for the Washington Senators and Philadelphia Athletics—to catch his repertoire. Castro wound up with a great windmill flourish, whirling his pitching arm overhead about six times. Obviously he considered himself an ace hurler, as the sportswriters say. Left-handers as a breed are eccentric, but Castro, a right-hander, looked kookier than any southpaw I have known.

I figured, "Let him have his fun," and watched him throw half a dozen pitches. The crowd was in an uproar. The students, ranged along the foul lines, were dancing with glee.

Suddenly Castro stopped throwing, glared at me, and barked the Spanish equivalent of "Batter up!"

I looked at the umpire but he only shrugged. "What the hell," I said, and stepped into the batter's box. I was not particularly anxious to defy Castro and his mob, because I knew the Latin temper to be an explosive force. Also, Castro's gunslinging buddy, Pedro Formanthael, was throwing me dirty looks from right field.

Castro gave me the hipper-dipper windup and cut loose with a curve. Actually, it was a pretty fair curve. It had a sharp inside break to it—and it came within an inch of breaking my head.

"Ball one!" said the umpire. Castro marched forward a few paces from the mound and stared daggers at him. The students expressed considerable displeasure. The umpire suggested to me that I had better start swinging or he would be compelled to call me out on strikes.

But I glanced at those students on the foul line and thought, "If I swing hard I'm liable to line a foul down there and kill somebody." I had to think fast because Castro, his floppy shirt billowing in the evening breeze, was already into his windup—a *super* hipper-dipper windup this time. I thought he would take off for the moon.

Finally he cut loose with a fast ball—a good fast ball, a regular bullet.

It came at me in the vicinity of the shins. Fortunately, I was a pretty fair bat handler, so I came around on the pitch with a short golf stroke and lofted a pop-foul over the heads of the students on the third-base line. I figured the best thing to do was to tap soft fouls into the stands.

Castro's third pitch was another fast ball. He really zinged it. It scorched its way straight for my eyeballs. I leaned away, gave my bat a quick lurch, and managed another pop-foul into the stands.

Castro had two strikes on me and he was stomping pompously around the mound as though he had just conquered Washington, D.C.

At that point, however, a new factor entered the picture. The Hoak temper.

I've got a wee trace of Comanche blood, you see, and I imagine I have a temper that can match any Latin's from Havana to Lima. To me, baseball is war. In 1956 I played winter ball in the Dominican Republic where I pleased the fans by hitting .394 and sliding into bases like a maniac. I am known there, even to this day, as Crazy Horse. When I played for Pittsburgh a broadcaster there named me The Tiger. Mind you, I don't care to fight Castro and 300 Cubans under any circumstances, but if I have a bat in my hands I know I won't be the only guy to get hurt.

So I turned to the umpire and announced, "I've got a major-league career and big money and good times ahead of me, and I am not going to stand here and let some silly punk in a pleated shirt throw at my skull. Now just get that idiot out of the game."

Here, still another factor entered the picture. The *umpire's* temper.

His name was Miastri and he was a fine umpire. He was such a firebrand that when he threw a player out of a game he often fined him on the spot, and when he fined a guy he would turn around and look up to the press box and announce the amount of the fine with vigorous hand signals. And now he had decided he, too, had had a bellyful of Castro.

He marched over to the *policía*, who were lazily enjoying the fun from the grandstands, and ordered them in no uncertain terms to clear the field. Down they came from the stands, riot clubs brandished at shoulder level.

A knot of cops moved briskly on pitcher Castro. Briefly, he made a show of standing his ground, but the cops shoved him off the mound. He shuffled meekly toward the third-base grandstands, like an impudent boy who has been cuffed by the teacher and sent to stand in the corner.

My final memory of him is one that somehow strikes me funny to this day. As he crossed the third-base line I happened to look at his shoes. He had dust on his black suede shoes.

Looking back, I think that with a little work on his control, Fidel Castro would have made a better pitcher than a prime minister.

DANA FRADON

Courtesy *The Saturday Evening Post* ©

"Young man! The Supreme Court of the United States has twice affirmed that baseball is a game, *not a* business! *Kindly act like it."*

THIS PIECE appeared in 1962. Its author doubtless still feels the same way.

The American League Is Tougher

RALPH HOUK
as told to **HARRY T. PAXTON**

EVERY TIME the New York Yankees win another pennant there are a lot of people who say, "But after all, they're playing in an easy league. In the National League the competition is much tougher."

I've been hearing this for years, and it always burns me up. I've been connected with nine Yankee pennant winners—first as a reserve catcher, then as a coach, and since 1961 as the manager—and I know how hard our ball club had to battle to win those American League championships. Even in years like 1960 and 1961, when the Yankees were able to pull away at the end, our final margins were deceiving, because those were hot races right into September. And we never met a National League club in the World Series that looked any rougher to us than the contenders we had to beat out in our own league. Truthfully, we sometimes had it much easier in the Series than during the regular season.

Yet somehow the National Leaguers have been able to put across the idea that it's harder to win pennants over there. They claim that their league has better balance and more overall strength. They've sold this theory to the fans—at least to the fans in their own cities—and they've sold it to many of the writers. I find this in talking to newspapermen during the season.

I guess it's human nature to build up your own group, and I'll have to credit the National Leaguers with doing a good job of it. But it pains me just the same, because what they're really doing is belittling the Yankees. They're saying that all those pennants we've won don't mean very much, because we didn't have much to beat.

One reason they've been able to get away with this argument is the tremendous amount of publicity that is given to the Yankees in the American League. Now, I think we do have the best team. Our players deserve all the praise they receive. But there's so much of this that it tends to downgrade the other clubs. People don't realize how strong the league as a whole is.

Look at how the standings of the two leagues read this year on July fifteenth with more than half the season played. In the National League the fourth-place team, St. Louis, was ten games out of first. In the American the ninth-place club, Kansas City, was closer than that. And Boston in eighth place was only six and a half games out.

We were first at that time, with just a one-game lead over Cleveland. There's no question that injuries played a part in the race up to then. If Mantle hadn't been out for a month, and if Ford hadn't had his troubles, along with Arroyo—why, we might have been in a little better position. And Detroit had been held back by Al Kaline's injury and Frank Lary's arm trouble.

But the biggest reason for the closeness of the American League race those first three months was the improvement of the other clubs. It was young ballplayers nobody ever heard of before who were making the difference. Fans and writers—and sometimes managers too—have a tendency to go by the established "names" in sizing up a ball club. They forget that there are always young players coming up who have a lot of ability.

That's been especially true in our league recently. The National League likes to talk up its individual stars, but if you check the record, I think you'll find that we've been developing more new ones lately.

Take the Minnesota Twins. Through mid-season they played much better ball than in 1961, when they finished a bad seventh. This spring you might have thought, "Well, they've got about the same team." And then they came up with this kid Rich Rollins, who hit and fielded so well that the American League players voted him to the All-Star team over established third basemen like Brooks Robinson of Baltimore and Cletis Boyer of our club. At second base they found another promising boy, Bernie Allen, to team up with their good-fielding young shortstop, Zoilo Versalles. And they got Vic Power to play first base. So all of a sudden they had a hot infield to go with a catcher like Battey and power hitters like Killebrew and Allison and good pitchers like Pascual.

Or take Cleveland. They've added young fellows like Luplow and Cline in the outfield. They've got a deep pitching staff and a strong bench. They have both right- and left-handed hitting power, which makes it tough for a manager to maneuver his pitching against them.

Last year we had the good luck to beat Cleveland fourteen out of eighteen ball games —although many of those games could have gone either way. This year they won nine of the first thirteen we played with them.

But the biggest surprise in the first half of 1962 was the Los Angeles Angels. They're one of the new "expansion" teams, and supposedly have a long building job ahead of them. Yet on July Fourth they were leading the league by half a game. I think this shows that the American League did a real good job in its expansion program. The National League clubs made darn sure that their new teams wouldn't get many good ballplayers, whereas in our league quite a few good ones went in the expansion draft. And that's helped to give us better balance than they have today.

Anyway, in July people were asking, "What's keeping the Angels up there?" Well, it was simply the fact that they had so many ballplayers who came into their own this year, such as Leon Wagner and Billy Moran and Lee Thomas and Bob Rodgers and Bo Belinsky.

So at mid-season we still couldn't tell who our chief competitors were going to be. Whether some of these surprise teams stayed in the race would depend on whether their youngsters could hold up all season. Meanwhile we knew that Baltimore, which gave us our chief opposition in 1960, and Detroit, which did the same in 1961, could still be rough. Chicago and Boston couldn't be counted out either. Nor could Kansas City be taken too lightly. They were leading the league in hitting, with fellows like Jiminez—another newcomer—and Siebern and Lumpe. And Washington, in tenth place, which gave the Yankees unexpected trouble last year, had enough pitching to make more trouble for us in 1962.

Does the National League offer competition like this from top to bottom? I certainly don't think so. In fact, I believe you could put any of our first-division clubs over there and they'd be right in the race. On the other hand, all but their very top teams would have a hard time making our first division.

Of course, the National League has good ballplayers too. We face some of them every year in the All-Star games. And I've always thought our personnel compared favorably with theirs. But actually, All-Star competition doesn't prove much about the relative strength of the two leagues—and I was saying so long before this year's games, in which I managed the American Leaguers.

Naturally you're trying to win. But you're handed a set lineup to start with, and then you try to give as many of the other fellows as possible a chance to play. Then there are restrictions on the use of pitchers. You just can't operate in a normal way.

One or two games are never a true test anyhow. Even a World Series can be misleading. Conditions are so different than in a full season of play. You're not using your entire personnel. You can start just your best pitchers, for one thing: I used only three starters in the 1961 Series. Over a pennant race you've got to be able to beat different types of ball clubs and pitchers and win in different types of parks. A World Series doesn't necessarily show your overall bench strength and maneuverability.

In the 1960 Series, when I was coaching under Casey Stengel in his last year with the Yankees, the Pittsburgh Pirates beat us in seven games. They may have had a lucky break or two, but they deserved to win. They made the plays and got the hits it took to beat us. Yet if they had been competing in the American League in 1960 I'm sure they wouldn't have finished ahead of us. I'm not so sure that they'd have finished ahead of Baltimore, either.

I felt the same about Cincinnati last year. We took the Series from them in five games, and they were a good ball club. But I don't believe they would have beaten out Detroit for second place in the American League.

I first came up to the Yankees in 1947 and I've been with them almost ever since, except for 1955–57, when I managed their American Association farm club at Denver. I think our league today is the strongest I've seen it. In the past there have been seasons when you could be pretty confident about beating some of the second-division clubs. But there's never been a year when I thought we had to concede anything to the other league on an all-around basis.

I have no doubt that the National League is better these days, too, because baseball has kept improving during the past fifteen years. The young ballplayers are getting a lot of special instruction from experts that clubs didn't furnish when I was a rookie. There are more players who can hit the long ball, and to try to keep them from doing it, new refinements in pitching and defense have been developed.

The front-office organizations have also been moving ahead. Naturally I think the Yankees have the best organization in the business, but the pattern everywhere is the same. I'll concede that there are wealthy owners and smart baseball men in both leagues. But I don't see how the National Leaguers could claim any edge over us.

Whenever one of their ballplayers switches to the American League and does well, they like to say that this proves our league is easier. But lately we've had quite a few of these cases going for us. Billy Pierce, who in 1961 had trouble breaking even in our league, went from the White Sox to San Francisco this year and immediately had great success as a starting pitcher. So did Don Larsen as a reliever. And Bob Shaw, who wasn't exactly burning up the American League, became quite a winner with Milwaukee.

Last season second baseman Frank Bolling was traded from Detroit to Milwaukee, and he made the National League All-Star starting lineup, which he had never done in the American League. The same deal brought Bill Bruton to Detroit, and he was quoted at first as saying he thought our league might be easier. Well, he's a ballplayer who has hurt our club at times, and we respect him. But the fact remains that whereas he averaged .276 as a hitter during his nine seasons in the National League, he batted only .257 for Detroit.

Naturally these interleague trades won't always work out in our favor. But it's happened so often lately that I don't imagine the National Leaguers would even want to raise the subject right now.

I know they won't agree with many of the things I've said here, but then I haven't agreed with a lot of the things they've said over the years. It's time I got it all off my chest. Sure, they've got a good league, but it's ridiculous for them to keep saying they're stronger than we are. The American League is better.

THE BELIEF, as expressed here, that the human arm was not designed to pitch a baseball is, medically speaking, absolutely true. Ever see a European try to learn to pitch?

Man with the Inhuman Arm

STAN HOCHMAN

IT IS DICK HALL's belief that the human arm was designed to write a sonnet . . . or hammer a nail . . . or add a column of figures . . . or hold a girl around the waist . . . or lift a glass that cheers, but it was not designed to hurl baseballs 60 feet six inches time after time after time.

"Dr. (John Royal) Moore has some interesting things to say about this," he said the other day. "Throwing overhand extends the elbow. The wrist must bend back farther than it should. The arm must come back more than it should.

"An arm doesn't develop to make this overextension. A pitcher operates his arm at 150 percent of optimum efficiency. The arm is resilient, though. It can stand abuse. But basically, it wasn't made to pitch."

Hall pitches for the Phillies, looking like the world's tallest windup toy. One week this season he hurled Tuesday, Wednesday, Saturday and Sunday, which is three times more than anyone thought he could pitch in one week. He won one game, saved two others. In the Saturday game he gave up a double, the first extra base hit off him in three weeks.

"I never kept track of anything like that," he said. "I didn't pay any attention to it. I had one stretch in Baltimore where I faced 28 batters without a hit.

"It lasted five games, and more than two and one-half weeks. I guess that was my no-hitter. No hits, no walks, no errors, no nothing."

Not bad for a guy who throws like a rusty robot. The Orioles sold him to the Phillies last winter. Maybe they thought that creaky windup was going to be outlawed. Or maybe they thought he was going to reach up to comb what's left of his hair one day and his arm was going to fall off at the elbow.

Chiefly as a reliever he won six games for the Phillies to the All-Star break and his ERA was a breathtaking 1.21. That spastic windup may have helped. "It may have something to do with them having trouble picking the ball up," he conceded.

"Stu Miller is a prime example. His motion is fabulous. The arm and shoulder come around and the ball doesn't. The ideal situation is to have the ball come at a different speed than it looks like you're throwing."

He does one other very important thing. He throws strikes. He walked only three men in the first half of the season. Last year he walked eight in 66 innings for Baltimore and four of those were intentional.

"I think about it," he said. "I give up a lot of hits. So the less people I put on base the safer it is. I've always had good control. As an eight-year-old I had good control.

"In the Mexican League one winter I started nibbling from the first pitch. There weren't any home-run hitters in the league. So I figured that even if I walked someone I could still come back and get the side out without getting in trouble.

"I discovered I was walking even fewer hitters. A pitcher faces a good hitter and he tries to get ahead of him. You think about throwing it down the middle and you won't. But if you try and throw it in a good spot, subconsciously, you'll have a better chance of putting it there."

Hall's subconscious, like his delivery, is a rare thing. But there is nothing offbeat about his theory of getting ahead of the hitters.

"Branch Rickey had a fellow keeping detailed statistics in Brooklyn," Hall recalled. "He kept track of batting averages when the hitter was ahead of the pitcher and when he was behind.

"What differences! A guy like Roy Campanella hit 120 points higher when he was ahead of the pitcher than when he was behind."

That's Hall, bland and businesslike as a bookkeeper. A head full of equations and an elbow tender as a love song. Meanwhile he keeps ambling into the furnace of close ball games and ambling right out again, unsinged.

"When the season ends," Jim Bunning said the other day, "Dick Hall will walk across the Atlantic Ocean." You could almost see the wheels churning . . . average temperature of the Gulf Stream, wind currents, navigational miles to Belfast.

"What I will do," he said, smothering a grin, "is fly to Miami and then walk across from there."

JOHN GALLAGHER

Courtesy *Sport* Magazine ©

THE ONLY TROUBLE with pinch-hitting, as the well-known Chicago writer Jerry Holtzman pointed out in this 1962 magazine piece, is to find a good man who likes the work.

Hitters in Waiting

JERRY HOLTZMAN

EITHER ADVANCED beyond his time or terribly frustrated—and possibly both—Oliver (Pat) Tebeau, manager of the Cleveland Spiders, tried a new experiment in the ninth inning of a National League game at Brooklyn in 1892. With his team trailing by two runs, he benched George Davies, his pitcher, and sent Jack Doyle, a reserve catcher, up to the plate to swing for him. Doyle responded with a single, advancing a runner to third. Thereby he became baseball's first pinch hitter.

Although the Spiders lost the game, 2–1, Tebeau really started something. By the end of that pioneering 1892 season a total of seven pinch hitters had been used in the major leagues. Last season the figure was 4,051, including forty-two men who were pinch-hitting *for* pinch hitters, a phenomenon of modern tactics in which a pinch hitter is sent up but immediately withdrawn for still another if the rival manager counters by changing pitchers.

Like relief pitchers, with whom they are often compared, pinch hitters have gained in stature and are no longer merely extra men on the bench. Pinch hitters were used in 97 percent of all major-league games last year, and most clubs now have men who specialize in coming off the bench cold to hit in clutch situations. A team will pay as much as $20,000 a year, perhaps more, to the player who can deliver consistently under these circumstances. Not many can.

Most major leaguers don't want to pinch-hit anyway. They prefer to play every day as starters. About the only men receptive to becoming pinch specialists are veterans anxious to prolong their careers and extend their pension credits. The few who adapt successfully can add anywhere from two to five years to their big-league longevity.

Or take the case of thirty-three-year-old Prentice (Pidge) Browne of the new Houston Colt .45's, who never had a look-in at the majors before. He spent a dozen seasons in the minors, including several stretches at Houston. After the city got its big-league franchise, he was signed on this year primarily as a left-handed pinch hitter. As of late June he had come through with nine hits—several of them game winners—in twenty-five official pinch at-bats. Manager Harry Craft was predicting that Pidge would break Sam Leslie's thirty-year-old National League record of twenty-two pinch hits in one season.

Pinch-hitting requires a rare combination of patience and fierce concentration. The pinch hitter's workday is short, usually lasting for only a minute or two and sometimes for just one swing. Many big-name stars have not been able to distinguish themselves in pinch roles.

The late Ty Cobb, whose .367 batting percentage is the highest of all time, averaged .247 as a pinch hitter. Babe Ruth's figure was a mere .200. Ted Williams, regarded as the best of the modern hitters, batted .316 in his final season of 1960 but had only a .053 pinch-hitting average, with a solitary single in nineteen at-bats. His lifetime average in pinch appearances was .271.

Mickey Mantle, whose experience in the role has been very limited, says simply, "I don't like to pinch-hit. I never did." Roger Maris, who did some of it at the start of his big-league career in Cleveland and Kansas City, is less emphatic. "I didn't mind—too much," he says, although he can't recall winning a game with a pinch hit.

Jerry Lynch of the Cincinnati Reds is easily the best pinch hitter in the majors today—he has been delivering at a .350 clip this season—

but he yields to nobody in expressing distaste for the assignment.

Of the scores of past and present pinch hitters who were interviewed for this article, one of the few who admitted to a liking for the job was big John Mize, a part-time first baseman and pinch swinger when the New York Yankees were winning five successive pennants from 1949 through 1953. The Yankees gave $40,000 to get the aging slugger from the Giants and paid him a salary in excess of $25,000. He was more than worth it.

Mize considers pinch-hitting easier than batting regularly. His reasoning is that the man who comes up in a pinch situation generally gets better pitches to swing at than in normal circumstances. "The pitchers were in a jam by the time I got in there," Mize explains. "The pressure was on them, not me. They couldn't fool around. They had to throw strikes."

Cincinnati's Lynch vigorously states the other side of the case: "The pinch hitter gets only one time at bat. He either does or he doesn't. The fellow playing regularly can strike out in the first inning, he can pop up in the fourth, but if he singles or doubles in a run or two in the sixth he's had a good day. With us there's no second chance."

If Lynch doesn't enjoy being a spot hitter, opposing pitchers are even less happy to see him come up. Manager Fred Hutchinson last year sometimes would have Jerry climb out of the dugout as if preparing to bat even when there was no intention of using him.

Just the sight of Lynch coiled in the on-deck circle was frightening to many pitchers. Admitted Elvin Tappe, the Cubs's head coach most of the 1961 season, "One look at him and our pitchers went to pieces. Even the guys in the bullpen began losing their stuff."

The injection of psychological warfare into the use of pinch hitters is nothing new. John McGraw of the Giants, one of the game's most original thinkers, was doing it back before World War I.

McGraw always made a real production out of sending up the fearsome Harry (Moose) McCormick. According to an account by Damon Runyon, McCormick wouldn't step into the batter's box "until after a three-minute delay during which time the trainer would massage his legs with a bat to create the proper circulation and atmosphere for the Moose to stride majestically to the plate and look the quaking pitcher in the eye."

"This isn't quite true," McCormick said a while ago at his home in Lewisburg, Pennsylvania. "The trainer used cocoa butter."

McCormick is a legend among pinch hitters, but neither he nor anybody else has had quite as devastating a single season as Jerry Lynch with Cincinnati last year. Lynch started off with three home runs in his first five tries and went on from there. All told, he made fifty-nine appearances as a substitute hitter in 1961 and was safe more than half the time, drawing twelve walks and delivering nineteen hits for a .404 pinch-batting average. More than half his hits were for extra bases.

Lynch's sustained success created one problem for manager Hutchinson. Should he continue to hold Jerry on the bench and use him only in the late innings, when a pinch hit in the right spot could tie or win a game? Or should he start Lynch in left field, gambling that his productivity in the normal four times at bat would outweigh his defensive shortcomings?

Lynch started only ten games during the first half of the season, but beginning in mid-August, he was in the regular lineup in twenty of thirty-one games. Had Hutch kept him in a reserve role all year long, Jerry undoubtedly would have broken most of the existing pinch-hitting records for one season.

After the Reds clinched the pennant on September twenty-sixth, Hutchinson said he would use Lynch as a pinch hitter in the Reds' remaining three games at Pittsburgh to give Jerry a shot at the record of six pinch homers in a season, set in 1932 by Johnny Frederick of the Brooklyn Dodgers.

Lynch had five pinch homers going into his final series, but was unable to add any more. Not only that, on the next-to-last day he took a called third strike for the first time in two seasons of heavy duty as a pinch hitter.

He argued the call heatedly, claiming that the pitch—thrown by Clem Labine—had missed the outside corner and should have been ball three. "It was one of those borderline pitches," Lynch said months later, relaxing with his family at their home in Allison Park, Pennsylvania. "I'm sorry for some of the things I said. Landes"—Stan Landes, the plate umpire—"was right in throwing me out."

It was not surprising that Lynch got so worked up about the decision. Most professional pinch hitters take the greatest pride not in how many hits they deliver but rather in how few times they strike out. Their object is at least to get a piece of the ball. Going down swinging is bad enough, but taking the third strike is unpardonable.

Bob Hale, an excellent pinch batter, illustrates the point. In 1960, when he was with Cleveland, he had five pinch hits in a row, tying an American League record set by John Mize. The record was tied again this year by Vic Wertz of Detroit. Hale finished 1960 with a total of nineteen, one short of Parke Coleman's league mark—since broken by Dave Philley. But that wasn't what gave Hale the greatest satisfaction. "I pinch-hit in seventy ball games," he said recently, "and I took only one third strike."

Hale went on waivers last August to the Yankees, and rode the bench with them to the pennant. It was, he concedes, an education just to sit in the Yankee dugout. Never had he been on a team with such depth. "Before, wherever I went I was the number-one pinch hitter. With the Yankees, I was number four." Johnny Blanchard, Bob Cerv and Hector Lopez all rated ahead of him.

The Yankees, clearing some of the fringe players from their roster shortly after the 1961 season, sent Hale down to Richmond. "They were overly generous," Hale said in Chicago, where he was working in the off season as a playground instructor. "I pinch-hit seven times and they still voted me two-thirds of a Series share." Then Hale, who is twenty-eight, added, "I'll be back. I'll hit .300 at Richmond, and one of the big-league clubs will sign me. There is always a spot for a good pinch hitter."

Elmer Valo, now a scout with the New York Mets, would be the first to agree. Last year, at forty, he was still in there swinging with the Phillies; it was his twentieth season in the majors. He had played longer than anyone else then active except Stan Musial and Early Wynn.

During his last four years Valo survived almost exclusively as a pinch hitter. As an American Leaguer in 1960 he got in eighty-one games as a substitute batsman, the first time a pinch hitter had appeared in more than half a season's quota of games. He produced hits at a .250 pace.

Another veteran a few months older than Valo is eager to keep going. He is Dave Philley, a saddle-faced Texan now with the Boston Red Sox, who connected for a record twenty-four pinch hits with the Baltimore Orioles last year. In 1958 with the Phillies he established still another mark with a string of eight consecutive pinch hits. He extended it to nine straight in his first appearance in 1959.

"It took me a couple of years to adjust to pinch-hitting," Philley says. "The toughest thing is learning to sit on the bench. Everyone wants to play. It's the natural thing. But I learned to sit. No one knows the pitchers like the pinch hitters. We watch 'em like hawks."

Pinch hitters fall into categories. Philley, for example, is a slap hitter who can be counted on to meet the ball. Men of this type are summoned for singles, and seldom for power. Others, such as Smoky Burgess of the Pirates, Charley Maxwell of the Tigers, Carl Sawatski of the Cardinals and Chuck Essegian of the Indians, are called on when the situation demands a long ball.

Catcher Burgess, often tapped for pinch duty in games he doesn't start, has a career total of eleven home runs as a pinch hitter—three short of George Crowe's major-league record of fourteen. Outfielder Essegian—often a regular starter this season—is the only man to hit two pinch homers in a World Series. He did it in 1959 for the Los Angeles Dodgers against the Chicago White Sox.

Bob Cerv of the Yankees, who has hit twelve pinch homers, and Vic Wertz of the Tigers are noted for their ability to bring in runners with sacrifice flies. Julio Becquer, late of the Minnesota Twins, and Bob Boyd, recently of the Milwaukee Braves, were in the speed-merchant class—an important pinch-hitting asset when the manager is anxious to avoid the double play.

Earl Torgeson, who concluded his long playing career with the Yankees last year, exemplifies still another breed. Torgie was primarily a "pinch looker"—almost always waiting out the pitcher and trying for a walk, which he often got. Such a man is ideal as a rally starter and is usually sent up to lead off an inning.

Most desirable of all is the versatile pinch hitter like Jerry Lynch who can be used under any circumstances—although preferably not with first base open, when the opposing manager can order an intentional base on balls, as happened in the third game of the 1961 World Series.

Lynch and Hale and most of the younger crop of pinch specialists prefer to swing at the first pitch—or the first "good" pitch, as they put it. "I'm swinging when I leave the bench," Hale has said, and Lynch declares, "I'm that way too. You've got to be aggressive."

Ron Northey, who developed into a remarkable pinch hitter at the tag end of his playing career several years ago, was different. He decided early that he would never swing at the first pitch. Beginning with Johnny Mize's premise that the pressure was on the pitcher,

Northey further reasoned that the first delivery would always be the pitch that was working best for the pitcher on that particular day.

Northey kept tabs. After two months he had established that eight times out of ten the first pitch to him wasn't thrown for a strike anyway. Mort important, by standing and watching it go by, Northey could study the speed and break of the ball. He knew this same pitch would appear again, usually at the moment when the pressure was greatest. "That was the pitch I would hit," Northey says.

Northey, who is now a coach with the Pittsburgh Pirates, twice led the major leagues in pinch-hitting. His 1956 season with the White Sox was his best. In thirty-nine official pinch at-bats he connected for fifteen hits—thirteen of them with two strikes against him—and drove in the winning run in the late innings of eight different ball games. Mickey Mantle, who won the American League's triple batting crown that season, drove in the winning run in only nine Yankee games.

The Dodgers missed a chance to pick up Northey from the Charleston club in the American Association the year before because they decided he had grown too fat. With a Dodger scout in the stands, Northey put on a great hitting show, but nothing happened.

"They want you," Northey was told by Danny Menendez, the Charleston owner. "But they said you've got to lose ten pounds."

Within four days Northey had pared off the weight, but the Dodger agent said he still was too heavy and didn't look good in a uniform. "What the hell do they want?" Northey asked Menendez. "A model or a ballplayer?"

Another memorable pinch hitter was James (Dusty) Rhodes, now trying at thirty-five to work his way back from the minor leagues. In his day, which wasn't too long ago, Rhodes became famous as the only pinch hitter ever to dominate an entire World Series as the New York Giants swept four straight from the Cleveland Indians in 1954. Rhodes won the first game with a three-run pinch homer in the tenth inning. His one-run pinch single helped to make the difference in a 3–1 game the next day. In the third game he contributed a two-run single to start the scoring. Dusty wasn't needed in the fourth game, which the Giants won going away.

"Rhodes thought he could hit anybody living," said Leo Durocher, who handled him. "And he did—that one year. I always tried to use him in the right spot, where they couldn't walk him. But I didn't put him in. He put himself in. When the number seven, eight or nine men were due to hit, he'd have his jacket off and be taking his practice swings. Then if we'd get a man on base he'd come over, spitting tobacco juice and saying, 'Hey, Skip. Me? Now?' "

Durocher doesn't rate Rhodes as the best pinch hitter he has seen, though. Leo picks two men who were active in his own playing days —Lew Riggs, of Cincinnati and Brooklyn, and Pat Crawford, who played for three National League clubs.

Everyone seems to have his own favorite. Dizzy Dean votes for Lefty O'Doul. The choice of Red Sox manager Mike Higgins, is Sheriff Dave Harris of the Senators. Charlie Grimm, who entered the majors prior to World War I, gives the nod to Moose McCormick. Clarence Rowland, a Cub executive who goes back even farther than Grimm, recalls another McGraw pinch hitter, Sammy Strang.

Some of the great pinch hitters, surprisingly enough, have been pitchers, such as Red Lucas, Red Ruffing and Jim Tobin of a generation ago, and Bob Lemon and Don Newcombe of more recent vintage. Red Lucas, now a tax collector in Nashville, Tennessee, had 107 pinch hits in sixteen years of National League service, the present career high.

The record is certain to tumble. As of a month ago, for example, Jerry Lynch had accumulated sixty-nine pinch hits since 1957. He has been at it on what could be considered a regular basis only since 1960. If Lynch doesn't remain a pinch specialist long enough to top Lucas, somebody else will, simple because there is so much more pinch-hitting nowadays.

Managers are completely sold on the practice. Some playing managers have been bold enough to pinch-hit themselves. American League president Joe Cronin slammed five pinch home runs for the Boston Red Sox in 1943. Lou Boudreau won two key games down the stretch with pinch hits while piloting Cleveland to the 1948 pennant.

Frank Frisch's last major-league hit came in a pinch role. His Cardinals, trailing the Braves by one run in the ninth, had the bases loaded with two out. Frisch was looking down the bench trying to decide whom to send up to the plate when a spectator yelled, "Hey, grandma, why don't you hit?" Frisch did, singling to win the game.

As a rule, however, the manager turns to a specialist to do the big job in the clutch. Perhaps the ultimate in rendering aid to a manager was achieved by Singing Sam Leslie, after establishing his National League record of twenty-two pinch hits for the Giants in 1932.

Following the season Leslie had Bill Terry, his boss, as a house guest in Pascagoula, Mississippi. One morning they were out fishing in a boat and Terry, who couldn't swim, fell overboard. As he had done so many times before, Leslie came through for his manager. He jumped in and brought Terry safely ashore.

WIDE WORLD

A MAN NAMED MAYS

Carried away by the record-breaking 535th home run of Willie Mays' career—which made him the greatest righthand home-run hitter of all time—umpire Chris Pelekoudas committed a most un-umpirelike act. In fact, he reported himself to the league president for doing what he did. The president said not to worry about it.

CHARLES DOHERTY, SAN FRANCISCO EXAMINER

This sequence shows Willie Mays doing something he personally developed into an occult science—avoiding collision with a fellow fielder while looking somewhere else. Here Mays and second baseman Chuck Hiller are both going for the same pop-fly. Note the way Mays instinctively swerves around Hiller as the latter goes for the catch. Hiller says he will always remember this play. To find out why, turn the page.

Mays, the ball in his glove, the start of a grin on his face, heads for the dugout as the astounded Hiller does one of the great double takes in baseball history. "The greatest catch I never made," he recalled afterward.

From *Papa Hemingway*

A. E. HOTCHNER

After the hamburger dinner, Adriana returned to the Gritti with us for the getaway party; Federico and a group of well-wishers were already waiting. Although I could tell he was occasionally in pain, Ernest stretched out on the couch and managed to enjoy himself. There was plenty to drink and someone had thoughtfully brought a portable phonograph. Along about midnight, for what reason I cannot now remember, I was called upon to demonstrate American baseball. It had something to do with a discussion Ernest was having with a British friend who was a cricket nut. Ernest suggested that a pair of his wool socks be rolled up and used as the baseball, and it was my bright idea to use the ornamental doorstop as a bat. The doorstops at the Gratti, like everything else there, are very elaborate. They are hand-carved mahogany with a heavy leaded base and a thin upright shaft that resembles a table leg. This shaft, when grasped at the end, with the round base at the top, made an excellent bat. Federico, who had seen baseball played, undertook the pitching assignment and I stationed myself at an improvised home plate.

I smacked the first pitch on a dead line to center field, and to my shocked surprise the baseball socks went sailing through the highly arched glass window and out into the Venetian night. The glass broke with a terrible clatter, and from the sidewalk below we heard angry voices. For a few minutes I basked in the glory of having belted a pair of wool socks so hard that they had shattered a glass window, but then we discovered that what had really happened was that the leaded base of the doorstop had come loose and gone flying out of the window along with the socks. I still have a piece of that glass, autographed by everyone who was there.

That was the end of the party; the next day when we checked out Ernest offered to pay for the broken glass.

"Ah, yes, the window," the manager said. "The flying saucer barely missed the nose of a gentleman who unfortunately is a member of the City Council. This gentleman, trembling with rage, came in with the disk, but we calmed him successfully. As for paying for the window, in the three-hundred-year history of the Gritti, no one, to our knowledge, has ever played baseball in any of its rooms, and in commemoration of the event, Signor Hemingway, we are reducing your bill ten percent."

If you find yourself in disagreement with the following, no one has the right to dispute you. But the author's credentials are unique. Joey Jay was the first Little League star to become a big-league star.

"Don't Trap Your Son in Little League Madness"

JOEY JAY
as told to LAWRENCE LADER

Only a half hour before game time in the last Eastern Regional Little League playoffs, the pitcher for Rhode Island's Smithfield All-Stars struck his head on the dugout roof and was rushed to the hospital. What happened then was a glaring sample of the frantic ambitions and ruthless drive for victory-at-any-cost of today's Little Leagues.

Five stitches were taken in the boy's scalp and drugs were given to ease his pain. Yet he still was sent in to pitch although he "appeared unsteady from the effects of the blow on his head," a local reporter observed. Another injured youngster started as catcher although he had sprained his hand two days before and had "great difficulty in even throwing the ball back to the pitcher."

No one could deny the courage of these 11- and 12-year-old boys. But to put injured youngsters through this ordeal, a risk few major-league managers would have taken with their players, not only infuriates me with the judgment of officials and managers, but typifies the dangerous values dominating the Little League today.

Similar pressure from victory-hungry managers and coaches gave ulcers to one 12-year-old Little Leaguer in Roslyn, New York. Another player in the same League had to be put on sleeping pills by his doctor.

"My coaches were brutally ambitious, only interested in the glory of an undefeated team," Tom Phillips of CBS Radio News, a former Little Leaguer, told me. "They drove us incessantly toward the town championship. After two good seasons, the pressure caught up with me when I was twelve. I choked up at the plate, couldn't swing at a third strike. One day the coach screamed at me in front of the crowded stands, 'If you don't get a hit, I'll drop you to the bottom of the batting order!' I cried myself to sleep that night."

The same frenzy to push their sons toward stardom turns many fathers into relentless tyrants. When a youngster was trapped off first base trying to steal during a Cincinnati Little League game, his father shouted, "Don't stand there, you fool!"

I've never seen such pain and shock on a boy's face. Friends told me he refused to play for weeks.

Some fathers have been paying their sons a dollar for each hit and higher sums for homers, a form of juvenile professionalism that disgraces the game.

I'm even more disturbed by the "farm" teams for boys of 6 to 8 which my 7-year-old son, Stephan, joined in Cincinnati last year. My wife kept complaining that Stephan was coming home tense and exhausted. I went to one game and watched angrily while the coach made a tired 6-year-old, who just couldn't get the ball over the plate, go back on the mound and keep pitching until he was ready to collapse.

I was equally disgusted with the way coaches tried to rubber-stamp Stephan and other kids into Mickey Mantles. Each time a kid swung, coaches would rush up to correct his stance, shift his feet, lower his shoulders. Instead of teaching fundamentals and fun, they were turning out a line of tin soldiers.

I decided then and there I didn't want my

son trapped in this Little League madness. I discouraged him from joining this year. This spring, instead, he'll be riding his bike, going on camping trips and occasionally playing pickup ball like any boy his age.

The deadly seriousness now enveloping organized baseball, junior style, has reached the point where a boy of 14 in Long Island's Senior Little League recently pitched a play-off in Kentucky after his father had collapsed and died of a heart attack. The boy flew back home for the funeral, returning immediately to Kentucky to play the outfield in the next game.

All these incidents are part of a frightening trend wrecking baseball for the kids. I saw Little League at its best when I was a boy and played in a league in Middletown, Connecticut, in 1948.

As the first Little Leaguer to become a major-league star, I think I'm a fair judge of how Little League has degenerated from its original goals. Our local league in 1948 concentrated on sportsmanship, character development, and above all, fun. We had no ambitious parents or coaches pushing us around like potentates. The season was short, only 12 games. We didn't give a hoot for schedules and batting orders. Sometimes we didn't bother with the score. If we could get in 21 innings by dusk, losing track of the score at 28–25, it made the game even more triumphant for the members of both teams.

We used the municipal field for regular games, and practiced when the whim struck us on a lopsided lot near home that ran downhill and kept the right fielder busy trying to keep his balance. No one handed us luxurious ball parks and equipment. Our bats were taped against splinters, our baseballs frazzled. If we didn't have enough gloves to go around, we borrowed some from the opposing team. The bases were often flat rocks or can tops. But games were such inexhaustible fun we often skipped lunch or kept a squashed sandwich in our pocket to munch between innings.

Another crucial difference between the Little League I knew and Little League today was that the responsibility rested in our hands, not with endless committees of parents and local administrators. When we wanted caps and shirts for our team, we went out and earned the money by delivering papers and mowing lawns. We weren't flooded with cups and prizes for every little accomplishment as is the fashion now.

If parents and coaches had tried to turn us into victory machines, we would have yelled bloody murder. We considered it an advantage to get away from the apron strings of home. Although my father had played pro ball with the old Boston Braves, he was wise enough never to force his baseball wisdom on me or the team. Only when I asked for help would he toss a ball with me in the back yard. When he drove me to the field, he watched a few minutes and disappeared.

We had coaches like Ed Collins, now principal of Woodrow Wilson High School in Middletown, who were trained to work with boys and were devoted to their development, not just to winning and championships. Such men were equally concerned with boys on the other teams. I remember one opposing coach coming over to congratulate me after a home run. Then he took the time to correct the dangerous sliding technique of one of my teammates. After the game, the coaches invited both teams out together for sodas.

In contrast to today's victory-hungry system, with teams revolving around their stars, we were allowed to switch positions frequently and learned every aspect of the game. Unlike today's frantic tryouts and discriminatory selection system, every boy who turned out got a chance to play. The only position I knew in the beginning was first base. Although we had a fine first baseman, the coach would move him to get me in the game. I tried every position that year until I determined to become a pitcher.

But what started as a glorious adventure for boys has grown into a monster of adult promotion and organization that literally straddles the globe. Masterminded by a headquarters staff at Williamsport, Pennsylvania, with a chain of command reaching to district, city and town administrators and parental committees, Little League baseball today almost makes the major leagues look like a two-bit operation. The United States alone boasts an empire of 33,000 teams and 5,800 leagues. Stretching overseas to such distant points as Turkey, Saudi Arabia, Japan and Eritrea are 400 more leagues with 100,000 boys.

The Little League proper admits boys of 9 to 12. The system has now added a Senior Little League for 13- to 15-year-olds. At the bottom is another hierarchy of "farm" leagues and "minor" leagues for boys who don't make Little League and even for tots like Stephan of 6 to 8. In many parts of the country Babe Ruth leagues compete with the original organization.

Little League tryouts, schedules and tournaments are run like an IBM machine. Many leagues play two and three games a week through spring and summer with practices in between. Training for some teams starts in winter in the gym. Then comes the ordeal of spring tryouts with each team limited to 15 players.

Former Little Leaguers have told me that one of their worst childhood memories is the recollection of watching coaches rating them for days in little black books until the boys learned if they made the team. The grueling selection system often starts young with League coaches bidding for the best future players. In Cincinnati farm teams that I observed, many managers scout the kids at 8. If they don't get picked for the League immediately, they're left out.

At the end of summer come three weeks of tournament competition. The best teams compete for the district championship, the state title, then the sectional and regional prizes. At the end of this grinding stretch lies the "World Series" at Williamsport. Four regional winners from the United States and one each from Canada, Latin America, Europe and the Pacific battle it out for the world championship.

The Williamsport headquarters reflects the growth of this colossus. Its 44 acres include a ball park almost equaling some in the major leagues for luxury, a sparkling, new administration building, an International Hall, three other Little League fields, a swimming pool, even a Little League Hall of Fame. Little League often resembles big business. Royalties pour in from products ranging from caps, shirts and electric scoreboards to the televising of its World Series. Some local leagues have advertising billboards at their fields. Almost all accept uniforms from local merchants in exchange for brandishing such legends as "Center Falls Cleaners" or "Joe's Hardware" on the backs of uniform shirts.

When I criticized Little League in a newspaper interview recently, I was afraid the fury of every fan would come crashing around my head. Then the mail came in, a flood of it. Surprisingly, almost every letter supported me enthusiastically. Parents, teachers, and many former Little Leaguers wanted these abuses brought into the open.

If I'm angry about the mess in Little League baseball, it's because I've grown up with the game since my mother used to wrap me in a blanket as a baby and drive me to the field in a pickup truck to watch my father playing semipro ball. I was lucky to be in Little League before it became so big-league. I owe it a lot. It helped me to go on to high-school ball, then American Legion and semipro ball, and the thrill of being signed by the Milwaukee Braves in 1953. After a year with Toledo, two years with Wichita and back to the Braves, I finally hit my stride when I was traded to the Reds and won 21 games in both the 1961 and 1962 seasons.

The most important factor in my development was that I could grow at my own pace. Nobody tried to make me a star at 12. In fact, it wasn't until my senior year at high school that I showed any real talent.

What happens today is that many Little Leaguers are burned out before maturity. I think this explains why Little League has had such limited impact on baseball, why it has failed to produce a gold mine of talent not only for the majors but for high schools and colleges as well. The fault lies in its concentration on immediate victories and premature glory, rather than on teaching basic skills and sound development. It has made the kids into robots, and squeezed the fun out of the game. It has pushed them too fast, and often destroyed the game for boys before their teens. Championships seem to come first, the youngsters last.

"Before I got into Little League, I used to spend my entire summers playing ball at the playground." Tom Phillips recalls. "But after I made the league with two or three tough games a week and practice in between, I spent my spare time around the house, just resting from the grind."

In this super-organized system, kids are often disciplined for missing a game and bawled out for being late to practice. It is little wonder that many are fed up with baseball by high school. "We had a 'County Champ' for the last number of years in Little League," Lewis H. Treen, principal of Crescent City, Florida, public schools, told me, "but we have had to drop high-school baseball because of lack of interest."

In the case of two Little League friends in Connecticut, I saw the dismal result of premature glory and success. Both boys had been pushed to stardom by their coaches. Everyone in town knew their names and anticipated each dazzling achievement. One boy played shortstop in the World Series at Williamsport, and had his picture in a national magazine. But by the time he got to high school, he was so exhausted by constant demands for new heroics, he never went out for the team. The other tried out in high school and failed. The shock of being a star at 12 and a flop at 15 stunned him for years, and crippled a promising baseball career.

What angers me most about Little League's win-at-any-cost frenzy is that too many boys are barred from baseball when every applicant should be playing. In a town like Ilion, New York, with a 10,000 population and only four teams, many boys are obviously excluded. When a village official complained to the league's directors, he was bluntly told they were interested in quality, not quantity. I can't think of anything worse than turning a recreation program into an elite society.

Further, I'm continually disturbed by the heartbreaks inflicted on youngsters relegated to the sidelines. "An 11-year-old boy was dressed in his uniform and bubbling with excitement at 10 A.M. for a game at 3 that afternoon," Dr. L. A. Will of Venice, Florida, described a typical case. "He sat there inning after inning and never left the bench while his whole family watched from the stands. I have never seen a more dejected or forlorn little boy in my life. He remained crushed for days, and never again played baseball with a Little League or any other ball team."

It appalls me how many coaches are frustrated athletes, hell-bent on producing winning teams to re-create their own dreams of vanished glory. Many fathers take over teams and consciously or subconsciously push their sons' careers. Their driving ambition has produced a new medical ailment, "Little League elbow." This is a calcium deposit resulting from excessive strain on bones not fully developed, and from the demands of coaches for curves, sliders and other trick pitches. Youngsters of Little League age should only be taught the basic rudiments of every position. Pitchers should be confined to learning fast balls and control.

"Knowledge of boys is far more important in managers and coaches than knowledge of baseball, although men who possess both qualities have the most to offer," Professor Charles A. Bucher of New York University's School of Education told me. "In this crucial, transitional age, a youngster needs fine teachers, worthy of emulation, not highly organized competition geared to state and world championships."

Although it would be unjust to indict many conscientious Little League officials who are dedicated to juvenile recreation, the selection standards for managers and coaches are often absurd. "A league president was presiding at an organizational meeting. He said, 'We need six managers. Who will volunteer?' The six who volunteered first were selected even though the president had never seen four of them previously," states Dr. Arthur A. Esslinger, dean of the University of Oregon's School of Health and Physical Education, and a member of the board of directors of Little League baseball. "Despite our good managers, we are all forced to admit that we have had too many poor ones."

It seems disgraceful that poor managers are often the result of Little League's isolation from community leaders. "Little League has to report to no one," laments one upstate New York official. "No corrective measures can be taken by town or village authorities, by the school or park recreation staffs."

I'm equally fed up with idiotic fathers who made the Little League hero a new status symbol not far below a Cadillac convertible. Often frustrated athletes themselves, living out their youthful fantasies, they drive their sons toward stardom to bring reflected glory on themselves. Two fathers I know in Cincinnati threatened their boys with extra chores if they didn't bring back the batting championship. At games the fathers become raging banshees, castigating their offspring for dropping a fly ball or missing a third strike.

Many mothers have also joined the Little League status race. I saw one mother shout at her boy as he left the field after an error, "Don't embarrass me again before everyone!" Mothers from opposing teams often trade insults in the stands over their sons' prowess. Neighbors end up feuding with each other.

In their mania for victory, adults can wreck the whole concept of sportsmanship. A guidance counselor in an upstate New York school told me, "The parents in the stands are sometimes unbelievable. Not all parents, of course, but a 10-year-old boy only has to hear one parent sound like a fool to question the moral values of all parents." This school official blames the managers equally. "Once, after a contested decision, out came both managers, and you could easily hear them swearing and screaming at the umpire. It was quite an example for my son to witness."

The grandiose ambitions of many Little Leagues today with their flamboyant grandstands, parades and banquets are all part of an absurd commercial exploitation of our youngsters. Invited to speak at the opening of one league near my Florida home, I found myself in a parade surrounded by bands, fire engines, and most incongruous of all, the local beauty queen. No one ever explained the connection between the opening of a baseball season for youngsters and the unveiling of her charms.

Many Little League ball parks, quite apart from Williamsport, are blatantly luxurious, with huge grandstands and dugouts, manicured infields cared for by paid maintenance staffs, even lights for night games. In Westport, Connecticut, Avon Park, Florida, Ardsley, New York, and Mt. Lebanon, a Pittsburgh suburb, to mention just a few, the Little League investment runs at least $10,000.

The hoopla reaches its peak at the end of the season with banquets, cups and trophies honoring everything from stolen bases to "best care of uniform." "Unbelievable!" says Ralph Sabock, head football coach of Worthington, Ohio, High School. "Junk all cups and trophies," adds Florida principal Treen, "unless they are for sportsmanship or the fellow who worked hardest." The New York guidance counselor concludes, "The perspective is way off—these Little League kids are taught false values before they even get to high school."

A high-school coach I know asked two former Little Leaguers to pick up the bases after practice. They looked at him as if he had lost his mind. Who were they to have to do this menial task? He soon discovered the Little League in his town had become the "Luxury League." As Little Leaguers, his pampered players had never even carried in the bats after practice.

The most obnoxious of all luxuries are the uniforms given by local merchants, which turn youngsters into commercial hucksters. While no one would deny these boys the thrill of being togged out like major leaguers, they would gain far more by earning their equipment at odd jobs than having everything handed them on a silver platter.

It's also infuriating to see the increasing exploitation of Little Leagues by press and radio and TV networks. Seizing on the antics of kids of 10 and 12 as if they were exhibitions in a three-ring circus, the news media splash pictures of premature heroes sliding into base as prominently as an international conference. I strongly question the value of televising the Little League World Series and thrusting kids of this age into national stardom. Televising even regional playoffs, as I have seen in Los Angeles, is just crude financial greediness.

The tragedy of this fabricated promotion is that it makes a travesty of children's happiness. The glory, the headlines, the super-stadiums, yes, even the red carpet that New York's City Hall literally spread before last year's Little League champs, have been concocted by ambitious adults using the kids for their own ends.

The youngsters, unfortunately, have entered their organization world as a high price. Not only must they survive the pressure and philosophy of their mentors, but they have sacrificed their independence—the wild and wonderful ever-changing freedom of preadolescence.

One of the most pitiful sights I have seen on a diamond was a 10-year-old Little Leaguer circling the bases after a home run, then planting himself at the plate, doffing his cap and bowing in all directions to the thunderous stands in an almost Chaplinesque imitation of Babe Ruth at the summit of his career.

"Let baseball with its glory and excitement come when they are 13 to 18," advises educator Treen. "Every age group has its own area of entertainment, and if we let them get out of balance, we are in for trouble."

Despite the dangerous growth of abuses which have made Little League a Disneyland caricature of baseball, I am certain that a program of simple reforms can restore its former goals and benefits.

First. League officials in each area must establish close links with school and park systems and recreation supervisors. Local leaders, skilled at working with boys, should guide the league toward community needs.

Second. Managers and coaches must be carefully selected, not from ambitious fathers and pseudo athletes, but from school staffs, recreation directors and other personnel trained in handling youngsters.

Third. Publicity and promotion should be cut to a minimum. No premature heroes should be built from youngsters. While I am not opposed to the league's World Series, the number of post-season championships and playoffs should be strictly curtailed.

Fourth. Investments in league ball parks should be set at a reasonable limit. Municipal and school fields should be used wherever possible. No games should be played under lights, no professional grounds keepers hired.

Fifth. Commercialism and advertising, particularly the purchase of uniforms by local merchants and local TV sponsorship, should be prohibited.

Sixth. Leagues should be open to every applicant, with tryouts and drafts abolished. Every team member should play at least one or two innings per game.

Seventh. Prizes should only be awarded to a team as a whole, or for individual character traits like sportsmanship.

Most of these objectives have already been met by a few model organizations, particularly the Kettering, Ohio, Little League, a blueprint for good juvenile recreation. With every applicant playing regardless of ability, the league now boasts 500 boys. All parents sit together along the first-base line, and follow a strict tradition of cheering both teams indiscriminately. No standings are kept, no scores published. Competition ends July 28 with no post-season playoffs or tournaments. "We pick our managers not from baseball stars, but from men who best handle youngsters," states Pat Irelan, a co-founder. "Smiles are what we're looking for, and we get lots of them."

This is the kind of Little League I hope my son can join, a league we should have in every city and town when the game has finally been returned to the kids.

JOHN GALLAGHER

Courtesy *Sport* Magazine ©

"How come you ain't playing my kid?"

JUST AS not all players achieved their fame in the major leagues, neither did all umpires. Yet this one is among the two or three best-remembered of all.

Steamboat Johnson

JAMES M. KAHN

THE MOST CELEBRATED of the minor-league veterans was Harry Samuel "Steamboat" Johnson, who died in 1950 after forty years of umpiring, the last thirty of them in the Southern League. Steamboat's career was a riotous one, frequently marked with violence on the giving as well as the receiving end, because "the Steamer," as Southern League fans got to call him, was fearless and not above getting in the first swipe himself if an assailant looked as though he was getting ready to let one go. In his own story of his life, which he published in 1935 under the title *Standing the Gaff*, he included a few vital statistics:

"I have rendered about one million decisions since I began umpiring in 1909. Something like four thousand bottles have been thrown at me in my day but only about twenty ever hit me. That does not speak very well for the accuracy of the fans' throwing."

No one intimidated Steamboat, and he was no more awed by the great names of baseball than he was by the obscure ones. In the spring of 1923 Ty Cobb, then managing Detroit, hired Johnson to umpire a ten-game exhibition series which the Tigers were to play with the St. Louis Cardinals in Augusta, Georgia. It was a series that had attracted tremendous interest throughout Georgia, with Cobb, its great native son, the champion batter of the American League, matched with Rogers Hornsby, the bright St. Louis star who was the champion batsman of the National League. Fans poured into Augusta from miles around and jammed the ball park for the opening game. It was hardly the ideal setting in which to forfeit a ball game, but that's precisly what Steamboat did in the sixth inning, when Cobb became embroiled in an argument with Cy Pfirman, the National League umpire and Johnson's partner. Cobb was ordered out of the game but refused to go. Instead, he went to his position in center field.

Pfirman came over to Johnson and told him he had put Cobb out of the game and that the Detroit manager would have to leave before the game went on. Johnson strolled out to center field and told Cobb he would have to leave, but Ty refused.

"I told Cobb that I was in a terrible position," Johnson said, "because I knew that if I forfeited the game he would fire me and I would lose out on the exhibition series. Cobb told me I was exactly right; that he would fire me if I forfeited the game.

"I then told Cobb that if he had not left the game by the time I returned to home plate I would forfeit the game to St. Louis. Ty warned me that if I forfeited the game the fans would mob me. I told him I would just as soon be killed on a ball field as anywhere else."

Upon reaching the plate, Johnson turned and saw that Cobb was still in center field, and so, removing his cap, and bellowing in the foghorn voice which had earned him his nickname, Johnson announced to the jammed stands that he was forfeiting the game to St. Louis because Cobb would not leave the field.

Neither Johnson nor Pfirman was assaulted as they walked across the field to their dressing room. They were pushed and jostled and all the buttons were torn off Pfirman's uniform coat, but they were otherwise unharmed. The admission money had to be refunded and Cobb came tearing into the umpires' dressing room to tell Johnson what he thought of him and to make good on his threat to fire him. Steamboat was very definitely on the spot, but later that evening as he was packing his things at his hotel to go back to his home in Memphis, Johnson got a phone call from Cobb, telling him that the rumpus was all over and that he should come back to finish out his contract, which he did.

It was of such scuffles, and more, year after year, that Steamboat's life story is comprised, but his honesty, courage and simplicity and the humor he usually brought to bear on even the most desperate situations in time earned him a unique place among minor-league umpires. He was not only regarded with esteem but actually was held in affection and became a Southern League hero and favorite, as well as a Southern League institution.

"Steamboat Johnson is as full of color as a circus parade," Ed Danforth, sports editor of the Atlanta *Georgian*, wrote of him. "He is one umpire who is a standout. He is a real attraction. Fans often come to the park just to see him work."

Johnson had one year in the National League —in 1914. At the end of the season his contract was not renewed. He was puzzled by it, never understood it, was a little bit hurt by it, and never quite got over it. It was an old and painful wound to his pride. But once he settled down in the Southern League and reconciled himself to a career of minor-league umpiring, he brought to it a quality of humor, personal authority and rugged individualism which was every bit as distinctive as that of Bill Klem in the National League.

Steamboat was proud of his voice and would announce the batteries before the game in coarse, vibrant syllables that quivered the rafters of the Southern League ball parks. He scorned the mechanical amplifiers and is reported to have brooded for quite some time after they eventually replaced the natural lung power of the umpires. He was likewise affirmative about his eyesight and would have his eyes examined regularly by an oculist and get a certificate attesting to their sharpness. He carried this in his uniform pocket and when a batter questioned his eyesight or he was otherwise referred to a a "blind robber," he would produce it.

"Read this, young man," he would say. "Twenty-twenty in each eye."

Steamboat lived in Memphis where, with his wife, he ran a restaurant, Steamboat Johnson's Eat Shoppe, a favorite place for cotton men. He was a popular and respected figure in his home town and finally, in 1949, when he was rounding out his thirtieth year in the Southern League, was paid an extraordinary compliment by Southern League fans when, on July 28 in New Orleans, they held a "night" for him.

In keeping with Johnson's most colorful performances and character, he made his appearance on the ball field to receive the homage of the fans, manacled to a policeman, wearing dark-blue glasses and led by a seeing-eye dog, a mite of a smooth-haired fox terrier. Three other Southern League umpires were present for the occasion and, to comprise part of the honors which were to go to Steamboat on his night, were permitted to reverse the usual procedure and boo the fans, which they did with enthusiasm and gusto. It remains a tribute to an umpire, hilarious as it was, unparalleled in minor-league history, a unique climax to a unique career.

Hug

JOHN KIERAN

THEY ALWAYS SAID that Miller J. Huggins was not the driving type of manager, but there was one man he drove too hard. That was Miller J. Huggins. He never spared himself, and the fatal testimony on that point is overwhelming. The Yankees were going nowhere. The race was all over. But Huggins, paying no attention to his own physical condition, worked and worried day after day on the problem of getting ready a better Yankee team for next year.

Even if the Yankees win everything in sight and set all sorts of new records next season, the price was too high. Far too high. Speaking of him only as a baseball manager and sticking to the cold facts and the printed records, Miller J. Huggins was by far the most successful manager of the modern era in baseball. Six pennants and three world championships in eight years. A team that won eight straight games to sweep through two World Series without a defeat. What other manager can point to a record like that?

Yet Huggins himself always said with that quizzical smile of his, "Great managers? Great players make great managers." That may be true, but some credit should go to the manager who recognizes a great player when he sees one.

For years Huggins had to battle against a tide of unpopularity. He had never been on a New York team before he came to manage the Yankees. He was a National League player and manager through all his career until he stepped into an American League dugout to take over the Yankees from Wild Bill Donovan.

He was not a glad-hander, not the hail-fellow-well-met type. He was reserved with strangers, quiet with acquaintances and only revealed himself to close friends. With those he knew and liked, Hug shed all his reserve. To the fans in general he must have seemed a serious and even grumpy fellow as he stalked up and down the coaching lines, a thin, nervous figure, with hunched shoulders that looked as though they were bowed with the weight of centuries. But to those who knew him behind the scenes and across the dinner table, he was a different man entirely. A ready and frequently witty talker, a student of men and a reader of books, a fellow who was frank, friendly and informal.

But on the surface and to the gaze of ordinary spectators, Huggins was just a sharp little fellow, shrewd enough to tell Colonel Jacob Ruppert and Colonel Til Huston what players to buy from the Boston Red Sox. When the Yankees won their first pennant in 1921 the fans gave great credit to the Ruppert and Huston bankrolls.

Even when the Yankees won in 1922 and again in 1923, the old argument still held good. The Ruppert checkbook was the answer to the Yankee pennants, according to the anti-Huggins crowd. But the crowd was getting smaller. Some had switched sides and others left the anti-Huggins brigade to take up a neutral position. After all, Hug was smart enough to know what players to buy, and every purchase or trade he made was a winning one. That, it was grudgingly admitted, was something.

The first championship machine began to creak here and clatter there and Hug tried to patch it up enough to last out the season of 1924. He couldn't quite make it. The team finished second. The next year came the grand crash and the sinking to a seventh-place berth. That was in 1925.

In 1926 Miller J. Huggins bobbed up with a team that won the American League pennant and lost the World Series by an eyelash. Exclusive of the pitchers, six out of eight regulars on that team were men who had never played on any other major-league team. Two of them, Koenig and Lazzeri, were green kids from the minors. Except for Ruth in right field and Dugan at third base, the players were men who had been picked from the minors by Yankee scouts and developed into a championship array by a Yankee manager.

That just about ended the debate over the ability of Miller J. Huggins. The scoffers ceased to scoff and the skeptics were convinced. The pennant-winning years of 1927 and 1928 merely served to bring in more evidence than was needed.

In winning his first three pennants Huggins had shown that he knew how to buy. In winning his last three, he showed that he knew how to build. He had the backing of Colonel Ruppert, of course, but John McGraw had the backing of C. A. Stoneham and Joe McCarthy had the backing of William Wrigley. McGraw and McCarthy are smart managers, but they have yet to equal the feat performed by Huggins. Then Dusty Miller rebuilt his club and drove it from seventh place to a pennant in one year.

There were other problems Huggins had to solve. He wasn't imposing in appearance and he couldn't control his players as Husk Chance used to do and Old Rough Carrigan did when he was younger. Huggins, a junior lightweight, had to solve his troubles in another way. It took him a few years, and there were some stirring battles that never went into the records, but the junior lightweight won over the heavyweights all along the line.

That's only part of the story, but perhaps it's enough. Here was a man who came into town with everybody giving him the cold shoulder and a few interested persons out gunning for him. Players, fans and writers were against him. He was a stranger in a strange town and he was given a sixth-place ball club to manage.

He won three pennants and the credit was given to somebody else. He smiled and said nothing. His team fell apart and he built another pennant-winning machine that won three times in a row. This time he got the credit.

Some of his high-priced and temperamental stars broke the rules of discipline and openly scoffed at his authority. He subdued the insurrection and ended up by being the complete master of the situation.

In Babe Ruth he had not only the biggest figure in baseball but one of the hardest problems to handle. They battled and it took a courageous chap to do what Huggins did. He handed an ultimatum to the most popular figure the game had ever known. Ruth was never a bigger fellow in his life than the day he admitted he was wrong and Huggins was right.

Huggins was a fine player and a remarkably successful manager, to which might be added the verdict of Babe Ruth: "He was a great guy, was Hug."

MOST READERS will be familiar with the works of Marvin Kitman, whose career seems to have been dedicated to the fine proposition that the more odd a man's behavior, the more strictly legal it becomes. Acting on this belief, he got himself nominated for President of the United States at the Republican convention in 1964—and, two years later, decided to buy himself a professional ballplayer for one dollar.

My Son the Outfielder, and My Major Leaguer, Dick Stuart

MARVIN KITMAN

I READ in the paper several weeks ago that a baseball player named Dick Stuart had been given his outright release by the New York Mets. As a free agent, the story explained, the first baseman was now able to make his own deals. Theoretically, anybody could hire a free agent by buying his contract for one dollar. I suddenly realized that an ordinary fan like me could become the first person on his block to own a private major-league ballplayer.

But I wasn't going to spend money to keep Stuart on the bench in front of my house in Leonia, New Jersey, as a mere status symbol. He would play ball every day with my son, the utility outfielder.

Stuart seemed an ideal tutor for my eight-year-old boy because I wanted somebody who wasn't perfect. A young ballplayer can be ruined psychologically by having to measure up to a perfectionist. To err is human, and Stuart's performance in the field proved that he was a regular fellow. His ability to turn a routine ground ball into a sports thrill had earned him the honorary title "Dr. Strangeglove." He liked working with kids, judging by the way he had fielded questions from boys on his *Stump Stuart* pregame TV show.

I was in the market for a major-leaguer because of what happened this spring in my son's first season of organized ball. His lifetime baseball record with the Petite Cleaners of the Leonia Skeeter League is not impressive. But scouting reports on my boy were encouraging. The only thing wrong with him, according to neighborhood bird dogs, is his father.

The boner I pulled as manager of his career was believing those psychological articles about the dangers of pushing your boy to star in the Little Leagues to gratify your own sick needs. When we talked about this in the hot-stove league last winter, the Petite Cleaners fathers agreed it was best to let the kids learn the game at their own speed. But on opening day, I discovered I was the only enlightened father who hadn't been taking his boy behind the ranch house at night to teach him everything he knew. Well, I would show them how a father *really* can encourage his boy to become a star.

The ex-Met slugger leads the league in self-confidence, so I wrote to him in his own language. "Congratulations," began my letter to Stuart at his home in Greenwich, Connecticut, where he was awaiting job offers. "I've decided to pick up your contract for 1967." To prove it was a firm offer, I enclosed my personal check for one dollar.

"Your duties will be to teach my boy the fundamentals of the game." I wrote, "especially fielding. With a man of your stature tutoring him I see no reason why he can't be ready for the majors within 12 years. None of the Little Leagues in New Jersey offer instruction in basic economics for young ballplayers, so this is an area where my son really can benefit from your wisdom. He endorsed Petite Cleaners by wearing the company's shirt all season without collecting a penny."

I closed by assuring my new ballplayer that I hoped to sit down with him as soon as possible to talk salary for 1967. "I'm sure we'll be able to work out a fair price for your services," I wrote, "based on the fact that you are currently unemployed. P.S. What size Petite Cleaners shirt will you need?"

Several days later I wrote him a second letter. "I hope your silence doesn't mean you're planning to be a holdout for 1967. Let's stop this haggling and come to terms. Incidentally, my son says that since I'm buying ballplayers, he would prefer Willie Mays."

A few days after that, the phone rang at my house. "It's somebody named Dick Stuart," my wife called out.

"I was out of town and just got your letter," Dick Stuart said. "How much money are you talking about for 1967?"

"Mr. Stuart, I've always been one of your great admirers," I said. "I'm the former president of the Dick Stuart Fan Club of Leonia. I resigned in protest when the club voted to change its name to the Ed Kranepool Fan Club after the Mets released you—"

My ballplayer interrupted, "How much money did you have in mind?"

"I've analyzed your career," I said, stalling while I figured how to explain to my wife that I had bought a major leaguer for the house when we didn't have a maid. "Branch Rickey said a winning player has to be hungry. By working for me, you could work yourself into proper financial condition."

Again Stuart asked about money.

"You only hit .218 for the Mets before they dropped you," I said.

"Do you realize I made $40,000 last season?" he asked. "And that a lot of clubs are still after me?"

Obviously Stuart, the master bargainer, was escalating his salary demands by mentioning offers he was getting to jump to Japanese baseball. "Don't think you're the only player who could help my boy," I said, as cold as any major-league magnate dealing with a hireling. "Dee Fondy and Wayne Terwilliger are also free agents."

"Why don't you teach the kid how to play ball yourself?" Stuart suggested.

"And have the kid hate me because I pushed him into baseball?" I asked. "I did show him how to take a cut at the ball before one game. He struck out every time. But that was just his way of rebelling against his father."

"Nobody can teach your boy how to play," Stuart said.

"Are you trying to tell me my son is hopeless?"

"I mean all you can do is *show* kids the fundamentals of the game. Not even Ted Williams could *teach* an eight-year-old. A kid has to mature first."

To break the impasse, I made a concrete offer. "I'm sure your account would prefer a deferred-payment deal. I'll give you fifty percent of the bonus the kid gets when he signs with a major-league club, plus the Cadillac."

Stuart shrewdly avoided saying no—and he left the door open by telling me to get in touch as soon as I figured out what I could pay him next year.

One solution to the high cost of owning a private major leaguer was to lease him to other fathers who wanted their sons to sit at the feet of a master. I had two days of Stuart's time booked for 1967 when I read that my ballplayer had been lured away by a cartel of West Coast oil and real-estate tycoons called the Los Angeles Dodgers.

Connie Mack once said, "You can't win them all." But I wasn't discouraged. I had a hunch Stuart might soon be a free agent again, and my strategy now was to play a waiting game. I wrote Stuart a letter congratulating him on his new job with the Dodgers. "Just a reminder that my offer still holds for next season. Spring training begins on April 1 at Sylvan Park in Leonia. I don't want to influence your decision, but Sylvan Park has a short left-field wall."

HERE IS A CHAPTER from Mr. Koppett's recent book, *A Thinking Man's Guide to Baseball,* that dares to ask the question: Who is the greater of the two mighty center fielders of our time? Dares to answer it, too.

The Great Debate: Mays or Mantle?

LEONARD KOPPETT

NEW YORK CITY has always enjoyed a lion's share of baseball history and glamour. The first real baseball club, of course, was the Knickerbocker Club of New York, which played the first recognized game in 1846. The dominant personalities of the two major leagues—John McGraw in the National and Babe Ruth in the American—operated in New York in their years of greatest achievement. There were 61 World Series between 1903 and 1964, and at least one New York team (including Brooklyn) took part in 37 of them; 13 times, the championship of baseball was decided in a "subway series," involving two New York teams.

The Golden Years ended, actually, in 1958, when the Dodgers and Giants set up shop in California, leaving the Yankees in lonely splendor. When the Mets came along four years later, they filled a great vacuum, but they didn't really replace the established rivalries the Giants and Dodgers had represented. The Yankees never did cash in on their position of monopoly while they were alone, and Met success at the gate was based on the return visits paid by Dodgers and Giants. This may have surprised a lot of casual observers and doctrinaire economists, but the explanation was simple: baseball fans live off argument, comparison, discussion, and opinion; with three teams in one city (two of them in the same league), there was an endless supply of material for barroom conversation, and a wide choice of loyalties; with only the champion Yankees around, what was there to argue about?

In many respects, therefore, the most Golden Year of all was 1951.

That year, for the only time in baseball history, all three teams finished first. The Yankees won the American League pennant, fighting off Cleveland in a tight battle through September; and the Giants, trailing the Dodgers by 13½ games in mid-August, caught them on the next-to-last day and finished in a tie for first. Then the Giants won the three-game play-off, on Bobby Thomson's three-run homer in the last of the ninth of the third game. And finally, the Yankees defeated the Giants in an eventful World Series, four games to two.

Among other things, Allie Reynolds pitched two no-hitters for the Yankees, and Joe DiMaggio played his final season; Gil McDougald hit a grand slam in the World Series; and the city had six 20-game winners—Vic Raschi and Eddie Lopat of the Yankees, Preacher Roe and Don Newcombe of the Dodgers, Sal Maglie and Larry Jansen of the Giants. The three managers—Casey Stengel of the Yankees, Leo Durocher of the Giants, and Charlie Dressen of the Dodgers—were three of the most talkative, colorful, controversial, and knowledgeable figures in the history of the game. It is small wonder, in a year like that, that 4,634,251 tickets were sold for games at the Yankee Stadium, Ebbets Field, and the Polo Grounds.

And yet, the most lasting effect of 1951 was none of those things. It was the arrival of two rookies, instantly recognized by the fans as superstars: Mickey Mantle and Willie Mays.

It is amazing how accurate the instincts of the dedicated fan can be. The bleacherites were far ahead of the experts in accepting Mantle and Mays as larger than life-size. The registered experts, well informed by baseball men who had seen Mickey and Willie in action, nevertheless clung to small hesitancies, reservations, doubts, and supercilious calm; they had to, after all, maintain their self-images as objective critics, even if they were willing to forgo their public pose as hard-to-impress New Yorkers.

But the fans made no such mistake, and indulged in no such delayed response. Their imaginations were inflamed as soon as they saw them—Willie, his cap flying off, catching the ball in that ridiculous fashion with his hands at his belt; blond Mickey, with blinding speed in his legs, swinging the bat from either side of the plate. The fans had no more trouble identifying baseball godhead when they saw it than an ancient Athenian would have had identifying a huge, bearded man with a bolt of lightning in his hand as Zeus; only an expert could miss it. (However, in fairness to the experts, it must be noted that most of them quickly switched status and began to react as fans.)

And so, the Great Debate began.

Who do you like better, Mantle or Mays? Which one is greater? Which one will be greater?

In bars, on street corners, in school hallways, in living rooms, in country clubs, in restaurants, at work, during lunch, over cocktails, in the subways and buses, and most of all around the ball parks, the discussion flourished.

Mantle could hit the ball farther than anyone, and do it lefty or righty—and still run faster than anyone. How could anyone top that? But Mays moved even better on a ball field, and made a new incredible catch every day—and also hit homers while maintaining a high average.

Fifteen years later, the argument had been settled in one sense, but more fascinating than ever in another. By 1966, Mantle had been crippled so often by a succession of injuries that his ability to play at all was in question, while Mays was accomplishing things in his mid-thirties that he had not done in his late twenties. From the standpoint of continuous, cumulative, and still fully effective achievement, Mays had come out ahead; but admiration for Mantle is stimulated by contemplation of what he might have done if granted the normal amount of freedom from injury.

Their careers followed quite different rhythms.

Mantle's buildup came first. Before the 1951 season, the Yankees conducted a "rookie school," an innovation at the time. That year, incidentally, the Yankees and Giants had arranged to "trade" training camps, and the Yankees were based in Phoenix, Arizona, while the Giants trained at the traditional Yankee site in St. Petersburg, Florida. By March, many tales had started to trickle back to New York about the "phenom" the Yankees had found.

He was nineteen years old, and his father had named him after Mickey Cochrane and had started training him as an infant. He had played half a season of professional baseball at Independence, Missouri, and then all of the 1950 season at Joplin, Missouri, as a shortstop. He had hit .383 with 26 homers and 136 runs batted in. He was shy and socially awkward, son of a lead miner from a small Oklahoma town. He was a switch-hitter, and incredibly fast.

In those days, few players made the jump from the low minors to the majors in one year. Even McDougald, who was to join the Yankees that season and become American League rookie of the year, was considered remarkable because he had come up from the Texas League, a double-A classification. But Mantle, who had played no higher than Class C at Joplin—that is, five steps below the majors—was already tabbed "can't miss."

He had, the most critical veteran observers admitted, two weaknesses. The physical one they shrugged off; from a football injury, he had osteomyelitis of the right leg—a persistent bone infection that could be controlled but might act up at any time. The other was his mental-emotional makeup: the young Mantle was simultaneously uncontrollably eager and stubborn. He was slow to learn, intent on hitting everything as far as he could, enraged with himself at every failure, capable of deep depression, and not at all analytic in his approach to the game.

The man most impressed by Mantle's potential was the Yankee manager, Casey Stengel. Looking at Mantle's physical equipment, and especially his ability to hit from both sides of the plate, Stengel saw the perfect player in the making. All the knowledge, slickness, and information Casey had accumulated in forty years of baseball would be imparted to this unformed but unlimited talent, and the mature Mantle would emerge as the monument of Stengel's career, his masterpiece.

So Mickey Mantle opened the season in right field at Yankee Stadium, wearing a very pointedly significant No. 6. Babe Ruth had worn No. 3, and Lou Gehrig No. 4, and both numbers had been "retired," never to be worn again by Yankee players. Joe DiMaggio was No. 5, and he was still the center fielder. The Yankees were making no bones about the progression they expected Mantle to maintain.

In his first Yankee game, a 5–0 victory over the Red Sox, Mickey's modest contribution was a single. The hitting star was another rookie, Jackie Jensen, who played left field.

But the burden was too great, the leap too wide. By mid-season, Mickey had bogged down in a strikeout streak. On July 15, with his average at .260, he was sent back down to Kansas City (then the triple-A farm club) to get straightened out. Despondent, he thought of quitting, but his father snapped him out of that by telling him, "If that's all the courage you have, go ahead and quit." In 40 games at Kansas City, Mickey batted in 50 runs, hit 11 homers, and batted .361. On August 24 he was back with the Yankees.

But when he came back, he didn't put on No. 6. He took No. 7, and wore it from then on.

Meanwhile, New York had remained unaware of Willie until May.

Jackie Robinson had become the first Negro major-league player only in 1947. The chief source for new talent, still being tapped, was the established Negro-league structure. In 1950, the Giants' organization signed Mays, who was nineteen years old and playing with the Birmingham Barons. He finished out that season at Trenton, New Jersey, in a Class B league, hitting .353. For 1951, he was assigned to Minneapolis, the top Giant farm club, in the American Association—the same league in which the Yankees had Kansas City.

By May 24, Willie was hitting .477.

Not .377.

.477.

And remember, this wasn't the low minors. This was the last step below the majors and, at that time, a considerably tougher league than the triple-A leagues now in existence. And yet, when the Giants called Willie up, it was for his fielding—and they were right.

The Giants' home field was the Polo Grounds, which had the largest center-field area in the majors, and Willie played center field in a way that had to be seen to be believed. (Eventually, tens of millions saw and believed.) His range was limitless, and his arm so strong that he could make effective throws from the most unlikely locations and from the most unlikely body positions. Because he could go back so well and so far, he could play closer to the infield, and catch innumerable possible singles—and still always get back to the boundary of the particular field to prevent a ball from going over his head for a double or triple.

The Giant management (Leo Durocher was the field manager) appreciated these qualities from prior knowledge (through reports)—and was confident that he would hit, too. The Giant players—especially the pitchers—saw for themselves in the first few days after his arrival. But even the fans recognized the full value of these magnificent skills, because it is a fact that they accepted Willie's greatness even before he did any real hitting in the majors. (He finished the year at .274, seven points higher than Mantle, and had 20 home runs.)

When Willie joined the Giants, they were just getting back to .500 after a disastrous start. Since the team's main assets were great pitching and Durocher-style opportunistic offense, the improved defense provided by Mays was exceptionally important. The Giants straightened themselves out—but the Dodgers were running away.

In mid-August the Giants began a 16-game winning streak. The day that Mantle rejoined the Yankees, the Giants won No. 12 of their streak. The Yankees, at that point, were a couple of games behind the Cleveland Indians and driving. Mays and Mantle, as individuals, were overshadowed by the steady stream of dramatic events as that season came to its end, but they played important roles in them. The day that the Yankees clinched the pennant, Reynolds pitched his second no-hitter; the Giants didn't win theirs until Thomson hit his home run—with Willie, admittedly scared, kneeling in the on-deck circle.

And so, on October 4, the World Series began with Willie Mays in center field for the Giants and Mickey Mantle in right for the Yankees. In the first game, both went hitless (Mickey walked once) as the Giants won. Mantle led off for the Yankees in the second game with a bunt single, and struck out in the third.

In the fifth, a routine play set the stage for the theme of the whole Mantle-Mays comparison. Mays, still hitless, hit a fly to right-center. Joe DiMaggio drifted to his left to catch it. Mantle eagerly raced over from right field to be alongside, back up, help, or catch it himself if necessary.

He was within 10 feet of DiMaggio when his right foot stepped on the wooden lid of a drainpipe imbedded in the outfield grass. His right knee buckled. He went down, as so many people have scribed it, "as if shot."

Mickey had a torn knee cartilage. He played

no more in that Series, and his legs were never 100 percent sound again. And no one remembers that Mays hit the ball that started Mantle's troubles.

Mays played out the Series with a .182 batting average, and the Yankees won it in six games.

In 1952 Willie played 34 games and then went into the Army, where he stayed through 1953.

In 1952 Mantle had to start slowly because of the knee operation he had undergone—and he was medically deferred from the draft. A certain segment of the public persecuted Mantle for many years on this score. Also, he had endured a spiritual crisis, his father's death at the age of forty-one.

DiMaggio had retired, and Mantle was heir apparent to the center-field job—but he wasn't ready physically, and opened the season in right field. In May, as his leg got stronger, he shifted to center. He had a fine year, hitting .311 and 23 homers, and the Yankees won another close pennant race. In a seven-game World Series against the Dodgers (the Giants had finished second), Mickey was spectacular, hitting .345. It was this World Series that established the idea nationally that Mickey was the next leader of the Yankees.

In 1953 a deteriorating, Mays-less Giant team finished fifth. The Yankees, however, won their fifth pennant in a row. Mantle, becoming famous for "tape-measure homers," hit .295, and hit a grand slam in the Series, as the Dodgers were beaten again, this time in six games.

When the 1954 season began, Mantle was fully established as a national sports hero. Willie, except to dedicated Giant fans and less secure Dodger fans with long memories, was just another promising player coming back from military service. And there was more to the publicity gap than the fact that the Yankees had just won five straight World Series while the Giants had faded with Willie away.

It must be realized that this was less than a decade after World War II. The recognition of teen-agers as a distinct class was relatively new—and Mantle had played in the majors as a teen-ager. Physically, he combined the most glamorous attributes of a classic hero—Herculean strength (those 500-foot homers), incredible speed (he could get down to first base in 3.1 seconds), good looks, youth, unprecedented versatility (there had never before been a switch-hitter with such power), and unlimited potential. If ever a "perfect" player was in the making, Mantle was the one—and it's hard to exaggerate how stimulating he was to the fans' imagination.

The degree of identification—always the basic ingredient in the creation of any superstar—was, in Mantle's case, of exceptional depth. His physical flaw, the bad leg, almost literally an Achilles' heel, only added to the drama.

And, of course, Mantle was white. This was only 1954, the year of the Supreme Court's school desegregation decision. Whatever more complicated guilts or resentments might arise in the collective mind later, at that time there was simply no comparison in emotional appeal. Willie was a Negro and, no matter how sincerely admired and enjoyed, could not arouse the same level of personal identification in whites that Mantle could.

Ten years later this factor meant much less, because the whole context of life was changing, and because each man's achievement had created an individuality beyond his outer aspect. But, at the beginning of 1954, neither man yet had any overwhelming achievement—just promise.

Then both started to make the promise good.

In 1954 the Giants won a pennant unexpectedly. They fought off the Dodgers and Braves, who were fundamentally more talented teams. The Giants had great pitching, and an experienced first-string lineup, but the real difference was Mays. In one sense, he gave the most remarkable performance of his entire career.

It was remarkable in this way: in June Willie went on a home-run spree, and by the end of July he was running well ahead of Babe Ruth's record pace of 1927. But his batting average was not too high, as he swung for the fences, and the way the Giants played, they needed more singles than homers. So Leo told Willie to stop swinging for homers, and to hit the ball to right field. In the team's first 99 games, Willie had hit 36 homers; in the last two months of the season, he hit only five more—but raised his average to .345 and won the league batting championship on the last day of the season.

The Giants went on to sweep the World Series in four straight games from the Cleveland Indians, who had finally beaten the Yankees by setting an American League record of 111 victories. Mays was the Most Valuable Player in the National League. Mantle had hit .300 and 27 homers for the Yankees, but he had been overshadowed.

From that point on, the Great Debate was firmly established.

In 1955 the Dodgers reclaimed the National League championship as the Giants finished a distant third—and Willie, with no reason not to swing for the fences, blasted 51 home runs, giving Ruth's record a good challenge most of the season.

In 1955 the Yankees started another string of pennants, which was to reach four. Mantle emerged as the American League home-run champion (with 37) and hit .306. (Mays hit .318.) But during the World Series, Mickey's legs kept him out of action more than half the time as the Dodgers (for the first time) won the world championship in seven games.

In 1956 Durocher was gone from the Giants, and they became a second-division club. Mays had one of his least distinguished batting records—.296, with 36 homers—but those who followed the Giants knew that he was performing new prodigies in the outfield every day. He also led the league in stolen bases, with 40, a department in which he was to lead for the next four years.

But Mantle, in 1956, hit the jackpot. He won the "triple crown"—batting title (.353), home runs (52), and runs batted in (130). Many of the home runs were of fantastic length. In the World Series, in which the Yankees got even with the Dodgers by winning the seventh game, Mickey hit three more homers. Now it was Mantle's turn to have an MVP award.

By now, several facets of the Great Debate had become well-established.

As base runners, both men were fabulous. Mantle never approached the statistical record of Mays in stolen bases, but there were two good reasons for it: the Yankees didn't play that kind of baseball, and there was no sense risking Mickey's vulnerable legs too much. (In 1956, when Willie stole 40 bases, the whole Yankee team stole 51.) But Mantle, when it was desirable, could steal as effectively as Willie, and over the years succeeded in about 80 percent of his attempts.

In fielding, Mays was obviously superior in skill—but Mantle could run so fast that he made up for much of the difference.

At bat, Mantle was obviously more dangerous, since he could turn around.

And in personality, there was a striking contrast. Mantle was always a figure tinged by tragedy, moody, at times frustrated, stubborn (he was still swinging for the fence every time, striking out too much), shy and suspicious, often troubled. His mainsprings were pride and determination. But he also had playboy tendencies, and was often mentioned in gossip columns.

Willie's mainspring was uninhibited joy. He played baseball with a cheerful abandon that made everyone who saw him smile involuntarily. With his squeaky voice and high-spirited laugh, he was the butt of playful gestures by teammates and rivals alike. He had an open manner, friendly, vivacious, irrepressible. Whatever his private insecurities, he projected a feeling that playing ball, for its own sake, was the most wonderful thing in the world; and when the major-league game was over, there was stickball to be played in the streets of Harlem.

Later, this changed. Willie, as he grew older, became more withdrawn and suspicious, more cautious, more vulnerable—and with plenty of reason. Life, both personally and professionally, became more complicated for him and he had his share of sorrow. He married, adopted a child, then went through a painful divorce. Mantle, on the other hand, became somewhat more expansive—at least, at times—as he matured. But the basic images always remained true: joyful Willie, unfortunate Mickey.

In 1957 the Giants finished their New York career (as a sixth-place club) and moved on to San Francisco. Willie hit .333 with 35 homers, and the New York public considered his departure a much greater loss than the franchise itself.

That left Mantle with the metropolis to himself—but even as Mays was leaving, Mantle was suffering another injury which was to have a lasting effect.

In 1957 Mantle was MVP again. (He hit .365 and 34 homers.) In the third game of the World Series against Milwaukee, Mickey was on second when the pitcher (Bob Buhl) tried to pick him off. It was a high throw, and Red Schoendienst, the second baseman, had to leap. He came down on Mantle's right shoulder.

Mickey finished that game (and hit a home run), but the shoulder was damaged. Gradually, from that point on, he developed more and more difficulty in throwing, and in batting left-handed. (From that side, the right shoulder is the front one, and the arm must be lifted higher to lead the bat; Mantle always was a better hitter right-handed, but this injury increased the difference.) Eventually—in 1965—the shoulder became so painful that he couldn't throw at all, or hit effectively, and he was ready to quit baseball. Only then, in January 1966, was surgery performed to remove bone chips and inflamed tendons, making it possible for him to continue.

How much this injury hampered Mantle can never be measured; it never got as much publicity as his legs, but it was a constant problem.

From 1958 on, the Great Debate lost its local intensity but gained a sort of diffuse momentum nationally. San Franciscans, believe it or not, resented Mays at first. Mantle, although he led the American League in homers in 1958 and 1960 (with 42 and 40), was dropping in all-around efficiency.

The Yankees didn't even win a pennant in 1959, and Stengel's regime ended when they pulled one out in 1960 but lost the World Series to Pittsburgh. Willie, meanwhile, played 1958 and 1959 in little Seals Stadium in San Francisco, while Candlestick Park was being built. His fielding brilliance, while no less effective for the club, was cramped and less noticeable to the public. And when the Giants moved into Candlestick in 1960, it turned out to be too large to hit many home runs in.

In those years, then, the debate cooled off, but it regained pertinence in 1961.

That was the year Mantle and Roger Maris went after Babe Ruth's record, and Maris got it. Roger hit No. 61 on the last day of the season, but Mantle wound up with 54 and kept pace until the last four weeks. Then Maris had 53, Mickey had 51, on September 5. Soon after that, a virus weakened Mickey, and kept him out of most of the World Series, but he won more finishing second than Maris did finishing first.

Maris carried two huge handicaps: the burden of attacking Ruth's hallowed record, and his own inability to deal with the pressures of instant fame. Commissioner Ford Frick added to his problem with a ridiculous ruling about "154 games" (since this was the first year of expansion and the 10-team league meant a 162-game schedule). To many fans, therefore, Maris became a target for resentment—and by reaction, Mantle became a hero in the eyes even of those who had criticized him up to then.

In Candlestick Park, that year, they moved the fences in, and Willie returned to the 40-homer class.

In 1962 Mantle was MVP again as the Yankees won the pennant for the tenth time in his twelve years with the club. A succession of leg injuries kept him from playing almost one-fourth of the time, but he hit .321 and 30 homers.

And they met again in the World Series, for the first time since their rookie year.

Willie had hit 49 home runs, and a key single in the ninth inning of the third play-off game at Los Angeles. This was another seven-game Series, and it ended with Willie on second base with the potential winning run as Bobby Richardson caught Willie McCovey's line drive for the final out of the 1–0 victory. As a confrontation, though, it was a bust: Mays hit .250 and Mantle .120.

In 1963, in June, Mantle suffered the injury that made him a semicripple for the rest of his career. Running into the wall in Baltimore, he broke a bone in his left foot, and also tore the knee cartilage. He missed two-thirds of that season, limped through 1964 and, in 1965, came to the point of retiring.

But Willie was getting his second wind as a slugger. Still superb, he was no longer quite the incredible outfielder he had been in the 1950s. As the team acquired more power, he did less base-stealing. His batting average stayed pretty stable—.314 in 1963 (the same as his lifetime average through 1965), .296 in 1964, and .317 in 1965. His home-run production, however, soared—38 in 1963, 47 in 1964, 52 in 1965. Early in 1966 Willie hit No. 512 of his career, breaking Mel Ott's National League record. Soon only Ruth's 714 was ahead of him.

At the end of the 1965 season, an interesting statistical coincidence showed up: Mantle and Mays had each played 2,005 games. Comparison was inevitable.

Mays had come to bat 220 more times.

Mantle had reached base 216 more times—because he had 1,464 walks to Willie's 949.

But Willie had a higher batting average, .314 to .306.

Willie had 32 more home runs, and 58 more runs batted in. He had almost twice as many stolen bases (276 to 145), but Mantle had a better percentage of success in stealing—81 percent to 76 percent. And Willie had hit into more than twice as many double plays (174 to 86).

But Mantle struck out much more—1,424 times (a major-league record, surpassing Ruth) to 893.

However, Mantle also broke Ruth's record for home runs in World Series play, with 18. (The Babe had 15.) Mays never did hit a World Series homer, in 17 games played.

Finally, in the very rudimentary category

of fielding statistics, Willie's big advantage showed. He played 1,987 games in the outfield, 65 more than Mickey—and made 980 more put-outs.

No one knows what a healthy Mantle might have done; still, in the early years, Mays surpassed him in rate of development. As a batter, Mantle was more dangerous and more consistent than Willie, who was notorious for all-on or all-off hot streaks and slumps. In effective speed, they were equal. Defensively, Mays was much, much better.

To players, Mantle has always been an object of special awe. They have been impressed not only by his exceptional strength and other abilities, but by his determination and courage in forcing himself to play—and to play so well with so many physical handicaps.

But the phrase usually applied to Willie is a sort of inarticulate appreciation: "Willie? He's just too much."

For myself, comparison isn't exactly equal, because I saw most of Mantle's career, but only pieces of Willie's since the Giants moved to California. Only a handful of players, in all baseball history, have been as important to winning teams, and have been able to contribute as much to eventual victory, rather than to statistics, as Mickey Mantle.

Willie, on the other hand, I can sum up very simply: he's the best baseball player I ever saw.

THE PILOT of a TWA plane, shuttling between Chicago and LaGuardia, which is hard by Shea Stadium, is supposed to have seen this game, coming and going, eight times. Here's baseball's "longest day."

1964: San Francisco Giants, 5, 8; New York Mets 3, 6

BARNEY KREMENKO

THIS WAS the longest day in the history of baseball.

This was the day that Pee Wee Reese, broadcasting the first game of a Cards-Reds doubleheader in St. Louis for the CBS Game of the Week, flew to New York in time to see the last few innings of the Mets-Giants 23-inning, doubleheader nightcap at Shea Stadium.

It was the day in which two tons of frankfurters and hamburgers were consumed by the Mets' record crowd of 57,037.

It also was the day in which the umpires thought they were amply supplied with baseballs when they started out with ten dozen, but wound up needing 22 dozen.

It was—to be exact—Sunday, May 31, when play began at 1:08 in the afternoon and didn't end until 11:25 that night.

The Giants won the doubleheader, taking the opener, 5–3, in regulation time and the nightcap marathon, 8–6. As one of the New York dailies, alluding to the Mets, headlined in huge capital letters:

WELL, YOU DON'T BEAT OUR GUYS IN A HURRY.

The elapsed—or actual playing—time for the doubleheader was nine hours, 52 minutes, a record.

Numerous other records were set—for most innings in one day (32), for the longest game by time (seven hours and 23 minutes in the 23-inning windup), for strikeouts and at-bats.

The huge crowd got more than time on its hands, however. The games were jam-packed with thrills and brilliant plays.

Through the day, there was a triple play engineered by shortstop Roy McMillan of the Mets, a steal of home by the Giants' Orlando Cepeda, the rare sight of Willie Mays forsaking center field for three innings to play shortstop, and all sorts of diamond treats.

The crowd took to the action with great enthusiasm, but as play went on and on, the stands began emptying. Nevertheless, there were still some 15,000 noisy, spirited New Breeders left at the finish.

These hardy souls did grow somewhat restless in the closing innings. A couple of fistfights broke out, but they were quickly brought under control.

There also was a paper fight in the lower stands behind home plate in which the combatants either rolled up or folded up bits of paper and tossed these missiles at each other. The result was a white cloud that distracted the players.

It brought a warning over the public-address system that anyone caught continuing the battle would be ejected as well as be faced with possible arrest. The announcement did the trick.

By and large, though, this was a happy crowd delighting in seeing baseball history being made.

There have been longer games in innings. The tops is the 26-inning, 1–1 tie waged by the Brooklyn Dodgers and Boston Braves in 1920. Twice there have been 24-inning games—between the Philadelphia Athletics and Boston Red Sox in 1906 and the A's and Detroit Tigers in 1945.

There also has been one other 23-inning game, a 2–2 tie between the Dodgers and Braves in 1939. Oddly enough, Casey Stengel, who skippered the Mets in this latest endurance test, also skippered the Braves in the '39 game.

After the Shea Stadium affair, the athletes—understandably—were all tuckered out, to say the least.

In both clubhouses, the players wearily trudged in and rested quietly on the stools in front of their lockers for long periods before showering.

"I know it's tiring to play 23 innings," said Alvin Dark, the Giants' manager. "But when you're a player and you win a game like this, you want to go out and dance."

However, the dancing spirit was not reflected in the looks or actions of the limp players.

Both games in the doubleton were close, well-played, exciting affairs.

A three-run homer by Jim Hickman gave the Mets a second-inning, 3–0 lead in the opener. But the Giants gradually wore down starter Alvin Jackson and, with the score tied at 3-all in the sixth, Cepeda stole home off knuckle-ball exponent Tom Sturdivant, who had just relieved Jackson.

That was enough to win for the Giants, but they added an insurance run in the ninth.

In the nightcap, the Giants got off winging and appeared to have an easy game when they rolled up a 6–1 lead by the third inning. This time it was the Mets' turn to come from behind.

They scored twice in the sixth inning to make it 6–3. Then, with two out and two on in the seventh, Joe Christopher sent a ball to deep center that just eluded Mays's grasp.

It hit Say-Hey Willie's glove, but fell over the fence for a three-run homer to tie the game at 6-all.

That's how the longest game in the matter of time was positioned. It took 16 more innings before the rival clubs could come to a decision.

Here, too, it happened with two out. Jimmy Davenport tripled. Cap Peterson, rookie infielder, was purposely passed to get to relief pitcher Gaylord Perry.

Dark, however, lifted Perry and called on Del Crandall to pinch-hit. The veteran catcher rifled an outside pitch to right field for the tie-breaking run. An infield roller which Jay Alou beat out for a hit brought the second run in the inning and the 8–6 Giant victory.

IF YOU THINK Ann Landers has advice only for the lovelorn, kindly think again.

"We Can't Afford a Lawyer"

ANN LANDERS

DEAR ANN: This letter is being written by seven baseball players, 11 and 12 years old. We can't afford a lawyer.

This afternoon we were playing ball in a lot behind this big house. I was at bat. The next thing I knew the ball sailed right through a great big plate glass window.

The owner of the house came running out like the place was on fire. We tried to explain it was an accident but the man said we had no business playing there in the first place. Then he took down all our names on a piece of paper.

Nothing has happened so far but we are going to have a meeting about it tomorrow. Do you think I should pay for the window because I was at bat? Is the pitcher partly to blame? Should the whole team pitch in? Or should the man be a real good sport and say, "Forget it, kids, I was young once myself?" —JR. CARDINALS.

DEAR JR. CARDS: I believe it would be very brotherly if the whole team pitched in and bought a new window.

It would be downright bright if you all went to the man and asked if you could earn some money by working on his lawn this summer—in shifts, say two or three at a time. Such a suggestion might jog his memory a little that he was young once himself.

"IT'S SIGNIFICANT," writes the late Mr. Lardner in this splendidly reasoned piece, "that the team with the highest income is the team that makes café-society news most often. By the same token, the Washington ball club should be cold sober."

The Baseball Playboy, Past and Present

JOHN LARDNER

"Avoid the hellish booze that makes a man's brain a mud puddle."—Billy Sunday, retired Chicago outfielder.

"A guy needs a little vacation now and then." —From the maxims of Shufflin' Phil Douglas, New York Giant pitcher.

"Tell Durocher I am tired of the way he is keeping me, like a bird in a cage."—Manifesto of Cletus Elwood Poffenberger, Brooklyn pitcher, 1939.

One night last May, as every baseball fan knows, the face of a private citizen collided with an object that was later described as the right fist of Hank Bauer, of the New York Yankees. If it was any fist of Bauer's at all, it had to be the right one. No right-handed ballplayer, when fighting, throws anything else. That goes without saying, and it explains why most ballplayers, as fighters, bat between .000 and .075.

But there were some curious points about this social adventure, apart from the fact that a ballplayer not only aimed a punch, but may even have landed one. The scene of the brawl was a New York nightclub, the Copacabana. Witnesses agree that both the thrower and the target were "feeling no pain" beforehand, which is an American slang phrase meaning that grain is distillable. Furthermore, there was not just one Yankee present at the revels, there were six, not counting wives.

The question that instantly rose to the newspaper reader's lips, when he saw the story next day, was, How come the boys were raising hell at night, in a nightclub, instead of playing baseball? Night ball was invented by Larry MacPhail in 1935. It is supposed to be one of the reasons why baseball today is a game for clean livers, instead of the lushes' picnic it was in the old days. The idea (though I don't say this is exactly what MacPhail had in mind) is that players nowadays are so busy playing ball all night, and sleeping or training their bodies for the game all afternoon, that they no longer have time for raising hell on the side.

Well, all right. So somebody slipped up and failed to schedule a night game on the date of Billy Martin's birthday, when Hank Bauer is supposed to have boosted his batting average at the Copacabana. But what are the true facts of the matter? Is there really less carousing in baseball now than there used to be? Is the player a cleaner, more wholesome type? Is the playboy rarer than he was? Is the quality of the game more spiritual? I think so.

The late Rabbit Maranville thought so too. He said that the modern game has a better moral tone. He began to say so in 1928.

"There is much less drinking now than there was before 1927," this great infielder would remark, "because I quit drinking on May 24, 1927.

"In my day, friend," the Rabbit added, "I was the best right-and-left-handed rum hound in the country."

In Maranville's prime, baseball clubs hired detectives, to shadow rumpots, as freely as they buy whirlpool baths and plastic helmets today.

The Rabbit himself used a different system of discipline. He became manager of the Cubs one time, to his own surprise and irritation, in mid-season of 1925. On the team's next road trip, the players sleeping in their Pullman berths were suddenly awakened at 2 A.M. by doses of cold water in their faces, as the Rabbit rolled up the aisle with a bucket yelling, "There will be no sleeping on this club under Maranville management!"

The record tells us that Rabbit was fired at an early opportunity, namely, the next time the owner saw him. The other managers—led by John McGraw, who operated the biggest stable of sleuths outside Scotland Yard—continued to fight sin with detectives. It was an old managerial custom, that went back to a time in baseball history when whiskey, not Wheaties, was the player's favorite breakfast food; when the best players—not just the good ones, but the greatest, King Kelly, Hoss Radbourne, Ed Delahanty, Rube Waddell—were thirty-third-degree alcoholics who all died young from devotion to their hobby. The relationship between playboy and private eye could be a loving one; some detectives brought sunshine into the sinner's life, as well as reports to the management. Shufflin' Phil Douglas' best friend for a while was a dick named Jim O'Brien, hired by McGraw to detach the Shuffler from his booze habit. One night in Pittsburgh, Douglas became separated from his shadow by accident. He waited outside the Giants' hotel until O'Brien caught up with him.

"I wanted to be sure we went into the lobby together," Douglas explained to friends, "so the hawkshaw would not get in trouble with McGraw for losing me."

I'm not saying, mind you, that detectives have vanished completely from the modern game. Or that the detective-player relationship cannot be a loving one even today—if the player has his way. As recently as 1948, there was a short outburst of sleuthing, when the Yankee club became suspicious that Joe Page and other players were leaving fingerprints on martini glasses. One of the detectives assigned to probe this deviltry was a handsome young lady; she scored high marks in the espionage trade when a Yankee player tried to pick her up at a bar, and, it is said, struck out.

There was also a spasm of detection in baseball in 1954. You'll recall that a private operative, trailing Granny Hamner, the Philly infielder, home at night by car, became the victim of a cutoff play when Hamner detected him, instead of vice versa. Hamner called the police, who arrested the shamus for carrying a gun. Robert Carpenter, Philly owner, declared later in some embarrassment that it was normal policy on his club at that time to have players shadowed (though not for the shadows to be pinched while on duty). What a player doesn't know, said Carpenter, won't hurt him. What an owner doesn't know might hurt him very much indeed.

If the Phils really were using detectives wholesale in 1954, I think it was a case of atavism, or reversion to ancestral habit. The club was losing, so Carpenter instinctively did what his baseball ancestors had done, when in trouble, and hired gumshoes. I doubt if there was much to detect, except lack of hitting. The modern ballplayer, as noted above, tends to be a wholesome type. Also, thanks to the increase of education in baseball, the player often is smarter than the detective. Also, he is hard to follow, when he does break loose. Don Larsen, in the spring of 1956, ran his automobile up a pole, where only the shrewdest sleuth could have followed him. The significance of the case was (1) that Larsen showed improved accuracy, and (2) that he was driving with no hands, a feature which later evolved into the no windup pitch and produced a perfect game in the World Series.

Night ball, higher education, pension plans, soda pop—they have all contributed to the decline of gaiety in baseball. Look at it this way. If you were to name an all-time All-Star team of playboys, would you put a single present-day player on it? My own team, and a strong, well-balanced one, would line up as follows:

Art Shires, first base.
Germany Schaefer, second base.
Rabbit Maranville, shortstop.
Pepper Martin, third base.
King Kelly, left field.
Ed Delahanty, center field.
Babe Ruth, right field.
Rollie Hemsley, catcher.
Rube Waddell, Phil Douglas, Grover Cleveland Alexander, Flint Rhem, pitchers.

There are critics who will insist that Hack Wilson, or Paul Waner, or Jim Thorpe, or Bugs Raymond, or this or that other classy reveler belongs in there. Jackie Robinson (judging by the newspaper selections of this noted handicapper of vice) might want to nominate the Milwaukee Club of 1956 in a body. Younger fans will plug for the Copacabana sextet, or holler, "What does Larsen have to do to prove his class, drive off a cliff?" Well, as regards the stars of the past, every picker is bound to have his own favorites. And, frankly, as regards the players of today and their powers of dissipation, I am skeptical. Can they raise hell over the full route? Can they violate a curfew in the clutch? Or do they want to live forever —you hear this ugly charge now and then— just to keep on cashing those new pension checks? In pre-pension days, Waddell and King Kelly had the good-fellowship to die at 37, Bugs Raymond at 30, Delahanty at 34.

In the case of the Braves of '56, Fred Haney has implied, and I am willing to take his word for it, that they were overrated as lushes. An outing once every week or so might well have been their limit. If these boys could shock Jackie Robinson (who, incidentally, doesn't drink and may be easily shocked), it is all for the best that Jack never knew King Kelly. On a world tour in the 1890s, the King told a British reporter politely that he had found that "a man can get as fine a little jag in London as he can in Boston." "Do you drink while playing baseball?" the reporter asked. "It depends on the length of the game," said Kelly.

In the case of Don Larsen, the subject's claim to recognition in this field is that he drove his automobile off the road during an early-morning nap. The great Delahanty (as strong a right-handed hitter as ever lived) chased a Michigan Central railroad train across the Niagara River on foot one night in 1903, and fell off the bridge into the rapids. It was his last performance, true, but it capped a notable career both on and off the field.

As for the Copacabana six, their record lacks consistency. In fact, in the cases of some of them, there is reason to think that theirs was a one-time gesture, like Bill Wambsganss' unassisted triple play—the kind of thing that gets nobody into the Hall of Fame by itself. Also, the Yanks of '57 were up against modern legal liquor, which is child's play compared with the 15-cent red-eye of the Kelly era, or the fresh-cooked prohibition dew on which Flint Rhem made his finest score. You may remember that Rhem, ace of the Cardinals' pitching staff, disappeared for 48 hours during a series at Ebbets Field in 1930. On turning up again, more or less intact, he told a story that made the blood run cold: Gangsters had kidnaped him, held him in a hotel room against his will, and forced him to drink "great quantities of liquor at the point of a gun."

The Cards won the pennant soon afterward. Good will became rampant in St. Louis, and Rhem drew a full paycheck. "We are in no position to disprove Rhem's story," said Branch Rickey admiringly. The great man never spoke a truer word.

This same quality of imagination is shared by all great playboys, on the field and off it. It marked the work of Germany Schaefer, of Detroit, who forced a change in the rule book one day some fifty years ago by stealing first base from second. It distinguished Rabbit Maranville, who once swam a river on his way back to the hotel because the nearest bridge was ten blocks west. It brought out the best in Pepper Martin, the time when Frank Frisch, Pepper's manager with the Gashouse Gang, narrowly escaped a brain concussion on the sidewalk in front of the Cardinals' hotel. A paper bag full of water, dropped from above, missed Frisch's skull by eight inches and splattered on the pavement. Without hesitation, the manager rushed into the lobby, rode the elevator twelve floors up, and burst into Martin's room, where Pepper was sitting by the window. "Don't you know you could have killed me by dropping that thing?" Frisch yelled. "Well, Frank," Martin said, "you wouldn't have wanted me to hold it there all day, would you, and tire out my arm?"

There was originality also in the work of C. E. "Boots" Poffenberger, the plump right-handed pitcher, who brightened the life of manager Leo Durocher with the Dodgers in the late 1930s. It's hard to leave Poffenberger off your All-Star playboy team; he misses only because of the competition from greater pitchers. (For one reason or another, probably because they don't work every day, pitchers have always led the field at hell-raising.) It was Boots who put the soul cry of the baseball individualist into words, when he decided to skip a game in Cincinnati, and gave Dolf Camilli this message to take to the clubhouse: "Tell Durocher I am tired of the way he is keeping me, like a bird in a cage." It was Boots who broke down the Dodger curfew in Philadelphia with the help of the battery of out-of-town clocks in the lobby of the Bellevue-Stratford Hotel. "You are two hours late!" shouted Larry MacPhail, catching the home-comer red-handed there one night. "Not by the time I go by, I ain't," said Poffenberger, pointing to the clock for Honolulu. The conversation left MacPhail at a disadvantage, and Boots went on to bed unmolested, at 8 P.M., Honolulu time.

Durocher relates that in Poffenberger's thirstiest year, 1939, Boots rigged a dummy one night in his berth on a train that was waiting in the station to take the Dodgers to Boston, and did not replace the bogus body with his own till 3 A.M. His object in boarding the train late was to give himself a few more hours at the soda fountain. This is just one of many reasons why the expert must pick Rube Waddell over Poffenberger on the All-Star team. The need to drink in a bar instead of in the Pullman berth itself is a modern weakness. Jim Crusinberry, the old-time baseball writer, has told of a night when Waddell, then with the Browns, took a bottle of bourbon to bed with him on a sleeper jump from Cleveland to St. Louis, and finished the bottle during the night. On the following afternoon, the story goes, Rube shut out Detroit with three hits.

Stamina at the water hole was part of the all-around genius of George H. Ruth. The Babe, on a trip to Washington in the 1920s, once made a deep impression on Al Schacht, who had roomed with Jim Thorpe in his time, and thought he knew a talent for firewater when he saw one. Ruth and other ballplayers were invited to a party by the Polish ambassador, a fan. With a doubleheader with the Yankees coming up the next day, manager Bucky Harris of the Senators assigned Schacht and Goose Goslin to attend the party and make sure that Ruth stayed up late and dampened his batting eye. Schacht and Goslin lasted as long with the Babe as they could, and then went home satisfied that Ruth by that time had become half man, half champagne. Schacht had a date to meet Ruth at the Yankee Hotel at 9 A.M. for a morning good-will visit to the patients in a local hospital. He dragged himself out of bed and went feebly to the hotel. At 9:30, Ruth appeared in the lobby—not from an elevator, but from the street, where a cab had just brought him home from the ambassador's party.

"Well, kid, let's go!" said the Babe to Schacht. "We got a great day for it!" After the hospital, the boys repaired to the ball park, where Ruth got two long hits in the first game of the doubleheader, and three in the second, as the Yankees copped both ends.

To revert to Billy Martin's birthday party, Copacabana, 1957, that event was notable, as I said before, for the fact that a ballplayer landed, or was thought to have landed, a punch. There are few punchers on the list of all-time playboys; the great Arthur Shires rules practically alone in this subdivision of hell-raising. In fact, to hear the great Shires tell it, he was no drinker, all fighter—and when he knocked out his manager, Lena Blackburne, of the White Sox, one day in the 1920s, it was because Blackburne had caught him drinking "a glass of ginger ale." Be that as it may, Shires could fight as well as he could play first base, which was just fairly well. His fame as an amateur swinger won him a short career in the professional ring during the off season. In his first and only bout for cash, Arthur stopped a person named Dan Daly in 21 seconds of the first round.

"Now get me this Gene Tunney," said Shires, alluding to the heavyweight champion of the world.

Before the Tunney match could materialize, Dan Daly began to circulate the rumor that he had gone to the tank. Daly was immediately barred from the ring for life, and, shortly afterward, the great Shires himself was suspended in 32 states, which was all the states that knew how to spell his name. Judge Landis, Commissioner of Baseball, then ordered Arthur to desist from boxing entirely, and Shires—after briefly considering an offer from an independent promoter to fight Landis for a $10,000 guarantee—agreed to an armistice.

The record shows that the White Sox fined Arthur $3,000 in one of his better years. The money, I should like to point out, was not assessed in one big dollop, for a one-shot performance, as was the case with the $1,000 fines the Yankees slapped on the birthday guests at the Copacabana. The White Sox fined Shires lightly but steadily. This, to my mind, is the measure of true consistency in a playboy; those big, inflated, single fines of today prove nothing about the class of the individual boozer, who may be merely a morning glory. Besides, if my information is correct, the large modern fines are often remitted under the table. We live in a hollow publicity-seeking age.

No ball club ever remitted a fine to Rollicking Rollie Hemsley, a catcher, night bird, and financial clay pigeon of true class. Perhaps no player in history was fined more regularly and thoroughly than Hemsley. Each of his years in the big time brought a thrill to the fans and to the club cashier. Suspense mounted as the season advanced: Who would finish ahead, Rollie or the ball club? Would his fines equal his income? To the best of my knowledge, though the management tore into his paycheck time after time with spikes high, Hemsley always nosed ahead at the wire, with margin enough for one more night out—which is the mark of a man of character. And character Rollie had, in both directions. When he cut out the sauce, it is said, no one ever cut it out more cleanly.

The modern fine, I've suggested, is a sign of inflation, of the age of big money, of the high cost of living. It does not reflect the real ability of the victim as a playboy. And the cost of living, it should be noted, has a good deal to do with the fact that alcoholism is not what it used to be in baseball, that drinking has declined. As most sociologists will agree, it's partly a question of the cost of booze. In the days of King Kelly and Delahanty, you could buy a scupper of whiskey for what is the price of a glass of good beer today. The hours were good in baseball in those days—two hours a day, in the afternoon—and a player with cash in his pocket and a social impulse could take a bath in grog after hours as freely as today's athlete takes a shower.

If baseball playboys are not what they were, the price could be the reason; ballplayers have always walked hand in hand with frugality. It's significant (anthropologists please copy) that the team with the highest income these days, the Yankees, is the team that makes the café-society news most often. By the same token, the Washington ball club should be cold sober. And if it is, it's a mighty lonesome ball club in its own home town—because the rest of Washington, D.C., leads the entire nation in licking up the stuff, per capita.

There are other pressures for wholesomeness today. The player must be clean-cut for television, in shape for his shot with Ed Sullivan. The public-appearance dodge was more relaxing in the old days. In the fall of 1914, the heroes of the miracle Boston Braves, having beaten the Athletics four straight in the World Series, went out to chase vaudeville money. Rabbit Maranville was playing Lewiston, Maine, one night, with his program of songs, funny sayings, and baseball highlights. The Rabbit got through two songs and three comical anecdotes without serious injury, through the good will of the audience.

"I will now demonstrate," he announced, "how I stole second base off Chief Bender in the first game of the Series."

He took off from the rear of the stage. His slide cleared the footlights, and landed him feet first in the bass drum in the orchestra pit. The Rabbit missed his next two weeks of booking, but not because of protests from the Anti-Saloon League. He had broken his leg in the drum, and needed time for repairs.

In the old days, the boys played hard.

THIS PARTIAL, if that's the word for it, account of the 1923 World Series simply helps to prove what needs no proof: There was only one Ring Lardner.

A World's Serious

RING LARDNER

Advance Notice

Sept. 30—All though they have been world serious practally every yr. for the last 20 yrs. this next world serious which is supposed to open up Wed. p.m. at the Polo grounds is the most important world serious in history as far as I and my family are conserned and even more important to us than the famous world serious of 1919 which was win by the Cincinnati Reds greatly to their surprise.

Maybe I would better exclaim myself before going any further. Well, a few days previous to the serious of 1919 I was approached by a young lady who I soon recognized as my wife, and any way this woman says would I buy her a fur coat as the winter was comeing on and we was going to spend it in Connecticut which is not genally considered one of the tropics.

"But don't do it," she says, "unless you have got the money to spare because of course I can get along without it. In fact," she added bursting into teers, "I am so used to getting along without this, that and the other thing that maybe it would be best for you not to buy me that coat after all as the sight of a luxury of any kind might prove my undoing."

"Listen," was my reply, "as far as I am conserned you don't half to prove your undoing. But listen you are in a position to know that I can't spare the money to buy you one stoat leave alone enough of the little codgers skins to make a coat for a growed up girl like you. But if I can get a hold of any body that is sucker enough to bet on Cincinnati in this world serious, why I will borrow from some good pal and cover their bet and will try and make the bet big enough so as the winnings will buy you the handsomest muleskin coat in New England."

Well friends I found the sucker and got a hold of enough money to cover his bet and not only that but give him odds of 6 to 5 and that is why we did not go out much in Greenwich that winter and not for lack of invitations as certain smart Alex has let fall.

I might also mention at this junction that they was a similar agreement at that serious between Eddie Collins the capt. of the White Sox and his Mrs. only of course Eddie did not make no bet, but if his team win, why he should buy the madam a personal sedan whereas if his team lost, why she would half to walk all winter. Luckily the Collinses live in Lansdowne, Pa., where you can't walk far.

Well friends I do not know what is the automobile situation in the Collins family at the present writeing as have not saw them of late but the fur coat situation in my family is practically the same like it was in 1919 only as I hinted in the opening paragraph of this intimate article, it is a d-a-m sight worse.

Because this yr. they won't be no chance for the little woman to offset her paucity of outdoor raps by spending the winter in the house. She is going to need furs even there.

Therefore as I say this comeing serious is the most important of all as far as we are conserned for Mother ain't the same gal when she is cold and after all is said and done what is home with mother in her transtrums?

So I and my little ones is hopeing and praying that the boys on who I have staked my winters happiness this yr. will not have no meetings in no hotel rooms between now and Wednesday but will go into this serious determined to do their best which I once said was the best anybody could do and the man who heard me say it said "You are dead right Lardner" and if these boys do their best, why it looks to me like as if the serious should ought to be well over by Sunday night and the little woman's new fur coat delivered to our little home some time Monday and maybe we will get invited out somewheres that night and they will be a blizzard.

The First Day

Oct. 5—Well friends you can imagine my surprise and horror when I found out last night that the impression had got around some way another that as soon as this serious was over I was planning to buy a expensive fur coat for my Mrs. and put a lot of money into same and buy a coat that would probably run up into hundreds and hundreds of dollars.

Well I did not mean to give no such kind of a impression and I certainly hope that my little article was not read that way by everybody a specially around my little home because in the first place I am not a sucker enough to invest hundreds and hundreds of dollars in a garment which the chances are that the Mrs. will not wear it more than a couple times all winter as the way it looks now we are libel to have the most openest winter in history and if women folks should walk along the st. in expensive fur coats in the kind of weather which it looks like we are going to have why they would only be laughed at and any way I believe a couple can have a whole lot better time in winter staying home and reading a good book or maybe have a few friends to play bridge.

Further and more I met a man at supper last night that has been in the fur business all his life and aint did nothing you might say only deal in furs and this man says that they are a great many furs in this world which is reasonable priced that has got as much warmth in them as high price furs and looks a great deal better. For inst. he says that a man is a sucker to invest thousands and thousands of dollars in expensive furs like Erminie, Muleskin, squirrel skin and kerensky when for a hundred dollars or not even that much, why a man can buy a owl skin or horse skin or weasel skin garment that looks like big dough and practically prostrates people with the heat when they wear them.

So I hope my readers will put a quietus on the silly rumor that I am planning to plunge in the fur market. I will see that my Mrs. is dressed in as warm a style as she has been accustomed to but neither her or I is the kind that likes to make a big show and go up and down 5th ave sweltering in a $700 hogskin garment in order so as people will turn around and gap at us. Live and let live is my slocum.

So much for the fur coat episode and let us hear no more about it and will now go on with my article which I must apologize for it not being very good and the reason is on account of being very nervous after our little ride from the polo grounds to park row. It was my intentions to make this trip in the subway but while walking across the field after the game I run into Izzy Kaplan the photographer and he says would I like to ride down in a car which him and his friends had hired so I and Grantland Rice got in and we hadn't no sooner than started when one of our fellow passengers says that we ought to been with them coming up.

"We made the trip from park row in 24 minutes," he says, "and our driver said he was going to beat the record on the return trip."

So we asked what had held them back comeing up and one of them said that the driver had kept peeling and eating bananas all the way and that he did not drive so good when both his hands was off the wheel. Besides that, they had ran into a guy and had to wait till the ambulance come and picked him up.

Well friends I will not try and describe our flight only to say that we did not beat the record but tied it and the lack of bananas didn't prevent our hero from driving with his hands off the wheel as he used the last named to shake his fists at pedestrians and other riff raff that don't know enough to keep off the public highways during the rush hour.

Most of the things I was going to mention in this article was scared out of me during our little jaunt. One of them however was the man from Toronto that stood in line with his wife from 8 pm Tuesday night till the gates opened Wednesday morning so as to be sure of good seats. According to officials of the club, they could of got the same seats if they had not showed up till a couple hours before the game, but if they had of done that, why the lady would not of had no chance to brag when she got back home. The way it is, why she can say to her friends, "Charley may not be much for looks, but he certainly showed me the night life of New York."

Dividing interest with this couple was a couple of heel and toe pedestrians that done their base circling stunt just before the start of the game. One of them was the same guy that done it before the first game last fall, but this time he was accompanied by a lady hoofer and it is not too much to say that the lady was dressed practically as though for her bath. Casey Stengel expressed the general sentiment in the following words, "If that is just her walking costume I would hate to see her made up for tennis."

The Second Day

Oct. 6—No doubt my readers has been tipped off by this time that the 2d game of the big serious was called on acct. of darkness but a great many of them may not know that the umpires and club owners was called a lot of different names which I will not repeat here but suffice it to say that none of them was honey, dearie and etc.

The boys that had paid $5.50 and up to see a ball game did not seem to think it was dark enough for the umps to step in and stop it. Personly I will not express no opinion as some of my best friends is umpires, but will merely state that I started out of the press box the instant it was over and by the aid of a powerful candle which I generally always carry to world serious games when Shawkey and Barnes is scheduled to pitch, why I was able to find my way down to the field where I run plum into A.D. Lasker who had forgot to light his headlights. Will further state that nobody who I passed on the way out to 8th avenue had yet put on their pajamas or made any other preparations that would indicate the fall of night and even when I got down to park's row, pretty near a hr. after the game's untimely end, I was still able to grope my way to the office by feeling along the sides of buildings and was seated right here at my typewriter writing this article before the hoot owls and nightingales begun to emit their nocturnal squawk.

However, one of our fellow passengers on the bus down town was Billy Evans, an umpire himself, and while he admitted that he had not saw none of the outfielders signalling to each other with flares, still and all he says the polo grounds is a terrible hard place for the athletes, and a specially the batters, to see a ball when they's the slightest twinge of darkness. As far as that is conserned there is 2 or 3 of the boys on each of the contending clubs than dont seem able to see the ball any too good even at high noon.

Anyway it means we are going to have a extra ball game to play over and some of we boys who predicted a short serious is being made to look like a monkey. Personly I was never so ashamed of myself since I picked Willard.

The general opinion amongst the writing boys tonight was that the game being a tie is a big help to one of the two teams but I forget which. It certainly aint no help to me and the only thing I liked about the day was the weather, which it would make a person sick to even talk about a fur coat in such weather, and it goes to show what a sucker a man would be to squander thousands and thousands of dollars in a costly fur garment and then may be have a whole winter of just such days like yesterday.

Personly I seen a girlie on the street last night wearing a linen duster and you have no idear how good they look on some people and keep you plenty warm too if you move around and dont stand still.

Well friends, I prophesied in these columns earlier in the week that Bob Shawkey would be a whole lot better this fall than he was last fall and that prophecy certainly come true, but the boy has still got the habit of pitching bad in the first innings and if I was running the Yank ball club here is what I would do. When it was Bob's turn to pitch, why just before the game started I would call Bob to one side and I would say, "well Bob it's the second innings all ready." If he believed it, why they would be nothing to prevent him from stepping right in and pitching his best from the start.

Jess Barnes pitched better than Bob at the start and not so good at finish. The way Jess pitched to Ruth did not seem to rouse unanimous enthusiasm amongst the bugs in the grandstand. Slow balls is what Jess feeds the Babe and the reason for same is because Babe dont hit slow balls out of the ball park. If Jess did not feed the Babe slow balls when he knows he cant hit slow balls so good, why that would make Jess a ½ wit and when he does feed the Babe slow balls, why it shows he is thinking. That is why the crowd hoots him for pitching slow balls, because the average baseball bug hates to see anybody think. It makes them jealous.

Well friends today is another day and may the best team win as I often say to Mother which is what I call the little woman when I am in a hurry and cant think of her name.

The Third Day

Oct. 7—Amongst the inmates of our heavily mortgaged home in Great Neck is 3 members of what is sometimes referred to as the feline tribe born the 11th day of last April and christened respectfully Barney, Blackie and Ringer.

These 3 little ones is motherless, as the lady cat who bore them, aptly named Robin Hood, took sick one June day and was give away by

Fred to a friend to whom he kindly refrained from mentioning her illness.

These 3 little members of the feline tribe is the cutest and best behaved kitties in all catdom, their conduct having always been above reproaches outside of a tendency on the part of Ringer to bite strangers knuckles. Nowhere on Long Island is a more loveable trio of grimalkins and how it pierces my old heart to think that some day next week these 3 little fellows must be shot down like a dog so as their fur can be fashioned into a warm winter coat for she who their antics has so often caused to screek with laughter. Yes boys the 3 little kittens is practically doomed you might say and all because today's game at the polo grounds was not called on account of darkness long before it started though they was no time during the afternoon when the Yanks could see.

I probably never would of heard of a cat skin coat was it not for an accidental introduction last night to a man who has did nothing all his life but sell and wear fur coats and who told me that no finer or more warmer garment can be fashioned than is made from the skin of a milk fed kitty.

"Listen," was the way he put it. "You would be a even worse sucker than you are if you was to squander thousands on thousands of dollars on the fur of a muskrat or a mule when you have right in your own asylum the makings of the most satisfactory and handsome coat that money can buy."

"Yes," was my reply, "but the fur of 3 kittens would make a mighty small coat."

"Small coats is the rage," was his reply, "and I personally seen some of the best dressed women in New York strolling up and down 10th avenue during the last cold snap with cat skin garments no bigger than a guest towl."

So while I said a few paragraphs ago that the result of this ball game spelled the doom of our little kitties, why as a matter of fact I have just about made up my mind to not buy no costly furs even if the Yankees does come through and bring me out on the right side of the public ledger. Whatever I win in bets on this serious I will freely give to charity.

I would try and describe the game to you in intimate detail was it not played in such darkness that I was only able to see a few incidence. Of these, few occurred in the 3rd innings and consisted of Whitey Witt getting caught asleep off of first base by a snap throw from one of the Smith brothers.

The dean of Cleveland baseball experts explained this incidence by saying that Whitey thought he was still with the Athletics. It is more likely however that Whitey was deceived by the darkness into believing it was his bedtime.

The next incidence come in the innings when the Babe tried to go from first to third on a wallop by Bob Meusel that got away from Frisch. Frankie pegged the ball to Heine Groh who stood in Babe's path to third but it was so dark that Babe crashed right smack into him and secured a rolling fall. For a minute it looked like they would be fisticuffs between the 2 famous athletes but Heine suddenly remembered the advice given him by his first school teacher, "never be a bully," and the fight was over before it begun.

Fifteen minutes before the start of the game the official announcer come up to the press box and said that McQuillan was going to pitch for the Giants. A minute later he come around again and said to make it Scott instead of McQuillan. McQuillan thus broke Fred Toney's record for the length of time spent in a world serious ball game.

I will close this article by making a apology to the boys to who I have give tickets for games no 1 and 3 and whose seats is in section 24 which is as far north as you can get without falling out of the grandstand. The gents who sold me these seats thought I was a close friend of the Meusel boys and might want to set out there myself and kid with them.

The End

Oct. 9—Well boys it looks like it was all over and the only complaint I have got to make is that the traffic regulations was not handled right.

The next time the Yankees takes part in a world serious they should ought to have a traffic policeman stationed between 1st and 2nd base and another traffic policeman stationed between home and 1st.

The former should tell the boys when it is ok to run to 2nd. And the latter must inform them that when a ground ball is hit to the infield in a world serious the general theory which has never been disapproved is to run on high speed to 1st base which is the base towards the right field from the home plate.

The lack of a adequate stop and go system is what lost this serious on the part of the Yanks. The final game of the serious was marked by the only incedence of brains exhibited by the Yanks during the whole serious.

In the 2nd innings with two boys on the

bases and one out Joe Bush passed Arthur Nehf to 1st base so as to get the head of the batting order up and not confuse the official scorers. This bit of thinking probably was responsible for nothing.

I will not try and dilate on the rest of the serious only to say that Charles A. Hughes and Eddie Batchelor of Detroit spent this a.m. at the Bronx Soo to try and see more animals. It is hard to satisfy the boys from Detroit.

All as I know what to write about on a occasion like this kind is a little incedence that come off. The 1st incedence that calls to mine is in regards to Tommy Rice of the Brooklyn Eagle. Tommy wrote 7,000 words in regards to the 1st game of the serious and page by page it blew out of the window in the costly apartment building in which Brooklyn experts lives, there is no telling what the loss to the world is on account of not being able to read Tommy's story to say nothing about the readers of the Eagle.

Now boys I suppose they is a few interested in whether the little woman is going to get a costly fur coat. The other day I wrote a story to the general effects that we was going to kill our cats and use their fur to make the costly garment. This story was not appreciated in the heavily mortgaged home. After a long argument the master of the house compromised and decided to not doom the little members of the finny tribe to death. Instead of that we are going to use a idea furnished by the same Eddie Batchelor, of Detroit, mentioned a few thousand words ago. Eddie's idears is to start a chain letter to all our friends and readers asking them to look around the old homestead and find their family albums and take the plush off the covers and send it to the undersigned and make a plush coat which everybody tells me is the most fashionable fur on the green footstool. The little woman can wear plush and a specially the red pigment but black and tan plush covers will be welcomed and this man tells me theys nothing more attractive than a black and red and tan blocked coat made out of plush albums.

I was going to say further in regards to the plush albums but Harry Frazee has just butted in with the story of his life. It seems like when Harry was a young man in Peoria his father said to him if you don't be wild and go into the theatrical business and stay around Peoria you will be as big a man as your uncle. So Harry looked at his uncle who was getting $125 per month staring at books.

"Well," says Harry, "I can get more than that catching runaway horses." So he is now catching runaway horses and selling them to the New York club.

As I now sit here and write I am surrounded by a corpse of experts just as ignorant as me and they don't seem to be none of them able to tell who is going to pitch tomorrow. Personally I think it will be Col. Ruppert and Huston.

CHARLES SCHULZ

4-28
Tm. Reg. U. S. Pat Off.—All rights reserved
Copr. 1963 by United Feature Syndicate, Inc.
WHERE? RIGHT HERE, THAT'S WHERE! RIGHT HERE ON PAGE THIRTY-ONE, SECTION THREE, RULE 6.12!
I LOVE A GOOD RHUBARB
SCHULZ

QUICK, NOW—who appeared in 27 World Series and 12 All-Star games?

From *Vaudeville*

JOE LAURIE, JR.

AFTER THE LAST GAME of the baseball season, all the topnotchers in the baseball world would take a crack at batting out a few vaudeville fungoes, and would stay just long enough to be struck out!

Hammerstein's was the baseball players' home plate! Most of them had to have acts built around them, full of regular vaude talent, to get 'em over. There were only a few who had talent. Some did monologues, some told about great plays and "inside stuff" of the big games they had been in, some danced, some did imitations, but most of them sang!

It was a natural for ballplayers to sing, because during training periods and before and after games they would get together and do a bit of "Sweet Adelining" in the clubhouse or on the hotel porch. They did this not only for their own amusement but with vaude dates in mind. There was big dough in show biz for pennant winners or those who stood out in a series or a season.

Mike Donlin and Mabel Hite were one of the first real baseball acts (Mabel Hite had a standard act as a great singing comedienne long before she married Mike). They had a number of acts in vaude. "Stealing Home" (in 1908, I think) was really a great act besides being a drawing card. In 1912 Mike did an act with the great comedian, Tom Lewis, who was the originator of the famous expression "Twenty-three" (to which they later added "Skiddoo"; it was not in the original George M. Cohan show, *Little Johnny Jones*). They finished with Tom Lewis on Mike's lap acting as a vent dummy and Mike doing the ventriloquist. He also did an act with Marty McHale, which proves that the guy made vaude his biz after his baseball career was over. Mike finally went to Hollywood and did bits in pics until he couldn't make home plate any more.

Charles Dooin (Philly National catcher) did songs and in 1910 did a singing and talking act in Dumont's Minstrels in Philly. Joe Tinker, the famous shortstop, started doing a monologue, and then did a skit, "A Great Catch," in an act with Sadie Sherman. Johnny Kling (catcher) did a monologue and a champ billiard exhibition act. The great Christy Mathewson and Chief Meyers (pitcher and catcher of the famous New York Giants) did a skit with May Tulley written for them by the famous sportswriter, Bozeman Bulger, called "Curves."

In 1911 Rube Marquard made his vaude debut at Hammerstein's, with Annie Kent. In 1912 he did an act with Blossom Seeley (then a headliner in her own right) in a skit, "Breaking the Record." They did the Marquard glide. I remember in this act he said to the audience, "You wished it on yourselves, so I got nerve enough to sing it alone" (and did it very well). Another act of theirs was "Nineteen Straight." In 1913 they did an act called "The Suffragette Pitcher," in which Blossom made Rube change into a dame's dress to pitch for her all-woman team. In 1917 Rube did a singing and talking act with Billy Dooley of the famous Dooley family.

John J. McGraw did a monologue on "Inside Baseball," and did very well, but didn't go for a vaude route, figuring he would have more fun at the Lambs. That same year (1912) there was the Boston Red Sox Quartette, with Marty Hale, Tom "Buck" O'Brien, Hugh Bradley, and Bill Lyons. Another quartette that year was Bill Gleason, George Crable, Tom Dillon, and Frank Browning in "Twenty Minutes in the Club House." Hugh Jennings did an act with Ben Smith (a vet blackface comic).

Capt. Adrian C. "Pop" Anson, the dean of baseball, went into vaude about 1913 and did a monologue, finishing up with a short dance. He liked vaude, because he came back in 1921 with his two beautiful daughters in a skit written for them by Ring Lardner with songs by Herman Timberg. George Stallings, the "miracle man of baseball," also did a monologue. Hank Gowdy and Dick Rudolph did a singing and talking act. I was at the party they gave Hank Gowdy up in Boston when he went into service in World War I. He was the first baseball player to enlist—a great guy.

There was a fellow by the name of George L. Moreland who billed his act "Baseballology"; he answered all questions about baseball from as far back as 1846. He showed stills of early baseball players, etc. He knew all the answers.

Waite Hoyt was practically raised in show biz, as his dad was an old-time minstrel man. In 1921 Waite went on the stage with a singing act; he had a very nice voice. About seven years later he took another vaude plunge (after his season), and had a gal playing the piano for him who didn't do so bad for herself in show biz since then; her name is Hildegarde! She also played for Mickey Cochrane, and when she left him the noted composer Freddy Coots played for Mickey (they did a swell act). In 1921 Babe Ruth did an act with Wellington Cross (Cross & Josephine), a fine artist; they had Cliff Dean at the piano. It's a funny thing about the Babe in vaude. When he was at his height in baseball and was getting a big salary in vaude, he didn't prove to be a drawing card, while Jack Dempsey was breaking all records. Showmen explained this by saying that people could see Babe Ruth anytime for a quarter or 50 cents, while it took at least three bucks to see Dempsey when he was fighting! They sold Irving Berlin's song, "Along Came Ruth," in the lobby of the Pantages houses when the Babe played them.

Vernon "Lefty" Gomez did a very funny monologue. In 1932 Al Mamiux (the Newark team manager) did a very good singing and talking act. A few years later, in his next time at bat in vaude, he had Jimmy Rule at the piano. There was an interclub quartette about 1925: George Crable (Brooklyn), Tom Dillon (Macon), Frank Browning (Detroit), and Billy Gleason (Galveston). My old friend Rabbit Maranville did an act with Eddy McHugh and he was as good on the stage as he was on the diamond. Coombs, Morgan, and Bender, World Series pitching heroes of the champ Athletics, did a skit assisted by Kathryn & Violet Pearl. Later Kathryn Pearl did an act with Chief Bender called "Learning the Game," by George Totten Smith with music by Arthur Behim.

Ty Cobb, Germany Schaefer, and Joe Tinker were all in vaude about 1911. Mike "King" Kelly did a monologue; he also was with Mark Murphy in "O'Dowd's Neighbors." Me and Aggie will never forget the time we played in Jersey City with Ford Frick; he was then a local radio sportscaster and sportswriter and was very popular locally. He did something like his broadcast for his act, but wanted some laughs to kinda lighten it up a bit. I gave him some gags (the wrong ones, because he got laughs with them; we should have kept them for ourselves in Jersey). Anyway, Ford didn't do bad, leaving vaude to become the czar of organized baseball. He is a swell guy in or out of vaude. We say he was a smart guy even back in those days; he knew vaude wouldn't last!

Many of the ballplayers who played vaude became sportscasters when radio got going, players like Bump Hadley (Yankee pitcher), Elbie Fletcher (Braves first baseman), Waite Hoyt, Frankie Frisch, Harry Heilman (great hitter), Gabby Street, Charles Gehringer (Hall of Fame guy), Fred Haney, and of course one of the greats, Dizzy Dean (who played the Roxy with his brother). And talking about sportscasters, we had Harry Howell, the curveball pitcher of the St. Louis Browns, explaining the movie of the Chicago-Detroit series in 1908.

And did you know that B. S. Muckenfuss, who is the owner of the great Inter-State Circuit with vaude theaters all through Texas and who played all the greats in vaude, was once the secretary of the St. Louis Cardinals? He followed E. F. Carruthers as general manager of Inter-State, and now owns it.

But I think the most remarkable man in baseball, as far as showmanship goes, is my pal Al Schacht, the "Clown Prince of Baseball." The guy belongs here because he played in vaude with his partner Nick Altrock (they were the originators of baseball clowning). In their act they did a lot of comedy bits and Al did what he calls the *pièce de résistance,* his imitation of Eddie Leonard singing "Roley Boley Eyes," which started the decline of vaude. The reason I say he belongs in a show biz story is that he has played to more people *personally* than *anybody* in or out of show biz! Sounds fantastic, but it's true. I am not counting the guys who appear on radio or TV, but *personal* appearances. Here is his record; figure it out for yourself. Al Schacht worked in baseball from 1910 to 1936 as a pitcher and coach and did clowning for the crowds on the side. He also appeared in twenty-seven World Series and in twelve All-

Star games. He has done his clown act all over the country every summer from 1937 till now. He did over 300,000 miles playing for our troops in Korea, New Guinea, East Indies, Philippines, Japan, Germany, Austria, Alaska, France, Iceland, etc., doing 790 shows and playing in 310 hospitals. Figure it out and tell me anyone that ever played to more people! And now as a restaurateur he even plays to crowds in his restaurant. A great clown and a great guy!

There were a lot of vaude actors who were great baseball fans. It was the favorite sport of actors, and many vaude road units had baseball teams which would play the stagehands of the towns (and get beat). Nearly all the big Broadway shows had teams representing them, and would sneak in a ringer pitcher, usually Sammy Smith, a song publisher who pitched in the big leagues, or Jack Conway, critic on *Variety*. I remember when the National Variety Artists were trying to get a team together to try and beat the Cohan & Harris team. The manager asked an acrobat, "Will you play third base?" and the acrobat said, "How big a jump is it?"

Yep, there were a lot of ballplayers in vaude; some hit home runs, and others went to the showers—followed by vaudeville!

TOMMY LEACH was an outfielder-third baseman for the great Pittsburgh teams of the early 1900s. In fact, as Tom Meany tells elsewhere in this volume, he was the man who hit into Red John Murray's famous "silhouette" catch. That was in 1909. Six years before that, in 1903, Leach and the Pirates played the Boston Red Sox in the first World Series. Here is his salute to that occasion, to "Nuf Sed" McGreevey, and to:

"That Damn 'Tessie' Song"

TOMMY LEACH

THAT WAS probably the wildest World Series ever played. Arguing all the time between the teams, between the players and the umpires, and especially between the players and the fans. That's the truth. The fans were *part* of the game in those days. They'd pour right out onto the field and argue with the players and the umpires. Was sort of hard to keep the game going sometimes, to say the least.

I think those Boston fans actually won that series for the Red Sox. We beat them three out of the first four games, and then they started singing that damn "Tessie" song, the Red Sox fans did. They called themselves the Royal Rooters, and their leader was some Boston character named Mike McGreevey. He was known as "Nuf Sed" McGreevey, because any time there was an argument about baseball he was the ultimate authority. Once McGreevey gave his opinion that ended the argument: nuf sed!

Anyway, in the fifth game of the Series the Royal Rooters started singing "Tessie" for no particular reason at all, and the Red Sox won. They must have figured it was a good-luck charm, because from then on you could hardly play ball they were singing "Tessie" so damn loud.

"Tessie" was a real big song in those days. You remember it, don't you?

> Tessie, you make me feel so badly,
> Why don't you turn around.
> Tessie, you know I love you madly,
> Babe, my heart weighs about a pound.

Yeah, that was a real humdinger in those days. Like "The Music Goes Round and Round" in the '30s. Now you surely remember *that* one?

Only instead of singing, "Tessie, you know I love you madly," they'd sing special lyrics to each of the Red Sox players: like "Jimmy, you know I love you madly." And for us Pirates they'd change it a little. Like when Honus Wagner came up to bat they'd sing:

> Honus, why do you hit so badly?
> Take a back seat and sit down.
> Honus, at bat you look so sadly,
> Hey, why don't you get out of town?

Sort of it got on your nerves after a while. And before we knew what happened, we'd lost the World Series.

THE FACT that in June of 1961, when this piece appeared in *Sport*, Nick Testa had played only three major-league innings in fourteen years of professional baseball fazed Mr. Testa not at all. Note the closing line of this article.

Portrait of a Baseball "Failure"

BILL LIBBY

NICK TESTA is considered a failure, which hurts him, as it would any of us. He accepts it and makes the best of it because he has his own life to live, and because there is nothing he can do about it. But it does hurt.

He is considered a failure because he is a professional baseball player, but not a big leaguer. It is a small stigma, and his friends, old and new, are nice about it. They smile when they see him and shake his hand. They ask him about the game's glamorous figures and offer him sympathetic words of encouragement.

But Nick is not blind to the pity they try to mask with their words. And the fact that pity even exists seems unfair to him. He would like to be Mickey Mantle or Stan Musial, but he is not. He is Nick Testa, 32 years old, who has been around. He is a solid athlete, but an unspectacular one. He brims with desire, but not big-league talent. And there are many more of his kind around than there are Mantles and Musials.

For fourteen years now, Nick Testa has pursued the dream of big-league success. Because he has articulated his dream, reached so high and settled for less, the stamp of "failure" is imprinted on him, rather than on those of us who have not quite made it either, but are only mechanics or clerks or office workers. If he ever had a chance, it is gone now. In those fourteen years in organized baseball, Nick has spent only one season in the majors. That was in San Francisco in 1958. He played only three innings of only one game, and without having had so much as a single time at bat he was banished to the bullpen, where he spent the remainder of the summer as a spare coach.

After that he returned to the minors—the bushes or the sticks, as they are stingingly called—where all this time he's bounced around from one team to another, one town to another, and never with one team in one town for as many as two complete seasons in a row.

Since 1946 Nick has played in places like Walden, Seaford, Trenton, Erie, Idaho Falls, Jacksonville, Fort Belvoir, Sioux City, Johnstown, Dallas, San Francisco, Omaha and Little Rock.

He has played two years of service ball and a dozen years of civilian ball in every type of league from class D to the majors, from the Pony League to the National League. He has played with young men on their way to stardom and old men on their way to obscurity.

He has played winters in Colombia and Nicaragua and Mexico and Panama. If they will take him, he will play next in Japan. He has played for big money and small change. He has played and will continue to play wherever he can get a game.

"Why do I do it?" Nick grinned, his leathery face gone soft, his eyes wistful. His voice was shy with confession. "I like to play ball," he said. "It's as simple as that.

"People think I'm a failure because I'm not in the big leagues. Let them. They're wrong, but I don't mind. I see them and the jobs they have, always the same and no excitement. Well, that's not for me. I play in Triple-A and Double-A leagues now, in big cities, nice cities. Not New York. Not Los Angeles. But big, nice cities. It's a good life. It's the life I want. How many people are getting to do what they've always wanted to do? Well, I am."

He's been playing ball, which is all he ever wanted to do, but now he has run out of guarantees that there will always be a team and a town for him the next season, or the season after that. He is the road-company Romeo, who is aging, and who is having trouble getting parts. He had two offers for 1961, one in the Eastern League and another in the Southern Association, so he's all right for this year. But what about next? He worries about that.

Testa is a ruggedly handsome young man, unmarried, who lives with his mother and sister in the Bronx, New York, between baseball seasons. He has the compact build of a boxer—which he almost was—short, but powerfully constructed. He is a skilled, strong-armed defensive catcher, but slow afoot and a mediocre hitter. He is shy, but honest and straight. He is intelligent, a college graduate with a Master's degree. He has other talents and could do other things.

Nick is licensed to be a physical-education teacher and he is trained to sell stocks and bonds, but he thinks such things are for when you are old and can no longer play baseball. He dreads them. He resists them by always finding another team to hang on another season, happy then, able to tolerate the pity of others, because he is playing ball.

"Sure I'd like to have made the majors to stay," Nick says. "No, I never had a real chance. I wouldn't complain, but you asked. No, I never hit much. Never the long ball, like they want. But I could always throw and handle pitchers, and when I was younger, if they'd given me a chance, I could have made it. Ah, well, it just didn't happen."

Although he is away from home more than he is home, he remains close to his mother and sister. Sister Theresa is perhaps his biggest rooter. She resents the pity of their neighbors and friends. "They ask me why Nicky doesn't give it up and quit," she said. "He tries to make them understand. I try to make them understand. Nick is making a good living doing what he wants to do most, and in big cities, like Dallas and Omaha, under nice conditions. I ask people who consider him a failure because he hasn't made the majors, if they are at the top of their professions. They're not, but they still don't understand."

Nick said, "I'm more of a celebrity in cities where I'm playing than I am at home among my own friends. Ballplayers are celebrities in the minors too, almost like in the big leagues, though more in some cities than in others. Usually the kids come after you for autographs. Girls are impressed with you, and the guys are too. Everyone knows you. You go on radio and television. They write stories about you in the newspapers.

"I'm not married. I have no big responsibilities. I make good money. I'm not gonna get rich, but I make good money. Kids coming up, unless they're bonus kids, starve in the minors—something like $300 a month, sometimes. Guys on the way down, especially if they were stars, may make a lot, maybe $1,500 a month. I'm somewhere in between. I guess the average is about $800 a month. Of course it's only for the five months or so of the season, but you can play winter ball too, or find work.

"I like the life. Not having security doesn't bother me. I don't mind moving around. I like being in different cities, always making new friends, which is easy for ballplayers. Conditions don't bother me. Playing fields, rooms, meals, expense money, buses, none of that bothers me. I'd play in a parking lot in any town, any time."

It all began for Nick on the same Bronx sandlots and at the same time it began for Rocky Colavito and Frank Malzone, who did make it big. Nick's parents came to New York from Italy during World War I. Nick's father was drafted on arrival and only afterward did he begin building a family. The Testas raised four children within a mile of the Yankee Stadium and the Polo Grounds. "Papa was never a baseball fan," Nick said. "But Mama was and still is. She used to root for the Yankees, for DiMaggio and Crosetti and Lazzeri. If DiMag had a bad day, she wouldn't give us our spaghetti for supper.

"I always wanted to play baseball. Since I was a kid, eight, nine years old, I figured I'd make my living at it, or in football or boxing or some sport. I was crazy about fighting. I did pretty well in the amateurs, including the Golden Gloves. Mom didn't know about it. She still doesn't. I used to work out with some small-time pros in the gym, and a couple of times I was approached to turn pro myself.

"I never did. Back in 1944 or 1945, during the war, the Giants did their spring training at Lakewood, New Jersey, and I used to hang out there. The fellas were nice to me, and they told me I had a future in baseball and was crazy to fool around with football and boxing."

On the sandlots Nick played football winters, sometimes two games in a row, and baseball summers, as many as five or six games a weekend. At thirteen he joined a semipro league and among his fellows were some declining veterans such as Danny Gardella. "I made two dollars a Sunday," Nick said. "They passed the hat and paid me off in dimes."

One afternoon in a championship semipro game in the Polo Grounds, Nick stood up so manfully under a heavy slide in a home-plate collision that a scout offered him an on-the-spot scholarship to Florida University. Nick accepted instantly.

In the autumn of 1945, Nick enrolled at the University of Florida, and the first free moment he got, he trudged to the athletic field, a catcher's mitt tucked under his arm. "I was a kid, green, just seventeen," he said. The warm sun beating down, baseball weather, he searched out the athletic director. "I'm Nick Testa," he said. "I've just enrolled."

"Glad to meet you," the fellow said. "Go down to the locker room and draw your uniform."

Alone Nick walked to the dressing room, stopping once to find out where uniforms were being issued. Reaching the window, Nick identified himself. Soon pads, clothes and cleats came thumping onto the counter.

"It was a football uniform!" Nick said. "They handed me a football suit. I'd been shanghaied! It was the first I knew that I was there on a football scholarship, not a baseball scholarship."

Looking back on it now, Nick can laugh. "That same day I was out butting heads in scrimmages. Freshmen could play varsity ball that year, so I played a little fullback, enough to get banged around. Later I had a good baseball season and all the way through, I attended classes and got good grades.

"During vacation that spring, I saw an ad in *The Sporting News* that Walden, New York, could use some baseball players. I threw a couple of balls and they signed me up. I put the name "Nick Warren" on the contract so as not to lose my amateur eligibility. I had a good year and I never went back to Florida. That fall I played football at Bergen Junior College in New Jersey, where a Giant baseball scout was coaching. In the spring of 1947, I signed a pro baseball contract with the Giants under my own name."

Nick was done with college sports then, but not with college. In off-season semesters, he attended the University of Delaware, and after graduation went to New York University to earn a Master's degree. All along the way, he made the dean's list regularly. He finished in 1956, roughly eleven years after that first day on the Florida campus.

In 1957, Nick took time out for two years in the Army. "I was just another soldier for four months until some general found out I was a ballplayer," he said. "They cut new orders for me and transferred me to Fort Belvoir. I spent the rest of my hitch playing ball summers and teaching physical education winters."

Since then it's been nothing but baseball for Nick. Early he realized that his catching would have to compensate for his weak hitting. So he became a holler guy, hustling, working on defense. He always could throw. "Oh, I'll make my errors," he said. "I get the ball and throw it. If I wanted to play it cool, I wouldn't make errors. But as it is, I've led a couple of leagues in assists, even if they don't run too much on me."

The only time he batted over .300 was in 1955, when he hit .311 at Wilkes-Barre. The lowest was .187 at Trenton in 1948. His lifetime average falls about halfway between these extremes. Two homers each at Wilkes-Barre and Seaford and Dallas are his best.

"I just hit those short drives to the outfield and hope they fall in," he said. "No one cares how much a catcher hits if he's got some power—ten or fifteen homers a year. But I just don't have the swing for it. I'm strong and I've tried, but it only fouls me up. I settle for trying to move the runner up. The best year I had in RBIs was 71 at Erie in 1949, but often as not I didn't play a full season. About seven different years I caught as many as 100 games."

Nick grinned and said he'd be satisfied to have sister Terry's batting ability. A handsome, amply curved young lady and a fine athlete, she gets along well with the players, who lure her on the field for pepper games and batting practice.

Terry loves to hit and has taken her cuts against Marv Grissom in San Francisco, and torn up the tarpaulin swinging away on high heels in Dallas, much to the rage of staid old club officials. "They get burned up," she said, laughing, "but I have fun."

"She's some hitter," Nick said. "At Dallas I threw her curves, fast balls—it didn't matter, she hit them all. She hit line drives—bang, whoosh!—she really hit screamers. She shook everyone up. Maybe I should have knocked her down. I should hit like she does!"

A lot of it has been fun for Nick. "I remember once in winter ball in Colombia, they were giving the guy ahead of me an intentional pass to get at me. I got so mad, I jumped in the batter's box before he was done. Has there been another time when a pitcher pitched to two men at the same time? Boy, was there a rhubarb!

"Actually, I haven't been in many rhubarbs. The only time I was ever thrown out of a game was at Jacksonville in 1952. I banged my catcher's mask around arguing with an ump on a call and he gave me the thumb." Nick grinned: "That was really unusual. Most times I don't get mad when I'm catching on calls on the pitcher, only when I'm batting."

After all these years, Nick is inclined to occasional clowning. Last summer in the Southern Association, when Stan Palys' slugging had earned him the nickname "the Animal," Nick donned a gorilla suit to greet Stan at home plate with a monkey hug.

Another time, in Rohoba, Delaware, Nick chased a skunk across the outfield, pegging baseballs at it. "He was holding up the game," he said. "The fans, there were about 100 of them, went wild. But what I couldn't figure out was why my teammates were chasing me. Later, they explained that a skunk first begins to give off an odor when it's frightened. They were afraid I'd catch it. Heck, I'm a city boy, I don't know about such things. But I know I got razzed."

There were no laughs for Nick in his one big chance. In 1956 he got his orders to report to the Giants the following spring. He had played at Dallas in 1956, hitting only .250, but driving in 50 runs, starring defensively and earning a place on the Texas League All-Star team.

That winter he was playing in storied Managua, Nicaragua, when his luck went bad. A home-plate collision knocked him into the hospital. He returned to action too soon, still weak. He felt sick and his body ached. When his condition deteriorated to the point where he couldn't raise his right arm, he worriedly returned to the States for a medical checkup.

Nick's leathery face grew soft with the memory of it. "They told me I had polio. I don't know. All I know is they said I had it in three muscles in my right side and was partially paralyzed. I lay in bed thinking I was going to blow my big chance. My only hope was when the doctors said exercise might bring me around. So I worked and worked with weights and calisthenics. I've always been a health addict, and in good shape, and maybe that helped. Anyway, by the spring I felt better.

"I'd never told the Giants, and my arm still wasn't right—in fact it wasn't completely better until last year—but I found I could just get by. I caught a lot of games that spring and hit about .260. Some guys noticed. They said, 'What's wrong, Nicky?' but I never told anyone. I didn't throw when I didn't have to and somehow I did get by.

"They had five catchers—Bob Schmidt, Valmy Thomas, Ray Katt, Roger McCardell and myself. When the season began, they swapped Katt to the Cards and optioned McCardell out. I couldn't believe it when I stuck, but it turned out to be the bench. I got into only one game, with the Cards in Seals Stadium. I went in in the eighth and Daryl Spencer broke it up with a homer in the eleventh, before I could get to bat. I'll never forgive him.

"I sat out in the bullpen, mostly, almost getting into a lot of games, wanting to, but dreading it; I could hardly throw. Cutdown day in May I expected to go, but they put me on the inactive list, made me a coach and left me in the bullpen. It was still the big leagues, so it wasn't so bad.

"I used to go out four hours before game time, and I was pretty much in charge until the regulars showed up. Anyone wanted extra work, I helped him out. Then I pitched or caught batting practice, and then warmed up the pitchers. Then when the game began, I went to the bullpen, ready to warm up the relievers.

"I've sat in a lot of bullpens in my time, and there's an art to it. There's not much work and it's a terrible seat. You can watch the game and chew the fat, but playing is the game, and if you're not playing, you got to do something else.

"Some guys sunbathe, even putting on sunglasses or suntan lotion. Or they sit up pretty straight with their arms crossed in front of their chests and sleep with their eyes closed, but from the dugout they look like they're studying the game. Why, in Milwaukee and Philadelphia they have to use phones because they can't see you good, and some of the guys even go in the back and lay down.

"You eat hot dogs and drink soda pop. The fans bring it to you and talk to you. In some parks, like St. Louis and San Francisco, you're real close to them. Lots of girls come out there, too. Actually, the bullpen coach is supposed to shoo the girls away, but I was real bad at it. I used to encourage them."

Nick attracts the girls, but shies from camp followers. He's short, just five-eight, 180 pounds, and darkly handsome in a physical, masculine way. He is neither all saint nor all sinner, but a deeply religious boy who does not smoke nor drink. He is a physical-culture enthusiast who protects his health and limits his recreational pursuit, but who is not distressed by the Army-camp, liberty-town excesses of many professional athletes.

"It's their own business," he said. "Night ball has a lot to do with it. When you're playing days and have to get out to the ball park early, you can't stay out all night. I'd rather have it that way, because with me playing comes first. Day call means a more normal routine. And free days pass slowly, and killing the hours, waiting for the night games, can be a hard, lonesome thing, and I've had a bellyful of it.

"But for most single fellows, night ball is more fun. They're through around 11 and they can go out and have a date, a few drinks, a little fun and sleep late the next day. There are always women for a ballplayer. Some of 'em are real nice girls and some guys marry them."

Sister Terry smiled wistfully. "Nicky dreads marriage," she said. "He's shy and very quiet, and he knows baseball, especially in the minors, is no life for a married man and for his family. Moving around to a different city every year, never knowing where, is no good. And being a thousand miles apart is cruel. It's easier not to have anyone."

Nick conceded the point. "I guess that's right," he said. "It's no good to be married and in the minors."

Nick lifts weights and does strenuous calisthenics and eats yogurt and takes vitamin pills. It all has a purpose, of course, to keep him fit for baseball. But being in shape to play and getting to play are two different things. Recently it has been harder for Nick to find a place to play. In the spring of 1960, he called up a friend, Bob Howsam, official of the Denver club, and asked for help. Denver didn't have an opening, but Howsam fixed Nicky up at New Orleans. It has been Nick's experience that friends in baseball are sympathetic and reliable and helpful. Nick was happy going into the Southern Association, because the league does little air travel.

"I admit I'm afraid of flying," Nick says. "It wasn't too bad in the big leagues—what is? They have big multi-engine planes, and if the weather is bad, they don't go. You feel safe. But in the minors, the weather doesn't matter. You just go. And those planes are so small. I guess I've been made nervous too often." He shrugged. "But it's just fear. I flew when I had to, to keep playing. You do things when you have to."

The New Orleans franchise was shifted to Little Rock in 1960, and Nick helped the team to a fast start. The team was in first place by mid-season. Nick was feeling strong and healthy again, catching almost all of the games and even hitting near .300. Opposing managers voted him the catcher with the best throwing arm in the league. They wrote colorful feature stories about him in the newspapers and put him on television.

"Then, all of a sudden, it was over," he said, looking hopelessly at his hands, bringing them up, past prayer, to rub his forehead. "They put me on the bench. They had one of those golden-haired boys—everyone always has one—who'd been hurt, and he came back, and another kid who'd quit, but then rejoined them. So there were reasons, but I couldn't understand not playing at all. The fans couldn't, either, and wrote up a petition asking why I wasn't playing. The club didn't answer the fans and they didn't say anything to me.

"When I finally realized I wasn't going to play any more, I went to them and asked for my release. But they said no. They did put me on the inactive list, but they kept my contract. I could've come home, but I'm a ballplayer, so I hung around. It was a long couple of months.

"The other players know how it is, and they understood, but I felt like excess baggage. Not playing is just awful. I've had a lot of it. You know, you spend six hours a day at the ball park, more for doubleheaders, what with long pregame warm-ups and long games, and if you're not playing, it's monotonous and a rough life."

The time may be coming, of course, when Nick Testa, thirty-two years old, will play no longer and will have to rejoin the civilian, workaday world. He's interested in the stock market and has invested much of his savings, but he doesn't think he'd like to sell. "I'm not aggressive enough," he said. He doesn't think he'll teach, either. "I'll never use the degree," he said. Then he shrugged the sad admission. "Well, maybe I will wind up teaching," he said. "But I don't even want to talk about it, or think about it. Not yet.

"Maybe, better, I'll wind up coaching or managing. You never know. In the minors of course. But that's all right. It's still baseball. It's still different every day, exciting, glamorous.

"Actually I don't want to coach while I'm still playing, not in the minors, because minor-league coaches have to do a tremendous amount of work and it drains you. But I wouldn't mind managing and playing."

Nick thinks that of the 20 or so managers under whom he's worked, Salty Parker was best. Maybe this is because Salty had Nick hitting cleanup one year at Dallas when Nick was hitting .193. Or, maybe, because Salty loved Nick and called him "terrific, a fellow who does everything like he was a .330 hitter." But Nick says he honestly believes Salty had most of what he considers the best managerial qualities. "If I ever manage," Nick said, "I want to be like Salty, treating each player like a man, working with him, trying to help him, teaching him to relax, which I think is the secret of this game. I'd like to try. I'd like to stay in baseball. I don't care what people say or whether they consider me a failure or not. I'd know I'm not, I'm happy."

Nick Testa shook his head as if to shake away sad thoughts. "I'll play this year," he said, "and I wish I knew already that I'd play next year, too. I've loved it ever since I was a kid and I love it as much now as I ever did. How long can I keep on playing? As long as Satchel Paige, maybe. Indefinitely. Forever. As long as they'll let me."

"I am a great believer in the sacrifice."

Courtesy *Playboy* Magazine ©

"Batter is agent of evil secret organization plotting to rule world. Stick me in his ear."

MANY WILL consider this a shocking piece. Many others will, after reading it together with John Updike's coverage of the same event on page 458 of this book, be even more shocked—and regret, perhaps, that they did not read the Updike first. Perhaps that is not a bad idea. Why not turn to the Updike now, then return to this one, written by a master at the baseball-writing craft, who was assigned, by the editors of *Sport* magazine, "to deliver benediction on Ted Williams."

1960: The Kid's Last Game

ED LINN

WEDNESDAY, SEPTEMBER 26, was a cold and dreary day in Boston, a curious bit of staging on the part of those gods who always set the scene most carefully for Ted Williams. It was to be the last game Ted would ever play in Boston. Not until the game was over would Williams let it be known that it was the last game he would play anywhere.

Ted came into the locker room at 10:50, very early for him. He was dressed in dark brown slacks, a yellow sport shirt and a light tan pull-over sweater, tastily brocaded in the same color. Ted went immediately to his locker, pulled off the sweater, then strolled into the trainer's room.

Despite all the triumphs and the honors, it had been a difficult year for him. As trainer Jack Fadden put it, "It hasn't been a labor of love for Ted this year; it's just been labor." On two separate occasions, he had come very close to giving it all up.

The spring-training torture had been made no easier for Ted by manager Billy Jurges. Jurges believed that the only way for a man Ted's age to stay in condition was to reach a peak at the beginning of the season and hold it by playing just as often as possible. "The most we can expect from Williams," Jurges had said, at the time of Ted's signing, "is 100 games. The least is pinch-hitting." Ted played in 113 games.

Throughout the training season, however, Ted seemed to be having trouble with his timing. Recalling his .254 average of the previous season, the experts wrote him off for perhaps the 15th time in his career. But on his first time at bat in the opening game, Ted hit a 500-foot home run, possibly the longest of his career, off Camilo Pascual, probably the best pitcher in the league. The next day, in the Fenway Park opener, he hit a second homer, this one off Jim Coates. Ted pulled a leg muscle running out that homer, though, and when a man's muscles go while he is doing nothing more than jogging around the bases, the end is clearly in sight.

It took him almost a month to get back in condition, but the mysterious virus infection that hits him annually, a holdover from his service in Korea, laid him low again almost immediately. Since the doctors have never been able to diagnose this chronic illness, the only way they can treat him is to shoot a variety of drugs and antibiotics into him, in the hope that one of them takes hold. Ted, miserable and drugged when he finally got back in uniform, failed in a couple of pinch-hitting attempts and was just about ready to quit. Against the Yankees, Ralph Terry struck him out two straight times. The third time up, the count went to 3-2 when Williams unloaded on a waist-high fast ball and sent it into the bullpen in right-center, 400 feet away.

The blast triggered the greatest home-run spurt of Ted's career. Seven days later, he hit his 500th home run. He had started only 15 1960 games and he had hit eight 1960 homers. When he hit his 506th (and 11th of the year), he had homered once in every 6.67 times at bat.

Cold weather always bothered Ted, even in his early years, and so when he strained his shoulder late in August, he was just about ready to announce his retirement again. He had found it difficult to loosen up even in fairly warm weather, and to complicate matters he had found it necessary—back in the middle of 1959—to cut out the calisthenics routine he had always gone through in the clubhouse. The exercising had left him almost too weary to play ball.

Ted started every game so stiff that he was forced to exaggerate an old passion for swinging at balls only in the strike zone. In his first time at bat, he would look for an inside pitch between the waist and knees, the only pitch he could swing at naturally. In the main, however, Ted was more than willing to take the base on balls his first time up.

He stayed on for two reasons. Mike Higgins, who had replaced Jurges as Sox manager, told him bluntly, "You're paid to play ball, so go out and play." The strength behind those words rested in the fact that both Williams and Higgins knew very well that owner Tom Yawkey would continue to pay Ted whether he played or not.

In addition, the Red Sox had two series remaining with the Yankees and Orioles, who were still locked together in the pennant race. Ted did not think it fair to eliminate himself as a factor in the two-team battle. He announced his retirement just after the Yankees clinched the pennant.

Four days earlier, Ted had been called to a special meeting with Yawkey, Higgins, Dick O'Connell (who was soon to be named business manager) and publicity director Jack Malaney. This was to offer Ted the job of general manager, a position that had been discussed occasionally in the past.

Ted refused to accept the title until he proved he could do the job. He agreed, however, to work in the front office in 1961, assisting Higgins with player personnel, and O'Connell with business matters.

The coverage of Ted's last game was at a minimum. It was thought for a while that *Life* magazine wanted to send a crew down to cover the game, but it developed that they only wanted to arrange for Ted to represent them at the World Series. Dave Garroway's *Today* program tried to set up a telephone interview the morning of the game, but they couldn't get in touch with Ted. The Red Sox, alone among big-league clubs, have offered little help to anyone on the public relations front—and never any help at all where Ted Williams was concerned. Ted didn't live at the Kenmore Hotel with the rest of the unattached players. He lived about 100 yards down Commonwealth Avenue, at the Somerset. All calls and messages for him were diverted to the manager's office.

The ceremonies that were to mark his departure were rather limited, too. The Boston Chamber of Commerce had arranged to present him with a silver bowl, and the mayor's office and governor's office had quickly muscled into the picture. By Wednesday morning, however, the governor's office—which had apparently anticipated something more spectacular—begged off. The governor's spokesman suggested the presentation of a scroll at Ted's hotel, a suggestion which Ted simply ignored.

The only civilian in the clubhouse when Ted entered was the man from *Sport*, and he was talking to Del Baker, who was about to retire, too, after 50 years in the game. Ted looked over, scowled, seemed about to say something but changed his mind.

Our man was well aware what Ted was about to say. The Red Sox have a long-standing rule—also unique in baseball—that no reporter may enter the dressing room before the game, or for the first 15 minutes after the game. It was a point of honor with Ted to pick out any civilian who wasn't specifically with a ballplayer and to tell him, as loudly as possible, "You're not supposed to be in here, you know."

Sure enough, when our man started toward Ted's locker in the far corner of the room, Ted pointed a finger at him and shouted, "You're not supposed to be in here, you know."

"The same warm, glad cry of greeting I always get from you," our man said. "It's your last day. Why don't you live a little?"

Ted started toward the trainer's room again, but wheeled around and came back. "You've got a nerve coming here to interview me after the last one you wrote about me!"

Our man wanted to know what was the matter with the last one.

"You called me 'unbearable,' that's what's the matter."

The full quote, it was pointed out, was that he "was sometimes unbearable but never dull," which holds a different connotation entirely.

"You've been after me for twelve years, that flogging magazine," he said, in his typically well-modulated shout. "Twelve years. I missed an appointment for some kind of luncheon. I forgot what happened . . . it doesn't matter anyway . . . but I forgot some appointment twelve years ago and *Sport* magazine hasn't let up on me since."

Our man, lamentably eager to disassociate himself from this little magazine, made it clear that while he had done most of *Sport's* Williams articles in the past few years he was not a member of the staff. "And," our man pointed out, "I have been accused of turning you into a combination of Paul Bunyan and Santa Claus."

"Well, when you get back there tell them what . . . (he searched for the appropriate word, the *mot juste* as they say in the dugouts) . . . what *flog-heads* they are. Tell them that for me."

Our man sought to check the correct spelling of the adjectives with him but got back only a scowl. Ted turned around to fish something out of a cloth bag at the side of his locker. "Why don't you just write your story without me?" he said. "What do you have to talk to me for?" And then, in a suddenly weary voice: "What can I tell you now that I haven't told you before?"

"Why don't you let me tell you what the story is supposed to be?" our man said. "Then you can say yes or no." It was an unfortunate way to put the question since it invited the answer it brought.

"I can tell you before you tell me," Ted shouted. "No! No, no, no."

Our man had the impression Williams was trying to tell him something. He was right. "Look," Williams said. "If I tell you I don't want to talk to you, why don't you just take my word for it?"

The clubhouse boy had come over with a glossy photo to be signed, and Ted sat down on his stool, turned his back and signed it.

Although we are reluctant to bring *Sport* into the context of the story itself, Ted's abiding hatred toward us tells much about him and his even longer feud with Boston sportswriters. Twelve years ago, just as Ted said, an article appeared on these pages to which he took violent exception. (The fact that he is so well aware that it *was* twelve years ago suggests that he still has the magazine around somewhere, so that he can fan the flames whenever he feels them dying.) What Ted objected to in that article was an interview with his mother in San Diego. Ted objects to any peering into his private life. When he holes himself up in his hotel, when he sets a barrier around the clubhouse, when he disappears into the Florida Keys at the end of the season, he is deliberately removing himself from a world which he takes to be dangerous and hostile. His constant fighting with the newspapermen who cover him most closely is a part of the same pattern. What do newspapermen represent except the people who are supposed to pierce personal barriers? Who investigate, who pry, *who find out?*

Ted's mother has been a Salvation Army worker in San Diego all her life. She is a local character, known—not without affection—as "Salvation May." Ted himself was dedicated to the Salvation Army when he was a baby. His generosity, his unfailing instinct to come to the aid of any underdog, is in direct line with the teachings of the Army, which is quite probably the purest charitable organization in the world. Even as a boy, Ted regularly gave his 30-cent luncheon allowance to classmates he considered more needy than himself, a considerable sacrifice since the Williams family had to struggle to make ends meet.

When Ted signed with San Diego at the age of seventeen, he was a tall, skinny kid (six-three, 146 pounds). He gave most of his $150-a-month salary toward keeping up the family house and he tried to build up his weight by gorging himself on the road where the club picked up the check. One day Ted was coming into the clubhouse when Bill Lane, the owner of the Padres, motioned him over. In his deep, foghorn voice, Lane said, "Well, kid, you're leading the list. You've got the others beat."

Ted, pleased that his ability was being noted so promptly, smiled and asked, "Yeah, what list?"

"The dining room list," Lane said. "Hasn't anyone told you that your meal allowance is supposed to be five dollars a day?"

Nobody had. "Okay, Bill," Ted said, finally. "Take anything over five dollars off my salary."

Bill did, too.

Even before *Sport* went into details about his background, the Boston press had discovered his weak point and hit him hard and—it must be added—most unfairly. During Ted's second season with the Sox, one reporter had the ill grace to comment, in regard to a purely personal dispute, "But what can you expect of a youth so abnormal that he didn't go home in the off season to see his own mother?"

When Williams' World War II draft status was changed from 1A to 3A after he claimed his mother as a dependent, one Boston paper sent a private investigator to San Diego to check on her standard of living; another paper sent reporters out onto the street to ask casual passersby to pass judgment on Ted's patriotism.

Reporters were sent galloping out into the

street to conduct a public-opinion poll once again when Williams was caught fishing in the Everglades while his wife was giving birth to a premature baby.

A press association later sent a story out of San Diego that Ted had sold the furniture out from under his mother—although a simple phone call could have established that it wasn't true. Ted had bought the house and the furniture for his mother. His brother—who had been in frequent trouble with the law—had sold it. The Boston papers picked up that story and gave it a big play, despite the fact that every sports editor in the city had enough background material on Ted's family to know—even without checking—that it couldn't possibly be true. It was, Ted's friends believed, their way of punishing him for not being "cooperative."

Ted had become so accustomed to looking upon any reference to his family as an unfriendly act that when *Sport* wrote about his mother, he bristled—even though her final quote was "Don't say anything about Teddy except the highest and the best. He's a wonderful son." And when he searched for some reason why the magazine would do such a thing to him, he pounced upon that broken appointment, which everybody except himself had long forgotten.

After Ted had signed the photograph the day of his last game, he sat on his stool, his right knee jumping nervously, his right hand alternately buttoning and unbuttoning the top button of his sport shirt.

When he stripped down to his shorts, there was no doubt he was forty-two. The man once called the Splendid Splinter—certainly one of the most atrocious nicknames ever committed upon an immortal—was thick around the middle. A soft roll of loose fat, drooping around the waist, brought on a vivid picture of Archie Moore.

Williams is a tall, handsome man. If they ever make that movie of his life that keeps being rumored around, the guy who plays Bret Maverick would be perfect for the part. But ballplayers age quickly. Twenty years under the sun had baked Ted's face and left it lined and leathery. Sitting there, Ted Williams had the appearance of an old Marine sergeant who had been to the battles and back.

Sal Maglie, who had the end locker on the other side of the shower-room door, suddenly caught Ted's attention. "You're a National Leaguer, Sal," Ted said, projecting his voice to the room at large. "I got a hundred dollars that the Yankees win the World Series. The Yankees will win it in four or five games."

"I'm an American Leaguer now," Sal said, quietly.

"A hundred dollars," Ted said. "A friendly bet."

"You want a friendly bet? I'll bet you a friendly dollar."

"Fifty dollars," Ted said.

"All right," Sal said. "Fifty dollars." And then, projecting his own voice, he said, "I like the Pirates, anyway."

Williams went back to his mail, as the others dressed and went out onto the field.

At length, Ted picked up his spikes, wandered into the trainer's room again, and lifting himself onto the table, carefully began to put a shine on them. A photographer gave him a ball to sign.

Ted gazed at it with distaste, then looked up at the photographer with loathing. "Are you crazy?" he snapped.

The photographer backed away, pocketed the ball and began to adjust his camera sights on Ted. "You don't belong in here," Ted shouted. And turning to the clubhouse boy, he barked, "Get him out of here."

The locker room had emptied before Ted began to dress. For Ted did not go out to take batting practice or fielding practice. He made every entrance onto the field a dramatic event. He did not leave the locker room for the dugout until 12:55, only 35 minutes before the game was scheduled to start. By then, most of the writers had already gone up to Tom Yawkey's office to hear Jackie Jensen announce that he was returning to baseball.

As Ted came quickly up the stairs and into the dugout, he almost bumped into his close friend and fishing companion, Bud Leavitt, sports editor of the Bangor *Daily News*. "Hi, Bud," Ted said, as if he were surprised Leavitt was there. "You drive up?"

A semicircle of cameramen closed in on Williams, like a bear trap, on the playing field just up above. Ted hurled a few choice oaths at them, and as an oath-hurler Ted never bats below .400. He guided Leavitt against the side of the dugout, just above the steps, so that he could continue the conversation without providing a shooting angle for the photographers. The photographers continued to shoot him in profile, though, until Ted took Leavitt by the elbow and walked him the length of the dugout. "Let's sit down," he said, as he left, "so we won't be bothered by all these blasted cameramen."

If there had been any doubt back in the

locker room that Ted had decided to bow out with typical hardness, it had been completely dispelled by those first few minutes in the dugout. On his last day in Fenway Park, Ted Williams seemed resolved to remain true to his own image of himself, to permit no sentimentality or hint of sentimentality to crack that mirror through which he looks at the world and allows the world to look upon him.

And yet, in watching this strange and troubled man—the most remarkable and colorful and full-blooded human being to come upon the athletic scene since Babe Ruth—you had the feeling that he was overplaying his role, that he had struggled through the night against the impulse to make his peace, to express his gratitude, to accept the great affection that the city had been showering upon him for years. In watching him, you had the clear impression that in resisting this desire he was overreacting and becoming more profane, more impossible and—yes—more unbearable than ever.

Inside Ted Williams there has always been a struggle of two opposing forces, almost two different persons. (We are fighting the use of the word schizophrenia.) The point we are making is best illustrated through Williams' long refusal to tip his hat in acknowledgment of the cheering crowds. It has always been his contention that the people who cheered him when he hit a home run were the same people who booed him when he struck out—which, incidentally, is probably not true at all. More to our point, Ted has always insisted that although he would rather be cheered than booed, he really didn't care what the fans thought of him, one way or the other.

Obviously, though, if he really didn't care he wouldn't have bothered to make such a show of not caring. He simply would have touched his finger to his cap in that automatic, thoughtless gesture of most players and forgotten about it. Ted, in short, has always had it both ways. He gets the cheers and he pretends they mean nothing to him. He is like a rich man's nephew who treats his uncle with disrespect to prove he is not interested in his money, while all the time he is secretly dreaming that the uncle will reward such independence by leaving him most of the fortune.

Ted has it even better than that. The fans of Boston have always wooed him ardently. They always cheered him all the louder in the hope that he would reward them, at last, with that essentially meaningless tip of the hat.

This clash within Williams came to the surface as he sat and talked with Leavitt, alone and undisturbed. For, within a matter of minutes, the lack of attention began to oppress him; his voice began to rise, to pull everybody's attention back to him. The cameramen, getting the message, drifted toward him again, not in a tight pack this time but in a loose and straggling line.

With Ted talking so loudly, it was apparent that he and Leavitt were discussing how to get together, after the World Series, for their annual post-season fishing expedition. The assignment to cover the Series for *Life* had apparently upset their schedule.

"After New York," Ted said, "I'll be going right to Pittsburgh." He expressed his hope that the Yankees would wrap it all up in Yankee Stadium, so that he could join Leavitt in Bangor at the beginning of the following week. "But, dammit," he said, "if the Series goes more than five games, I'll have to go back to Pittsburgh again."

Leavitt reminded Ted of an appearance he had apparently agreed to make in Bangor. "All right," Ted said. "But no speeches or anything."

A young, redheaded woman, in her late twenties, leaned over from her box seat alongside the dugout and asked Ted if he would autograph her scorecard.

"I can't sign it, dear," Ted said. "League rules. Where are you going to be after the game?"

"You told me that once before," she said, unhappily.

"Well, where are you going to be?" Ted shouted, in the impatient way one would shout at an irritating child.

"Right here," she said.

"All right."

"But I waited before and you never came."

He ignored her.

Joe Cronin, president of the American League, came down the dugout aisle, followed by his assistant, Joe McKenney. Through Cronin's office, the local nine-o'clock news-feature program which follows the *Today* program in Boston had scheduled a filmed interview with Ted. The camera had already been set up on the home-plate side of the dugout, just in front of the box seats. Cronin talked to Ted briefly and went back to reassure the announcer that Ted would be right there. McKenney remained behind to make sure Ted didn't forget. At last Ted jumped up and shouted, "Where is it, Joe, dammit?"

When Ted followed McKenney out, it was the first time he had stuck his head onto the field all day. There were still not too many fans in the stands, although far more than would have been there on any other day to watch a seventh-place team on a cold and threatening Wednesday afternoon. At this first sight of Ted Williams, they let out a mighty roar.

As he waited alongside interviewer Jack Chase, Ted bit his lower lip, and looked blankly into space, both characteristic mannerisms. At a signal from the cameraman, Chase asked Ted how he felt about entering "the last lap."

All at once Ted was smiling. "I want to tell you, Jack, I honestly feel good about it," he said, speaking in that quick charming way of his. "You can't get blood out of a turnip, you know. I've gone as far as I can and I'm sure I wouldn't want to try it any more."

"Have we gone as far as we can with the Jimmy Fund?" he was asked.

Ted was smiling more broadly. "Oh, no. We could never go far enough with the Jimmy Fund."

Chase reminded Ted that he was scheduled to become a batting coach.

"Can you take a .250 hitter and make a .300 hitter out of him?"

"There has always been a saying in baseball that you can't make a hitter," Ted answered. "But I think you can *improve* a hitter. More than you can improve a fielder. More mistakes are made in hitting than in any other part of the game."

At this point Williams was literally encircled by photographers, amateur and pro. The pros were taking pictures from the front and from the sides. Behind them, in the stands, dozens of fans had their cameras trained on Ted, too, although they could hardly have been getting anything except the number 9 on his back.

Ted was asked if he were going to travel around the Red Sox farm system in 1961 to instruct the young hitters.

"All I know is that I'm going to spring training," he said. "Other than that, I don't know anything."

The interview closed with the usual fulsome praise of Williams, the inevitable apotheosis that leaves him with a hangdog, embarrassed look upon his features. "I appreciate the kind words," he said. "It's all been fun. Everything I've done in New England from playing left field and getting booed, to the Jimmy Fund."

The Jimmy Fund is the money-raising arm of the Children's Cancer Hospital in Boston, which has become the world center for research into cancer and for the treatment of its young victims. Ted has been deeply involved with the hospital since its inception in 1947, serving the last four years as general chairman of the fund committee. He is an active chairman, not an honorary one. Scarcely a day goes by, when Ted is in Boston, that he doesn't make one or two stops for the Jimmy Fund somewhere in New England. He went out on the missions even on days when he was too sick to play ball. (This is the same man, let us emphasize, who refuses to attend functions at which he himself is to be honored.) He has personally raised something close to $4,000,000 and has helped to build a modern, model hospital not far from Fenway Park.

But he has done far more than that. From the first, Williams took upon himself the agonizing task of trying to bring some cheer into the lives of these dying children and, perhaps even more difficult, of comforting their parents. He has, in those years, permitted himself to become attached to thousands of these children, knowing full well that they were going to die, one by one. He has become so attached to some of them that he has chartered special planes to bring him to their deathbeds.

Whenever one of these children asks to see him, whatever the time, he comes. His only stipulation is that there must be no publicity, no reporters, no cameramen.

We once suggested to Ted that he must get some basic return from all this work he puts into the Jimmy Fund. Ted considered the matter very carefully before he answered: "Look," he said finally, "it embarrasses me to be praised for anything like this. The embarrassing thing is that I don't feel I've done anything compared to the people at the hospital who are doing the important work. It makes me happy to think I've done a little good; I suppose that's what I get out of it.

"Anyway," he added thoughtfully, "it's only a freak of fate, isn't it, that one of those kids isn't going to grow up to be an athlete and I wasn't the one who had the cancer."

At the finish of the filmed interview he had to push his way through the cameramen between him and the dugout. "Oh——," he said.

But when one of them asked him to pose with Cronin, Ted switched personalities again and asked, with complete amiability, "Where is he?"

Cronin was in the dugout. Ted met Joe at the bottom of the steps and threw an arm around him. They grinned at each other while the pictures were being taken, talking softly and unintelligibly. After a minute, Ted reached over to the hook just behind him and grabbed his glove. The cameramen were still yelling for another shot as he started up the dugout steps. Joe, grinning broadly, grabbed him by the shoulder and yanked him back down. While Cronin was wrestling Ted around and whacking him on the back, the cameras clicked. "I got to warm up, dammit," Ted was saying. He made a pawing gesture at the cameramen, as if to say, "I'd like to belt you buzzards." This, from all evidence, was the picture that went around the country that night, because strangely enough, it looked as if he were waving a kind of sad goodbye.

When he finally broke away and raced up to the field, he called back over his shoulder, "See you later, Joe." The cheers arose from the stands once again.

The Orioles were taking infield practice by then, and the Red Sox were warming up along the sideline. Ted began to play catch with Pumpsie Green. As he did—sure enough—the cameramen lined up just inside the foul line for some more shots, none of which will ever be used. "Why don't you cockroaches get off my back?" Ted said, giving them his No. 1 sneer. "Let me breathe, will you?"

The bell rang before he had a chance to throw two dozen balls. Almost all the players went back to the locker room. Remaining on the bench were only Ted Williams, buttoned up in his jacket, and Vic Wertz. One of the members of the ground crew came over with a picture of Williams. He asked Ted if he would autograph it. "Sure," Ted said. "For you guys, anything."

Vic Wertz was having his picture taken with another crew member. Wertz had his arm around the guy and both of them were laughing. "How about you, Ted?" the cameraman asked. "One with the crewmen?"

Ted posed willingly with the man he had just signed for, with the result that the whole herd of cameramen came charging over again. Ted leaped to his feet. "Twenty-two years of this bull——," he cried.

The redhead was leaning over the low barrier again, but now three other young women were alongside her. One of them seemed to be crying, apparently at the prospect of Ted's retirement. An old photographer, in a long, weatherbeaten coat, asked Ted for a special pose. "Get lost," Ted said. "I've seen enough of you, you old goat."

Curt Gowdy, the Red Sox broadcaster, had come into the dugout to pass on some information about the pregame ceremonies. Ted shouted, "The devil with all you miserable cameramen." The women continued to stare, in fascination, held either by the thrill of having this last long look at Ted Williams or by the opportunity to learn a few new words.

A Baltimore writer came into the dugout, and Ted settled down beside him. He wanted to know whether the writer could check on the "King of Swat" crown that had been presented to him in his last visit to Baltimore. Ted wasn't sure whether he had taken it back to Boston with him or whether the organization still had it.

"You know," he told the writer, "Brown's a better pitcher now than he's ever been. Oh, he's a great pitcher. Never get a fat pitch from him. When he does, it comes in with something extra on it. Every time a little different. He knows what he's doing."

Ted is a student of such things. He is supposed to be a natural hitter, blessed with a superhuman pair of eyes. We are not about to dispute this. What we want to say is that when Ted first came to the majors, the book on him was that he would chase bad balls. "All young sluggers do," according to Del Baker, who was managing Detroit when Ted came up. "Ted developed a strike zone of his own, though, by the second year."

When Ted took his physical for the Naval reserve in World War II, his eyes tested at 20/10 and were so exceptional in every regard that while he was attending air gunnery school he broke all previous Marine records for hitting the target sleeve. But Ted has a point of his own here: "My eyesight," he says, "is now 20/15. Half the major-leaguers have eyes as good as that. It isn't eyesight that makes a hitter; it's practice. *Con-sci-en-tious* practice. I say that Williams has hit more balls than any guy living, except maybe Ty Cobb. I don't say it to brag; I just state it as a fact. From the time I was 11 years old, I've taken every possible opportunity to swing at a ball. I've swung and I've swung and I've swung."

Ted always studied every little movement a pitcher made. He always remained on the bench before the game to watch them warming up. From his first day to his last, he hustled around to get all possible information on a new pitcher.

It has always been his theory that we are all creatures of habit, himself included. Pitchers, he believes, fall into observable patterns.

A certain set of movements foretells a certain pitch. In a particular situation, or on a particular count, they go to a particular pitch. There were certain pitchers, Ted discovered, who would inevitably go to their big pitch, the pitch they wanted him to swing at, on the 2-2 count.

And so Ted would frequently ask a teammate, "What was the pitch he struck you out on?" or "What did he throw you on the 2-2 pitch?"

When a young player confessed he didn't know what the pitch had been, Ted would grow incredulous. "You don't know the pitch he struck you out on? I'm not talking about last week or last month. I'm not even talking about yesterday. Today! Just now! I'm talking about the pitch he struck you out on just now!"

Returning to his seat on the bench, he'd slump back in disgust and mutter, "What a rockhead. The guy's taking the bread and butter out of his mouth and he don't even care how."

In a very short time, the player would have an answer ready for Williams. Ted always got the young hitters thinking about their craft. He always tried to instruct them, to build up their confidence. "When you want to know who the best hitter in the league is," he'd tell the rookies, "just look into the mirror."

Among opposing players, Williams was always immensely popular. Yes, even among opposing pitchers. All pitchers love to say, "Nobody digs in against *me*." Only Ted Williams was given the right to dig in without getting flipped. Around the American League, there seemed to be a general understanding that Williams had too much class to be knocked down.

Waiting in the dugout for the ceremonies to get under way, Ted picked up a bat and wandered up and down the aisle taking vicious practice swings.

The photographers immediately swooped in on him. One nice guy was taking cameras from the people in the stands and getting shots of Ted for them.

As Ted put the bat down, one of them said, "One more shot, Teddy, as a favor."

"I'm all done doing any favors for you guys," Williams said. "I don't have to put up with you any more, and you don't have to put up with me."

An old woman, leaning over the box seats, was wailing, "Don't leave us, Ted. Don't leave us."

"Oh hell," Ted said, turning away in disgust.

The redhead asked him plaintively, "Why don't you act nice?"

Ted strolled slowly toward her, grinning broadly. "Come on, dear," he drawled, "with that High Street accent you got there."

Turning back, he stopped in front of the man from *Sport,* pointed over his shoulder at the cameramen and asked, "You getting it all? You getting what you came for?"

"If you can't make it as a batting coach," our man said, "I understand you're going to try it as a cameraman."

"What does *Sport* magazine think I'm going to do?" Ted asked. "That's what I want to know. What does *Sport* magazine think I'm going to be?"

Speaking for himself, our man told him, he had not the slightest doubt that Ted was going to be the new general manager.

"*Sport* magazine," Ted said, making the name sound like an oath. "Always honest. Never prejudiced."

At this point he was called onto the field. Taking off his jacket, he strode out of the dugout. The cheers that greeted him came from 10,454 throats.

Curt Gowdy, handling the introductions, began: "As we all know, this is the final home game for—in my opinion and most of yours—the greatest hitter who ever lived. Ted Williams."

There was tremendous applause.

"Twenty years ago," Gowdy continued, "a skinny kid from San Diego came to the Red Sox camp . . ."

Ted first came to the Red Sox training camp at Sarasota in the spring of 1938. General manager Eddie Collins, having heard that Ted was a creature of wild and wayward impulse, had instructed second baseman Bobby Doerr to pick him up and deliver him, shining and undamaged.

It was unthinkable, of course, that Ted Williams would make a routine entrance. Just before Doerr was set to leave home, the worst flood of the decade hit California and washed out all the roads and telephone lines. When Williams and Doerr finally arrived in Sarasota, ten days late, there was a fine, almost imperceptible drizzle. Williams, still practically waterlogged from the California floods, held out a palm, looked skyward, shivered and said in a voice that flushed the flamingos from their nests, "So this is Florida, is it? Do they always keep this state under a foot of water?"

Williams suited up for a morning workout out in the field, jawed good-naturedly with the fans and got an unexpected chance to hit when a newsreel company moved in to take some batting-cage shots.

The magic of Ted Williams in a batter's box manifested itself that first day in camp. The tall, thin rookie stepped into the box, set himself in his wide stance, let his bat drop across the far corner of the plate, wiggled his hips and shoulders and jiggled up and down as if he were trying to tamp himself into the box. He moved his bat back and forth a few times, then brought it back into position and twisted his hands in opposite directions as if he were wringing the neck of the bat. He was set for the pitch.

And somehow, as if by some common impulse, all sideline activity stopped that day in 1938. Everybody was watching Ted Williams.

"Controversial, sure," Gowdy said, in bringing his remarks about Ted to a close, "but colorful."

The chairman of the Boston Chamber of Commerce presented Ted a shining, silver Paul Revere bowl "on behalf of the business community of Boston." Ted seemed to force his smile as he accepted it.

A representative of the sports committee of the Chamber of Commerce then presented him with a plaque "on behalf of visits to kids' and veterans' hospitals."

Mayor John Collins, from his wheelchair, announced that "on behalf of all citizens" he was proclaiming this day "Ted Williams Day." The mayor didn't know how right he was.

As Mayor Collins spoke of Ted's virtues ("nature's best, nature's nobleman"), the muscle of Ted's upper left jaw was jumping, constantly and rhythmically. The mayor's contribution to Ted Williams Day was a $1,000 donation to the Jimmy Fund from some special city fund.

Gowdy brought the proceedings to a close by proclaiming, "Pride is what made him great. He's a champion, a thoroughbred, a champion of sports." Curt then asked for "a round of applause, an ovation for No. 9 on his last game in his Boston." Needless to say, he got it.

Ted waited, pawed at the ground with one foot. Smilingly, he thanked the mayor for the money. "Despite the fact of the disagreeable things that have been said of me—and I can't help thinking about it—by the Knights of the Keyboard out there (he jerked his head toward the press box), baseball has been the most wonderful thing in my life. If I were starting over again and someone asked me where is the one place I would like to play, I would want it to be in Boston, with the greatest owner in baseball and the greatest fans in America. Thank you."

He walked across the infield to the dugout, where the players were standing, applauding along with the fans. Ted winked and went on in.

In the press box, some of the writers were upset by his gratuitous rap at them. "I think it was bush," one of them said. "Whatever he thinks, this wasn't the time to say it."

Others made a joke of it. "Now that he's knighted me," one of them was saying, "I wonder if he's going to address me as Sir."

In the last half of the first inning, Williams stepped in against Steve Barber with Tasby on first and one out. When Barber was born—February 22, 1939—Ted had already taken the American Association apart, as it has never been taken apart since, by batting .366, hitting 43 home runs and knocking in 142 runs.

Against a left-hander, Williams was standing almost flush along the inside line of the batter's box, his feet wide, his stance slightly closed. He took a curve inside, then a fast ball low. The fans began to boo. The third pitch was also low. With a 3-0 count, Ted jumped in front of the plate with the pitch, like a high-school kid looking for a walk. It was ball four, high.

He got to third the easy way. Jim Pagliaroni was hit by a pitch, and everybody moved up on a wild pitch. When Frank Malzone walked, Jack Fisher came in to replace Barber. Lou Clinton greeted Jack with a rising liner to dead center. Jackie Brandt started in, slipped as he tried to reverse himself, but recovered in time to scramble back and make the catch. His throw to the plate was beautiful to behold, a low one-bouncer that came to Gus Triandos chest high. But Ted, sliding hard, was in under the ball easily.

Leading off the third inning against the right-handed Fisher, Ted moved back just a little in the box. Fisher is even younger than Barber, a week younger. When Fisher was being born—March 4, 1939—Ted was reporting to Sarasota again, widely proclaimed as the super-player of the future, the Red Sox' answer to Joe DiMaggio.

Ted hit Fisher's 1-1 pitch straightaway, high and deep. Brandt had plenty of room to go back and make the catch, but still, as Williams returned to the bench, he got another tremendous hand.

Up in the press box, publicity man Jack Malaney was announcing that uniform No. 9 was being retired "after today's game." This brought on some snide remarks about Ted wearing his undershirt at Yankee Stadium for the final three games of the season. Like Mayor Collins, Malaney was righter than he knew. The uniform was indeed going to be retired after the game.

Williams came to bat again in the fifth inning, with two out and the Sox trailing, 3–2. And this time he unloaded a tremendous drive to right center. As the ball jumped off the bat, the cry "He did it!" arose from the stands. Right fielder Al Pilarcik ran back as far as he could, pressed his back against the bullpen fence, well out from the 380-foot sign, and stood there, motionless, his hands at his sides.

Although it was a heavy day, there was absolutely no wind. The flag hung limply from the pole, stirring very occasionally and very faintly.

At the last minute, Pilarcik brought up his hands and caught the ball chest high, close to 400 feet from the plate. A moan of disappointment settled over the field, followed by a rising hum of excited conversation and then, as Ted came back toward the first-base line to get his glove from Pumpsie Green, a standing ovation.

"Damn," Ted said, when he returned to the bench at the end of the inning. "I hit the living hell out of that one. I really stung it. If that one didn't go out, nothing is going out today!"

In the top of the eighth, with the Sox behind 4–2, Mike Fornieles came to the mound for the 70th time of the season, breaking the league record set by another Red Sox relief star, Ellis Kinder. Kinder set this mark in 1953, the year Williams returned from Korea.

As Fornieles was warming up, three teenagers jumped out of the grandstand and ran toward Ted. They paused only briefly, however, and continued across the field to the waiting arms of the park police.

Ted was scheduled to bat second in the last of the eighth, undoubtedly his last time at bat. The cheering began as soon as Willie Tasby came out of the dugout and strode to the plate, as if he was anxious to get out of there and make way for the main event. Ted, coming out almost directly behind Tasby, went to the on-deck circle. He was down on one knee and just beginning to swing the heavy, lead-filled practice bat as Tasby hit the first pitch to short for an easy out.

The cheering seemed to come to its peak as Ted stepped into the box and took his stance. Everybody in the park had come to his feet to give Ted a standing ovation.

Umpire Eddie Hurley called time. Fisher stepped off the rubber and Triandos stood erect. Ted remained in the box, waiting, as if he were oblivious to it all. The standing ovation lasted at least two minutes, and even then Fisher threw into the continuing applause. Only as the ball approached the plate did the cheering stop. It came in low, ball one. The spectators remained on their feet, but very suddenly the park had gone very quiet.

If there was pressure on Ted, there was pressure on Fisher, too. The Orioles were practically tied for second place, so he couldn't afford to be charitable. He might have been able to get Ted to go after a bad pitch, and yet he hardly wanted to go down in history as the fresh kid who had walked Ted Williams on his last time at bat in Boston.

The second pitch was neck high, a slider with, it seemed, just a little off it. Ted gave it a tremendous swing, but he was just a little out in front of the ball. The swing itself brought a roar from the fans, though, since it was such a clear announcement that Ted was going for the home run or nothing.

With a 1-1 count, Fisher wanted to throw a fast ball, low and away. He got it up too much and in too much, a fast ball waist high on the outside corner. From the moment Ted swung, there was not the slightest doubt about it. The ball cut through the heavy air, a high line drive heading straightaway to center field toward the corner of the special bullpen the Red Sox built for Williams back in 1941.

Jackie Brandt went back almost to the barrier, then turned and watched the ball bounce off the canopy above the bullpen bench, skip up against the wire fence which rises in front of the bleachers and bounce back into the bullpen.

It did not seem possible that 10,000 people could make that much noise.

Ted raced around the bases at a pretty good clip. Triandos had started toward the mound with the new ball, and Fisher had come down to meet him. As Ted neared home plate, Triandos turned to face him, a big smile on his face. Ted grinned back.

Ted didn't exactly offer his hand to Pagliaroni after he crossed the plate, but the young catcher reached out anyway and made a grab for it. He seemed to catch Ted around the wrist. Williams ran back into the dugout and ducked through the runway door to get himself a drink of water.

The fans were on their feet again, deafening the air with their cheers. A good four or five minutes passed before anybody worried about getting the game under way again.

When Ted ducked back into the dugout, he put on his jacket and sat down at the very edge of the bench, alongside Mike Higgins and Del Baker. The players, still on their feet anyway, crowded around him, urging him to go out and acknowledge the cheers.

The fans were now chanting, "We want Ted . . . we want Ted . . . we want Ted." Umpire Johnny Rice, at first base, motioned for Ted to come out. Manager Mike Higgins urged him to go on out. Ted just sat there, his head down, a smile of happiness on his face.

"We wanted him to go out," Vic Wertz said later, "because we felt so good for him. And we could see he was thrilled, too. For me, I have to say it's my top thrill in baseball."

But another player said, "I had the impression—maybe I shouldn't say this because it's just an impression—that he got just as much a kick out of refusing to go out and tip his hat to the crowd as he did out of the homer. What I mean is he wanted to go out with the home run, all right, but he also wanted the home run so he could sit there while they yelled for him and tell them all where to go."

Mike Higgins had already told Carroll Hardy to replace Ted in left field. As Clinton came to bat, with two men out, Higgins said, "Williams, left field." Ted grabbed his glove angrily and went to the top step. When Clinton struck out, Ted was the first man out of the dugout. He sprinted out to left field, ignoring the cheers of the fans, who had not expected to see him again. But Higgins had sent Hardy right out behind him. Ted saw Carroll, and ran back in, one final time. The entire audience was on its feet once again, in wild applause.

Since it is doubtful that Higgins felt Williams was in any great need of more applause that day, it is perfectly obvious that he was giving Ted one last chance to think about the tip of the hat or the wave of the hand as he covered the distance between left field and the dugout.

Ted made the trip as always, his head down, his stride unbroken. He stepped on first base as he crossed the line, ducked down into the dugout, growled once at Higgins and headed through the alleyway and into the locker room.

He stopped only to tell an usher standing just inside the dugout, "I guess I forgot to tip my hat."

To the end, the mirror remained intact.

After the game, photographers were permitted to go right into the clubhouse, but writers were held to the 15-minute rule. One writer tried to ride in with the photographers, but Williams leveled that finger at him and said, "You're not supposed to be here."

Somehow or other, the news was let out that Ted would not be going to New York, although there seems to be some doubt as to whether it was Williams or Higgins who made the announcement. The official Boston line is that it had been understood all along that Ted would not be going to New York unless the pennant race was still on. The fact of the matter is that Williams made the decision himself, and he did not make it until after he hit the home run. It would have been foolish to have gone to New York or anywhere else, of course. Anything he did after the Boston finale would have been an anticlimax.

One of the waiting newspapermen, a pessimist by nature, expressed the fear that by the time they were let in, Ted would be dressed and gone.

"Are you kidding?" a member of the anti-Williams clique said. "This is what he lives for. If the game had gone 18 innings, he'd be in there waiting for us."

He was indeed waiting at his locker, with a towel wrapped around his middle. The writers approached him, for the most part, in groups. Generally speaking, the writers who could be called friends reached him first, and to these men Ted was not only amiable but gracious and modest.

Was he going for the home run?

"I was gunning for the big one," he said with a grin. "I let everything I had go. I really wanted that one."

Did he know it was out as soon as it left his bat?

"I knew I had really given it a ride."

What were his immediate plans?

"I've got some business to clean up here," he said. "Then I'll be covering the World Series for *Life*. After that, I'm going back to Florida to see how much damage the hurricane did to my house."

The other players seemed even more affected by the drama of the farewell homer than Ted. Pete Runnels, practically dispossessed from his locker alongside Ted's by the shifts of reporters, wandered around the room shaking his head in disbelief. "How about that?" he kept repeating. "How about that? How about that?"

As for Ted, he seemed to be in something of a daze. After the first wave of writers had left, he wandered back and forth between his locker and the trainer's room. Back and forth, back and forth. Once he came back with a bottle of beer, turned it up to his lips and downed it with obvious pleasure. For Ted, this is almost unheard of. He has always been a milk and ice-cream man, and he devours them both in huge quantities. His usual order after a ball game is two quarts of milk.

Williams remained in the locker room, making himself available, until there were no more than a half-dozen other players remaining. Many of the writers did not go over to him at all. From them, there were no questions, no congratulations, no good wishes for the future. For all Ted's color, for all the drama and copy he had supplied over 22 years, they were glad to see him finally retire.

When Ted finally began to get dressed, our man went over and said, "Ted, you must have known when Higgins sent you back out that he was giving you a final chance to think about tipping the hat or making some gesture of farewell. Which meant that Higgins himself would have liked you to do it. While you were running back, didn't you have any feeling that it might be nice to go out with a show of good feeling?"

"I felt nothing," he said.

"No sentimentality? No gratitude? No sadness?"

"I said *nothing*," Ted said. "Nothing, nothing!"

As our man was toting up the nothings, Ted snarled, "And when you get back there tell them for me that they're full of . . ." There followed a burst of vituperation which we cannot even begin to approximate, and then the old, sad plaint about those twelve years of merciless persecution.

Fenway Park has an enclosed parking area so that the players can get to their cars without beating their way through the autograph hunters. When Ted was dressed, though, the clubhouse boy called to the front office in what was apparently a prearranged plan to bring Williams' car around to a bleacher exit.

At 4:40, 45 minutes after the end of the game and a good hour after Ted had left the dugout, he was ready to leave. "Fitzie," he called out, and the clubhouse boy came around to lead the way. The cameramen came around, too.

The locker-room door opens onto a long corridor, which leads to another door, which in turn opens onto the back walks and understructure of the park. It is this outer door which is always guarded.

Waiting in the alleyway, just outside the clubhouse door, however, was a redheaded, beatnik-looking man, complete with the regimental beard and the beachcomber pants. He handed Ted a ball and mentioned a name that apparently meant something to him. Ted took the ball and signed it.

"How come you're not able to get in?" he said. "If they let the damn newspapermen in, they ought to let you in." Walking away, trailed by the platoon of cameramen, he called out to the empty air, "If they let the newspapermen in, they should have let him in. If they let the newspapermen in, they should let everybody in."

He walked on through the backways of the park, past the ramps and pillars, at a brisk clip, with Fitzie bustling along quickly to stay up ahead. Alongside of Williams, the cameramen were scrambling to get their positions and snap their pictures. Williams kept his eyes straight ahead, never pausing for one moment. "Hold it for just a minute, Ted," one of them said.

"I've been here for 22 years," Ted said, walking on. "Plenty of time for you to get your shot."

"This is the last time," the cameraman said. "Cooperate just this one last time."

"I've cooperated with you," Ted said. "I've cooperated too much."

Fitzie had the bleacher entrance open, and as Ted passed quickly through, a powder-blue Cadillac pulled up to the curb. A man in shirt-sleeves was behind the wheel. He looked like Dick O'Connell, whose appointment as business manager had been announced the previous night.

Fitzie ran ahead to open the far door of the car for Ted. Three young women had been approaching the exit as Ted darted through, and one of them screamed, "It's him!" One of the others just let out a scream, as if Ted had been somebody of real worth, like Elvis or Fabian. The third woman remained mute. Looking at her, you had to wonder whether she would ever speak again.

Fitzie slammed the door, and the car pulled away. "It was him," the first woman screamed. "Was it *really* him? Was it *him*?"

Her knees seemed to give away. Her girl friends had to support her. "I can't catch my breath," she said. "I can hear my heart pounding." And then, in something like terror: "I CAN'T BREATHE."

Attracted by the screams, or by some invisible, inexplicable grapevine, a horde of boys and men came racing up the street. Ted's car turned the corner just across from the bleacher exit, but it was held up momentarily by a red light and a bus. The front line of pursuers had just come abreast of the car when the driver swung around the bus and pulled away.

There are those, however, who never get the word. Down the street, still surrounding the almost empty parking area, were still perhaps 100 loyal fans waiting to say their last farewell to Ted Williams.

In Boston that night, the talk was all of Williams. Only 10,454 were at the scene, but the word all over the city was: "I knew he'd end it with a home run . . ." and "I was going to go to the game, but–"

In future years, we can be sure, the men who saw Ted hit that mighty shot will number into the hundreds of thousands. The wind will grow strong and mean, and the distance will grow longer. Many of the reports of the game, in fact, had the ball going into the center-field bleachers.

The seeds of the legend have already been sown. George Carens, an elderly columnist who is more beloved by Ted than by his colleagues, wrote:

"Ted was calm and gracious as he praised the occupants of the Fenway press penthouse at home plate before the game began. Afterwards he greeted all writers in a comradely way, down through his most persistent critics. In a word, Ted showed he can take it, and whenever the spirit moves him he will fit beautifully into the Fenway PR setup."

Which shows that people hear what they want to hear and see what they want to see.

In New York the next day, Phil Rizzuto informed his television audience that Ted had finally relented and tipped his hat after the home run.

And the *Sporting News* headline on its Boston story was:

SPLINTER TIPS CAP
TO HUB FANS AFTER
FAREWELL HOMER

A New York Sunday paper went so far as to say that Ted had made "a tender and touching farewell speech" from home plate at the end of the game.

All the reports said that Ted had, in effect, called his shot because it was known that he was shooting for a home run. Who wants to bet that, in future years, there will not be a story or two insisting that he *did* point?

The legend will inevitably grow, and in a way it is a shame. A man should be allowed to die the way he lived. He should be allowed to depart as he came. Ted Williams chose his course early, and his course was to turn his face from the world around him. When he walked out of the park, he kept his eyes to the front and he never looked back.

The epitaph for Ted Williams remains unchanged. He was sometimes unbearable but he was never dull. Baseball will not be the same without him. Boston won't be quite the same either. Old Boston is acrawl with greening statues of old heroes and old patriots, but Ted has left a monument of his own–again on his own terms–in the Children's Cancer Hospital.

He left his own monument in the record books too. For two decades he made the Red Sox exciting in the sheer anticipation of his next time at bat.

He opened his last season with perhaps the longest home run of his career and he closed it with perhaps the most dramatic. It was typical and it was right that the Williams era in Boston should end not with a whimper. It was entirely proper that it should end with a bang.

So, the old order passeth and an era of austerity has settled upon the Red Sox franchise.

And now Boston knows how England felt when it lost India.

From the remarkable collection of musical Americana assembled by Harry Dichter of Philadelphia, comes this portfolio of yesteryear's baseball songs.

HURRAH FOR OUR NATIONAL GAME.

WALTER NEVILLE.

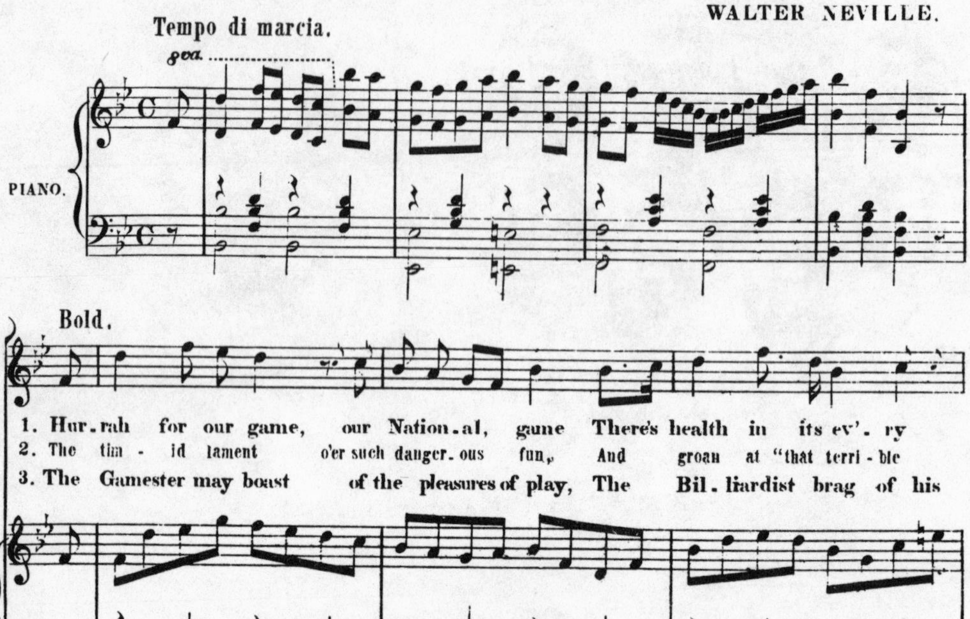
Tempo di marcia.
8va
PIANO.
Bold.
1. Hur-rah for our game, our Nation-al, game There's health in its ev'-ry
2. The tim-id lament o'er such danger-ous fun, And groan at "that terri-ble
3. The Gamester may boast of the pleasures of play, The Bil-liardist brag of his
bound. A thrill of de-light in its ve-ry name, A
ball," The la--zy ones shrink from making "a run" And
cue. The Horse jock-y gabble of next rac-ing day. The
4796

* The upper line in the accompaniment may be omitted if thought proper, as the remaining line will be found sufficient.

joy in its sim - plest sound; It lends new strength to our
cow - ards are fear - ing a fall, But give us the dash of a
Yacht - man discourse of the Blue. The pa - trons of Rack - et may
rall:
a tempo.
har - dy race, And its pleas - ures are nev - er tame, _ _ Then
strong "home strike" And we laugh such fol - ly to shame: _ _ Take
feast on its joys, Whilst Crick - et its lovers in - flame, _ _ Cro - -
rall:
here's to the bat, the ball, and the base, Hurrah for our National Game.
all other sports and do what you like But leave us our Na - tional Game.
- quet's very well for young ladies and boys But give us the National Game.
24796

Home Run Galop.
To The
Atlantic Club of Chicago
THE BOYS WHO MAKE 'EM
By F. W. Root.
CHICAGO
Published by ROOT & CADY 67 Washington St

To the Members of the
UNION BASE BALL CLUB
CHAMPIONS OF MISSOURI.
UNION BASE BALL CLUB MARCH
Composed by
T. W. Brown
HON. MEMBER
MUSICAL AMERICANA
HARRY DICHTER
5458 Montgomery Ave.
Philadelphia 31, Pa.
SAINT LOUIS.
Published by RICH. J. COMPTON 205 Fourth Str.

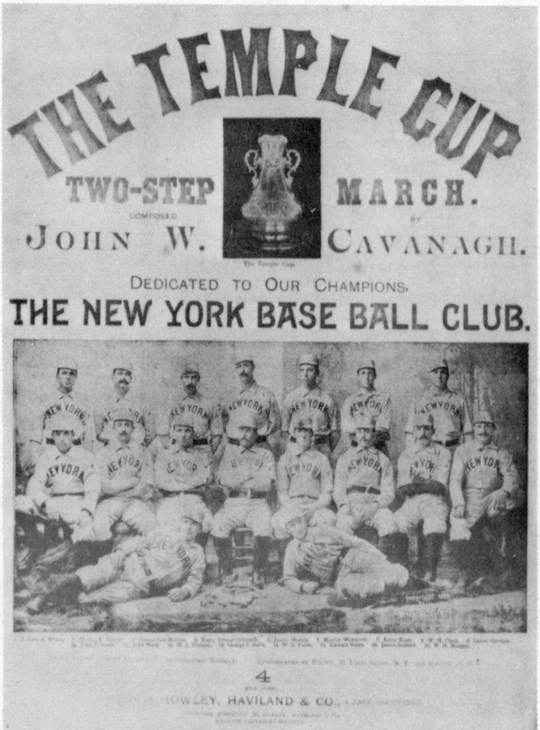
THE TEMPLE CUP
TWO-STEP MARCH.
COMPOSED BY
JOHN W. CAVANAGH.
The Temple Cup
DEDICATED TO OUR CHAMPIONS.
THE NEW YORK BASE BALL CLUB.
4
HOWLEY, HAVILAND & CO.

Compliments of
F. W. Helmick.
TALLY ONE FOR ME
BASE BALL SONG & CHORUS
WORDS AND MUSIC BY JOHN T. RUTLEDGE.
MUSICAL AMERICANA
HARRY DICHTER
5458 Montgomery Ave.
Philadelphia 31, Pa.
PUBLISHED BY F. W. HELMICK, CINCINNATI, O.
No. 50, West Fourth Street.

The Quality of Courage, subtitled "True Stories of Heroism and Bravery," was a remarkable book by Mickey Mantle, published in 1964. No finer segment within that book exists than the tribute to Fred Hutchinson, who was then dying of cancer.

Brave and Honest Hutch

MICKEY MANTLE

COURAGE IS so much a part of some people's nature that you almost forget about it—until something happens that jars you into a new realization of it. Take Fred Hutchinson.

In 1937, when he was eighteen, Hutch was a great pitching star in the Pacific Coast League (he won twenty-five games and lost seven), which in itself was quite an achievement. The Pacific Coast League was a very fast league in the days before the majors expanded to California. It was about the closest thing to big-league baseball that you could find. There were plenty of good young players on the way up, and plenty of good older players on the way down, who could have been playing still in the majors, except that they enjoyed being regulars in the Coast League more than they did sitting on the bench in the big leagues. For a kid of eighteen to star in this company took not only ability but toughness, heart, and competitive drive.

Fred Hutchinson had all of that, and some to spare. He was a determined man even then. His father was a doctor in Seattle and Hutch's brother Bill followed in his father's path and studied medicine, too. But Fred decided early that he wanted to be a ballplayer, and I guess that settled that. According to people from Seattle, when a Hutchinson makes up his mind there isn't much that anyone can do to change it.

There is a famous story about Fred's father that illustrates this. The doctor, who died several years ago, was a community leader, and back when Seattle first had trolley cars he was in the front of a running battle that went on about fare raises. It seems that the trolley company raised the fare and that Dr. Hutchinson and other people didn't care for the idea. There were protest meetings and petitions, and committees were sent to municipal hearings and all that sort of thing. Nothing much happened and the fight died down. Except for Dr. Hutchinson. He wasn't about to give in.

One night he was downtown and he got on a trolley car to go back home to the Hutchinson's neighborhood, which was several miles away. He dropped the old fare (I think it was a nickel) in the box. The driver said, "Sorry. The fare has been raised." It was now a dime, let's say. Dr. Hutchinson said, "This is the fare I have always paid." The driver shrugged his shoulders and said, "I'm sorry, but it's been raised." Dr. Hutchinson said, "You mean, the money I have put in there is not enough?" The driver said, "That's right." Dr. Hutchinson said, "You mean, if I don't pay more I will have to get off and walk home?" The driver said, "I guess so." Dr. Hutchinson said, "Give me back my money." The driver did and Dr. Hutchinson got off the trolley and walked home.

But he didn't just walk home. He walked home on the trolley tracks, right in front of the trolley. It was his way of calling attention to the dispute over the fares, and he made the most of it. The trolley couldn't get past him, and it wasn't going to knock him down and run over him, and nobody was going to move Dr. Hutchinson off the tracks. (Knowing Fred, I can believe that; anyone who ever saw Hutch get mad will tell you that a Hutchinson is not a man to mess with.)

The doctor walked home, his head high and his jaw out, and all the trolleys on the line pulled up behind him, trailing along like a kid's wooden choo-choo train, and they didn't get moving on normal schedule again until Dr. Hutchinson reached home and walked off the street. I don't know what the result was—I guess the fare stayed raised—but I know this, that of all the people involved in the fuss over the trolley fare, Dr. Hutchinson fought longest and hardest and best. He was a man who believed in his principles and he didn't give in.

His son Fred had the same qualities from the time he first played baseball. He was brought up to the major leagues by the Detroit Tigers before he was twenty, and while he never was as great a star in the majors as he was in the minors, he was a key man on the Tiger staff for several years. He was also a good hitter, which figures, because most of all Hutch was a competitor, a man who was never afraid of the idea of winning and who would do everything he could to win. Some people are kind of afraid of winning; the idea of trying to win seems to embarrass them. Not Hutch. Winning was what he expected to do. Losing was a mistake.

When Fred was named manager of the Detroit Tigers in 1952, people who didn't know him were surprised. For one thing, he was young—only thirty-three. For a second, he had had no managing or coaching experience. And for a third, he was a pitcher—and very few major-league managers have been pitchers. Lots of catchers and infielders have been managers, and some outfielders, but only a handful of pitchers.

But to everybody who knew Hutch, it seemed absolutely right. As a manager he was a natural, a man others looked up to. There have been few men in baseball who have been praised as a man by as many people as Hutchinson. It isn't just that everybody liked him—a lot of baseball players are well liked by their teammates and by managers and by the front office and by fans, and yet do not have the qualifications of a manager. A manager has to be respected, too, and no one was ever more respected than Hutch.

He got the Tigers from last place to fifth in a couple of seasons. Later, he managed the St. Louis Cardinals and moved them from seventh to second in two years. He took over the Cincinnati Reds when they were in the second division—two seasons later they won the National League pennant.

All this doesn't mean that Hutch was the greatest manager ever to run a major-league team, but nobody ever got more out of his players. It's probably because Hutch was always completely honest with everybody—and players know that. Hutch was never afraid to speak his mind—to anybody—and he didn't sneak around corners to do it. It takes a lot of courage to be honest all the time. Think of the times when you've bent the truth a little to get out of an awkward or embarrassing situation.

There was a time when Hutch was managing the Cardinals when he had a run-in with August A. Busch, Jr., the owner of the team. Mr. Busch was concerned with the Cardinals' attendance, which had fallen off a bit, and he was bothered because the Cardinals were not as colorful a team as they used to be. He wanted a good team, but he wanted a colorful team, too. Now, the Cardinals had a rookie first baseman at that time, a very tall, graceful guy who had a strange way of fielding his position. He would stretch his arms out wide, like a net, and if there was a chance of a bunt, say, he would sort of crouch and lean over and as the pitcher threw he would come scurrying in toward the plate.

It was a wild sight, this big tall man bent over with his arms spread, racing in across the infield. The crowd loved it. The only thing was, the first baseman wasn't much of a ballplayer. He had had several chances and had proved that he couldn't hit major-league pitching, and Hutch benched him.

A few days later Mr. Busch and Frank Lane, who was general manager of the Cardinals then, and Hutch, and perhaps a couple of other club officials, had a meeting to discuss the team. Mr. Busch kept bringing up the name of the rookie first baseman. Hutch said he wasn't good enough. Busch thought maybe they should play him anyway because the crowd enjoyed seeing him in the field, the way he spread his arms and all. Hutch said he couldn't hit, that he wasn't a major-league ballplayer. Busch said maybe so, but he certainly was colorful and the crowd got a lot of laughs out of him and perhaps the Cardinals should play him anyway. Hutch looked at Mr. Busch, who was his boss, you remember, and said, "If you want a clown to play first base, why don't you hire Emmett Kelly?" (Kelly was the famous sad-faced "bum" of the Ringling Brothers-Barnum and Bailey circus.) That sort of ended the meeting. It wasn't a polite answer, and it certainly wasn't diplomatic. But it was honest. And Hutch was right. The colorful first baseman never did make it in the majors.

When you are as honest as Hutch, you expect everybody else to be honest, too. And that means you *expect* a ballplayer to do his honest best, all the time. It takes effort, and it takes courage, to do your honest best all the time. I think every major-league ballplayer *thinks* he is doing his best, but sometimes without realizing it a player will ease off and let down a little. But not if he was playing for a guy like Hutchinson. Not for long.

A fellow named Jim Davis, a good left-handed knuckleballer who pitched for the Cubs and the Cardinals and the Giants several years ago, once told a story about himself that showed how players felt about Hutchinson. Jim said, "I think I know why players do well for Hutch. I remember one game I was pitching, and we were a couple of runs ahead in the middle of the game. There was one out, and a fellow got a hit, and then I got behind on the next man. I was thinking to myself, if this guy gets on base I'll really have to bear down on that next batter. Then I happened to glance over at the dugout and there was Hutch, up on the top step, glaring at me. I thought to myself, oh boy, I better bear down on *this* guy or Hutch is gonna be out here. He made you work hard without saying anything."

Everybody in baseball knew Hutch from the time he first broke in and knew the kind of man he always was. I guess we all took him for granted and forgot what a special man he was until something happened to remind us all over again. I mean his illness.

In early 1964 there was a story in the papers one day that said that Fred Hutchinson had had a physical examination and that something was wrong with his chest. Right away people who knew him began to worry, as you always do when you think something might be seriously wrong with someone you know well. Hutch flew from his home in Florida to Seattle to consult with his brother Bill, the doctor. He had chest X-rays and more examinations. Then a medical report was issued, stating that Hutch had a "malignancy" and that he would undergo special treatment.

I felt sick when I heard that. "Malignancy" means cancer. Some people wondered why the medical report was so outspoken, and they wondered if Hutch knew what he had.

They didn't have to wait long. Reporters were politely trying to find out more information. Instead of hiding, or staying out of sight someplace and letting his brother or some other doctor talk to the press, Fred Hutchinson talked to the reporters himself. He told them what the doctors had told him, what treatment he would undergo, what his chances were. He said he had found out about it at Christmastime and that it was like having a rug pulled out from under you. "One day you're fine," he said, "and the next day you have cancer." He didn't use the word "malignancy." He was still the same old Hutch. He grinned that little half grin of his at the reporters, told them the truth, and didn't try to fool them or himself or anybody.

It takes courage to be that honest. It takes courage, and lots of it, to be a man like Fred Hutchinson. Happily, courage like that rubs off on other people. One of the reporters said, "I thought I would feel sorry for Hutch. Instead, I feel—I don't know—proud. I feel proud to be a human being because Hutchinson is one. I mean, *he* has cancer but instead of letting me feel sorry for him he makes me feel good just because I know him. What a man he is."

AT THE TIME this book was completed, early during the 1967 season, Juan Marichal owned the best career won-and-lost percentage of any pitcher in either major league in the entire twentieth century.

From *A Pitcher's Story*

JUAN MARICHAL *with* CHARLES EINSTEIN

TUESDAY, AUGUST 23, 1966 . . .

This will be, in one very real sense, the most important game I have ever pitched.

Important, because now everyone has said it:

Marichal pretends to be injured . . . he cannot pitch in the clutch . . . he cannot win late in the season.

It is six days since I last tried to pitch—that game against the Cardinals where I went two innings and left, behind 3–0 in the score.

In the meantime, the Braves have come and gone, and I still have not pitched against them, not for a single moment, this entire season.

My left ankle is still puffed, and there is still pain, but now I have pitched only one complete game in the past month, and in that same period of time have won only one game, an inning-and-a-third of relief pitching.

My salary is $75,000 a year (they offered me less because, they said, "You did not win for us late in the season.").

The standings, on this August 23 of 1966, say:

	W.	L.	P.	G.B.
PITTSBURGH	73	50	.593	–
SAN FRANCISCO	74	51	.592	–
LOS ANGELES	70	53	.569	3

Nothing will be right tonight, except that I must pitch. I know this.

Do the Braves have a habit of roughing me up? So do the Cincinnati Reds. And tonight, it is the Reds we must play at Candlestick Park.

In the dressing room, before the game, a quiet, gray-haired man walks over to talk to me at my locker. His name is Eugene Solovieff. I myself, and others among the Giants, think of him as one of the miracle men. He is the doctor who fixed Orlando Cepeda's knee, when everyone else had given up. Orlando was born with that knee deformed, and he has injured it repeatedly in his lifetime, but now he says to the doctor, "It is stronger than it has ever been, the knee, even before I started to play baseball."

"How is it?" Dr. Solovieff says to me.

"See for yourself," I say, and he looks at my foot.

"The swelling is down," he says.

"It is still there," I say.

"Maybe that is good," he says.

"Good?"

"Yes."

"Why good?"

"Because," he says, "personally I think you can pitch."

"Oh."

"I have not said that when I did not feel it," he says.

"I know."

"And that being the case," he says, "perhaps it is just as well you have a little bit of swelling, because after this long a time without pitching regularly in turn, you could be perfectly healthy but still be rusty and have your timing off and so forth. This way you have something to remind you, and so you will pitch carefully instead of recklessly."

"I have heard of doctors for the body," I say, "and doctors for the mind. Also doctors for the soul. Which are you?"

"All things work together," he says.

"That is what Doc Bowman used to say," I said. "Also a priest I know."

"Then that is a good sign," he said, "because when you talk that way it means you want to pitch."

"How can you say that?"

"Because you are talking about the body and the soul and the mind."

"What else is there to talk about?"

He stood up. "Your foot," he said, and laughed, and went away.

I called after him. "Doc?"

He turns around and comes back.

"I have confidence," I said.

"I know it," he said.

"I would have more confidence," I said, "if Willie Mays were playing tonight."

"They say he is resting," Dr. Solovieff said. "By now, he has got to rest from time to time. You know that."

"I was only referring to my own confidence," I said.

"He'll be there," Dr. Solovieff said, "if you need him." He started away again, then turned once more. "Which you won't." Then he left for good.

Outside, when it is time for me to take my warm-ups, I use the area beside home plate. I would prefer the higher mound in the bullpen, but it is too windy out there. Nearby, McCovey is playing catch with somebody. He says to me, "How's the foot?"

"I'm not sure," I say. "How is yours?"

"Terrible," he says, which is true, for he has bad feet as a rule, even when he is healthy, and tonight one of them is very bad.

I take my warm-ups off the corner of the rubber (the side that in a game is nearer first base). For a while, some years ago, other managers, led by Charlie Dressen when he was with Milwaukee, complained that this was illegal. The rule says that when the pitcher starts his delivery, the foot not on the rubber (meaning the left foot, if you are a right-handed pitcher) must be behind the rubber. When you deliver from the very corner of the rubber, as I do, your rear foot is off to the side. It is not behind the rubber. It is behind the imaginary line you could draw if you extended the rubber. They buck this all the way up to Mr. Giles, the president of the league, and he is the one who decides that my delivery is legal.

I prefer the corner of the rubber because it gives me an "angle" for pitching away from left-handed hitters; also, it helps my slider break away from right-handed hitters. It is something that is personal with me; I do not recommend it for youngsters learning how to pitch.

Right now, I am no longer certain even I know how to pitch.

And it is time for the game to begin, and the Reds send Harper up to lead off, and the night is cool and so is the crowd. Not so cool, perhaps, as for the St. Louis game last week, when one of them yelled, "Sober up, Marichal!" at me between pitches in the second inning, but still a little doubtful, waiting to be shown.

Harper fouls off strike one. I come in low—too low—with the next pitch, and I begin to dig a hole in front of the rubber—Russ Hodges and Lon Simmons, the Giants' broadcasters, call it "landscaping" when I do this—and this time, now, I take my high kick and get strike two, swinging, with a good curve ball. Back of home plate Tom Haller says, loudly, "Good pitch!"—almost in relief, he says it.

Now I go to the fast ball, and it is there—not the true express, but enough of it, and Harper fouls it. Then another foul tip, then ball two on a change-up, high and inside, another foul on a slider, ball three on a curve, low outside, a foul on another curve. And now the not-so-fast fast ball, and Harper swings down on it and he is an easy out, Fuentes at short to McCovey at first.

I go to three balls and no strikes on Rose, the next hitter. Then I hit the outside corner with the high-kicking fast ball for the called strike. Two fouls, then Rose slaps a hard grounder into the hole on the right side. Maxie Lanier is over there, kneels down, and throws Rose out at first.

My first pitch to Pinson is a strike. He lines the second one to McCovey and the inning is over.

Eighteen pitches for that first inning, which is a lot of pitches to just three men—but Dr. Solovieff was right. I feel that I can pitch. That is the important thing.

For us, in the home half of the first, Fuentes beats one out, back to the box, for an infield single. Gabrielson pops up and Hart takes a called third strike, with Fuentes stealing second on the sequence. Then McCovey gets a Pappas pitch that he likes and hits it into the bleachers in right field and the Giants are ahead, 2–0.

What is in my mind as I face Johnson, leading off the second for Cincinnati, I will never know. I want to throw him the not-so-fast fast ball, because I suppose that will kind of set him up in reverse for the faster pitch to follow, but what happens is simply that he strokes it over the fence for a home run. A stupid pitch with nothing on it, not even any intelligence, and now our lead is 2–1.

Now Helms comes up and he has the same idea and goes for the first pitch, but this one had something on it, and he flies to Brown, playing center in place of Mays.

Now the hitter is Shamsky. He has thirty-nine hits this season, and sixteen of them have been home runs! In one game recently, he got three home runs in three times at bat, after entering the game as a pinch hitter!

We give him two straight change-up curves for strikes, then go to the fast ball for strike three called. The reaction is predictable on all sides. The crowd loves it, Shamsky hates it, and Cardenas, the next hitter, asks to look at the ball. Marichal must be spitting on it.

Cardenas goes out on a foul pop to McCovey.

Alou, playing right field tonight, singles to begin the home half of the second inning, but Brown grounds into a double play and Lanier also grounds out to Cardenas, and I am back out there pitching in a hurry, which I do not mind. At night especially, and especially at Candlestick Park, too long a rest between innings can stiffen your arm.

My arm! I hadn't even thought about that part of me, up till now.

Coker leads off the third for Cincinnati. Here they go for the first pitch again, and he singles to left field. Pappas comes up, tries to bunt, argues that he didn't swing, and finally bunts the third strike foul for an automatic strikeout.

Now Harper, and he hits it good, down the right-field line—just fair, but well hit. Alou does a great job in the "mystery corner"—we call it that because you can't see in there from the infield: it is a pocket in foul territory, between the end of the right-field stands and the fence, where they keep the batting cage. I have seen outfielders disappear in there and then seen the ball come out, all by itself, with the outfielder still out of sight. Once I saw big Frank Howard go in there and he didn't come out and neither did the ball. I don't know what they were doing in there together.

But Alou brings the ball out fast, so fast that Coker has to stop at third, and Harper, who would have had a triple, has to settle for a double.

Rose is up now. He flies to short left. Fuentes goes back, Gabrielson comes in. The rule in such cases, definitely the rule when there is a man on third, is that the outfielder, not the infielder, must make the catch. The reason is simple. The outfielder is coming in, therefore has the momentum for the throw to the plate in case the man on third tries to score after the catch. The infielder, going away from the plate, would have to stop and set himself before throwing. So obediently, Fuentes shies away, and Gabe catches it, and Coker bluffs but doesn't come in.

Pinson at bat now. We jam him inside with two straight pitches, both called balls. Now he is looking for the outside pitch, so we come inside again, for the third straight time, and he swings and misses. Now we go for the outside corner with the fast ball, and umpire Weyer calls strike two. And now we want to put him away with the inside pitch, down low, but it is too low—in fact, it rolls a little bit away from Haller, and from my follow-through I come racing in to cover the plate, but Coker decides not to try to come in. If Coker was Willie Mays he would already be in the dugout and the score would be tied, but it is no rap on Coker to say he is not Willie Mays. I remember the poems that the rival newspapermen in Los Angeles and San Francisco turned out, back some five years or so ago, when the Los Angeles group, talking about Willie Davis and Tommy Davis and Maury Wills, said:

The difference in Davises
Is seen in many skills
For Tommy is not Willie
And Willie is not Wills!

To which, the San Francisco group responded:

The difference in Davises
Is seen in many ways
For Tommy is not Willie
And Willie is not Mays!

Anyway, now we have 3-and-2 with Pinson at bat and men on second and third and two out, and I do not want to walk Pinson with Johnson next up, so we go to the best money pitch we can have in this situation against this hitter—the screwball—and all he can do is late-hit it into an easy fly ball to Gabrielson in left.

Hitters are funny people. They react in strange ways. Bat them in an unusual place in the order, one they are not used to, and they can look just awful. Throw a man a nothing ball, like I threw Johnson in the second inning when he got the home run, and he can be a tiger the rest of the game even though you are pitching great stuff at him.

Bear in mind what I have just said, for it has two applications in the game we are now playing.

For my part, I am first at bat for the Giants in the last of the third, and the crowd gives me a hand for the way we got out of the top half of the inning. I have moments of pride in my hitting, as I have already said, but they do not pay me $75,000 a year on account of my bat.

Many people want to know why pitchers cannot hit. The answer to that is simple. Most people cannot hit. That is, they cannot hit major-league pitching. The only man who can make it to the major leagues without being able to hit is a pitcher. Thus, the number of pitchers who can't hit.

Personally, I *like* to hit. And I go after Pappas' first pitch and put up a little fly ball that might drop in, in very short right field, but Harper comes tearing in and gives it the one-handed somersault-catch treatment. Then Fuentes fouls out and Gabrielson grounds out and it is the top of the fourth, and we go back now to what I said just before about hitters having a hot spell, because my first pitch to Johnson is the best pitch I have thrown in a month. An absolutely tremendous high fast ball inside, and he swings and misses, and there is *no way* any hitter can handle that particular pitch. If you could throw it eighty-one times a game, I think you would have twenty-seven strikeouts, and everybody could go home. But I cannot throw it eighty-one times a game, and neither can anyone else, yet I am pitching well to Johnson, and get him one ball and two strikes, and the next pitch is a good one and Johnson hits a double to left field. Now you see what I am saying when I talk about somebody having the hot bat, and this is why it was so important to get Pinson out the inning before instead of walking him and having Johnson up with the bases loaded.

Now Helms is at bat, and he lines one back off my right foot, and there is an explosion of pain as the ball goes off my foot. Turning, I see Fuentes grabbing the ricocheting ball and throwing to McCovey at first in time to get Helms. Johnson goes to third on the play.

Then I am down on one knee, and Doc Hughes and manager Franks are out there, and Franks is moaning, "First the left foot, now the right! First the left foot, now the right!"

"Can you stand up?" Doc asks me.

"I think so," I said.

"First the left foot, now the right," Franks said.

"At least it will have to cure my limp," I said, being very logical about it. Nobody laughed, which was just as well. I had not really intended it to be funny.

"We'll come get you," Franks says.

"No," I say. For I have got to stay in this game. I have got to pitch. I have got to win.

I try a few pitches, and Weyer, the umpire, says, "All right, girls. I'll serve tea."

"When a pitcher is hurt," Franks says to him, "you have the right to . . ."

"Blow it, Manager," Weyer says. "Go back and sit down where you were. Play ball!"

Now Shamsky is the hitter, with one out and Johnson on third, and we get him for strike three swinging with the fast ball. Now the right foot is throbbing so I can hardly notice the left. I go to the sidearm curve against Cardenas, which puts the least strain on the feet—imagine, a pitcher using the deliveries that are least harmful to his feet!—but we are missing with them, so I go back to the overhand and Cardenas jerks the thing over the right-field fence and we are behind 3–2. Just like that.

Then Coker just does beat out a deep ground-ball single to Lanier. We concentrate on Pappas and he flies out to Alou in right.

I go to the bench and sit down next to Mays. He says, "It cured your limp."

"I already tell Herman that," I said.

Ordinarily, Mays would laugh, but now he takes a new stick of gum and puts it in his mouth and unbuttons the top button of his jacket. If he has anything to say about it, we are going to win this one. His confidence in me is such that he picked tonight to try to get some rest by not playing. So far, I have repaid that confidence by throwing two home-run balls for a 3–2 Cincinnati lead.

Hart leads off for us in the bottom of the fourth, and for the second straight time, Pappas strikes him out. Remember what I said about the man batting in the strange position. Jimmy, out of position in the order, feels the strain of needing to get on base so McCovey can have somebody to drive in. He is not used to this.

Now Pappas walks McCovey, and then he walks Haller, and then he goes to a count of two balls, no strikes on Alou. At this point, Pappas' last seven pitches have been balls, and Bristol, the Cincinnati manager, is alarmed. He is alarmed, I think, not so much that the last seven pitches have been balls, but that the last two have been to Alou, because it is almost impossible to fall behind the count when Jesus Alou is hitting. In all of 1966, appearing in 110 games, he will receive only nine bases on balls. In 1965, it took so long for him to get his first walk that when it happened we all yelled from the dugout to the umpire to call time so we could present him with the ball. The fact is, Alou swings at anything. He does not believe in the base on balls.

In fact, while Bristol is going out to talk to Pappas, Mays stands up in our dugout and takes off his jacket. Nothing is said to him, or by him. It is simply taken for granted. If Alou now walks, to load the bases, there goes Willie's night off. He will put himself in to bat for Brown, next due up, and then will play center field in Brown's place the rest of the evening.

But Alou takes care of that, and of many other things. On the next pitch, once Bristol has had his talk with Pappas and returned to the Reds' dugout (with a nervous glance at the hastily heating bullpen in left field), Alou singles to left field, scoring McCovey, aching foot and all, with the tying run.

Now with a tie score and men on first and third with one out, the situation has changed. Just as silently as he got up, Willie Mays now sits down. He may get the night off after all. Ollie Brown, the rookie, will hit for himself.

And Ollie Brown does. He hits the first pitch Pappas throws—hits it more than four hundred feet over the right-center fence, for a three-run homer, and from being tied at 3–3, the Giants now are ahead 6–3.

It does something for us. More important—to me, much more important—it does something for me. From the fourth inning on, I will permit just two singles, one (of course) to Johnson (even though I thought I had him struck out), and the other to Ruiz, pinch-hitting for the Reds' second pitcher. The course the game will take becomes so obvious that manager Franks takes out McCovey at the start of the eighth inning, even though McCovey is scheduled to lead off for us in the last of the eighth, and puts in Burda to play first base instead, so McCovey does not have to aggravate his foot any more than he already has.

Doubles by Burda and Alou give us another run in the last of the eighth, and that is the final score.

Given the boost of that 6–3 lead, I pitched the fifth inning on just four throws. Harper, swinging at the first pitch, grounded back to me on two hops. Rose hit an 0-and-1 pitch on an easy arc to Gabe in left. Pinson swung at the first pitch, and also flied to Gabrielson.

Starting off the Giant half of the sixth, Ron Herbel gets up in the Giant bullpen and starts to throw. Going in to the top of the eighth, Linzy gets up and joins him. But there are no problems. I retire the last eight men I face, getting Rose and Shamsky on swinging third strikes. Even Johnson—the last time I see him, he fouls out to Burda, now playing first in place of McCovey.

The last batter of the game is Coker. By now there is that great feeling of being in charge. On a count of one ball and one strike, we go to the great slow curve ball—the one that seems to be bending every inch of the way between the mound and the plate—and Coker swings and misses. Then we jam him and he grounds out to Hart at third to end the game.

The Giants are back in first place.

I have given all the reasons why this game was so important, not only to the Giants, but to me myself. I hope I have made it clear. But there is little time to think about it afterward, because I am ordered to the hospital right away to have precautionary X-rays taken of my right foot.

At the hospital they take the X-rays, and they look at what they call the "wet plates," and they ask me to stay until the X-rays dry.

"Why?" I said. "Do you see a break?"

"I do and I don't," the doctor said, and called in two other doctors.

Together they stared at the X-rays, and then at me, and then at my foot. Then back at the X-rays and back at me and back at the foot.

Finally, the plates were dry and they all looked again.

I said, "Do I have a broken foot?"

"Yes and no," one of the doctors said.

"What do you mean, yes and no?"

"I mean yes and no."

"Oh," I said.

"What does not make sense," the doctor said, "is that the X-ray shows a break, but it did not happen tonight."

"I know," I said. "It happened four years ago, at Los Angeles. That is why my foot is malformed the way it is."

"I have followed the Giants," the doctor said, "but I never heard of you having a broken foot."

"I tried to tell them it was broken," I said, "but they did not believe me. They said, 'Oh, it is late in the season and Marichal never pitches well late in the season.' "

The doctor said, "How many games have you won since then? Ninety?"

"Something like that, I suppose."

"You won ninety games on a broken foot? It didn't bother you?"

"My other foot has been bothering me. If it was not so late, I would ask you to X-ray my left foot as well as my right."

"I do not wish to X-ray your left foot," the doctor said.

"That is because you have no instructions to X-ray my left foot," I said.

"It is not because I have no instructions to X-ray your left foot," the doctor said. "It is because I am afraid of what the picture will show. It will turn out you have won ninety games on *two* broken feet, and I do not wish to have to be the doctor to say this in a report, because they will make me out to be a publicity seeker."

"It is a good thing," I said to him, "that you were not around the time I got mumps."

JOHN GALLAGHER

Courtesy *Sport* Magazine ©

"He's a great handler of pitchers!"

FROM *The Glory of Their Times* comes this warm and wonderful reminiscence by one of the two or three greatest left-handed pitchers of all time. I guess all of us have had a Mr. Frisbee in our lives at one point or another.

How Come I'm Called "Rube"?

RUBE MARQUARD

MY NICKNAME being what it is, you probably automatically assume I must have been a country boy. That's what most people figure. But it's not so. Fact is, my father was the chief engineer of the city of Cleveland, and that's where I was born and reared.

Then how come I'm called "Rube"? Well, I'll get to that. But let me tell you about my father first. Like I say, he was the chief engineer of the city of Cleveland. As far as he was concerned, the only important thing was for me to get a good education. But as far back as I can remember, all I could think of, morning, noon and night, was baseball.

"Now listen," Dad would say, "I want you to cut this out and pay attention to your studies. I want you to go to college when you're through high school, and I don't want any foolishness about it. Without an education you won't be able to get a good job, and then you'll *never* amount to anything."

"I already have a job," I'd say.

"You've got a job? What are you talking about?"

"I'm going to be a ballplayer."

"A ballplayer?" he'd say, and throw his hands up in the air. "What do you mean? How can you make a living being a ballplayer? I don't understand why a grown man would wear those funny-looking suits in the first place."

"Well," I'd answer, "you see policemen with uniforms on, and other people like that. They change after they're through working. It's the same way with ballplayers."

"Ha! Do ballplayers get paid?"

"Yes, they get paid."

"I don't believe it! Ballplayers are no good," he'd say, "and they never will be any good."

And with that he'd slam the door and go outside and sit on the porch, and not talk to me for the rest of the evening.

The thing is, I was always very tall for my age. I had three brothers and a sister, and my sister was the shortest of the five of us. She grew to be six feet two. So I was always hanging around the older kids and playing ball with them instead of with kids my own age. When I was about 13 I used to carry bats for Napoleon Lajoie and Elmer Flick and Terry Turner and a lot of the other Cleveland Indians. They weren't called the Indians then. They were called the Cleveland Bronchos and then the Naps, after Napoleon Lajoie.

Then later I even pitched a few games for Bill Bradley's Boo Gang. Bill Bradley was the Cleveland third baseman—one of the greatest who ever lived—and he also barnstormed with his Boo Gang after the season was over. So by the time I was only 15 or 16 I knew a lot of ballplayers, and I had my heart set on becoming a big leaguer myself.

One of my friends was a catcher named Howard Wakefield. He was about five years older than I was. In 1906 he was playing for the Waterloo club in the Iowa State League, and that spring—when I was only 16—I got a letter from him.

"We can use a good left-handed pitcher," the letter said, "and if you want to come to Waterloo, I'll recommend you to the manager." I think Howard thought that I was at least 18 or 19, because I was so big for my age.

I wrote the manager, asking for an advance for a train ticket, but when no money came, I just took off. I left home and bummed my way to Waterloo, Iowa. I was 16 years old, and I'd never been away from home before. It took me five days and five nights, riding freight trains, sleeping in open fields, hitching rides any way I could. My money ran out on the third day, and after that I ate when and how I could.

Finally, though, the freight slowly drew into the Illinois Central station at Waterloo, Iowa, and just before it came to a stop I jumped off and went tumbling head over heels right in front of the passenger house. I hardly had time to pick myself up off the ground before the stationmaster grabbed me.

"What do you think you're doing?" he growled. "Come on, get out of here before I run you in."

"No," I said, "I'm reporting to the Waterloo ball club."

"You're what?" he says. "My God, did you ever wash your face?"

"Yes I did," I said, "but I've been traveling five days and five nights, and I'm anxious to get to the ball park. Where do the ballplayers hang around?"

"At the smoke shop," he said, "down the street about half a mile. If you walk down there, probably whoever you're looking for will be there."

So I thanked him and told him I'd see that he got a free pass to the ball game as soon as I got settled, and started off for the smoke shop. It turned out that two brothers owned the smoke shop, and they also owned the ball club. One of them was behind the counter when I walked in. He took one look at me and let out a roar.

"What are you doing in here?" he yelled. "This is a respectable place. Get out of here."

I told him I was going to pitch for the ball club.

"Are you kidding?" he said. "Who in the world ever recommended you?"

"Howard Wakefield did."

"Well," he said, "Wakefield is in back shooting billiards. We'll soon settle this!"

"I'd like to go back and see him," I said.

"Don't go back there," he shouted. "You'll drive everybody out. Did you ever take a bath?"

"Of course I did," I said, "but I've bummed my way here, and I haven't had a chance to clean up yet."

So he called to the back, and in a minute out came Howard. "Holy Cripes!" he said. "What happened to you?"

I was explaining it to him when in came Mr. Frisbee, the manager, and I was introduced to him.

"Keokuk is here tomorrow," he said, "and we'll pitch you."

"Tomorrow? You want me to pitch tomorrow after what I've been through?"

"Tomorrow or never, young fellow!"

"All right," I said. "But could I have five dollars in advance so I can get a clean shirt or something?"

"After the game tomorrow," he said, and walked away.

So Howard took me to his rooming house, and I cleaned up there and had something to eat, and they let me sleep on an extra cot they had.

The next day we went out to the ball park, and I was introduced to the players and given a uniform that was too small for me. The Keokuk team was shagging balls while I warmed up, and they kept making comments about green rookies and bushers, and how they'd knock me out of the box in the first inning. Oh, I felt terrible. I had an awful headache, and I was exhausted. But I was determined to show them that I could make good, and I went out there and won that game, 6–1.

After the game I went to Mr. Frisbee and said, "Well, I showed you I could deliver the goods. Can we talk about a contract now?"

"Oh," he said, "Keokuk is in last place. Wait until Oskaloosa comes in this weekend. They're in second place. They're a tough team, and if you can beat them then we'll talk."

"Can't I get any money, any advance money, on my contract?" I asked him.

"You haven't got a contract."

"All right," I said, and I didn't say another word.

That evening, when it got dark I went down to the railroad station, and the same stationmaster was there.

"Hey," he said, "you pitched a fine game today. I was there and you did a great job. What are you doing back here? Did you come to give me that free ticket you promised me?"

"No, I'm sorry," I said. "I'm going back home to Cleveland, and I want to know what time a freight comes by." And I explained to him everything that had happened.

He was very nice to me, and after we talked a while he said, "Look, this train comes in at one o'clock in the morning, and the engine unhooks and goes down to the water tower. When it does, you sneak into the baggage compartment, and meanwhile I'll talk to the baggageman before the engine gets hooked up again. Then when the train pulls out and is about five miles out of town, he'll open the baggage door and let you out."

So that all happened, and when we were five miles out of town the door opened, and the baggageman appeared. I talked with him all the way to Chicago, and as we got close to the yards, he said to me, "OK, you better get ready to jump now. There are a lot of detectives around here, and if you're not careful they'll grab you and throw you in jail. So once you get on the ground, don't hesitate. Beat it away from here as fast as you can."

The baggageman must have told the engineer about me, because we slowed down to a crawl just before we approached the Chicago yards, and off I jumped. I got out of there quick and took off down the street. I don't know what street it was, and I'm not sure where I was headed, but I do remember that I was awfully tired. It was the middle of the morning, and I had hardly slept a wink the night before.

I'd walked about three or four blocks when I passed by a fire-engine house. Evidently all the firemen were out at a fire, because the place was empty. I was tired, so I went in and sat down. Well, they had a big-bellied iron stove in there, and it was warm, and I guess I must have fallen asleep, because the next thing I knew a couple of firemen were shaking me and doing everything they could to wake me up. They called me a bum and a lot of other names, and told me to get out of there or they'd have me thrown in jail.

"I'm no bum," I said, "I'm a ballplayer."

"What, you a ballplayer! Where did you ever play?"

So I told them: Cleveland, around the sandlots, and in Waterloo, Iowa, too. And I told them all about it.

They still didn't really believe me. They asked me did I know Three-Fingered Brown, Tinker, Evers, Chance, and all those fellows.

"No," I said, "I don't know them. But someday I'll be playing with them, or against them, because I'm going to get in the big leagues."

"Where are you going now?" they asked me.

"Back home to Cleveland."

"Have you got any money?"

"No."

So they got up a little pool of about five dollars and said, "Well, on your way. And use this to get something to eat."

I thanked them, and as I left I told them that someday I'd be back. "When I get to the big leagues," I said, "I'm coming out to visit you when we get to Chicago."

And home I went. I played around home all the rest of that summer, and then the next summer, 1907, I got a job with an ice-cream company in Cleveland. I made $25 a week: $15 for checking the cans on the truck that would take the ice cream away, and $10 a Sunday, when I pitched for the company team. It was a good team. We played the best semipro clubs in the Cleveland area, and I beat them all. I was only 17, but I hardly lost a game.

Then one day I got a postal card from the Cleveland ball club, asking me to come in and talk to them. Mr. Kilfoyl and Mr. Somers, the owners of the club, wanted to see me. I went in and told them, "I'm not signing with you or anybody else until I hear what you're offering. I've been taken advantage of before, and it's not going to happen again. I know a lot of ballplayers, and they always tell me not to sign with anybody unless I get a good salary. They all tell me you better get it when you're young, 'cause you sure won't get it when you're old."

"That's a lot of nonsense," Mr. Kilfoyl said. "Don't you worry. We'll treat you right. We'll give you a hundred dollars a month. That's a wonderful offer."

"I think he'll be overpaid," Mr. Somers says.

"I don't think that's so wonderful," I said "And as for being overpaid, I get that much right now from the ice-cream company, and in addition I get to eat all the ice cream I want."

They wouldn't increase their price, and I wouldn't reduce mine, so I left and went home. On the way home, though, I stopped in this sporting-goods store at 724 Prospect Avenue. It was owned by Bill Bradley and Charlie Carr, and was a popular hangout for ballplayers. Bill Bradley, of course, played third base for Cleveland, and Charlie Carr managed and played first base for Indianapolis in the American Association.

When I walked in the door, Bill Bradley said, "Hello, Big Leaguer, I understand the boss wants to sign you up."

"Not me," I said, "he wouldn't pay me as much as I already make with the ice-cream company."

"You know, I manage the Indianapolis club," Charlie Carr said to me.

"I know that."

"How would you like to sign with me?"

"You're in the minor leagues," I said. "If a major-league club won't pay me what I want, how could you do it?"

"How much do you want?"

I took a deep breath. "Two hundred a month."

"Wow! You want all the money, don't you!" he said.

"No, but you want a good pitcher, don't you?"

"Yes."

"Well," I said, "I'm one."

And darned if he didn't agree to it. So right then and there I signed my first professional contract, with Indianapolis of the American Association.

When I got home that night I had to tell my Dad about it, because I was to leave for Indianapolis the next day. Oh, that was a terrible night. Finally, Dad said, "Now listen, I've told you time and time again that I don't want you to be a professional ballplayer. But you've got your mind made up. Now I'm going to tell you something: When you cross that threshold, don't come back. I don't ever want to see you again."

"You don't mean that, Dad," I said.

"Yes, I do."

"Well, I'm going," I said, "and someday you'll be proud of me."

"Proud!" he said. "You're breaking my heart, and I don't ever want to see you again."

"I won't break your heart," I said. "I'll add more years to your life. You wait and see."

So I went to Indianapolis. They optioned me out to Canton in the Central League for the rest of the 1907 season, and I won 23 games with them, which was one-third of all the games the Canton club won that year.

The next year I opened the season with Indianapolis and pitched the first game against Kansas City. I won, 2–1, and that evening the story in the Indianapolis *Star* read like this: "The American Association season opened up today, and it was a beautiful game between two fine teams. Each had great pitching, with an eighteen-year-old right-hander pitching for Kansas City and an eighteen-year-old left-hander for the home team. The right-hander with Kansas City looks like he's going to develop into a great pitcher. They call him Smoky Joe Wood. But we have a left-hander with Indianapolis who is going places, too. He resembles one of the great left-handed pitchers of all time: Rube Waddell." And from that day on they nicknamed me "Rube."

I had a wonderful season that year with Indianapolis. I pitched 47 complete games, won 28 of them, led the league in most strikeouts, least hits, most innings pitched, and everything. Occasionally what I'd do would be reported in the Cleveland papers, and friends of mine would tell me that they'd pass by the house and see Dad sitting on the porch.

"Well, Fred," they'd say—that was my dad's name, Fred—"did you see what your son Rube did yesterday?"

"Who are you talking about?" he'd say. "Rube who?"

"Your son, Richard."

"I told him baseball was no good," my Dad would reply. "Now they've even gone and changed his name!"

Anyway, I had a terrific year with Indianapolis, like I said. Late in the season we went into Columbus, Ohio, and Charlie Carr came up to me before the game.

"Rube," he said, "there are going to be an awful lot of celebrities here at the game today. The American and National leagues both have an off day, and they're all coming to see you pitch. If you pitch a good game, I may be able to sell you before the night is out."

"For how much?" I asked.

"I don't know," he said, "but a lot. It depends on what kind of game you pitch."

"Will you cut me in?"

"No, I won't," he said. "You're getting a good salary, and you know it."

"OK," I said, "I was only kidding anyway."

"I don't want you to get nervous today," he said.

"Nervous? Have I ever been nervous all season?"

"No," he said. "I've been in baseball a long time, and I never saw anything like it. I never saw a kid like you, who can beat anybody and is so successful."

"Well," I said, "the reason I'm so successful is because I can beat anybody."

I went out there that day, and I pitched one of those unusual games: no hits, no walks, no runs, no errors. Twenty-seven men faced me, and not one of them got to first base. And that evening they put me up for sale, with all the big-league clubs bidding on me, like a horse being auctioned off. The Cleveland club went as high as $10,500 for my contract, but the Giants went to $11,000, and I was sold to them. At that time that was the highest price ever paid for a baseball player.

I reported to the New York Giants in September of 1908, as soon as the American Association season was over. I was 18 years old and I was in the big leagues!

I came up too late in the season to make a trip to Chicago with the Giants that year, but the next season we made our first trip to Chicago the second week in June. And the first thing I did, as soon as I got there, was to make a beeline for that firehouse.

The only one there when I first got there was the lieutenant. I walked up to him and said, "Lieutenant, do you remember me?"

"Never saw you before in my life," he said.

"Well, remember about three years ago you caught me sleeping back of that stove there?"

"Oh, are you the kid from Cleveland that said he's a ballplayer?"

"Yes. Remember me? My name is Marquard, Richard Marquard."

"Of course. What are you doing here?"

"I'm in the big leagues," I said. "I told you when I got to the big leagues I was coming out to visit you."

"Well, I'll be darned," he said. "Who are you with?"

"Why, I'm with the New York Giants."

And boy, for years after that, whenever the Giants would come to Chicago, I'd go out to that firehouse. I'd sit out front and talk for hours. The firemen would have all the kids in the neighborhood there . . . and all the families that lived around would stop by . . . and it was really wonderful. Everybody was so nice and friendly.

I was in the big leagues for 18 years, you know, from 1908 through 1925. I was with the Giants until 1915, with the Dodgers for five years after that, with Cincinnati for one year, and then with the Boston Braves for four. And I loved every single minute of it.

The best years of all were those with the Giants. I don't mean because those were my best pitching years, although they were. In 1911 I won 24 games and lost only 7, and in 1912 I won 26. That's the year I won 19 straight—I didn't lose a single game in 1912 until July 8! That record has stood up for a long time now. Over 50 years.

It was wonderful to be a Giant back then. Take Mr. McGraw. What a great man he was! The finest and grandest man I ever met. He loved his players, and his players loved him. Of course he wouldn't stand for any nonsense. You had to live up to the rules and regulations of the New York Giants, and when he laid down the law you'd better abide by it.

I'll never forget one day we were playing Pittsburgh, and it was Red Murray's turn to bat, with the score tied in the ninth inning. There was a man on second with none out. Murray came over to McGraw—I was sitting next to McGraw—and he said, "What do you want me to do, Mac?"

"What do I want you to do?" McGraw said. "What are you doing in the National League? There's the winning run on second base and no one out. What would you do if you were the manager?"

"I'd sacrifice the man to third," Murray said.

"Well," McGraw said, "that's exactly what I want you to do."

So Murray went up to the plate to bunt. After he got to the batter's box, though, he backed out and looked over at McGraw again.

McGraw poked his elbow in my ribs. "Look at that so-and-so," he said. "He told me what he should do, and I told him what he should do, and now he's undecided. I bet he forgot from the bench to the plate."

Now, in those days—and I guess it's the same now—when a man was up there to bunt, the pitcher would try to keep the ball high and tight. Well, it so happened that Red was a high-ball hitter. Howie Camnitz was pitching for Pittsburgh. He wound up and in came the ball, shoulder high. Murray took a terrific cut at it, and the ball went over the left-field fence. It was a home run, and the game was over.

Back in the clubhouse Murray was happy as a lark. He was first into the showers, and out boomed his wonderful Irish tenor, singing "My Wild Irish Rose." When he came out of the shower, still singing, McGraw walked over and tapped him on the shoulder. All of us were watching out of the corner of our eyes, because we knew the Little Round Man—that's what we used to call McGraw—wouldn't let this one go by without saying *something*.

"Murray, what did I tell you to do?" McGraw asked him.

"You told me to bunt," Murray said, not looking quite so happy any more. "But you know what happened, Mac. Camnitz put one right in my gut, so I cow-tailed it."

"Where did you say he put it?"

"Right in my gut."

"Well," McGraw said, "I'm fining you one hundred dollars, and you can try putting that right in your gut too!" And off he went.

Oh, God, I never laughed so much in my life! Murray never did live that down. Years later something would happen, and we'd yell to Murray, "Hey, Red, is that right in your gut?"

Then later on, you know, I was traded to the Dodgers. Well, really, I traded myself. I didn't seem to be able to get going in 1915, although I pitched a no-hitter in April, and McGraw started riding me. That was the year we were favored to win the pennant and wound up last. So McGraw wasn't very happy. After I'd taken about as much riding as I could stand, I asked him to trade me if he thought I was so bad.

"Who would take you?" he said.

"What do you mean?" I said. "I can still lick any club in the league." Heck, I wasn't even twenty-six years old yet.

"Lick any club in the league?" McGraw said. "You couldn't lick a postage stamp."

"Give me a chance to trade myself, then," I said. "What would you sell me for?"

"Seventy-five hundred dollars," he answered.

"OK," I said, "can I use your phone?"

"Sure," he said. We were both pretty mad by that time.

So I got hold of the operator and asked her to get me Wilbert Robinson, manager of the Brooklyn club. See, Robbie had been a coach with us for years before he became the Dodger manager in 1914. After a while she got Robbie on the phone.

"Hello," he says.

"How are you, Robbie?" I said.

"Fine," he said. "Who is this?"

"How would you like to have a good left-handed pitcher?"

"I'd love it," he said. "Who is this? Who's the man? Who are you going to recommend?"

"I'm going to recommend myself."

"Who are you?"

"Rube Marquard."

"Oh, what are you kidding around for, Rube?" he said. "I have to go out on the field, and I don't have time to fool around."

"No, I'm serious," I said. "McGraw is right here, and he says he'll sell me for seventy-five hundred dollars. Do you want to talk to him?"

"Of course I do," Robbie said. And right then and there I was traded from the Giants to the Dodgers.

And, of course, we—the Dodgers, that is—won the pennant the next year, and I had one of the best years I ever had. I think I had an earned-run average of about 1.50 in 1916. And then we won the pennant again in 1920. So everything worked out pretty well.

One day, when I was pitching for Brooklyn, I pitched the first game of a doubleheader against Boston and beat them, 1–0. I was in the clubhouse during the second game, taking off my uniform, when the clubhouse boy came walking in.

"Rube," he said, "there's an elderly gentleman outside who wants to see you. He says he's your father from Cleveland."

"He's not my father," I said. "My father wouldn't go across the street to see me. But you go out and get his autograph book and bring it in, and I'll autograph it for him."

But instead of bringing in the book, he brought in my dad.

"Boy, you sure are a hardhead," he said to me. "You know I didn't mean what I said ten years ago."

"What about you, Dad?" I said. "You're as stubborn as I am. I thought you never wanted to see me again. I thought you meant it."

"Of course I didn't," he said.

After we talked a while, I said, "Did you see the game today?"

"Yes, I did," he said.

"Where were you sitting?" I asked him.

"Well, you know the man who wears that funny thing on his face?"

"You mean the mask? The catcher?"

"I guess so. Well, anyway, I was halfway between him and the number one—you know, where they run right after they hit the ball."

"You mean first base?"

"I don't know," he said. "I don't know what they call it. I was sitting in the middle there."

"How many ball games have you seen since I became a ballplayer, Dad?"

"This is the first one," he told me.

Well, he stayed in New York with me for a few weeks, and we had a great time. Finally he had to go back to Cleveland. After he'd left, the newspapers heard about my dad, and they wanted to know his address back home. So I gave it to them, and doggone if they didn't send reporters and photographers to Cleveland to interview him.

They took his picture and asked him a lot of questions. One of the things they asked him was whether he had ever played very much baseball himself.

"Oh, of course I did, when I was younger," he told them. "I used to love to play baseball. I used to be a pitcher, just like my son Richard —I mean like my son Rube."

"Are you proud of your son?" they asked him.

"I certainly am," Dad said. "Why shouldn't I be? He's a great baseball player, isn't he?"

In the May, 1911, issue of *Pearson's* magazine appeared an article entitled "Outguessing the Batter," and here is an excerpt from it. The author was somewhat of an expert, you'll agree.

From *Outguessing the Batter*

CHRISTY MATHEWSON

Many things have been said and written about pitchers outguessing batters, and batters outguessing pitchers, and to tell the truth there has always been a question in my mind about the outguessing proposition. I have seen so many instances where guesses went wrong—so many hundreds of instances—that I am about the last human being in the world to pose as an oracle on the subject of pitching psychology. Nevertheless, there certainly is a lot of psychology about pitching a baseball. Joe Tinker, the clever little shortstop of the Chicago club, is a man with whom I have fought many battles of wits, and I am glad to acknowledge that he has come out of the fuss with flying colors on many occasions. There was a time when Tinker was putty in my hands. For two years he was the least dangerous man on the Chicago team. His weakness was a low curve on the outside, and I fed him low curves on the outside so often that I had him looking like an invalid every time he came to the plate. Then Joseph went home one night and did a little deep thinking. He got a nice long bat and took his stand at least a foot farther from the plate, and then he had me. If I kept the ball on the inside edge of the plate, he was in a splendid position to meet it, and if I tried to keep my offerings on the outside, he had plenty of time to "step into 'em." From that day on Tinker became one of the most dangerous batters I ever faced, not because his natural hitting ability had increased, but because he didn't propose to let the pitcher do all the "outguessing."

Baseball as It Used to Be

ROSCOE McGOWEN

THE DECADE which began shortly after World War I and ended with the stock-market crash of 1929 was later dubbed by some sportswriter—who was overcome by nostalgia, romanticism and/or pure corn—the Golden Age of Sports. The acerbic and iconoclastic J. Westbrook Pegler had a decidedly different designation. He called it The Era of Wonderful Nonsense.

Maybe it was a golden age for sports but it couldn't be proved by that baseball team in Brooklyn—the inimitable, unforgettable Dodgers. Any chance they may have had to become a part of this golden age died with Charles Hercules Ebbets in the early spring of 1925. With the death of Ebbets, the club's president and controlling owner, chaos and confusion enveloped the entire outfit.

To the stockholders the situation was sad and painful, but to the unbiased observer, such as a baseball writer (if a baseball writer *can* be called unbiased), the doings of the Dodgers became a source of never-ending wonder and delight.

A lot of people remember the Dodgers who won pennants in the forties and fifties with reasonable regularity. Not so many now recall the Dodgers of the twenties and thirties who went 21 years without a pennant.

I remember the Dodgers when they were the Robins, named after their manager from 1914 through 1931, Wilbert Robinson, the rotund, rollicking and beloved Uncle Robby.

I remember when Uncle Robby and his wife, "Ma" Robinson, would sit in a taxicab outside Ebbets Field surrounded by fans who were loudly assailing him for his managerial moves in the game just lost. Robby would stoutly defend what he called his "strategy," but sometimes Ma would side with the fans, whereupon the argument ended abruptly in Uncle Robby's growling to the driver to "get t' hell outa here!"

When the Robins went to spring training at Clearwater, Florida, in 1925, they rated among the elite of baseball. They had finished second in 1924, giving John McGraw's Giants a tough battle. They had two of the better pitchers in the majors, Dazzy Vance (28-6) and Burleigh Grimes (22-13), in the '24 season.

Both were holdouts. Vance, who lived in Florida, was around the field frequently, but Grimes was sticking close to his Minerva, Ohio, home until getting some indication that his terms would be met.

This was my first trip to a baseball training camp and I was the only morning paper (New York *News*) represented. Somebody from one of the afternoon papers got the bright idea of sending Grimes a wire asking when and if he would sign and report. Burleigh's reply, sent collect, was several hundred well-chosen words. It told us virtually nothing and it cost us about five bucks.

Vance's eventual signing of a three-year contract could have been fun for me had I been more enterprising—or more ruthless. It happens that I was an expert telegrapher, an accomplishment of which my afternoon-paper colleagues were unaware. The afternoon writers didn't want to relinquish the monopoly they had enjoyed on big news stories. So, although Vance agreed to terms sometime in the early afternoon, they decided to keep the story for the afternoon papers of the next day. Most of their stories were filed early and were being transmitted by 6 P.M.

At about that hour I dropped into the Western Union office, where old Abe Yeager, sports editor of the Brooklyn *Eagle*, and young Tom Meany, of the Brooklyn *Times*, were sitting—probably on guard to see that the lone morning newsman didn't get back of the counter and read their copy.

As I leaned on the counter and talked casually to Abe and Tom, my ear caught the Vance story crackling over the wire in the singing Morse of the operator. I listened, still talking to Abe and Tom, until I had virtually all the story. Then, instead of sauntering carelessly up the street to the Postal (there was a Postal Telegraph Company then) and filing the tale to the *News* for a clean scoop—as I should have done—I turned to the pair and said, "What's this about Vance signing?"

It was almost like setting off a giant firecracker beneath their bench. Their expressions were ludicrous in their astonishment. "How could this guy know about Vance?" they seemed to be thinking. But Abe, although still puzzled, wasn't about to let me in on the story.

"Why," he said, "we have an agreement here that anything that happens after 6 o'clock belongs to the evening papers; what happens before that time the morning papers get."

I was a soft touch, perhaps because Abe was such a really nice little guy. Anyway, I agreed to go along with their arrangements on news splits, ignoring the obvious fact that the story must have broken sometime before six o'clock for all of them to have written such complete pieces.

The players then were quartered at a somewhat decrepit hostelry on Clearwater's main street called the Cleveland Hotel. There was one exception. The sophisticated and ruggedly handsome Jack Fournier, along with his beautiful young blond wife Helen, were permitted to put up at the Gray Moss Inn, which normally wouldn't let a ballplayer through the servants' entrance. Jack frequently got into his tux for dinner, which probably overawed even the stuffy patrons and management of the inn. Uncle Robby and Ma also stopped at the inn.

Zach Wheat, then 37 and nearing the end of an illustrious career, had a young rookie player assigned to room with him. The theory was that some of Wheat's baseball savvy and all-round class might rub off on the younger fellow. What happened was something quite different.

One night Wheat, a somewhat early-to-bed chap, was in his bed with the lights out but still awake when his young roomie came softly into the room about midnight. He stood still for a full minute, then moved closer to Zach and peered down at him. Apparently satisfied that Wheat was asleep, the rookie stealthily lifted Wheat's trousers from the chair they were draped over, took out the wallet and removed a bill from it. Then he carefully replaced the wallet and trousers as he had found them.

Since the room faced the street there was light enough for Wheat to see all this, although of course he didn't know how much the boy had taken. The fellow's next move was to go to one of the windows, pull down the shade, insert the pilfered bill and roll it up in the shade. Then he went to bed and soon was snoring.

Wheat thereupon arose, went to the window, got the bill (it was a five), pulled the blind back as it had been and went back to bed.

The rookie must have been greatly puzzled about that missing five, and Wheat left him that way. He told nobody of the incident for several years, long after the rookie had returned to the minors.

In 1929, when I was working for *The New York Times,* I witnessed a baseball novelty. Everybody interested in baseball has heard of "the strings," the strike zone gadget for pitchers which Branch Rickey is always credited with having originated. Actually, Uncle Robby beat Rickey to the idea in 1929, just as even earlier he had beaten Lou Boudreau to the "Williams shift."

At Clearwater the Dodgers had a batting cage, an oblong affair perhaps 60 feet long and 25 feet wide, completely covered and enclosed by a netting. There the hitters could belt balls freely without the chance of losing any. But they had to have a live pitcher, since mechanical pitchers had not been invented. It was in this cage that Robby set up his contraption, only instead of strings he used two long, heavy bags like boxers use. The bags were suspended the width of home plate apart, with the top and bottom of the strike zone indicated by markings.

With this setup completed, Uncle Robby announced a contest for his pitchers. "You'll each be allowed 25 pitches," he told them, "and the feller that throws the most strikes I'll give 25 dollars."

Robby said nothing about the type of pitches—curve balls, change-ups or what have you—just that they be strikes. Privately he was confident that Vance, his prime favorite, would easily win the 25 bucks.

But a big brash rookie right-hander, hitherto the wildest pitcher in camp, proceeded to put more than 20 of his pitches in the strike zone and pocketed the prize money.

This was Louis Norman Newsom, the famous Bobo, who adorned the rosters of at least eight major-league clubs over more than two decades.

After paying off Newsom, Uncle Robby abruptly called off any further competition. "Don't do 'em any good, anyway," he grumbled.

About that Williams shift Robby came up with. I remember a day in that old Philadelphia bandbox known as Baker Bowl, with the Dodgers and Phillies involved in something decidedly not a pitchers' battle. Fred (Cy) Williams came to bat one inning with the bases empty. Uncle Robby promptly shifted his infielders and outfielders far to the right. For Cy, like his namesake, Ted, was normally a dead pull hitter. It wasn't the first time Robbie had used this shift either. I had seen it before but this time the results were different.

Baker Bowl, for those unfamiliar with this long-gone ball park, had a very short right field, probably less than 250 feet, with a very high tin-covered wall. From the left-field foul line to center field was a considerable expanse.

Previously Cy had always played the percentages and pulled the ball, frequently hitting it off or over the wall. But when he saw the tremendous overshift—the third baseman was near second base, the left fielder was in center field and everybody else far to the right—he decided to try to cross up Uncle Robby.

He succeeded even better than he hoped. With perfect timing Cy lined the ball into left field about 20 feet inside the foul line. But he started laughing as he started running and as his mirth increased his speed diminished. What could easily have been an inside-the-park homer became a triple when Cy, reaching third, sat down on the bag and laughed hilariously.

Uncle Robby was not amused.

Somehow, the Dodgers always seemed to have problems in Boston. Perhaps their most hilarious day there was on April 15, 1931, Uncle Robby's final year as manager. It was only the second day of the season. That spring Uncle Robby had brought up from the Macon, Georgia, club a young outfielder named Alta Cohen, son of a Newark, New Jersey, rabbi. Al was 20, agile and ambitious, was anxious to play and that day got his chance.

The game wasn't going well for the Dodgers. The ineffable Babe Herman was playing right field and, in Uncle Robby's opinion, had failed to catch a couple of catchable balls. Babe was having a bit of trouble with what Casey Stengel used to call "Old Joe Wind, my fifth outfielder."

On the bench in the top of the fifth inning, Robby voiced his complaints to Herman, whereupon the Babe flared and said, "If you got somebody can play it better, put 'em in. I'm through."

And Herman left the bench and headed for the clubhouse. Meanwhile Ike Boone, a good hitter but no gazelle afield, had batted for Robby's pitcher. Ike, noting Herman's departure, took it upon himself to go out to right field when the inning ended.

Meanwhile Robby, who had been brooding about his quarrel with Babe, one of his favorites, suddenly awoke to Boone's presence in right field. "Hell's fire!" he spluttered. "He can't play there. Who've I got?"

Young Cohen, more eager than ever, was sitting right beside the manager. "I can play right field, Mr. Robinson." he said.

"Uh, eh, what—oh, yeah, go on out there," said Robby.

In case it isn't clear to the reader—and it wasn't clear either to any of the Braves or the Dodgers at the time—it should be explained that since Boone batted for the pitcher and Cohen replaced Boone, Cohen also had to bat in the pitcher's spot, while the new Dodger pitcher, who happened to be Freddy Heimach and a good hitter, had to bat in Herman's No. 4 spot.

But as the sixth inning opened, the eager Cohen came to the plate in Herman's spot and promptly singled to left center. Neither manager Bill McKechnie nor his field captain, Rabbit Maranville, was aware of the error. Had the Braves appealed to the umpire an automatic out would have resulted. But once the following Dodger finished his batting turn the thing couldn't be called. The inning ended without the Dodgers scoring.

I was highly in favor of letting the confusion continue on the theory that since the Dodgers were losing anyway, things might become even funnier. But one of my press-box colleagues yelled down until he attracted a Dodger's attention and explained what had happened.

So, instead of Heimach coming to bat in the pitcher's spot in the seventh, young Cohen was up again, this time where he belonged. He singled again to the same spot and later scored the Dodgers' third and last run. (The Braves had nine runs.)

No sooner had Alta reached the bench again than he sidled up to Uncle Robby and excitedly asked, "Do both them hits count, Mr. Robinson?"

The afternoon papers had quite an overnight story, and Quentin Reynolds, then covering the Dodgers for the New York *World-Telegram,* probably produced the best one, which was written in the form of a letter to Cohen's mother.

But it developed later that night that all the hilarious happenings of the day were not perpetrated by the Dodgers nor all of them encompassed by Reynolds' story. The Western Union added its zany bit.

Some dazed employee delivered Quent's story to Mrs. Cohen in Newark instead of to his paper and about 3 o'clock in the morning Reynolds got a frantic phone call from the night desk man. "Where's your story?" the man wanted to know.

"I filed it long ago," replied Reynolds.

Then he had a thought that perhaps the Western Union had taken things too literally. A recheck uncovered the story, and it was delivered to the paper.

Because of a shift in baseball writers on the *News* in 1928 I was sent to spring training with the Giants at Augusta, Georgia, a memorable year for several reasons.

It was the spring when a local bootlegger sold the writers what he solemnly assured them was "real golden cawn likkah," but which was so loaded with fusel oil that, after downing a draft, it was risky to bring a flame close enough to light a cigarette.

It was the spring when the late Bozeman Bulger and I opposed Dick Vidmer and the late Buck O'Neill at golf every morning on the Augusta Country Club course—and thereby hangs a tale.

The writers, ten of us, were quartered in a mansion, complete with housekeeper, a block or so above the Partridge Inn, where we took our meals. In our tremendous living room there was a blackjack game going every night. One night the game didn't end but Boze was on hand in his car promptly at 7 o'clock to take us golfing. I was the only member of the foursome who had had no sleep.

After the 18 holes I had to cover the workout of the noble athletes and report thereon to meet an early deadline.

At 6 o'clock, feeling that a few minutes' shuteye would set me up for the night's little game of skill and chance, I went to my room and asked Frankie Graham to call me at 6:30, so I could make the inn dining room before its 7-o'clock closing time. Later Graham said he really forgot to call me, but I never was quite sure. Anyway, I was suddenly awakened by Rud Rennie tugging at my shoulder. "Hey, Mac," he said urgently, "look what time it is. If you want dinner you'll have to hurry." And he held up my watch, which he had thoughtfully set at 6:40. A bit groggy, but very conscious of hunger, I hustled into my clothes and down the street. Halfway there I had an odd feeling that something wasn't quite right. It was too dark. And in front of the inn, where I could see the clock in the lobby, I found out what was wrong. It was 11:40 P.M.

Sometime in August of 1928, after leaving the *News,* I became sports editor of the Brooklyn *Standard Union,* and was more or less back with the Dodgers, where perhaps I belonged. That year the Yankees and the Cardinals were the pennant winners and the *Standard Union* management, aiming for new promotional gimmicks, signed Uncle Robby to cover the World Series. Murray Robinson was to be Robby's ghost, but after the first two games in New York, a threat of appendicitis prevented Murray's going to St. Louis. Another staff man, John Thorp, was sent in Murray's stead. It was a tactical error.

We got through the first day in St. Louis fairly well, although Robby already had hooked up with one of his good friends and favorite drinking companions, the late W. O. (Bill) McGeehan, as well as Henry Farrell, sports editor of the United Press. Henry was a pugnacious imbiber and took an instant dislike to Uncle Robby's ghost-writer.

Robby had a large suite at the old Buckingham Hotel (now the Kingsway). I was quartered there and it was also where McGeehan and Farrell spent virtually all their stay in St. Louis.

It was the second day that brought trouble. Judge Landis stopped everything by calling off the fourth game because of wet weather—and at 10 o'clock the sun was shining and it was a beautiful day. But a day off was fatal to the Robinson-McGeehan-Farrell triumvirate, not to mention the ghost-writer.

When Uncle Robby took a drink of bourbon it was what Col. Bill Pipp (Wally's father) called a "cow's mouthful"; in other words, half a tumblerful. Even Robby couldn't stay up under many of those, while McGeehan and Farrell couldn't even begin to compete.

As soon as the judge called off that game, Jack Kofoed and I went out to some country club and played 18 holes of golf. And when I got back to the Robinson suite, I wished I hadn't. For all I had to do then was invent and write Robby's story, write an overnight piece and a broad-gauge column. The next day that all had to be repeated, plus writing a full running story for that day's paper.

When the Series ended—fortunately the Yankees took it in four straight—I was able to complete my various jobs, still with no help from either Robby or his ghost.

Sometime the next day Uncle Robby, with Thorp still at his side, knocked on the door of his suite at the St. George Hotel in Brooklyn. Mrs. Robinson opened the door, glared at Robby and, before he could take a short breath, snapped, "You certainly are a mess!"

Robby summoned his last vestige of dignity. "Ma," he said with slow and exaggerated distinctness, "I want you to meet Mr. Thorp."

Ma turned a withering glance on Thorp. "You're a mess, too!" she said, and slammed the door in their faces.

Babe Herman was a lot of laughs to the writers. But Uncle Robby and the other Dodgers found Herman no laughing matter in 1930, the last year that Robby's team had a run for the pennant. Twice that season two players hit balls out of the park that had to be scored as singles because each time a runner was passed between first and second base.

And the base runner who was passed? Herman, of course.

On May 30, 1930, in the fourth inning of a morning game at Ebbets Field, Del Bissonette hit a towering fly over the right-field screen. Herman, standing well in on the grass, stood watching the ball while Bissonette, not sure but what it might hit the screen, was hotfooting it for extra bases. Del was out and his homer became a single.

On September 15, the same year in the same ball park, Dodgers vs. Reds, Glenn Wright hit a liner to deep left center—a ball obviously not catchable—and raced hard for extra bases. Herman was off first base in the same position as on May 30 and Glenn passed him. The ball took a second bounce over the low barrier into the old bleachers. Such bouncers were home runs in those days, but not this one; it was just another single.

Uncle Robby might well have had his pennant that year but for crippling injuries to two key players within three days in September, Rube Bressler and Johnny Frederick.

Tragedy sometimes hit the Dodgers, temporarily belying the general belief that was built up and fostered by writers, that all Dodgers were fun-loving screwballs. I remember a September night in St. Louis in 1935. The Dodgers had split a doubleheader, winning the second game, which was a moral victory for the troupe then managed by Casey Stengel. All the writers had been invited to the Stengel suite, partly by way of mild celebration and partly because Mrs. Stengel's brother was there.

It must have been near midnight when the phone rang and one of the writers answered. It was a wire-service man with the shocking news that Len Koenecke, an outfielder Casey only that day had told was going to the minors, had been killed in a plane accident.

"I don't believe it," said Casey in shocked disbelief. "How can it be true?"

The newsmen wanted to talk to Stengel but he refused to talk to anybody.

It isn't needful here to rehash the sad details, more than to say that Koenecke had chartered a private plane to take him from Detroit to Buffalo and, once aloft, had tried to grab the controls and crash the plane. One of the two pilots, fighting for their lives, had crushed Len's skull with a fire extinguisher.

Stengel seemed to feel he was being blamed in some way. But he only made his position suspect by refusing to talk to the newsmen of the wire services. Here is something that Casey will be hearing for the first time, so far as I know.

A Dodger official called me aside and asked if I would attempt to pose as Stengel on the phone and call the A.P. man in St. Louis. I did make the call, giving a fair imitation of Stengel's gravelly voice and careless syntax. I said that I (Casey) had been mighty upset but was sorry not to have talked to the man earlier. Koenecke was praised as a player and a man and deep regret was voiced at his tragic death.

The A.P. reporter apparently did not question Stengel's identity. He asked the pseudo Casey a few sympathetic questions and received answers in kind. The story, quoting Stengel, went out, and that ended the unpleasant speculations that had arisen because of Casey's silence.

In 1941, under Leo Durocher, the Dodgers won their first pennant in 21 years. On Thursday, September 25, Whit Wyatt shut out the Braves, 6–0, in Boston for the clincher and we all boarded a train for New York. Then the madness started. The boys took over the dining car, champagne began flowing and clothing began to suffer.

Pee Wee Reese and Cookie Lavagetto, youngsters then, each wielded a jackknife to cut off all neckties just below the knot. Singer Tony Martin, a real baseball fan and Leo's friend, lost his tie and his shirt. Other shirts were ripped off. Mrs. Dixie Walker's bowl-shaped hat was too great a temptation and had a bottle of champagne poured into it.

After we had passed New Haven the conductor came in and asked if anybody wanted the train to stop at the 125th Street station. "Not on your life," Durocher said. "I want everybody to stay on till we get to Grand Central, where all those Brooklyn fans are waiting."

We'll skip the fans' welcome at Grand Central, where outgoing trains were delayed from 30 minutes to an hour because of the throng, and turn to Larry MacPhail, the Dodger owner. It was Larry's plan to get himself in the limelight by taking a large party of newsmen and photographers to 125th Street, where he would board the train and arrive at Grand Central, in a manner of speaking, as the grand marshal at the head of his troops.

When the train whisked by the uptown station MacPhail was the maddest man in or out of captivity.

And Durocher was basking in the adulation of the fans at Grand Central, completely unaware of what he had done to his boss.

Much later, MacPhail showed up at Leo's hotel room. Let Leo tell it.

"I'm feelin' pretty good," he said afterward. "Here I've won a pennant and I figure Larry's gonna pat me on the back and tell me what a great manager I am. So when he came in, I wait. He glares at me, his face getting redder and redder, then he busted out.

" 'You're fired!' he yelled.

"Then, while I'm speechless, he gives me hell for telling the conductor not to stop at 125th Street. I don't get a word in," Leo went on, "and when he left me that night I wasn't the manager of the Dodgers, as far as I knew."

Of course, as the records show, the firing didn't stick, any more than several others the fiery Larry imposed on Durocher afterward.

I recall many Dodger ups and downs.

I remember when the Dodgers were flying back from Cherry Point, North Carolina, in 1944, after a game at that U.S. Marines' base. The team was in a C-47 (the peacetime DC-3). The plane ran into very rough weather, lost radio contact, got lost and finally landed at Norfolk, Virginia, with 30 minutes' gas left. Luis Olmo, the Puerto Rican outfielder, talked to me about his terrifying experience when the plane was dropping as much as 200 feet, then bouncing up.

"Sometimes," Luis said with a slight shudder, "sometimes she go down, I no think she come up again."

Typical of the old Dodgers.

It's interesting how many baseball greats vote for Honus Wagner as the best of them all. Bill Klem, for instance, in the first *Fireside Book of Baseball;* Sam Crawford, elsewhere in the pages of this *Third Fireside;* and, in this piece by the late Tom Meany, no less an authority than John J. McGraw.

The Flying Dutchman

TOM MEANY

It is quite possible that there never was anybody in baseball so enamored of a controversy as John McGraw. The old Oriole attracted trouble as tall buildings attract lightning. He did more than that. He went out of his way to find trouble. McGraw was consistent only when it pleased his own ends to be so and he sometimes took the opposite side of a discussion merely to provoke and promote an argument, which he dearly loved.

There is no telling how many arguments McGraw provoked by his flat statement that John Honus Wagner was the greatest ballplayer who ever lived. There were many who believed the admiration of the Giant manager to be politic: He gave the accolade to Wagner because he was a National Leaguer, to offset the claims for Ty Cobb and, later, for Babe Ruth.

It could be so. Cobb, the firebrand outfielder of the Tigers, seemingly had many qualities which the Pirate shortstop lacked. On behalf of Ruth it may be said that his impact upon the game of baseball was greater than that of any other single athlete upon any single sport. Babe made them change the game. Neither Wagner nor Cobb did that.

Whether it was league loyalty or an honest opinion, McGraw until the day he died maintained that Wagner, bowlegged old Honus, was the greatest ballplayer he had ever seen. Boosters of Cobb, or of Ruth, could marshal all the statistics, all the facts and all the figures, but McGraw merely smiled and said, "Wagner was the best." Sometimes he didn't smile when he said it, either.

McGraw's contention always was that, all other things being equal, an infielder has it all over an outfielder, a pitcher or a catcher in value to a team. Maybe that was because Mac himself had been an infielder. If you grant McGraw that premise, then you must concede him the whole argument, too, for nobody ever disputed Wagner's claim to being the greatest infielder the game had ever known. The place of Honus among the all-time greats is secure. It is only that many object to Wagner being ranked Mr. Big over Cobb and/or Ruth.

Like some other great ballplayers, Wagner was so good he didn't know where he belonged. He once took a fling at pitching and whenever he got the ball over the plate, he would usually strike out the hitter. On the Pirate team which won the 1902 pennant, after Wagner had been a big leaguer for five seasons, he was still trying to orientate himself. He played 45 games at shortstop that year, 59 games in the outfield and 31 at first base.

By 1909, however, Wagner had settled down seriously to the business of playing short and he was playing it as nobody played it before or since. Modern fans, in discussing Honus, talk in terms of his hitting and his power and, less frequently, of his speed, good enough for him to lead the National League five times in stolen bases. Rarely is Wagner's fielding mentioned today, but it was his defensive skill which drew the greatest raves in his playing days.

Honus could go anywhere for a ground ball. No shortstop, or so McGraw always contended, could go "into the hole" as far as Wagner, that is, go to his right for ground balls, to field what ordinarily would have been base hits between the shortstop and the third baseman. Wagner played low, hugging the ground, his back almost on a parallel with the ground like a halfback awaiting the signal. He had not only a strong arm but a versatile one. He could throw from any position, throw overhand or underhand or sidearm and always get something on the ball.

Wagner's hands were like hams. Old-timers around Pittsburgh tell the tale that one day in 1902, when Honus was serving at first base for the Pirates, he stuck his hand in the back pocket of his pants to deal himself a chaw of tobacco and couldn't extricate his hand. He had to make the play at first base one-handed and then call time until his hand could be cut loose from his pocket.

In addition to his outsized hands, another physical peculiarity which assisted in making Wagner the greatest shortstop was his long, simianlike arms. He had a great reach and quick, agile hands, which was one of the reasons Honus did part-time service at first base.

Wagner, a right-handed hitter, held his left hand a few inches up from the handle of the bat, his right hand a palm's length away from the left. It is a rare and unusual grip. No other batter of importance, in the entire history of baseball, ever gripped a bat in this fashion, with one exception. The lone exception was Ty Cobb. Neither even knew the other employed this grip until, as their leagues' leading hitters and the stars of their representative clubs, they were asked to pose together before the 1909 World Series!

Wagner stood well back in the box and, with his hands-apart grip, could choke up when he wanted to hit to right or to bunt, and he could, of course, swing from the end of the bat, too. Because of his perfect control of the bat, Honus was able to hit wide pitches, low ones and high ones. He was as dangerous on bad balls at the plate as another National Leaguer, Joe Medwick, was to be three decades later. Wagner led the National League in hitting eight times, and although his home-run output was not extraordinary, even in those days of the dead ball, he was a powerful hitter who twice led the league in triples and eight times in doubles. Outside of home runs, he holds all the total National League batting records—hits, doubles, triples, total bases, and runs.* Wagner batted .300 or better for seventeen National League seasons and had passed his fortieth birthday before he fell below that mark.

One evening in Pittsburgh, after a Dodger-Pirate game, there was a twilight game scheduled between the Homestead Grays, a well-known Negro team, and the Green Cab Company. Some of us in the press box lingered to watch an inning or two of the game, principally because Wagner was playing first base for the cabbies. On his first time at bat, Honus tripled to the top of the exit gate in right center in Forbes Field. In all the games I have seen at that park in a quarter of a century, that exit gate was cleared only once, by Bill Terry with the Giants. And this was in 1927 when Honus hit the top of it, when he was fifty-three years old!

Ed Barrow, the man who changed Babe Ruth from a pitcher to an outfielder, was the discoverer of Wagner. Back in 1895, Barrow went out to Mansfield, Pennsylvania, to look at a ballplayer named Wagner—Al, a brother of Honus. He found out that the bloods of the town were down by the railroad track having a "stone throw." Honus—or John Peter Wagner, as he was known in those days—was throwing stones with such vim, vigor and vitality that Barrow decided he had come upon a natural. He forgot all about Al and signed Honus.

Barrow at the time was running the Paterson, New Jersey, Club in the Atlantic League. He had Wagner finish out the season with Warren, Pennsylvania, in the Iron and Oil League and brought him to Paterson in 1896. Barrow sold him to Barney Dreyfuss of the Louisville club the next season for $2,200. Louisville was then in the National League and remained in the league until the franchise was transferred to Pittsburgh in 1900.

With all of his physical assets, Wagner also was blessed with the perfect temperament for a ballplayer. He was neither a hothead nor a loafer, just a stolid, easygoing German who loved to play ball and could play it superbly. And he played it in the National League for twenty years, always with the same club.

When, after an absence of sixteen years, Wagner returned to the Pirates as coach in 1933, they had a parade and a banquet for him, plus a civic reception in, of all places, Brooklyn! The banquet was held in Coney Island, at the Half Moon Hotel, and among the speakers was the minister who had taught Honus in Sunday school. After the banquet broke up, I found Wagner munching a hot dog at a sidewalk stand on Surf Avenue. It seemed that the guest of honor had been so busy signing autographs that he hadn't had time to eat at the banquet!

Wagner, of course, wasn't the only man on

* This piece was written in 1948. Since then, thanks in the main to Stan Musial, Wagner no longer leads all these categories.—Ed.

that 1909 Pirate team. It was managed by Fred Clarke, an outfielder whom Barrow, the discoverer of Wagner, considered the finest competitive ballplayer he had ever seen. And Barrow saw plenty of Ty Cobb, remember. Clarke managed Wagner at Louisville and had Honus playing for him in all the fifteen years he managed the Pirates. Clarke won four pennants for the Pirates, finished second five times, and was in the second division only twice.

Clarke was a kid delivering papers in Des Moines, Iowa, when Barrow, circulation manager of the paper, first saw him. Ed liked his aggressiveness then, liked it even more when Fred turned to baseball. It was because of this friendship that Barrow sold Wagner to Dreyfuss. Big-league clubs were after the Flying Dutchman and Barrow wanted him to go to a man whom he admired.

Clarke was a playing manager, a left fielder, and he had an average of .315 for a career that spanned twenty-one seasons. Fast, he was not only a good defensive outfielder but a distinct threat on the bases. Twice he stole sixty bases and eight times he stole thirty or better. Fred was considered one of the real inspirational managers of all time, a scrappy, aggressive pilot and a topflight ballplayer as well.

A decade after he had left the Pirates, to become a prosperous rancher in Winfield, Kansas, Clarke came back to sit on the bench in 1926. The Bucs, after winning the World Series in 1925, were torn by internal dissension and Fred was requested to come back "and straighten out the boys." The boys resented Clarke's return, for ballplayers of the present have little regard or respect for those of the past. Yet even then Clarke, mellowed by age and softened by prosperity, spoke with the voice of authority, the crisp incisiveness of the born leader.

Clarke won pennants with the Pirates in 1901, 1902 and 1903—but then the Giants of John McGraw and the Cubs of Frank Chance began muscling in on his territory. It was six years before he was able to knock off the Cubs in 1909, breaking what would have been a run of five straight pennants for Chance, who had won for Chicago in 1906, 1907 and 1908 and was to win again in 1910.

In the outfield with Clarke on the 1909 Pirates was Tommy Leach, a speedy fly chaser but not a .300 hitter, and Chief Wilson. Clarke was the only left-handed hitter among them. Leach occasionally went to third, a ... which Clarke used several player... Bobby Byrne had the positi... the time the World Series came around. John (Dots) Miller played second and Bill Abstein was the first baseman. Bill was a classy fielder but a weak hitter, and when he fanned nine times in the World Series, Owner Dreyfus fired him.

George Gibson, who years later was to be a Pirate manager himself, did virtually all of the Pittsburgh catching. A good, sound receiver, Gibbie handled pitchers well.

Although the pitching leader of the Pirates that season was Howie Camnitz, who won twenty-five games and lost six, Clarke came up with a real sensation in Babe Adams, a freshman. Adams, a big, stalwart right-hander, was as good a control pitcher as the game ever knew. In this first year as a regular, Babe walked only twenty-three men in 130 innings. Just twenty-one when he became a regular, Adams was pitching winning ball for the Pirates when he was almost forty.

In addition to Camnitz and Adams, Clarke had Vic Willis, 22-game winner, Lefty Leifield, who won nineteen, and Nick Maddox, a right-hander who won thirteen. Deacon Phillippe, who was born at the marvelously named hamlet of Rural Retreat, Virginia, but began pitching in Minnesota, was near the end of the string now but managed to win eight games while losing three. In the very first World Series ever played, in 1903, the Deacon won three games for the Pirates and lost two.

Pittsburgh opened the 1909 campaign with a 1–0 victory over the Cubs, the team it had to beat for the pennant, but then slumped and hit the cellar in late April. A week later the Pirates were in front again and they stayed there for the entire pennant race! It was not, however, a romp, for Chance's Cubs breathed heatedly on the necks of the Bucs from start to finish. The Peerless Leader was fighting for his fourth straight pennant and made quite a battle of it. Chicago won 104 games, yet lost the pennant by a margin of six and a half games.

Followers of the Pirates were certain ... was going to be a big season whe... won a doubleheader from the ... cago on May 2. It was ... one of the historian... "the first time t... way of sh... boys ...

season. The Memorial Day holiday was celebrated with morning and afternoon games, and Adams, going to the relief of Phillippe in the morning game, received credit for winning it. With a short break for lunch, Babe came back and went all the way in the afternoon game, winning that, too!

It was here that the Pirates got really rolling. They reeled off fourteen straight victories before Christy Mathewson and the Giants stopped them on June 16. About six weeks later, the Pirates repaid that stumble by beating Matty, 3 to 0, after he had won thirteen straight. Nick Maddox pitched that one.

One of the big events in 1909 was the formal opening of beautiful Forbes Field, in the heart of Schenley Park. The ball park was called a million-dollar plant even then, and there is no telling what it would cost now. Two-tiered ball parks were considered real snazzy then, but Barney Dreyfus built three tiers, although the top deck contained only box seats.

No ball park in the majors has as pretty a background as Forbes Field, which, incidentally, was named after the British general who founded the town in pre-Revolutionary times. The rolling hills of Schenley Park stretch behind the right- and center-field fences, while to the left may be seen the Carnegie Museum, the University of Pittsburgh's Cathedral of Learning and some of the buildings of Carnegie Tech.

Dreyfuss was proud of his park, and no advertisement ever marred the blue-black of his fences, save during World War I when he permitted the painting of a legend on the left-field fence recommending that the patrons buy war bonds and war savings stamps. Years afterward, when it rained, the tracing of the letters would gleam through the glistening fence.

Forbes Field was dedicated on June 30 before a remarkable crowd of 30,338, but the holiday was marred no little by the thoughtlessness of Ed Reulbach of the Cubs, who beat Willis and the Pirates by 3 to 2. Crowds of over 30,000 were remarkable in this day, but these Pirates of Clarke were drawing everywhere. They attracted a crowd of 30,600 to the Polo Grounds for a weekday doubleheader on July 9. And beat the Giants both games, too.

In addition to the dedication of Forbes [illegible] there were a couple of other unusual [illegible] Pirates in 1909. On May 20 in [illegible] Wagner who remembered the bowlegged, hawk-nosed Honus from the days when he had played in Paterson, presented a loving cup to him. And friends of Dots Miller, Wagner's partner in the Bucco keystone combination, having no desire to be outdone, gave a diamond ring to Dots.

Clarke, who was nearing the end of the trail as a regular, made news of an unusual sort when he apologized publicly for a criticism he had made of members of the National Commission for the ruling they made on a protested game involving Pittsburgh. It was unlike the fiery Fred to be apologetic to anybody, even the National Commission, the body then holding the powers later to be vested in Kenesaw Mountain Landis and A. B. Chandler. Clarke worded his apology in masterful prose.

"When I protested the ruling of the National Commission, I had no intention of impugning the honesty, integrity, or intelligence of the members of the commission," said Clarke. "I just didn't like their decision."

It was in 1909, too, that Red John Murray, Giant outfielder, made a catch at Forbes Field considered by those who saw it to be the most spectacular ever made. There is no gainsaying that it is difficult to evaluate defensive plays in baseball. Hits can be measured in terms of distance or in terms of the runs they bring in or the circumstances under which they are made.

Not many saw the catch Red Murray made against the Pirates, for it was merely a Monday afternoon at Forbes Field. Those who did, however, could still describe it thirty years later. The Giants and Bucs were tied, 2 to 2, in the last of the eighth, there were two out and two on. One of those sudden August thunderstorms had come out of the Alleghenies to darken the field. The rain had not yet fallen, but it was only a matter of minutes, or even of seconds.

The ballplayers were scarcely distinguishable on the field below. Crack! A ball sailed into right center, driven by Tommy Leach. It was seemingly an extra base hit, judging by the sound, for by now none could follow the ball or the players. Suddenly there was a great flash of lightning, which illuminated all of the vast reaches of Forbes Field in an eerie, white light. It did more than that—it virtually spotlighted Murray leaping in the air to make a one-handed stab of the ball high above his head. On the heels of the flash, almost instantly, came the reverberating roar of a mighty thunderclap and the field and the athletes were swallowed in an inky darkness, while the heavens opened and the rain cascaded down. The game, of course, never was resumed, and it remained a 2–2 tie, while Murray's catch remained an anecdotal tidbit, ever treasured by those who had seen it.

The late Sid Mercer, one of the charter members of the Baseball Writers Association, told me that for some time after, traveling on the Pullmans, the Giants would douse all the lights and somebody would strike a match to reveal Murray posed, tableaulike, in the position in which he had made the sensational catch.

Although the Cubs kept doggedly in pursuit of the Pirates, it was no dice, even though Chance's team won 104 games, five more than had sufficed to bring the 1908 championship to Chicago.

Wagner was the only .300 hitter on the club when the year was over, leading the National League with a mark of .339. Yet this was a team of great deeds on the basepaths. Honus bow-legged his way around the bases to steal thirty-five times. The gritty Clarke, now a veteran of thirty-eight years, stole thirty-one bases, while Tommy Leach bagged twenty-seven and Chief Wilson seventeen, a total of seventy-five stolen bases for the three regular outfielders alone.

When Hughie Jennings brought his Tigers, and Cobb, into Forbes Field to open the World Series, he received a double surprise. One was that Clarke elected to start with his freshman ace, Babe Adams. The other surprise was that the youngster tamed the Tigers rather easily, holding them to one run and five singles. The lone Detroit tally came in the first inning.

There was great interest among the fans over the expected duel of the stars, Wagner and Ty Cobb, who had led the American League in batting with .377. It was the first time in World Series history that the two league batting champions faced each other in the fall classic, and it has happened only once since in all the intervening years. Cobb went hitless against Adams, although Leach made a great running catch on him with two on in the seventh, depriving Ty of what might have been a homer. Honus made one hit, a double, which led up to the final Pittsburgh tally.

Adams treated Cobb with respect in the first inning and walked him, the Georgia Peach eventually bringing home the only run the Tigers were destined to get against Babe that day. Clarke, who had hit only three home runs in the entire season, tied the score in the fourth by belting one into the right-field seats against George Mullin, who had won twenty-nine games during the season for Detroit. In the end, however, it was Mullin's defenses which betrayed him, for the Tigers made four errors, including one by Cobb.

Since the Tigers had won pennants in 1907 and 1908, this opening game at Forbes Field was their eleventh World Series appearance under Jennings, and all Hughey had to show for the eleven games was one tie against the Cubs in the opener of the 1907 Series, a twelve-inning game, and one victory over the Cubs in the third game of the 1908 set. It was getting rather monotonous.

In an effort to do something about it, Jennings pitched Wild Bill Donovan in the second game in Pittsburgh. Bill had been plagued all season with a sore arm, but Wild William was ready for this one. The Bucs climbed all over Bill for two runs in the first inning, but after that he slammed the door on them. A walk to Bobby Byrne and doubles by Leach and Dots Miller gave the Pirates two in the first, but Donovan held them to three hits for the balance of the game.

Meanwhile the Tigers were most familiar with Howie Camnitz, Clarke's 25-game winner. He finally was chased in the third and relieved by Vic Willis. Cobb gave Willis something to remember him by. While Vic was deciding upon how to pitch to George Moriarty, Ty stole home. It was Charley Schmidt, the Detroit catcher, who did most of the flailing in this game, getting two singles in the clutch which knocked in four runs as Donovan triumphed by 7 to 2.

The shift from Forbes Field to Bennett Park in Detroit was startling in more ways than one. The attendance in Pittsburgh had averaged 30,000 and the weather had been of an Indian-summer salubrity. It had rained the night before and in the aftermath of the storm blistering gales had come down the Michigan peninsula. Only 18,277 braved the elements to see a sloppy ball game in which Nick Maddox staggered home ahead of a trio of Detroit pitchers by a score of 8 to 6. Ed Summers, who started for the Tigers, was knocked out in the first inning, while the Buccos were piling up five runs.

Despite the looseness of play, Wagner and Cobb both had good days in the third game. Honus made three hits and stole three bases while Cobb, with a single and a double, knocked in half of Detroit's six runs and made a fine running catch of Dots Miller's texas leaguer in short center.

As a footnote to the weather conditions in

Detroit, it should be mentioned that Bill Klem, National League umpire, wore an overcoat. Even more remarkable was the behavior of Dr. Frederick A. Cook, a self-styled polar explorer from Brooklyn who had reportedly just returned from a successful voyage to the North Pole. Dr. Cook was one of the personages who graced the game with his presence, but the alleged Arctic adventurer left halfway through the game. "Too cold," he explained. It may have been his lack of ruggedness this day at Bennett Park which set in motion the machinery that was later to expose him as a charlatan who had never reached the Pole at all.

It was even colder for the fourth game, but George Mullin warmed the Tiger fans with a 5–0 shutout which evened the Series once more. Lefty Leifield started but was lifted for a pinch hitter after Detroit had scored all its runs. Deacon Phillippe, the hero of the 1903 Series, finished for Pittsburgh, pitching four scoreless innings and allowing only one hit, a single by Moriarty.

The cold weather apparently followed the athletes to Pittsburgh, but it didn't chill young Adams, for Babe won his second game of the Series, beating Ed Summers 8 to 4. There were three home runs in this game, two by the Tigers, Davy Jones and Wahoo Sam Crawford, but the payoff home run was a belt by Clarke, his second of the Series. It came in the seventh with two on and broke a 3–3 tie, setting up the ball game for the Pirates.

Back went the Series to Detroit for the sixth game, and this time the freezing temperatures kept the crowd down to 10,535 persons. George Mullin started for Detroit and it looked as though the Pirates were all set to become World's Champions when they tore into Mullin for three runs, a two-bagger by Wagner being the key blow. Vic Willis couldn't stand either the icy blasts or the Tiger bats and eventually bowed out, by which time Detroit had gone ahead 4 to 3. Howie Camnitz came in and yielded another run.

It was in the ninth that the Bucs came to life. Dots Miller and Bill Abstein opened with singles, and on Wilson's bunt Schmidt, the Detroit catcher, threw poorly to Tom Jones at first. Miller scored on the error, Abstein reached third and Wilson second. With none out, the Pirates were in a position where they could take the lead on a single and doubtless the championship as well.

Mullin saw to it that the single wasn't forthcoming, aided and abetted by strange base running on the part of the Pirates. To complicate the situation for Mullin, Jones at first had been injured in the tangle when Schmidt threw badly and Crawford came in from center to take his place, with Davy Jones moving from left to center and McIntyre coming in as the left fielder.

Crawford hardly got the first baseman's mitt on when he had a play coming up. Gibson hit to him and Sam threw out Abstein at the plate, Wilson holding second. Clarke sent up Ed Abbaticchio to bat for Phillippe. Ed fanned and Wilson was doubled up trying to steal third on the play, ending the ball game.

After this disappointment, Clarke went back to his first love again, the youngster Adams. Babe went against the Tigers and the veteran Donovan in the seventh game and brought home the bacon in the best of all possible ways, with a shutout. And a convincing 8–0 shutout, at that.

Donovan was wild and the Tiger pitchers who followed him were no better. Meanwhile, Adams was the boss man. He walked only one and held what was considered the best hitting team in baseball at the time to six scattered hits.

While Adams with his three victories was, of course, the pitching hero of the Series, all the more so because he was not a big winner during the season, it was, in the long run, a team victory for the Pirates. They ran wild on Jennings' catchers, Charley Schmidt and Oscar Stanage, stealing eighteen bases. And although Wagner and Leach were the only Pirates to hit .300, manager Clarke had delivered two home runs where they would do the most good. The mighty Cobb was held to a .231 average, and only Jim Delahanty, the second baseman, of all the Tiger sluggers, reached the .300 class against Pittsburgh pitching.

It was, for the Flying Dutchman, for the fiercely competitive Clarke and for all of the others of that gallant Pirate crew, the last World Series, the end of an era. Of them all, only Babe Adams was to be still active when the Pirates got into a World Series again, sixteen years later.

Pittsburgh fans can always look back on 1909 with fond recollections. It was the year that Forbes Field was opened and the year that the Pirates gave them something to fly from the flagpole—a World's Championship banner.

WHEN *The Saturday Evening Post* reprinted extracts from *The Glory of Their Times,* it used this condensed version of the piece by one of the authentic old-time greats, a Cahuilla Indian named Chief Meyers. He was in his mid-eighties when Lawrence Ritter taped his observations—and just as sharp as when he caught for the Giants in the World Series of 1912.

"I Am Like an Old Hemlock"

CHIEF MEYERS

YOU KNOW, those fellows back there, they *thought,* they used their head in baseball a whole lot. They talked baseball morning, noon, and night. Baseball was their whole life. We had old pitchers, like Joe McGinnity, who'd go out and pitch two games in an afternoon. Pitch a doubleheader! He did that a number of times.

Nowadays the pitcher wastes so much time out there it's ridiculous—fixing his cap . . . pulling up his pants . . . rubbing his chin . . . wiping his brow . . . pulling his nose . . . scratching the ground with his feet. And after he does all that, he looks all around at the outfield, and then he st-a-a-a-res in at the catcher giving the sign. Why, he's afraid to throw the darned ball! And with this modern jackrabbit ball, I don't know as I blame him.

They waste an hour or so every day that way. We *always* played a game in less than two hours. Never longer. Two hours used to be considered a long game, really a long game. We played a lot of games in an hour and a half. I played in one that took only 58 minutes. Nowadays, a three-hour game isn't at all unusual.

I'm not saying anything disparaging about the athletes of today. They're just as good and just as fast now as they ever were. In fact I think they're faster. But they've got so much to work with that we didn't have. The equipment, for instance. Our gloves were like a motorman's mitt. Now they're similar to a lacrosse net. You just catch the ball in the net.

Another big difference between today and yesterday is that the ballplayers are all businessmen now. They've got agents and outside interests and all that sort of thing. We played for money too. Naturally. That's how we made our living. But mostly we played just for the love of it. Heck, most of us would have paid *them* just to let us play. We loved baseball.

I don't blame the modern players for making it while the making's good. I'm not belittling them. Why wouldn't they get the money? We never got it. I guess in a way we were just dumb eggs. We played for practically nothing. My top was about $6,000. Matty never made more than about $8,000. Well—that's the way it was then.

The world seems to be turned all upside down today. Progress, they call it. The radio and the television and all, brainwashing the children and teaching them to cheat and steal and kill. Always violence and killing. I think it's an awful bad example for the youngsters. Why can't they teach people about the good things of life instead?

In the old days, you know, a shake of your hand was your word and your honor. In those days, if anything was honest and upright, we'd say it was "on the square." Nowadays they've even turned that word around: Now it means you don't belong, you're nothing. "Square deal" is no more. You're a "square." Where do they get that stuff, anyhow? It just doesn't make sense—at least not to me, it doesn't.

I guess I'm like the old warrior chief of the great Six Nations, who announced his retirement by saying, "I am like an old hemlock. My head is still high, but the winds of close to a hundred winters have whistled through my branches, and I have been witness to many wondrous and many tragic things. My eyes perceive the present, but my roots are imbedded deeply in the grandeur of the past."

FOR THE average fan, this system of scorekeeping is the best we have seen, combining as it does a thorough and graphic picture of what goes on together with a pleasing simplicity.

How to Keep Score

D. J. MICHAEL

YOU CAN CALL this the "typewriter" method of keeping score at a ball game—simply because the only characters and symbols needed are all to be found on a typewriter keyboard. (That doesn't mean you have to take a typewriter to the park with you, and if you want to add a few extra symbols of your own, we'll suggest a few here. But the idea is, this is supposed to be easy to learn, not hard.)

The standard way of numbering positions is used: 1—pitcher; 2—catcher; 3—first baseman; 4—second baseman; 5—third baseman; 6—shortstop; 7—left fielder; 8—center fielder; 9—right fielder.

We will use numbers for other purposes too. A raised "2" or "3" will indicate second or third base, and ordinary numerals (always followed by letters) will indicate hits, so that 1C is a single to center, 2LC is a double to left center, 1 followed by a little 4 would indicate that the batter beat out a grounder to the second baseman for a hit, 3R would be a triple to right, HR and a lower-case "r" would be a home run to right.

We can tell at a glance if our use of numbers is being used to show defensive or offensive information, because on defensive plays, and only on defensive plays, we use hyphens. Therefore, 6-3 means the hitter grounded out, short to first. 0-3 means he grounded out to the first baseman unassisted. F-7 means he flied out to left. L-5 means he lined out to the shortstop. 1-6-3, unless in a double-play situation, which we will describe in a few moments, would mean he grounded one off the pitcher's glove, the shortstop picked it up, and threw him out, with the pitcher also receiving credit for an assist. Thus a batter whose box reads 2R, followed immediately by a small 9-4-5, would be one who doubled to right field and was thrown out trying to stretch it to a triple, right fielder to second baseman to third baseman.

If the same play read 2RE9, we would know it was a double to right with the hitter advancing to third when the right fielder messed up the ball for an error. If the same play read 2R followed by 9-4-E5, we would know he got to third when the third baseman dropped the relay throw for an error.

An exclamation point following a fielder's number shows an outstanding play. A lower-case "r" indicates a running catch. You can also use arrows pointing up or down to show if a hit or a catch was very deep or very short. And you can put a little flag on your "F," so it looks like a sixteenth note in music, to indicate a fly ball that was caught in foul territory.

Pick-off or rundown plays are indicated just the way you'd expect, with a small series of numbers, connected by hyphens, to show who handled the ball.

To show a run scored we use a heavy dot (•). To show a run batted in we show a little circle (o). Thus, a grand-slam home run to left would be: $\mathrm{HRL}^{\mathrm{oo}}_{\mathrm{oo}}$•. Or, if we saw $1\mathrm{C}^{\mathrm{o2t}}$, we would know that the hitter singled to center to drive in a run and took second on the throw to the plate (2t).

A strikeout is known as a "K," and since the catcher always gets the put-out (unless he drops the third strike and has to throw the man out at first), we record it as K-2. If it was a swinging third strike, we make it K-2s.

The letter "s" has various meanings too, readily distinguishable in context. It can indicate a steal, as in W^{s2}, meaning the hitter walked, then stole second. F-7s^{o} would indicate a sacrifice fly to left. 2-4s would be a bunt sacrifice, with the hitter being retired, catcher to the second baseman covering first.

Raised hyphen-connected numbers *before* the play is annotated indicate the count on the hitter at the time. Thus $^{3\text{-}0}$2C indicates the batter doubled to center on a 3-and-0 pitch. We use these only to indicate an unusual count.

Any batter's performance that results in an out at some other base while he (the batter) is safe at first is indicated by the use of an "x." This accounts both for force and non-force plays. Say there's a man on first and the hitter forces him at second, shortstop to second baseman. Show this by putting 6-4x in the hitter's box. Or say with a man on second the hitter bounces back to the pitcher, and the pitcher gets the base runner at third. The use of 1-5x will show that. If the pitcher on the same play elected to go to third and wound up getting nobody, then put FC$_1$, meaning a fielder's choice on the ball back to the pitcher.

That FC$_1$ indicates routinely that the man on second advanced one base to third. If on the other hand he had held up at second and still no play was made anywhere, we'd show FC$_1$#, the last symbol indicating that the ordinarily expected advance did not occur. We also use the symbol "#" after a hitter has reached base to show that he was replaced by a pinch runner. Thus W#$^{s2\bullet}$ would mean that Jones walked, Smith went in to run for him, and it was Smith, not Jones, who stole second and went on to score the run.

The use of the symbol "#" *before* a man's performance is recorded means that, while not a starter, he was already in the game when he came to bat for the first time.

Two uses also are made for the symbol "/." If it appears before a hitter's performance, it indicates a pinch hitter. If used after, it indicates that a runner moved up an extra base on what the hitter did. Thus /L-8 means a pinch hitter came up and lined out to the center fielder. But L-8/ means the hitter lined out to the center fielder with a base runner moving up after the catch. 1C/ is a single to center that sends the runner on first around to third. (A similar notation is not needed if the runner scores from second on a single, since the "o" for a run batted in will show that.) o-3/ would show the hitter grounding out to first unassisted while another base runner moves up.

An extraordinary, but wholly plausible, notation might be //o-3// which would show the following: With men on first and second, a pinch hitter was announced, then recalled and replaced by a second pinch hitter, who grounded out to first while both base runners advanced.

One thing a typewriter can't do is draw a circle, but you and I can do that. A circle around a "W," for instance, indicates an intentional walk. Or, in the notation 4-5x$^{2\text{-}4}$, you might circle the "2-4" to separate it from the other numbers. In the above example, our hitter reached first safely on an out at another base, then was out stealing, catcher to second baseman.

In recording errors, we always use the capital letter E, followed if you wish by a lowercase "f," "t" or "g" to show whether the error was on a muffed fly, a throw, or a grounder. If a man makes two errors on the same play, show it as E5E5; if the first error got the hitter to first and the second got him all the way to third, show it as E5E5^{3}, the little "3" at the end showing he wound up on third base.

Double plays are indicated by underlining. Remember the illustration we gave above, of 1-6-3 showing a ball off the pitcher's glove that the shortstop picked up and threw to first for the out? Well, with a man on first, if the play showed as 1-6-3, it would indicate a double play, pitcher to short to first. If it showed as 1-6-3/ it would mean they tried for the man at second, missed him, but still were in time to get the hitter at first, with the last symbol showing that the base runner moved up.

Pitching notations include "WP" and "BK" for wild pitch and balk, just as "PB" means a passed ball charged to the catcher. Advances for men on base at the time such things happen should be shown by a little number (either "2" for second, "3" for third, or "•" for home) connected by a curving arrow to the "PB" or "WP" or whatever in the hitter's box to show the moment and the reason the advance occurred.

A change in pitchers is shown by *double underlining* in between hitters' boxes. (We prefer to use a long line for a double play, and two short lines: = for a change of pitchers. With reference to a double play, incidentally, it is seldom necessary to show an extra number to denote both a put-out and an assist for the same man. L-4-6 shows a line drive to the second baseman who then tossed to the shortstop for the second out before the runner could get back to second. L-4 all by itself shows the second baseman caught the liner, then ran and touched second himself for the double play. The notation 6-3 means the hitter was out short to first; 6-3 means he grounded into a double play, the shortstop stepping on second, then throwing to first.)

In writing out the lineups to begin with, we like to use standard abbreviations, rather than numbers, for positions—Jones, ss; Hall, cf; etc. In recording substitutions as the game goes on, we continue this:

Jones, ss
Wilson B5 rf6
Archer R7 3b8
Vincent B9
Kelly 3b10

That unusual example puts together most of what can happen. Jones started the game at shortstop. Wilson batted for him in the fifth and went to right field in the sixth. Archer went in to run for Wilson after the latter reached base in the seventh, then went in to play third base in the eighth. Vincent batted in the ninth. Kelly went in to play third in the tenth. (If you run out of space, put the extra names at the bottom and connect them with outside borderlines to the right spot in the order.)

(Note, you can tell from this that we're talking about the home team! If it were the visiting team, Wilson's line would read "B5 rf5" and Archer's "R7 3b7," since the same inning would still be going on when they went into the field.)

At the bottom of each inning column, we put four numbers—0000, 0101, 3521, or whatever—to indicate, in order, runs scored, hits, errors, and men left on base.

We could give a few typical innings here, but would prefer not to do so, because the temptation would be to crowd in all various possibilities and thus make the scorecard look overwhelmingly complicated. Which is exactly what is *not* the point, for of all the complete scorekeeping systems we know, this is the least complicated and easiest to learn.

In this book, see, this millionaire hotelman dies and leaves all his property to the Soviet Union. All his property just happens to include the Chicago White Sox.

From *A Pennant for the Kremlin*

PAUL MOLLOY

People often told Bratton they wondered why he didn't have an ulcer. The wonderment came from regular visitors to Comiskey Park in Chicago. Watching the destinies of the unpredictable White Sox, so adroit at squeaking through one-run victories and blowing five-run leads, was often an ulcerous hazard, and the afflicted marveled at Bratton's composure under duress. Bratton loved to tip his ever-present dark glasses to the top of his head and explain that he once had an ulcer but it was located in his left arm. And he had left that arm near Mount Cassino long ago.

His philosophy was that he had enough things on his mind without cluttering it up with worry.

But the thing on his mind this moist Sunday afternoon in Yankee Stadium was responsible for the fresh teeth marks in the temples of his glasses. He wasn't worried—yet—but he was in meditation. Not about the Yankees winning the first game of the doubleheader; not about the off-and-on rain that had already delayed the second game twice; not even about Mrs. Bratton who got lonely when he went on the road and shortened the waiting with long afternoons in the movie houses, trying to overcome her depression.

He was concerned with last night's first encounter with Mikhail Deborin. The Russian had been businesslike and gentlemanly (though he could understand why Beadle had swung at Bukharov), but to learn that he was no longer team manager was upsetting. At least, it didn't look as if he would remain in charge. What Deborin had said was that he would take over as chairman of the club, and Bratton would become its deputy chairman. As far as Bratton was concerned, the title was almost obscene, and in the locker room he had warned the players—a man can't be placid all the time—that the first one to call him deputy chairman would be fined a hundred dollars.

Aware that Deborin didn't know the first catechism of baseball, Bratton was fairly sure he would at least be calling the shots on the field. But a fact was a fact: after nine years as boss, he was now a second banana.

With the fifth inning out of the way, Bratton was surprised to see Deborin, buttoned up to the neck in a raincoat, walk into the dugout. But the shocker was to see Bukharov follow him in.

Frequently during the first game the mammoth crowd had kept up a clamorous, handclapping we-want-Deborin cry in the stands. The fans were curious to see the foreigner sent from Moscow to manage the colorful Sox. Eventually they assumed he was not yet ready (or he was afraid) to make his public debut, and the din had subsided. Now Bratton hoped his visitors would stay inside the dugout and not venture onto the field.

"We have some points?" Deborin asked, looking about for a seat on the bench.

The Sox had just been retired in order. "No," Bratton said, "it's nothing to nothing."

"That is good," said Bukharov, motioning to the bat boy to give him his seat. "Then nothing has happened that we should have seen." Several players looked at each other in mute disbelief. "I wouldn't say that," Bratton said. "We lost the first game."

"I was all afternoon in your museum," Deborin explained. "It is very beautiful, all those paintings. Tasia, she is still there."

"That's nice," Bratton said, irked at the Yankees' first run on a walk and two successive hits. "They've just gone ahead."

"We must equal our opponents," said Deborin, noticing a new stampede of clouds. "But it is sad that the clubs engage themselves in such a climate."

"There are seventy-five thousand people out there," Bratton said, "and a little rain doesn't bother them."

The Sox came to bat at the top of the seventh and Bratton was seized with a small elation when Beadle led off the inning with a walk. It soon subsided, however, for the next man struck out and the third was retired on an infield popout. Adding to the gloom was Deborin's poorly timed curiosity about the club's financial condition. He kept distracting Bratton with questions about player salaries, pay increases and bonuses (which he called production incentives). Suddenly, while Deborin was asking about travel expenses, Bukharov grabbed his arm and whispered hurriedly in his ear.

Deborin glared at home plate. "That man!" he shouted. "Call him back!"

"Who?" Bratton asked.

"That man with the stick!" Deborin said, pointing excitedly to the batter. "At once call him to me!"

Bratton bounded up the dugout steps, called time out and motioned to Salvatore Castinez, his shortstop who was digging in at the plate. Castinez, a Puerto Rican in his second year with the Sox, shrugged his massive shoulders and walked slowly back to the dugout.

"This is Sal Castinez," Bratton said. "He's one of my good hitters. What's the big idea?"

"What did you do?" Deborin asked, his nostrils a-quiver.

Castinez tapped a chunk of mud off his cleats "Who? Me?"

"You!"

"When?"

"When you go to your position. What did you do?"

"I didn't do nothin'," Castinez said nonchalantly. "What d'you mean?"

"You did like this," Deborin yelled, his hand flying to his head and then to his chest.

"Oh, that," Bratton laughed. "He was making the sign of the cross."

"Aha!" Bukharov said in Deborin's ear, but this time out loud. "The sign of the cross. As I told you!"

"This will stop," Deborin said. "You will not do that. Never!"

"Just a minute," Bratton said. "What's wrong with his making the sign of the cross?"

"I forbid. No more."

"Oh, come on, now. It's something he likes to do when he comes up to bat."

Deborin fixed Bratton in his dark glasses. "Tell me, my friend, what does it mean?"

Bratton stuck his hand in his back pocket, and thought for a moment. "Well, to be honest, it doesn't mean a damn thing if he can't hit."

"Of course," Bukharov said, lurking behind Deborin.

The plate umpire, holding a soggy protector away from his chest, marched up to the dugout as the rhythmic hand-clapping started up again. "What's going on here?" he demanded. "Get a batter up there and make it fast!"

Bratton patted Castinez on the rump and nodded toward the plate.

"Do not forget," Deborin said as Castinez left, "no cross." He turned to Bratton. "This is a place for the contest of athletes," he said. "This is not a church place. I am not permitting such things when I am chairman of the club."

Bratton idly wondered what Deborin would say if he learned that the Yankee land they were standing on, all six acres of it, was owned by the Knights of Columbus. "I can't see that it hurts anything," he said.

Ignominiously, Castinez struck out.

Deborin spoke almost with relish. "I do not see that it is helping," he said.

"Christian superstition," Bukharov muttered, getting back to his seat.

The Yankees held on to their one-run lead until the top of the ninth when the Sox put a man on first. Beadle flied out, and again it was Castinez's turn at bat. This time he made no outward gesture as he reached the plate but, unnoticed, he traced a tiny cross in the wet sand with the end of his bat. On the first pitch, his huge shoulders seemed to shudder as the bat swung on a low, inside throw and the ball soared in a mighty arc and struck below the lip of the left-field fence, three hundred and ten feet away.

Deborin was on his feet. "You see!" he shouted, as the base runner galloped home from first. "You see what he does without your stupid sign of the cross!"

Castinez, a grin cracking his somber mulatto face, looked like a black gazelle as he bounded to third standing up. But his triumph was brief. Slapping his glove urgently, the Yankee second baseman called for the ball, caught it and smugly stood on the bag. The umpire's arm shot out as if to detach the hand. "Runner is *OUT!*" he bawled.

Castinez was downcast when he stepped into the dugout. 'I thought I touched the base," he said. "It was all this mud, on my shoes."

Bratton smiled and put his arm over Castinez's shoulder. "You crazy Catholic," he said in a low tone. "But anyway, you tied it up."

The game went into extra innings and if Bratton had any doubt about Deborin's acquaintance with the game, they were dispelled in the top of the eleventh. Ken Powers, who had gone hitless in the first game and got on base in the second only through a Yankee error, banished one ball from the game forever. Quite possibly unseamed, it hurtled over the towering fence as if determined to try for the Harlem River while Deborin put his hands to his head, groaned and gave the bench a vigorous kick.

Seeing him, Bukharov groaned too, and uttered a Russian curse as the players stared in awed admiration at Powers, and Bratton hustled out of the dugout to greet him. Beadle opened his mouth to free a whoop but stopped at the sight of the Russians.

"You guys crazy?" he said.

"Such excellence of striking the ball," Deborin sighed, "and all wasted."

"What d'you mean, wasted?"

"The ball—it has vanished."

"For God's sakes, we got a homer! We won the game!"

Deborin watched the players file out to shake Powers' hand. "We have made the point?"

"Even when the ball is gone?" Bukharov asked.

"Oh, brother," Beadle said. "It's a home run! We beat 'em, don't you understand, we win!"

Beadle started to unbutton his shirt. "By the way," he said, "how's your daughter?" Deborin just glared at him, and said nothing.

When Bratton returned from the showers, Deborin and Bukharov were waiting near his locker. He noticed that for the first time since his arrival Bukharov, though still unsmiling, looked a little less unpleasant. Bratton himself was in good spirits for the Sox had split the four-game series while Cleveland was routing Detroit. Now the Sox were in sole possession of third place, six games from the Yankees and three behind the second-place Baltimore Orioles; but Detroit had fallen to fourth, seven games behind the pace.

"Tonight," Deborin said, "we have a meeting in your hotel, after supper."

"Another conference?" Bratton said, slipping into his trousers.

"You will teach me tonight the sport of baseball. I wish to know everything."

Bratton buckled his belt and smiled. "I've been in it a long time, and I'm still learning. You want to learn it all in one night?"

"There is not much time. We must proceed with quickness."

"All right. I'll do the best I can."

"You will find me a good student. Your Mr. Dewar, he will bring to me the cards from the gums. I will study them much and bring them to the meeting."

Bratton had heard of the cards. "I meant to tell you about that," he said. "You won't need them. I've copied all the information down in a special book I keep. It's a lot simpler than carrying all those cards around."

"That is good. You are much alert, like a true deputy chairman."

As they were leaving, Bratton said, "I would appreciate it, Mr. Deborin, if we could skip that deputy chairman business."

"Your title, you do not like it?"

"Well, it doesn't sound right for baseball."

"You would prefer foreman?"

"Hell, no."

"Shop controller?"

"That's not what I had in mind."

"I suggest, then, collective planner?"

"That isn't it, either. You see—"

"I have it! Supervisor of the personnel."

"You don't understand. I figure—"

"Mr. Bratton, you must find a title and then like it. I would say, then, director of production."

"No. All that stuff's okay in your factories back home. But this is a baseball team."

"Then I wait your thought."

"I think assistant manager would be all right."

"Assistant manager, hmmm. . . . Then I am the manager, yes?"

"Yes, Mr. Deborin," Bratton said. "You're the manager."

Bratton hadn't really minded the idea of a meeting in his room. The team had a Monday layover, anyway, before opening in Baltimore for the windup of the road trip.

He wondered, though, if Deborin ever went anywhere alone. At the game, this afternoon, he had brought Bukharov with him (or had Bukharov brought him?). He had him in tow again tonight. And Ambassador Galynin was along, too. And so was Tasia.

But he was grateful for Tasia's presence. With all those dour Russian faces around, it was a relief to have a pretty girl in the group. He sneaked the quick, practiced look of the middle-aged male at her legs, as she sat, and decided they were just the way he liked legs.

He was pleased, too, that Mike Dewar was on hand. Good old Dewar, who had thought of the blackboard to illustrate the bull session and ordered vodka to soothe the Soviet breast.

Deborin lost no time proposing a toast. "I drink to our glorious union," he said, raising his glass. Neither Dewar nor Bratton was sure if the reference was to the Soviet Union or the ball team, and they didn't care to ask.

After more toasts, to Childers' memory and Baltimore's defeat, Bratton suggested as delicately as he could that Bukharov, at future games, might enjoy himself more in the stands. He sweetened the proposal by offering to supply the tickets, but Deborin wouldn't hear of it. He needed Bukharov as a consultant, he said, and Bukharov's place was in the dugout.

"But we're a little crowded down there," Bratton protested. "After all, there's twenty-five players on the roster; then there's the coaches, the trainer, the bat boy, and—"

"What you call the bat boy," Deborin interrupted, "that is necessary?"

Bratton assured him it was.

"Your Voice of America," Bukharov sneered, "it does not tell us that you have still child labor in this country. This was abolished in the Soviet Union many years ago."

Patiently, Bratton and Dewar explained the child labor laws. It was a revelation to the Russians that not only was young Jerry Thiel's education not neglected, but he would be entering college on a sports scholarship. Apparently satisfied, Deborin raised a glass again. "I drink to your children," he said.

Bratton noticed that on each toast the Russians, except for Tasia, downed their glasses. He would have preferred sipping but he felt etiquette ordered that he follow suit. The glasses were refilled. "And I drink to your children," he said.

Dewar felt a new courage warming up his blood, poured himself another and glanced slyly at Tasia. "I'll drink to your child anytime, Mr. Deborin," he said. Deborin was silent, but a soupçon of a blush brushed Tasia's cheeks.

Bratton drew a baseball diamond on the blackboard and reconstructed the afternoon plays at Yankee Stadium to dramatize his lecture. His discourse on the home run fascinated the group, especially Deborin who inquired about the distance of Powers' blow.

"It cleared the fence," Bratton said, "and at that point the fence is three hundred and twenty-five feet from the plate."

"The fences are the equal distance in Chicago?" Deborin asked.

"No. All parks aren't built the same. At Comiskey Park, the fences are four hundred and fifteen feet at center field, and three hundred and fifty-two at left and right."

"You said Komisky," Galynin interrupted. "This is Russian?"

"No," Bratton smiled. "The Comiskeys are an old Irish family. They founded the Chicago White Sox."

"Once when I was Ambassador to Turkey," Galynin went on, "there was in my employ a translator who was called Anasta Komisky. He was not an Irish. He was a Russian."

Deborin was impatient. "It is more important to discuss the fences," he said. "In Chicago, we shall move them closer."

"What for?" Bratton asked.

"So our club will strike more hammers."

"Homers," Dewar said unsteadily.

"We'll get more homers," Bratton said, "but so will the other guys."

"I would not have thought this," Bukharov said, trying to ease the awkward moment.

" 'Course not," Dewar giggled. "Why don't you propose a toast to the homer and sickle?"

Bratton was embarrassed but, surprisingly, Galynin seemed amused. "I drink to your Mr. Powers," he said.

Bratton excused himself and went to the bathroom, where he poured out the vodka and replaced it with water. When he returned, he ticked off the roles of each position on the field. This done, Tasia was puzzled on one point: "I do not understand why you need three bases. It would be simpler, would it not, with only one base three times as long?"

Bratton explained that this would eliminate about ninety percent of the action, including the excitement of running, sliding, the pick-off and base stealing.

"They steal the bases?" Deborin said in disbelief.

"We got the smartest base stealers in the league," Dewar said, pointing the bottle at the Russians.

Bukharov leaned into Deborin's ear again. "It is the mark of decadence in this country," he said, looking to Galynin for approval. "Crime is everywhere."

"And now we learn it is even in the athletics," Galynin said sadly. "This is very serious."

Again Bratton had to explain, and again his monologue was climaxed by a toast, and again

Bratton prudently went to the bathroom for water. "To the glorious pilferers of the bases," Deborin said, when Bratton returned.

"You lost me there," Dewar said happily, "but I'll drink to that."

When the meeting broke up, Bratton said he hoped Deborin had learned some basics of the game.

"I learn something tonight," Deborin said at the door. "I learn you know your subject much. I shall have confidence in my absence."

"Your absence?" Bratton wondered.

Deborin disclosed he wouldn't accompany the team to Baltimore because he would be busy with arrangements to take up residence in Chicago. The ambassador had already enlisted the help of the attorney Leonard Daniels (now on the committee running the Russian-owned Childers project) and Daniels had assigned a Miss Wiley to turn the Presidential suite of the Childers-Chicago Hotel into a home for the Deborins. Bukharov and two Russian bodyguards, Galynin revealed darkly, would occupy an adjoining suite.

"Bodyguards?" Bratton said. "You're joking!"

"We do not make the joke," Galynin said, with some tartness. "We have done much reading of Chicago and we know of the situation of the gangsters there. My government is taking all precautions for the safety of Mr. Deborin and his daughter."

After they left, Dewar spread himself on the couch and closed his eyes. Bratton loosened Dewar's tie and took off his shoes. Then he removed the glasses and bottles and, undressing, began to think about Baltimore and the Orioles. He also wondered about the team meeting that Beadle, as player representative, had called for next week. And he hoped that Deborin's first public appearance, in Comiskey Park, would be free of incidents.

With an effort, Dewar opened one eye and laughed. "To the glorious pilferers of the bases," he said. "Piffle!" Then he fell asleep.

JIMMY HATLO

Courtesy King Features Syndicate ©

JIM MURRAY, whose home paper is the Los Angeles *Times*, is regarded by many, and deservedly so, as the best sports columnist to acquire syndication in the past decade. His delivery might be described, stylistically, as mid-century stand-up-comic: he machine-guns his readers with one-liners, as the following column, written in May of 1966, makes clear.

This is great vintage Murray. It is also an example of what must be a general reaction to those horrible scoreboards that have sullied the new era of stadium building. And it is also, we think, the only piece in the three volumes of the *Fireside* baseball library that mentions that (ugh!) forbidden word: golf.

Triumph for Virtue

JIM MURRAY

TEXAS AGAIN. Just Rhode Island if you take the hot air out. Oklahoma, if you leave out the lies. A state that was settled by 5 million people, 2 million cows, and a Virginia posse. America's Big Rock Candy Mountain where the cows and Cadillacs all have long horns on the front and where you have one mink for the party and the other to dry the dishes.

I came here partly to see a golf tournament, and partly to escape exploding scoreboards, between innings messages and electronic cheerleaders. Golf is the one place where a birdie doesn't touch off a sound system approximating the Battle of Verdun, and where the loudest sound you hear is the guy jangling coins to distract a player he bet against.

I caught the Giants-Dodgers opener before I left, but I had trouble concentrating on the game (so did Willie McCovey) what with the organist throwing in song hits from 1909 and a message board which not only listed name, rank and serial number of everyone who attended the game, but gave such dramatic social notes as the fact that the right fielder's sister had married the plumber, that there were parts of Alaska bordering on the Arctic Circle, and that the world is round.

All I require of a scoreboard is the score and the inning. If I want the social rambles of the players' families I'll get the collected works of Dorothy Kilgallen. I expect some night the scoreboard will begin serializing *War and Peace* or *Victory at Sea.*

The ball game was the biggest triumph for virtue since the last Bobbsey Twins novel. Juan Marichal, who was what you might call "a good hitting pitcher" (but not to his face) got what the old Louisa May Alcott books would call his "just desserts."

Don Drysdale, a man of probity, who never hits anybody with any object bigger than a baseball, pitched to Willie McCovey like he owed him. The only pitch he fooled McCovey on all night was one to second base. Willie has a little difficulty keeping interested in the ball game between times at bat—which doesn't make him unique, except that he was on base between times at bat most of the night. They may have to bring him black coffee the next time he gets on.

The Dodgers won the game because the Giants played Maury Wills in the ninth inning as if he were going for Mel Ott's record. The only three guys in the ball park who didn't know he was going to bunt were the Giant pitcher, shortstop and third baseman. It was one of Maury's tape-measure jobs—two feet on the fly and 20 more on the trickle. The Giants treated it as if they heard it ticking.

Willie Mays threw so many base runners out he may lead the entire Giant infield in assists. Willie Davis pioneered a new way to come into third base—as if he were third in line at the Roxy. He must have thought he had a ticket. Willie Mays threw the ball at 100 mph. And Willie went in at 20 mph. Willie needs a course in calculus. Mays should play in handcuffs to even things up a bit. He threw out Drysdale, too, but Don runs as if he were climbing a rope ladder. It takes him 15 steps just to clear his dropped bat.

He did manage to hold the Giants to three hits an inning on several occasions, but the Giants acted all night as if they owned the dice. If they did, they dropped them. They look like the 1927 Yankees at bat, and the 1906 Harvards in the field.

GEORGE LICHTY

Courtesy Publishers-Hall Syndicate ©

"You owe me a dime, Pop! . . . I TOLD you the last words of the Star-Spangled Banner were 'play ball' . . . !"

THE LIMERICK, that exceptional art form within the English language, finally finds its way into the *Fireside* library—from the pen of the master.

An Ump's Heart

OGDEN NASH

There once was an umpire whose vision
Was cause for abuse and derision.
He remarked in surprise,
"Why pick on my eyes?
It's my heart that dictates my decision."

WIDE WORLD

A view of the old Huntington Avenue ballpark in Boston where the Red Sox (then known as the Pilgrims) met Pittsburgh in the first World Series in 1903. The years since then have produced a parade of memorable scenes at Series time. Some of the highlights follow.

UNDERWOOD AND UNDERWOOD

UNASSISTED TRIPLE PLAY

The climax to Bill Wambsganss' famous unassisted triple play (Cleveland versus Brooklyn in 1920) as he tags Brooklyn's stunned, unresisting Otto Miller for the third out.

THE GOOSE

Wearing a mourning band for the late Christy Mathewson, Goose Goslin raps one in classic form in the 1925 Series.

UNITED PRESS INTERNATIONAL

EUROPEAN PICTURE SERVICE

A 1919 RE-CREATION

In the old days crowds used to follow Series action on mechanical flashboards. It was the old-style version of television—sometimes more accurate. This one was in Times Square, New York.

CAUSE AND EFFECT

In the top photo, Joe Medwick of the Cardinals slides into Detroit's Marvin Owen, "nicking" him (as one contemporary 1934 account put it) on the right foot. When Medwick went to left field in the next inning, the angry Tiger fans threw so many things at him (bottom) that Commissioner Landis, watching from the stands, removed him from the game for his own safety.

WIDE WORLD

THE FLOOD GATES OPEN

Al Smith (top photo) playing left field for the White Sox in the 1959 World Series, gets an unexpected drink. Bill Mazeroski (bottom) climaxes an unbelievable final game of the 1960 Series against the Yankees by hitting the tie-breaking homer.

WIDE WORLD

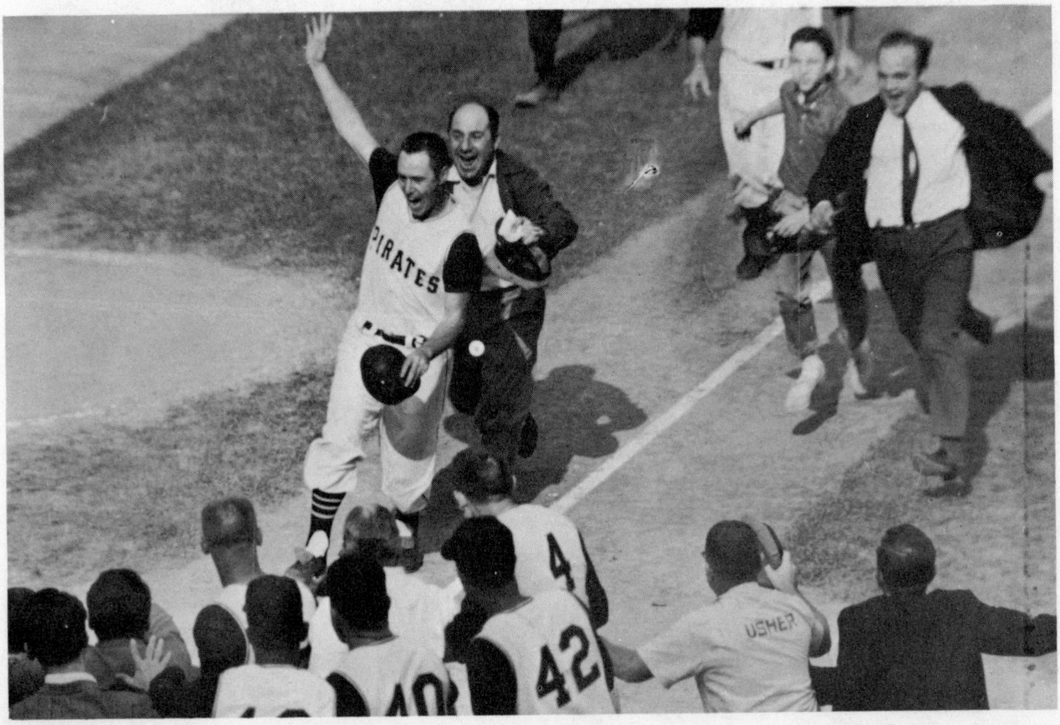

WIDE WORLD

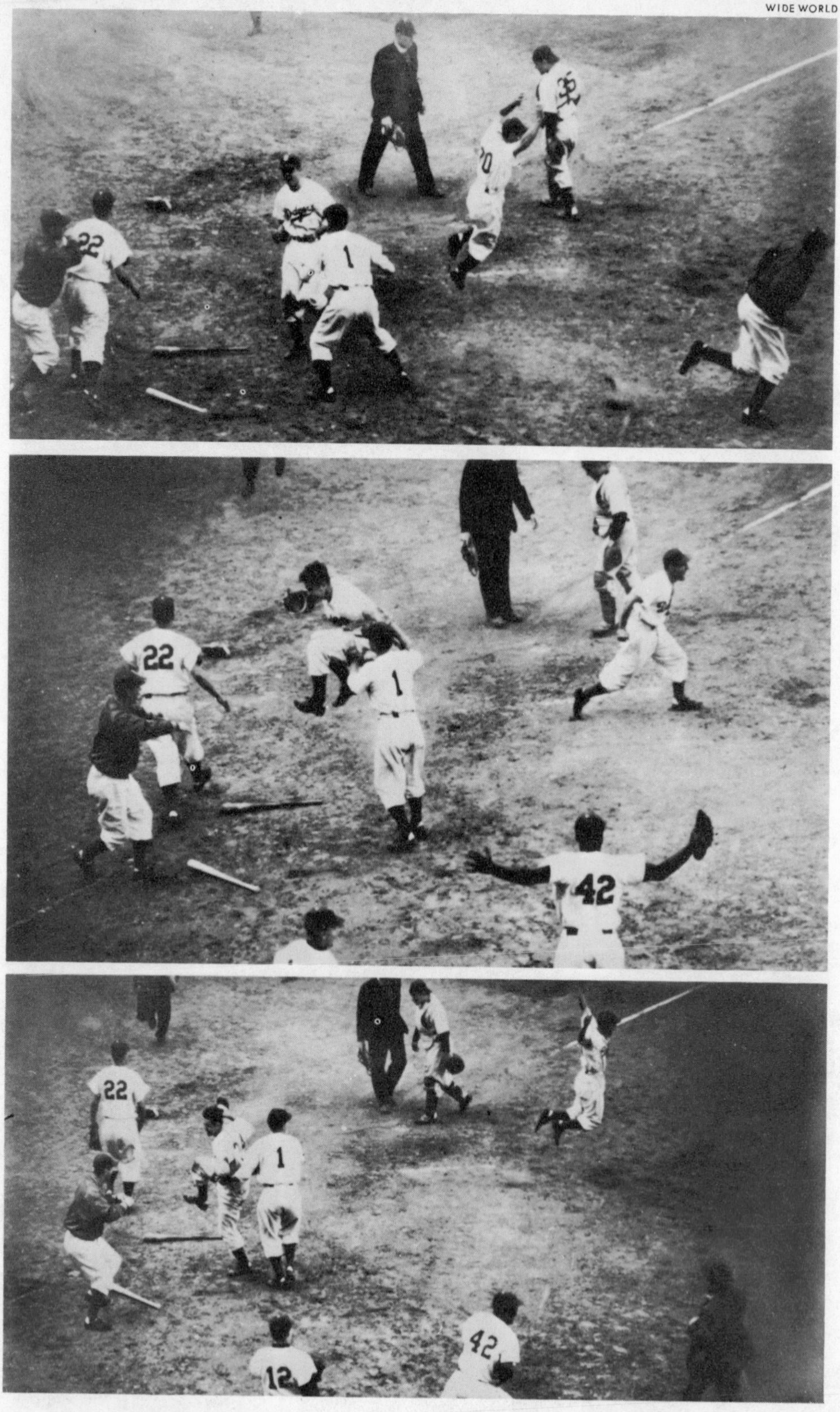

JOY! JOY! JOY!

1947: Brooklyn's Eddie Miksis scoring the game-winning run on the Cookie Lavagetto double that broke up Yankee Bill Bevens' no-hitter with two out in the ninth.

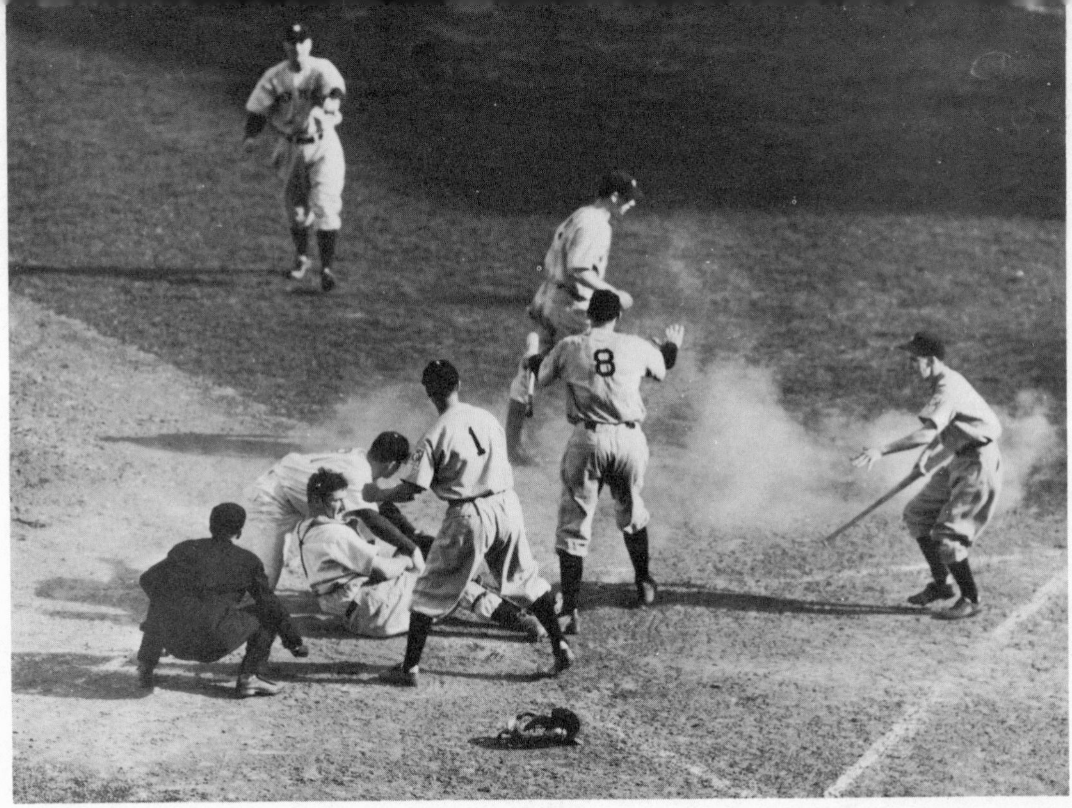

HORROR! HORROR!

1938: Cincinnati catcher Ernie Lombardi executes his historic "swoon" while lying at home plate with the ball untouched as two key Yankee runs score (above). And no joy but further horror in Brooklyn, this time in 1941, as catcher Mickey Owen fails to hold the game-ending third strike on Tommy Henrich.

WIDE WORLD

WIDE WORLD

COPPING THE CAP

What did the St. Louis Cardinals do with their winning shares from the 1967 World Series? Bought new caps for 1968, that's what.

THAT LIFE imitates art no one may deny—and baseball has a way of proving it every time you turn around. The first *Fireside Book of Baseball* presented, for example, James Thurber's fictional account of a pinch-hitting midget, and then pictorial proof of the way it came true at St. Louis ten years later. And Mark Harris' fictional pitcher-writer, Henry Wiggen, called "Author" by his teammates (see the Harris entries in the first and second *Fireside* books) was followed, in a few years' time, by the real-life pitcher-writer, Jim Brosnan, called "Professor" by his teammates (see the Brosnan entry in this book).

Perhaps even more startling, for the fact that it came true almost the moment it was published, was this *Saturday Evening Post* serial, which ran for three weeks in the pages of that magazine beginning with the issue of July 29, 1950 . . . just in time, that is, for the final stages of the pennant race. Author Frank O'Rourke made a halfhearted attempt to disguise names—the real-life Phillies became known as the Quakers; the real-life catcher Andy Seminick, who played with that year's club, may not have a fictional counterpart, but there's a catcher named Andy Semick in this story; and so on: Ashburn-Ashton, Sisler-Sipler, Hamner-Hammett, Konstanty-Constanty, Waitkus-Watkens. Players on the other National League clubs keep their real names.

And the pennant race hangs on the last two games with the Dodgers.

The Philadelphia Phillies of 1950, pennant winners in a race that hung on the last two games with the Dodgers, had it easier than a lot of people must have thought.

All they did was follow Mr. O'Rourke's script.

Here it is, every word complete as it appeared at that time—and as it was read then by an audience which, we can only surmise, had to include the Phillies.

Bonus Rookie

FRANK O'ROURKE

1.

JIM RAMSEY walked from the Fort Harrison Hotel along the dropping curve of a street that passed between the city auditorium and the municipal pier, staring at the vivid coloring of this strange world and breathing the alien odors of salt water and tropical flowers, and tidal mud drying on the back-bay flats; and then, secure in momentary anonymity, turned south behind a large church where the shuffleboard courts offered comparative solitude for his troubled thoughts.

He had come down alone from Minnesota yesterday on the late plane and was guided through signing the hotel register and meeting Semick, the first-string catcher, and the manager, Billy Lawson. He had liked Semick immediately, but Lawson was everything he had read about and feared.

Lawson had turned aggressively from the desk in that often-pictured fighting-cock pose and glared at him appraisingly. Lawson was short and heavy, with a growing bald spot and the droop of a double chin, a vitriolic and rough old-timer with a lifetime of baseball savvy and little regard for bonus rookies. Lawson spoke briefly and sent him upstairs to meet his new roommate, a rookie catcher named Shane, up from Toronto.

He had entered the room and found Shane rubbing oil into a new yellow mitt. Shane was massaging the stiff ball pocket furiously, and his sharp stare examined Ramsey with angry belligerence. He gave the mitt a slap and said, "Ramsey?"

"Yes," Ramsey said. "Glad to know you, Shane."

Shane ignored his outstretched hand, and Ramsey wondered why Lawson had paired him with a man who plainly cared nothing about forming the slightest friendship.

Trying to be civil, he said. "That's a nice mitt."

Shane tossed the mitt into a corner. "It's new. Like a lot of things in baseball. If it turns out good, I'll be surprised." Shane was including everything new in baseball since the war, but most of all, bonus rookies.

"Maybe I'm wrong," Ramsey said stiffly, "but I guess you don't want to room with me, do you?"

Shane said, "You guess right," and left the room, leaving Ramsey with the beginning of a situation he had to face; and the worst part was he couldn't blame Shane too much.

Shane had sweated five years at minor-league pay and was up with a six-thousand-dollar contract at most, facing a tough fight to stick as third-string catcher behind Semick and Lorenson; while he, the bonus rookie, had signed for twenty-five thousand the previous summer and was up with the minimum salary of five thousand. Surpassing the money angle, the Quakers had to keep him on the squad because of the bonus rule, while Shane might prove his worth and still be optioned back to Toronto, so the bonus rookie could fill the twenty-fifth spot on the roster. The old-timers, with the exception of someone like Shane, didn't resent the bonus rookie as an individual, but the boy was the object of wild spending and unfair ruling, and could not escape the harsh words and feeling of bitter resentment.

All this, Ramsey thought, was their argument. His side was equally important to him. He realized that signing for a bonus meant relinquishing any chance of gaining experience in the minors, but the money meant fulfillment of plans he had only dared dream in the past. So, like fifty others, he had signed and gone to the Quakers' Class B club in an Eastern league and finished the half season with twelve wins and two losses. He looked like a natural on paper, but he was woefully ignorant and in no way ready for the big show. And worst of all, the old fear of hitting a batter was growing daily in his mind. Two years ago, in his own Minnesota amateur league, he had got in a bad hole and pitched full speed for the first time, hitting the batter on the leg and putting that man, a good friend, in the hospital for two weeks. After that the phobia had grown until he was unable to use his greatest speed; and it was a compliment to his latent ability that, pitching under wraps, he had still shown so much speed the Quaker scout offered the bonus immediately. He had taken the money, knowing he was not being completely honest, but feeling that his fear was only a momentary problem.

Filled with his bitter thoughts, Ramsey left the hotel, walked over to the shuffleboard courts and sat down on a bench. He did not see the girl until she sat beside him. The white-haired man on the near court made a shot, and the girl called, "Good one," and smiled when Ramsey turned. "It was a good shot, wasn't it?" she asked.

Ramsey said, "Yes," and watched the white-haired man move across the court. The girl said, "Nice day, isn't it?"

"Yes," Ramsey said shortly.

She grinned and pushed long legs far out on the platform. She was an exceedingly plain girl, but her smile was pleasant. She said, "I'll make a guess."

"I don't get you," Ramsey said.

"You're a ballplayer. I know the look. How do you like Clearwater?"

"Why?" Ramsey said. "You live here?"

"Most of the year. What do you play?"

"Pitch."

"And your home?"

"Minnesota," Ramsey said sharply, "and seeing as how you're so damned curious, I'm twenty-three, weigh two hundred pounds, got all my teeth, like a couple of beers after a game, and anything else you want is in the Quaker front-office file." He paused then, feeling better for unloading anger, and said, "I'm all wound up. I'm sorry."

"I knew you were," she said calmly. "You're Ramsey, the bonus rookie. We've read about you. We're Quaker fans. My dad always felt cheated in me. He wanted a ballplayer."

"I've got a sister," Ramsey said sheepishly. "She always wanted to be a boy until last year."

"And then, she grew up?"

Ramsey knew why he felt relieved. This girl wasn't a camp follower like so many he had seen in Class B ball the past year, hanging around the parks and trying to date players.

He said, "Yes, she got married."

"I thought so. Say, practice starts soon for you."

Ramsey glanced at his watch. He said, "I'll have to go. You come to the games?"

He was moving away when she called, "Yes, and good luck."

The white-haired man chuckled and watched Ramsey out of sight. He said, "Who was he, Sue?"

"Ramsey, the bonus rookie. I like him."

"Think he'll look you up again?"

"I hope so," Sue said. "He's tough and scared and pretty nice. How often do you meet someone like that, Dad?"

Ramsey felt the silent antagonism in that first practice; it was in Lawson's face and curt, sharp words as he drove them through the workout. Ramsey loosened up and shagged balls and finally pitched to Semick in the bullpen.

Ramsey had the feeling of being a fifth wheel, a spare tire, something added to this smooth machine as an afterthought, and already forgotten in the steady rush of activity covering the field. He showered quickly and walked alone to the hotel and wandered through the garden.

Going to dinner that night, Semick met him in the lobby and said, "Eat with me," and led the way to a table. Not until dessert did the big catcher light a cigar and smile contentedly.

"Look at that Shane head for the lobby," Semick said. "Regular ladies' man, they tell me."

"He'll pass," Ramsey said. "Andy, what's his inside story? You know what I mean. Why does he hate my guts?"

"No secret," Semick said. "Three years ago he had a fine chance to stick with another club and got bounced to make room for a bonus rookie. Shane figures the bonus rule cost him two years of major-league pay, plus time for his pension. I've heard a lot about him the last three years, after the Quakers bought him and sent him to Toronto. He's a good catcher, smart and tough, a hitter in any league. But he hates the rule and naturally he doesn't like bonus rookies. Speaking of girls, how about you?"

"No special one," Ramsey said.

Semick nodded gravely. "Good idea. Save your money and wait for the right one. You're staying with Ashtons this summer, aren't you?"

"Yes," Ramsey said, "and lucky to get a regular home. I don't like hotels."

"You met Neil Ashton today. Mrs. Ashton is swell too. You'll feel like she's your own mother taking care of the house. You'll get along fine, them from Nebraska and you from Minnesota."

"I hope so," Ramsey said.

Semick talked on, asking about Minnesota, and Ramsey told him about the lakes and the baseball played in the small towns. The evening passed quickly and Ramsey went upstairs at nine o'clock. He read for two hours and fell asleep after eleven; and then morning came swiftly, breakfast tasted better, and practice began in dead earnest. The days blended together in a hazy period of hard work that gradually cleared before his curious eyes.

Earling, the pitching coach, drove them through unending workouts and drills. Ramsey watched the regulars and began to appreciate the effort expended to stay on top, and worked doubly hard himself on fielding and conditioning. He threw batting practice in turn and pitched in the first squad game with Shane behind the plate. The Quaker regulars hit everything he pitched, booming drives to the fences and beyond, scoring seven runs in his three-inning turn. His fast ball didn't hop and his curve hung like a crippled duck, but all Earling said was "Take your shower," and turned to follow the play. He showered and walked downtown, moving automatically around the block to the shuffleboard courts, feeling utterly dejected and worthless.

He found the same bench and sat heavily, and was staring blankly at the ground when someone said, "I had a hunch you'd be here," and sat beside him. He noticed the white-haired man on the near court and wondered if time was reversing itself.

"You didn't look around today," she said. "Our box is behind the bench."

"I'm sorry," Ramsey said, "I—"

"My name is Sue Johnson," she said. "This is my father. . . . Dad, come on over."

The white-haired man shook hands and said, "Hello, Jim. Feeling bad?"

"You saw me," Ramsey said. "I stunk."

"And then some," Sue Johnson said. "You looked like a bum." She grinned. "What's the matter? Want me to soft-soap your pride?"

"Now, Sue," Mr. Johnson said.

"Don't Sue me," she said. "He did look terrible, but we know why. . . . You know, don't you, Jim?"

"I was scared," Ramsey said. "I'm green. My curve stinks."

"You two fight it out," Mr. Johnson said. . . . "Sue, ask Jim to do something with us after practice."

"If you'll run along," she said pointedly, "I'll get to that part."

Mr. Johnson vanished behind the courts, and Ramsey felt decent enough to sit straight and swallow part of his anger.

"Feel any better?" she asked.

"Some," Ramsey said. "I needed a little straight talk."

"That's the only way I like to talk," she said. "Straight out. You're wondering why I'm so forward, aren't you? Because I like you. I think you'd be nice to know. I don't know you yet, and you don't know me. I'll meet you here tomorrow after the game, and we'll see if we can't find out why."

He watched the Quakers work steadily into shape as batting eyes sharpened and bodies moved toward a fluid smoothness of play. He pitched twice in squad games and received the same treatment that had marked his first appearance, and Sue's friendship alone made the growing pressure bearable. As he saw her in the passing days, he realized that she was not plain. In Sue's face were strength and humor and deep understanding.

Ramsey told her of his home and past life, of finishing high school in 1944 and going into the Army, then working for his parents on their Gull Lake resort. He had wanted to buy his own resort, but this was a long way off until the bonus money was tossed in his face like a gift from heaven, and then he could not turn such a chance down.

Sue spoke of her own family as though their lives were close and similar. Her mother had died ten years ago and her father sold his business in their small city near Quaker City, and moved here to stay, with three months allotted to going north for the games in Quaker City and New York.

Shane caught him in the squad games, played excellent ball and outhit Semick and Lorenson at this early time; if only his own efforts were half as good, Ramsey thought enviously. He was rounding into shape and his arm had never felt better, but the Quakers hit everything he pitched and drove him crazy on the bases.

He was thoroughly disgusted with himself, and Lawson seemed to concur, leaving him behind with the extra pitchers while the team played away from home. He worked out those afternoons and pitched short batting practices, and was conscious of the team as individuals for the first time, possibly through the medium of their absence. He had studied their pictures in past years, but in the flesh they were entirely different.

Only Semick was the same, a squarely built man with big forearms and powerful wrists. Semick was rough and untiring in a game, afraid of no man at the plate, harsh with his voice when the team needed that stringent lift. Off the field, he was possibly the best-liked man on the squad.

Ramsey watched them all and saw the team take form, and understood that no team could be entirely compatible with so many distinct personalities. Infielders fighting for the same position did not chum together, and pitchers on the doubtful list were never too friendly. One man might rub another the wrong way for no logical reason, but Ramsey knew the petty differences were forgotten when they stepped on the field. There, playing as a unit, they had a deep and vigorous spirit of teamwork. Ramsey watched them all and hoped he could become a part of their life, accepted and used as a valuable cog in the machine, and not a hanger-on, unable to carry his own weight while forcing a good man off the roster.

Lawson started him against the Reds and he lasted two innings; and facing the Cards three days later, he could not conquer his old fear and throw at full speed when he needed it badly. Slaughter and Musial homered in the first inning, and that was all.

Today, the thirtieth of March, he dressed slowly in the clubhouse, thinking of the game. He was starting against the Senators, his last time out in the Grapefruit League, and he wasn't good enough. The folks back home were calling the Quakers his teammates, he knew, and that was not true. He was a boy masquerading as a man among men, and most of them nursed that silent grudge.

He warmed up in the bullpen, throwing to Semick, and made the walk as the P A system announced the lineups, and the umpires moved into position.

Everything was clear today, too clear. The field seemed brighter and greener, the Senators smoother than they really were. The leadoff man settled in the box, and Ramsey took his signal for the pitch. Today, he thought, would mean a great deal. Lawson had given him valuable hours from the precious stock of days, pumped knowledge into his head, treated him with rough coldness, showing plainly that he did not expect any bonus rookie to come through. Today he had to show something. He remembered the last time he had pitched at full speed, and wondered if he dared this afternoon. Thinking in this way, remembering that terrible moment in the past, he delivered the ball with a full-bodied sweep.

The batter leaped backward, throwing his body down and away from the pitch, and from the Senators' bench came a roar of protest. Shane made a stabbing catch and blocked the ball, chased it down the first-base line, and came to the mound. Ramsey was sweating with the old fear, rubbing his fingers across his shirt, knowing that he had not thrown with full strength, yet could not control the ball.

Shane said, "What the hell are you trying to do, Ramsey? Kill somebody?"

"Sorry," he said. "It slipped."

"Control," Shane said sharply. "Remember? Get the little white ball in there, dope. All right, let's start over."

Lawson, sitting in the press-box shade, turned to Cy Perry, the catching coach. "You see that?"

"Told you he hadn't opened up," Perry said. "Nobody realizes how fast he is."

"He can't control the speed," Lawson said sourly. "He's scared to death of something. Look at him. Sweating blood after one pitch. Afraid he'll hit somebody. Why don't they send me men instead of kids?"

"He's strong," Perry said mildly. "He didn't throw that one full power, and it's the fastest ball I've seen this spring. You can't cross him off, Billy."

"How true," Lawson said. "He's got our money and we're stuck with him, have to give him time we can't spare."

"He's scared and green," Perry said. "But there's a pitcher if we can bring it out."

Ramsey pitched to the target, and the Senators went down in order, the third batter standing tautly alert, watching for the wild pitch. They weren't getting set against him, and Ramsey considered this fact between innings, wondering if another fast wild pitch, thrown well outside, might not keep them loose and jumpy. But he couldn't take the chance; the ball might slip, and then he'd be watching another man go down and writhe in agony. He pitched through the second inning, allowing one single, but no runs, and moved into the third with part of his nervous fear blotted out.

The leadoff man singled and the next batter bunted. Ramsey fielded the dribbler along the third-base line and got the batter as the runner advanced to second.

Shane came from his backup position and said, "You think maybe you could put some smoke on the ball again?"

"I can't control it," Ramsey said. "You know that."

"Throw it outside," Shane said. "They're digging in again. Got to keep 'em loose."

He felt his body tighten when Shane called for the outside pitch. He threw and the ball went high and outside, sailing up and against the edge of Shane's mitt. Shane faked the runner back to second and called, "All right, come to me now." For a moment, he thought Shane was going to grin and offer encouragement, and then he saw the catcher's face, tight-lipped and entirely sullen. Shane called for the fast ball inside, over the wrists, and he checked the runner, felt the urge rise in his chest, and threw with full strength and terrific follow-through.

The third-base coach shouted, "Drop!" and the batter fell away, bat flying high in the air as Ramsey saw the ball strike a shoulder and carom high against the grandstand screen. He ran for the plate as Dascoli called the dead ball and Shane bent over the batter, now rolling with pain in the dust.

Someone gave him a rough push and said, "Stay away, gold plate, we'll take care of our men."

He watched the Senators' trainer work over the batter, long fingers probing. "Nothing broken," the trainer said, and looked savagely at Ramsey. "By the grace of God!"

"I—" Ramsey said. "It—"

"Bonus rookies!" someone said.

"That's enough," Lawson spoke behind him. "Come on, Ramsey."

Ramsey followed him across the grass to the clubhouse, into the quiet of the private office.

Lawson closed the doors and motioned to a chair and said, "What's the matter? Afraid you beaned him?"

"Yes," Ramsey said. "I thought for a minute—"

"Why haven't you opened up before?" Lawson asked bluntly.

"I can't control it," Ramsey said.

"On that last pitch," Lawson said. "You give it everything?"

"Just about," Ramsey said. "I'm sorry."

"Listen," Lawson said. "Did you ever throw wide open, back home?"

"Once."

"What happened?"

"I hit a guy," Ramsey said.

"And then?" Lawson said sharply. "Come on, spill it."

"Two years ago," Ramsey said. "The bases were full and I had a one-run lead with two outs. I got a two-two count on the batter—

their best hitter—and I let one go. I hit him in the left leg. He couldn't walk for two weeks."

"So you got scared?" Lawson said.

"I knew him," Ramsey said. "They play ball for fun. I couldn't hit a bunch of nice guys who had to work on Monday morning."

"This is the big show," Lawson said sharply. "You took our money. You wanted to come in. And the only way you stick up here is by beating the other guy's brains out. You've been holding back. I stand for that from no man on my team. I want your best, nothing less. From now on, pour that ball through."

"And kill somebody?" he said thinly. "You want me to do that?"

"Look," Lawson said impatiently. "You've got a phobia. You hit a boy back home and you think these ballplayers are going to stand up there and let you break their heads open. Wake up! You're pitching against the fastest reflexes in the world. Keep that fast ball low and bear down."

"But I can't hold it there," he said. "I've tried."

"How long?" Lawson said scornfully. "Ten throws behind the barn on Saturday. Bah! I'm talking about practice. Not one week or a month, but all season. When we hit Quaker City, you go to work. Conditioning every day, bullpen work, on the road and at home. We've got too much money invested to give up on you. You'll sweat blood all summer, but you'll lick that fear if you've got the guts. Toward the end of the season I'll start you, and then I want to see you go out there and mow 'em down." Lawson laughed mirthlessly. "You've got just one asset right now—speed, more than anybody in the league—but it's worthless if you can't bear down. All right, get your shower."

He left the clubhouse at the game's end and walked alone to the hotel, thinking of Lawson's words. Shane had needled him into pitching full speed, and he wanted to hurt Shane as badly as that batter's shoulder must be aching now. A few inches, he thought miserably, and the man could be dead. And Shane laughed, urged him on, until he made a fool of himself; and now Lawson had seen that speed and he was facing a brutal summer until he mastered this fear. He entered the lobby and Semick came from the desk.

"Come back here," Semick said, guiding him to a quiet corner. "Let's have some plain talk. I don't think a man on this team holds a personal grudge against you—maybe one, but I'm not thinking about him. What I'm worried about is this: You're a bonus rookie and it's riding you into the ground. You want to make good, but you don't know where to start. Have you got the guts to work, really work?"

"You know I have," Ramsey said. "But look how I pitch. I'll never learn everything."

"You think so now," Semick said, "but it'll come. Not very fast, but one day you'll stand out there and find it. I'll tell you something else, Jim. You can't play just because it's a good living and you've got the ability to stay up. Sure, baseball is big business now. We've got just so many years to make good money. I'm practical about it. But I love this game and I play to win, and as long as I can go out there and catch, I'll give everything I've got to win. Think it over, Jim. Later on you'll either feel like I do or it won't make any difference."

Semick's words were all too clear. Ramsey wondered if he would ever have that feeling in his heart, knowing it had to come before he could stand beside Semick and be half the man the catcher was. He left the hotel after dinner, trying to muster his troubled thoughts, and finally called Sue.

"Hello," Ramsey said. "Is Sue there?"

"She has a date tonight, Jim," Mr. Johnson said. "What's the matter? Did she promise you?"

"No, sir," Ramsey said. "I just wanted to say good-bye."

"I know," Mr. Johnson said gravely. "We hoped you would, Jim."

Ramsey was suddenly in a painful rush. He said, "Thanks, Mr. Johnson," and ran outside and flagged a taxi. They crossed the causeway and Ramsey gave both cafés quick inspection, looked into the ice-cream stands, and finally stood disconsolately on the sidewalk, calling himself a fool. She might be in any of a dozen places along the beach or in Tampa. The driver called, "Where to?" and Ramsey said, "Pull down to the drugstore," and walked the hundred steps and bought a package of gum. He turned then and saw her in a booth, regarding him curiously.

"Sue!" Ramsey said.

"What are you doing over here so late?" Sue asked.

"You sit still," Ramsey said. "Right there!"

He ran outside, paid the driver and tipped him too much, and then joined Sue. He said, "I called your house. Your dad told me you had a date."

"I went to a show with Mrs. Riggs," Sue said. "So Dad said I had a date!"

And then he was watching her, seeing her for the first time, it seemed. Her hair was soft about her quiet face with the wide-set eyes clear beneath the heavy brows, and her mouth, wide and firm, a lovely and honest mouth sculptured against the tan of her face.

"I'll have to take this just one way," Sue said severely. "You've developed a sudden interest in me, is that it? So you began touring the beach to see who I was dating? Well—"

"Yes," Ramsey said. "Don't you like the idea?"

"Do I!" Sue said. "It's the nicest thing that ever happened to me!"

"Listen," Ramsey said. "About not calling sooner. I felt lousy after I hit that guy. I was coming out after the game, but then I wanted to hide. I finally felt better and called."

"Is that the best you can do?"

"No," Ramsey said. "I can do a lot better. I can tell you that I don't like the idea of you dating anybody else, anywhere."

"Is that an order?"

"I can't order you around, Sue."

She was smiling, and Ramsey couldn't tell if she was serious or just fooling. He said, "I don't know how we got started talking this way, but I like it."

"So do I," Sue said. "I told you that the first day."

"What?"

"That I liked you."

"Say," Ramsey said. "You're wearing lipstick."

"Is that a crime?"

"I never saw you wear it before," Ramsey said. "It looks nice."

"Mr. Alexander wants to close up," Sue said. "Walk home with me. You don't make sense tonight. I've asked some pertinent questions and all you do is notice my lipstick. There's only one thing to do about that."

They left the drugstore and walked slowly along Mandalay into the mid-block darkness. She turned then and kissed him firmly, and then walked more slowly, holding his arm tightly.

"Somebody had to do something," Sue said. "But don't expect me to do all the leading."

"I won't," Ramsey said.

"One month gone," Sue said softly. "Bingo, just like that. But I'll see you in June."

"If they don't send me home."

"You?"

"Don't kid me, Sue," Ramsey said. "You saw me pitch today. I nearly killed a man. I've got the speed, but I can't control it. And there's a lot more I haven't told you."

"I knew something was wrong," Sue said. "Dad kept saying you hadn't opened up. Want to tell me, Jim?"

Ramsey told her everything, from the moment he hit the man back home, on through the fear that had grown and hobbled his speed until that one wild pitch today. He said then, "I've got to lick it, Sue, or there's no use going on."

"Don't think that way," Sue said. "Now you've got me upset. I can't help you on the field, but if you don't make good, I'll—" She stopped talking abruptly.

"I'll do my best," Ramsey said.

"That's not enough. You've got to try more than your best. And don't think that because I kissed you, I—"

"I don't."

"Well, you'd better! Do you think I go around kissing everybody I know?"

"I don't know what you think," Ramsey said, "but I want to see you every day from now on. Is that what you're trying to say?"

"That's what I mean, Jim," she said. "And I'd better drive you to the hotel before we start acting like a pair of fool kids. Let's take our time and see how we feel in June."

"I know how I'll feel," Ramsey said. "But I'll wait."

Ramsey felt the increased tempo of play as they moved north, a tension that placed an imprint on every man. He lasted one inning against Baltimore, and running north to Quaker City that night, Lawson paused beside his seat and said, "Wet weather bother your arm?"

"No, sir," he said. "I don't mind it."

"Looked like it today," Lawson said moodily. "You weren't bearing down. Remember, from now on, you won't pitch much. You'll practice, though, plenty of that."

Ramsey read a magazine and tried to sleep, and was caught in the excitement of arrival, meeting Neil and Genevieve Ashton and driving across the immense, sprawling city to his summer home. In a matter of minutes he was sitting down to a late dinner, feeling more natural than he had in a month.

He and four other young players filled the house this year, now that Robbie Ashton and Robbins were married and in their own homes; and it came to Ramsey, feeling the sincere warmth of this household, that the Ashtons loved the game as much as any player, to come here for half the year after their own son no longer needed them. And best of all, he thought, he was away from Shane.

The night before opening day he slept soundly, surprising himself. He rose eagerly to dress and eat and drive with the others to the stadium.

His hands were sticky with sweat as he dressed and listened to the talk run quietly through the big dressing room.

He followed Semick across the corridor and up the tunnel onto the field and faced the full power and corrosive quality of the capacity crowd, the largest he had ever seen. The stadium was different today. The chalk lines seemed whiter and straighter and the stands extended upward into some infinite cavern of shadowy faces and waving arms and loud, impatient voices. And then time was slipping by, hitting was finished, and he was in the dugout, watching Lawson meet the umpires and Billy Southworth at home plate following the opening-day ceremonies and flag raising, and Henchman was lifting his arms in the first pitch.

Ramsey saw a classical game that day, one of those swift battles that became fluid in motion and agonizing in the closing minutes as pressure mounted and the outcome rode on every pitch. Henchman won that game, 2 to 0, and Ramsey felt the lift of their spirits around him as the crowd roared happily. Another season was under way.

Ramsey rode the bench and watched the Quakers sweep their opening series and make the short road trip around the Eastern circuit; and with this rush that carried them to the top, his own life was set firmly in routine. He worked daily in the bullpen and chased balls during pregame batting practice, and wondered if Lawson would give him a chance to pitch. They came home for three games with the Pirates, won two, and jumped into a big three-game lead with one of those rare hitting streaks every team has during the season. Berglund was coasting behind a ten-run lead in the fifth when Lawson called the bullpen.

Cy Perry turned from the phone and said, "Warm up, Ramsey. . . . And you, Shane. . . . Ramsey, don't open up. It's too cold."

He pitched to Shane and made the long walk to the mound with the P A system blaring their names. The wind was colder now, and people were leaving the stands. Hopp stepped into the box, and Ramsey thought, *A tough one to face the first time,* and pitched at Shane's dabbing mitt. Hopp hit his third pitch into the right-field stands, twenty rows up, and jogged around the bases while Shane brought a new ball to the mound.

"Come on," Shane said thickly. "Show some smoke."

"Perry said no," he said.

"Your funeral," Shane said. "You're not in the sticks now."

Shane began talking fiercely behind the plate as Kiner stepped in. *Kiner,* he thought, wondering if the big man had a weakness. He had to bear down, and he felt the fear trickle through his fingers. His pitch sent Kiner doubling back and down as Shane made a brilliant save high outside. Kiner dusted his hands and grinned faintly at Bill Stewart behind the plate. *Got to throw it hard,* he thought; *can't baby it in there.* He delivered, grunting with the force of his swing and wrist snap, and stood openmouthed, watching the ball lift and drop into the left-field stands. Kiner had taken picks on his second pitch. He had to bear down, and he was afraid.

Shane came out, walking stiff-legged, and said, "You're dogging it. Throw the ball hard, Ramsey. Can you do that one little thing?"

"I'll throw," he said. "You catch."

He pitched to Westlake, and froze with terror as Westlake dropped beneath the head-high ball, then bounced up, shouting angrily to the umpire in protest. Shane said something and Westlake nodded and took a slightly deeper position in the box. Shane called for the fast ball outside, and delivering to the mitt, Ramsey felt his body tighten and his arm refuse to obey; at the last moment he eased off and the ball went in slow and outside, a cripple that hung and begged to be hit as Westlake refused to hit the bad pitch. Shane asked for a new ball and came to the mound.

"You yellow louse," Shane whispered fiercely "I saw you ease up. Come on, show me some stuff."

He couldn't answer, knowing he was wrong. Shane gave him a quick, contemptuous look and trotted back to the plate. He took the fast-ball signal and wanted to throw the ball through Shane's mitt, through that mask, into that face, knock Shane on his back and stand over him and laugh.

He pitched without thought and the count ran full, three and two, as he drove the batter back and then up, the pitches going inside and high, one cutting the outside corner, fast and alive. Shane was shouting and the entire infield seemed to be directly behind him, pouring their practiced invective against the batter and the Pirate's bench, as if the score were tied and the game hinged on every pitch. He saw Westlake crouch and edge forward in the box, wiggling hips and shoulders, daring him to clip the inside corner; and he came around with the pitch, forgetting everything, wanting that strikeout more than any in the past. The ball went in, caught some vagrant air current, or so it seemed, and at the last moment, with Westlake leaning over the plate, body straining in a question-mark pose, sailed in and against the left shoulder. In that quick, horrified moment, Ramsey saw the ball rebound from Westlake in a high arc, and saw Westlake spin and drop, legs kicking helplessly across the dusty plate.

He remembered Lawson leading him from the mound, saw Westlake get uncertainly to wobbly feet and then trot to first, and was safely in the dugout's protective cover as Thomas took the mound and Lorenson went in for Shane.

He sat on the bench and said, "I didn't mean to. I thought I was all right," and swallowed thickly.

Perry sat beside him, and Semick brought a cup of water and forced it between his fingers.

"Drink," Semick said.

He tilted the cup and felt water clear his throat; and Lawson came from the field and stared at him. "He's all right," Lawson said. "A sore shoulder. Take your shower."

Stepping from the dugout into the tunnel entrance, in full view of the adjoining box seats, he heard her voice calling and saw her half standing, one hand outstretched, eyes worried and dark. He said, "How—" and then Shane pushed him from behind and said, "Don't block traffic. Move out."

He ran to the dressing room, shame building a miserable lump in his throat, wondering why Sue had come north so early; and then he was dressed and running from the room and meeting her in the empty corridor, holding her tightly and trying to speak.

He said, "How come?"

"I wanted to see you," she said. "Dad agreed. So we closed the house and headed north."

"And saw me today," Ramsey said bitterly.

Sue squeezed his hand and said, "You've improved a lot, Jim."

"Sure," he said. "I hit them harder now."

"Your control is better," Sue said. "It is!"

"Don't soft-soap me," Ramsey said.

"But you pitched good ball for a while," Sue said. "I'm proud of you for that, Jim."

"You're lonesome," Ramsey said. "Nobody else is."

"But you haven't licked it yet, have you?"

"You saw me," Ramsey said shortly. "Let's talk about something else. We're leaving right away for the West, you know."

"You're not facing the trouble," Sue said. "Either you lick this fear or you'll lose a lot more than the chance to pitch."

Ramsey said, "What do you mean?"

"You know what I mean," Sue said. "If a man lets one thing lick him, then he'll be afraid when other tough problems come along. And I could never respect a man who refused to fight, Jim. Now I'll drive you to the train."

Lawson dropped heavily into his chair and remembered the pitches started with full back swing and then delivered with what appeared to be a deliberate change-up motion on the follow-through.

He said, "You see it?"

"Yes," Perry said. "The kid's scared he'll bean somebody."

"He's yellow," Lawson said harshly. "Damn this bonus rule. Now I've got to keep him and baby him, and hope he comes through."

"He's a good kid," Perry said gently. "He's got everything it takes, plus more speed than anybody suspects. He wasn't throwing more than three quarters on that one to Westlake, and Westlake didn't drop much too soon. I say keep working him hard and he may lick it."

"Sure," Lawson said, "and I'll be around ten years if we don't win a pennant. Like hell! By the way, I'm switching Shane and Ramsey on road trips from now on. Ramsey will room with Lorenson."

"Good idea," Perry said.

"I hate to admit I'm wrong," Lawson said tightly. "I was, there. All right, work the hell out of him all summer. Better grab your shower. I'll see you at the train."

Lawson remained in his private office standing pinkly bare on the black rubber matting, visualizing the season ahead. They were in first place today, but that meant nothing, for the Dodgers were coming fast. He considered the hot months and doubleheaders, and wondered if they had enough to outlast the Dodgers; it would be a vicious fight to the final two-game series with the Dodgers, a series that could settle the race. The Quakers were short on pitching, and he was saddled with a useless rookie in the twenty-fifth spot when he ought to have a cagey veteran from their Triple A farm.

Ramsey could not sleep that night, measuring himself in the mirror of his own mind. Lawson knew, had to know, and so did the coaches and Semick, and soon the entire team would understand that Ramsey was gun-shy, afraid to open up.

He lay tense and wide-eyed in the swaying berth, feeling every bump and ripple in the roadbed, and finally slipped down to the dark, cold aisle and walked to the washroom. He was leafing through a magazine when the curtains parted and Shane stepped into the washroom.

"What's the matter?" Shane said. "Can't sleep?"

"You're not pounding any pillows," Ramsey said shortly.

"I will," Shane said. "From now on. With a new roomie."

"That's mutual," Ramsey said. "I hope we both sleep better."

"Don't worry," Shane said. "My conscience is clear."

Ramsey said, "Don't rub it in, Shane. I know when I goof off."

Shane drew deeply on his cigarette and tossed it into the spittoon under the washbowls. His hands were clenched in his robe pockets, forming knotty bulges beneath the slick blue cloth.

Shane said, "So does everybody else."

"Don't rub it in," Ramsey repeated quietly, "I said that once."

"And if I do?" Shane asked.

Ramsey got up quickly. "You want to stay in here? Say so and I'll leave. Otherwise you get out and I'll stay."

"Maybe I want to do both," Shane said. "Then what?"

"You're a fool," Ramsey said. "You keep needling me deliberately. Get out of the way. I'm going to bed."

He started for the door and Shane refused to step aside. Their shoulders met solidly as Ramsey passed, and Shane drove one fist into his body and leaped around, facing him, arms up.

"You want the whole room?" Shane said wildly.

Ramsey turned and felt his anger dissolve into cold rage, body slipping into the crouch, and feet moving soundlessly as his arms came up and he watched Shane's left arm and jaw. They stood two arm lengths apart and Ramsey feinted with his left and moved in; and from the doorway Semick said softly but sharply, "Hold it, both of you! You damned fools!"

Semick leaped from the door in their moment of frozen surprise, elbowing between them and pushing Ramsey onto the leather seat while holding Shane roughly by his robe.

"I got here one punch late," Semick said in a low voice, "but soon enough. If you want to fight, wait until October and pick a spot a thousand miles away where the sportswriters don't come out of the woodwork. I'm not asking for promises. Shane, I'm telling you flat out. . . . Ramsey, I'm telling you. This business stops right here, between the three of us. . . . Shane, you go to bed and cool off."

Shane rose slowly and said, "All right, Semick," and left the washroom. Wind from the car end sifted coldly through the swaying curtains and touched Ramsey's hot face.

"Sorry I had to get tough, Jim," Semick said.

"I—" Ramsey said.

"I know," Semick said. "No use repeating the reasons. We all know them. Let's talk about today when you let up on those fast balls. You can't get the best of it, can you?"

"Not yet," Ramsey said miserably. "Every time I bear down, I get scared to death. Andy, what am I going to do?"

"First off," Semick said, "have you thought about our chance for the pennant? We've got the hitting, the best infield, and just enough pitching. Get that—just enough pitching, no more. And that's where you come in, Jim."

"Me?" Ramsey said. "I'll never make it this year."

"Maybe you won't," Semick said, "but you've got to try, work like hell every day, all summer. Think about the last month, work toward getting yourself as far along as you can. You might have to start. Who knows? And if you don't give everything getting in shape, trying to break this jinx, you won't be honest with yourself and the team. Jim, when you open up, nobody in the league has more speed. Newcombe, Barney—they can't fog it through any faster."

"But they've got control."

"You can get it," Semick said sharply. "It'll be a tough summer. You'll get so sick of throwing in the bullpen, you'll want to quit. It's up to you, I guess, when we come down to brass tacks. Now grab some shut-eye."

Lawson sat wearily in his compartment, drinking a cold beer, rubbing one flat hand over his balding head. He had been unable to eat dinner and now, at midnight, could not regain the appetite he urgently needed. He thought of Ramsey and swore softly. He had used Ramsey that afternoon as any manager would pitch a rookie in a loose game; and when Ramsey seemed to find himself after a shaky start and pitched the blinding fast balls that surprised everyone, including himself, Lawson had felt the rare, wonderful hope that a pitcher was coming into his own. But he had been wrong; and worse, had left Ramsey in one pitch too long. Now two months' work might be thrown down the drain. The kid didn't have guts, he thought sourly, and they expected Lawson to work miracles with that kind of green talent. But tonight, ready to give up on Ramsey, a vagrant long-forgotten memory tugged at his mind, some connection between Ramsey and long ago that finally came clear.

He sat straighter and thought of that day twenty-one years ago when the biggest gamble in baseball had paid off and ultimately cinched a World Series. The memory of Ehmke walking out that afternoon and beating the Cubs, setting the Series record for strikeouts, would never dim; and most important was the daring of Mack, with three great pitchers, planning his coup for two months, and starting Ehmke against a team of sluggers. That had taken courage, and faith, and confidence. Lawson found his mind working in strange channels, against his better judgment tonight, counting pitchers and considering the remaining games to play; and placed on a small platform opposite those men was his confused, uncertain evaluation of Ramsey.

He dreaded the thought of any one regular pitcher being hurt and put out of play for a week, two weeks or more; that could blast their chances without recourse. And with this thought, always foremost in his mind, was the inevitable pattern of their final twenty games, when his pitchers would be weary and every game a dogfight. That last month would be a succession of juggling his staff, picking the right pinch hitter, bringing in the best relief man, until each game became a nightmare and the regular rotation vanished under grim necessity. When that time came, with one game easily spelling defeat or victory, it was painfully and clearly possible they could fight down the stretch and face that final two-game series with the Dodgers, completely stripped of fresh pitchers, and not only the bugaboo of starting pitchers with insufficient rest but sending them below peak against the Dodgers, who, by then, would know each pitcher all too well.

Lawson had these thoughts and slowly, in a mind that was orderly and sensible, came the possibility, the wild gamble. It might occur at any time in the final two weeks of the season; and it might not happen if the Quakers dropped from the race or, which was more unlikely, cinched the pennant early.

Lawson slapped the serving table and said aloud, "By damn! It's worth planning for!"

"What is?" Semick said, entering the compartment.

"Sit down," Lawson said, "I want to tell you a story. I've got to tell somebody right now, tonight."

2.

The pattern was forming now; even the sportswriters were predicting the ultimate finish. The Dodgers were growing stronger, but the Quakers had that indefinable quality called spirit, fight or just plain guts. They continued to win with less hitting than two of the second-division clubs. They finished the Eastern swing in Brooklyn, and Ramsey suffered intensely, watching Newcombe and Roe whip the Quakers twice and give the Dodgers a three-game lead as they started the second Western swing.

The Quakers played steady baseball and surged through the Western trip on fine pitching and a sudden burst of hitting by Anderson and Sipler, who won half the games with timely hits. They took a key game from the Cards, closed within half a game on the Dodgers; and came home to maintain that pace and tie the Dodgers for the lead on July Fourth.

The Dodgers moved in for three games, and all the seats were gone before the first ball was pitched. He began to understand the surging brutality of a crowd in that series; it was a controlled lust that bellied forth in wall-rocking sound and clapping hands and seventy thousand shoes pounding on the concrete aisles. But most of all, it was a wild-eyed look about the fans as a whole, a kind of Hydra-headed stare that followed every move on the field and seemed to dare and push the team without cessation. The series itself was as near a donnybrook as Ramsey had ever witnessed back home, where mass battles occurred regularly on the small-town fields. They won the first game, lost the second and took the third in fourteen innings, Henchman going all the way against Roe and staggering through when Anderson homered in the last of the fourteenth with two outs and nobody on. That gave them a one-game lead, and they finished the home stand in first place.

Ramsey wondered if the Dodgers would crack, but the Quakers made the short Eastern trips and kept winning, and the Dodgers matched them every game. The third Western swing was on them before he realized the passage of time; again it was saying good-bye to Sue, riding the Pullmans, eating food that became tasteless from regularity, going to the stadiums, playing in the strength-sapping, wet heat of midsummer, going on, never stopping. Always tomorrow, he thought, always another game to win.

He saw the pressure on that Western swing; it was a visible substance that colored all faces and changed all bodies. He saw it in Henchman's face and in the left-hander's body as the precious pounds sloughed off and Henchman became all muscle and bone, and skin drawn tightly over cheeks and nose, burned nearly black from the sun. He saw it in Henchman's eyes, most of all, where the longing to win that pennant glowed more brightly every day. This was Henchman's ninth year in the majors without a pennant. He saw it in Henchman, too much of it, for it made the usually smiling, quiet man a stranger who retired more deeply into lobby chairs and smoked too fast and talked only when spoken to.

He saw it on Hammett's body, perhaps the most perfect set of muscles and reflexes in the league; it came in a continual tenseness that moved Hammett on and off the field with that catlike, nervous pace, the long, graceful hands rubbing against something, tossing a coin, holding a ball, lifting a glove and bat. He saw it in Semick's face, a gradual tightening of mind and body against the final month in which the catcher must lift and carry his pitchers, and pray against injury that would place the burden on Lorenson and Shane, not because of jealousy of their possible success, but through that selfless desire to win that made Semick want to take the team in his two hands and play all positions.

He saw it in Ashton, a sudden deepening of the angular face lines and the constant movement of the center fielder on and off the field, a man Ramsey's own age, growing older faster than he should, fighting off a hitting slump and coming up to .300, playing as though every out, every base, meant the flag.

He saw it in the faces of Perry, and Benson, and Baker and Earling; and with them it was a sameness of narrow-eyed alertness, of deepening wrinkles, a knowledge of what was coming, ingrown and repeated so many times that pressure had become a way of life for them, a kind of opium they hated for its use of their bodies, but a habit that only death would break.

And finally he saw it in Lawson's face, for Lawson carried them all on his back, in his mind, in his heart and hopes and dreams. And this pressure became the face wrinkles and transverse forehead lines and mouth never relaxed and body hunched with thought and, if you cared to look into them, the eyes filled with all the worry and anger and hope and care, too much for a dozen men, but not enough for Lawson, who in his heart and in his mind combined shrewdness with sheer, angry fight, to carry them on day after day. He saw the pressure and wished he could assume part of each man's load, having none himself, and the last night in St. Louis he glanced in the mirror and saw a stranger's face, and knew the truth. He was no longer the bystander, no matter the days on the bench; he had his share, and he was changing inwardly, and he would never be the same.

They came home for the long home stand in the middle of August, one game behind the Dodgers, with every pitcher tired and every player exhausted. One day of rest, he thought, could never bring them back, but he was wrong. They seemed, each man, to bring forth unsuspected hoards of strength and apply it in little spots and dabs as needed; and the games came on relentlessly and they won and lost, and the Dodgers set the pace as the rest of the field dropped behind and out of contention. They finished the home stand and started the Eastern swing in a deadlock, played on through and came into Brooklyn for three games that had all the tightness of a World Series.

He threw each day with increasing anger at himself, bearing down and blazing the ball at Shane or Perry or Lorenson, throwing always at the outside corner, watching his pitches go high and low and inside, gritting away thought of failure to come back and pitch again. He threw fifty games in the bullpen, he decided, and every one a loss. His curve was breaking now as he had hoped it might someday, coming in and falling off the table; not good enough, but much better. But he did not feel this subtle change that came during the Dodger series, for he sat in the dugout and climbed the railing and shouted and pounded his hands throughout those games. This could be the pennant, he knew, if one team cracked, but again it was a split series. The Dodgers took the opener, and Robbins won the second; and in the third Beyer pitched his game of the year, a blazing duel with Newcombe that went eleven scoreless innings before Watkens dropped the squeeze bunt for the winning run.

He saw Beyer that day, the picture of a man

who hated every batter, who scowled at them and, time after time, drove them back with inside balls that cut through the box and sent them into the dirt; and he saw Beyer shake batters loose and hit the outside corner, and bring in the curve, and do what Semick said you had to do—play with them, hate them all, push them out, bring them in, keep them jumping, and give them the pay-off with everything you had in your mind and body. He saw Beyer in the dressing room after that game, unable to get off the bench for his shower half an hour later, sitting head down while the trainer worked his shoulder and arm muscles, breathing in the deep, gulping pants of the completely spent man, yet so happy his face burned with pride when he finally stood and went to the showers.

They came home for a week, and now it was September, suddenly and unbelievably, into the first ten days, with the final Western swing to play, and then home for five games—three with the Giants and the final two with the Dodgers. Those games had been sold out for two weeks and they played to near-capacity crowds against the Braves and Giants in that week at home. Henchman won his game and Beyer followed suit the next day. Robbins lost a heartbreaker to the Giants, a two-hitter that went against him, 1 to 0, when Hammett made his first error in thirty-two games and allowed the run. He saw Hammett cry in the dressing room after that game, tears of rage and self-accusation, as the Dodgers won in Boston and climbed within half a game of the lead; and the next night, in their last game at home before heading West, Hammett singled three times and smashed a double with the bases full to blast the Giants with a one-man attack.

Ramsey undressed slowly that night and wondered if he might get a chance to pitch twice the following year.

Lawson tapped his shoulder and said, "Come inside," and led him to the office. The door closed, Lawson said bluntly, "You're staying home this last three weeks. I want you at the park every morning at ten. There'll be a catcher to work with. Neil Ashton will drive you down. Run more, get your legs in perfect shape. Make your workouts longer, warm up slower. When you get warm, take off all the wraps. Throw low and throw hard. Mix the curve in. I want you to get in as much work as possible before you go home. That's all."

He hadn't realized until then, leaving the stadium, how much the team meant to him, being with these men each day, unable to help on the field, but fighting through every out with them. He wondered if Lawson had given up on him. He walked blindly to the car and tossed his packed bags into the back seat.

Sue said, "What's the matter?"

"I'm not making the trip," he said bitterly. "Lawson wants me to stay home and work. Sure, work. He doesn't want me around, that's all."

"Where to, then?"

"Anywhere," he said. "I feel lousy, Sue."

"I thought," Sue said softly, "we might drive down and see them off."

He felt the shame color his face. He said, "I'm a damned fool. Of course, we should."

They drove across the city and walked quickly through the crowded station, down the ramp, and onto the familiar platform; and he stood beside the gate and shook hands and wished them luck until the last group passed and the porter closed the gate.

Some of them showed surprise and others betrayed a new interest and feeling in their eyes, and Semick stopped to place one hand on his shoulder and say "Hold your thumbs for for us, Jim. And work hard back here. You hear me, boy."

He drove to the stadium with Neil the next morning and met Riley, a middle-aged man, squat and red-faced, veteran of fifteen minor-league years, now running his own business in the city and scouting part-time for the Quakers. Riley was all business, thorough and competent, and Ramsey ran two laps around the deserted walls, threw easily with Riley and Neil, and then settled down to the serious work. He warmed up with greater caution and did not bear down until his undershirt was wet and his face became red from effort; and then he pitched to Riley's black mitt for twenty minutes before Riley called, "Now open up, Jim."

He had dreaded this moment, and his first pitch sailed over Riley's head and thudded against the screen. Riley's face remained impassive as he reached for another ball and said, "Aim for the mitt, Jim. Low and hard."

Ten minutes later he wiped sweat from his face and said, "That's enough," and turned away disconsolately. He had tried desperately, but the old fear clung in his mind. He could throw hard and exercise good control, but hard was not sufficient, not when he could blaze it through and match any pitcher in the league. He said, "I stink," and turned away.

Neil got up and looked at Riley, and said,

"See you tomorrow, Bill," and walked with Ramsey across the vacant field to the stands.

"You saw me," Ramsey said. "I'm okay until I open up. Then I blow sky-high."

"Maybe I shouldn't say this," Neil said, "but do you realize how far you've come this summer?"

"About two feet," he said. "If that."

"No," Neil said. "Your curve is good, Jim. You can throw a fast ball in there that half the pitchers in this league would love to have. And there's the difference. The guys who don't have the fast ball, the big pitch for the tight spot, have got the other stuff to go with. They've got the good curve and the change-up, and the knuckler, half a dozen pitches, plus experience and savvy. So they get by. But you can't, and we know it, and you've got all that speed if you could only lay it in there. And the funny thing is, I think you can."

"How?" he said. "Tell me that, and I'll give you anything you want."

"So would Lawson," Neil said. "But give me time. Maybe I'll think of something."

"Like hiccups," he said. "Shock me when I'm not looking."

"That's an idea," Neil said, a small grin lifting his mouth corners. "I was thinking more along the lines of a hatpin. Well, grab your shower and let's get home for the game."

The Quakers had gone west with a one-game lead, and as the days passed and the Dodgers followed them around the circuit, neither team faltered in the all-important stretch drive. Ramsey worked doggedly in the mornings, feeling no improvement, stayed beside the radio through the afternoon games, with Sue joining him every day; and going to dinner with Sue before the Quakers played at night, coming home to listen as the innings slipped by and the Quakers continued to drive.

They lost the first game in Cincinnati, and Brooklyn won in St. Louis, again deadlocking the race, but the next day Henchman pitched a three-hitter while the Cards took Roe's measure to give the Quakers that precious one-game lead. They won the rubber game and moved to Pittsburgh for three final games with that club.

Lawson was working his pitchers on a vicious schedule, starting the big four in rotation, with Constanty pitching relief nearly every day as the games grew tighter. Henchman needed four days' rest, and Ramsey could see that man, growing thinner, more tired, but hanging on, giving everything. Robbins could last, Beyer would not falter, but Berglund's arm might not stand the strain. Ramsey dreamed at night, waking in a cold sweat whenever he envisioned injury striking the team at this time. If Hammett was hurt, he thought, if Henchman or Beyer was hurt, everything might go down. "If" was the big word. "If" and "luck." Luck had smiled on them all year, and now the days were slipping away and he prayed that nothing would happen.

They sat beside the radio and listened to the first game in Pittsburgh, Berglund pitching and Semick behind the plate. In Chicago the Dodgers were trailing the Cubs two runs in the fourth. He thought, *This can be the big break,* and listened impatiently as the Pirates went down in order, another inning passed, another, and Berglund was working on a shutout in the ninth with one away, and the announcer was saying quickly between innings, "The Cubs scored twice in the eighth and now lead the Dodgers four to two."

"We can do it," he said. "We can do it, Neil."

Neil shredded an unsmoked cigar between thick fingers and shook his head. "Wait. Anything can happen."

He listened as Berglund got the lead off man on a fly ball. The next batter struck out. He felt the tenseness leave his muscles, and decided to see a movie with Sue that night; and then the announcer's voice was saying, "It looks as if Berglund will wrap up his sixteenth win. Kiner is set in the box and here's the pitch. . . . It's a high foul on the third-base side. . . . Semick's after it. . . . He's close to the dugout. . . . Look out! . . . Semick fell into the dugout and I can't tell if he caught the ball. . . . He's getting up now, but they're holding his shoulders and—Yes, he caught the ball, and there's your ball game. . . . The Quakers' trainer and Billy Lawson are helping Semick off the field. . . . This could be an expensive foul ball for the Quakers. We'll let you know as soon as possible about Semick's ankle . . . for I'm sure the injury, if any, is an ankle."

They waited silently, listening to the recapitulation of the game, the final score from Chicago, which left the Dodgers only one game behind; and then the announcer said, "We've just got word from the Quakers' dressing room. This is bad news for Quaker fans. Semick has sprained his right ankle—how badly we do not know at this time but it is almost certain he will not be able to catch tomorrow. Billy Lawson will undoubtedly start Stan Lorenson. This is—"

Neil Ashton said, "The luck ran out."

"Maybe," Jim said. "Maybe it isn't too bad."

Neil shook his head. "That doesn't matter, Jim. It's the feeling. Semick lifted that team. Sometimes a club comes back stronger, sometimes they fold up. You never know. I'll call the front office to let us know just as soon as word comes from Pittsburgh."

Neil hurried to the phone and Ramsey stared at the radio, wanting to curse and kick the room apart, give both his ankles to Semick if that would help. He was completely, utterly sick, and he went from the house and stood in the back yard, alone and hating the world, thinking of Semick and how the Quakers would play tomorrow. Lorenson would, and could, catch as well as Semick, and Shane was there to back up, but Semick had that spark, that feeling he gave to the team which could not be matched. Ramsey turned and smashed one hand against the house wall, and wanted to cry.

The office called at seven that evening and they sat unmoving around the table, until Neil came from the hall and said, "It isn't a bad sprain, but he can't catch for three days, maybe four. He's flying home tonight for treatment. Lorenson catches tomorrow."

"We'll meet the plane," he said. "Can we Neil?"

"Sure," Neil said. "He's due in at ten."

Dinner was tasteless and uneaten after that. Ramsey drove Neil's car to Sue's, got her, and returned to pick up Neil; they reached the airport half an hour early and found the publicity director, Babe Allen, and the owner, Bob Chambers, outside against the fence, with the team's doctors. Ramsey stood apart and listened to the talk until the Pittsburgh plane came in and swung around on the apron. The door opened and he saw passengers waiting while the pilots and the stewardess helped Semick down the steps. He stood beside the gate, and Semick, hopping on one foot, supported by Babe Allen and the doctors, came through the gate, face drawn in a tight white mask.

He said, "Andy," and Semick turned, saw into and through him, and then forced a smile.

"Hey, Jim," Semick said. "How are you, boy?"

"Fine," he said thickly. "I—"

"We've got to check this ankle," Semick said. "I'll see you in the morning."

He called, "You coming out to the park?" and heard Semick answer, "Where else?" and then the crowd was thickening as they helped Semick through the rotunda to the waiting car. Sue touched his arm and they followed slowly, and drove home in late night traffic, through downtown, then on the tree-shadowed streets that seemed far from all stadiums.

"He looked so tired," Sue said.

"They're all tired," Neil said shortly. "Tonight was something to remember when the wise guys talk about all that easy money the big leaguers make for playing a foolish little game. Do you think all the money in the world would make a man go through what Semick has this summer, what he's done the last two weeks? Look at his face. You saw it. Think that money can pay for the pressure? They don't make it fast enough. And he's coming to the park tomorrow, and you know why. Because he wants to help Jim if he can and never mind the ankle. That's something they'll never pay for with money."

He could think of no words while they drank coffee and ate a midnight lunch, and driving Sue home, her hand resting lightly on his shoulder, he tried to discount Neil's words against the bigger facts of baseball as it lived to day, and could not. Baseball was big business, he knew that, with millions of dollars at stake. Players fought for the highest possible salaries and owners considered all players and coaches and managers, in too many cases, as valuable chattels rather than individuals. It was a tough game with no quarter, and once a man slipped he went down and there was always someone coming up to take his place.

A man had to make it while he could; his years were numbered in the big show; his body was all he possessed; he had to measure it against time and salaries, and make it stretch as long as possible. But under this hard core of business and too much publicity and completely heartless buying and trading and selling to improve a team, was the other part of baseball that no one would ever understand but men like Semick, who gave everything they had in mind and body and something called soul to win the game, that little game the kids played on the back lot back home.

He remembered Semick's words spoken so long ago in the spring, about having to love the game above all else if a man expected to be honest with himself; and those words rang true tonight, and would from this time on, whether he made good or failed. Semick had something in his heart that too many other players had missed along the line, and this quality was the thing Semick would carry with him throughout his life, long after he had been forgotten, the sure and solid knowledge that he gave with love while others gave with one hand in the pocketbook. A man had to live with his conscience, for what else did he have, when all was said and done, and Semick would rest easy all his life.

When they reached the bullpen the next morning, Semick was already sitting on the bench, ankle wrapped tightly and cushioned on his crutch. Semick grinned and said, "Now, this is the life, Neil. Lying around in the sun, pitching a few balls, getting fat and sassy. How do you stand it?"

"It's tough," Neil said, "but I bear up."

Ramsey knelt beside the ankle and looked at Semick questioningly. "How is it, Andy?"

"Why lie?" Semick said soberly. "I gave it a bad twist, Jim. Doc worked two hours last night. I'll get treatments every morning and afternoon. The swelling is going fast, plenty of black showing up, but it's tender. If I was your age"—Semick's face tightened—"then it would respond in a hurry. Now, I don't know. That was a damned-fool play, all my own fault."

"If the swelling is gone," Ramsey said hopefully, "maybe you'll be set for the last two games."

"We'll see," Semick said. . . . "All right, show me some stuff. I've been chewing the fat with Bill Riley. He says you're still wild when you bear down."

"I'm sorry, Andy," he said. "I can't help it."

"Your curve better?"

"Yes," he said. The curve is coming fine."

"Well, get at it," Semick said. "I'll be giving you hell every time you slip. The honeymoon is over."

Semick sat back against the wall, smoking a big cigar and rubbing his fingers over the smooth crutch wood, pushing them deliberately from their own angry sadness over his ankle, making this effort with a cost Ramsey could not measure. He warmed up slowly, while Semick talked with Neil, and said, "I'm loose, Bill," and saw Semick's eyes lift and watch him closely.

Riley crouched and gave him the target, knee high, and he came around with a full, swinging pitch. The ball went true, into the waiting mitt, and Semick nooded approval. "That's it. Wait a minute, Jim."

Semick hobbled behind him and leaned on the crutch, watching every pitch from hand to mitt on the same plane. Ramsey threw a dozen fast balls and then broke the curve fast.

Semick said, "The curve's all right. Now open up."

He squeezed the ball and his fingers whitened, feeling Semick's eyes on him, watching every move. He kicked up and gave the pitch everything in his body; it moved Riley's mitt high and outside, tipping off the edge and slamming loudly against the screen.

Semick said, "Again."

He threw for ten minutes, alternating curves and fast balls, while Semick stood motionless and called for each pitch, offering no comment as the fast balls made Riley jump and move like a monkey. He threw one last hopeful ball that made a white blur and fleeting shadow, socking into the mitt a foot high.

Semick said, "That's enough," and hobbled back to the bench. He slipped into his jacket and stood before them while Riley and Neil lit cigarettes and held the match for Semick's cigar.

"I know what you think," Semick said suddenly. "You get the call and the big one has to come, and you remember that guy back home, and the ones you hit this summer. I can see it in your shoulders, Jim. Your fingers squeeze the ball too tight. That's one thing. You kick too high because you're afraid you won't come down on the follow-through far enough to keep the ball low. And you know the ball has to be low. What if you had to pitch one of these last games and the team depended on you, believed in you? What then?"

"I'd do anything to help," Ramsey said. "You know that, Andy. But I'd louse it up."

"You'll make it," Semick said. "I can tell you that now, Jim. Not this year, maybe not even next year. But you will. There's no pressure on you, time means nothing; you'll get over this jinx, this phobia or whatever they call it. But I don't like to see you get over it that way. You're wasting time. You've got everything it takes, and the fastest ball in this league. Lick that one little thing and you can go out there today and win. If I thought beating you over the head with a bat would help, I'd be on you twice a day. But that won't do it. Come on, let's get out of here."

He felt the disappointment in Semick's voice, a rage directed against the ankle and the turn of luck, and against him for failing. He followed them across the field and down the tunnel to the dressing room, and again time overtook and passed them through that day. Semick left them to meet the doctors and they went home, ate lunch and waited beside the radio. Sue came over and kissed him quickly, and took the nearest chair; and the game came with the announcer's voice sharper today, filled with a personal worry that could not be concealed.

The Quakers won that game, with Lorenson catching magnificent baseball and collecting two hits in the rallies that scored the runs. The Dodgers were all over the Cubs, winning from the first inning, and Ramsey could see that scoreboard in Pittsburgh, and the Quakers turning, looking and digging in. They came from behind to tie in the fifth, dropped back two runs as Kiner homered in the seventh, and scored three in the eighth to gain and hold the lead.

Lawson used five pitchers and two pinch hitters in that day's game, and Ramsey saw the worry grow in Neil's eyes. They had maintained the one-game lead, but now all rotation was ruined for the duration of the season, all pitchers were tired and facing six more games in which any and all had to stand ready to deliver.

He pitched again the next morning, and talked with Semick, and listened to the final game with the Pirates, walking from the room when the Pirates scored six runs in the eighth inning and cinched the win. The Dodgers won in Chicago and the precious game lead was gone.

Lawson used four pitchers that day. And Lorenson did not hit.

They met the train next morning and Ramsey stood outside the gates and saw them pass, and had to turn away. Never again would he misjudge the meaning of pressure; it was on their faces, indelibly stamped, but they came up the ramp fast and eager, as if ready to step out on the field and play now, all day, all night, if they needed that much to win. The first game with the Giants was the next night, the second another night game, and the last in the afternoon; the schedule was tripping them now, cutting hours from rest between the second night game and the afternoon game the following day. The Giants were fresh, he knew. They had no pressure. Durocher had saved his three best for this series, as all managers did. Ramsey thought of Jansen, and whoever else Durocher would pick, and wished that he could help. But all he could do was go out and throw to a catcher, watch his fast ball go wild, and sit in the dugout, useless in the uniform he loved.

Semick wasn't waiting the next morning when they reached the stadium. He ran one lap and threw easily to Riley for twenty minutes, and finally Semick hobbled across the field and through the bullpen gate.

"Sleeping late?" he asked.

Semick bent beside the bench and picked up a bat, and stared sober-faced across the dusty ground. Jim wondered if Semick had got bad news about the ankle or was preparing to give him everlasting hail Columbia.

"You loose?" Semick asked sharply.

"Just about," he said. "Five more."

Semick said, "Throw them."

He pitched five balls and felt his arm come loose and ready; and stepped behind the rubber, waiting and wondering. Semick hefted the bat carelessly and rubbed the trademark lines and threw his cigar against the screen; tobacco shreds broke and fluttered limply to the ground.

"Did you see them come home yesterday morning?" Semick said. "Sure you did. They looked whipped? You know they didn't. They're playing on nerve and guts. Listen, Jim. Henchman hasn't kept food down for three days. You see him crawling for a bed? Lorenson's got a bruise on his meat hand half an inch deep and big as a tin cup. He'll catch. You see Hammett and Smith and Ashton and Anderson? They've played every game this year. Anderson's got a charley horse that doubles him up. Ashton's lost ten pounds. Hammett can't sit still ten seconds. You think they care? You know what they want, how much they've given to win this pennant. You've felt it, I know you have. And you want to pitch? You said you'd try anything, didn't you? Well, this is as good a time as any to call your bluff. Let's see you bear down, Jim. Let's see you cut loose. This is the road down the middle, right here, a few lousy feet. And this is the fork in the road. The men go one way, the boys go another. You can't stall along on the cushion forever. Show me your stuff!"

He had never heard Semick talk in this way before, harsh and thin, with the voice of a total stranger and yet his best friend. He did not understand, and then he saw Semick hobble painfully to the plate and stand in the righthand batting box, about six inches back from the inside corner, balancing on the crutch and his one good leg, holding the bat up and behind his thick shoulder.

He stared and wondered what Semick wanted, and waited for him to move away, and then Semick spoke in a snarling voice, "Well, damn it! Let's see what you've got!"

And then he knew. He saw Riley's face behind the plate, carved in red stone, silent and fading white. He saw Neil leaning forward on the bench, hands clasped and grinding together, face impassive and waiting. He looked at Semick and saw the white plate and the dust and the six short inches from rubber to body; and in that distance, which meant nothing in its emptiness and was less than a man's finger span, was everything he had to face. Not tomorrow, or next month, or next year; that was no good and Semick knew it, and he knew it deep inside. The only way was the tough way, and he either had it within him and brought it out now, or could do just one thing: turn around and walk across that field and take off the uniform and go home.

He looked at Semick and saw the ball going down with the killing speed he knew he possessed, going wild and hitting the man, who could not move if he wished, and would not move for heaven or earth in this moment. He felt his right toe on the rubber and saw his arm drop from the glove, holding the ball, fingers so white the bones made their dull shadow beneath the skin. Then he could not stop, but moved back and around, left leg kicking up and out, shoulders tensing and fingers tearing the very seams out of the ball, then coming down and feeling the ball go faster than he had ever thrown before, knuckles scraping dirt deeply as he followed through and stood in this half-suppliant position, eyes closed and blood running from the knuckles rasped cruelly across the dirt.

"All right!" Semick said bitingly. "Throw it again! And keep throwing!"

And then he could look up. He saw the mitt on the outside corner, a foot higher than it should be, but steady and black, with the ball in the pocket, and Riley's face behind the blackness of the mitt, no longer white, but growing red with some feeling he did not comprehend. Semick stood unmoving beside the plate, bat back, crutch tight under his right shoulder.

"Throw it again!" Semick said. "What's the matter? Is the yellow running down your legs? You were a foot off! Put it in the target!"

Riley threw the ball and he caught it, and stood for a moment behind the rubber; and then he wanted to throw his glove over the screen and kick the screen out and do a dance. He felt it going, and his face worked convulsively with this new freedom that had come the hard way, the only way, and was not complete, but coming into his arms and body and, most of all, into his heart. He toed the rubber and pitched at the mitt, which looked bigger now, bearing down and feeling the surge of power in his shoulder as the ball went in and thudded against the mitt, straight to the pocket and blurred with its speed.

"That's better!" Semick said. "Keep throwing!"

He did not remember how long he threw to the mitt, but suddenly his arm was hot and tired, and Semick held up one hand and dropped the bat and said, "I think that'll do it," and staggered as he turned to the bench.

Ramsey ran as Neil came off the bench, and when he held Semick's arm, he looked down at the catcher's brown, scarred hands and saw the white-and-red marks on the palms and fingers, the oblong flattened marks where the hands had gripped the bat handle so tightly that all circulation had been cut off.

"Andy," he said. "Andy!"

"Well, pitcher," Semick said, and this time his voice cracked with pent-up strain, "welcome home."

He sat in the dugout that night and the next, and the third afternoon, no longer a stranger to these men. They didn't know yet, he thought, and this was no time to babble about a new-found strength, but he felt as if this team was his, and he was a part that could not help them this year, but would make up everything in years to come. He worked in the bullpen and Semick hobbled out each afternoon and stood behind him and said, "Take it easy. Not all the way. You've got it now. Bring it along."

And then he was part of the bench, yelling himself hoarse as Lawson brought the Quakers through that series undefeated. He never knew how they won the three games against fresh pitching, especially the last game, with Jansen going for the Giants after a full week's rest. Beyer started the first game, but could not last, and Lawson sent Constanty and Robbins and finally Berglund to the mound, as Durocher countered with everything on the Giant bench, in a game that saw the lead change five times before Anderson broke it up in the last of the ninth, a storybook finish with the bases full and the single dropping into center one short step before Thomson's desperation dive.

They took the second as Lawson started Robbins, and the Giants hit like madmen, with only the fielding saving runs and cutting off half a dozen rallies. Lawson used five pitchers that night, and Hammett played a game Ramsey never forgot. The shortstop handled twelve chances and started four double plays, and one was impossible, even when they saw him make the stop and throw. They won the afternoon game with Henchman going eight innings in a reversal of the other games, a scoreless duel against Jansen that saw Henchman unable to come out for the ninth and Constanty pitch his sixth straight day to hold the deadlock for Willy Smith in the last of the ninth. Smith hit the first pitch into the centerfield stands; and as the third-sacker ran the bases and they rushed to the plate, the scoreboard showed the eighth inning in Brooklyn. The Braves had scored three runs and led three to two, and ten minutes later Babe Allen burst into the dressing room and shouted the good news. The Dodgers had lost and the Quakers had the one-game lead.

He stood beside Semick and felt wonderful, and then thought, *Who will Billy pitch against the Dodgers tomorrow?* and knew why the voices had quieted so suddenly across the room. Shane came from his locker and they looked at each other, a brief moment, and Shane grunted and left the room.

Semick murmured, "He'll be great if he can ever lick himself," and hobbled into the private office, opening the door and showing Ramsey, for a second, the faces inside and the cigar smoke and the lack of all jubilation over the Dodgers' defeat. He saw Neil signal from the corridor and left the room.

Lawson sat behind the desk and held both hands flat on the table, and this applied force was not enough to conceal the trembling that moved up the forearms and vanished beneath the flaring white sleeves. Lawson stared at Semick and breathed deeply, cautiously, as if testing his lungs and finding them intact; and then found a cigar and lit it carefully. Earling sat with Cy Perry in the far corner, their hands filled with the charts, eyes wandering to the floor and across the room. Benson's face twitched as he began undressing, one hand moving upward to rub his bald pink head with a slow, painful gesture.

"The ankle," Lawson said. "Can you go, Andy?"

"Not tomorrow, Billy," Semick said.

"The last one?"

Semick nodded and stared beyond Lawson at the blank wall. "I could, but it isn't worth the chance. I can't let you try it."

"All right," Lawson said. "You're the doctor, Andy. I wouldn't want to hurt it permanently."

Semick murmured, "Thanks, Billy," and then moved his right hand across his body in a short, quick gesture, as if relaying some secret, shared fact between them.

Lawson's face moved with an old thought and he said, "Did he lick it?"

Semick lifted the crutch and stared at the rubber tip, and then said faintly, "Yes, Billy."

"You mean that?"

"Everything, Semick said. "He's ready."

Lawson moved his head quickly in a negative, silencing gesture. "All right, Andy," he said, as if unable to believe Semick's words. Lawson turned then, facing the others, and said, "Let's face it, George. Who starts tomorrow?"

Lawson listened to their speech that seemed to loosen the nearly unbearable tension for a few minutes; and in his mind, hidden so deeply that he dared not express himself to them, and afraid that Semick might accidentally betray the confidence, was the idea that had formed long ago and was no longer a foolish, wild chance, but very likely the only thing he could do if the Dodgers won tomorrow's game and placed the pennant on the block that final day. He had no pitchers left—everyone knew that—and he could not have used them differently and stayed in the race. They were dog-tired, even sick, and after tomorrow there was no one remaining for the final game. No one but . . . Lawson closed his eyes, weighing the chance, knowing the risk to the team, considering that risk above his own future, which could fall to pieces completely and forever if his gamble failed. He had to sleep on it, he thought, and make the final decision tomorrow after the game, if the Dodgers won.

Shane had dinner in a downtown café and wandered aimlessly through the shopping district, staring into show windows and moving with the early-evening crowd, thinking of the team. He had expected the Quakers to finish in the first division, even second, but this surge was something he could not understand; and he knew too well that somewhere on the Western swing, playing those bitterly fought games day after day, the team had got away from him. It was a sensation of dryness in his chest, watching them as individuals on the field, at the plate, in the hotel at night, and seeing them come together in a cohesive unit that included only those men who were giving all their strength and part of their future health to this pennant drive, and he was not among those present. He wanted the pennant, and his part had been important to the whole. He had caught games when Semick and Lorenson needed rest, he had hit in the clutch, he had given the team his strength and skill, but inside, where Shane lived with himself, the truth was self-evident. He had not given enough, and he could not find the reason, wanting now to feel their spirit of oneness.

He had watched Lorenson in the trainer's room after the game today, sitting under a lamp while Wecheck worked on the bruised right hand. Lorenson was white-faced, and when Wecheck pressed too long on the palm, over the thick brown calluses, the big man winced and then coughed to cover the pain. Shane saw this, from the medicine cabinet across the room, and wondered if Lorenson was a damned fool.

Shane thought of the money riding on these final two games and wanted to tell Lorenson what he considered to be stupidity—namely, catching with a bad hand that might drop a crucial throw and lose the game. Shane wanted to catch the final games, not for the honor and the glory, or whatever the romanticists called it, but to protect an investment he was already counting; and with this desire was the overriding and undimmed wish to show Ramsey what he could do in the big clutch with the pressure on tighter than a can lid. He was satisfied with himself tonight. He would be back next year, he felt, and a good many years following, as Semick grew too old and Lorenson needed help in the long grind; and the big money was coming now, with the Series split hanging in the balance tomorrow and the last day. He was satisfied, and told himself that Shane was a lucky guy, and underneath he was entirely and miserably unhappy.

Shane turned into a movie and sat for half an hour, watching the ghost shadows, and left without knowing the picture's name or the faces of the actors, and took a taxi to the apartment, where he made a pot of coffee and undressed, and sat in the kitchen's small, cramped breakfast nook, the evening papers before him, filled with the usual headlines and twenty-odd stories concerning the two big games. The city was caught in the pennant fever, he knew, and the World Series could not excite more interest and hope and sound than these last games with the Dodgers.

The vagrant thought touched his mind that all over the country tonight, reading a thousand papers filled with the same words, fifty million baseball fans were wondering how the big players spent this night before the big games.

Shane remembered his own youth, the fall of the 1940 Series, how he had lain sleepless the better part of a night, praying that the Tigers would win the pennant and give Rowe a chance to pitch once more in a Series. He had visualized the players on that night as sitting sternly in their homes, listening to radio music, eyes closed to avoid strain, saving themselves for the next day, living in a vacuum-packed world, guarded from molestation by cops and fed through a tube to protect their churning stomachs. And tonight, across the country, another crop of boys held the same thoughts and dreams, and Shane sat in his apartment with a cup of black coffee, made too strong and needing the woman's touch, unable to sleep and worried about tomorrow with a selfishness that excluded him from the inner circle of his own team.

When a taxi horn blared below in the street, Shane got up and threw the empty cup against the wall and went to bed.

3.

Ramsey ate silently that night, sitting again with the others as they had eaten at this table for six months, each in his own place, with Neil and Genevieve surveying them gravely. He remembered the talk of other nights, the laughter and jokes, the arguments about where to go and what to do, and who was the girl who cruised past in the convertible that afternoon—a full hour of happy, casual talk—but tonight there was an unnatural intentness upon food, so that dinner was finished and everyone had moved to the living room within a half hour.

Sue arrived at eight-thirty, and they sat together on the porch, holding hands and saying very little, listening to the odd word scraps coming through the open door and windows from the living room.

He heard Galliant excuse himself and go upstairs at ten, and the others followed within twenty minutes. Above their heads the room lights threw yellow rectangles on the lawn, remained so for a few minutes, and then snapped off. Genevieve clattered dishes in the kitchen and Neil joined them on the porch to sit on the top step, back against the corner post, smoking a cigar and staring into the night. Jim had not told Sue about pitching to Semick and finding part, if not all, of himself. Neil, for some reason, had given him strict orders not to boast before he was certain; and tonight

Neil wiggled restlessly against the corner post and finally spoke.

"Might not be my business," Neil said, "but what have you two planned?"

"Nothing," Sue said. "Yet."

Neil drew a huge red spark in the darkness. "Time, I'd say, to start."

Ramsey said, "I've been scared to mention it to her, Neil. I'm glad you did. Maybe she'll give me an answer before a witness."

"You know how I feel," Sue said. "So does Neil. But I want to be sure."

"About Jim?" Neil asked.

"Not Jim," Sue said quickly. "You know what I mean, Neil."

"I should," Neil said dryly. "Listening to you two rub noses on this porch all summer. If you're worrying about Jim making himself into a pretty fair country-style pitcher, I'll tell you a little secret. Just between me, Semick, Lawson, Earling, Perry, Benson and Baker, not to mention Jim and a few baseballs squeezed out of shape, we kinda think he'll come through."

"Then he's licked it?" Sue said. "And you didn't tell me?"

"I didn't say that," Neil said. "I said Jim was going to make it. So, in case you're worrying about the groceries and the rent and the income tax and the furniture and a few thousand other odds and ends, don't. Just set the date and give us fair warning, so we can all think up some original present and end up buying sixteen toasters and half a dozen waffle irons."

Sue said, "You've got a lot of nerve, Neil Ashton," and Ramsey felt her fingers tighten on his hand as the laughter overrode severity.

"Always did have," Neil said. "Out around Tilden, Nebraska, I'm a tough man before the draw and after the chips are down. . . . I'm going to bed. Jim, don't you stay up too late."

Neil closed the front door, and Ramsey turned and kissed her, and wanted to tell about Semick and felt that it was too soon. *Later,* he thought; *sometime next year, when I really prove I can lick it.*

She moved against his arm and said, "When, you big lug?"

"This winter," Ramsey said. "You set the date."

"I will," Sue said. "Let's wait until—" and they both sat in silence, thinking of tomorrow.

"I feel pretty good tonight," Ramsey said. "I'm wound up tighter than a dollar watch, don't let me fool you, and I won't slow down until this is over. I'm happy enough to like everybody, even Shane."

"You never really hated him," Sue said softly. "Did you?"

Ramsey said, "No, Sue. It was always pity, I know that now. I'd give a lot to see him change. He could be a wonderful guy."

"I'm going home," Sue said. "Good night. I'll see you at the game."

He had orders to be at the stadium before eleven and finish his workout by eleven-thirty, and Neil drove with him across the city and led the way through a throng already mobbing the gates. He dressed and made the long walk to the bullpen and found Semick, in uniform, without the crutch, waiting impatiently.

Semick limped to the plate and threw a new ball and said, "Let's get at it, Jim. Show me that stuff, boy."

He felt wonderful and said, "Better get two sponges, Andy," and then warmed up slowly and threw fast for ten minutes, feeling the blessed difference, the relaxation and confidence, as he jarred Semick from shoulders to heels with a dozen blazing fast balls. He was far from steady, he knew, and his control lacked an inch here and there, but he was coming fast. He would work this fall at home, he thought, and take Sue to Clearwater on their honeymoon and work out early next spring, and really show them something next year.

Semick said, "That's it, Jim. Button up and be here tomorrow at eleven."

As he walked across the field, staring at the stands, nearly filled at eleven-thirty, the pressure came down tight and hard and vicious, blotting out all personal happiness and dreams as he reached the dugout and stepped into the beginning of the game.

He saw the familiar routine progress as the Quakers and Dodgers took their workouts, then the infield practice, and Lawson moved deliberately along the base line, watching everything, calm as stone outside, but unable to conceal the tension in his fingers and moving eyes, kicking pebbles with his spikes as he walked. Everything was the same, yet filled with a difference today, a tightness on the field and a sound from the crowd that had no similarity to other games.

Baker ran the infield through a fast workout, and suddenly the announcer's voice blared through the stands and rolled across the field, giving the lineups. Lawson was starting Beyer with two days' rest, plus relief the day before, but no one could doubt his decision. Beyer would start and go to the limit of his endurance, and then the others would come on and hope they had enough left to win this game and cinch the pennant.

He knew that Roe was pitching today for the Dodgers, with two days' rest, and Shotton was saving Newcombe for the final game, betting everything on the batting power of his team to win this one and then come back with Newcombe in the final.

Lawson came into the dugout and stood beside him for a moment and said, "Feel okay?" and moved away. Shane stood beside him at the railing, face strained and dark-eyed, big hands clamped over the rail. He felt no animosity today for Shane, and did not move until Beyer pitched to Cox, a called strike, and then sat back on the bench as the game began.

He was lost in the game then, as Beyer and Roe started in strong fashion, and the crowd roared with every play and hit. Roe was having a day, that was painfully clear after the first inning, and Beyer was pitching his heart out, bearing down on every ball.

They raced through four innings of up-and-down-and-out baseball, and Beyer showed the strain when he went to the mound for the fifth. Campanella worked a full count and fouled two pitches, and singled to center field; and Constanty and Henchman began throwing in the bullpen without command. Lorenson called the pitchout and Reese lunged for the ball as Watkens and Smith rushed in and then stopped on the fake. Reese looked at two pitches, and Ramsey felt the strength leave Beyer's arm as surely as if he stood out there himself. Reese swung on the next pitch as Campanella broke for second. The ball skittered over the grass and Galliant made the play to first as Campanella hit second in a cloud of dust. Lawson was up, brushing past them to the step, hand sliding along the rail, knuckles white. *One break*, Ramsey thought; *one is all anyone will need today.*

Roe came from the dugout and selected a bat, and Ramsey saw the pitcher step into the box, and knew then that Shotton was going with the lanky left-hander all the way. Beyer wiped his face and dusted his fingers on the rosin bag, and pitched cannily, putting Roe in a quick hole and slipping the curve ball past for the strikeout; and Cox came up, as Lawson glanced toward the bullpen and then studied Beyer intently. Lorenson turned and Beyer waited, and Lawson gave the signal, playing all percentage to the finish. Beyer threw the four outside pitches and Cox ran to first and stood there, hands cupped, shouting encouragement to Hermanski coming in.

Beyer again wiped his face, and then his hands, and used the rosin bag. *Stealing seconds,* Ramsey thought, *trying to find it in his arm once more.* Lawson moved suddenly, and then seemed to weigh the odds, and remained still on the dugout step. Beyer checked the runners and made his pitch, and the ball was a streak over second, dropping free and rolling as Campanella rounded third and Ashton scooped the short hop on the dead run and threw to the plate.

Ramsey felt the railing crack beneath them as Campanella and the ball met, and Stewart stood over the play, arms out and palms down. Campanella was safe, there was no question, and Lorenson was out of the dust and holding Cox at second; behind second base Ashton slammed one fist into his glove, and Ramsey saw the angry tears glint as Ashton turned and dropped back into position. And then Lorenson was calling time and coming to the dugout, right hand stiff and red.

Ramsey saw Wecheck work over the hand and heard Lorenson say, "The toe got it. It's numb, Billy; I can't move the fingers."

"Nothing broken," Wecheck said quickly. "Try again, Stan."

"No use," Lorenson said. "I'll be all right tomorrow, Billy. I'll be all right then. But I'll louse it up if I stay in now. I'm sorry, Billy. I'm so damned sorry."

Lorenson began to cry, and Lawson pushed him gently toward the tunnel and called, "Shane."

Shane passed him, and he said, "Give 'em hell, Clark," and Shane's eyes met his for a brief moment, and then Shane was running to the plate and the announcer's voice gave the change. Ramsey thought, *He can do it; he's got to do it,* and then Beyer was pitching with that momentary rest, forcing Snider to ground out and end the inning. They came off the field on the dead run, and Beyer was helped into his jacket as Smith swung three bats and went to the plate.

Beyer looked up and called, "Billy," and Lawson came from the step and said, "What's the matter, Russ?"

"One more," Beyer said. "Maybe I can, maybe not, Billy. Better have somebody ready. I don't have it any more."

He felt that game slipping away, even though Anderson tied it in the seventh with a long home run. Beyer lasted the sixth, and Henchman came out for the seventh, staggered through, with a fine double play by Galliant saving another run; and in the eighth the Dodgers broke through.

It was sudden and brutal, with Snider tripling and Robinson doubling. Lawson called time and Berglund came in, and Furillo singled to right field, scoring Robinson with the third run. Berglund steadied then and retired the side, but the damage was done. They could not break through in their half of the eighth, and after Berglund had pitched beautiful ball to stop the Dodgers cold in the ninth, Ramsey watched luck turn away. Ashton singled to start the last chance, Hammett drove a curving, skittering smash into the hole between first and second on the hit-and-run, and Robinson made a diving one-hand stab, rolled over and up, and threw to Hodges for the out. Watkens doubled down the right-field line and Ashton came across, and then Anderson hit a ball up and out, and Hermanski backed against the wall and leaped and made the catch, falling and making the throw-in as Watkens tagged up and raced to third. Smith was walked on purpose, and Sipler smashed another ball that looked like the best hit of the day, but Snider ran out and back and took it against the right-center-field wall to end the game and put them where they were on April nineteenth, all even and going away, with tomorrow the final pay-off.

Jim had been deadened by sound and tension, and he did not think of tomorrow until after he showered and sat miserably on the bench, trying to console himself by thinking that tomorrow was another day and luck could not treat them in this way forever; and then he remembered the pitching and was completely frightened and sick. The Dodgers had Newcombe, rested two days—enough for that big man to come back and go the distance—and Newcombe had beaten them four out of six starts during the year. And what did they have, he thought, as everyone in this silent room was thinking. Beyer was exhausted, Henchman and Berglund would not be fresh, could not be, and Robbins had come back with one day's rest after pitching in seven of their last nine games. Constanty had been saved today and could go at least three innings in relief tomorrow, but Constanty was possibly more tired than any other man on the staff. The others had no chance. Lawson would have to start Robbins and pray for the breaks.

Ramsey wanted to smash the bench and the locker line, do something, anything, and in this moment hated himself with bitter intensity for standing before them, strong and fresh, able to pitch twenty innings, but unable to offer himself for such a game. He would come out tomorrow morning and throw fifty useless balls and put on his jacket and watch what seemed to be the inevitable, and what good would that do? He got up and kicked savagely against the bench and left the dressing room. From the office door Semick watched him go and turned inside where Lawson sat at the scarred desk, holding an unlit cigar and staring blindly at the opposite wall.

"What do you say, Billy?" Semick asked softly.

Lawson looked up and shook his head and murmured, "Tomorrow, Andy. Don't ask me now."

"Sure," Semick said gently. "But believe me, Billy, he's ready."

Lawson crushed the cigar in his fingers and let the crumpled pieces drop on the desk. He said, "Can he go five, Andy? If he can, we've got a chance."

"He'll go all the way," Semick said, "or nothing."

Lawson nodded and moved his head, and Semick went away into the dressing room and stood over Shane, face intent and thoughtful. He said, "I knew you had it, Clark. Thanks."

Shane looked up and said, "Ah," and then bit his lower lip and said, "You mean that?"

"I don't talk for fun," Semick said. "Sleep tonight, Clark. You know what I mean . . . Stan can't do it tomorrow. He'll offer, but that hand's swollen twice up now."

Semick moved away and Shane sat, head down, staring dully at his dirty, wet hands and stained pants. He was confused and sick with an unknown fear. He would catch tomorrow. They did not need to worry about how he could catch if Lorenson couldn't go; he would catch the game of his life. For somewhere in the last four innings, crouching behind the plate, calling signals and talking to the pitchers, he had lost part of that lonely feeling. He had found himself thinking only of the team and the game, with no thought for the money. He was going soft, he thought bitterly, but the feeling remained.

Ramsey barely touched his meal that night, and could not stay in the living room longer than five minutes. He went to the porch, and Neil came from the house and said, "We'll have a lunch later on, Jim," and sat heavily on the top step. This was the worst part, he decided, this living through the night and the morning, waiting for tomorrow afternoon. He heard them going upstairs to their rooms and hoped that Galliant could sleep. The second baseman was playing magnificent ball, but the pressure was getting him, too, and tomorrow was something altogether unfair for Galliant, in his first year, to face. But Galliant would face it and come through. He felt that, and then he could see Lawson across town in his own home, and could not guess or even feel the depth of that man's emotions on this night.

He thought the time would never pass, but eleven came and Neil said, "Time to eat," and he followed dutifully to the kitchen and ate two sandwiches and drank half a quart of milk, and then went to bed. He finally slept, waking twice in the gray morning hours, and getting up at nine when Genevieve called from the stairs. He was hungry this morning and ate decently and left the house with Neil and made the drive across the city. Dressed and crossing the field, he stopped suddenly at the bullpen gate and looked at Neil and thought, *He has given me all this time, this help, and his own son must need something today.*

He felt a wave of guilt and said, "I never have thanked you for everything. Neil. Robbie—"

"Robbie and I understand," Neil said. "Robbie is over the hump, Jim. He'll be all right today. And don't thank me. You don't have to. I guess we understand each other without a lot of words."

He grinned and tossed his jacket on the bench, and turned to greet Semick, who came through the gate and nodded without expression.

Semick said, "We'll warm up good, Jim. Not too much speed. Just throw and get loose all the way."

"All right," he said. "How's the ankle?"

"No," Semick said shortly. "Come on, let's throw."

He seemed to have better control on this last day, as if all the months had come together in a final peak and presented him with a small reward of confidence and good control. He threw to the mitt and felt the sweat come, and then opened up three-quarters speed for a dozen pitches.

Semick said, "Give me two more," and he threw perfectly to the steady mitt. "Put on your jacket," Semick said. "Put a towel around your neck."

Semick seemed to be laboring with some problem too great for any one man, and when they reached the dugout and he saw the faces and heard the crowd above and around them, he could not believe that such tension existed. Yesterday had been a time he would never forget; and today was all the pressure, the nights, the games, the past months rolled into two short hours yet unspent, impossible to foresee and live through, but he would, watching every pitch and play. He thought of Robbins and wondered how he would react in that man's place; and then he wanted to give Robbins his own strength in some way, so that Robbins could pitch and last and win this game.

He knew that Lawson had refused to name the starting pitcher, but the papers had examined the situation with cold logic, and the only choice was Robbins. He had to agree. Robbins was the only man left—tired and nervous, but the only one. And Lorenson might not be able to come back. He looked around and saw Shane, and wanted to go over and say something, but Shane would only laugh and turn away.

Time was gone then, through the workouts and the infield practice for the Quakers, and the Dodgers moved across the field and began their last workout, talking loudly, throwing with a seeming lack of all tension; and across the triangle Newcombe came out and began warming up. Lawson stood before the dugout and spoke with Lorenson and Wecheck, and then turned and nodded to Shane, who whitened and spoke some soundless word. High above in the press box, the writers looked down, waiting, and as Shane moved out to the warm-up plate, the announcer finished the Dodgers' lineup and began calling the Quakers in their regular order: Ashton, Hammett, Watkens, Anderson, Smith, Sipler, now Galliant, moved up to seventh, and then Shane in the catcher's spot. And Lawson stood before the dugout and faced the field and seemed to freeze in a terrible moment of silence, one hand holding the pencil, the other twisting the small white lineup cards with the ninth line still blank, as if looking back on the long night and morning, and coming to a final decision. Semick was suddenly beside him, hand hard on his shoulder, watching Lawson; and he was cold with fear for some reason; and then Lawson turned as the clock read twelve minutes to go, and looked down and said, "Ramsey, warm up!"

Jim felt Semick's rough hand dig into his shoulder and he thought there were no words in his mind, only murmuring from above, and then he saw Lawson's face and understood everything that had happened in the past. He tried to speak, and the shock touched down into his chest and stomach, and he felt Semick's hands pushing him toward the step. And then he had to be alone for a minute, two minutes. He looked up at Lawson and said thickly, "Wait," and ran blindly for the tunnels and down through the shadows and across the empty corridor into the dressing room, past the lockers into the lavatory and over the nearest bowl; and then he was sick until he gasped for breath and stood up, finally able to breathe. He bent over the next bowl and washed his face and hands, and thought, *Don't think; don't try to think,* and then he was walking steadily through the tunnel onto the field, and Semick was waiting to remove his jacket and push his glove into his left hand.

Semick said, "You've got ten minutes. Take your time. You're almost warm now. Throw to the mitt. Don't look up. Don't look at the field. Throw to the mitt. You understand, Jim, there's just you and Shane and that mitt."

He came from the dugout shadow and stepped on the rubber and faced Shane, and saw the stunned unbelief on Shane's face; and then he heard the roar, and as it died away in an equally stunned sound, the announcer's voice came hoarsely and unsteadily over the speakers, "Pitching for the Quakers, Number Forty-six, Ramsey! Number Forty-six, Jim Ramsey!"

He stared at the mitt and threw, and Shane took the ball, returned the throw, and stood white-faced behind the plate. He threw for an eternity, it seemed, hearing the voices rising and the words a jumble of incoherent sound, but clear in their meaning. Lawson was crazy, they were saying; Lawson had cracked up. Ramsey! Not Ramsey! That was giving it to them on a platter. He pitched and kept his head down, and his arms came loose and hot beneath the shirt; and then Lawson had his arm, turning him, and Shane came trotting to walk with them toward the plate.

"You know your signals?" Lawson asked.

He nodded, and Shane said, "Same ones, Ramsey."

"All right," Lawson said in an utterly calm and expressionless voice. "I've made a lot of mistakes. I'll make some more. I put you two together in the spring. I know how you've felt. Maybe I've been wrong about that, I don't know. But you're catching, Shane. . . . Ramsey, this is your ball game. Pitch for us, Ramsey; pitch as long as you can. Every inning you can last means more chances for us. . . . Shane, I want speed. . . . Ramsey, you've got it, boy. Now you know how much you've got. They don't know. Show them. All right, let's go!"

Lawson turned away and for one moment Ramsey stood beside Shane, closer than a million brothers had ever stood through the years, and Shane whispered, "I'm catching a game, Ramsey. Let's see you stay with me."

He nodded, unable to speak, and made the walk and turned and threw eight times. He bent over and held the rosin bag between his fingers and felt the fat sack crush and almost split. The ball went down to second and came around, and they were up and standing with him, and the ball was in his hand. They did not speak now; they looked at him, and then he was alone on the mound and Cox was stepping in, and Shane gave the signal for the fast ball through the middle, and time now stood still within his chest.

He toed the rubber and moved his arm, up and around, and then he could see the mitt alone, waiting, and he came down with explosive force, muscles bunching and uncoiling in the long whip as he felt the ball leave his finger tips, straight and hard and true. Cox stood with bat poised, head snapping around and following the white blur as the mitt moved upward and swallowed the pitch; and then Shane was throwing and talking, a strange note in his voice, and behind the mound came the sudden, completely surprised shout from his infield. He had touched the outside corner with a belt-high pitch, and Cox was turning and dusting both hands, glancing at the dugout, and again facing him with some new feeling of respect and shock in his face.

Ramsey took the signal and pitched, and Cox swung, coming around and falling with the force of a missed strike as the ball went in above the knees; and then he had the sensation of power and the feeling of coming from the darkness into the light. He was shaking with a nervous fear, and he knew his control was not good, but he could throw, he could put all power on the ball and his body remained loose and confident.

He missed the corner with two pitches and Cox fouled another, and now Shane was moving around and throwing to Watkens, slowing him down, and Watkens crossed to the grass edge and tossed underhanded and said, "All the time, Jim. All the time in the world." He turned and faced Cox, and saw the signal for another low fast ball; and this pitch slipped as he came down, splitting the plate at the shoulders as Cox poked and missed, and turned out of the box, surprise plain on his face. He heard the roar and saw, in uncertain, oblique silhouette, the Quakers up and lining the railing, shouting unheard below the crowd sound, every man with him now.

He thought, *Let me last six innings if I can have the luck,* and faced Hermanski with no elation at the strikeout, as if that piece of miraculous luck was only a matter of Cox's unpreparedness for his speed. They would come up with their eyes open from this time on, choking if necessary, going for the good pitch, waiting him out; and suddenly he didn't care. He could pitch all day and night if Lawson spoke the word.

Hermanski looked at three pitches—a strike and two balls—and Shane called an inside pitch, the first one. This was the unconscious test he had been waiting for, he knew that, forming the invisible alignment between fingers, toes, body and the inside corner of that small plate. He threw and saw Hermanski leap back, falling away and dropping on stiff spread hands and buttocks, bat rolling in the dirt, as Shane lunged and speared the high pitch; and Ramsey felt no fear, only an overpowering hatred for the batter, who had no name in his mind and represented all the batters who came on forever, as Semick had spoken of them in the long ago.

He took the throw and saw Shane's face, worried behind the mask, and saw Shane call for another inside pitch on the belt. He came down and saw the ball slant in, then hop, and disappear into Shane's waiting mitt as Hermanski lifted both arms and sucked in his belly, standing thoroughly loose and unsettled; then he was pitching in a narrow world that contained only himself, the batter and Shane, throwing at the big yellow mitt, vaguely aware of the black-clad arm rising in the strike call or remaining incumbent as he missed the zone.

He lost Hermanski on the three-two pitch and Snider faced him, digging in and swinging from the heels on his first pitch, fouling the ball into the stands far down the line. He pitched inside and Snider topped the ball as crowd sound lifted in panic, hung on a high note and burst into a choked, lifting roar as Galliant scooped and flipped the flat, burning peg to Watkens for the out. He took the ball from Watkens and mumbled his thanks, and they nodded grimly, and Robinson stepped into the box.

Shane was talking hoarsely, moving his shoulders and giving the signs, dabbing with his mitt and crouching in the umpire's slanting shadow. Robinson took the strike, looked on and back at the ball on the outside, and seemed to swing as he released the third delivery. He saw the ball, topped, rolling in the grass along the third-base line, and came on the run, lifting it and turning, then feeling it bobble in his fingers. He held it then, watching Hermanski reach third and Robinson cross first as the roar came down and beat upon his head.

He was frightened again, not for himself, but for the team. He straddled the rubber and took the sign, saw Robinson dancing, tempting the throw, and tried to ignore the dangerous threat. Robinson faked the steal as he pitched a strike to Furillo; and then Shane was calling for the pitchout and he was checking first, stopping his arms at the belt, and losing a precious second as he threw wide. Robinson was running and he ducked just in time as Shane's bullet peg grazed his head and hit Hammett's waiting glove. Robinson came in and made his slide, hooking outside and away from the tag, safe by that split second.

Hermanski did not risk trying to go in from third on the play.

Ramsey cursed himself and thought, *I've got to last,* and pitched again. Furillo ran up the full count, and he missed the corners and Furillo trotted to first as the crowd protested, calling for another pitcher, losing their astonishment and momentary joy, seeing this game thrown away in the first moments. Hodges waited and took two pitches, and Shane made the return throws slower, faking to second as Robinson leaped and ran off the bag, never still and always dangerous.

He had a two-two count then, and Hodges was taking the sign from the coach, and Shane crouched, shouting to him, giving the second signal set as Robinson bent at second and watched the plate. He caught the curve sign, the first one, and came up and down, released the ball with full snap and good finger action, and saw it go in and duck suddenly as Hodges swung, tried to check, and ended in a half-faced motion, bat dangling helplessly while Stewart called the strike. And then he was moving toward the dugout and Hammett had his arm and they were talking, and he heard the words, but they meant nothing yet. He felt Semick push him into the jacket and lead him to the dugout's blessed shelter, and the game was moving too fast.

Lawson paused beside him and said, "Take your time, Jim," and was gone toward third base as Ashton stepped into the box.

Newcombe was hot and steady, and he

watched the Quakers go down in order; and then he was in the sunlight, growing brighter overhead as a wind came over the left-field wall and touched his face; and clouds moved sluggishly to the south and west, breaking away and showing blue sky. He pitched to the mitt that seemed to be the one important object in a world gone mad with sound and movement he had come upon too soon and could not understand. He fanned Campanella on four pitched balls, and Reese fouled off half a dozen pitches and missed the fastest ball he had thrown to that moment; and then Newcombe stepped in, and Shane was talking it up, face breaking from sober tenseness and finding a new face, eyes and mouth shining with a joy the mask bars could not hide.

Newcombe missed a bad pitch, looked at two balls, took the sign to take and watched the strike split; and struck out on his fast ball through the middle, swinging late and moving away before Shane tossed the ball along the lane and turned to the dugout. Willy Smith was rubbing his arm and shouting, "We'll get 'em for you, Jim!" and Ashton stood beside him, face moving with pent-up emotion that came out in the blue eyes and thin mouth that had not smiled for a week. He had no thought of the strikeouts, and along the bench, far away, someone said, "Let's start it, Del," and the bench was up, shouting and pounding the rail, calling for the rally.

Anderson flied to center field and Willy Smith grounded to Hodges at first, and Sipler drove a liner into left center, a sinking ball that curved to the right and was dropping in and away when Snider crossed before Hermanski, with inches to spare, and took it off the grass and rolled over and over, coming up with the catch.

Jim went out and took the ball from a damp spot just off the grass, and rosined his fingers, and then he was pitching against time, feeling the importance of every out, conscious that the Dodgers were waiting him to the limit, judging him, starting from scratch in this last game, with no form chart to work on, but learning fast with the desperateness that came with the game and showed on every face. Cox crowded the plate and Shane called inside and low, and he watched Cox's leaping legs do the split as the ball got away and sailed through the box. Cox was up, shouting wordlessly at him, and Milt Stock was protesting loudly from the third-base box; and Lawson stood unmoving beside the step, face carved in some unknown stone.

He walked Cox, and Hermanski bunted his first pitch toward first. He came over, and stopped as Shane shouted, "Eddie!" and he saw Watkens field the ball in one smooth motion and make the quick, turning throw to Galliant covering first for the out as Cox slid into second. Shane glanced at the dugout, but Lawson gave no sign, and he pitched to Snider and felt his first bad ball slip off and go in, fat and white, down the middle. The bat was around and the ball over his head, a rifle shot going up and out. He ran automatically to back up third base and saw Ashton, running with the wind's speed, come into the wall, bounce off and drop on one knee, then move along the wall base and take the ball, that lost carrying speed and dropped in for the out. Cox was holding between second and third, and raced back to second as Ashton made the long true throw to the infield. He saw Ashton moving into position, limping momentarily, then covering the limp with a fast trot, and he thought of the wall and Ashton's career, and found more power than ever before in his pitch to Robinson. Shane called for the curve and he caught the corner for the second strike, and then Shane called the curve again, and he hoped for luck as it went in, hung for one agonizing moment, then dropped under the swinging bat for the strikeout.

When he reached the dugout, Semick sat beside him, rubbing his arm gently for no reason, watching the field and talking softly about things he did not hear and would never remember, but the words came through to his mind in a soothing flow, and he sat back under their sound as Lorenson began calling for the run, the one run they all wanted. But Newcombe was pitching that game a man had somewhere in his body, and Galliant could not touch the the fast ball. And then Semick was saying, "Don't try to hit. Stand back and swing, but don't lean in," and he was at the rack, taking a bat, any bat, and watching Shane fly to short left field. He stepped into the box and Campanella's voice came up from behind, talking to Newcombe, and the fast ball exploded under his wrists, and another, and he swung blindly at the third delivery, missing a foot, as Newcombe came off the mound before his swing was finished. He threw the bat to the bat boy, and moved down the line for his glove; and the roar was no longer as wild and high-pitched, but rather a continuous sound that beat down on the field and would not stop.

Furillo singled on his first pitch, a line drive

to right field, and he heard the sigh pass along the stands and wondered why; and then Hodges was faking the bunt and hitting the next pitch, another single into center on the hit-and-run, and Furillo was under the fast throw at third, safe by a long yard, and Hodges was holding at first. Jim came from behind third and saw Constanty coming off the bullpen bench, and then he wanted to stay in. He was strong and he felt his power, and he could not let them down now. Shane called time and came to the mound, and they stood close together for the first time in weeks, with a nearness that had no relation to any words or actions between them in the past.

Shane said, "You all right?"

"I'll pitch," he said. "I'll pitch."

Shane's face was queer, or perhaps it was his own face and vision. Shane said, "Give me everything. We've got to knock them down now. They're swinging free."

He nodded, heard the words and understood clearly. Campanella stepped in and Shane dabbed for the inside pitch on the belt, and he gave it with full power and a rising hatred, the ball past Campanella before the squat catcher threw himself backward and sat in the dirt, holding the bat and staring wordlessly at the mound. Campanella dusted his hands and came back, and Shane called for the curve. He saw it go in and fade away from the swinging bat, and then he felt a surge of joy. They would not dig in on him, no one, ever again. He fanned Campanella on two more pitches, and Reese poked at the ball twice, evidently on order, as Shane drove him back with the called inside third pitch. He threw the curve and Reese let it go, and Stewart called the ball. And then Shane was turning, rising up and roaring, shaking his right arm with the ball, and Lawson was out of the dugout and he stood on the mound and watched them gesture and argue, and finally it was over and Shane, from behind the plate, winked humorlessly and signaled for the fast ball. He threw and missed the corner, and missed again, and Reese trotted to first as the bases filled with one away.

He turned and dusted the rosin on his fingers, and saw the infield move back and get set for the double play; and Newcombe came up to bat for himself. No pinch hitter, he thought, not for Newcombe. Shane talked to him and he heard the voice now, clear and strong. "With me, Jim boy! Come now! Come on, boy, here we have him! Push him back and set him down!"

And he threw for the called strike, and again for the strike; and Shane was signaling for the curve. He threw and saw the ball dip, and Newcombe, coming around from the heels, expecting the fast one, smashed it to his right, a wicked drive that hit the grass edge as he threw himself too late and thought, *It's gone,* and rolled on his belly as Hammett made the scoop near second, tossed to Galliant, and Galliant pivoted and leaped above the flying spikes of Reese coming in at full speed, and beat Newcombe to the bag with a wrist throw that Watkens took stretched flat, only his toe touching the bag. Galliant fell, rolling on one shoulder, went over and sat in the dust, and Hammett threw his glove away to the grass and came in shouting, "They can't beat us! Come on! Come on!"

He thought, *It wasn't me,* and then he felt their hands on his back and saw their faces, and knew what it was he had missed and seen and longed for with all his heart through the bitter, aching, meaningless months. They were talking to him, and moving in the dugout as though they could not sit still, and he was no longer on the outside, but with them all the way, inside at last.

He sat and watched Ashton drag the bunt toward second and beat the frantic throw from Hodges to Robinson by an unseen distance visible only to the umpire's eyes and extended arms. He thought, *Get one, just one,* and Hammett laid the sacrifice before the plate and pushed Ashton to second on the out.

Watkens stepped in and touched his cap and made the little cross on his chest with one hand, and hit the ball over Reese's stretching glove into left-center field for the single and the run, as Ashton, only a blur of white on the base lines, rounded third and hit the plate in a headfirst dive, throwing dust in a huge cloud and rolling free and safe as Watkens went to second on the throw-in. They were going wild behind him and pillows began to bounce against the lower railing, and he saw the team beating Ashton's back and shouting to Watkens, and he thought, *So they never feel this kind of emotion in the big show,* and knew that was a lie.

Newcombe hitched his pants and fanned Del Anderson, and Smith sent Furillo to the wall with a long drive for the third out. But they had the run.

He went out and made the warm-up throws, and felt that nothing mattered now; he could go on forever. He knew the fifth and sixth innings were going, then gone, as he pitched to

Shane's mitt and walked men, and saw them miss and turn away, and three times the hits smashed beyond him into the outfield, held to singles by Ashton and Anderson. And when he stood to begin the seventh, and Semick took his jacket and touched his arm gently, he heard someone saying far away, "Eleven, we want twelve," and moving to the mound, realized it was the crowd, talking in one great voice about some number he cared nothing for and did not understand.

He faced Hodges and wondered absently if he could go on this way, pushing the balls past that dangerous bat. Hodges was tense now, as tight and narrow-eyed as the faces behind him on the field, and Hodges hit the second pitch into left, a long, lazy fly ball that hit the wall above the fielder's leaping body and arm, and gave Hodges two bases standing up. Constanty and Henchman—a half dozen of them—were throwing in the bullpen, and he thought, *We can do it now,* and hoped he might last just one more inning. He pitched to Campanella, and Shane called the curve balls, four in a row, breaking all the rules. Campanella topped the fourth curve and Galliant made the put-out at first; and then he seemed to lose the control with Hodges dancing off third. He walked Reese, and Newcombe crouched and moved, and crowded and went back, and he threw wild on the three-two pitch to fill the bases.

Shane called time and came to the mound and said, "You all right?"

"Fast balls," he said thickly. "Let me go."

"Come to me," Shane said. "Come to me, boy."

And then he was pitching to the mitt, hearing the protesting roar against his ears, losing track of the count and caring nothing about any count, throwing only to the mitt that seemed to grow smaller as the moments passed and the first shadow came to his feet and slipped beneath them across the infield. He saw Cox turn away, and thought, *Two down,* and pitched on. And then Hermanski was fouling pitches, and crowding up, and the ball was in the air behind second, and Hammett was under and waiting and making the catch. He stood on the mound for a moment, arm loose and hanging like a rope, but strong, and Shane came from the plate and took his hand and walked with him to the dugout.

Semick held his jacket, and as he slipped inside and fumbled for the buttons, Shane stood before him, eyes wet and filled with deep understanding.

"Look," Shane said brokenly. "I don't know how to say it. . . . I—"

He said, "Six outs to go, Clark."

And then Shane smiled, and he took the hand and shook it for a long time, and Shane said, "That's all that matters, after all. Six outs to go. We'll get 'em, Jim. We'll get 'em."

He was suddenly aware of faces as he sat in the dugout, and the Quakers went up and came back, unable to find Newcombe again. He saw Lawson at third, talking and standing firm, and Semick beside him, face shining with some secret happiness; and when he went out for the eighth, he turned and looked into the solid bank of faces and colors, and saw Sue sitting small and silent beside her father. She lifted one hand, a short gesture, and Ramsey nodded and turned away. He could do it now, he thought, and then everything was bad as Snider singled and Robinson waited for, and got, the walk, and Furillo dumped the bunt for the sacrifice that advanced both runners. Hodges popped to third base and he had the big two outs, and then he missed the corner and Campanella trotted down to first; and they were full again, and he wondered how long the luck would last.

He pitched to Reese and the ball dribbled straight to the mound, and he had it and turned and threw, and wanted to cry with pain and rage as Watkens dived and knocked it down, and Reese was safe as Snider crossed with the tying run. He wanted to find a hole or run and hide from them, and he could not look up until he felt Shane's fingers biting cruelly into his left arm, and then Shane said, "We'll get it back, Jim. Pitch to me. That's all you have to do. Just pitch to the mitt. You hear me, boy. Pitch to the mitt!"

"The mitt," he said thinly. "I'll pitch, Clark."

He waited and watched the commotion in the Dodger dugout, and Newcombe came out again, and he thought, *They're going all the way with him. They think they'll win it in the end.* He fanned Newcombe on three pitched balls, and heard the roaring, lifting sound and the number twelve repeated as he reached the dugout.

Shane swung three bats and stood beside him and said, "I'm getting on. Boost me around."

He saw Shane take two balls and meet the next pitch squarely, lining the ball into right center for a long single, rounding first and slowing up as Hermanski reached the ball and straightened before throwing; and then Shane was going, running in great plunging strides, throwing his body in a long headlong dive at second base, swinging inside the line and catching the bag; and spinning around and under Reese, upending the shortstop as ball and runner met and the dust obscured all view. He was standing, staring across the infield, as the umpire's arms went down and out in the safe sign. Benson was shouting from first base, and Lawson was facing in from the third-base coaching box, calling to Shane as the catcher stood and dusted his pants and shook one fist in the air.

"Lay it down if you can," Semick said behind him.

He hadn't caught the signal, and he took the bat from Semick's hand and went to the plate. He felt no pressure now, or maybe he was beyond that mortal feeling, in another world where the tension and pressure were the normal, and the even side of life was something that you saw and never experienced. He tried to bunt the first pitch and missed, and then stepped out of the box and rubbed his hands, and remembered everything. He watched Newcombe's arm go up and the ball was coming, a flash of light. He turned and dropped the bat calmly and felt wood strike and sound true, and then he was running for first and feeling the ball pass him for the out, but Shane was into third safely, and now they had the big chance.

He came back to the dugout, watching the field, and pushed into the jacket as Ashton pounded the plate twice and settled for the pitch. And now, he thought, here was the big one. Here was the payoff for the months and years, for all of them, each man wishing he could be at the plate instead of Ashton, knowing that each man would kill anyone who tried to push him away.

They had to walk Ashton, he knew that, and Newcombe threw wide and Ashton ran to first, face twisted with anger, and stood on the bag, shouting at Shane across the infield, then turning a suddenly wicked and harsh tongue on Newcombe. Hammett was up, calm and sober-faced, and Ramsey watched this final duel between the two men, the fine pitcher and the shortstop who was deadly in the clutch.

Newcombe was pitching his heart out, and the Dodger infield was back, playing for the double. Hammett lifted two fouls and waited out to the full count; and Newcombe missed the corner on the last pitch. Hammett ran to first as Ashton moved to second, and Watkens stepped in. He thought that this was somehow right, in a way, for Watkens to have this chance; and as he held breath and came off the heels of his shoes against the railing, Watkens met the first pitch and he saw the ball go up and out, not far enough to clear, but far enough for everything they needed. Hermanski was against the wall, and Shane was poised on third, and as the ball dropped and was caught, Shane came down the line, arms pumping, head down and unseeing, running into and across the body of Campanella, who blocked and waited for the throw that came too late. Campanella was down, rolling, and Shane was safe; and Newcombe had the ball and held Ashton at third.

Shane came into the dugout, face a black mask of dirt and sweat, and took his arm and said, "There's your run, Jim! Now we do it, boy! Now we do it!"

Anderson flied to center field, but no one seemed to groan; and he crossed the white line and pitched to the mitt; and now the sound was passing all comprehension and he was vaguely aware of police moving down the aisles and lining the last railing before the box seats. Shane pegged and the ball came around, and Smith was placing it in his glove, and they were all close around him, with the smell of the dirt and the dust and the sweat, and their faces shining through this grimy set of unnatural masks; and the words came from them all in a kind of muted gabble that meant nothing and yet meant everything to him. He turned and faced Cox, and now he saw only the yellow mitt, stained with black, held open for him behind the plate.

Cox hit the first pitch, and he turned and saw the ball dropping, rolling, out of Hammett's last diving stab, for the single; and he saw the bullpen alive with moving figures, and Lawson was up on the step, watching him; making no sign, just watching. He pitched to Hermanski and saw the ball drop to the right, and took it with his bare hand and made the throw to first, straight and hard and true. Cox was on second and he did not care now. He had made a throw and they could not call him yellow in the clutch. He pitched to Snider, and now he felt the ache in his arm, and the control was going for a brief moment. Snider waited out the full count, and then he had to get over a part of the plate, and the bat sound was flat and loud as the ball was down the third-base line, kicking up the fine white chalk, going out and over the bag into left field; and he saw Smith going over and bringing the gloved hand down backward, against the ball, smashing it to the ground, then on it and throwing, the ball passing his face and curving as it hopped in that dirty, low throw; and Watkens was stretching and snapping that black mitt, and the ball disappeared and Snider was out as Cox rounded third and pulled up. He turned to Smith and tried to speak, and Smith shook a white face stained with grime and backed away into position. From the dugout steps Lawson nodded, and Shane called time and came to the mound.

"Walk this one," Shane said. "We got to play the percentage. You all right?"

"All right," he said.

"Count," Shane said harshly. "Count to five for me, Jim!"

He said, "One . . . two, three, four . . . five . . . six—"

"You're all right," Shane said. "You and me, Jim!"

He walked Robinson, and then he realized the truth. Lawson was signaling to Shane, and Shane was nodding and crouching behind the plate. He straddled the mound, and Shane shook his head, and he stepped out and toed the rubber, and pitched wide. Robinson was gone, flying toward second, and Shane faked the peg and held the ball as Cox dived back to third; and then he was pitching outside, walking Furillo, filling the bases, going to the end of the string; and Hodges was stepping up, and he saw the crowd standing, leaning forward, and wondered if they weren't tired by now, for he was, deadly tired.

He pitched to the mitt, always that yellow mitt, and Hodges seemed reluctant. He threw a strike to follow that ball, and the second ball, and the strike, and then the ball; and Shane called time and they stood together on the mound with the others around them, and Lawson moving swiftly over the grass and stopping on the edge of the circle, watching them all with a kind of exhausted, understanding compassion.

"Jim," Shane said, "this is my mitt, boy. This is the mitt. Pitch to me, Jim. One more time. Give me all you'll ever have."

He said, "One more time," and looked at Lawson, and Lawson opened his mouth, and then shut it quickly and smiled and turned away.

He waited, and now there was no sound, now he heard nothing, and his toe scraped the rubber and he saw the mitt come up and face him, yellow and dirty, the pocket black and deep, with Shane's face behind, quiet now, and seemingly beyond all emotion. He thought of many things, all beyond his eyes, and saw only the mitt as his arm came up and he delivered with all his body behind this one ball. He saw Hodges tense and swing, the bat coming around, and he was sick with fear, and then it was gone, under the bat and into the mitt, and Shane was throwing his mask and running across the roiled, shadowed dirt and bruised grass, leaping on him and swinging him around.

He was moving toward the dugout and people were all around him, and Semick was pounding his back and yelling, face incandescent with joy, streaming frank tears and grinning through those tears that seemed to touch him inside and fill him with the full heat of Semick's happiness.

He saw Shane turn and stand beside the step, jostled and pushed by people; and then Sue was holding him and they were helped through the last crowded, wild rush into the tunnel.

She was crying, and he said, "What's the matter?" and she tried to laugh and finally said, "Nothing, you big lug! I'll be waiting in the car!"

And then he was sitting on the bench while the dressing room went completely mad about him, and Shane came beside him and sat heavily, holding the mitt between two hands.

Shane said, "Remember this mitt, Jim?"

"Yes," he said, remembering that afternoon; and then he saw that Shane was thinking into the past and he remembered. He said, "Is that the one you had in the room the first day?"

"Yes," Shane said softly. "It was new, like a lot of things in baseball. It's the best mitt I'll ever have."

JOHN GALLAGHER

Courtesy *Sport* Magazine ©

"You caught my yo-yo!"

Courtesy *Sport* Magazine ©

"Yes, this is the bullpen. And who is this calling, please?"

BECAUSE OF the nature of the two pieces Jack Orr contributed to the *Fireside Book of Baseball* and the *Second Fireside Book of Baseball*, the editor's forenote to his article in the second book mentioned the possibility that Mr. Orr was preoccupied with failure in Philadelphia. You can scrub the Philadelphia part of it.

Busts of the Training Camps

JACK ORR

SPRING IS the time of year a baseball writer comes down with an occupational disease known as superlativitis. The attack comes as the man is covering training-camp activities in some winter haven in California, Florida or Arizona. You know he has caught the bug when he gets the compulsion to write shimmering prose about the promise shown by young, inexperienced ballplayers in camp. His copy starts to be dotted with such observations as: "Nineteen-year-old Thurman Buster fields his position with the grace of a Hal Chase," or "Young Bill Cunnythumb is the fastest pitcher these old eyes have seen since Lefty Grove," or "With his pair of hands, Harry Fumble may be our best second baseman since Charlie Gehringer." In fact that Buster, Cunnythumb and Fumble eventually wind up in the Arizona-Texas League doesn't bother the writer; he returns the following spring, even if they don't, and raves about a new collection of rookies.

No matter how hard-boiled and hard-to-please a writer may be the rest of the year, he seems to leave his critical capacities back north, along with the wife, kiddies and snow shovel, when he goes to spring training. Possibly because of the warm sun and the luxurious mode of living, he becomes a patsy for the first youngster who throws a called strike past Pete Castiglione. A couple of years ago a rookie named Ellis Deal struck out DiMaggio in an exhibition game and the feat drew sighs from his manager and bold headlines in the papers. To date, Deal has credit for one win and one loss in big-league competition.

The writers aren't altogether at fault. From the moment they get off the train at the club's conditioning spot, they are exposed to this sort of thing from owners, managers, hotel cigarette girls, bat boys, advertising agency representatives and a vacationing shoe executive from Johnson City, New York. Everybody is given to exalted praise about the kid outfielder who looks like O'Doul, about the pitcher who, in Leo Durocher's classic phrase, has a curve that "breaks like a ball falling off a pool table," and the catcher who hit .821 in the Cuban League and who can't possibly miss. The "can't miss" tag gets a big play each spring.

Even normally astute baseball men have been known to sing lustily about rookies even before a ball is thrown in anger. Branch Rickey once said that a young man named Marvin Rackley "looks like the new Waner." The only way Rackley resembled Waner was that they were both males, for the rookie got into only 18 games with the Dodgers in his freshman year and hit .222.

Rogers Hornsby, a tough man to fool and a hitter's severest critic, was heard last spring saying that Jim Rivera, who had hit .352 in the Pacific Coast League in 1951, would burn up the majors. Rivera hit almost a hundred points less than that. Joe McCarthy, who certainly owns a sagacious baseball mind, took a couple of looks at a tall, skinny shortstop named Jack Phillips when the Yankees trained at Atlantic City in 1945 and pronounced him one of the great prospects of our time. "Right now he's better than Marion," quoth Joe, and this was when Marty was Mr. Shortstop himself. This is the same Jack Phillips who eventually came up as a first baseman, was waived into the National League and who last year was run off the bag at Pittsburgh by a kid named Tony Bartirome. McCarthy pulled another beaut during the war when he praised the veteran Bill Zuber as a potential 17-game winner. Zuber never won more than eight a year the rest of his playing days.

Leo Durocher once predicted a brilliant future for Dixie Howell, who was never to catch a game for the Dodgers. For the past three springs, Leo has had a running love affair with Gail Henley, a big strong kid out of the University of Southern California. Leo announced each year that Henley would break down National League fences. Each year Henley wound up in Sioux City. Now Leo will have to find a new "can't miss" prospect, for last winter the Giants gave up on Henley and sold him to Tulsa.

In 1950 the Yankees had another USC graduate, Jim Brideweser, who hit .400 in Florida and played shortstop as if they invented the position with him in mind. Yankee officials were muttering about the greatest since Wagner. Jim wound up in San Francisco that year and he's still riding the Yankee bench. Cleveland writers raved about a pitcher named Red Fahr last year—he did his pitching for Ottawa. At the same time the Giants were taking Cooperstown measurements for Roger Bowman and he wound up working for Ottawa, too. And so it goes.

One year some of us whipped up what we call "Ye Manager's Springtime Glossary," in which there is no mention of second division, erratic infielders, bases on balls or big dummies who never throw to the right base. Our list was as follows: 1) "Look at that kid hit; and he's just a baby." 2) "I know Johnny Jolted lost 14 and won two last year, but it's going to be different." 3) "These pitchers have shown me so much that it's going to be tough to cut any one of them." 4) "We may not win it, but they'll know we're in the race." There were others. (Somebody spotted a young catcher last spring and made this comment: "Know what I like about him? He squats just like Campanella.")

Anyway, with our numbered glossary, a reporter who dallied too long at extracurricular diversions and missed the daily meeting with the manager could get a quick fill-in from a colleague. It made note-taking easier, too.

They don't all turn into busts, of course. Possibly the two greatest rookie finds of the decade were Pete Reiser and Mickey Mantle. There are those who covered the Dodgers' camp in 1941 who insist there never was one as good as Reiser when he broke in. ("Until Willie Mays came along," Durocher says today, "Reiser was the greatest prospect I ever saw.") The first 11 times he batted in spring exhibitions, Reiser hit safely. It appeared they'd never get him out and everybody came home starry-eyed and raving about him. If Reiser hadn't had the habit of banging into fences, they say he'd still be the best around. In 1942, for instance, when he injured himself running into a Sportsman's Park wall, Reiser was hitting .382. He had won the hitting title the year before, the youngest (22) player ever to do it.

And then there was Mantle. A month after they first saw him in training at Phoenix, Arizona, two springs ago the writers had turned the kid into a national institution, like Howdy-Doody. Now everyone figures he will make people forget half the baseball stars enshrined in Cooperstown.

But Mantles and Reisers come along very seldom. There are many more Clint Hartungs, or lesser copies thereof, in the training camps. Hartung was possibly the most fabled rookie of them all. He had been scouted in a high-school game in Brownsville, Texas, but before he could draw a breath in organized ball, he was drafted. Word bounced back to the Giants about big Clint's fabulous .566 Army hitting average and they heard that he was pitching no-hit games every hour on the hour. In 1947 he was a civilian again and he was the biggest news in the baseball world.

"We got into Phoenix around noon," one of the writers recalled recently, "and, naturally, our big story was the new guy. The Giants were living in a motel up the road then and all of us rushed out to see this Paul Bunyan character. We spotted some ballplayers hanging around one of the cabins and we went over and asked what was up.

"'Shh,' one of them said, 'don't make any noise. He's sleeping.' You'd have thought they were talking about the President or somebody. Pretty soon we were tiptoeing around and whispering, too."

It wasn't many weeks later, however, that nobody would have objected if you played a bass drum outside his hotel-room window at 3 A.M. For though he burned up the Grapefruit League and reams of copy were written about him (Tom Meany wondered if Hartung would stop at the Polo Grounds at all. "He should go straight to Cooperstown," Tom said.), his talent as both a hitter and a pitcher just missed. He had a couple of good days, but the sad fact seemed to be that he couldn't hit the curve and wasn't much of an outfielder and was only a so-so base runner. As a pitcher he had a high, hard one, but not much else. The legend perished as suddenly as it had appeared.

There's a sequel, sad in some ways, to the Hartung story. A couple of springs later, Bill Roeder, a baseball writer for the New York *World-Telegram & Sun*, did a piece for his paper on the tragedy of Clint Hartung, the faded phenom. Roeder had him standing silent and alone beside the pinball machine in a hotel lobby. The piece was so good that one of the wire services picked it up and sent it around the country. At the time the Giants had broken camp and were traveling through Texas. In each town, as it happened, the local paper saved the Roeder piece for publication the day the club came to town.

So Hartung read about his tragic self in Dallas and again in San Antonio and again in Houston. On the fifth day, big Clint could stand it no longer. He went up to Roeder, grabbed him by the lapels and said, "Look. When the hell you gonna stop writing this same story about me every day?"

Seven years earlier there had been another well-publicized Giant who didn't stand up under the ballyhoo which accompanied him north. He was Johnny Rucker and baseball men still wonder why he didn't make it. This was 1940 and the first time Bill Terry saw the 23-year-old youngster get down to first base, he became very excited indeed. The newspapers and magazines described Rucker as the fastest man in the game, a once-in-a-lifetime rookie. Rucker knocked the stuffing out of the ball in exhibitions.

On the bench before the opening day game, Terry waved at Rucker and told newsmen, "We may be looking at the start of the career of one of the greatest ballplayers we've ever seen." Rucker went 4-for-0 in the opener and when his average settled down to a cozy .188 a month or so later, he was benched. Rucker never did find himself and though he played for the Giants in the war years, he never approached the ballplayer everybody thought he was that first spring.

The Giants seem to have a knack for coming up with fizzling phenoms. Besides Hartung and Rucker, there were such blooming spring flowers as Mose Solomon (who ended up playing only two games in the majors), Len Koenecke and, of course, Andy Cohen.

Cohen is quite a story. John McGraw had traded Rogers Hornsby to the Braves after the season of 1927 and young Cohen was being groomed to take over. There was a good deal of grumbling from the fans and at the New York baseball writers' show that year, they sang:

"All the Kelleys and the Cohens
Can't begin to fill the brogans
That Hornsby filled so well at second base."

Cohen hit in the spring and when the Giants played the Braves at the Polo Grounds in the first game of the season, the kid had a hot day, fielding five chances and getting two hits, one of which won the game. Giants players were so enthusiastic that they carried Cohen off the field on their shoulders, a rarity even in those days. But that was the only day Cohen out-heroed Hornsby; Rog hit .387 for Boston while Cohen's season mark was .274.

There are scores of other cases of springtime beauts who never could make it in the big leagues. Many of them were victims of superior pitching, as in the legend of the rookie's letter to his mother halfway through spring training. "Be home real soon, Mom," the letter said, "they're beginning to throw the curve."

Lou Novikoff, the Russian strong man who used to say that he was bewildered about not being able to hit in the majors, was another case. He would knock down the walls in the minors, look good in spring training and then flop dismally when he saw National League pitching. "I can't understand it," he once said. "I feel so strong that I could tear that ball in half."

Possibly in some of these cases too much ballyhoo did have an injurious effect on the players. But if so, the fault lies at the doorstep of club owners. It was their idea in the first place to train away from home and stimulate early spring enthusiasm among the fans. Owners had noticed that interest in baseball was slow getting going. Sometimes it took fans a month to whip up any interest, and if the club got off badly, they never showed up at all. Training away from home—and having newspapermen filing daily dispatches—provided an ideal solution to the problem.

In that respect, things worked out just fine. Athletes did their conditioning in the most pleasant climate possible. Writers didn't have to strain at all to think up adjectives to put in front of the names of the rookies. The managers obliged with we-can't-miss-this-year statements. The fans ate it up. With their baseball appetites whetted, they waited impatiently for opening day and their first glimpse of the new phenoms.

What the publicity did to the young athletes is hard to say. In some of the case histories recorded here it is likely that youngsters of certain temperaments were overcome by the publicity and, as a result, never reached their potential. It seems more likely, though, that they would have flopped anyway—clippings or no clippings.

Take the case, for instance, of one Buck Tanner, a young pitcher who tried to make the Dodgers. Though he never pitched a ball in the big leagues his name is a famous one among sportswriters, who refer to him as "Two Installment" Tanner, much to the discomfort of Arthur Patterson, now promotion and publicity head of the Los Angeles Dodgers, about whom the story is told.

This was a wartime year, 1943, and Red was covering the Dodgers' training sessions at Bear Mountain for a New York paper. Though the club stayed at Bear Mountain, it worked out in an armory at West Point, where, one day, newsmen were standing around the hitting cage, swapping lies and insulting each other. On the other side of the hall, a big rawboned pitcher started warming up. He looked strong and every time the ball plopped into the catcher's mitt, it made a thunderous noise. Patterson listened and his eyes popped. He decided that he had discovered the fastest pitcher since Van Lingle Mungo. Later, Patterson cornered the kid and peppered him with questions. When he sat down to write it, Red let the story get away from him and it was so long that his paper had to run it in two installments on consecutive days.

Well, Tanner, whose fast one didn't sound quite so fast without the booming echo of the armory going for him, was cut loose a couple of days later, and if he ever did get to Ebbets Field, he had to pay his way in. But his memory goes on.

To underscore again the imagination that goes into these early spring dispatches, the story should be told of the day last year when the Giants had their opening drill of pitchers and catchers. It was a thin day for newspaper copy and one writer decided to go with Max Lanier, the new man who had been acquired in the Eddie Stanky deal. The writer squeezed enough comment out of Durocher to knock out his lead: " 'If Max Lanier can continue to show me what he showed me today, he'll win 14,' manager Leo Durocher told this reporter."

What Lanier had shown that day consisted of a half-hour pepper game and three laps around the outfield.

THERE'S A nostalgia all its own to this one, now that the Dodgers have turned into veteran Californians. Remember?

Leave Us Go Root for the Dodgers, Rodgers

DAN PARKER

Murgatroyd Darcy, the belle of Canarsie,
Went 'round with a fellow named Rodge.
At dancing the rhumba or jitterbug number,
You couldn't beat Rodge at this dodge.
Throughout the cold weather, the pair danced together,
But when the trees blossomed again,
Miss Murgatroyd Darcy, the belle of Canarsie
To Rodgers would sing this refrain:

Leave us go root for the Dodgers, Rodgers,
That's the team for me.
Leave us make noise for the boisterous boys
On the B.M.T.
Summer or winter or any season,
Flatbush fanatics don't need no reason.
Leave us go root for the Dodgers, Rodgers,
That's the team for me.

George Plimpton is well-known for his book *Paper Lion,* in which he tested personally what it was like to play professional football. A few years before that, though, he had already done the same thing in baseball, and written a book about that too, called *Out of My League.* With *Sports Illustrated* putting up a $1,000 prize to be split among the American or National League team that got the most hits off him, Plimpton set out to pitch once through each batting order just before a post-season All-Star game at Yankee Stadium. Needless to say, he didn't survive the experiment—didn't even get through the National League hitters—and Ernest Hemingway said later, after reading *Out of My League,* "It is the dark side of the moon of Walter Mitty."

From *Out of My League*

GEORGE PLIMPTON

Ernie Banks was followed in the batter's box by Frank Thomas, then playing for the Pittsburgh Pirates. He was the only batter I faced who loomed over the plate. Despite a large, homely, friendly face over which his blue plastic helmet perched like a birthday paper hat, Thomas' size made him look dangerous; he had an upright batting stance, which made him easier to pitch to than Banks, but the bat looked small and limber in his hands, and when he swung and missed one of my first pitches to him, I imagined I heard the bat sing in the air like a willow switch. For the first time the batter's box seemed close to, and I could understand why many pitchers manipulate the follow-through of their pitching motion, which brings them in toward the plate by as much as six feet, so that the glove can be flicked up to protect the head in the event of a hard shot toward the mound. You never can tell. In 1947 Schoolboy Rowe threw in a pitch toward Stan Musial and back came the top half of a bat cracked directly in two, whirring at him with the speed and directness of a boomerang, and struck him a brutal blow on the elbow of his upflung arm. Even batters worry about crippling a pitcher over that distance. A hard-hit line drive, after all, will cover those 60 feet 6 inches in one-fifth of a second. Babe Ruth had nightmares of such a thing, and there's a body of thought which believes his fear of smacking down a pitcher was why he changed his batting style (he was originally a line-drive hitter in the early days with Baltimore) and started swinging from the heels of his pipestem legs to get loft and distance.

According to my statistician in the stands, it was the seventh pitch that Thomas whacked in a long high arc, very much like that of a Ruthian home run, deep into the upper deck in left field. The ball looped in at the downward end of its trajectory, and above the swelling roar of the crowd I could hear it smack against the slats of an empty seat. The upper deck was deserted and it was a long time before a scampering boy, leaping the empty rows like a chamois, found the ball and held it aloft, triumphant, the white of it just barely visible at that great distance.

The ball was hit well over 400 feet, and after the roar that had accompanied its flight had died down, you could hear the crowd continue buzzing.

My own reaction, as I stood on the mound, was not one of shame, or outrage. Perhaps it should have been, particularly following my difficulties with Banks, but actually my reaction was one of wonderment at the power necessary to propel a ball out of a major-league park. I could hardly believe a ball could be hit so far.

Later that afternoon in the locker room I asked Billy Pierce, the great White Sox southpaw, about the effect of the home run on the pitcher. He'd been talking about the major-league curve ball, what a marvelous and wicked weapon it was at its best, and the unwelcome shift into the batter's province threw him off. "Home runs?" he said in a high, querulous voice. He shrugged. "Well, the effect of the damn things depends upon their importance in any given game," he said reflectively. "Look at Branca." He thought for a while and then he said, "But when that ball sails out of the park, even if it doesn't mean a damn thing, you just feel awful stupid."

Pierce's mention of Branca, of course, was in reference to Bobby Thomson's home run off the Brooklyn speed pitcher in the Miracle of Coogan's Bluff playoff game in 1951. In the films of that stupendous moment you see Branca wheel to watch the flight of the ball that lost Brooklyn the pennant, then start slowly for the dugout, but almost running finally to get out of that wild public demonstration into privacy where he could project that scene over and over again in his imagination, never quite believing it, puzzled that the script wouldn't change and the ball curve foul or into an outfielder's reach. An enterprising photographer got into the Dodger dressing room—it was barred to the press but he got in somehow—and took a picture of Branca within minutes of his disaster. The photograph, a strange one, shows him face down and prostrate on a flight of cement steps—as if he'd stumbled on the bottom step and fallen face forward, his body absolutely as stiff as cordwood with grief. The effect of that home run finished Branca, practically speaking, as a pitcher. Afterwards he toyed with the idea of changing his uniform number, which was 13, but he never did. Perhaps he knew that nothing would help him.

I found I couldn't explain the effect of Frank Thomas' home run, at least not to Pierce, because in actual fact I felt a certain sense of pride in that home run. Every time I return to Yankee Stadium—to a football game, for example—I automatically look up into the section where the ball hit (it was section 34), remembering then that I felt no sense of stupidity but in fact enjoyed a strong feeling of identification with Thomas' feat—as if I was his partner rather than opposing him, and that between us we'd connived to arrange what had happened. It was as if I'd wheeled to watch the ball climb that long way for the upper deck and called out, "Look, look what I've helped engineer!"

It wasn't a reaction I could have explained to Pierce without being accused of being in sympathy with the enemy. Besides, he was back on pitchers, talking about curve balls, the gloomy consideration of Branca, and the batter and his prowess postponed, laid away in the shadows, as he described a bright and cheerful world full of pitching splendors.

"You've got to see Donovan's curve," he said eagerly. "Can't tell about the curve on TV. Got to catch it, try to catch it, to see what the thing does. It breaks so you can almost hear it."

So we talked comfortably about pitching. I told him that I'd thrown one curve ball that afternoon. "It was the first pitch I threw to Frank Robinson," I said. "It almost ran up the foul screen. It got away from me."

"I see," said Pierce. "So *that's* what it was."

Later that afternoon, Gil Hodges, the Dodger first baseman, complained that I had thrown him a curve ball. He followed Thomas in the lineup, and despite the fact that he hit the curve ball for a sharp single to short center, he spoke to me reproachfully. He told me he didn't think curve balls were allowed.

I was surprised at the high respect major leaguers hold for the curve ball and how they hate to bat against it. If a curve is hit safely, the batter attributes his success less to his own ability than to being given the chance to take advantage of a fault in the curve itself. "That hook hung up there just long enough," he will say later in the dugout, meaning that he was able to get his bat around on the ball before it broke. Any player who professes to prefer taking his swipes against curve balls is looked upon with suspicion. And indeed in the history of the majors only a few players have had the reputation of preferring to see curves thrown at them: Hornsby, for one, Rollie Hemsley, Moose Skowron, Roy Sievers, Ducky Medwick, and Al Simmons, these last two despite both having the fault of stepping away from the pitch with the forward foot, falling away "into the bucket"—supposedly suicidal against the curve. They compensated for their faulty swings with amazing eyes and quick strong wrists. There are others, of course, who do well against curve-ball pitchers, but nonetheless the curve has always been better known for destroying reputations. Jim Thorpe, for example, probably the greatest athlete who ever lived, never stuck in the majors because a curve ball fooled him too often. A rookie's classic letter from the training camp begins: "I'll be home soon, Ma. The pitchers are starting to curve me."

Frankly, I don't remember throwing Hodges a curve ball. But I remember other things about his lengthy tenure at the plate, right from the beginning as he stepped into the batter's box, hitching up his baseball pants, reaching out then and rubbing up the fat part of his bat as he set himself, picking again at those pants as if about to wade into a shallow pond. He has outsized hands which you notice when he stands in at the plate. They span over twelve inches, and Pee Wee Reese, his captain, used to say of him, in connection with those big hands, that he only used a glove for fielding at first base because it was fashionable. They call him Moon, and I remember how he looked, the rather beefy pleasant face under the blue helmet, and the blue piping of the Dodger uniform, and while I don't remember throwing him a curve, I remember the line-drive single he hit, how easy and calculated his swing, and how sharp that hit of his was going out.

JOHN GALLAGHER

Courtesy *Boys' Life* ©

"I don't know much about this guy as a hitter. Let's see what it says on his bubblegum card."

Courtesy King Features Syndicate ©

Ripley's Believe It or Not!
PHIL CAVARRETTA
of the Chicago Cubs
RETIRED FROM BASEBALL
IN 1953
AFTER HAVING PLAYED IN
EXACTLY 1953 GAMES
CHICAGO
GOODLOE ROGERS a semi-pro catcher
MADE AN UNASSISTED TRIPLE PLAY
-Pontiac, Mich.
JAMES HILL
of Fort Wayne, Ind.
HAS NO LEGS
YET HE PLAYS BASEBALL!
BABE RUTH
USED 170 BATS EACH SEASON
BILL TERRY NEEDED ONLY 2 BATS TO
LEAD THE NATIONAL LEAGUE'S HITTERS IN 1930

THE FOLLOWING account appeared in *Sporting Life*, which was the *Sporting News* of its day.

1905: Waseda 12, Sherman Institute 7

R. S. RANSOM

THE MEETING of the little brown men from the realms of the Mikado and the red men from Sherman Institute at Fiesta Park in Los Angeles, May 20, under the management of Walter Hempel, marked an epoch in the history of our national game which is deserving of more than passing mention in the columns of America's greatest Base Ball paper. For the first time a Base Ball game was played by teams whose players were from two races that have adopted a sport heretofore distinctively that of the white man. And victory rested with the men from across the sea because of their all-around superiority in every department of the game, coupled with the steadiness and excellence of Kono's masterly work in the pitcher's box. This young man is a marvel, and his work a revelation to our twirlers, who consider themselves overworked if called on to pitch two games during a single week. Already the Japs have played three games here—May 17, winning from the L. A. High School team by the score of 5 to 3; May 18, when Caucasian triumphed over Mongolian, Occidental winning by a score of 6 to 5, and May 20, when Red and Brown met, with disaster to the Native Sons by a score of 12 to 7. In all these contests Kono, a veritable iron man, did the twirling, showing marked improvement in each successive game.

All these contests were witnessed by large crowds, the attendance at the Jap-Indian game being by far the largest of the series. During this game, which stands as an event unique in the annals of Base Ball, the Orientals from Japan had it over the Aborigines during all stages of the game, with the exception of the sixth inning, when the Sherman braves with a whoop broke from the reservation and went tearing madly about until six of them had scored before Field Marshal Hashido and his aides drove them back.

The Japanese players represent the Waseda Imperial University and are being sent on a tour of the United States at the expense of the government. They have been coached by Fred Merrifield, an American, who is a professor in the university. When he first introduced the American game, he was startled by the rapid manner in which the brown men picked it up. They were playing good amateur ball in no time. As they improved, a trip to the United States was talked of, and finally the government made the appropriation. The touring party includes: I. Abe, manager; Fred Merrifield, coach and trainer; K. Hashido, shortstop and captain; M. Obara, center field; U. Suzuki, left field; K. Shishiuchi, right field; K. Oshikawa, second base; S. Izumitani, first base; S. Morimoto and S. Tachihara, substitutes. After completing their engagements on this Coast the team will go to Chicago.

When it comes to handling the ball, these little brown men are all stars, but when it comes to a wise interpretation of the rules they get up against it. The other day the Japs were playing a tight game against Stanford. With a Jap on first base, no outs and the score tied, the Jap at bat hit the ball straight into the air back of first base. The runner on first crouched for the start and the minute the catch was made, zing! he was off for second. Of course he was thrown out by something like forty feet, and when their traveling Jap Base Ball coach was asked to unravel this play, he responded something like this: "Well, you see, sar, the rule he say the runner he shall not proceed until the ball he is catch. So he wait for the ball to be catch and then he go down to the number-two base. Is it not correct to follow the rules of the game?"

And the sport who asked the question went away and batted his head against an oak tree. The Japs have the old Indian trick of "sighting" with the ball before throwing it. Some of them have wonderful wings, their pitcher having the most marvelously developed arm ever seen in a pitcher's box.

As indicative of the aptitude shown by the Japanese players in the development of the game, it can be said that when they arrived in this country the "bunt" was entirely unknown to them. After their first game a class in instruction was held, with the result that this style of playing was at once assimilated, and the brown men "worked the trick" successfully thereafter.

HERE IS one of Grantland Rice's earliest works, printed in the Atlanta *Journal* in the first decade of the twentieth century. No one else in all the history of baseball journalism would have dreamed of writing this one—let alone having it published. But there was only one Granny Rice. (*N.B.*—First night game in recorded history.)

The Slide of Paul Revere

GRANTLAND RICE

Listen, fanatics, and you shall hear
Of the midnight slide of Paul Revere—
How he scored from first on an outfield drive
By a dashing sprint and a headlong dive—
'Twas the greatest play pulled off that year.

Now the home of poets and potted beans,
Of Emersonian ways and means,
In Base Ball epic has oft been sung
Since the days of Criger and old Cy Young—
But not even fleet, deer-footed Bay
Could have pulled off any such fancy play
As the slide of Paul Revere, which won
The famous battle of Lexington.

The Yanks and the British were booked that trip
In a scrap for the New World Championship—
But the British landed a bit too late,
So the game didn't open till half past eight,
And Paul Revere was dreaming away
When the umpire issued his call for play.

On, on they fought 'neath the Boston moon
As the British figured—"Not yet, but soon"—
For the odds were against the Yanks that night,
With Paul Revere blocked away from the fight—
And the grandstand gathering groaned in woe,
While a sad wail bubbled from Rooters' Row.

But wait—Hist! Hearken! and likewise hark!
What means that galloping near the park?
What means that cry of a man dead sore?
"Am I too late? Say, what's the score?"
And echo answered both far and near,
As the rooters shouted, "There's Paul Revere!"

Oh, how sweetly that moon did shine,
When P. Revere took the coaching line!
He woke up the grandstand from its trance,
And made the bleachers get up and dance—
He joshed the British with robust shout
Until they booted the ball about—
He whooped and he clamored all over the lot
Till the score was tied in a Gordian knot.

Now, in this part of the "Dope Recooked"
Are the facts which history overlooked—
How Paul Revere came to bat that night
And suddenly ended the long-drawn fight—
How he singled to center and then straight-away
Dashed on to second like Harry Bay—
Kept traveling on with the speed of a bird,
Till he whizzed like a meteor rounding third—
"Hold back, you lobster"—but all in vain—
The coaches shouted in tones of pain—
For Paul kept on with a swinging stride,
And he hit the ground when they hollered "SLIDE!"

Spectacular plays may come and go
In the hurry of Time's swift ebb and flow—
But never again will there be one
Like the first American "hit and run."
And as long as the old game lasts you'll hear
Of the midnight slide of P. Revere.

WE HAVE here the spectacle of a writer (Robert Riger) working with a baseball figure (the late and great Branch Rickey) to produce a profile of another baseball figure. All to the good. Ban Johnson too often goes overlooked by baseball historians. Mr. Rickey chooses rightfully not to ignore him. That last is an understatement.

Ban Johnson

BRANCH RICKEY *with* ROBERT RIGER

WHEN I WAS ASKED to choose sixteen immortals for my book, *The American Diamond,* many names passed through my mind. The very first one was Mr. Byron Bancroft Johnson, founder and first president of the American League. For seventeen years, Ban Johnson was the czar of baseball in America. He ruled the game. Charles Comiskey had made him president of the Western League in 1893. Even then, at twenty-nine years of age, Ban Johnson had conceived the idea of a second major league. He became baseball's first successful major-league expansionist.

Professional baseball in 1890 was in the doldrums. Ownership was not too far removed from racketeers. Previously the Western League had a balanced schedule but not much besides to give it dignity in organization or order in the stands or decency in appearance and action on the field. Umpires almost needed physical protection, and Ban Johnson took care of that. He was a new force on the baseball horizon. He had character and ideals and he loved the game. Greedy owners were just above being counterparts of ward politicians. Not many ladies attended the games. Ban Johnson changed that too. He believed that attendance of women at games guaranteed the dignity of the game and its economic future.

The National League said there weren't enough players for another league, and the press at the time supported that position. Johnson frequently answered, "There are not enough players for the last-place club in the National League either."

This czar of baseball was a dominant personality, domineering indeed in a crowd of clashing partisans. I have been with him in meetings when he reminded me of my grandfather, who on one occasion was visiting my father at our old country home. In midafternoon I had accompanied Grandfather and my father as they went over to view the timber on the twelve acres of the Shelpman tract which had been recently purchased by my father. The question was should the timber be cut and the ground cleared. It was a subject for considerable discussion that evening, and at an hour late for me, a youngster of ten years, Grandfather said to my father, "Frank, we will take a 'belly rest' on this thing and discuss it further tomorrow morning." The next morning at breakfast, Grandfather did discuss the question, referring to the kind of timber, the stage of growth, and the amount and price of the marketable product. I will never forget his final remark. "Frank," said he, "that's the way I think it is and that's the way it is," and he came down with a bang on the table with his fist. And that's the way it was. The timber stood. That was Ban Johnson as he always was in controversy. He made the decisions. He ruled the roost, but he never stopped to crow over it. When one battle was won, he was immediately high-headed for another.

He was a college baseball player, a debater, a law student, a reporter, a ruggedly opinionated advocate of whatever he believed in. Above all, he was a tireless finder and maker of facts to preface every undertaking. The other fellows' facts were to be questioned or modified or disregarded. He dreamed baseball almost aloud, but his dreams did not require psychiatric mastery to find the cause. He was a supersalesman of ideas—a persuader with economic inducements and a finished organizer in new fields.

He never intentionally deceived. However, it can be said that he might let an adversary stumble along with less than all the facts. To illustrate: Mr. Johnson was responsible for the illustrious George Sisler coming from the University of Michigan to St. Louis. Pittsburgh had a paper claim to George's services, but Johnson knew the rules better, strange to say, than Mr. Dreyfuss, president of the Pittsburgh club. George P. Codd, mayor of Detroit, and Judge James Murfin, president of the board of regents of the university, knew the law points and the moral issue involved and vigorously pleaded the university's case for George's free agency. George's eligibility to represent the university in intercollegiate athletics was at stake. The National Commission made up of the presidents of the American and National leagues and Mr. August Herrmann, president of the Cincinnati club, had to have more than right on its side in order to make a decision. Johnson supplied it. He stood viciously pat on the free agency of the player because of the nonconforming with a deadline date for the promulgation of a contract signed long since by a seventeen-year-old high-school boy. George was made a free agent. The Sisler case made a file of over 100,000 words covering a period of eighteen months.

Mr. Johnson had time for the minutest detail as well as for big business, such as bringing the Shibes into Philadelphia, financier Charles Somers into Cleveland, Charles Comiskey into Chicago, Robert Lee Hedges into St. Louis, and all the others. And bringing Sisler into the American League was not a very minute detail to Mr. Johnson. The organization of a new league to compete with and excel the old one was a succession of battles. He started with the Western League—then came changes here and there with invasion of National League territory. It took more than planning ability to launch the American League in 1901. Johnson was a very great tactician. He could handle the weapons on the field and he could call the plays. However, he was not given to negotiation on choosing a field for battle. That kind of strategy never occurred to him. He took conditions as he met them—face to face, as he marched headlong toward his objective. He fought where he met the enemy. If he met him, as he did in St. Louis, he armed himself with the Milwaukee franchise of the old Western League and pocketed the support of the Cincinnati buggy maker, Mr. R. L. Hedges, and then he said out loud to the National League, "St. Louis is a member of the G-R-E-A-T American League." He signed players from the old Cleveland club and from the St. Louis Cardinals and called the club the Browns. And the battle was on, and the time and the place were whenever and wherever he met opposition. In contest he was never taken by surprise—contest is not the right word; battle is the word. He never expected quarter and he never gave any. Victory gained, he was, strange to say but very true, fair and generous in terms of settlement and then instant in pursuit to establish a permanent peace—but largely on his own terms.

He had friendly help in writing the National Agreement of Professional Baseball, but Ban Johnson wrote it. It is still, in effect, the basic written medium of order and control in organized baseball.

No victory was ever sought with the idea of destroying anything helpful to the game. The objective was always the good health of baseball, to make it highly respected by the public and profitable to the owners.

He was a great friend of the players, and continuously, in speeches and private conversations, he set out the extraordinary features of the game, inviting youth to be interested in making it a lifelong career. Ban Johnson would have been very proud of the present commissioner's eulogistic brochure dealing with the professional game. He made the game into what is now an acceptable profession. Very few professions place moral and physical requirements so high or economic and social requirements so low.

Byron Bancroft Johnson would debate, not too conciliatingly, Dr. Alexis Carrel's statement that "in general, athletes are not intelligent." The two would not agree on what constituted intelligence, but Johnson would concede "in general" the great scientist's contention that the habit of logical thinking produced it. Johnson would viciously oppose any adverse comment on any phase of the game from any critic.

He would admit that a game played once a week might offer the emotional thrill of anticipating the next play, but not that it could equal the thrills of the daily game of baseball. Football is indeed a very great game in our country, but the punt is one of the few situations that offer no alternative. The kicker might run with it—he might, but not likely. The spectator is engaged only with the effect of the kick. All other offensive plays are complex. In baseball, the public does not have many alternatives to anticipate. The batter will either bunt or hit, and he can only run in one direction when he does either. It is a simple game but deeply profound. It holds suspense almost continuously, and it holds forth seven days a week for seven months, professionally. It is the recreational refuge for trial and trouble and tribulation and all the other alliterative t's of our time. Johnson was right in his analysis of the game and his constant prophecy about its deserving future.

The job of the offense is to score, and just about 100,000,000 of our people know the alternative means of doing it. The job of defense is to defeat the score, and the tactics of placement and pitch are so well known to the same 100,000,000 that the defensive as well as the offensive game makes grandstand managers out of many spectators and listeners-in. Whatever the great game is, Ban Johnson helped make it so, and it would not be so if he had not been.

Johnson was only thirty-three when he wrote his first bulletin to the American League club owners in 1901. His long-range concept of baseball conduct and operation was indelibly reflected in two paragraphs of that bulletin, dated May 8, 1901. It read in part:

> The Club Managers are requested to institute such reforms as will shorten the games. In some cities of the American League the games have been long drawn out, and there has been much complaint. The catchers hereafter will play up behind the bat throughout the game. This is a standing order.
>
> CLEAN BALL is the MAIN PLANK in the American League platform, and the clubs must stand by it religiously. There must be no profanity on the ball field. The umpires are agents of the League and must be treated with respect. I will suspend any Manager or player who uses profane or vulgar language to an Umpire, and that suspension will remain in force until such time as the offender can learn to bridle his tongue. Rowdyism and profanity have worked untold injury to base ball. To permit it would blight the future of the American League. This bulletin you will please hand to your Manager so that he may impart its contents to the players.

He preserved and extended the self-respect of players and management and administrative employees. He removed saloons as the meeting place for baseball conferences. He brought men of high character and ample means into the game as owners. He made it possible for players to be accepted in good hotels. He banned liquor from the stands. He made umpiring a respectable and dignified profession. He unpopularized profanity on the field. He changed personal associates off the field.

He established acceptance of professional baseball in the high echelon of our social structure, believing that it would easily percolate down through the strata of culture, even finally including the lowest as well as the best. He democratized a large segment of American life—making the game the social and economic leveler of *everybody*. Neither money, nor name, nor inheritance, nor dress, nor anything except color had much to do with who sat next to whom. If the player could bunt with rare skill, the conversation was pooled without personal background determining its direction or content. A bank president exchanged views with a bricklayer.

He painted the old parks and built new ones. He was bold in adventure. He was the leading man in my early life who impressed me as having little use for people who could and didn't. At our very first meeting in 1913—an informal one—I was seated opposite him at a convivial table with a dozen present, when following a distant uncomplimentary remark about one of his club managers, he loudly ejaculated, "No you don't—no you don't," and pointing jerkingly at the manager, he said, "He's my boy, he's my boy." He had no patience with anybody's views contrary to his own.

He proved the naked fallacy of not enough players. He was the earliest advocate of the now trite truth that goodness in competitive sport is relative; that if a club wins in its class or league, it is a good club, so says the public. If it loses, it is not so good, so says the public. Pittsburgh won the World Series from the great New York Yankee team in 1960. Western Pennsylvania said it was the greatest team ever. The whole country agreed. The same Pittsburgh club, almost to a man, finished sixth the very next year. It was regarded as "no good" throughout the country and most certainly in western Pennsylvania. "Goodness" in professional baseball competition and in public appeal depends simply upon whether or not somebody else is better.

Johnson never lost the right to loyalty, but he signally did lose it. His almost compulsory demotion by the owners from his executive functions as president of the American League killed him. That is a long story. He had given birth to the American League and he nurtured it to a long dominance over the National

League, which he almost hated. He never called his league the American League. He always said it, the G-R-E-A-T American League.

He is, almost exclusively, to be credited with the exposure of the Black Sox scandal in Cincinnati in 1919. There never would have been a publicized exposure except for Mr. Johnson's continuous investigation. His probity and his honor gave him no hesitant choice to bring to justice some very great players in his own, the G-R-E-A-T American, league. Following the World Series White Sox scandal of 1919, baseball became panicky. The owners felt that the professional game had lost public confidence. It reached out for a savior and decided to supplant the old National Commission with a new boss, to be called the Commissioner of Baseball. Unfortunately for himself, Mr. Johnson opposed the election of a commissioner, wishing instead that the civil law should handle the matter and thus substantiate and restore public confidence. He lost Mr. Comiskey's friendship—for the Old Roman, as Comiskey was called, could not bring himself to believe that his "boys could do any wrong." He resented Johnson's investigation, and in the fight that followed, Johnson lost the support of the American League owners—all except Mr. P. D. C. Ball of St. Louis. He gave no consideration to any future results to himself, and after he was retired by the American League, he refused the offer of payment of $320,000 still due on his contract as president of the American League. The making or amassing of money was no part of Ban Johnson's life. He lived for the American League and the game of baseball.

If he had been the leader of the proposed Continental League, it would surely be in existence today as a third major league of eight clubs. He would never have accepted the promises of the American and National leagues in Chicago, August 6, 1959, to absorb the eight owners and cities of the Continental League. I doubt if he would have accepted the invitation to meet with them.

Mr. Johnson was never a compromiser. He prepared for exigency like Napoleon and went down like him. He fought like Grant "along this line" and no other. Almost sad to say, he never tolerated a Henry Clay in his close acquaintanceship. He was blatantly "pooh" with compromise. He had many negotiating battles outside of courts of law, and except for the loss of McGraw to the New York Nationals, he never to my knowledge bore a scar. A federal injunction against Lajoie kept the player out of Philadelphia for a time, but he continued to play for Cleveland in the G-R-E-A-T American League as Mr. Johnson wished. He bore no scar.

He died rejected by his tearful erstwhile friends—an anticlimactic end. He died lonely and alone. His contribution to the game from the beginning, and always, is not closely equaled by any other single person or group of persons. He set the stage for baseball to become our G-R-E-A-T national game.

He is my first choice as a baseball immortal.

A GOOD NUMBER of years ago, a prominent movie actor opened a closet door in his Beverly Hills home and showed me a baseball bat. "This," he said, "is the one Babe used to hit the sixtieth home run. He gave it to me personally." I looked at him. There must be 600 of those bats in existence, I thought. And of course I was right.

Except that I was wrong.

The Time He Hit One for Me

JHAN ROBBINS

FIFTEEN YEARS AGO Babe Ruth stood at home plate in Yankee Stadium for the last time. The occasion was the 25th anniversary of the "house that Ruth built." High point of the ceremonies was the retirement of No. 3—the uniform number Ruth made famous. The microphones could not pick up the weak whisper of the ailing Babe's acknowledgments, but cheers of tribute rolled down from the stands. Only two months later many of the same fans stood in line for hours to shuffle slowly past his black-draped casket at home plate.

I was among them. I was then married with children of my own, but as I looked up at the strips of bleacher seats I remembered the day in 1934 when I sat up there, a stubby teenager, confidently waiting for the Babe to fulfill his personal promise to hit one for me.

On that morning I could hardly wait for my mother to finish packing my lunch. "There!" she said, tucking a banana into the paper bag and knotting a string around it. "Mind your manners, behave yourself and don't let anyone cough germs on you!"

I knew I was too excited to eat and I'm sure she knew it, too. I was off to interview Babe Ruth for my school newspaper and to see the Yankees play the Cleveland Indians. I was 14 and unquestionably one of the "thousands of dirty-faced kids" that New York City's Mayor Jimmy Walker said represented the Babe's highest responsibility.

Perhaps he was right. My friends and I had heard Ruth condemned in some quarters as undisciplined, loose-living and not bright. Yet I don't think there is any athlete on any modern playing field who means as much to today's youngsters as Babe Ruth meant to us.

We worried about him. We knew his playing days were nearly over. His absurdly spindly legs were straining beneath the weight of his roly-poly body. Crippled by a bad knee, he could no longer sprint and he covered little ground in the outfield.

Although it was only mid-June, his younger teammate, Lou Gehrig, had hit 18 home runs. Yet Ruth was still a beautiful sight at home plate. Gracefully arched fly balls flowed effortlessly from a bat that seemed merely an extension of his body. He was baseball, and to me baseball was life itself.

Caught up in a sweating, pushing crowd, I edged my way to Yankee Stadium's bleacher entrance. I knew nothing about press passes in those days. I bought a bleacher ticket. Then I showed a gate guard a carbon copy of my English teacher's elaborate request to "admit a serious student of journalism" to interview the Babe, along with the three-line response signed by Yankee owner, Colonel Jake Ruppert, saying, "Mr. Ruth will expect you."

The guard thrust a thumb over his shoulder at a gate marked "Press." I followed signs that led to the shadowy humid Yankee locker room. Famous faces popped out of the gloom. Vernon "Lefty" Gomez sat on a bench, cussing lightly over a broken shoelace. Frankie Crosetti, Red Ruffing and Earl Combs were huddled in an apparently serious argument. Tony "Poosh-'em-up" Lazzeri leaned against the wall slowly flexing his knees. I puzzled for a moment over the identity of Art Jorgens, a substitute catcher.

Then a deep voice bawled from a corner,

"Hey, Jorgens, maybe today you'll get your chance—Dickey looks pretty sick to me!"

I turned and dropped my lunch bag. It was the Babe. He was wearing a pair of brightly striped undershorts. I was surprised to see how tall he was. His pink moon face, lined and drooping even before the game, peered down at me like an underpowered streetlamp. He was drinking soda pop and gulping handfuls of salted peanuts.

I said I had come to interview him and offered my credentials. He waved them aside.

"Fine!" he said. "Have a swig." My mother had cautioned me about germs but this was the great Bambino. I seized the cool, slippery green bottle and drank deeply.

"To what," I asked choking, "do you owe your success?"

He chuckled. "Good, clean living," he said. I wrote it down.

I knew he was hoping to retire to a manager's job and that most sports critics considered it an absurd dream. Only that morning a columnist had written, "Babe can't even manage himself," and referred to his inability to remember signals. I mentioned the problem and was all but floored by a startling bellow of rage.

"That's the trouble with you newspaper guys," Ruth shouted. "You never forget the past! You never give a guy credit for learning anything! Maybe I lived it up in my time but don't forget I did the papers a favor—I gave you plenty to write about!

"I've settled down now," he went on. "All I want is a chance. You know I never made a wrong play on the field in my whole life. I know how to win and I can make other players do the same!"

It was about a half hour until game time, yet he straddled a bench and began to talk about his childhood. Some of the story I already knew from my conscientious study of newspaper clips.

"My old man was a bartender," he said. "I was chewing tobacco by the time I was seven. I was drinking hard whiskey when I was ten. My mother died when I was fifteen. Most of my life was in and out of St. Mary's."

He meant St. Mary's Industrial School in Baltimore. A Catholic institution for orphans and neglected children, it was nonsectarian and had also at one time sheltered singer Al Jolson. There George Herman Ruth, Jr., had learned shirt-making and tailoring—and to play baseball.

He told me that he had started as a southpaw catcher. One day he tossed a practice ball to the shortstop, who fell down complaining that Ruth had broken his hand. They made Ruth a pitcher.

Following my teacher's advice, I asked him to describe his greatest thrill in baseball. I expected him to talk about the big-league home runs that had won him world fame. Instead he replied, "The 29 and two-thirds scoreless innings I pitched in the World Series for the Red Sox." Next, he said, was the 587-foot hit he had in Tampa, Florida, in the spring of 1919.

"I wasn't even born!" I exclaimed reverently. The Babe reached for another bottle of pop and downed it with a swift gurgle. I remembered the stories about his near death in Asheville, North Carolina, in 1925 when he collapsed at the railway station after consuming a dozen sodas and fifteen hot dogs on a brutally hot day. He was hospitalized and declared in such bad shape that an English newspaper had published his obituary. Now, I nervously sought to keep him talking. I asked him what he thought about when he was in the batter's box.

"Well, you're all alone out there," he answered slowly. "You're expected to belt it. You don't want to let anybody down. But I don't worry about how I'm going to hit. I don't bother trying to outguess the field. I think about the pork chops I had the night before and if there shoulda been more salt in the barbecue sauce. Or I wonder if Claire will like that watch I just bought her as a surprise present. Or if I look good in a tux. But the second the pitcher rears back everything goes out of mind but that ball. What I see is the heart of it. That's what I lean into."

I knew that the Babe always made dramatic copy. He told me about the wisecrack he had made while negotiating his 1932 contract. Colonel Ruppert had said that Ruth's 1931 salary—$80,000—was more than President Hoover's. Ruth had said, "I had a better year."

We talked about his batting slump. He hadn't had a hit in his last 17 trips to the plate. He told me it was just tough luck.

The other players rose, stretched and began moving out to the field. I rattled on desperately: "I read that you have a prize bull terrier. My uncle has a bull terrier, too."

He grinned. "My manager, Joe McCarthy, looks like a bull terrier. You can print that."

He stood and headed for the field door. "So long, keed," he said. "You going to see the game?"

"Oh, yes!"

"Well, sit tight," he said, "and I'll show you I still got plenty. I'll hit one just for you!"

I forgot I was a "newspaper guy." "Honest?" I gasped.

"Promise," he said. "I'll stamp your name right on the ball."

I still have the faded, dog-eared yellow copy paper on which I recorded the interview. At the bottom is my thoroughly unprofessional conclusion: "The Babe great as ever," I wrote, "and I am about to go down in history!"

The sun was bright and the temperature, as I climbed into the stands, was in the 90s. It had rained lightly that morning and clouds of steam rose from the turf. I made myself a sun helmet from a section of newspaper and, together with a crowd of 15,000, cheered the Yankees and booed the Indians.

Ruth walked his first turn up. Not his fault, I told myself, and I glared at the cowardly opposing pitcher. The next time up Babe struck out. He swung mightily at the third pitch, lost his balance and fell heavily on his bad knee. I was too far away to see his face but I winced with a real pain.

A bushy-haired man in front of me howled, "Ya bum! Why dontcha quit, ya good-for-nothin' has-been!" As Ruth made his way to right field, the man yelled again, "Why don't they turn ya out to pasture?"

I leaned forward slightly and somehow the wad of gum I was chewing fell in the man's hair. I started to tell him what had happened when he bellowed, "Hey, Ruth, want me to bring a rockin' chair out for ya?"

I didn't mention the gum.

Two innings later an infield pop-up stretched out Ruth's no-hitting streak, but Gehrig hit a clean single scoring Earl Combs, and the Yankees went ahead, 6–3.

Then it happened. Ruth came up at the end of the eighth inning. A hush settled over the wilted spectators. Those who were on their way out stopped in the aisles. It was clear from any point in the stadium that the Babe was straining at the plate, tense and scowling.

I can still hear the crack of leather as the ball took off on the first pitch, high and black against the glaring blue sky. I leaped to my feet screaming with joy. This one was for me. The ball skimmed to the right, along the first-base line, headed for the fence with speed and height to spare. No successful rocket-firing at Canaveral has generated more pride and fellowship in the human heart than I felt at that moment. The Babe could do anything—he was the greatest!

At the last moment a gust of wind pushed the ball across the foul line. Ruth lined out to first on the next pitch.

Although the game ended with a Yankee victory, I walked out of the park, downcast. It was that pitcher, I muttered to myself. He didn't give Babe anything good to hit. I decided to wait for Ruth outside the clubhouse. If I felt bad, I reasoned, imagine how he felt.

Ruth emerged onto the sidewalk freshly shaved and even more pink-cheeked than before the game. He was wearing a silk shirt, a bow tie and a bright plaid jacket and smoking a big cigar. I stopped him as he plunged toward a waiting Cadillac.

"Gee, Babe!" I said. "I'm sure sorry! You're still tops even if you didn't hit that homer you promised me. Thanks for trying."

He glanced at me, puzzled. Then he remembered. "I didn't feel so good today," he said, grinning. "I had a bellyache. Maybe too much beer and sour pickles?" He pounded my shoulder. "But tell you what. I'll hit one for you tomorrow! Absolutely! First chance I get! You can take my word for it! Okay?"

He grabbed my scorecard out of my hands and scribbled his name on it. I couldn't speak. He had let me down with his empty boasts and futile promises—and he could kid about it! The Babe returned the card with a flourish. He stepped into the limousine, bellowed a joke at the driver and was driven away.

The subway ride back to my home on the outskirts of Brooklyn took an hour and 25 minutes. I jammed the autographed scorecard in my pocket. What good was his signature if he couldn't face up to the truth? He was through! He had almost made a fool of me but not quite—I could see through him now.

The following day was also hot but dry and very clear. I wasn't at the ball park. My sister and I were detailed to wash windows. As I wrung the chamois, I thought about the Babe. I felt my sense of outrage disappear and a great tenderness toward the aging Ruth took its place. It was no disgrace to be a has-been. Nothing could dim the luster of a batter who could hit 60 homers in a single season. If he needed to believe he still could do so, it was all right with me. I'd cheer him until he could no longer lift a bat.

There were no Yankee radio broadcasts in those days. I kept slipping down to the corner newsstand to wait for the early sports edition. At last it came, hurled from a truck, and the news vendor cut the cord around the bundle. High in the left-hand corner of the front page was the second-inning score: New York 5—Chicago 0. And a big black headline read: BABE BLASTS GRAND SLAMMER.

I saw Babe Ruth play only a few more times. My family moved to the Southwest for four years and by the time we returned his career was over. Now my sons and their friends ask me about him. I hardly know what to say. He was a great ballplayer. He was also self-indulgent, dissolute and a braggart. Still, he helped me to discover compassion and that it is necessary to separate love from idolatry. He was the first person to treat me like a real "newspaper guy," and to make me feel as though I could be one. Years later, having had more complicated conversations with Presidents, prime ministers and politicians, I still look back on it as a pretty good interview.

I'm glad Commissioner Frick ruled that Roger Maris' 61 home runs in a 162-game season is a separate record and that Babe Ruth's 60 homers in 154 games still stands. I wonder, sometimes, about the home-run ball he hit the day after I talked to him. I suppose it is still a treasured souvenir on someone's bookshelf. But I shall always believe it has my name on it.

THE BY-LINE of Arthur Robinson goes back fifty years, I suppose, but that is not important. (I can recall my father telling me once, "George Jessel really isn't that old—it's just that he started to reminisce at the age of four.") What *is* important is the delights Mr. Robinson has offered his readers over the years.

Casey's Daughter at the Bat

ARTHUR ROBINSON

A WORLD SERIES begins and ultimately it ends and for the fans the game's the thing. But for old baseball men—managers, scouts, players and newspapermen—the Series is also a time for the gathering of the clan, a time for the remembrance of things past, the clinking of friendly glasses, the telling of tall tales and the singing of old songs in crowded hotel rooms long after the last man in each game is out.

It is also the time—inevitably—when an amiably exhilarated veteran of the baseball wars will launch himself, with practically no encouragement whatever, into a recitation of "Casey at the Bat."

With gestures.

Men with the voices of slide trombones and the eloquence of road company Hamlets have become hoarse reciting the great poem since Ernest Lawrence Thayer, a young graduate of Harvard, wrote it in 1888.

Although Thayer set the stage in his epic for a heroic climax, he avoided the cliché of a happy and triumphant ending. Sophocles and the other ancient Greek dramatists whom Thayer had studied at Harvard were like that, too.

With two out in the ninth, two men on base and the score 4 to 2 against Mudville, the Mighty Casey took two called strikes. Then he swung cyclonically at the next pitch and missed.

And that was the old ball game.

There was no joy in Mudville. Mighty Casey had struck out. In the clutch.

The big bum.

Some years ago I analyzed the great poem in print and came to the conclusion that Thayer, although a great poet, was a lousy reporter and obviously knew very little about the finer points of the game.

He would have been fired as a rank incompetent if he had worked for any of the ogres who have been my managing editors. Thayer didn't even mention the name of either the opposing team or the pitcher who struck out the Mighty Casey.

And what was Casey's first name? Nor did Thayer say what kind of a pitch it was that the Mighty Casey took his cut at for the last strike. And why didn't the opposing pitcher give Casey, the greatest of home-run hitters, an intentional base on balls? Flynn was on third and Blakey on second and first base was open.

If Babe Ruth had a stomach ache—and he did have a famous one—the Bambino's public would be told about it in full detail. Thayer tells us nothing about Casey, the Man. Didn't he ever interview Casey in the clubhouse after a game or associate with him off the field?

Not until Franklin P. Adams published *Innocent Merriment*, a voluminous anthology of light verse about 25 years ago, did I learn that the Mighty Casey was married and had a daughter named Patricia.

FPA's anthology contained a poem by Al Graham called "Casey's Daughter at the Bat."

She was a softball player and the star of a team called The Mudvillettes.

Graham, obviously a compassionate man, felt Pat was entitled to redeem the family name. She had suffered much in her childhood. People pointed her out on the street as the daughter of That Man who had failed Mudville in a pinch. Her schoolmates tormented her during recess with nasty reminders of her father's failure.

The poor kid.

Graham did everything his lively imagination could contrive to give Patricia a break. He discovered that Casey's teammates all had daughters and that they, too, were outstanding softball players.

The old familiar names reappear in Graham's poem. Cooney's daughter Brenda is known as "Lefty." Burrow's pride and joy is "Babs." Myrna Flynn didn't have a nickname but Hedy Blake is called "Flatfoot."

Again it is the ninth inning. Two are out. The score is 4 to 2 against the Mudvillettes. Myrna and Flatfoot have both hit safely.

And when the dust had lifted, there on third and second base
Perched a pair of Mudville cuties, each a-powdering her face.

* * *

Then from the howling mamas in the stand in back of first
Went up a weird, unearthly scream, like a Tarzan crazed with thirst;
Like a million screeching monkey-fans, like a yowling giant cat;
For Casey, Patsy Casey, was advancing to the bat!

* * *

There was ease in Patsy's manner as she stepped up to the plate;
There were curves in Patsy's figure, and a bounce in Patsy's gait;
And when responding to the screams she lightly doffed her hat,
No Casey fan could doubt 'twas Mighty's daughter at the bat.

* * *

She took a called strike. Then another.

And now they see her daub a bit of powder on her nose;
They watch her put fresh lipstick on—a shade called Fleur de Rose;
And now the pitcher holds the ball, and now she lets it go:
And now the air is shattered by *another* Casey's blow."

* * *

Oh, somewhere there are softball fans who scream and yell and shout;
There's still no joy in Mudville—Casey's daughter has struck out."

DeWolf Hopper, an old-time musical comedy star, is said to have recited the original poem 10,000 times. I heard him myself many years ago. So did Casey Stengel.

"I recite it myself once in a while," Stengel has said, "but it's not the same."

Sometime I hope to hear Talullah Bankhead recite the Graham sequel. I'm sure she'd break your heart.

JACKIE ROBINSON'S BOOK *Baseball Has Done It,* edited by Charles Dexter, is a remarkable compendium of both the history and the circumstances of the Negro in baseball. It was Robinson, of course, who broke baseball's color line in 1945, when Branch Rickey assigned him to the Montreal club of the International League as the first Negro ever to play officially in organized ball. Youngsters of today find it hard to believe there ever was a time when things were different than they are now. But it is worth remembering.

From *Baseball Has Done It*

JACKIE ROBINSON
***edited by* CHARLES DEXTER**

July 4, 1906
In no other profession has the color line been drawn more rigidly than in baseball. Colored players are not only barred from white clubs; at times exhibition games are canceled for no other reason than objections raised by a Southern player. These Southerners are, as a rule, fine players, and managers refuse to book colored teams rather than lose their services.

The colored player suffers great inconveniences while traveling. All hotels are generally filled from garret to cellar when they strike a town. It is a common occurrence for them to arrive in a city late at night and to walk around for several hours before finding lodging.

The situation is far different today than it was in the 1870s, when colored players were accommodated in the best hotels in the country. The cause of this change is no doubt the sad condition of things from a racial standpoint today. The color question is uppermost in the minds of Americans at the present time.

The average pay of colored players is $466 a year, compared to an average of $2,000 for white major leaguers and $571 for white minor leaguers. The disparity in salaries is enormous when it is apparent that many colored stars would be playing in the majors but for the color line.

This picture was drawn by Sol White in 1906 in his *History of Colored Baseball.* With minor modifications it was true in 1945 when I was on the Kansas City Monarchs of the Negro National League. Sol White was a hero of Negro baseball in the 1880s and 1890s, a .400 hitter on the original Cuban Giants and later manager of the invincible Philadelphia Giants. In the yellowed pages of his little book are valuable instructions in hitting and pitching, the histories of many fine teams of the times, as well as an exhortation to Negro youths to play hard, cleanly, and with respect for their opponents and the game.

According to White, baseball came late to Negroes. Bud Fowler was the first Negro to play on an otherwise white team, starring at second base for the New Castle champions of western Pennsylvania in 1872.

By 1880 twenty Negroes were on minor-league rosters. I was not the first Negro in the major leagues. In 1884 Fleetwood Walker caught 41 games for the Toledo Mudhens of the big-league American Association, while his brother Weldon played the outfield in six games.

That June the Chicago White Stockings rolled into Toledo for an exhibition game. They were champions of the rival National League, a bruising crew of sluggers, four of whom batted over .340. Their manager and first baseman was Cap Anson, who would turn handsprings in his grave if he knew that I share a niche with him in baseball's Hall of Fame.

During his 27-year big-league career Anson played all nine positions. He batted over .300

in 22 seasons; his average was .394 in 1894, when he was forty-three years old. He was a great ballplayer but a heartless man.

In 1884 the nation was still recovering from the aftermath of the Civil War. Southern senators and congressmen were whipping up a fury of bigotry against Negroes in much the same vituperative language that many Southern demagogues use today. Whether Cap Anson was poisoned by their venom I do not know, but he walked on the field in Toledo that June day, saw the Walker brothers in uniform and stalked off, taking his team with him. A large crowd was in the stands. Charlie Morton, Toledo's manager, promised to fire the Walkers the next morning. The game was played.

Thereafter Anson saw red at the mere mention of a Negro in baseball. He launched a one-man crusade to rid the game of all but whites.

The following season John Montgomery Ward of the New York Giants watched George Stovy fan fifteen batters in an Eastern League game and recommended Stovy's purchase. When Anson heard about the pending deal, his howls of rage could be heard from Chicago to New York. Negotiations were called off. Stovy spent the remainder of his career in segregated ball.

Anson's vendetta reached a climax in the winter of 1887–88. He appeared at major- and minor-league meetings, urging the adoption of a rule that would require owners to fire Negroes on their rosters and never again to contract with them. None was then in the majors; twenty-five in the minors were deprived of their jobs, among them Sol White and Weldon Walker.

Walker had played for Akron in the Tri-State League in 1887. He refused to take banishment lying down. His letter to President George McDermitt of the Tri-State League is a relic of one man's struggle for equality in that far-off day:

I have grievances, sir. I question whether my individual loss serves the public good. I write you not because I have been denied making my bread and butter, but in the hope that the league's action will be reserved. The rule that you have passed is a public disgrace! It casts derision on the laws of Ohio, the voice of the people, which says that all men are equal. There is now the same accommodation for colored and white men and women in your ball parks, and the same disposition is made of the moneys of both. I would suggest to your honorable body that if your rule is not repealed, you should make it criminal for black men and women to be admitted to your ball parks.

There should be some sounder cause for dismissal, such as lack of intelligence or misbehavior. Ability, intelligence, should be recognized first, last and at all times by everyone. I ask this question—why was this rule passed?

Weldy Walker received no reply.

John J. McGraw loved victory so passionately that he would have ordered his pitchers to dust off his grandmother if she'd been a .350 hitter with a home-run bat. As the third baseman of the rough and tough Baltimore Orioles of the 1890s he had been one of an invincible crew. But as their manager in the infant American League in 1901 he was in desperate need of players. That February he went to Hot Springs, Arkansas, to drown his worries in the thermal baths.

On a diamond near McGraw's hotel two Negro teams were playing. His eye was caught by the smart hitting and slick fielding of a copper-skinned second-sacker, Charlie Grant. After the game McGraw invited Grant to his suite.

Grant was a Negro, under contract to the Chicago Columbia Giants. He emerged from McGraw's suite a full-blooded Indian chief and an Oriole.

Newspapers reported Grant's signing. On March 5 a delegation of Chicago Negroes arrived in Hot Springs. As Baltimore baseball writers watched, they presented a floral tribute to their hero.

The following day McGraw received a telegram from National League president Nick Young, reminding him of the anti-Negro rule adopted at Cap Anson's instigation in 1888.

McGraw released Grant later that day.

In the long years between the late 1880s and the mid-1940s dark-skinned Americans played ball in a world of their own. Hundreds of independent Negro teams sprang up in the 1910s, some booking as many as 200 games a year. Leagues were formed, dissolved, and re-formed. During the sports-conscious 1920s, the Negro National League and the Negro American League took firm root east and west. It was *apartheid* as in South Africa, except that occasionally a big-league team, barnstorming after the season, met a Negro team and had a heck of a time holding its own. Negro ball was almost a carbon copy of the white game, with a regular schedule, an annual All-Star game and World Series. Attendance was high, often over 20,000 at World Series contests. Among those present were many enthusiastic white fans.

Negroes regarded their stars as the equals if not the superiors of many whites whose names they read daily in the box scores. In those days we had our own press, our theaters, churches and, of course, our segregated schools. Some progress toward integration in sports was taking place in the 1930s as Jesse Owens triumphed in the 1936 Olympics and during Joe Louis' dignified reign as heavyweight king. But organized baseball was closed to us.

Few of our own diamond stars were known to white fans. Josh Gibson, the hammering home-run slugger, and Satchel Paige received occasional comment on white sports pages. Negro teams played in big- and minor-league parks, but white newspapers seldom reported their doings.

As for Negro fans—they longed to see the Homestead Grays or Kansas City Monarchs pitted against white world champions. How would Josh Gibson fare against Lefty Grove or Carl Hubbell? Could Satch stop Babe Ruth or Jimmy Foxx? No one will ever know.

Terris McDuffie was one of the many top-notch Negro hurlers of that period, a burly right-hander with a busy baseball brain. Says Terris:

I'm Alabama-born and Florida-raised. Back in '29, when I was 18, I enlisted and they put me on the ball team at Fort Benning, Georgia. I was just a beginner. I played the outfield when I wasn't pitching for the regimental club, the 24th Infantry it was. The Colonel wanted winning sports teams, so he got officers to come down from West Point to coach us in special duties like baseball, basketball and track. Well, Satchel Paige and the Birmingham Black Barons—that's the team Willie Mays was on later—come over to play us. Satch must of liked what he saw of me. He told me he was going to keep his eye on me. The day he pitched at Fort Benning he threw so hard an average hitter couldn't get his bat around for a full swing. The only way to hit Satch was to choke the bat and half swing—that's how quick he was! In all my years I never seen anyone who threw like him. Feller? No comparison! By the time Satch got on the Indians with Feller in '48 he'd lost his fast ball, but he knew so much about pitching he could still make big leaguers look silly.

When I finished my Army bit in '31 the Barons signed me. I pitched against Satch in '37 when he was with the Kansas City Monarchs and I was on the Newark Eagles. He shut me out, 6 to 0. That winter he fixed for me to go to Puerto Rico. I faced him on the Puerto Rico All-Stars . . . he was on an all-star colored team from the States. I beat 'em 4 to 0 with one hit. I lost two other games to Satch years later in Mexico. I concentrated on control. I had a sinker, a slider, a curve and different speeds and a good fast ball. My favorite pitch was my sliding sinker. I never had to use off-pitches like the knuckler or sneaky slow stuff. I started 27 games with the Eagles in '38 and finished 'em all without relief, 27 complete games in succession! I played the outfield days when I wasn't pitching. That year I was the Most Valuable Player in the Negro National League. In '41 with the Homestead Grays I won 27 games and lost 5.

After the war I was getting the highest pay in the East, though not as high as Satch in the American League out West. I had a contract for $800 a month, with a $2,000 bonus at the end of the season, about $6,000 a year. That's not much compared to what the boys were getting in white ball, so when the Pasquel brothers offered me higher pay to jump to their Mexican League, I jumped along with Sal Maglie, Lou Klein, Max Lanier, Mickey Owen, Fred Martin and Danny Gardella. In Mexico I played on mixed teams with players of big reputations in the majors for the first time. Well, as you know, the Mexican League didn't last long, and by 1950, when it broke up, the colored leagues in the States were busting up because the majors were taking their best players. I was forty or forty-one then, but I won the Most Valuable Player award in Venezuela, pitching for Caracas in '51. The next year I went to Santo Domingo and won their MVP award, too. Just before the '54 season the big push for colored stars was on in the States. I was forty-five but my arm was still good, so the Dallas Eagles of the Texas League sent for me. That was the only time I pitched for a mixed team. My stuff was as good as ever. I worked in 14 games, won three, lost four and held my earned-run average down to 3.04. Then I badly injured my leg, could hardly walk on it for three or four years, and was finished. All told I played 24 years in professional ball.

Our home runs were not made off the jackrabbit ball. Our hitters lambasted a ball inferior to the one used in the majors. We had no soreheads, swelled heads or braggarts. We trained in March like big leaguers, but we didn't travel like them. If they'd traveled in cars and buses like we did, lost nights on the road trying to reach the next town, riding until game time the next day, eating the wrong food, how long do you think those highly touted stars would've lasted? We stood more wear and tear and hard knocks than them.

What's happening in baseball today is very impressive. I'm glad our boys are getting a chance to prove what they can do. I think they're extraordinary. They give fans what they want, they believe in themselves; they produce.

Bill Yancey is one of the few stars of Negro ball now employed in the big leagues. In the 1930s he was the All-Star shortstop for the Philadelphia Giants, New York Lincoln Giants and the all but invincible Hilldales of Darby, Pennsylvania. Wintertimes he was the stone-wall guard of the famous Renaissance Five which was recently admitted en masse to basketball's Hall of Fame. Today he is a scout for the New York Yankees, his most impressive protégé Al Downing, the strikeout prodigy.

I was born in Philadelphia and attended Central High from 1918 to 1922 but couldn't play on the basketball or baseball teams because I was a Negro. In fact, I never played on an organized team until after I was graduated.

The Philadelphia Giants tried me out in 1923, but I was too inexperienced to make the Negro big leagues then. They were owned by Bert Williams, who'd broken the Broadway color line with the Ziegfeld Follies. *We had no Negro minor leagues to develop players in so I had to do my own developing where I could. I caught on with the Boston Giants as a shortstop. I didn't master that position until '28 when John Henry Lloyd, old Pop Lloyd—they've named a ball park for him in Atlantic City—taught me position play, showed me the right moves on the pivot, and how to work cutoffs and relays.*

In 1929 I signed with the Lincoln Giants and was the first Negro player to put his foot on the grass at Yankee Stadium. We were scheduled to meet the Baltimore Black Sox in the first Negro game at the Stadium. I suited up early, ran out to right field and stood where the Babe stood and pretended to catch fly balls like him. Then I took a bat and went to the plate and pretended I was hitting one into the right-field seats like him. It was a bigger thrill than hitting my own first home run against the Paterson Silk Sox back in '24.

Thirty years ago Negro ball was at its peak. The Lincoln Giants often beat the Bushwicks when they were barnstorming with stars such as Lou Gehrig, Jimmy Foxx and others. White baseball writers didn't cover our league games although we often drew 10,000 to 15,000 fans and filled Comiskey Park in Chicago for our 1934 All-Star game, which was run off as smoothly and was certainly as well played as the big-league show.

No one scouted me. No one scouted Josh Gibson. I've seen 'em all since the 1920s and Josh was the greatest right-hand hitter of all time, including Jimmy Foxx and Rogers Hornsby. Take Foxx—Josh could wrap him up! They say that Jimmy's homer to the last box in the third tier in left field at Yankee Stadium was the longest blow ever made there. I was playing in the Stadium against Josh's Homestead Grays when he lifted one two stories over the bullpen and out of the ball park! The Grays used Griffith Stadium in Washington while the Senators were on the road. That old park was the toughest in the majors on home-run hitters. But Josh hit eight homers in ten games in one span, more than all the Senators hit in 77 games. Josh had great pride. Dizzy Dean often pitched post-season games against Negro teams Josh played on. One day the crowd was small and Diz was in a hurry to get away. He would never have done this in a regular game, but this was only an exhibition, so before the ninth inning he called to Josh, "Let's get the side out quick and get the heck out of here! Let three strikes go past you, will ya, Josh?" "Okay with me," grinned Josh. So Diz fogged one up to the plate. Josh swung. The ball went winging far over the fence. Josh laughed as he jogged around the bases. "That's more fun than taking three strikes!" he called to Diz.

Josh earned the top salary in the Negro leagues, $1,000 a month. He was still catching for the Homestead Grays in '47, the year Jackie Robinson became a Dodger. He was tickled to death the color line was broken, but he was a frustrated man, too old for the majors. Poor Josh let himself go. He got fat and quit in '48. Two years later he died.

THE EVENT recounted here is simply this: a record that has stood unchallenged for nearly half a century.

Sunny Jim Bottomley

HAROLD ROSENTHAL

SUNNY JIM BOTTOMLEY came up to the St. Louis Cardinals in the early '20s and was part of a then-radical experiment squashed by unfavorable reaction from both fans and rival players. Branch Rickey, St. Louis manager, had placed numbers on the backs of his players but had to back off when customers and visiting teams alike tossed ear-curling remarks about what sort of company this placed the Cardinal players in.

Almost a half century later Rickey wrote, "I did not mind the public criticism. That sort of thing has not often changed any program I thought was good.

"But the effect upon the team was bad and 'busted up' team morale completely. The players were embarrassed all the time. They really didn't want to show themselves on the field. Because of the continuing embarrassment to the players, the numbers were removed."

So the system of identifying ballplayers as known today was shelved until the start of the '30s when suddenly baseball officials, players and fans alike wondered how in the world the game had ever gotten by without some system of easy, instant identification.

There was never any mistaking Jim Bottomley, however, numbered or otherwise. The rangy Cardinal first baseman wore his working clothes with a special insouciance. He turned an ordinary baseball cap into a figurative plumed hat, and his flannel shirt and pants made it appear as though his teammates were running around in gunny sacks. And in 1924, on a midweek September afternoon, he tailored for himself a remarkable record which still stands—a dozen runs batted in during a single nine-inning game.

Just how extraordinary this record is can best be realized by a quick comparison with a recent World Series record. In 1960 Richardson, of the Yankees, won himself a sports car and a raise with his Series performance, rated superior to anything else that happened in the seven-game Series. Richardson's payoff performance was a dozen runs batted in during the *entire Series* with Pittsburgh!

Equally remarkable about Bottomley's effort was the nonchalance with which it was received. Not only was it shunted for other sports news of that particular day, but it didn't even rate a headline.

The prime news was the United States' beating England in international polo on Long Island, with the Prince of Wales watching. In the Polo Grounds the Giants were driving for their fourth straight pennant under McGraw. Washington was hustling toward the flag in the American League under the direction of its boy manager, Bucky Harris. If anyone was silly enough to be concerned about what was happening at Ebbets Field, let 'em go dig it out of the box score.

Wilbert Robinson was the leader of the Brooklyn flock at the time, and he was plenty concerned with what was happening. His club had racked up fifteen straight victories (including four straight doubleheaders) in a streak which had ended on Labor Day. Brooklyn was only a game or two behind the Giants.

From a more personal viewpoint, Jim Bottomley was engaged in assaulting a twin record which Uncle Robbie, a catcher with the Old Orioles, had flaunted so proudly: eleven runs batted in, with seven hits in seven at-bats.

The first half of the record fell, the second still stands. Bottomley got six for six.

His efforts for the afternoon included three singles, a double and two homers. One of his homers cleared the bases after Uncle Robbie had ordered Rogers Hornsby passed purposely to pitch to Sunny Jim. The strategy was fairly sound. Hornsby was en route to a .424 season, his greatest. Years later, when he was to taunt Roger Maris with "You didn't hit in one year what I hit in two," he was almost correct.

Bottomley, however, was en route to his greatest day. The Dodgers used five pitchers; Bottomley nailed each one. His two homers were stroked off Art Decatur. Others who got into the act were Rube Ehrhardt, Jimmy Hollingsworth, Gormer Wilson and Cameo Jim Roberts. (Roberts came from Cameo, Alabama.)

Bottomley was a fine hitter, a .309 lifetime performer, but 1924 was not one of his big homer years. His two off Decatur amounted to one-seventh of his season's total. A few years later he lashed enough to share the National League homer crown with Hack Wilson and win the Most Valuable Player crown.

The Cards won that particular game, of course, by a rousing 17–3 count, and the contest was completed in less than two hours. This included the time needed to fan the spark back into the field announcer who had collapsed on his megaphone when the Cards racked up four runs in the opening inning and chased Ehrhardt without his being able to retire a man.

If the papers weren't aware of the significance of Bottomley's record, Uncle Robbie certainly was. The next afternoon Bottomley, a friendly fellow, stopped by the Dodger dugout to pick up some chewing tobacco from Uncle Robbie. Robbie promptly chased him and meant it.

"You'll get no more chews from me," sputtered the old Oriole. "Do you know what you did to me yesterday? You chased me right out of the record book. Now get outta here!"

WITH THE COMING of the tape recorder, journalism has taken on a new look, and the spoken word has become as much a part of the archives as the written. In the case of baseball broadcasts, that means, of course, the *unrehearsed* spoken word.

Anyone who has heard Russ Hodges' description of Bobby Thomson's "homer heard 'round the world" in 1951 knows how brilliant and dramatic such treatment can be, in the right hands (or mouth). And Dodger broadcaster Vince Scully gives us further proof here, in his description of the final inning of Sandy Koufax' perfect game.

Koufax' masterwork was his fourth no-hitter in four straight years (Bob Hendley, who pitched against him this night, threw a one-hitter but no cigar). And as you read Scully's spontaneous description, it will become hard to believe that this wasn't written, but is indeed the unrehearsed spoken word instead.

1965: Los Angeles Dodgers 1, Chicago Cubs 0

VINCE SCULLY

THREE TIMES in his sensational career has Sandy Koufax walked out to the mound to pitch a fateful ninth when he turned in a no-hitter. But tonight, September 9th, 1965, he made the toughest walk of his career, I'm sure, because through eight innings he has pitched a perfect game. He has struck out eleven, has retired 24 consecutive batters.

And the first man he will look at is catcher Chris Krug—big, right-handed hitter—flied to center, grounded to short.

Dick Tracewski is now at second base; and Koufax ready—and delivers: curve ball for a strike—0-and-1 the count to Chris Krug.

Out on deck to pinch-hit is one of the men we mentioned as a "possible": Joe Amalfitano. Here's the strike-one pitch: fast ball, swung on and missed, strike two.

And you can almost taste the pressure now. Koufax lifted his cap, ran his fingers through his black hair, and pulled the cap back down, fussing at the bill. Krug must feel it too, as he backs out, heaves a sigh, took off his helmet, put it back on, and steps back up to the plate.

Tracewski is over to his right to fill up the middle. Kennedy is deep to guard the line. The strike-two pitch on the way: fast ball outside, ball one. Krug started to go after it but held up, and Torborg held the ball high in the air trying to convince Vargo, but Eddy said, "No, sir."

One-and-two the count to Chris Krug. It is 9:41 P.M. on September the ninth. The 1-2 pitch on the way: curve ball tapped foul off to the left of the plate. The Dodgers defensively in this spine-tingling moment: Sandy Koufax and Jeff Torborg—the boys who will try to stop anything hit their way: Wes Parker, Dick Tracewski, Maury Wills and John Kennedy—the outfield of Lou Johnson, Willie Davis and Ron Fairly.

There are 29,000 people in the ball park and a million butterflies; 29,139 paid. Koufax into his windup and the 1-2 pitch: fast ball, fouled back out of play.

In the Dodger dugout Al Ferrara gets up

and walks down near the runway, and it begins to get tough to be a teammate and sit in the dugout and have to watch.

Sandy back of the rubber now, toes it. All the boys in the bullpen straining to get a better look as they look through the wire fence in left field. One-and-two the count to Chris Krug. Koufax, feet together, now to his windup, and the 1-2 pitch: ball, outside, ball two. [*The crowd boos*]

A lot of people in the ball park now are starting to see the pitches with their hearts. The pitch was outside. Torborg tried to pull it in over the plate, but Vargo, an experienced umpire, wouldn't go for it. Two-and-two the count to Chris Krug. Sandy reading signs. Into his windup, 2-2 pitch: fast ball got him swinging! Sandy Koufax has struck out twelve. He is two outs away from a perfect game.

Here is Joe Amalfitano to pinch-hit for Don Kessinger. Amalfitano is from southern California, from San Pedro. He was an original bonus boy with the Giants. Joey's been around, and as we mentioned earlier, he has helped to beat the Dodgers twice. And on deck is Harvey Kuenn.

Kennedy is tight to the bag at third. The fast ball for a strike: 0-and-1 with one out in the ninth inning, 1 to 0 Dodgers.

Sandy ready, into his windup, and the strike-one pitch: curve ball tapped foul, 0-and-2, and Amalfitano walks away and shakes himself a little bit, and swings the bat. And Koufax, with a new ball, takes a hitch at his belt and walks behind the mound. I would think that the mound at Dodger Stadium right now is the loneliest place in the world. Sandy, fussing, looks in to get his sign; 0-and-2 to Amalfitano —the strike-two pitch to Joe: fast ball, swung on and missed, strike three!

He is one out away from the promised land, and Harvey Kuenn is coming up. So Harvey Kuenn is batting for Bob Hendley. The time on the scoreboard is 9:44, the date September the ninth, 1965. And Koufax working on veteran Harvey Kuenn.

Sandy into his windup, and the pitch: fast ball for a strike. He has struck out, by the way, five consecutive batters, and this has gone unnoticed.

Sandy ready, and the strike-one pitch: very high, and he lost his hat. He really forced that one. That was only the second time tonight where I have had the feeling that Sandy threw instead of pitched, trying to get that little extra, and that time he tried so hard his hat fell off. He took an extremely long stride toward the plate, and Torborg had to go up to get it. One-and-one to Harvey Kuenn. Now he's ready: fast ball high, ball two.

You can't blame the man for pushing just a little bit now. Sandy backs off, mops his forehead, runs his left index finger along his forehead, dries it off on his left pants-leg. All the while, Kuenn just waiting.

Now Sandy looks in. Into his windup, and the 2-1 pitch to Kuenn: swung on and missed, strike two. It is 9:46 P.M. Two-and-two to Harvey Kuenn—one strike away.

Sandy into his windup. Here's the pitch: *swung on and missed, a perfect game!*
[*Long wait as crowd noise takes over.*]

On the scoreboard in right field it is 9:46 P.M. in the city of the angels, Los Angeles, California, and a crowd of 29,139 just sitting in to see the only pitcher in baseball history to hurl four no-hit, no-run games. He has done it four straight years, and now he capped it: on his fourth no-hitter, he made it a perfect game.

And Sandy Koufax, whose name will always remind you of strikeouts, did it with a flourish. He struck out the last six consecutive batters. So, when he wrote his name in capital letters in the record book, the "K" stands out even more than the "O-U-F-A-X."

One of the most scholarly contributions to the literature of baseball was the book *Baseball—the Early Years*, by Harold Seymour, published in 1960 by the Oxford University Press. The chapter from that book selected for reproduction here touches on a phase of the game not otherwise alluded to, I believe, elsewhere in the *Fireside* library.

The Great Player Revolt

HAROLD SEYMOUR

The revolt of the players in the Brotherhood War of 1890 was the climax of their long-festering resentment against the policies of the owners. The reserve clause and its abuses, limitations on salaries, arbitrary fines, the blacklist, and the absence of effective means of redress all played their part in provoking the revolt. As far back as 1880, the New York *Mercury* recommended that the players "rise up in their manhood and rebel," and the Cincinnati *Enquirer* predicted that one day they would. For that matter, from the very inception of the National League there were periodic rumors that the players were planning to organize. But the owners and their spokesmen always dismissed such reports as highly unlikely.

They were proved wrong. In 1885 William H. Voltz, then a Philadelphia sportswriter, tried to form a protective association with the primary object of establishing a benefit fund for sick and needy players. But little came of this first effort. It lacked a militant program, and besides, Voltz, as an outsider, did not have the confidence of the players. They were suspicious of his motives.

Taking up where Voltz left off, nine members of the New York Giants formed a local chapter of the Brotherhood of Professional Base Ball Players on October 22, 1885. Their objectives were to protect and benefit themselves collectively and individually, to promote a high standard of professional conduct, and to foster and encourage the interests of baseball. Among the signatories were stars like Buck Ewing, Roger Connor, and Tim Keefe. They chose John Montgomery Ward for their president.

Ward, a man overlooked by labor historians, played a highly influential role in baseball's labor relations. He was a rarity among the players of his era: a college graduate. After playing ball at Penn State he turned professional in 1877 and became a first-class pitcher, helping Providence to the pennant in 1879 and leading the league with 44 won and 18 lost. After an arm injury forced him to quit pitching, he became a star shortstop. Later he managed Brooklyn and New York. While playing with the Giants Ward took a law degree at Columbia University and eventually became a successful attorney. Like Joe DiMaggio much later, he surprised his public by voluntarily quitting baseball while he was still a leading player.

His background, unquestioned leadership ability, and popularity made Ward a well-equipped spokesman for the players. Under his energetic direction, Brotherhood chapters were soon set up in various National League cities, and toward the end of the 1886 season the organization publicly announced its existence.

The news caused no great stir. A baseball paper welcomed the Brotherhood as "sorely needed" to offset the "simply shameful" abuses many managers forced upon the players. Even the National League took the announcement in stride, Nick Young going so far as to praise the Brotherhood as an organization of the most reputable players in the game and therefore worthy of respect and consideration. Up until a year before the trouble began, the Brotherhood was tolerated by the league, which only asked that it use its influence for the general good of its members and the game.

Yet there were signs the players were growing more bold, and some of the more articulate among them were beginning to speak out. *The New York Times* carried a statement by one of them at the time the salary limitation rule was passed:

> The time has arrived when the players must take some action in the matter. . . . Legislation has been solely in the interests of the clubs. The players have been ignored at every meeting, and restrictions one after another have been placed upon them until now they can stand it no longer. The first piece of injustice was adopting the reserve rule. A club can engage a player, reduce his salary to $1,000 and compel him to play for that sum, although he may have a standing offer of five times that amount elsewhere. . . . Stockholders of clubs will find before long that they have placed the last straw on the camel's back. We make the money, and it is only just that we ought to get a fair share of the profits.

When Fred Dunlap was sold to Pittsburgh, he astonished Detroit president Stearns by having the temerity to ask for half the selling price. In 1889 a couple of player strikes occurred spontaneously, one over the incident of Yank Robinson and the dirty pants which has already been described.

Ward himself published a scathing attack on organized baseball in 1887. He bitterly criticized the buying and selling of players and the blacklisting of those who would not sign at club terms. He condemned the one-sided contract as a means of instituting serfdom in baseball, and denounced the reserve clause as an ex post facto law, a product of the owners' distrust of each other. While he did not call for its repeal in so many words, he did say that baseball should return to ordinary business practices and allow supply and demand to regulate salaries, and he predicted that improvement would come only "when the law of the land governs the game."

By 1887 the Brotherhood, with an estimated membership of some ninety players, felt strong enough to seek formal recognition by the league and to negotiate contract reform. Nick Young and the owners were willing to discuss the contract but, like other business leaders of their day, unwilling to accord the Brotherhood official recognition as a union. The league branded the players' group a secret organization, and said it preferred to bring about reform by the "old and usual means"—to which Ward replied, "What ones?"

Nevertheless, the league authorized Young to write Ward that it was willing to meet with him and some of the players to learn their objectives. Conceivably, Spalding influenced this step, because he was an exception among the owners in that he was willing to recognize the Brotherhood and sit down with their representatives to discuss the contract. At any rate, a players' committee of Ward, Ned Hanlon, and Dennis Brouthers* appeared at a league meeting and asked that players have full salary figures written into their contracts, and that none be reserved at a reduced salary.

The players succeeded in obtaining a new type of contract, which incorporated the terms of the reserve specifically, rather than by general reference to the National Agreement, as was the case up to then. But the league stalled over the question of writing in full salary figures, because it would necessitate repealing the limitation rule. This, of course, was an admission that many players were being paid more than the rule allowed. The league argued that to repeal the rule, it would have to get the consent of the American Association—which it promised to do at the spring meeting of the Board of Arbitration. Hailing Ward's work during negotiations, the *Sporting News* called him "the St. George of baseball, for he has slain the dragon of oppression."

But after the players had signed their contracts for the season of 1888, the league told them that nothing could be done about the limitation rule because the Association refused to surrender it. After the season, the league also ignored the request not to reserve men at lowered salaries, with the excuse that since the limitation rule could not be repealed, the rest of the bargain was also nullified.

This setback, while disappointing, made little real difference. The limitation rule was largely a dead letter anyway, and few players were actually reserved at reduced salaries. As for the reserve clause itself, the players were by no means dead set against it. During negotiations with the league they could offer no substitute for it. To the contrary, Ward allegedly supported it, and the player representatives conceded not only the league's right of reservation but its authority to reserve players of disbanded or expelled clubs in order to make it "easy" to replace them and "preserve the autonomy of the League."

* A fourth player, Arthur Irwin, was an alternate.

Certainly Ward was no radical. He once said that the "gravest offense" a player could commit was to break his contract. A year before publishing his strong magazine article, he was reported in *Sporting Life* as saying that he believed the reserve would not be attacked, and that the majority of players felt it was necessary, although it had been abused. Then in his book, published the year after his article, he went so far as to accept the reserve as an evil necessary to stabilize the game and protect the capital of investors. Furthermore, during negotiations the players were willing to accept a system of graduated fines for "dissipation," ranging from twenty-five to one hundred dollars, and they even agreed to blacklisting after a player's fourth offense. So it is conceivable that had the owners been more willing to conciliate, or at least to let matters continue in the same manner for a while, the eruption of 1890 would have been avoided.

Instead, they crowded the players still more and brought to an end the rather joyless honeymoon with the Brotherhood. In the off season of 1888, when the men were scattered in their homes or, like Ward and Hanlon, off on Spalding's world baseball tour, the owners put through the Brush Classification Plan described earlier, under which players were to be grouped according to skill and paid on that basis.

When Ward heard about classification, his first impulse was to leave the exhibition tour and return home at once. However, he completed the trip, possibly persuaded by Spalding. As soon as he returned, Brotherhood men held secret conferences, and predictions of a player strike were freely circulated. The players did consider striking, but decided against it, because many of them already had signed their contracts for the next season and were afraid that if they broke them they would lose public support. Instead, at a Brotherhood meeting on May 19 they appointed a grievance committee for the purpose of trying to negotiate with the league once more.

In June the committee petitioned President Young to repeal classification and to end the practice of selling players. The league assigned a three-man committee headed by Spalding to talk matters over, but on June 25 Spalding and Ward met alone. Spalding dismissed the issue as not important enough for immediate action, and maintained with some plausibility that it could wait until the regular league meeting in the fall. Ward disagreed, and cautioned that, while the Brotherhood was not threatening anything yet, the league would be unwise to put the players off. When Tim Keefe, secretary of the Brotherhood, heard of this setback, he warned that the players' organization would take action, adding ominously, "The league will not classify as many as they think."

Strike talk revived, only to bring scoffs from the owners. Day of the Giants called it "nonsense," and Spalding discounted it as "a Little Bluebeard story." Soden of Boston said the idea was "absurd," adding, however, a threat to use strikebreakers, because his club had made a business contract with the public to furnish them baseball and he was not going to "close up shop"! The owners did not know it, but the players were already planning something far more drastic than some isolated strikes. Two facts point this way. First, a general strike for the Fourth of July was actually considered, but voted down. Second, Ward succeeded in holding back Jack Rowe and Deacon White, who were threatening to test the reserve rule in the courts.

These two stars were sober, steady men who had saved their money and were prepared to invest in the Buffalo club, an International League club at that time. The trouble was that they had been sold to Pittsburgh a short time before they bought into the Buffalo club. Fred Stearns, Pittsburgh president, insisted on his property rights, and said the players would play in Pittsburgh or "get off the earth." The players avowed that they owned the Buffalo club and they were going to play for it; White made the pungent remark, "No man can sell my carcass, unless I get at least half." But, after a letter from Ward, the players gave in and reported to Pittsburgh in mid-season. The contents of the letter have never been revealed, but in all likelihood Ward advised the men to lie low for the same reason that the strike was probably called off. Ward and the Brotherhood leaders did not want to disturb matters while they were preparing something far bigger—a league of their own.

When they received the final provocation of the Classification Plan, and saw that Spalding and the league were stalling negotiations, the players decided that matters had gone far enough. For some time they had been aware that a number of wealthy men were prepared to back them in forming a new organization. Foremost among those anxious to enter baseball was Albert L. Johnson, brother of Cleveland's renowned reform mayor, Tom L. Johnson. Al, like Tom, was very much involved in urban transportation. The two of them were operating a couple of streetcar lines in the Cleveland area. Streetcar companies were always interested in having ball parks or other amusement parks along their routes. In Johnson's case a ball park would give him two businesses, each enhancing the profits of the other. As he admitted later, he had "visions of millions of dollars of profit." He had "seen streetcars on the opposition street road loaded down with people going to games and it occurred to me here was a chance for a good investment as I could get grounds on a streetcar line owned by my brother and myself." Like his brother, Al Johnson also had a strong streak of idealism. When he learned about the reserve clause and the so-called laws of baseball, he is said to have exclaimed, "If the league can hold a man on a contract for any or all time that it may desire, when it simply guarantees to him ten days' pay (for that is everything in the world it does for the players), why, then the laws of our land are worse than those of any other nation on earth, and instead of progressing, as we suppose that every civilized country is struggling to do, the sooner we turn back the better."

A genuine baseball enthusiast, Johnson knew many ballplayers and often met with them socially. It was natural that Ned Hanlon should sound out Johnson during the summer of 1889 on the Pittsburgh club's second trip to Cleveland. The Brotherhood representative met with the Cleveland businessman at his hotel and told him how the league had "broken faith" with the players. Hanlon presented Ward's idea for getting backers for a new league in which they and the players would share the profits. The plan could be put through, said Hanlon, if Johnson would help.

Johnson was interested immediately, and asked to discuss the matter further with some of the other players. After this was done, he agreed to do everything in his power to put the scheme across. That summer, meetings were held with the players of other league clubs when they came to Cleveland to play. Johnson posted a man in the corridor of the Hollenden to keep anyone else from breaking in on the discussions, and he took the added precaution of paying off the policeman on the corner so that he would not report the comings and goings of all the ballplayers. In these meetings, players of the various clubs were apprised of plans and given a chance to express their views about them.

Next a contract was prepared and players were signed. To gauge their possible attendance, the Brotherhood got Cub Stricker, Cleveland second baseman, to watch the turnstiles at his park. Johnson followed up his Cleveland meetings with a trip to several league cities, including Boston, New York, and Philadelphia, to sign up more players and to make final arrangements with people who were willing to invest in the new venture. Thus by the end of the summer most of the organizational groundwork was finished.

That the owners remained in the dark while all this was going on was a tribute to the skill of the Brotherhood leaders in controlling the men. The first intimation that something more than a strike was afoot did not come until early September when A. G. Ovens, correspondent for *Sporting Life,* managed to get one of the players to talk, and learned enough to break a story about a "widespread plot." After the story broke, Johnson's brother Will verified it. Although he had been sworn to secrecy along with the others, Will felt justified in speaking now that the news had leaked.

The surprise of the league men was exaggerated somewhat by *Sporting News,* whose editor, Al Spink, was sympathetic toward the players' organization. He chortled in the columns of his paper that the magnates were "wild" and that Spalding was "in conniption fits." But the league owners made calm public statements. Nick Young said that the season had been full of scares and that the league would proceed as usual. Although Spalding was not prepared for such a "ponderous plot," he was not so disconcerted as to miss a chance for a propaganda blow at the players. He branded the Brotherhood "an oath-bound, secret organization of strikers," and questioned whether the public would have confidence in such an outfit. In a "confidential" letter to Mills, he said that, as far as he knew, the players had absolutely no grievance against the league, and he was rather amused at their great efforts to find some cause for complaint. Nevertheless, he agreed with Mills that there was room for improvement in the way baseball was run, although the game was safer in the hands of the league than it would be in those of the players collaborating with a lot of "soreheads and speculators." In later years, when he looked back on these events, Spalding placed chief blame on businessmen who, with the help of star players, wanted to break into baseball and exploit it for their own gain.

In his next move the able Chicago owner tried to force the issue with Ward. He wrote the Brotherhood leader asking when the players' grievance committee could resume talks with National League representatives. But

Ward was also skilled at playing cat-and-mouse. He replied that since the league had failed to answer the players' proposals satisfactorily early in the season, the committee had been dismissed, and the issue would now have to be placed before the entire Brotherhood. Now the league knew it was definitely in trouble, and the teams began quietly signing some young players. As the Cincinnati *Enquirer* predicted, there were "piping times ahead" for baseball.

Early in October, Ward abandoned all secrecy and told his boss, John B. Day, of the Brotherhood's intentions. That month Brotherhood players failed to follow baseball custom as they refused to sign contracts for the coming year. Spalding, who was highly indignant, threatened his reserved players with injunctions to prevent them from jumping to other teams. On November 4, 1889, thirty or forty players convened in New York City. Ward opened the meeting by reciting the failure of the previous summer's negotiations. The players received a good laugh from a telegram from Mr. Bright, the turnstile manufacturer, who was already bidding to supply Brotherhood parks. The following day the Brotherhood and their backers, in joint session, formed a Players' National League of Base Ball Clubs and spelled out the business relationship between them.

The venture was unique in the American business world. Farmers' and workers' cooperatives were an old story in America, but the Players' League went them one better. It was a democratic alliance of workers and capitalists in which both were to participate in the governing and share in the profits of the enterprise. It was a startling contradiction of traditional communist dogma that capitalists always formed a united front against workers. Here was a group of capitalists, associated with employees, preparing to wage a bitter fight against other capitalists!

The Players' League planned to invade seven National League cities—Boston, New York, Brooklyn, and Philadelphia in the East, and Pittsburgh, Cleveland, and Chicago in the West. Jack Rowe and Deacon White, with additional local backing, brought in the Buffalo club to complete an eight-club circuit.* Each club was controlled by its own local eight-man board, four elected by the players and four by the "contributors," as the backers were sometimes called. They chose officers and looked after the financial affairs of each club.

For the first time since the breakup of the old National Association in 1875, players were going to share in the administrative end of the game. The Players' League was to be governed by a "senate" of sixteen men, two from each club—one chosen by the players, the other by their backers. The senate was to select a president and vice president from its own ranks and bring in an "outsider" for secretary-treasurer at $4,000 a year. It was to be a tribunal in all matters of league welfare and was to have final decision on all appeals from local boards and players.

The economic blueprint of the Players' League at first called for all profits and losses to be pooled and shared by all clubs in common, but this idea, attributed to Ward, was soon rejected in favor of putting each club on its own financial feet. Gross receipts from each game were to be shared fifty-fifty between home and visiting clubs, but the home club could keep profits from concessions.

Each club was to deposit its share of gate receipts in its own fund, out of which all obligations were to be met in a specified order of priority. First, all running expenses were to be paid. After that came players' salaries, because at first the backers refused to assume personal liability for them. They soon changed, agreeing to guarantee salaries and establishing a fund of $40,000 as insurance. Next, each club was to contribute $2,500 to the league as its portion of a $20,000 prize fund, to be allotted on a descending scale to each club, depending on where it finished in the pennant race. First prize was $7,000.

These commitments discharged, the backers and players could dip into additional profits, if any—the first $10,000 to the former, depending on the amount of stock held, and the second $10,000 to all league players, share and share alike. Any additional money was to be split equally between the clubs and the players. This meant that profits had to climb above $20,000 before one club began supporting another.

Both the reserve and classification rules were discarded, but players signed three-year contracts at the same salaries they received in 1889. In cases where classification had caused pay reductions, players were to receive their 1888 salaries. No player could be released until the end of the season, and then only by majority vote of his club's board of directors. Players could also purchase stock in their clubs, and many did so. The hated blacklist was aban-

* Washington and Indianapolis were originally included, but their franchises were transferred to Buffalo and Brooklyn.

doned, but those guilty of drunkenness or corrupt practices were liable to severe penalties.* This was a more liberal deal for the players. But although the reserve clause and classification rule were discarded, their restrictive effect remained—an admission that an arrangement akin to the reserve was necessary to stabilize the business. Players were still tied to their clubs, although for a limited time, and salaries were frozen at old classification levels.

A committee drew up a constitution for adoption at the next meeting on December 16. At that time Col. Edwin A. McAlpin, New York real-estate operator, was elected president of the Players' League; John Addison, Chicago contractor, vice president; and Frank H. Brunell, former sportswriter, secretary-treasurer. The financial backers of the Players' League had an opportunity to get into a new business without having to start from scratch. Unlike Henry V. Lucas and his associates in the Union Association, the Brotherhood backers were acquiring the player assets of their competitors with relatively little initial outlay.

Securing sites and building ball parks were comparatively simple for the Players' League. There were plenty of open spaces available in those days, and a fence and wooden stands could be put up inexpensively and almost overnight—quite a different situation from the problem that would confront anybody trying to establish a new league in these days of high real-estate prices and enormous construction costs for elaborate stadia.

National League spokesmen were quick to point out weaknesses in the Players' League setup. They mentioned that players were binding themselves to go wherever assigned, relying on the uncertainties of gate receipts for their salaries. They even sneered at the $40,000 salary guarantee of the Players' League investors, A. G. Mills calling it a "fake substitute" for the "no-gate-receipts-no-salary clause." John T. Brush vouchsafed that he would be glad to sign players under such conditions.

At their first meeting the Brotherhood published a "manifesto" aimed at winning public support. In forceful phrases the Brotherhood declared its position, reviewed player relations with the National League, and recited the failure of arbitration efforts:

> There was a time when the League stood for integrity and fair dealing; today it stands for dollars and cents. . . . Players have been bought, sold or exchanged, as though they were sheep, instead of American citizens. Reservation . . . became another name for property-rights in the player. By a combination among themselves, stronger than the strongest trusts, they [the owners] were able to enforce the most arbitrary measures, and the player had either to submit or get out of the profession.

The formation of the Players' League was said to have brought "consternation and commotion" among National League owners, who could see their expensive "stock in trade, their teams," about to disappear. Knowing they must prepare themselves for an all-out fight against the "outlaw" league, they appointed a three-man war committee, John I. Rogers, Philadelphia owner, who was also an attorney; John B. Day of the New York Giants; and Al Spalding, the most influential figure in the league.

Spalding had to be on the committee. His name was synonymous with the National Game, since his career had spanned its growth from early professional days. As one of the founders of the National League, he had a hand in bringing an end to the old National Association. An excellent organizer, skilled diplomat, and first-rate promoter, he was known at home and abroad through his baseball interests and his sporting goods enterprises. As his wordly success grew, he took on the appearance, air, and even the girth of the successful businessman of his era. His penchant for pious remarks won for him such nicknames as "the Messiah." Yet, he always had an eye for the main chance and unfailingly acted to further his business interests, which he placed above "sentiment." Withal, his massive contribution to baseball in the formative years of the business cannot be denied. He was a formidable antagonist for John Ward and the Players' League.

Spalding's hand was at once apparent in the work of the War Committee. It immediately circulated an "Address to the Public" to counteract the Brotherhood Manifesto. The wordy document recalled the "untarnished record" of the National League and emphasized its role in eliminating corruption. It defended the reserve clause as the savior of the game in the league's early desperate struggle for solvency. By checking competition, the reserve had been instrumental in raising the incomes of clubs and players alike; however, the league denied making large profits. It was nonsense to speak of "bondage" and "slavery," because league players had never been sold without

* Players also took a prescribed oath to promote the objectives of the Brotherhood and to assist each other in distress.

either their consent or their financial gain. The league rebuked the players for refusing to confer at the end of the season, and denounced the conduct of the Brotherhood as "false," "mendacious," and "evasive." Then, with a typical Spalding touch, the statement charged that the Brotherhood had "no moral foundation and must perish," and promised that the National League would "fight for supremacy."

The Brotherhood answered the league Address with a statement which went over the same ground as its Manifesto. The propaganda battle was going full tilt. The press joined the argument and kept at it throughout the strife-torn year of 1890. There was much newspaper criticism of the players. One paper predicted their defeat almost before the Players' League was under way, and ridiculed the appearance of the players at their first meeting. It reported them dressed in fur-lined overcoats, silk hats, and patent-leather shoes, carrying gold-headed canes, wearing five-thousand-dollar brilliants in their neck scarves, smoking Rosa Perfectos or Henry Clays at twenty-five cents apiece, but wearing no gloves because it was too much trouble to pull them on over the "flashlights" that encircled their crooked, broken fingers. The parting jibe was:

> Don't mistake them for the poor, miserable, overworked, underpaid, haggard, starving slaves of the League tyrants. Nor is it a meeting of the Vanderbilts, Goulds, etc.; it is but a gathering of the Brotherhood men.

An especially severe critic of the players was Henry Chadwick, the veteran sportswriter. As editor of *Spalding's Guide,* a semiofficial league organ, he accused the players of issuing a "revolutionary pronunciamento," and charged them with secrecy, ingratitude, and a desire for "self-aggrandisement." Chadwick asserted that two-thirds of the players would never have revolted had they not been forced into line by the "terrorism" characteristic of all revolutionary movements. We can be charitable toward Chadwick for making extravagant statements; he wrote them in the heat of conflict. It is more difficult to countenance the opinion expressed thirty years later by a sportswriter who eventually became secretary of the New York Giants—that the Brotherhood was a "bolshevik movement which merely preceded the Russian Revolution"!

Naturally, Ward was singled out for a full measure of personal criticism. He was the "master-mind" behind the baseball "secessionists." The Cincinnati *Enquirer* changed his name to John Much-Advertised Ward and accused him of wanting a new league so he could take off on "oratorical flights." The players as a group were denounced for repaying a generous league by "snatching away" the business of their employers and giving it to others. "Now that you are on your own," they were warned, "your little sprees, escapades, until early hours in the mornings, and drunkenness on the ball field won't be excused as readily as it once was."

The St. Louis *Sporting News,* destined to become the "Bible of baseball," championed the cause of the players. It boldly proclaimed that it preferred their friendship to the paid advertising of Spalding. It took particular delight in needling the Chicago owner. Recalling that he had himself been a contract-jumper, it made fun of his "pomp and bluster," and charged that he had "skinned" the fans on his score card and cushion "racket." As for A. G. Mills, his initials stood for "Awful Gall." At the root of the trouble, said *Sporting News,* was the "mean, niggardly, close-fisted acts" of the league owners, who had treated the players in a "high-handed manner" and now "squealed to the public."

The popular weekly *Sporting Life* also joined the players' side, much to A. G. Mills's distress. Mills was "amazed" at the "tirades" of its editor, F. C. Richter, against the reserve clause, which he had once favored. Mills said that, although he disapproved of much that the league had done, the "indefensible" attack of Ward and others forced him to speak out. He entertained Richter at dinner a number of times, once remarking that "after [dinner], arming ourselves with cigars, I proposed to wipe up the floor with you on the baseball question!" Always mindful of public relations, Mills suggested that the league owners could do themselves some good if they would follow his example and put on a "feed" for newspapermen.

Organized labor also supported the players. To Major Samuel L. Leffingwell, a trade unionist, the issue was whether capital would rule despotically over baseball as it would like to do in other industries, and he urged the players to join either the AFL or the Knights of Labor, where they would have a million skilled men behind them. But the players did not respond to the invitation.

As in all organized baseball's trade wars, much of the struggle revolved around the effort of each side to gain control of as many players as possible. Right after the Brotherhood's first convention, Ward hastened to the Middle West to persuade players to stay behind the Brotherhood. He must have done a good job, for a newspaper survey of fifty players showed that with the exception of "Judas" Glasscock, a "spy" and "informer," the men were standing by the Brotherhood "like rocks." Before the end of December, seventy-one league players, sixteen association men, and four minor leaguers were reported to have signed with the Players' League. A couple of months later Secretary Brunell was claiming 188 men, whereas the National League, according to him, had only "about 20 deserters and a bunch of unknowns." The Pittsburgh Nationals, for example, were supposed to have signed "a crowd of stiffs," with only "four ballplayers in the lot."

Some players changed sides as often as three times, but the Players' League gained control of most of them. According to one estimate, the league succeeded in holding only thirty-eight of its players. Many of its best men deserted, among them Charles Comiskey and Connie Mack. John K. Tener, who later became governor of Pennsylvania, joined the new league. The outstanding exception was Cap Anson, whose ownership of stock in the White Sox may have influenced his decision. The league filled the gaps in its ranks by purchasing released players and taking on the best minor leaguers. It picked up a few more replacements from among the more than 300 rag, tag and bobtail from various parts of the country who applied for jobs.

But the league never quit trying to win back its regulars. Hurried reforms and fat financial inducements were held out. To match the Brotherhood, the league offered three-year contracts, repealed classification, and modified the system of selling players to give them more voice in the assignment of their contracts. Players were also allowed to appeal fines and penalties to league directors. Clubs even agreed to pay expenses home for players released while on the road. And in spite of Nick Young's earlier statement that the league would not "place a premium on desertion and unfaithfulness" by "buying off" stars, owners were soon busy offering them bribes. On Spalding's own admission his colleagues assigned him the dirty work of tempting King Kelly with $10,000 to desert the Brotherhood. Doubtless in a dilemma, Kelly left the secret rendezvous, took a walk to think it over, and returned with a refusal.

During the war season Mills instigated a similar attempt to break the solidarity of the players and undermine their league. This time Buck Ewing was the target. Mills drafted a statement for Ewing to sign and sent it to J. Walter Spalding, Al's brother, cautioning him to keep the matter secret. In the document Ewing would declare that he intended to return to the Giants next season because the Players' League could not win, and that he did not like to see money poured into a losing cause. He would also say that he did not think continuing the war was in the best interests of baseball. Mills thoughtfully left space on the paper for the signatures of any others who could be persuaded to desert.

Ewing was the player chosen not only because he was a star but because he had expressed sympathy for his employer, John B. Day, on the eve of the players' revolt. Later on, there were stories about a carriage ride under cover of darkness, a clandestine meeting in the back room of a dimly lighted Westchester cigar store, and a proposal for another secret meeting at an obscure railroad stop—all arranged by Cap Anson. The scheme fell through because Ewing reneged when other players refused to join him. Ewing denied everything when confronted, claiming that he was merely spying for the Brotherhood and had told Al Johnson everything that was going on. However, the players were unconvinced and for some time they refused to have anything to do with him.

The struggle for players between the rival leagues hit the American Association hard. In a shrewd bid for association neutrality, Ward promised at the outset that its players would remain untouched. In fact, he went to a special association meeting December 4 to explore the possibility of amalgamating the Players' League and the association. The rumor was that the two circuits would combine their teams in certain cities to form a single ten-club league. Von der Ahe did a little flirting with the Players' League on his own. At first his attitude toward the war was that capitalists should "stick together" against labor; but inside of a month he was quoted as favoring the Brotherhood and hoping for their success. Al Spink claimed afterward that he had convinced Von der Ahe to support the Players' League and that some dickering had taken place. However, Ward, in sizing up the Browns' owner, said they could "use his financial backing" but he "would injure our cause" because "he talks too much."

For a while the National League was very much worried that an "unnatural alliance" between the association and the Players' League might materialize. Mills was convinced that the association was negotiating with the "players' gang," and he strongly urged that "someone should do something to keep the American Association in line." But, fortunately for the National League, nothing came of all this. The result was that the association was soundly buffeted by the other two parties to the baseball triangle. The Players' League raided it, and the war strategy of the National League weakened it. To strengthen its own circuit, the league dumped its Washington and Indianapolis clubs, replacing them with Cincinnati and Brooklyn of the association. In the course of these shifts the Players' League was able to pick up many of the men involved. All told, the insurgents captured about thirty association players. Mills complained that such "looting" was completely unjustified, even if the National League was wrong—and he thought it was right—in taking Cincinnati and Brooklyn.

Although the league opened the season of 1890 seriously weakened by the loss of so many players, it nevertheless boldly revamped its schedule so that its games would conflict with those of the Players' League in the cities where both leagues were represented. It also increased the visiting teams' share of the gate receipts from the usual 25 to 40 percent in order to give a lift to its weaker clubs. Both sides strove to make their opening-day games as attractive as possible, and the profusion of banners and flags made each opener look like a circus. Each side went to any lengths to hurt the other. As usual, truth was the first casualty, as Spalding later admitted:

> If either party . . . ever furnished to the press one solitary truthful statement as to the progress of war from his standpoint; if anyone at any time . . . made true representation of conditions in his own ranks, a monument should be erected to his memory.

The Players' League bid for the use of National League grounds, forcing the incumbent either to pay more rent, obligate itself to a longer lease, or both. On its part, the National League attempted to undermine the Players' League by trying to buy into its clubs.

The struggle spilled over into the courts. National League owners tried to get injunctions to prevent their employees from jumping to the Players' League. This move again placed the baseball contract, and therefore the long-debated reserve clause, in the spotlight of legal contention. League officials entered litigation with the assurance of their noted corporation lawyers—Evarts, Choate & Beman—that they would be victorious. Choate was the famous attorney who once disdained taking a labor case, saying that if a big strong Irishwoman wanted to sweat in a bakery more than ten hours a day, that was a private affair between her and her employer. Mills had an equally confident legal opinion of the league's chances. But as it turned out, the courts were overwhelmingly on the side of the players.

The first test came in January 1890, when the New York Giants club was denied an injunction against Ward on the grounds that his 1889 contract did not fix the terms and conditions of his next contract contemplated by the reserve clause. Justice O'Brien ruled that when the terms of a contract are indefinite or uncertain, specific performance cannot be ordered. He decided that Ward's contract was wanting in fairness and mutuality because it bound the player not only for the current playing season but year after year, so that he always had to commit himself a year in advance under the same terms, as long as he played ball, whereas the club could terminate the contract on ten days' notice. O'Brien concluded: "We have the spectacle presented of a contract which binds one party for a series of years and the other party for ten days, and of the party who is itself bound for ten days coming into a court of equity to enforce its claims against the party bound for years."

While action against Ward was still pending, the Giants tried for an injunction against Buck Ewing and failed again. Judge Wallace ruled that the baseball contract was merely "a contract to make a contract if the parties agree," but as a basis for damages or enforcement of specific performance it was "wholly nugatory." Wallace differed with Judge O'Brien, however, in deciding that the terms of the reserve were definite; it was the lack of mutuality in the contract which led him to deny the injunction.

Again in March the league suffered another legal defeat, this time in Pennsylvania, when the Philadelphia club tried to keep George Hallman from joining the Players' League. Judge Thayer decided against the plaintiff on essentially the same grounds as in the Ward and Ewing cases. It seemed to him that for $1,400 a year Hallman had sold himself to the club for life; yet he had no claim on it for more then ten days. As Thayer saw it, Hallman was "absolutely at their mercy, and may be sent adrift at the beginning or in the middle of a season, at home or two thousand miles from it, sick or well, at the mere arbitrary discretion of the plaintiffs, provided only they give him ten days' notice."

In cases like these, where ballplayers have

jumped their contracts to play for other teams, clubs seeking relief have often pleaded the English doctrine laid down in the case called *Lumley* v. *Wagner*, which involved not baseball players but instead a singer who was the daughter of the famous composer Richard Wagner. According to the precedent established in the classic case, the law cannot compel specific performance under a personal service contract, but it can keep the party guilty of a breach of contract from performing for another—if his services are of a special, unique, and extraordinary character. In the Ward, Ewing, and Hallman cases, the courts decided that the absence of mutuality in the baseball contract prevented them from restraining the players. But in another Brotherhood case, the doctrine of *Lumley* v. *Wagner* was upheld, and the owners were successful in securing an injunction. This case concerned John Pickett of the association's Kansas City club.

The club had bought Pickett from St. Paul in May 1889 for $3,300. Pickett received $800 of the purchase price and $340 a month, even though he was out half the season because of sickness. He signed to play with Kansas City again in 1890, this time for $2,200, but several months later notified the club that he intended to break the agreement, giving as his excuse Kansas City's transfer from the American Association to the Western Association, a minor league. He also argued that the club had released other players with whom he wanted to play and, mindful of the uncertainties of minor-league ball in those days, said he was afraid his salary might not be forthcoming. What he was really after was a chance to play with the Players' League.

The court brushed aside Pickett's explanation with the observation that "his ingratitude was shown to be equal to his bad faith." Applying the *Lumley* v. *Wagner* principle, Judge Arnold decided that, while Pickett could not be forced to play for Kansas City, he could be enjoined from playing elsewhere. However, Pickett played second base for the Philadelphia Players' League club, where the court had no jurisdiction.

Hoping to forestall future legal objections to the contract, the league experimented with a reworded agreement giving clubs the "option" of renewing player contracts for an agreed-upon number of years. But in practice the effect was the same as the reserve clause, since players were required to sign contracts with identical renewal features.

Court victories did not mean that the Players' League won the war. In the long run, the gate receipts would decide. Here competition was ruinous for both sides, and Nick Young frankly predicted that "someone had to go to the wall." Each league falsified attendance figures for propaganda purposes. Again the ingenious Spalding demonstrated his astuteness. He secretly stationed his own agents at Players' League gates to keep count, and then discredited his opponents by publishing their inflated figures alongside those of his checkers!

In view of the phony attendance figures compiled on both sides, it is highly unlikely that the published totals of 980,887 for the Players' League as against 813,678 for the National League are worth much. Probably the combined attendance of both warring leagues was less than that enjoyed by the National League alone the year before. Interest in the game declined as the public became more and more disgusted with the chaotic state of baseball affairs. Fans grew increasingly tired of reading and hearing about the political and business problems of the game, and longed for a return to stability so that they could concentrate on the pennant race. And of course with another league in the field, the money that was taken in had to be divided three ways instead of two, leaving that much less for each.

The Players' League had the advantage of being something new to baseball, and it boasted most of the established players. But even though it doubtless outdrew the National League, by July it ran into trouble. Not one game out of six was drawing enough to cover the cost of playing it, and it was necessary to assess all member clubs an extra $2,500 apiece. According to Secretary Brunell's estimate, the Players' League finished the season with a total deficit of $340,000, of which $215,000 was invested in plants, leaving an operational loss of $125,000.

The National League was in a bad way, too. Figures given out on losses varied all the way from $231,000 to $500,000. Pittsburgh was a particularly heavy drag on the League. It lost the staggering total of 114 games, winning only 23, for a miserable percentage of .168. New York was hardest hit. After finishing first in 1889, the club was stripped of its stars by the Players' League. Knowing the importance of having a strong entry in the metropolis, the National League engineered a deal transferring some players from its abandoned Indianapolis club, among them stars such as Amos Rusie, Jack Glasscock, and Jesse Burkett. But even with these reinforcements the club was in such poor condition that John B. Day sent out a secret call for help to the other magnates in July, telling them that he must have $80,000 at once or he would be forced to sell out to the Players' League. Spalding and the other "dazed" owners realized that New York must be saved "at all hazards" or the war would be lost, so they bailed out Day. The Spalding brothers took $25,000 worth of stock, some of which they parceled out to others, including Anson; Soden of Boston put up the same amount; John T. Brush canceled $25,000 in notes which he held against the sale of his Indianapolis stars; and F. A. Abel of Brooklyn, a professional gambler, and Al Reach of Philadelphia contributed $6,250 apiece. Day insisted on retaining $20,000 worth of stock for his "sacrifice."

Worse yet, Cincinnati gave up the battle in October when Aaron Stern cut his losses and sold the club for $40,000 to a syndicate of Players' League owners. Stern indignantly replied to being branded "league traitor" by saying there was nothing wrong in selling out for a good price. It was a choice between sacrificing baseball or giving up his more profitable clothing business.

As the 1890 season ended, all three majors were deeply drained by the losses they had suffered. As Spalding reported, "Not in the twenty years' history of professional club organizations was there recorded such an exceptional season of financial disaster and general demoralization as characterized the professional season of 1890." The somber prospects of baseball were cleverly described in a parody which put full blame on the players:

Who Killed Baseball?

Who killed baseball? "I," said John Ward: "of my own accord, I killed baseball."
Who saw it die? "We," said the slaves; "from our own made graves, we saw it die."
Who'll make its shroud? "I" said Buck Ewing, "I'll do it well, I'll do the sewing, I'll make its shroud."
Who'll dig its grave? "I," said Brunell, "I'll do it well, I'll dig its grave."
Who'll be the parson? "I," said Cub Stricker, "I'll let her flicker, I'll be the parson."
Who'll carry the link? "I," said Jay Faatz;* "I watched the gates, I'll carry the link."
Who'll be chief mourner? "I," said Tim Keefe; "I'm filled with grief, I'll be chief mourner."
Who'll sing a psalm? "I," said Comiskey; "though it's rather risky, I'll sing a psalm."
Who'll toll the bell? "I," said "King Kell."; "I'll toll it like ——, I'll toll the bell."
And now all the cranks have forgotten the game
And the ex-slave perceives that D. Mud is his name.

* Non-playing manager of the Cleveland Players' League team.

Courtesy *The Saturday Evening Post* ©

"I understand the Mets already have an eye on him."

Courtesy *The Chicago Tribune* Syndicate ©

*"Notice how their pitcher warms up?
The catcher is on the other side of the fence."*

The *Second Fireside Book of Baseball* reproduced just enough of Harry Simmons' knotty problems to whet reader appetites for more. So here are half a dozen more, illustrated as ever by the inimitable Willard Mullin. Note: Answers follow each problem in each instance, but no fair peeking.

So You Think You Know Baseball!

HARRY SIMMONS *and* WILLARD MULLIN

Timing is of the essence of baseball. The cutoff play, the underhand flip, the pick-off—all demonstrate the importance of split-second action in our national sport. Yet it can be overdone. In the following hypothetical situation, a player's attempt to save time raises a question of legality.

Say the White Sox are host to the Red Sox in Comiskey Park. The visitors are ahead, 4–3, as they come up for their turn in the eighth. Don Buddin leads off with a single, but the next batter fans. Gary Geiger then hits a slow bounder to the right of second and the baseman makes a neat pickup near the bag, where Shortstop Luis Aparicio is already waiting for the toss.

The baseman, realizing that he will not have time to complete a double play if he flips to Luis or touches the base himself, plunks the ball into Luis's outstretched glove without letting go of it. Then he whirls and throws to first base in time to beat Geiger to the bag for a double play. Or is it a double play? How would you call it?

No double play. Buddin is safe at second.

The ball must be securely held by the fielder. Section 2.00 (tag) of the rules says, in part, "A tag is the action of a fielder in touching a base with his body while holding the ball securely and firmly in his hand or glove. . . ."

* * *

It's a rare ball game that doesn't offer some comedy relief. Almost every contest produces a caustic, leather-lunged fan, or customers risking a suit of clothes for a souvenir foul ball, or a bizarre twist to a play on the field.

The following play, set forth hypothetically here, actually occurred elsewhere and left the stands in hysterics.

The Cardinals and Reds are meeting in the first inning of a twin bill at the Crosley Field, Cincinnati. Grammas, St. Louis shortstop, lays a puny bunt down the first-base line to start the game. The Redleg catcher pounces on the ball and gives chase.

Grammas is getting away when the catcher dives at him from behind and accidentally stuffs the ball into his hip pocket. Grammas pulls ahead and the catcher loses his grip on the ball.

Realizing the significance of the unaccustomed lump on his flank, Grammas goes merrily around the bases while the Redlegs watch in consternation. Grammas carefully tags each base and crosses the plate with a home run. Or does he? How would you call it?

No homer, this. The ball is out of play when controlled by the offensive team, as it is in this case. Play ceases at the moment of the innocent interference. Charge the Redleg catcher with an error and give no hit to Grammas. Put him on first base, however, because of the catcher's error.

* * *

The tricky situation described below has confused both fans and players repeatedly. Let's see if you know the answer.

Say it's the top of the eighth at Los Angeles, with the Braves leading the Dodgers 6 to 1.

Bobby Avila opens with a spanking single to left. The Braves' pitcher than lifts a pop-up to Charley Neal at second base, tosses his bat down in disgust and jogs toward first.

Neal gets under the pop. Noticing the Brave pitcher's lazy pace, he traps the ball cleverly and throws to Gil Hodges at first base. Hodges tags Avila, who is still standing on first, then touches the bag just before the Milwaukee pitcher sprints up to it.

The Dodges claim a double play, but the Braves maintain that in this situation a runner cannot be put out while standing on the base. How would you call it?

It's a double play, all right. Because a force play was created when Neal trapped the ball, Avila is no longer entitled to first base and is liable to be put out.

The procedure must be exact, however. Had Hodges touched the base before tagging Avila, the force would have been removed and Avila would not be out. (See Section 2.00: "A force play is a play in which a runner legally loses his right to occupy a base by reason of the batter becoming a base runner.")

* * *

If you have to blow off steam in baseball, don't throw things. Here is the hypothetical case of a player who did, causing quite a ruckus.

Say it's the White Sox and Tigers in the last half of the fifth in a close game at Briggs Stadium, Detroit. Harvey Kuenn opens with a screaming double down the right-field line. Al Kaline gets nicked by an inside pitch and takes his base. Charlie Maxwell then lifts an infield pop. As a Sox baseman runs toward it, the umpire calls, "Infield fly, if fair!"

The Sox baseman gets under the ball in fair territory, but it merely touches his glove, then bounces and rolls into foul ground. In disgust, the baseman flings his mitt at the ball, hitting it and stopping the roll.

Kaline and Kuenn halt at second and third, respectively, while Maxwell legs it to first base. But you, as umpire, can't let them stay there. What would you do?

Call Maxwell out, and send Kuenn and Kaline around to score.

Two rules, in quick succession, govern this play:

Maxwell is automatically out when the umpire calls an infield fly and the ball is touched in fair territory (See Section 6.05e: "A batter is out when an Infield-Fly is declared.")

When the baseman's thrown mitt touched the batted ball, it entitled both Kuenn and Kaline to three bases. (See Section 7.05c: "Each runner, including the batter-runner, may, without liability of being put out, advance three bases, if a fielder deliberately throws his glove at and touches a fair ball.") The rule continues: "The ball is in play and the batter may advance to home base at his peril," but this must be disregarded in the case of an Infield Fly.

* * *

Is the catcher an infielder? A lot may depend on the answer. Here, in a simulated big-league setting, is a major problem over the catcher's status.

Let's say Los Angeles and Cincinnati are tied, 1–1, as the Reds come to bat in the top of the fourth at Los Angeles. With one away, Ed Bailey laces a double along the left-field line. He goes to third as Orlando Pena grounds out.

Roy McMillan then lifts a dinky pop-up in front of the plate. Dodger catcher Joe Pignatano lunges for the ball, but it twists down between his outstretched hands, untouched.

Now the ball takes a freak backward hop toward the third-base foul line. While still in fair territory, it hits Bailey on the seat of the pants as he sprints home.

That puts it squarely up to you as the umpire. Is catcher Pignatano "an infielder"? If so, Bailey is saved by Section 7.08f of the Playing Rules, which says a base runner is out when hit by a batted ball *only* if the ball strikes him "before it has touched or passed an infielder." But if the catcher is not an infielder, Bailey is plainly out. How would you call it?

Although there is something to be said for the claim that the catcher is an infielder, major-league umpires are instructed to call the base runner out on a play like this one.

* * *

The hidden-ball trick isn't the only debatable play which may befuddle a ball game. Take this one:

Say the Pittsburgh Pirates lead the Los Angeles Dodgers, 5–3, as the Dodgers come to bat in the sixth.

John Roseboro opens with a single and moves to second on an infield out. After Hodges draws a walk, Roseboro goes to third.

Hodges reaches second when Carl Furillo grounds out to the Pirate first baseman for the second out.

Here manager Alston sends in a pinch hitter, but gets no results. With two strikes on him, the hitter swings and misses a third. He heads glumly back to the bench, failing to notice that the Pirate catcher has dropped the ball. The catcher, seeing the batter returning to his dugout, picks up the ball and rolls it gently to the mound.

But the Dodger bench roars to the batter to run to first. He does, without a play being made on him, while Roseboro and Hodges cross the plate to tie the score. The Pirates thereupon rise up and claim the batter is out for leaving the basepath and not running straight to first.

If you were the umpire, how would you rule?

The batter is not out, and the runs count.

When two are out, if the ball is not held by the catcher after a third strike, the batter must be tagged or thrown out at first base. (Sections 6.05j and 6.09b.) A runner may not be called out for leaving the basepaths unless he does so to avoid being tagged. (Section 7.08a.)

* * *

BIL KEANE

Courtesy Register & Tribune Syndicate

THERE ARE two authentic surprises in this excerpt from *My Greatest Day in Baseball.* Did you know that the immortal George Sisler was a pitcher before he was a first baseman?

That's surprise number one. Number two is the name of the right fielder: Baby Doll Jacobson. *Baby Doll Jacobson?!?!*

1915: St. Louis Browns 2, Washington Senators 1

GEORGE SISLER
***as told to* LYALL SMITH**

EVERY AMERICAN KID has a baseball idol. Mine was Walter Johnson, the "Big Train." Come to think about it, Walter still is my idea of the real baseball player. He was graceful. He had rhythm and when he heaved that ball in to the plate he threw with his whole body just so easy-like that you'd think the ball was flowing off his arm and hand.

I was just a husky kid in Akron (Ohio) High School back around 1910–11 when Johnson began making a name for himself with the Senators and I was so crazy about the man that I'd read every line and keep every picture of him I could get my hands on.

Naturally, admiring Johnson as I did, I decided to be a pitcher and even though I wound up as a first baseman my biggest day in baseball was a hot muggy afternoon in St. Louis when I pitched against him and beat him. Never knew that, did you? Most fans don't. But it's right. Me, a kid just out of the University of Michigan beat the great Walter Johnson. It was on August 29, 1915, my first year as a baseball player, the first time I ever was in a game against the man who I thought was the greatest pitcher in the world.

I guess I was a pretty fair pitcher myself at Central High in Akron. I had a strong left arm and I could throw them in there all day long and never have an ache or pain. Anyway, I got a lot of publicity in my last year in high school and when I was still a student I signed up one day to play with Akron.

I didn't know at the time I signed that contract I was stepping into a rumpus that went on and on until it finally involved the National Baseball Commission, the owners of two big league clubs and Judge Landis.

I was only 17 years old when I wrote my name on the slip of paper that made me property of Akron, a club in the Ohio-Pennsylvania League and a farm club of Columbus in the association. After I signed it I got scared and didn't even tell my dad or anybody 'cause I knew my folks wanted me to go on to college and I figured they'd be sore if they knew I wanted to be a ballplayer.

In a way, that's what saved me, I guess. For by not telling my dad he never had a chance to okay my signature and in that way the contract didn't hold. The way it worked out, Akron sold me to Columbus and Columbus sold me to Pittsburgh, and all the time I was still in high school and hadn't even reported to the team I signed with! Wasn't even legally signed, the way it turned out.

They wanted me to join the club when I graduated from high school, but I was all set to go to Michigan, so I said "no" and went up to Ann Arbor. Well, to make a long story short, the story came out in the open there and when the whole thing was over I had been made a free agent by the old National Commission and signed up with Branch Rickey who at that time was manager of the St. Louis Browns.

I pitched three years of varsity ball up at Michigan and when I graduated on June 10, 1915, Rickey wired me to join the Browns in Chicago. Now, all this time I was up at school I still had my sights set on Walter Johnson. When he pitched his 56 consecutive scoreless innings in 1912 I was as proud as though I'd done it myself. After all, I felt as though I had adopted him. He was my hero. He won 36 games and lost only seven in 1913 and he came back the next season to win 28 more and lose 18. He was really getting the headlines in those days and I was keeping all of them in my scrapbook.

Well, then I left Michigan in 1915 and came down to Chicago where I officially became a professional ballplayer. I hit town one morning and that same day we were getting beat pretty bad so Rickey called me over to the dugout.

"George," he said, "I know you just got in town and that you don't know any of the players and you're probably tired and nervous. But I want to see what you have in that left arm of yours. Let's see what you can do in these last three innings."

I gulped hard a couple of times, muttered something that sounded like "thanks" and went out and pitched those last three innings. Did pretty good, too. I gave up one hit but the Sox didn't get any runs so I figured that I was all right.

Next day, though, I was out warming up and meeting more of the Browns when Rickey came over to me. He was carrying a first baseman's glove. "Here," he said. "Put this on and get over there on first base."

Well, nothing much happened between the time I joined the club in June until long about the last part of August. Rickey would pitch me one day, stick me in the outfield the next and then put me over on first the next three or four. I was hitting pretty good and by the time we got back to St. Louis the sportswriters were saying some nice things about me.

They were saying it chiefly because of my hitting. I'd only won two-three games up to then. I still remember the first one. I beat Cleveland and struck out nine men. Some clothing store gave me a pair of white flannels for winning and I was right proud of them. Didn't even wear them for a long time, figured they were too fancy.

As I was saying, we got back to St. Louis late in August. Early one week I picked up a paper and saw that a St. Louis writer, Billy Murphy, had written a story about Washington coming to town the following Sunday and that Walter Johnson was going to pitch.

I was still a Johnson fan and I guess Murphy knew it, for when I got about halfway through the story I found out that he had me pitching against Johnson on the big day, Sunday, August 29.

That was the first I knew about it and I figured it was the first manager Rickey knew about it, for here it was only Tuesday and Murphy had the pitchers all lined up for the following Sunday.

Well, he knew what he was talking about, because after the Saturday game Rickey stuck his head in the locker room and told me I was going to pitch against Johnson the next day. I went back to my hotel that night but I couldn't eat. I was really nervous. I went to bed but I couldn't sleep. At 4 A.M. I was tossing and rolling around and finally got up and just sat there, waiting for daylight and the big game.

I managed to stick it out, got some breakfast in me and was out at Sportsman's Park before the gates opened. It was one of those typical August days in St. Louis, and when game time finally rolled around it was so hot that the sweat ran down your face even when you were standing in the shadow of the stands.

All the time I was warming up I'd steal a look over at Johnson in the Washington bullpen. When he'd stretch way out and throw a fast ball, I'd try to do the same thing. Even when I went over to the dugout just before the game started, I was still watching him as he signed autographs and laughed with the photographers and writers.

Well, the game finally started and I tried to be calm. First man to face me was Moeller, Washington's left fielder. I didn't waste any time and stuck three fast ones in there to strike him out. Eddie Foster was up next and he singled to right field. Charley Milan singled to right-center and I was really scared. I could see Mr. Rickey leaning out of the dugout watching me real close so I kept them high to Shanks and got him to fly out to Walker in center field. He hit it back pretty far though, and Foster, a fast man, started out for third base. Walker made a perfect peg into the infield but Johnny Lavan, our shortstop, fumbled the relay and Foster kept right on going to score. That was all they got in that inning, but I wasn't feeling too sure when I came in to the bench. I figured we weren't going to get many runs off Johnson and I knew I couldn't be giving up many runs myself.

Then Johnson went out to face us and I really got a thrill out of watching him pitch. He struck out the first two Brownies and made Del Pratt fly to short center. Then I had to go out again and I got by all right. In the second inning, Walker led off with a single to center field and Baby Doll Jacobson dumped a bunt in front of the plate. Otto Williams, Washington catcher, scooped it up and threw it ten feet over the first baseman's head. Walker already was around second and he came in and scored while the Baby Doll reached third.

I think I actually felt sorry for Johnson. I knew just how he felt because, after all, the same thing had happened to me in the first inning. Del Howard was next up for us and he singled Jacobson home to give us two runs and give me a 2–1 lead.

Well, that was all the scoring for the day, although I gave up five more hits over the route. Johnson got one in the first of the fifth, a blooper over second. I was up in the last of the same inning and I'll be darned if I didn't get the same kind. So he and I were even-up anyway. We each hit one man, too.

There wasn't much more to the game. Only one man reached third on me after the first inning, and only two got that far on Johnson.

When I got the last man out in the first of the ninth and went off the field, I looked down at the Washington bench hoping to get another look at Johnson. But he already had ducked down to the locker room.

I don't know what I expected to do if I had seen him. For a minute I thought maybe I'd go over and shake his hand and tell him that I was sorry I beat him, but I guess that was just the silly idea of a young kid who had just come face to face with his idol and beaten him.

THE TITLE of this piece is at once truly authentic (especially in the chapter context of author Robert Smith's genial history of the game, in his book called *Baseball*), and at the same time oddly contradictory. This was the Depression. But there was nothing depressing about the main characters, Pepper Martin and Dizzy Dean.

Can You Spare a Dime?

ROBERT SMITH

NINETEEN THIRTY-ONE was the year in which sore-footed young ex-salesmen, unfrocked executives, paper millionaires, businessless businessmen, and laborers with no labor to do found themselves reminded on street radios (with an apologetic semi-laugh for telling an old joke) that "there are no rich people any more" and that, if there was to be an end to the hunger which was lapping so close, they—the dispossessed themselves—must reach down into their empty pockets and "share" what they did not have with the unidentified hordes of pitiful folk who had even less.

Men who were waking in a tremble in the morning, to give a quick thanks that they still had jobs, more often than not rode into the shop or office to hear a solemn talk from a suddenly sober and early-rising executive about the need for a wage cut, a payless payday, and a percentage contribution to the national fund for the unemployed.

But the people were comforted by the fact that the man they had made President on a "four-more-years-of-prosperity" platform was, if not in person, then at least through the medium of his ghostly spokesman, expressing "continuing anxiety for the maintenance of the national standard of living." The standard of living meanwhile was fighting a losing battle without appreciating what great men stood in its corner, or just outside it, urging it on. The United States Steel Company set the style for every other major industry by dealing out a 10-percent pay cut. People who had saved for a rainy day, in the good old American style, were left out in the rain as banks defaulted.

There were, however, at least in the minds of those who ate regularly, if somewhat less sumptuously than before, greater threats abroad in the land than mere starvation. William Green of the American Federation of Labor, in the face of Lord knows what temptation, refused to surrender the laboring man to the dread languors of the dole—or "unemployment insurance," as those crackpots who favored the scheme persisted in naming it. And leading politicians and newspaper commentators railed against the foolish fear that was keeping people from buying things. Nobody was ever going to be better off, they insisted, unless each one of us went right out and started to buy something—anything—right now, to get the cash to flowing again. One or two, in response to this plea, may have sent a few pennies trickling down the dry stream bed, but they were not enough to unleash the floodwaters nearly everyone had been wallowing in only a few years before.

But at least, in those dreary days, when a man might be asked three times in the same block if he had a dime to spare, and when he had to stare out of car windows at overwhelming posters where big overalled men with their oversize hands in their pockets promised him "I Will Share," there were some mighty good ball games to watch or to listen to.

The National League had given up the lively ball, so that in the National League parks the games on exhibition were more in keeping with the times—without inflated batting averages, overlong hits, or bloated scores. And it was in keeping with the times that the baseball hero of 1931 should be a dirty-faced, underpaid, hungry-looking center fielder who had entered baseball on the rods of a freight car. Many a man who had spent the whole morning and part of the afternoon wearily slapping his thinned-out shoe soles against strange pavements, stiffly smiling at erstwhile friends who now wished he would crawl off somewhere and leave them in peace, endlessly listening to his own pallid voice as it tried to recite, without anxiety, its possessor's qualifications for some stingy employment, discovered in the broadcast of the 1931 World's Series a sweeter anodyne than drink. Edging in among the crowd before some enormous bulletin board, he could look a well-fed neighbor in the eye and talk baseball with him as if together they owned the earth. He could yell with the unrestraint of a man whose meals were assured for months uncounted. He could groan and shake his head over strikeouts, errors, and other woes petty enough for the rich to recognize. And when the victory came, he could grasp the arm of the man near him and, in the few last moments before the man became a wary stranger, remind him loudly of the things they had just learned together—how the game was won and lost, how close disaster came, how great, how unbelievably great this little Pepper Martin was!

Pepper in that Series was indeed unbelievably great. Most fans had hardly heard his name in the season before the Series began; and the previous season he had been just a bench rider, an athletic spare tire, kept in case of emergency. In this Series he was the hero three times over. In one game he did enough to enshrine him for a year in the records of the Series. Then in the next game, and in the next, he showed new skill, new daring, new proof that the fellow at the very bottom of the heap was sure to have his day.

Some of the feats he performed were stunts that fans of another day had come to look for in championship baseball—feats which the return of the dead ball had resurrected. Others were mighty deeds with the bat which properly belonged to the modern age.

In the first game, which Philadelphia won, as most fans expected they would, Pepper Martin got three solid hits off Lefty Grove, who was then at the top of his skill and strength. In the second game, which St. Louis won, Martin made two hits, stole two bases, and scored the only two runs. He ran the bases in a manner so heedless of his physical safety that he had the fans screaming with excitement. He slid into bases on his chest, smearing the dirt on himself and his uniform, spurting it high along the base lines, risking a broken nose, a split skull, cracked ribs.

Pepper got on base in the second inning of the second game by lining a single into left field. He rounded first base as Al Simmons rather lazily fielded the ball on the bounce. Simmons slipped to one knee and bobbled the ball a little as if he were trying to find the handle. Pepper kept right on going to second, flinging himself safely into the base with the abandon of a maniac. He took a big lead on second, backing away from the base so that he could keep his eye on both pitcher and second baseman. When big George Earnshaw, the Philadelphia pitcher, started his throw to the plate, Martin broke for third, again landing safely in his breakneck fashion, despite the lightning throw of Mickey Cochrane, who was then supposed to be the best catcher in either league. Wilson, the batter, then drove the ball to deep right center, where Mule Haas caught the ball on the run. Martin scored easily after the catch. He had moved himself into scoring position by his own dash and daring.

In the seventh inning Martin singled again. When he broke for second, he had Mickey Cochrane so nervous that Cochrane heaved the ball almost into the outfield, and Martin again slid safely into the base. Wilson, next at bat, sent an easy roller to the shortstop; but while Wilson was being thrown out at first, Martin charged on to third and stood in scoring position once more. Gabby Street, the St. Louis manager, then put out the sign for the old running squeeze play, which had been laid in mothballs ever since the advent of the lively ball. As soon as George Earnshaw committed himself to the pitch, Martin broke at top speed for home. Gelbert, the St. Louis shortstop, bunted the ball toward the pitcher. Earnshaw was on top of the ball in a flash and flipped it backhanded to Cochrane. It came in just too high, however, and Martin's tough, wiry frame dove under it for the second run.

When the Athletics brought the Series back to their home town and back to the lively ball, experts thought surely their obvious superiority would begin to tell. St. Louis had won one game because a mediocre outfielder had played over his head. Now he had certainly spent his nickel.

But the air in Philadelphia agreed with Pepper Martin, and he liked the lively ball. In the second inning of the third game, Pepper came to bat with one man on base and one out.

He swung on Grove's first pitch for a clean single over second base. Bottomley, who had been on first, went all the way to third. Then another relic of old-time "inside" baseball was pulled out of the attic—the hit-and-run play this time. Wilson, the batter, played his part neatly. The ball went right into the hole left by the second baseman. Wilson reached first, Bottomley scored, and Martin arrived safely at third. Gelbert then sent a long hard liner (this American League ball did take a ride!) straight into the hands of the Philadelphia right fielder —but the ball had carried so far that again Martin scored easily after the catch.

In the fourth inning it was Martin again. Chick Hafey opened the St. Louis inning with a single to center field. Then Pepper came up, took a good look at Lefty Grove's famous fireball, and lambasted it from here to Sunday. It rode fast and far toward the right-field scoreboard while the Philadelphia fans, all yelling for Pepper now, stood up and howled: "Home run! Home run!" The ball, however, struck just a foot short of the top and bounced back into play. Hafey was held on third while Martin made two bases. The next two batters went out. Then old Burleigh Grimes (he was thirty-eight) drove out a single that scored both Martin and Hafey. The St. Louis Cardinals won that game 5–2 and were leading the Series two games to one.

The Athletics won the fourth game 3–0, to tie up the Series. But once more Martin blazed into the box score and made sportswriters dream up new adjectives for him. Except for Martin, Earnshaw would have had a no-hit game. Martin made two hits, one a two-bagger, and stole a base. On Pepper's first visit to the plate Earnshaw had fanned him, and that made Pepper grit his teeth. "I'm going to sock this guy and sock him plenty," he growled to his teammates. He socked him, too; but no one else did. And even though Martin stole a base after his first hit, the Cardinals went scoreless.

The next day, Pepper won the game for St. Louis. He made three hits, one of them a home run, and drove in four of the five St. Louis runs.

In this game, Gabby Street, apparently convinced now that Martin was no flash in the pan, had moved the little center fielder up to fifth place in the batting order. (He had been batting seventh.) In the fourth inning he swung at a ball and missed, stepped out of the batter's box, picked up a handful of gravel and tossed it into the box ahead of him, then stepped back into the box and hit a home run. Frisch was on base at the time, so this meant two runs for St. Louis.

At this point in the game Pepper Martin's wife burst into tears. "He's always been a hero to me," she said. "When we were in grammar school I stood on a soapbox to cheer him. . . . Now when the crowd starts to yell for him my eyes get misty."

In the eighth inning Pepper made his twelfth hit of the Series, tying a major-league record, and sending in still another run. He tried to steal second this time, but Cochrane nailed him with a perfect throw. When Pepper went out to the center field a fan greeted him by flinging a shower of torn-up scorecards over the rail. The tatters fluttered down all over the grass. Pepper, illustrating another superstition, called time and spent five minutes picking up every last scrap of paper. He liked to have the grass all clean behind him.

When the teams returned to St. Louis, and the home-town crowds came out to yell for Pepper, his hitting streak came to an end. St. Louis lost the sixth game 8–1, and Pepper got on base only once, with a base on balls.

In the last game, St. Louis won the World's Championship, but Martin had gone into eclipse. He got a base on balls on the first trip to the plate and immediately stole second base. That seemed to finish him. He went out on a pop fly the next time, grounded out after that, then struck out for his last time at bat. Just to show whose Series it was, in the last half of the ninth inning, with two out and the tying runs on base, Martin ran in from deep center to make a one-handed catch of Max Bishop's high fly, thus ending the game and the Series.

Martin was mobbed when the Series was over. People from all over the country had poured presents upon him: rifles, hunting trophies (Martin's two hobbies were deer hunting and automobile racing), and a big red pepper. Commissioner Landis, his ruddy face made even ruddier by excitement, grabbed Martin's hand and told him fervently, "I wish I could change places with you, Martin."

Martin, having seen too much of the world to lose his balance, replied immediately, "O.K. If you'll swap your fifty thousand a year for my forty-five hundred."

After the Series, Martin started on a vaudeville tour. The Series had paid him an extra $4,500, and his vaudeville contract gave him $1,500 a week. His advisers urged him to cash in while the cashing was good. He might not have so many more years in baseball. . . .

Pepper put in four weeks on the stage, then quit with five weeks to go.

"I ain't no actor," he said. "I'm a ballplayer. I'm cheating the public."

Martin, though a conscientious and scrappy ballplayer for several more seasons, never quite attained the same heights again. He was, however, a member of one of the most famous teams of this period—the St. Louis Gashouse Gang of 1934. On this same team were two other men, who, with Lou Gehrig and Joe DiMaggio, became the most widely noted ballplayers of the post-Babe Ruth era. They were Dizzy Dean, whose real name was either Jerome Herman or Jay Hanna, and Leo Durocher, who later became the manager of the other famous team of the time—the Bums of Brooklyn.

Dizzy Dean won his first fame as a pitcher when he was a soldier in the Regular Army, a neurotic, footloose boy, the son of a sharecropper who had been a semipro ballplayer. When, after pitching a number of victories for his Army team, Dean was offered thirty dollars a week to play for a semipro club in San Antonio, his father managed to secure Dizzy's discharge. In 1929 Dean won sixteen straight for the San Antonio club, and in the fall he was picked up by a St. Louis scout and signed to play for the St. Louis farm team in Houston. He was shifted in the spring, however, to another St. Louis farm, St. Joseph, Missouri, where he made an immediate success, not only by his pitching but by his swaggering manner, his willingness to pitch into a fight, his complete good nature, and his public eccentricities —which were still a marketable item in those days.

He went back to Houston before the end of the 1930 season, when he was the idol of all St. Joseph and the despair of the St. Joseph manager, who had had to pick up his IOUs, pay his carelessly contracted hotel bills, and even get him out of jail. With Houston, Dean continued to win (and to cut up) and he was taken up by the parent club in time to pitch a three-hit shutout against the Pittsburgh Pirates just before the season ended. St. Louis won the championship that year, but Dean was not eligible for the World's Series and so missed, by a matter of weeks, his first chance to cash in properly on his really unmatched ability.

The following spring he made a name for himself, in the St. Louis training camp, as a bigmouth with a swelled head, for he talked his own ability up continually and in any company; and he tried, in the matter of keeping hours, to imitate a few of the great stars, whom he knew he could equal. His habit of signing IOUs for the club to pick up was forestalled, and he was taught to limit himself to a dollar a day; but he refused to yield to the type of discipline Manager Gabby Street felt was good for a young recruit and good for the club. He was too damn fine a pitcher for that sort of treatment, Dizzy insisted, and, so insisting, he found himself sent back to Houston for "seasoning."

It is possible that his nature might have made it impossible for him ever to get through a training season with a big-league club, although one look at him was all a man needed in those days to see that he was one of the greatest who had ever played the game. In Texas, however, he married a smart, patient, and devoted girl who gave him the sort of private buildup and sound advice most boys of that type need to keep them even with the world. Dizzy was not, as a few wisecrack specialists of the day propounded, a man who was in love with himself. He was almost typical of the boy who has not quite grown out of an uneasy childhood, where his only hope for matching his fellows is through almost tearful bragging, lying, fighting, inventing of romantic backgrounds and adventures that never took place.

Dean had been a raggedy little cotton picker when he should have been going to school; and when he should have been living in a secure home, running with playmates he had known since he could talk, he was traveling in a ramshackle car with his father and brothers from one backbreaking job to the next. The Army to him had been a refuge, where a kid could get regular meals, shoes, clean clothes, and a proper bed to sleep on.

His ability with a baseball was the only thing Dean owned, when he was a kid (he was only nineteen when he signed first with Houston), that offered him a chance to vaunt himself on fairly equal terms with boys who had been to school, had known clean clothes, and had taken meals for granted. His boasting, when he was breaking in to baseball, was almost hysterical—fantastic far beyond belief, haphazard to the point of senselessness. He gave himself two different names and three different birthplaces in his eagerness to create a background and a personality that people would want to hear about. He contradicted himself, made promises he sincerely meant to keep, and broke them immediately because he sincerely thought he was doing right to change his mind.

Steering him through this morass of adolescent antics were two people he had been lucky to meet: his wife, who was determined that her Dizzy was going to win the good things he deserved, and a newspaper writer named J. Roy Stockton, who realized how much ability the boy possessed and who owned the patience, the good nature, and the human sympathy to see, through Dizzy's vainglorious babbling, the essential sweetness of the boy's nature.

For Dizzy Dean was not only the finest baseball pitcher of modern times, but an unusually intelligent boy with a great fondness for people, a sharp wit, and, at the bottom of his heart, an honest desire to work his head off for the people who liked him.

In this era, between the end of the Hoover regime and the entry of the United States into the Second World War, there were several distinct types of successful professional ballplayers; and it is well to remember in judging them that practically all of them were still boys, many very poor boys, and that most of them had to grow up in the public prints, with each silly boast, thoughtless threat, and angry recrimination baked into hard type and left for the world to stare at.

Without his fiery speed ball and his sharp-breaking curve, Jerome Herman Dizzy Dean would have been just a goodhearted and unhappy little braggart, cheated by poverty of a chance to develop his better-than-average mind. As he grew older, he became somewhat shrewd about his own eccentricities and saw to it that his priceless publicity did not wither and die. But he learned, too, that just being Dizzy Dean out loud was not what made people love and admire him—that he had to work hard and win ball games. So he worked hard and won ball games; and people bought toothpaste carrying his name, paid money for his pictures, gave their kids clothing with his name inscribed, or fed them the breakfast food that the comic strips said Dizzy Dean consumed.

He was at his most attractive when he talked about his brother Paul (who was called "Daffy" only by the sports writers). Paul, three years younger than Jerome, had a lightning-fast ball and excellent control. His three-quarters overhand pitching motion was almost the duplicate of Dizzy's, but he did not have Dizzy's spectacular curve—or Dizzy's penchant for talking loudly, loosely, and endlessly. Without his eccentric brother, he'd have been merely a very good pitcher. But to Dizzy he was "faster than me," "better than I ever was," and compared to Paul, said Dizzy, "I'm just a semipro." He saw to it that Paul got his rights, too. He even threatened a strike unless Paul's salary was increased. And Paul repaid his interest by returning the admiration sevenfold and sticking to Dizzy in whatever tempestuous stunt the older Dean felt he had to turn to.

When Dizzy went on strike against appearing in exhibition games or being shown off like a prize dog, Paul went on strike, too, and acted just as angry. When Dizzy repented and came back to work twice as hard, Paul too bore down and won a row of ball games.

Typical of Dizzy Dean's antics, which won him the dislike of a number of people who were not inclined to make allowances, was his childish lobbing of the ball up to Pittsburgh batters in a game where he thought the rest of the team wasn't trying. One of his most famous stunts—made more famous because he did it all over again in front of a photographer—was his tearing up two uniforms (Paul helped him) when manager Frank Frisch suspended him and his brother after they had refused to take the field unless a fine was rescinded. Frisch kept both Deans out of the game after that, in spite of popular clamor, until Dizzy sought the aid of Landis. Landis, after hearing the story, told the Dean brothers quite frankly what a pair of spoiled kids they looked like. And Dizzy, swallowing his pride and his threats with dignity equal to Babe Ruth's, set to and pitched for Frisch some of the finest games of his career.

Dizzy was a good hitter. He loved baseball enough to play any position, and he knew enough about the game to have been valuable anywhere. But he was most valuable to his club in the pitching box. They got their money's worth from Dizzy, too. Not only did he pull countless customers in at the gate; with the aid of Paul, he pitched the Cardinals into a pennant they had practically abandoned hope of winning. That was the year he and Paul won forty-nine games between them. Toward the end of that season, one Dean or another was pitching almost every day.

To see Paul and Dizzy pitch a doubleheader was like seeing the same man do a perfect job twice. From the center-field bleachers it was not easy to tell them apart. They were built alike and were about the same size. Their motions were nearly identical, both smooth, almost effortless sweeps of the arm halfway between sidearm and overhand. To a batter, there was not much to choose between that streaking fast ball of Paul's and the crackling curve that Dizzy could pour in.

Dizzy shortened his own career by pitching when he had to favor a broken toe. The toe had been hurt when he was pitching his heart out in an All-Star game. When his better nature was appealed to, Dizzy was as generous with his skill and strength as he was with his money. And with money he was another of those who "did not know the value of a dollar" —just as if a kid who had worked from dawn to dark for a grudging fifty cents did not know more about what money was and wasn't worth than any news writer alive.

Dizzy got into many a row, with his own teammates, with opponents, with newspapermen, and with the president of the league. He could take a licking with good grace, and he could dish one out. And when he locked horns with the president of the league, he did not exactly come in second. This last set-to came about because Dizzy, harried by a sudden new ruling which forced him to make a distinct pause after his pre-pitching stretch and before sending the ball to the plate, made extra-long pauses which delayed the game interminably. The umpire penalized him for this; and afterward Dizzy found occasion to declare publicly that umpire George Barr and president Ford Frick were "a pair of crooks." Frick, he went on to say, was "our great little president —but a pain in the neck to me."

For this *lèse-majesté,* Frick suspended Dean and ordered him to New York. Dean denied making the remarks. A newspaper reporter insisted he had. Frick, who, like many other men, thought that a boy becomes a man when he gets a wad of money, insisted on a "written retraction." He wrote it and asked Dean to sign it. But there Dean balked. "I ain't signing nothing," he announced. And he did not sign it, either. Frick lifted the suspension, apparently realizing at last that you could no longer kick a man out of the game just for losing his temper at the boss.

Perhaps not the high point of his career, but certainly the episode that becomes him best, was his fulfillment of a promise to a hospital full of crippled kids to strike out Bill Terry, who was then playing manager of the Giants. The kids had assured Dizzy they would be listening to the radio account of the game, and Dizzy said he would, if possible, fan Terry with the bases full. In the ninth inning of the game next day, with two out and the Cardinals one run ahead, the first two men hit safely. The next man was Critz and after him came Terry. Critz got a base on balls. Dean walked toward Terry and smiled. "I hate to do this, Bill," he said. "But I done promised some kids I'd fan you with the bases full. That's why I walked Critz."

Then Dizzy went back to the mound and poured his fast ball through for two quick strikes. With two strikes on a good hitter, the traditional—and safest—thing to do is to waste a ball; that is, give the batter a chance to hit a bad ball. But Dizzy fogged the next one, waist-high, across the center of the plate, and Terry just stared at it. That was strike three. Dizzy came chuckling in to the bench.

"Bill never figured I'd dare put that last one right through the middle," he explained.

Dizzy, when his arm was gone, managed to keep pitching for a time on his craft. And perhaps he could have held a baseball job for many years more, with his brains and hitting power. He chose, however, to accept an offer to broadcast baseball games over the radio; and his local following, as he flaunted his personality on the air, remained as large as ever. So great was his influence on the small fry of St. Louis that a schoolteacher once gently reproved him for using "ain't" on the air.

"Shucks," said Dizzy. "Everybody knows what 'ain't' means!"

Dean played a little baseball, too, on barnstorming tours with Satchel Paige, the best-loved and best-known Negro star of recent days. In various small towns throughout the West, Dizzy would pitch for one team and Old Satch for the other. Neither one had even a suggestion of his old speed and curves, but they were good enough to throw two or three fairly successful innings against semipros. And Dizzy, grown paunchy from lack of training, loved to knock the ball from here to there. He hit a triple against Satchel once, and arrived at third so out of breath that he could hardly stagger. "I've got to stop hitting that ball so fur!" he laughed.

HOW TO FIELD THE BALL: THE EXPERT

Third baseman Cletis Boyer exhibits, in the sequence on this and the following page, the magic that makes fans gasp. Diving for the ball, throwing a strike across the diamond to first while still on his knees, he gets his man with daylight to spare.

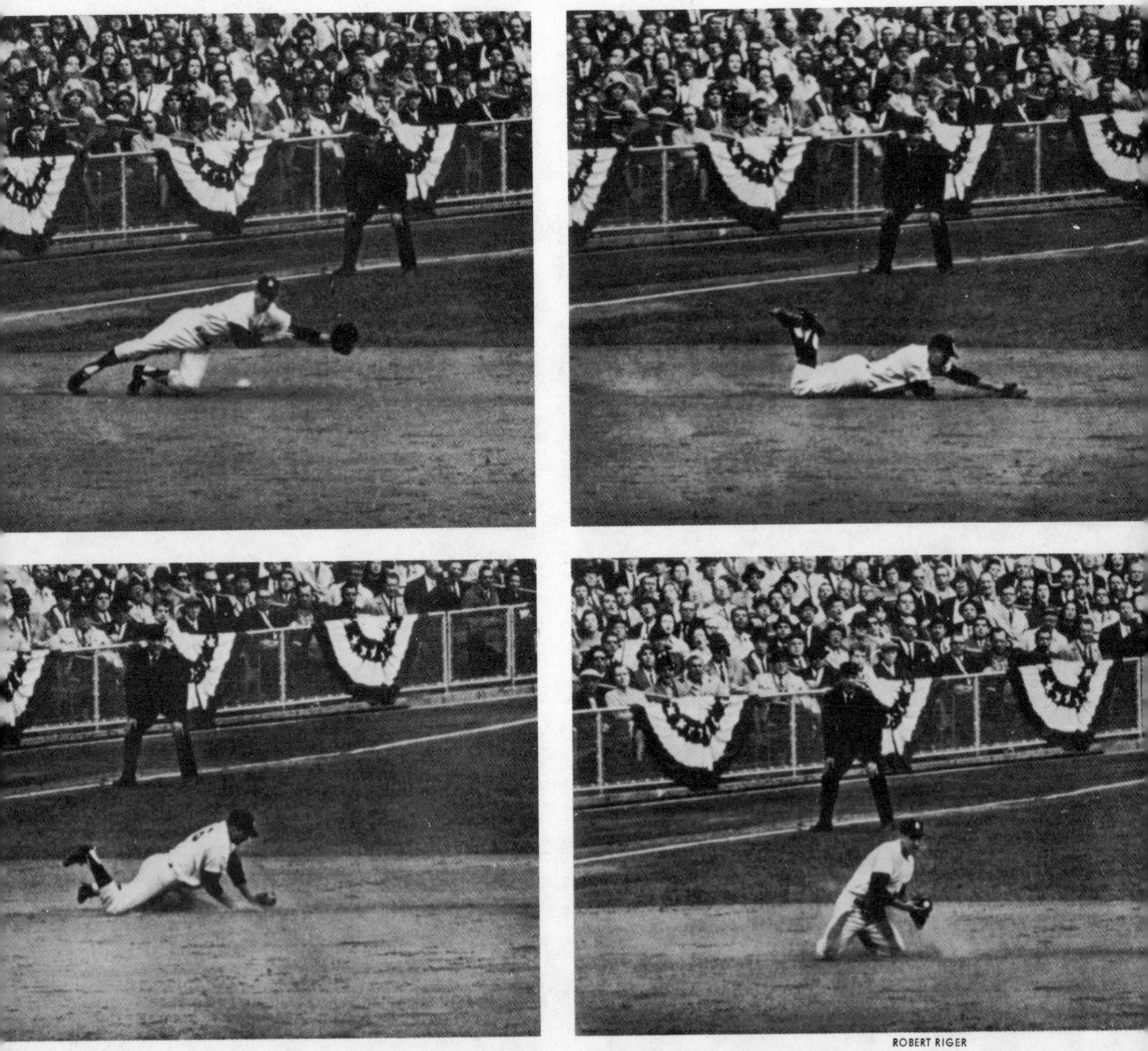

ROBERT RIGER

14

HOW TO FIELD THE BALL: THE FUTURE EXPERT

This young man is not Cletis Boyer. Not yet, anyway. But turn the page...

But turn the page...

ROBERT RIGER

…ooops!

ONE OF THE THINGS that earned Red Smith his reputation as the best sports columnist in the business was his willingness to try anything once. Details:

Baltic Cooperstown

RED SMITH

THEY PLAYED a ball game here last night, and if there's a stone left upon a stone in Cooperstown today, it's an upset. What the Finns did to the game that Doubleday did not invent shouldn't happen in Brooklyn. Not even under its Finnish name, *pesapallo*.

Although *pesapallo* is only about thirty years old, it is a monstrous infant that has grown up to be Finland's national sport. It was invented by Lauri Pihkala, a professor who wears a hearing aid and believes his game was modeled on baseball. Somebody must have described baseball to him when his battery was dead.

"Well," explained a tolerant Finn, "he took baseball and, ah"—he paused to grope for a word meaning "adapted"—"and, ah, mutilated it," he said.

Somebody then performed the same service for the English language while composing program notes to explain *pesapallo* to foreigners.

"The batsman, or striker," wrote this Helsinki Rud Rennie, "must try by power of hit of his own and team-fellows to run from base to base with home-base as final objective. The striker is allowed three serves; i.e., a serve rising at least one-half meter above his head and falling, if not connected by the bat, within base-plate with a diameter of 60 cm."

If that doesn't make you see the game with vivid clarity, there seems little use of further elucidation. Stick around, though, if you've nothing better to do.

Pesapallo hasn't yet achieved Olympic status and was presented merely as an exhibition for about twenty-five thousand spectators in Olympic Stadium. Two nine-man teams came trotting in from the outfield in single file, converged in a V at home plate, and removed caps. Their captains stepped forward and shook hands with the referee, a joker in cinnamon brown carrying a bat, possibly in self-defense. The players wore baseball uniforms, white for one team, malevolent red for the other.

Four other jokers in brown did a lockstep onto the field. These were "assistant controllers" or base umpires. A tasty shortcake in gay peasant costume threw a ball out to the referee and dropped a deep curtsy. The referee fired the ball—which is about the size and weight of a ten-cent "rocket"—to the server and blew a long blast on a police whistle. The game was on.

A *pesapallo* field is a lopsided pentagon 298 feet long and 131 feet wide at its broadest. The pitcher stands across the plate from the batter and tosses the ball straight up like a fungo hitter. Base runners all act like Dodgers gone berserk.

That is, they start for third base and then get lost. First base is just where Phil Rizzuto likes to place his bunts; in Yankee Stadium it would be between third base and the mound. If Finns didn't use chalk lines instead of fences, second base would be against the right-field wall. Third is directly opposite, on the left-field boundary. The route from there home is a dogleg to the left. The plate is a trash-can cover, two feet in diameter.

The pitcher may fling the ball as high as he chooses, but if it doesn't drop on the garbage-can lid it's outside the strike zone. Two successive faulty serves—they must be consecutive—constitute a walk, but the batter goes to first only when there are no runners aboard. Otherwise the runner who has advanced farthest takes one more base.

The batter gets three strikes, but nobody is required to run on a hit except on the third strike. Players are retired only on strikeouts, pick-offs, or throws that beat them to a base. On a fly that is caught, the batter is only "wounded"; he is not out.

A wounded man just stands aside and awaits his next turn at bat. One who has been put out may not bat again in the same inning; if his turn comes around, they skip him. An inning ends after three put-outs or after all nine men have batted without scoring a run. (This can happen if enough men are wounded.)

That's about all, except that over the fence would be a foul ball if there were a fence. Hits must bounce in fair territory. A Ralph Kiner would be a bum in *pesapallo;* a Leo Durocher, whose fungo stick is a squirrel rifle that can brush a fly off an infielder's ear, would be a Finnish Willie Keeler.

This game progressed at bewildering speed, with the ball practically always in motion. There is no balk rule. The server would fake a toss for the batter and whip the ball to a baseman on an attempted pick-off. The baseman would fake a throw back and try the hidden-ball play. Infielders, outfielders, and the pitcher-catcher, they heaved that apple around with the sleight-of-hand of the Harlem Globetrotters.

They played the hit-and-run, with the batter clubbing the ball into the earth like a man beating a snake, then standing still at the plate while the base runners sprinted across the landscape. Everybody showboated frantically. Base umpires lifted cardboard signs to signal "safe" or "out," and the referee announced decisions on his whistle in a sort of Morse code of dots and dashes.

Finally a guy named Eino Kaakkolahti slapped a bounding ball past one infielder, through a second infielder, and past an outfielder, with one runner on base. It was a triple, which counts as a home run in Finland. That was as much as one foreigner could take.

In the first *Fireside Book of Baseball* there appeared an aerodynamic study of a curve ball as tested in the wind tunnel of a modern aircraft company. It had nothing on old Will White, back in 1877, as this excerpt from a classic book by the legendary A. G. Spalding will show. Mr. Spalding's 542-page account of America's National Game (that was its title) was published in 1911 and today is a collector's item.

The Non-Conversion of Colonel Joyce

ALBERT G. SPALDING

Arthur Cummins, of Brooklyn, was the first pitcher of the old school that I ever saw pitch a curved ball. Bobby Matthews soon followed. This was in the early seventies. Both men were very light, spare fellows, with long, sinewy wrists, and having a peculiar wrist-joint motion with a certain way of holding the ball near the fingers' ends that enabled them to impart a rotary motion to the ball, followed by a noticeable outward curve.

In 1874 Tom Bond inaugurated the present style of pitching or, rather, underhand throwing, with its in-curves and out-shoots. This style of delivery was then in violation of the straight-arm pitching rules, but umpires were disposed to let it go, and thus gradually, in spite of legislation, the old style gave way to the new.

In the first year of the existence of the National League several of its pitchers began the delivery of the curved ball, that is, a ball which, after leaving the pitcher's hand, would curve to the right or left, and could be made to deceive the batsman by appearing to come wide of the plate and then suddenly turn in and pass over it; or, appearing to come directly over the plate, to shoot out, missing it entirely.

The result of this work on the part of the pitcher was to make hitting much less frequent and small scores characterized all well-played games. In 1877, as a result of the curved ball, a hot controversy arose into which many scientists were drawn. Distinguished collegians openly declared that the "curved ball" was a myth; that any other deflection of a thrown ball than that caused by the wind or opposing air-currents was impossible. Men high up in the game clung strenuously to the same opinion. Col. J. B. Joyce, who had been a ruling spirit in the old Cincinnati Red Stockings, held to this view. It was absurd, he claimed, to say that any man could throw a ball other than in a straight line. A practical test was made at Cincinnati in the presence of a great crowd to convert the Colonel. A surveyor was employed to set three posts in a row, with the left-hand surface of the two at the ends on a line with the right-hand surface of that in the middle. Then a tight board fence about six feet high was continued from each end post, also bearing on the straight line drawn. Will White, one of the most expert twirlers of the day, was selected to convert Col. Joyce. The test took place in the presence of a big crowd and was a success in everything but the conversion. White stood upon the left of the fence at one end, so that his hand could not possibly pass beyond the straight line, and pitched the ball so that it passed to the right of the middle post. This it did by three or four inches, but curved so much that it passed the third post a half foot to the left. Col. Joyce saw the test successfully performed, but he would not be convinced.

For years under the late J. G. Taylor Spink, *The Sporting News*—bible of baseball, as it was called, most correctly—combined old faithfulness with young ideas. Five of those ideas are presented here in the form of five of Mr. Spink's editorials, each of which appeared at least half a dozen years ago.

Five Editorials

J. G. TAYLOR SPINK

NO GAME TODAY—SNOW!

Baseball is fighting a losing battle with spring—or rather late-winter—weather. Several openings the first week of the season were postponed or marred by snow. Other games were played in miserable chilling winds and rain.

It seems rather ridiculous to send a club to Florida or Arizona to acclimate it to warm weather and then bring it back to the refrigerated northern weather of early April. Perhaps the most daring of all was the effort of several clubs to open their seasons at night when the temperature is roughly 20 degrees cooler than it is in the afternoon—and in early April neither is any bargain.

Naturally baseball will answer with two statements—that with the expanded schedule the season must open as early as it does and that no one has ever been able to change the weather.

Something has to be done, however. Attendance not only is meager on these miserable days and nights but some fans, who braved it for one game, swear they won't come back until June.

The Sunday before the season opened, the Cardinals and Phils played to an overflow crowd of better than 15,000 in perfect weather in Atlanta.

Why, for the first two weeks of the season, until the weather responds in the North, couldn't the teams play regularly scheduled games in the South? They should draw big crowds.

TIME NOW RIPE FOR INTER-LOOP SLATE

If the major leagues had not expanded in the last two years, interleague play probably would be a reality today. Proponents of interleague play, headed by Hank Greenberg, have been beating the drums for their favorite project since the mid-'50s and had been slowly gaining support.

The whole idea was shelved, however, when the American took in two new franchises in 1961 and the National duplicated it in 1962. There was enough trouble, it was said, putting together a 162-game package for the majors without further complicating it with an inter-loop bracketing.

The 162-game schedule is proving unwieldy. The players are bitter over the loss of sleep, the overnight jumps halfway across the country, the lack of open dates and the pileup of doubleheaders. They have asked for a return to a schedule close to the old 154-game one.

In the meantime, the interleague boosters have taken up the cudgels again. This should be a good time to do something about it.

Inter-divisional play is a strong point in both professional football and basketball. It can be just as important to baseball.

ROTATE UMPS DURING GAME

Like the weather, everybody talks about the umpires, but nobody ever seems to do much for them. Certainly, it is startling to realize that in a game or a season their job is tougher than that of the ballplayer.

A player is on his home grounds half of the season. An umpire is always on the road. A player sits down for half a game. An umpire is on his feet through the whole proceedings.

This situation came into bold relief in the long game at Detroit when the four umpires had to stand for seven hours. Umpire Bill McKinley, who worked the plate, couldn't sleep that night because his legs ached too much.

There have been instances of umpires, burdened with cumbersome protective equipment, having been overcome by heat.

Since there are four umpires assigned to each game, why couldn't some relief be offered the umpires? In that game at Detroit, for instance, where there was almost no scoring for some 16 innings, one of the umpires on the bases could have been dispatched to the clubhouse to don equipment so he could replace the man back of the plate. Similarly, in hot weather, umpires might be allowed to spell the hot job back of the plate. This isn't weakness on the part of umpires. It's merely common sense.

N. L. IGNORES DANGER SIGNS IN LONG SKED

The National League, at its meeting in conjunction with the second All-Star game, made it plain that it is not going to trim its schedule for 1963. The league voted in favor of another 162-game schedule, even in the face of strong evidence that this is not an unmixed blessing.

In the first year of the 162-game operation, the National has had a couple of close brushes with airline problems, has brought teams into the next town completely exhausted after all-night rides through the air. Certainly the second All-Star game offered living proof that players are used up now with two months of the schedule still to go.

Twi-night doubleheaders, night games on getaway night and long strings of contests without a day of rest are still piling up on the clubs. The players have protested, but the National plans to go right ahead.

This, of course, is the league's privilege. It should be noted, however, that the league has been warned that ultimately the longer schedule may create more headaches than financial blessings.

TOUR BY HALL OF FAME MEMBERS PROPOSED

Four more distinguished men of baseball—Edd Roush, Bill McKechnie, Bob Feller and Jackie Robinson—were inducted into the Hall of Fame at Cooperstown on July 23. Previously, *The Sporting News* had expressed its pleasure over their election to membership. All four have merited it.

The tiny New York community of Cooperstown always is swollen far beyond capacity on Hall of Fame Day. Visitors come from all over the country. The shrine itself has an ever-increasing number of visitors each summer.

Yet, it is a fact that only a tiny fraction of baseball fandom ever has the chance to visit Cooperstown. It is remote. In addition, the best baseball fan is the man who works hard at his job; he has neither the time nor the resources to visit the Hall of Fame.

We wonder if it wouldn't be a good idea—since many fans can't go to the shrine—to bring the shrine to the fans. In other words, put the inductees on tour for a week or so after the actual installation days. Let them visit major- and minor-league parks, to meet the fans and let them see some of the trophies which are installed at Cooperstown.

On July 9, 1958, hearings were held in Washington by the Subcommittee on Antitrust and Monopoly of the Committee of the Judiciary of the United States Senate. The Subcommittee was considering H.R. 10378 and S. 4070, to limit antitrust laws so as to exempt professional baseball, football, basketball and hockey. Before them as an expert witness came Casey Stengel, whose verbal cuneiform has added the word "Stengelese" to our language. They say there was nothing like it, in all the history of Congressional hearings, since the time the midget sat in J. P. Morgan's lap.

From *The Congressional Record*

CASEY STENGEL

SENATOR KEFAUVER: Mr. Stengel, you are the manager of the New York Yankees. Will you give us very briefly your background and your views about this legislation?

MR. STENGEL: Well, I started in professional ball in 1910. I have been in professional ball, I would say, for forty-eight years. I have been employed by numerous ball clubs in the majors and in the minor leagues.

I started in the minor leagues with Kansas City. I played as low as Class D ball, which was at Shelbyville, Kentucky, and also Class C ball and Class A ball, and I have advanced in baseball as a ballplayer.

I had many years that I was not so successful as a ballplayer, as it is a game of skill. And then I was no doubt discharged by baseball in which I had to go back to the minor leagues as a manager, and after being in the minor leagues as a manager, I became a major-league manager in several cities and was discharged, we call it discharged because there was no question I had to leave.

And I returned to the minor leagues at Milwaukee, Kansas City and Oakland, California, and then returned to the major leagues.

In the last ten years, naturally, in major-league baseball with the New York Yankees; the New York Yankees have had tremendous success, and while I am not a ballplayer who does the work, I have no doubt worked for a ball club that is very capable in the office.

I have been up and down the ladder. I know there are some things in baseball thirty-five to fifty years ago that are better now than they were in those days. In those days, my goodness, you could not transfer a ball club in the minor leagues, Class D, Class C ball, Class A ball.

How could you transfer a ball club when you did not have a highway? How could you transfer a ball club when the railroad then would take you to a town, you got off and then you had to wait and sit up five hours to go to another ball club?

How could you run baseball then without night ball?

You had to have night ball to improve the proceeds, to pay larger salaries, and I went to work, the first year I received $135 a month.

I thought that was amazing. I had to put away enough money to go to dental college. I found out it was not better in dentistry. I stayed in baseball. Any other question you would like to ask me?

SENATOR KEFAUVER: Mr. Stengel, are you prepared to answer particularly why baseball wants this bill passed?

MR. STENGEL: Well, I would have to say at the present time, I think that baseball has advanced in this respect for the player help. That is an amazing statement for me to make, because you can retire with an annuity at fifty and what organization in America allows you to retire at fifty and receive money?

I want to further state that I am not a ballplayer, that is, put into that pension fund committee. At my age, and I have been in baseball, well, I will say I am possibly the oldest man who is working in baseball. I would say that when they start an annuity for the ballplayers to better their conditions, it should have been done, and I think it has been done.

I think it should be the way they have done it, which is a very good thing.

The reason they possibly did not take the managers in at that time was because radio and television or the income to ball clubs was not large enough that you could have put in a pension plan.

Now I am not a member of the pension plan. You have young men here who are, who represent the ball clubs.

They represent the players and since I am not a member and don't receive pension from a fund which you think, my goodness, he ought to be declared in that, too, but I would say that is a great thing for the ballplayers.

That is one thing I will say for the ballplayers, they have an advanced pension fund. I should think it was gained by radio and television or you could not have enough money to pay anything of that type.

Now the second thing about baseball that I think is very interesting to the public or to all of us that it is the owner's own fault if he does not improve his club, along with the officials in the ball club and the players.

Now what causes that?

If I am going to go on the road and we are a traveling ball club and you know the cost of transportation now—we travel sometimes with three Pullman coaches, the New York Yankees and remember I am just a salaried man, and do not own stock in the New York Yankees, I found out that in traveling with the New York Yankees on the road and all, that it is the best, and we have broken records in Washington this year, we have broken them in every city but New York and we have lost two clubs that have gone out of the city of New York.

Of course, we have had some bad weather, I would say that they are mad at us in Chicago, we fill the parks.

They have come out to see good material. I will say they are mad at us in Kansas City, but we broke their attendance record.

Now on the road we only get possibly 27 cents. I am not positive of these figures, as I am not an official.

If you go back fifteen years or so if I owned stock in the club, I would give them to you.

SENATOR KEFAUVER: Mr. Stengel, I am not sure that I made my question clear.

MR. STENGEL: Yes, sir. Well, that is all right. I am not sure I am going to answer yours perfectly, either.

SENATOR O'MAHONEY: How many minor leagues were there in baseball when you began?

MR. STENGEL: Well, there were not so many at that time because of this fact: Anybody to go into baseball at that time with the educational schools that we had were small, while you were probably thoroughly educated at school, you had to be—we only had small cities that you could put a team in and they would go defunct.

Why, I remember the first year I was at Kankakee, Illinois, and a bank offered me $550 if I would let them have a little notice. I left there and took a uniform because they owed me two weeks' pay. But I either had to quit but I did not have enough money to go to dental college so I had to go with the manager down to Kentucky.

What happened there was if you got by July, that was the big date. You did not play night ball and you did not play Sundays in half of the cities on account of a Sunday observance, so in those days when things were tough, and all of it was, I mean to say, why they just closed up July 4 and there you were sitting there in the depot.

You could go to work someplace else, but that was it.

So I got out of Kankakee, Illinois, and I just go there for the visit now.

SENATOR CARROLL: The question Senator Kefauver asked you was what, in your honest opinion, with your forty-eight years of experience, is the need for this legislation in view of the fact that baseball has not been subject to antitrust laws?

MR. STENGEL: No.

SENATOR LANGER: Mr. Chairman, my final question. This is the Antimonopoly Committee that is sitting here.

MR. STENGEL: Yes, sir.

SENATOR LANGER: I want to know whether you intend to keep on monopolizing the world's championship in New York City.

MR. STENGEL: Well, I will tell you. I got a little concern yesterday in the first three innings when I saw the three players I had gotten rid of, and I said when I lost nine what am I going to do and when I had a couple of my players. I thought so great of that did not do so good up to the sixth inning I was more confused but I finally had to go and call on a young man in Baltimore that we don't own and the Yankees don't own him, and he is doing pretty good, and I would actually have to tell you that I think we are more the Greta Garbo type now from success.

We are being hated, I mean, from the ownership and all, we are being hated. Every sport that gets too great or one individual—but if we made 27 cents and it pays to have a winner at home, why would not you have a good winner in your own park if you were an owner?

That is the result of baseball. An owner gets most of the money at home and it is up to him and his staff to do better or they ought to be discharged.

SENATOR KEFAUVER: Thank you very much, Mr. Stengel. We appreciate your presence here. Mr. Mickey Mantle, will you come around? . . . Mr. Mantle, do you have any observations with reference to the applicability of the antitrust laws to baseball?

MR. MANTLE: My views are just about the same as Casey's.

STAN HUNT

"It's turned on. Top of the sixth, no score, two men on, two out, Willie Davis up, one ball, one strike."

JOHN GALLAGHER

Courtesy *Sport* Magazine ©

This exercise in writing against a deadline not only recounts in sterling fashion a memorable All-Star game but imprisons in one sentence what may be the best capsule tribute ever made to Willie Mays's all-around skills: "The only center fielder who could have caught it just happened to hit it."

The 1959 All-Star Game

BOB STEVENS

Handcuffed his first three times up, Willie Mays broke loose from his shackles with a triple in the eighth inning today and left the American League for dead.

The incomparable Giant shattered a 4-to-4 tie by ripping into a Yankee Whitey Ford serve and driving it 420 feet into right-center field to score Hank Aaron and do all sorts of other interesting things.

The high hit eluded the desperately clutching glove of Detroit's Harvey Kuenn to give the National Leaguers a 5–4 victory over the Americans in the 26th annual All-Star classic.

It also snapped a two-game winning streak by the Americans, reduced their all-time edge to 15–11, and made it a rather complete day for the San Francisco Giants by sending southpaw Johnny Antonelli into the winners' circle.

The other Giant in this spectacular didn't do so well, however. Orlando Cepeda went four times to the well and got clobbered by the bucket each time. He failed to get the ball past the first line of defense, and totaled five outs as the result of a double play, two pops to shortstop and a foul to first base.

The first six innings were almost completely pitcher-dominated and then the hitters took charge. The Americans snapped a 1–0 drought created by a first-inning home run by Eddie Mathews off Early Wynn with a four-bagger over the wall by Al Kaline off Lew Burdette with two out in the fourth, and it was 1–1.

The Americans tied into Pittsburgh's Roy Face, the 12-0 relief pitching phenom, driving him out of sight with a three-run explosion in the eighth for a 4–3 and then here comes Willie.

Ford, the Yankee southpaw, was greeted by an eighth-inning opening single up the middle by St. Louis' Ken Boyer, and Pittsburgh's Dick Groat successfully sacrificed.

Milwaukee's undeniable Aaron collected his second single, a roaring job over shortstop, to score Boyer for 4–4, and Mays was convoyed to the plate by the throaty roars of 34,763 restless, expectant customers who contributed $104,303.46 to the players' pension fund.

Ford worked carefully but not too well on the unsmiling Willie. With the count two balls and one strike, he got a fast ball high and away and Mays attacked it. Kuenn gave it an honest pursuit, but the only center fielder in baseball who could have caught it just happened to hit it.

As Aaron pounded home, Willie, looking back, loped easily into third and there no longer was a Ford in the future. Whitey went to the garage, and Bud Daley, the Kansas City southpaw with the withered right arm, took the mound. Chicago's Ernie Banks and Cepeda were his easy victims.

Antonelli didn't have to work hard to receive credit for the victory, his first in five All-Star appearances. He came to the rescue of the well-massaged Face in the eighth with three runs across and Americans lurking off second and third bases.

Johnny A. walked Washington's Roy Sievers, then got Chicago's Sherm Lollar to ground into a force at third to end the inning. He was the pitcher of record when the Nationals, with Mays delivering the coup de grace, demolished the Ford in the bottom half of the round.

Willie's rocket was the ninth and last hit

by the victors, one more than the power-packed Americans could total during this exciting two-hour-and-30-minute battle. And if you didn't like this one, for the first time in the game's history you can get a shot at an encore when the same casts collide again in the Los Angeles Coliseum on August 3.

Don Drysdale, the great Los Angeles Dodger side-wheeler, went the first three innings for the Nationals and nailed nine in a row, striking out four with an unforgettable performance.

Wynn, the 39-year-old White Soxer, did almost as well. Mathews, second up, smashed a home run deep into the right-field seats, his first All-Star HR in his fourth game. And Banks doubled in the second. Milwaukee's Burdette was fidgeting around the mound when the Americans tied it in the fourth on Kaline's number-two iron-type line-drive home run over the left-field bricks.

Yankee Ryne Duren, the myopic flame-thrower, went the next three innings for the Americans and escaped unscathed, although Mays was lucky to do the same. Duren flattened him in the fourth just before striking him out.

Jim Bunning of Detroit was minding the store when the Nationals broke loose for two runs and a 3—1 lead in the seventh, and in this round Kuenn grew wee little goat's horns.

Banks doubled, barely missing an all-the-wayer as the ball crashed into the light tower just to the right of the scoreboard. Cepeda went out to shortstop, a limp loft, and Wally Moon took a called third strike.

Del Crandall collected his first All-Star hit, a single, and Banks galloped across. Kuenn foolishly tried to throw out Ernie at home, something a rifle couldn't have done, and Del waddled unchallenged down to second.

Crandall scored behind Pittsburgh Bill Mazeroski's ensuing bolt into left field, and it was that giveaway run that prevented this one from going into extra innings.

Face, who has a fabulous 17-0 relief-job record dating back to last year, retired the side in the seventh and had two down in the eighth when he became unglued.

Nellie Fox singled, Kuenn walked, and Cleveland's Vic Power singled to tally the Fox. Ted Williams, making his fifteenth, and probably his last, All-Star appearance, walked as Face seemed quite content to keep all pitches away from the big man from Boston.

Pittsburgh fans, bitter in their disappointment at the failure of their civic and national hero, let out a pitiful groan when San Francisco-born Gus Triandos, the Baltimore backstop, banged a double off the embattled Face to drive ElRoy out of the box and drive across Kuenn with the tying run and Power with the go-ahead tally.

After Willie's game-winning blow, the Americans gave Chicago's Don Elston fits before finally succumbing. Don wiped out Frank Malzone on a pop to Banks and struck out Minnie Minoso of Cleveland.

Then came a little excitement.

Fox missed a ninth-inning right-field home run by inches before singling and going to second on a wild pitch. Kuenn, trying desperately to make up for his throwing goof two innings earlier, crashed one far over the left-field wall, again just barely foul.

Harve then fouled out to third baseman Boyer and pounded his bat savagely into the ground in a fit of monumental frustration as Boyer settled under the ball that ended it all.

WE LABEL THIS a profile, for so it is—a stark characterization of an all-time baseball immortal in the last year of his life.

Ty Cobb's Wild Ten-Month Fight to Live

AL STUMP

EVER SINCE SUNDOWN the Nevada intermountain radio had been crackling warnings: "Route 50 now highly dangerous. Motorists stay off. Repeat: *Avoid Route 50.*"

By 1 in the morning the 21-mile, steep-pitched passage from Lake Tahoe's 7,000 feet into Carson City, a snaky grade most of the way, was snow-struck, ice-sheeted, thick with rock slides and declared unfit for all transport vehicles by the State Highway Patrol.

Such news was right down Ty Cobb's alley. Anything that smacked of the impossible brought an unholy gleam to his eye. The gleam had been there in 1959 when a series of lawyers advised Cobb that he stood no chance against the sovereign State of California in a dispute over income taxes, whereupon he bellowed defiance and sued the commonwealth for $60,000 and damages. It had been there more recently when doctors warned that liquor would kill him. From a pint of whiskey per day he upped his consumption to a quart and more.

Sticking out his chin, he told me, "I think we'll take a little run into town tonight."

A blizzard rattled the windows of Cobb's luxurious hunting lodge on the crest of Lake Tahoe, but to forbid him anything—even at the age of seventy-three—was to tell an ancient tiger not to snarl. Cobb was both the greatest of all ballplayers and a multimillionaire whose monthly income from stock dividends, rents and interest ran to $12,000. And he was a man contemptuous, all his life, of any law other than his own.

"We'll drive in," he announced, "and shoot some craps, see a show and say hello to Joe DiMaggio—he's in Reno at the Riverside Hotel."

I looked at him and felt a chill. Cobb, sitting there haggard and unshaven in his pajamas and a fuzzy old green bathrobe at 1 o'clock in the morning, wasn't fooling.

"Let's not," I said. "You shouldn't be anywhere tonight but in bed."

"Don't argue with me!" he barked. "There are fee-simple sonsofbitches all over the country who've tried it and wish they hadn't." He glared at me, flaring the whites of his eyes the way he'd done for twenty-four years to quaking pitchers, basemen, umpires and fans.

"If you and I are going to get along," he went on ominously, *"don't increase my tension."*

We were alone in his isolated ten-room $75,000 lodge, having arrived six days earlier, loaded with a large smoked ham, a 20-pound turkey, a case of Scotch and another of champagne, for purposes of collaborating on Ty's book-length autobiography—a book which he'd refused to write for thirty years, but then suddenly decided to place on record before he died. In almost a week's time we hadn't accomplished thirty minutes of work.

The reason: Cobb didn't need a risky auto trip into Reno, but immediate hospitalization, and by the emergency-door entrance. He was desperately ill and had been even before we'd left California.

We had traveled 250 miles to Tahoe in Cobb's black Imperial limousine, carrying with us a virtual drugstore of medicines. These included Digoxin (for his leaky heart), Darvon (for his aching back), Tace (for a recently-operated-upon malignancy of the pelvic area), Fleet's compound (for his infected bowels), Librium (for his "tension"—that is, his violent rages), codeine (for his pain) and an insulin needle-and-syringe kit (for his diabetes), among a dozen other panaceas which he'd substituted for doctors. Cobb despised the medical profession.

At the same time, his sense of balance was almost gone. He tottered about the lodge, moving from place to place by grasping the furniture. On any public street, he couldn't navigate 20 feet without clutching my shoulder, leaning most of his 208 pounds upon me and shuffling along at a spraddle-legged gait. His bowels wouldn't work: they impacted, repeatedly, an almost total stoppage which brought moans of agony from Cobb when he sought relief. He was feverish, with no one at his Tahoe hideaway but the two of us to treat this dangerous condition.

Everything that hurts had caught up with his big, gaunt body at once and he stuffed himself with pink, green, orange, yellow and purple pills—guessing at the amounts, often, since labels had peeled off many of the bottles. But he wouldn't hear of hospitalizing himself.

"The hacksaw artists have taken $50,000 from me," he said, "and they'll get no more." He spoke of "a quack" who'd treated him a few years earlier. "The joker got funny and said he found urine in my whiskey. I fired him."

His diabetes required a precise food-insulin balance. Cobb's needle wouldn't work. He'd misplaced the directions for the needed daily insulin dosage and his hands shook uncontrollably when he went to plunge the needle into a stomach vein. He spilled more of the stuff than he injected.

He'd been warned by experts from Johns Hopkins to California's Scripps Clinic—that liquor was deadly. Tyrus snorted and began each day with several gin-and-orange-juices, then switched to Old Rarity Scotch, which held him until the night hours, when sleep was impossible, and he tossed down cognac, champagne or "Cobb Cocktails"—Southern Comfort stirred into hot water and honey.

A careful diet was essential. Cobb wouldn't eat. The lodge was without a cook or manservant—since, in the previous six months, he had fired two cooks, a male nurse and a handyman in fits of anger—and any food I prepared for him he pushed away. As of the night of the blizzard, the failing, splenetic old king of ballplayers hadn't touched food in three days, existing solely on quarts of booze and booze mixtures.

My reluctance to prepare the car for the Reno trip burned him up. He beat his fists on the arms of his easy chair. "I'll go alone!" he threatened.

It was certain he'd try it. The storm had worsened, but once Cobb set his mind on an idea, nothing could change it. Beyond that I'd already found that to oppose or annoy him was to risk a violent explosion. An event of a week earlier had proved *that* point. It was then I discovered that he carried a loaded Luger wherever he went and looked for opportunities to use it.

En route to Lake Tahoe, we'd stopped overnight at a motel near Hangtown, California. During the night a party of drunks made a loud commotion in the parking lot. In my room next to Cobb's, I heard him cursing and then his voice, booming out the window.

"Get out of here, you ——heads!"

The drunks replied in kind. Then everyone in the motel had his teeth jolted.

Groping his way to the door, Tyrus the Terrible fired three shots into the dark that resounded like cannon claps. There were screams and yells. Reaching my door, I saw the drunks climbing each other's backs in their rush to flee. The frightened motel manager, and others, arrived. Before anyone could think of calling the police, the manager was cut down by the most caustic tongue ever heard in a baseball clubhouse.

"What kind of a pest house is this?" roared Cobb. "Who gave you a license, you mugwump? Get the hell out of here and see that I'm not disturbed! I'm a sick man and I want it quiet!"

"B-b-beg your pardon, Mr. Cobb," the manager said feebly. He apparently felt so honored to have baseball's greatest figure as a customer that no police were called. When we drove away the next morning, a crowd gathered and stood gawking with open mouths.

Down the highway, with me driving, Cobb checked the Luger and re-loaded its nine-shell clip. "Two of those shots were in the air," he remarked. "The *third* kicked up gravel. I've got permits for this gun from governors of three states. I'm an honorary deputy sheriff of California and a Texas Ranger. So we won't be getting any complaints."

He saw nothing strange in his behavior. Ty Cobb's rest had been disturbed—therefore he had every right to shoot up the neighborhood.

About then I began to develop a twitch of the nerves, which grew worse with time. In past years, I'd heard reports of Cobb's weird and violent ways, without giving them much credence. But until early 1960 my own experience with the legendary Georgian had been slight, amounting only to meetings in Scottsdale, Arizona, and New York to discuss book-writing arrangements and to sign the contract.

Locker-room stories of Ty's eccentricities, wild temper, ego and miserliness sounded like the usual scandalmongering you get in sports. I'd heard that Cobb had flattened a heckler in San Francisco's Domino Club with one punch; had been sued by Elbie Felts, an ex-Coast League player, after assaulting Felts; that he boobytrapped his Spanish villa at Atherton, California, with high-voltage wires; that he'd walloped one of his ex-wives; that he'd been jailed in Placerville, California, at the age of sixty-eight for speeding, abusing a traffic cop and then inviting the judge to return to law school at his, Cobb's, expense.

I passed these things off. The one and only Ty Cobb was to write his memoirs and I felt highly honored to be named his collaborator.

As the poet Cowper reflected, "The innocents are gay." I was eager to start. Then—a few weeks before book work began—I was taken aside and tipped off by an in-law of Cobb's and one of Cobb's former teammates with the Detroit Tigers that I hadn't heard the half of it. "Back out of this book deal," they urged. "You'll never finish it and you might get hurt."

They went on: "Nobody can live with Ty. Nobody ever has. That includes two wives who left him, butlers, housekeepers, chauffeurs, nurses and a few mistresses. He drove off all his friends long ago. Max Fleischmann, the yeast-cake heir, was a pal of Ty's until the night a house guest of Fleishmann's made a remark about Cobb spiking other players when he ran the bases. The man only asked if it was true. Cobb knocked the guy into a fish pond and after that Max never spoke to him again. Another time, a member of Cobb's family crossed him—a woman, mind you. He broke her nose with a ball bat.

"Do you know about the butcher? Ty didn't like some meat he bought. In the fight, he broke up the butcher shop. Had to settle $1,500 on the butcher out of court."

"But I'm dealing with him strictly on business," I said.

"So was the butcher," replied my informants. "In baseball, a few of us who really knew him well realized that he was wrong in the head—unbalanced. He played like a demon and had everybody hating him because he *was* a demon. That's how he set all those records that nobody has come close to since 1928. It's why he was always in a brawl, on the field, in the clubhouse, behind the stands and in the stands. The public's never known it, but Cobb's always been off the beam where other people are concerned. Sure, he made millions in the stock market—but that's only cold business. He carried a gun in the big league and scared hell out of us. He's mean, tricky and dangerous. Look out he doesn't blow up some night and clip you with a bottle. He specializes in throwing bottles.

"Now that he's sick he's worse than ever. And you've signed up to stay with him for months. You poor sap."

Taken aback, but still skeptical, I launched the job—with my first task to drive Cobb to his Lake Tahoe retreat, where, he declared, we could work uninterrupted.

As indicated, nothing went right from the start. The Hangtown gunplay incident was an eye-opener. Next came a series of events, such as Cobb's determination to set forth in a blizzard to Reno, which were too strange to explain away. Everything had to suit his pleasure or he had a tantrum. He prowled about the lodge at night, suspecting trespassers, with the Luger in hand. I slept with one eye open ready to move fast if necessary.

At 1 o'clock of the morning of the storm, full of pain and 90-proof, he took out the Luger, letting it casually rest between his knees. I had continued to object to a Reno excursion in such weather.

He looked at me with tight fury and said, biting out the words: "In 1912—and you can write this down—I killed a man in Detroit. He and two other hoodlums jumped me on the street early one morning with a knife. I was carrying something that came in handy in my early days—a Belgian-made pistol with a heavy raised sight at the barrel end.

"Well, the damned gun wouldn't fire and they cut me up the back."

Making notes as fast as he talked, I asked, "Where in the back?"

"Well, dammit all to hell, if you don't believe me, come and look!" Cobb flared, jerking up his shirt. When I protested that I believed him implicitly, only wanted a story detail, he picked up a half-full whiskey glass and smashed it against the brick fireplace. So I gingerly took a look. A faint whitish scar ran about five inches up the lower left back.

"Satisfied?" jeered Cobb.

He described how, after a battle, the men fled before his fists.

"What with you wounded and the odds three to one," I said, "that must have been a relief."

"Relief? Do you think they could pull that on *me? I went after them!*"

Where anyone else would have felt lucky to be out of it, Cobb chased one of the mugs into a dead-end alley. "I used that gunsight to rip and slash and tear him for about ten minutes until he had no face left," related Ty, with relish. "Left him there, not breathing, in his own rotten blood."

"What was the situation—where were you going when it happened?"

"To catch a train to a ball game."

"You saw a doctor, instead?"

"I did nothing of the sort, dammit! I played the next day and got two hits in three times up!"

Records I later inspected bore out every word of it: on June 3, 1912, in a blood-soaked, makeshift bandage, Ty Cobb hit a double and triple for Detroit, and only then was treated for the knife wound. He was that kind of ballplayer through a record 3,033 games. No other player burned with Cobb's flame. Boze Bulger, a great old-time baseball critic, said, "He was possessed by the Furies."

Finishing his tale, Cobb looked me straight in the eye.

"You're driving me into Reno tonight," he said softly. The Luger was in his hand.

Even before I opened my mouth, Cobb knew he'd won. He had a sixth sense about the emotions he produced in others: in this case, fear. As far as I could see (lacking expert diagnosis and as a layman understands the symptoms), he wasn't merely erratic and trigger-tempered, but suffering from megalomania, or acute self-worship; delusions of persecution; and more than a touch of dipsomania.

Although I'm not proud of it, he scared hell out of me most of the time I was around him.

And now he gave me the first smile of our association. "As long as you don't aggravate my tension," he said, "we'll get along."

Before describing the Reno expedition, I would like to say in this frank view of a mighty man that the greatest, and strangest, of all American sport figures had his good side, which he tried to conceal. During the final ten months of his life I was his one constant companion. Eventually, I put him to bed, prepared his insulin, picked him up when he fell down, warded off irate taxi drivers, bartenders, waiters, clerks and private citizens whom Cobb was inclined to punch, cooked what food he could digest, drew his bath, got drunk with him and knelt with him in prayer on black nights when he knew death was near. I ducked a few bottles he threw, too.

I think, because he forced upon me a confession of his most private thoughts, that I knew the answer to the central, overriding secret of his life: was Ty Cobb psychotic throughout his baseball career?

Kids, dogs and sick people flocked to him and he returned their instinctive liking. Money was his idol, but from his $4-million fortune he assigned large sums to create the Cobb Educational Foundation, which financed hundreds of needy youngsters through college. He built and endowed a first-class hospital for the poor of his backwater home town, Royston, Georgia. When Ty's spinster sister, Florence, was crippled, he tenderly cared for her until her last days. The widow of a onetime American League batting champion would have lived in want but for Ty's steady money support. A Hall of Fame member, beaned by a pitched ball and enfeebled, came under Cobb's wing for years. Regularly he mailed dozens of anonymous checks to indigent old ballplayers (relayed by a third party)—a rare act among retired tycoons in other lines of business.

If you believe such acts didn't come hard for Cobb, guess again: he was the world's champion pinchpenny.

Some 150 fan letters reached him each month, requesting his autograph. Many letters enclosed return-mail stamps. Cobb used the stamps for his own outgoing mail. The fan letters he burned.

"Saves on firewood," he'd mutter.

In December of 1960, Ty hired a one-armed "gentleman's gentleman" named Brownie. Although constantly criticized, poor Brownie worked hard as cook and butler. But when he mixed up the grocery order one day, he was fired with a check for a week's pay—$45—and sent packing.

Came the middle of that night and Cobb awakened me.

"We're driving into town *right now,*" he stated, "to stop payment on Brownie's check. The bastard talked back to me when I discharged him. He'll get no more of my money."

All remonstrations were futile. There was no phone, so we had to drive the 20 miles from Cobb's Tahoe lodge into Carson City, where he woke up the president of the First National Bank of Nevada and arranged for a stop-pay on the piddling check. The president tried to conceal his anger—Cobb was a big depositor in his bank.

"Yes, sir, Ty," he said, "I'll take care of it first thing in the morning."

"You goddamn well better," snorted Cobb. And then we drove through the 3 A.M. darkness back to the lake.

But this trip was a light workout compared to that Reno trip.

Two cars were available at the lodge. Cobb's 1956 Imperial had no tire chains, but the other car did.

"We'll need both for this operation," he ordered. "One car might get stuck or break down. I'll drive mine and you take the one with chains. You go first. I'll follow your chain marks."

For Cobb to tackle precipitous Route 50 was unthinkable in every way. The Tahoe road, with 200-foot drop-offs, has killed a recorded eighty motorists. Along with his illness, his drunkenness, and no chains, he had bad eyes and was without a driver's license. California had turned him down at his last test; he hadn't bothered to apply in Nevada.

Urging him to ride with me was a waste of breath.

A howling wind hit my car a solid blow as we shoved off. Sleet stuck to the windshield faster than the wipers could work. For the first three miles, snowplows had been active and at 15 mph, in second gear, I managed to hold the road. But then came Spooner's Summit, 7,000 feet high, and then a steep descent of nine miles. Behind me, headlamps blinking, Cobb honked his horn, demanding more speed. Chainless, he wasn't getting traction. *The hell with him,* I thought. Slowing to first gear, fighting to hold a roadbed I couldn't see even with my head stuck out the window, I skidded along. No other traffic moved as we did our crazy tandem around icy curves, at times brushing the guardrails. Cobb was blaring his horn steadily now.

And then here came Cobb.

Tiring of my creeping pace, he gunned the Imperial around me in one big skid. I caught a glimpse of an angry face under a big Stetson hat and a waving fist. He was doing a good 30 mph when he'd gained 25 yards on me, fishtailing right and left, but straightening as he slid out of sight in the thick sleet.

I let him go. Suicide wasn't in my contract.

The next six miles was a matter of feeling my way and praying. Near a curve, I saw taillights to the left. Pulling up, I found Ty swung sideways and buried, nose down, in a snowbank, his hind wheels two feet in the air. Twenty yards away was a sheer drop-off into a canyon.

"You hurt?" I asked.

"Bumped my —— head," he muttered. He lit a cigar and gave four-letter regards to the Highway Department for not illuminating the "danger" spot. His forehead was bruised and he'd broken his glasses.

In my car, we groped our way downmountain, a nightmare ride, with Cobb alternately taking in Scotch from a thermos jug and telling me to step on it. At 3 A.M. in Carson City, an all-night garageman used a broom to clean the car of snow and agreed to pick up the Imperial—"when the road's passable." With dawn breaking, we reached Reno. All I wanted was a bed and all Cobb wanted was a craps table.

He was rolling now, pretending he wasn't ill, and with the Scotch bracing him, Ty was able to walk into the Riverside Hotel casino with a hand on my shoulder and without staggering so obviously as usual. Everybody present wanted to meet him. Starlets from a film unit on location in Reno flocked around and comedian Joe E. Lewis had the band play "Sweet Georgia Brown"—Ty's favorite tune.

"Hope your dice are still honest," he told Riverside co-owner Bill Miller. "Last time I was here I won $12,000 in three hours."

"How I remember, Ty," said Miller. "How I remember."

A scientific craps player who'd won and lost huge sums in Nevada in the past, Cobb bet $100 chips, his eyes alert, not missing a play around the board. He soon decided that the table was "cold" and we moved to another casino, then a third. At this last stop, Cobb's legs began to grow shaky. Holding himself up by leaning on the table edge with his forearms, he dropped $300, then had a hot streak in which he won over $800. His voice was a croak as he told the other players, "Watch 'em and weep."

But then suddenly his voice came back. When the stickman raked the dice his way, Cobb loudly said, "You touched the dice with your hand."

"No, sir," said the stickman. "I did *not.*"

"I don't lie!" snarled Cobb.

"I don't lie either," insisted the stickman.

"Nobody touches my dice!" Cobb, swaying on his feet, eyes blazing, worked his way around the table toward the croupier. It was a weird tableau. In his crumpled Stetson and expensive camel's-hair coat, stained and charred with cigarette burns, a three-day beard grizzling his face, the gaunt old giant of baseball towered over the dapper gambler.

"You fouled the dice, I saw you," growled Cobb, and then he swung.

The blow missed, as the stickman dodged, but, cursing and almost falling, Cobb seized the wooden rake and smashed it over the table. I jumped in and caught him under the arms as he sagged.

And then, as quickly as possible, we were put into the street by two large uniformed guards. "Sorry, Mr. Cobb." they said, unhappily, "but we can't have this."

A crowd had gathered and as we started down the street, Cobb swearing and stumbling and clinging to me, I couldn't have felt more conspicuous if I'd been strung naked from the neon arch across Reno's main drag, Virginia Street. At the street corner, Ty was struck by an attack of breathlessness. "Got to stop," he gasped. Feeling him going limp on me, I turned his six-foot body against a lamppost, braced my legs and with an underarm grip held him there until he caught his breath. He panted and gulped for air.

His face gray, he murmured, "Reach into my left-hand coat pocket." Thinking he wanted his bottle of heart pills, I did. But instead pulled out a six-inch-thick wad of currency, secured by a rubber band. "Couple of thousand there," he said weakly. "Don't let it out of sight."

At the nearest motel, where I hired a single, twin-bed room, he collapsed on the bed in his coat and hat and slept. After finding myself some breakfast, I turned in. Hours later I heard him stirring. "What's this place?" he muttered.

I told him the name of the motel—Travelodge.

"Where's the bankroll?"

"In your coat. You're wearing it."

Then he was quiet.

After a night's sleep, Cobb felt well enough to resume his gambling. In the next few days, he won more than $3,000 at the tables, and then we went sight-seeing in historic Virginia City. There as in all places, he stopped traffic. And had the usual altercation. This one was at the Bucket of Blood, where Cobb accused the bartender of serving watered Scotch. The bartender denied it. Crash! Another drink went flying.

Back at the lodge a week later, looking like the wrath of John Barleycorn and having refused medical aid in Reno, he began to suffer new and excruciating pains—in his hips and lower back. But between groans he forced himself to work an hour a day on his autobiography. He told inside baseball tales never published:

". . . . Frank Navin, who owned the Detroit club for years, faked his turnstile count to cheat the visiting team and Uncle Sam. So did Big Bill Devery and Frank Farrell, who owned the New York Highlanders—later called the Yankees.

". . . . Walter Johnson, the Big Train, tried to kill himself when his wife died."

". . . . Grover Cleveland Alexander wasn't drunk out there on the mound, the way people thought—he was an epileptic. Old Pete would fall down with a seizure between innings, then go back and pitch another shutout."

". . . . John McGraw hated me because I tweaked his nose in broad daylight in the lobby of the Oriental Hotel, in Dallas, after earlier beating the hell out of his second baseman, Buck Herzog, upstairs in my room."

But before we were well started, Cobb suddenly announced we'd go riding in his 23-foot Chris-Craft speedboat, tied up in a boathouse below the lodge. When I went down to warm it up, I found the boat sunk to the bottom of Lake Tahoe in 15 feet of water.

My host broke all records for blowing his stack when he heard the news. He saw in this a sinister plot. "I told you I've got enemies all around here! It's sabotage as sure as I'm alive!"

A sheriff's investigation turned up no clues. Cobb sat up all night for three nights with his Luger. "I'll salivate the first dirty skunk who steps foot around here after dark," he swore.

Parenthetically, Cobb had a vocabulary all his own. To "salivate" something meant to destroy it. Anything easy was "soft-boiled," to outsmart someone was to "slip him the oskafagus," and all doctors were "truss-fixers." People who displeased him—and this included almost everyone he met—were "fee-simple sonsofbitches," "mugwumps" or (if female) "lousy slits."

Lake Tahoe friends of Cobb's had stopped visiting him long before, but one morning an attractive blonde of about fifty came calling. She was an old chum—in a romantic way, I was given to understand, of bygone years—but Ty greeted her coldly. "Lost my sexual powers when I was sixty-nine," he said, when she was out of the room. "What the hell use to me is a woman?"

The lady had brought along a three-section electric vibrator bed, which she claimed would relieve Ty's back pains. We helped him mount it. He took a twenty-minute treatment. Attempting to dismount, he lost balance, fell backward, the contraption jackknifed and Cobb was pinned, yelling and swearing, under a pile of machinery.

When I freed him and helped him to a chair, he told the lady—in the choicest gutter language—where she could put her bed. She left, sobbing.

"That's no way to talk to an old friend, Ty," I said. "She was trying to do you a favor."

"And you're a hell of a poor guest around here, too!" he thundered. "You can leave any old time!" He quickly grabbed a bottle and heaved it in my direction.

"Thought you could throw straighter than that!" I yelled back.

Fed up with him, I started to pack my bags. Before I'd finished, Cobb broke out a bottle of vintage Scotch, said I was "damned sensitive," half apologized, and the matter was forgotten.

While working one morning on an outside observation deck, I heard a thud inside. On his bedroom floor, sprawled on his back, lay Ty. He was unconscious, his eyes rolled back, breathing shallowly. I thought he was dying.

There was no telephone. "Eavesdroppers on the line," Cobb had told me. "I had it cut off." I ran down the road to a neighboring lodge and phoned a Carson City doctor, who promised to come immediately.

Back at the lodge, Ty remained stiff and stark on the floor, little bubbles escaping his lips. His face was bluish-white. With much straining, I lifted him halfway to the bed and by shifting holds finally rolled him onto it, and covered him with a blanket. Twenty minutes passed. No doctor.

Ten minutes later, I was at the front door, watching for the doctor's car, when I heard a sound. There stood Ty, swaying on his feet. "You want to do some work on the book?" he said.

His recovery didn't seem possible. "But you were out cold a minute ago," I said.

"Just a dizzy spell. Have 'em all the time. Must have hit my head on the bedpost when I fell."

The doctor, arriving, found Cobb's blood pressure standing at a grim 210 on the gauge. His temperature was 101 degrees and from gross neglect of his diabetes, he was in a state of insulin shock, often fatal if not quickly treated. "I'll have to hospitalize you, Mr. Cobb," said the doctor.

Weaving his way to a chair, Cobb angrily waved him away. "Just send me your bill," he grunted. "I'm going home."

"Home" was the multimillionaire's main residence at Atherton, California, on the San Francisco Peninsula, 250 miles away, and it was there he headed later that night. With some hot soup and insulin in him, Cobb recovered with the same unbelievable speed he'd shown in baseball. In his heyday, trainers often sewed up deep spike cuts in his knees, shins and thighs, on a clubhouse bench, without anesthetic, and he didn't lose an inning. Grantland Rice one 1920 day sat beside a bedridden, feverish Cobb, whose thighs, from sliding, were a mass of raw flesh. Sixteen hours later, he hit a triple, double, three singles and stole two bases to beat the Yankees. On the Atherton ride, he yelled insults at several motorists who moved too slowly to suit him. Reaching Atherton, Ty said he felt ready for another drink.

My latest surprise was Cobb's eighteen-room, two-story richly landscaped Spanish-California villa at 48 Spencer Lane, an exclusive neighborhood. You could have held a ball game on the grounds.

But the $90,000 mansion had no lights, no heat, no hot water.

"I'm suing the Pacific Gas & Electric Company," he explained, "for overcharging me on the service. Those rinky-dinks tacked an extra $16 on my bill. Bunch of crooks. When I wouldn't pay, they cut off my utilities. Okay—I'll see them in court."

For months previously, Ty Cobb had lived in a totally dark house. The only illumination was candlelight. The only cooking facility was a portable Coleman stove, such as campers use. Bathing was impossible, unless you could take it cold. The electric refrigerator, stove, deepfreeze, radio and television, of course, didn't work. Cobb had vowed to "hold the fort" until his trial of the P.G.&E. was settled. Simultaneously, he had filed a $60,000 suit in San Francisco Superior Court against the State of California to recover state income taxes already collected—on the argument that he wasn't a permanent resident of California, but of Nevada, Georgia, Arizona and other way-points. State's attorneys claimed he spent at least six months per year in Atherton, thus had no case.

"I'm gone so much from here," he claimed, "that I'll win hands down." All legal opinion, I later learned, held just the opposite view, but Cobb ignored their advice.

Next morning, I arranged with Ty's gardener, Hank, to turn on the lawn sprinklers. In the outdoor sunshine, a cold-water shower was easier to take. From then on, the back yard became my regular washroom.

The problem of lighting a desk so that we could work on the book was solved by stringing 200 feet of cord, plugged into an outlet of a neighboring house, through hedges and flower gardens and into the window of Cobb's study, where a single naked bulb hung over the chandelier provided illumination.

The flickering shadows cast by the single light made the vast old house seem haunted. No ghost writer ever had more ironical surroundings.

At various points around the premises, Ty showed me where he'd once installed high-voltage wires to stop trespassers. "Curiosity seekers?" I asked. "Hell, no," he said. "Detectives broke in here once looking for evidence against me in a divorce suit. After a couple of them got burned, they stopped coming."

To reach our bedrooms, Cobb and I groped our way down long, black corridors. Twice he fell in the dark. And then, collapsing completely, he became so ill that he was forced to check in at Stanford Hospital in nearby Palo Alto. Here another shock was in store.

One of the physicians treating Ty's case, a Dr. E. R. Brown, said, "Do you mean to say that this man has traveled 700 miles in the last month without medical care?"

"Doctor," I said, "I've hauled him in and out of saloons, motels, gambling joints, steam baths and snowbanks. There's no holding him."

"It's a miracle he's alive. He has almost every major ailment I know about."

Dr. Brown didn't reveal to me Ty's main ailment, which news Cobb, himself, broke late one night from his hospital bed. "It's cancer," he said, bluntly. "About a year ago I had most of my prostate gland removed when they found it was malignant. Now it's spread up into the back bones. These pill-peddlers here won't admit it, but I haven't got a chance."

Cobb made me swear I'd never divulge the fact before he died. "If it gets in the papers, the sob sisters will have a field day. I don't want sympathy from anybody."

At Stanford, where he absorbed seven massive doses of cobalt radiation, the ultimate cancer treatment, he didn't act like a man on his last legs. Even before his strength returned, he was in the usual form.

"They won't let me have a drink," he said indignantly. "I want you to get me a bottle. Smuggle it in in your tape-recorder case."

I tried, telling myself that no man with terminal cancer deserves to be dried up, but sharp-eyed nurses and orderlies were watching. They searched Ty's closet, found the bottle and over his roars of protest appropriated it.

"We'll have to slip them the oskefagus," said Ty.

Thereafter, a drink of Scotch-and-water sat in plain view in his room, on his bedside table, under the very noses of his physicians—and nobody suspected a thing. The whiskey was in an ordinary water glass, and in the liquid reposed Ty's false teeth.

There were no dull moments while Cobb was at the hospital. He was critical of everything. He told one doctor that he was not even qualified to be an intern, and told the hospital dietician—at the top of his voice—that she and the kitchen workers were in a conspiracy to poison him with their "foul" dishes. To a nurse he snapped, "If Florence Nightingale knew about you, she'd spin in her grave."

(Stanford Hospital, incidentally, is one of the largest and top-rated medical plants in the United States.)

But between blasts he did manage to buckle down to work on the book, dictating long into the night into a microphone suspended over his bed. Slowly the stormy details of his professional life came out. He spoke often of having "forgiven" his many baseball enemies, then lashed out at them with such passionate phrases that it was clear he'd done no such thing. High on his "hate" list were McGraw; New York sportswriters; Hub Leonard, a pitcher who in 1926 accused Cobb and Tris Speaker of "fixing" a Detroit-Cleveland game; American League president Ban Johnson; onetime Detroit owner Frank Navin; former Baseball Commissioner Kenesaw Mountain Landis; and all those who intimated that Cobb ever used his spikes on another player without justification.

After a night when he slipped out of the hospital, against all orders, and we drove to a San Francisco Giants-Cincinnati Reds game at Candlestick Park, 30 miles away, Stanford Hospital decided it couldn't help Tyrus R.

Cobb, and he was discharged. For extensive treatment his bill ran to more than $1,200.

"That's a nice racket you boys have here," he told the discharging doctors. "You clip the customers and then every time you pass an undertaker, you wink at him."

"Good-bye, *Mr.* Cobb," snapped the medical men.

Soon after this Ty caught a plane to his native Georgia and I went along. "I want to see some of the old places again before I die," he said.

It now was Christmas Eve of 1960 and I'd been with him for three months and completed but four chapters. The project had begun to look hopeless. In Royston, a village of 1,200, Cobb headed for the town cemetery. I drove him there, we parked, and I helped him climb a windswept hill through the growing dusk. Light snow fell. Faintly, Yule chimes could be heard.

Among the many headstones, Ty looked for the plot he'd reserved for himself while in California and couldn't locate it. His temper began to boil. "Dammit, I ordered the biggest damn mausoleum in the graveyard! I know it's around here somewhere." On the next hill, we found it: a large marble, walk-in-size structure with "Cobb" engraved over the entrance.

"You want to pray with me?" he said gruffly. We knelt and tears came to his eyes.

Within the tomb, he pointed to crypts occupied by the bodies of his father, Professor William Herschel Cobb, his mother, Amanda (Chitwood) Cobb, and his sister Florence, whom he'd had disinterred and placed here. "My father," he said reverently, "was the greatest man I ever knew. He was a scholar, state senator, editor and philosopher. I worshiped him. So did all the people around here. He was the only man who ever made me do his bidding."

Arising painfully, Ty braced himself against the marble crypt that soon would hold his body. There was an eerie silence in the tomb. He said deliberately: "My father had his head blown off with a shotgun when I was eighteen years old—*by a member of my own family.* I didn't get over that. I've never gotten over it."

We went back down the hill to the car. I asked no questions that day.

Later, from family sources and old Georgia friends of the baseball idol, I learned about the killing. One night in August of 1905, they related, Professor Cobb announced that he was driving from Royston to a neighboring village and left home by buggy. But, later that night, he doubled back and crept into his wife's bedroom by way of the window. "He suspected her of being unfaithful to him," said these sources. "He thought he'd catch her in the act. But Amanda Cobb was a good woman. She was all alone when she saw a menacing figure climb through her window and approach her bed. In the dark, she assumed it to be a robber. She kept a shotgun handy by her bed and she used it. Everybody around here knew the story, but it was hushed up when Ty became famous."

News of the killing reached Ty in Augusta, where he was playing minor-league ball, on August 9. A few days later he was told that he'd been purchased by the Detroit Tigers, and was to report immediately. "In my grief," Cobb says in the book, "it didn't matter much. . . ."

Came March of 1961 and I remained stuck to the Georgia Peach like court plaster. He'd decided that we were born pals, meant for each other, that we'd complete a baseball book beating anything ever published. He had astonished doctors by rallying from the spreading cancer and, between bouts of transmitting his life and times to a tape recorder, was raising more whoopee than he had at Lake Tahoe and Reno.

Spring-training time for the big leagues had arrived and we were ensconced in a $30-a-day suite at the Ramada Inn at Scottsdale, Arizona, close by the practice parks of the Red Sox, Indians, Giants and Cubs. Here, each year, Cobb held court. He didn't go to see anybody; Ford Frick, Joe Cronin, Ted Williams, and other diamond notables came to him. While explaining to sportswriters why modern stars couldn't compare to the Wagners, Lajoies, Speakers, Jacksons, Mathewsons and Planks of his day, Ty did other things.

For one, he commissioned a noted Arizona artist to paint him in oils. He was emaciated, having dropped from 208 pounds to 176. The preliminary sketches showed up his sagging cheeks and thin neck.

"I wouldn't let you calcimine my toilet," ripped out Ty, and fired the artist.

But at analyzing the Dow-Jones averages and playing the stock market, he was anything but eccentric. Twice a week he phoned experts around the country, determined good buys and bought in blocks of 500 to 1,500 shares. He made money consistently, even when bedridden, with a mind that read behind the fluctuations of a dozen different issues. "The State of Georgia," Ty remarked, "will realize about one million dollars from inheritance taxes when I'm dead. But there isn't a man alive who knows what I'm worth." According to the *Sporting News,* there was evidence upon Cobb's death that his worth approximated $12 million. Whatever the true figure, he did not confide the amount to me—or, most probably, to anyone except attorneys who drafted his last will and testament. And Cobb fought off making his will until the last moment.

His fortune began in 1908, when he bought into United (later General) Motors; as of 1961, he was "Mr. Coca-Cola," holding more than 20,000 shares of that stock, valued at $85 per share. Wherever we traveled, he carried with him, stuffed into an old brown bag, more than $1 million in stock certificates and negotiable government bonds. The bag never was locked up. Cobb assumed nobody would dare rob him. He tossed the bag into any handy corner of a room, inviting theft. And in Scottsdale it turned up missing.

Playing Sherlock, he narrowed the suspects to a room maid and a man he'd hired to cook meals. When questioned, the maid broke into tears and the cook quit (fired, said Cobb). Hours later, I discovered the bag under a pile of dirty laundry.

Major-league owners and league officials hated to see him coming, for he thought their product was putrid and said so, incessantly. "Today they hit for ridiculous averages, can't bunt, can't steal, can't hit-and-run, can't place-hit to the opposite field and you can't call them ballplayers." He told sportswriters, "I blame Frick, Cronin, Bill Harridge, Horace Stoneham, Dan Topping and others for wrecking baseball's traditional league lines. These days, any tax-dodging mugwump with a bankroll can buy a franchise, field some semipros and get away with it. Where's our integrity? Where's *baseball?*"

No one could quiet Cobb. Who else had a lifetime average of .367, made 4,191 hits, scored 2,244 runs, won 12 batting titles, stole 892 bases, repeatedly beat whole teams single-handedly? Who was first into the Hall of Fame? Not Babe Ruth—but Cobb, by a landslide vote.

By early April, he could barely make it up the ramp of the Scottsdale Stadium, even hanging onto me. He had to stop, gasping for breath, every few steps. But he kept coming to games—loving the sounds of the ball park. His courage was tremendous. "Always be ready to catch me if I start to fall," he said. "I'd hate to go down in front of the fans."

People of all ages were overcome with emotion upon meeting him; no sports figure I've known produced such an effect upon the public.

We went to buy a cane. At a surgical supply house, Cobb inspected a dozen $25 malacca sticks, bought the cheapest, $4, white-ash cane they had. "I'm a plain man," he informed the clerk, the $7,500 diamond ring on his finger glittering.

But pride kept the old tiger from ever using the cane, any more than he'd wear the $600 hearing aid built into the bow of his glasses.

One day a Mexican taxi driver aggravated Cobb with his driving. Throwing the fare on the ground, he waited until the cabby had bent to retrieve it, then tried to punt him like a football.

"What's your sideline," he inquired, "selling opium?"

It was all I could do to keep the driver from swinging on him. Later, a lawyer called on Cobb, threatening a damage suit. "Get in line, there's five hundred ahead of you," said Tyrus, waving him away.

Every day was a new adventure. He was fighting back against the pain that engulfed him again—cobalt treatments no longer helped—and I could count on trouble anywhere we went. He threw a saltshaker at a Phoenix waiter, narrowly missing. One of his most treasured friendships—with Ted Williams—came to an end.

From the early 1940s, Williams had sat at Ty Cobb's feet. They often met, exchanged long letters on the art of batting. At Scottsdale one day, Williams dropped by Ty's rooms. He hugged Ty, fondly rumpled his hair and accepted a drink. Presently the two greatest hitters of past and present fell into an argument over what players should comprise the all-time, All-Star team. Williams declared, "I want DiMaggio and Hornsby on my team over anybody you can mention."

Cobb's face grew dark. "Don't give me that! Hornsby couldn't go back for a pop fly and he lacked smartness. DiMaggio couldn't hit with Speaker or Joe Jackson."

"The hell you say!" came back Williams jauntily. "Hornsby outhit *you* a couple of years."

Almost leaping from his chair, Cobb shook a fist. He'd been given the insult supreme—for

Cobb always resented, and finally hated, Rogers Hornsby. Not until Cobb was in his sixteenth season did Hornsby top him in the batting averages. "Get . . . away from me!" choked Cobb. "Don't come back!"

Williams left with a quizzical expression, not sure how much Cobb meant it. The old man meant it all the way. He never invited Williams back, nor talked to him, nor spoke his name again. "I cross him off," he told me.

We left Arizona shortly thereafter for my home in Santa Barbara, California. Now failing fast, Tyrus had accepted my invitation to be my guest. Two doctors inspected him at my beach house by the Pacific and gave their opinions: he had a few months of life left, no more. The cancer had invaded the bones of his skull. His pain was intense, unrelenting—requiring heavy sedation—yet with teeth bared and sweat pouring down his face, he fought off medical science. "They'll never get me on their damned hypnotics," he swore. "I'll never die an addict . . . an idiot. . . ."

He shouted, "Where's anybody who cares about me? Where are they? The world's lousy . . . no good."

One night later, on May 1, Cobb sat propped up in bed, overlooking a starlit ocean. He had a habit, each night, of rolling up his trousers and placing them under his pillow—an early-century ballplayer's trick, dating from the time when Ty slept in strange places and might be robbed. I knew that his ever-present Luger was tucked into that pants roll.

I'd never seen him so sunk in despair. At last the fire was going out. "Do we die a little at a time, or all at once?" he wondered aloud. "I think Max had the right idea."

The reference was to his onetime friend, multimillionaire Max Fleischmann, who'd cheated lingering death by cancer some years earlier by putting a bullet through his brain. Ty spoke of Babe Ruth, another cancer victim. "If Babe had been told what he had in time, he could've got it over with."

Had I left Ty that night, I believe he would have pulled the trigger. His three living children (two were dead) had withdrawn from him. In the wide world that had sung his fame, he had not one intimate friend remaining.

But we talked, and prayed, until dawn, and then sleep came; in the morning, aided by friends, I put him into a car and drove him home, to the big, gloomy house in Atherton. He spoke only twice during the six-hour drive.

"Have you got enough to finish the book?" he asked.

"More than enough."

"Give 'em the word then. I had to fight all my life to survive. They all were against me . . . tried every dirty trick to cut me down. But I beat the bastards and left them in the ditch. Make sure the book says that. . . ."

I was leaving him now, permanently, and I had to ask one question I'd never put to him before.

"Why did you fight so hard in baseball, Ty?"

He'd never looked fiercer than then, when he answered. "I did it for my father, who was an exalted man. They killed him when he was still young. They blew his head off the same week I became a major leaguer. He never got to see me play. But I knew he was watching me and I never let him down."

You can make what you want of that. Keep in mind what Casey Stengel said, later: "I never saw anyone like Cobb. No one even close to him. When he wiggled those wild eyes at a pitcher, you knew you were looking at the one bird nobody could beat. It was like he was superhuman."

To me it seems that the violent death of a father whom a sensitive, highly talented boy loved deeply, and feared, engendered, through some strangely supreme desire to vindicate that father, the most violent, successful, thoroughly maladjusted personality ever to pass across American sports. The shock tipped the eighteen-year-old mind, making him capable of incredible feats.

Off the field, he was still at war with the world. For the emotionally disturbed individual, in most cases, does not change his pattern. To reinforce that pattern, he was viciously hazed by Detroit Tiger veterans when he was a rookie. He was bullied, ostracized and beaten up—in one instance, a 210-pound catcher named Charlie Schmidt broke the 165-pound Ty Cobb's nose. It was persecution immediately heaped upon the deepest desolation a young man can experience.

Yes, Ty Cobb was a badly disturbed personality. It is not hard to understand why he spent his entire life in deep conflict. Nor why a member of his family, in the winter of 1960, told me, "I've spent a lot of time terrified of him . . . I think he was psychotic from the time that he left Georgia to play in the big league."

"Psychotic" is not a word I'd care to use. I

believe that he was far more than the fiercest of all competitors. He was a vindicator who believed that "Father was watching" and who could not put that father's terrible fate out of his mind. The memory of it threatened his sanity.

The fact that he recognized and feared this is revealed in a tape recording he made, in which he describes his own view of himself: "I was like a steel spring with a growing and dangerous flaw in it. If it is wound too tight or has the slightest weak point, the spring will fly apart and then it is done for. . . ."

The last time I saw him, he was sitting in his armchair in the Atherton mansion. The place still was without lights or heat. I shook his hand in farewell, and he held it a moment longer.

"What about it? Do you think they'll remember me?" He tried to say it as if it didn't matter.

"They'll always remember you," I said.

On July 8, I received in the mail a photograph of Ty's mausoleum on the hillside in the Royston cemetery with the words scribbled on the back: *"Any time now."* Nine days later he died in an Atlanta hospital. Before going, he opened the brown bag, piled $1 million in negotiable securities beside his bed and placed the Luger atop them.

From all of major-league baseball, three men and three only appeared for his funeral.

WIDE WORLD

BIG MOMENT

Hope and doubt mix in Chuck Hiller's face as he watches his hit drop in for the first grand-slam homer in National League World Series history (1962).

FREELANCE PHOTOGRAPHERS GUILD

THE OLD...

Above, the old grandstand at the old Polo Grounds in New York. For a close-up of its most famous denizen, John J. McGraw, see photo at right.

WIDE WORLD

WIDE WORLD

THE NEW...

Left, the Astrodome at Houston. Another new park, D.C. Stadium in Washington (below), had a famous fan at its inaugural in 1962. Speaking of Presidents and baseball, turn the page...

WIDE WORLD

This famous Homer C. Davenport drawing depicts the legend that Honest Abe was playing baseball when first informed that he had been nominated for the Presidency. "Tell the gentlemen," Mr. Lincoln is supposed to have said, "they will have to wait a few minutes till I get my turn at bat."

THIS SIXTH-CENTURY experiment, alas, never came off, for the various players were to become caught up in the devastating carnage wrought by Launcelot's love for Guinevere. More's the pity.

From *A Connecticut Yankee in King Arthur's Court*

MARK TWAIN

AT THE END of a month I sent the vessel home for fresh supplies, and for news. We expected her back in three or four days. She would bring me, along with other news, the result of a certain experiment which I had been starting. It was a project of mine to replace the tournament with something which might furnish an escape for the extra steam of the chivalry, keep those bucks entertained and out of mischief, and at the same time preserve the best thing in them, which was their hardy spirit of emulation. I had had a choice band of them in private training for some time, and the date was now arriving for their first public effort.

This experiment was baseball. In order to give the thing vogue from the start, and place it out of the reach of criticism, I chose my nines by rank, not capacity. There wasn't a knight in either team who wasn't a sceptered sovereign. As for material of this sort, there was a glut of it always around Arthur. You couldn't throw a brick in any direction and not cripple a king. Of course, I couldn't get these people to leave off their armor; they wouldn't do that when they bathed. They consented to differentiate the armor so that a body could tell one team from the other, but that was the most they would do. So, one of the teams wore chain-mail ulsters, and the other wore plate armor made of my new Bessemer steel. Their practice in the field was the most fantastic thing I ever saw. Being ball-proof, they never skipped out of the way, but stood still and took the result; when a Bessemer was at the bat and a ball hit him, it would bound a hundred and fifty yards sometimes. And when a man was running, and threw himself on his stomach to slide to his base, it was like an ironclad coming into port. At first I appointed men of no rank to act as umpires, but I had to discontinue that. These people were no easier to please than other nines. The umpire's first decision was usually his last; they broke him in two with a bat, and his friends toted him home on a shutter. When it was noticed that no umpire ever survived a game, umpiring got to be unpopular. So I was obliged to appoint somebody whose rank and lofty position under the government would protect him.

Here are the names of the nines:

BESSEMERS	ULSTERS
KING ARTHUR.	EMPEROR LUCIUS.
KING LOT OF LOTHIAN.	KING LOGRIS.
KING OF NORTHGALIS.	KING MARHALT OF IRELAND.
KING MARSIL.	KING MORGANORE.
KING OF LITTLE BRITAIN.	KING MARK OF CORNWALL.
KING LABOR.	KING NENTRES OF GARLOT.
KING PELLAM OF LISTENGESE.	KING MELIODAS OF LIONES.
KING BAGDEMAGUS.	KING OF THE LAKE.
KING TOLLEME LA FEINTES.	THE SOWDAN OF SYRIA.

Umpire—CLARENCE.

The first public game would certainly draw fifty thousand people; and for solid fun would be worth going around the world to see. Everything would be favorable; it was balmy and beautiful spring weather now, and Nature was all tailored out in her new clothes.

THIS SPLENDID ARTICLE was done by a truly fine writer, John Updike, in the pages of *The New Yorker* following the 1960 season. In the forenote to the Ed Linn piece earlier in this book, we suggested that you read this one by Updike before the one by Linn, and I think if you do it in that order, you will see why. Both pieces report the same event—Ted Williams' last game—and, speaking of the Updike, Herbert Warren Wind has written: "It is easy to picture Williams reading it with enormous pleasure—he read (and remembered) practically everything written about him—and saying to himself as he nodded his head, '*This* fellow has got it right.'" Mr. Linn confirms, in his article, that Williams *did* read—and remember—practically everything written about him. I do not want to guess at the Williams reaction to the Linn piece, and neither, I suspect, will Herbert Warren Wind. But I think the presence of these two stories in the same book gives an authentic added dimension to the event, and one that is rewarding and unique.

Note the agreement between Linn and Updike on the salient features (such as the cap-tipping)—an agreement by no means shared by others who were also there. I wasn't there. I'll have to go with Updike and Linn.

1960: Hub Fans Bid Kid Adieu

JOHN UPDIKE

FENWAY PARK, in Boston, is a lyric little bandbox of a ballpark. Everything is painted green and seems in curiously sharp focus, like the inside of an old-fashioned peeping-type Easter egg. It was built in 1912 and rebuilt in 1934, and offers, as do most Boston artifacts, a compromise between Man's Euclidean determinations and Nature's beguiling irregularities. Its right field is one of the deepest in the American League, while its left field is the shortest; the high left-field wall, 315 feet from home plate along the foul line, virtually thrusts its surface at right-handed hitters. On the afternoon of Wednesday, September 28, as I took a seat behind third base, a uniformed groundkeeper was treading the top of this wall, picking batting-practice home runs out of the screen, like a mushroom gatherer seen in Wordsworthian perspective on the verge of a cliff. The day was overcast, chill, and uninspirational. The Boston team was the worst in twenty-seven seasons. A jangling medley of incompetent youth and aging competence, the Red Sox were finishing in seventh place only because the Kansas City Athletics had locked them out of the cellar. They were scheduled to play the Baltimore Orioles, a much nimbler blend of May and December, who had been dumped from pennant contention a week before by the insatiable Yankees. I, and 10,453 others, had shown up primarily because this was the Red Sox's last home game of the season, and therefore the last time in all eternity that their regular left fielder, known to the headlines as TED, KID, SPLINTER, THUMPER, TW, and, most cloyingly, MISTER WONDERFUL, would play in Boston. "WHAT WILL WE DO WITHOUT TED? HUB FANS ASK" ran the headline on a newspaper being read by a bulb-nosed cigar smoker a few rows away. Williams' retirement had been announced, doubted (he had been threatening retirement for years), confirmed by Tom Yawkey, the Red Sox owner, and at last widely accepted as the sad but probable truth. He was forty-two and had redeemed his abysmal season of 1959 with a—considering his advanced age—fine one. He had been giving away his gloves and bats and had grudgingly consented to a sentimental ceremony today. This was not necessarily his last game; the Red Sox were scheduled to travel to New York and wind up the season with three games there.

I arrived early. The Orioles were hitting fungoes on the field. The day before, they had spitefully smothered the Red Sox, 17–4, and neither their faces nor their drab gray visiting-team uniforms seemed very gracious. I wondered who had invited them to the party. Between our heads and the lowering clouds a frenzied organ was thundering through, with an appositeness perhaps accidental, "You *maaaade* me love you, I didn't wanna do it, I didn't wanna do it . . ."

The affair between Boston and Ted Williams has been no mere summer romance; it has been a marriage, composed of spats, mutual disappointments, and, toward the end, a mellowing hoard of shared memories. It falls into three stages, which may be termed Youth, Maturity, and Age; or Thesis, Antithesis, and Synthesis; or Jason, Achilles, and Nestor.

First, there was the by now legendary epoch when the young bridegroom came out of the West, announced, "All I want out of life is that when I walk down the street folks will say, 'There goes the greatest hitter who ever lived.'" The dowagers of local journalism attempted to give elementary deportment lessons to this child who spake as a god, and to their horror were themselves rebuked. Thus began the long exchange of backbiting, bat-flipping, booing, and spitting that has distinguished Williams' public relations. The spitting incidents of 1957 and 1958 and the similar dockside courtesies that Williams has now and then extended to the grandstand should be judged against this background: the left-field stands at Fenway for twenty years have held a large number of customers who have bought their way in primarily for the privilege of showering abuse on Williams. Greatness necessarily attracts debunkers, but in Williams' case the hostility has been systematic and unappeasable. His basic offense against the fans has been to wish that they weren't there. Seeking a perfectionist's vacuum, he has quixotically desired to sever the game from the ground of paid spectatorship and publicity that supports it. Hence his refusal to tip his cap to the crowd or turn the other cheek to newsmen. It has been a costly theory—it has probably cost him, among other evidences of good will, two Most Valuable Player awards, which are voted by reporters—but he has held to it from his rookie year on. While his critics, oral and literary, remained beyond the reach of his discipline, the opposing pitchers were accessible, and he spanked them to the tune of .406 in 1941. He slumped to .356 in 1942 and went off to war.

In 1946 Williams returned from three years as a Marine pilot to the second of his baseball avatars, that of Achilles, the hero of incomparable prowess and beauty who nevertheless was to be found sulking in his tent while the Trojans (mostly Yankees) fought through to the ships. Yawkey, a timber and mining maharajah, had surrounded his central jewel with many gems of slightly lesser water, such as Bobby Doerr, Dom DiMaggio, Rudy York, Birdie Tebbetts, and Johnny Pesky. Throughout the late forties, the Red Sox were the best paper team in baseball, yet they had little three-dimensional to show for it, and if this was a tragedy, Williams was Hamlet. A succinct review of the indictment—and a fair sample of appreciative sports-page prose—appeared the very day of Williams' valedictory, in a column by Huck Finnegan in the Boston *American* (no sentimentalist, Huck):

> Williams' career, in contrast [to Babe Ruth's], has been a series of failures except for his averages. He flopped in the only World Series he ever played in (1946) when he batted only .200. He flopped in the play-off game with Cleveland in 1948. He flopped in the final game of the 1949 season with the pennant hinging on the outcome (Yanks 5, Sox 3). He flopped in 1950 when he returned to the lineup after a two-month absence and ruined the morale of a club that seemed pennant-bound under Steve O'Neill. It has always been Williams' records first, the team second, and the Sox non-winning record is proof enough of that.

There are answers to all this, of course. The fatal weakness of the great Sox slugging teams was not-quite-good-enough pitching rather than Williams' failure to hit a home run every time he came to bat. Again, Williams' depressing effect on his teammates has never been proved. Despite ample coaching to the contrary, most insisted that they *liked* him. He has been generous with advice to any player who asked for it. In an increasingly combative baseball atmosphere, he continued to duck beanballs docilely. With umpires he was gracious to a fault. This courtesy itself annoyed his critics, whom there was no pleasing. And against the ten crucial games (the seven World Series games with the St. Louis Cardinals, the 1948 play-off with the Cleveland Indians, and the two-game series with the Yankees at the end of the 1949 season, winning either one of which would have given the Red Sox the pennant) that make up the Achilles' heel of Williams' record, a mass of statistics can be set showing that day in and day out he was no slouch in the clutch. The correspondence columns of the Boston papers now and then suffer a sharp flurry of arithmetic on this score; indeed, for Williams to have distributed all his hits so they did nobody else any good would constitute a feat of placement unparalleled in the annals of selfishness.

Whatever residue of truth remains of the Finnegan charge those of us who love Williams must transmute as best we can, in our own personal crucibles. My personal memories of Williams begin when I was a boy in Pennsylvania, with two last-place teams in Philadelphia to keep me company. For me, "W'ms, lf" was a figment of the box scores who always seemed to be going 3-for-5. He radiated, from afar, the hard blue glow of high purpose. I remember listening over the radio to the All-Star Game of 1946, in which Williams hit two singles and two home runs, the second one off a Rip Sewell "blooper" pitch; it was like hitting a balloon out of the park. I remember watching one of his home runs from the bleachers of Shibe Park; it went over the first baseman's head and rose meticulously along a straight line and was still rising when it cleared the fence. The trajectory seemed qualitatively different from anything anyone else might hit. For me, Williams is the classic ballplayer of the game on a hot August weekday, before a small crowd, when the only thing at stake is the tissue-thin difference between a thing done well and a thing done ill. Baseball is a game of the long season, of relentless and gradual averaging-out. Irrelevance—since the reference point of most individual games is remote and statistical—always threatens its interest, which can be maintained not by the occasional heroics that sportswriters feed upon but by players who always *care;* who care, that is to say, about themselves and their art. Insofar as the clutch hitter is not a sportswriter's myth, he is a vulgarity, like a writer who writes only for money. It may be that, compared to managers' dreams such as Joe DiMaggio and the always helpful Stan Musial, Williams is an icy star. But of all team sports, baseball, with its graceful intermittences of action, its immense and tranquil field sparsely settled with poised men in white, its dispassionate mathematics, seems to me best suited to accommodate, and be ornamented by, a loner. It is an essentially lonely game. No other player visible to my generation has concentrated within himself so much of the sport's poignance, has so assiduously refined his natural skills, has so constantly brought to the plate that intensity of competence that crowds the throat with joy.

By the time I went to college, near Boston, the lesser stars Yawkey had assembled around Williams had faded, and his craftsmanship, his rigorous pride, had become itself a kind of heroism. This brittle and temperamental player developed an unexpected quality of persistence. He was always coming back—back from Korea, back from a broken collarbone, a shattered elbow, a bruised heel, back from drastic bouts of flu and ptomaine poisoning. Hardly a season went by without some enfeebling mishap, yet he always came back, and always looked like himself. The delicate mechanism of timing and power seemed locked, shockproof, in some case outside his body. In addition to injuries, there were a heavily publicized divorce, and the usual storms with the press, and the Williams Shift—the maneuver, custom-built by Lou Boudreau, of the Cleveland Indians, whereby three infielders were concentrated on the right side of the infield, where a left-handed pull hitter like Williams generally hits the ball. Williams could easily have learned to punch singles through the vacancy on his left and fattened his average hugely. This was what Ty Cobb, the Einstein of average, told him to do. But the game had changed since Cobb; Williams believed that his value to the club and to the game was as a slugger, so he went on pulling the ball, trying to blast it through three men, and paid the price of perhaps fifteen points of lifetime average. Like Ruth before him, he bought the occasional home run at the cost of many directed singles —a calculated sacrifice certainly not, in the case of a hitter as average-minded as Williams, entirely selfish.

After a prime so harassed and hobbled, Williams was granted by the relenting fates a golden twilight. He became at the end of his career perhaps the best *old* hitter of the century. The dividing line came between the 1956 and the 1957 seasons. In September of the first year, he and Mickey Mantle were contending for the batting championship. Both were hitting around .350, and there was no one else near them. The season ended with a three-game series between the Yankees and the Sox, and, living in New York then, I went up to the Stadium. Williams was slightly shy of the four hundred at-bats needed to qualify; the fear was expressed that the Yankee pitchers would walk him to protect Mantle. Instead, they pitched to him—a wise decision. He looked terrible at the plate, tired and discouraged and unconvincing. He never looked very good to me in the Stadium. (Last week, in *Life*, Williams, a sportswriter himself now, wrote gloomily of the Stadium, "There's the bigness of it. There are those high stands and all those people smoking—and, of course, the shadows. . . . It takes at least one Series to get accustomed to the Stadium and even then you're not sure.") The final outcome in 1956 was Mantle .353, Williams .345.

The next year, I moved from New York to New England, and it made all the difference. For in September of 1957, in the same situation, the story was reversed. Mantle finally hit .365; it was the best season of his career. But Williams, though sick and old, had run away from him. A bout of flu had laid him low in September. He emerged from his cave in the Hotel Somerset haggard but irresistible; he hit four successive pinch-hit home runs. "I feel terrible," he confessed, "but every time I take a swing at the ball it goes out of the park." He ended the season with thirty-eight home runs and an average of .388, the highest in either league since his own .406, and, coming from a decrepit man of thirty-nine, an even more supernal figure. With eight or so of the "leg hits" that a younger man would have beaten out, it would have been .400. And the next year, Williams, who in 1949 and 1953 had lost batting championships by decimal whiskers to George Kell and Mickey Vernon, sneaked in behind his teammate Pete Runnels and filched his sixth title, a bargain at .328.

In 1959, it seemed all over. The dinosaur thrashed around in the .200 swamp for the first half of the season, and was even benched ("rested," manager Mike Higgins tactfully said). Old foes like the late Bill Cunningham began to offer batting tips. Cunningham thought Williams was jiggling his elbows; in truth, Williams' neck was so stiff he could hardly turn his head to look at the pitcher. When he swung, it looked like a Calder mobile with one thread cut; it reminded you that since 1953 Williams' shoulders had been wired together. A solicitous pall settled over the sports pages. In the two decades since Williams had come to Boston, his status had imperceptibly shifted from that of a naughty prodigy to that of a municipal monument. As his shadow in the record books lengthened, the Red Sox teams around him declined, and the entire American League seemed to be losing life and color to the National. The inconsistency of the new superstars—Mantle, Colavito, and Kaline—served to make Williams appear all the more singular. And off the field, his private philanthropy—in particular, his zealous chairmanship of the Jimmy Fund, a charity for children with cancer—gave him a civic presence somewhat like that of Richard Cardinal Cushing. In religion, Williams appears to be a humanist, and a selective one at that, but he and the Cardinal, when their good works intersect and they appear in the public eye together, make a handsome and heartening pair.

Humiliated by his '59 season, Williams determined, once more, to come back. I, as a specimen Williams partisan, was both glad and fearful. All baseball fans believe in miracles; the question is, how *many* do you believe in? He looked like a ghost in spring training. Manager Jurges warned us ahead of time that if Williams didn't come through he would be benched, just like anybody else. As it turned out, it was Jurges who was benched. Williams entered the 1960 season needing eight home runs to have a lifetime total of 500; after one time at bat in Washington, he needed seven. For a stretch, he was hitting a home run every second game that he played. He passed Lou Gehrig's lifetime total, then the number 500, then Mel Ott's total, and finished with 521, thirteen behind Jimmy Foxx, who alone stands between Williams and Babe Ruth's unapproachable 714. The summer was a statistician's picnic. His two-thousandth walk came and went, his eighteen-hundredth run batted in, his sixteenth All-Star Game. At one point, he hit a home run off a pitcher, Don Lee, off whose father, Thornton Lee, he had hit a home run a generation before. The only comparable season for a forty-two-year-old man was Ty Cobb's in 1928. Cobb batted .323 and hit one homer. Williams batted .316 but hit twenty-nine homers.

In sum, though generally conceded to be the greatest hitter of his era, he did not establish himself as "the greatest hitter who ever lived." Cobb, for average, and Ruth, for power, remain supreme. Cobb, Rogers Hornsby, Joe Jackson, and Lefty O'Doul, among players since 1900, have higher lifetime averages than Williams' .344. Unlike Foxx, Gehrig, Hack Wilson, Hank Greenberg, and Ralph Kiner, Williams never came close to matching Babe Ruth's season home-run total of sixty. In the list of major-league batting records, not one is held by Williams. He is second in walks drawn, third in home runs, fifth in lifetime averages, sixth in runs batted in, eighth in runs scored and in total bases, fourteenth in doubles, and thirtieth in hits. But if we allow him merely average seasons for the four-plus seasons he lost to two wars, and add another season for the months he lost to injuries, we get a man who in all the power totals would be second, and not a very distant second, to Ruth. And if we further allow that these years would have been not merely average but prime years, if we allow for all the months when Williams was playing in sub-par condition, if we permit his early and later years in baseball to be some sort of index of what the middle years could have been, if we give him a right-field fence that is not, like Fenway's, one of the most distant in the league, and if—the least excusable "if"—we imagine him condescending to outsmart the Williams Shift, we can defensibly assemble, like a colossus induced from the sizable fragments that do remain, a statistical figure not incommensurate with his grandiose ambition. From the statistics that are on the books, a good case can be made that in the *combination* of power and average Williams is first; nobody else ranks so high in both categories. Finally, there is the witness of the eyes; men whose memories go back to Shoeless Joe Jackson—another unlucky natural—rank him and Williams together as the best-looking hitters they have seen. It was for our last look that ten thousand of us had come.

Two girls, one of them with pert buckteeth and eyes as black as vest buttons, the other with white skin and flesh-colored hair, like an underdeveloped photograph of a redhead, came and sat on my right. On my other side was one of those frowning, chestless young-old men who can frequently be seen, often wearing sailor hats, attending ball games alone. He did not once open his program but instead tapped it, rolled up, on his knee as he gave the game his disconsolate attention. A young lady, with freckles and a depressed, dainty nose that by an optical illusion seemed to thrust her lips forward for a kiss, sauntered down into the box seats and with striking aplomb took a seat right behind the roof of the Oriole dugout. She wore a blue coat with a Northeastern University emblem sewed to it. The girls beside me took it into their heads that this was Williams' daughter. She looked too old to me, and why would she be sitting behind the visitors' dugout? On the other hand, from the way she sat there, staring at the sky and French-inhaling, she clearly was *some*body. Other fans came and eclipsed her from view. The crowd looked less like a weekday ball-park crowd than like the folks you might find in Yellowstone National Park, or emerging from automobiles at the top of scenic Mount Mansfield. There were a lot of competitively well-dressed couples of tourist age, and not a few babes in arms. A row of five seats in front of me was abruptly filled with a woman and four children, the youngest of them two years old, if that. Someday, presumably, he could tell his grandchildren that he saw Williams play. Along with these tots and second-honeymooners, there were Harvard freshmen, giving off that peculiar nervous glow created when a quantity of insouciance is saturated with insecurity; thick-necked Army officers with brass on their shoulders and lead in their voices; pepperings of priests; perfumed bouquets of Roxbury Fabian fans; shiny salesmen from Albany and Fall River; and those gray, hoarse men—taxi drivers, slaughterers, and bartenders—who will continue to click through the turnstiles long after everyone else has deserted to television and tramporamas. Behind me, two young male voices blossomed, cracking a joke about God's five proofs that Thomas Aquinas exists—typical Boston College levity.

The batting cage was trundled away. The Orioles fluttered to the sidelines. Diagonally across the field, by the Red Sox dugout, a cluster of men in overcoats were festering like maggots. I could see a splinter of white uniform, and Williams' head, held at a self-deprecating and evasive tilt. Williams' conversational stance is that of a six-foot-three-inch man under a six-foot ceiling. He moved away to the patter of flash bulbs, and began playing catch with a young Negro outfielder named Willie Tasby. His arm, never very powerful, had grown lax with the years, and his throwing motion was a kind of muscular drawl. To catch the ball, he flicked his glove onto his left shoulder (he batted left but threw right, as every schoolboy ought to know) and let the ball plop into it comically. This catch session with Tasby was the only time all afternoon I saw him grin.

A tight little flock of human sparrows who, from the lambent and pampered pink of their faces, could only have been Boston politicians moved toward the plate. The loudspeakers mammothly coughed as someone huffed on the microphone. The ceremonies began. Curt Gowdy, the Red Sox radio and television announcer, who sounds like everybody's brother-in-law, delivered a brief sermon, taking the two words "pride" and "champion" as his text. It began, "Twenty-one years ago, a skinny kid from San Diego, California . . ." and ended, "I don't think we'll ever see another like him." Robert Tibolt, chairman of the board of the Greater Boston Chamber of Commerce, presented Williams with a big Paul Revere silver bowl. Harry Carlson, a member of the sports committee of the Boston Chamber, gave him a plaque, whose inscription he did not read in its entirety, out of deference to Williams' distaste for this sort of fuss. Mayor Collins presented the Jimmy Fund with a thousand-dollar check.

Then the occasion himself stooped to the microphone, and his voice sounded, after the others, very Californian; it seemed to be coming, excellently amplified, from a great distance, adolescently young and as smooth as a butternut. His thanks for the gifts had not died from our ears before he glided, as if helplessly, into "In spite of all the terrible things that have been said about me by the maestros of the keyboard up there . . ." He glanced up at the press rows suspended above home plate. (All the Boston reporters, incidentally, reported the phrase as "knights of the keyboard," but I heard it as "maestros" and prefer it that way.) The crowd tittered, appalled. A frightful vision flashed upon me, of the press gallery pelting Williams with erasers, of Williams clambering up the foul screen to slug journalists, of a riot, of Mayor Collins being crushed. ". . . And they *were* terrible things," Williams insisted, with level melancholy, into the mike. "I'd like to forget them, but I can't." He paused, swallowed his memories, and went on, "I want to say that my years in Boston have been the greatest thing in my life." The crowd, like an immense sail going limp in a change of wind, sighed with relief. Taking all the parts himself, Williams then acted out a vivacious little morality drama in which an imaginary tempter came to him at the beginning of his career and said, "Ted, you can play anywhere you like." Leaping nimbly into the role of his younger self (who in biographical actuality had yearned to be a Yankee), Williams gallantly chose Boston over all the other cities, and told us that Tom Yawkey was the greatest owner in baseball and we were the greatest fans. We applauded ourselves heartily. The umpire came out and dusted the plate. The voice of doom announced over the loudspeakers that after Williams' retirement his uniform number, 9, would be permanently retired—the first time the Red Sox had so honored a player. We cheered. The national anthem was played. We cheered. The game began.

Williams was third in the batting order, so he came up in the bottom of the first inning, and Steve Barber, a young pitcher who was not yet born when Williams began playing for the Red Sox, offered him four pitches, at all of which he disdained to swing, since none of them were within the strike zone. This demonstrated simultaneously that Williams' eyes were razor-sharp and that Barber's control wasn't. Shortly, the bases were full, with Williams on second. "Oh, I hope he gets held up at third! That would be wonderful," the girl beside me moaned, and, sure enough, the man at bat walked and Williams was delivered into our foreground. He struck the pose of Donatello's David, the third-base bag being Goliath's head. Fiddling with his cap, swapping small talk with the Oriole third baseman (who seemed delighted to have him drop in), swinging his arms with a sort of prancing nervousness, he looked fine—flexible, hard, and not unbecomingly substantial through the middle. The long neck, the small head, the knickers whose cuffs were worn down near his ankles—all these points, often observed by caricaturists, were visible in the flesh.

One of the collegiate voices behind me said, "He looks old, doesn't he, old; big deep wrinkles in his face . . ."

"Yeah," the other voice said, "but he looks like an old hawk, doesn't he?"

With each pitch, Williams danced down the base line, waving his arms and stirring dust, ponderous but menacing, like an attacking goose. It occurred to about a dozen humorists at once to shout, "Steal home! Go, go!" Williams' speed afoot was never legendary. Lou Clinton, a young Sox outfielder, hit a fairly deep fly to center field. Williams tagged up and ran home. As he slid across the plate, the ball, thrown with unusual heft by Jackie Brandt, the Oriole center fielder, hit him on the back.

"Boy, he was really loafing, wasn't he?" one of the boys behind me said.

"It's cold," the other explained. "He doesn't play well when it's cold. He likes heat. He's a hedonist."

The run that Williams scored was the second and last of the inning. Gus Triandos, of the Orioles, quickly evened the score by plunking a home run over the handy left-field wall. Williams, who had had this wall at his back for twenty years, played the ball flawlessly. He didn't budge. He just stood there, in the center of the little patch of grass that his patient footsteps had worn brown, and, limp with lack of interest, watched the ball pass overhead. It was not a very interesting game. Mike Higgins, the Red Sox manager, with nothing to lose, had restricted his major-league players to the left-field line—along with Williams, Frank Malzone, a first-rate third baseman, played the game—and had peopled the rest of the terrain with unpredictable youngsters fresh, or not so fresh, off the farms. Other than Williams' recurrent appearances at the plate, the *maladresse* of the Sox infield was the sole focus of suspense; the second baseman turned every grounder into a juggling act, while the shortstop did a breathtaking impersonation of an open window. With this sort of assistance, the Orioles wheedled their way into a 4–2 lead. They had early replaced Barber with another young pitcher, Jack Fisher. Fortunately (as it turned out), Fisher is no cutie; he is willing to burn the ball through the strike zone, and inning after inning this tactic punctured Higgins' string of test balloons.

Whenever Williams appeared at the plate—pounding the dirt from his cleats, gouging a pit in the batter's box with his left foot, wringing resin out of the bat handle with his vehement grip, switching the stick at the pitcher with an electric ferocity—it was like having a familiar Leonardo appear in a shuffle of *Saturday Evening Post* covers. This man, you realized—and here, perhaps, was the difference, greater than the difference in gifts—really intended to hit the ball. In the third inning, he hoisted a high fly to deep center. In the fifth, we thought he had it; he smacked the ball hard and high into the heart of his power zone, but the deep right field in Fenway and the heavy air and a casual east wind defeated him. The ball died. Al Pilarcik leaned his back against the big "380" painted on the right-field wall and caught it. On another day, in another park, it would have been gone. (After the game, Williams said, "I didn't think I could hit one any harder than that. The conditions weren't good.")

The afternoon grew so glowering that in the sixth inning the arc lights were turned on—always a wan sight in the daytime, like the burning headlights of a funeral procession. Aided by the gloom, Fisher was slicing through the Sox rookies, and Williams did not come to bat in the seventh. He was second up in the eighth. This was almost certainly his last time to come to the plate in Fenway Park, and instead of merely cheering, as we had at his three previous appearances, we stood, all of us—stood and applauded. Have you ever heard applause in a ball park? Just applause—no calling, no whistling, just an ocean of handclaps, minute after minute, burst after burst, crowding and running together in continuous succession like the pushes of surf at the edge of the sand. It was a somber and considered tumult. There was not a boo in it. It seemed to renew itself out of a shifting set of memories as the kid, the Marine, the veteran of feuds and failures and injuries, the friend of children, and the enduring old pro evolved down the bright tunnel of twenty-one summers toward this moment. At last, the umpire signaled for Fisher to pitch; with the other players, he had been frozen in position. Only Williams had moved during the ovation, switching his bat impatiently, ignoring everything except his cherished task. Fisher wound up, and the applause sank into a hush.

Understand that we were a crowd of rational people. We knew that a home run cannot be produced at will; the right pitch must be perfectly met and luck must ride with the ball. Three innings before, we had seen a brave effort fail. The air was soggy; the season was exhausted. Nevertheless, there will always lurk, around a corner in a pocket of our knowledge of the odds, an indefensible hope, and this was one of the times, which you now and then find in sports, when a density of expectation hangs in the air and plucks an event out of the future.

Fisher, after his unsettling wait, was wide with the first pitch. He put the second one over, and Williams swung mightily and missed. The crowd grunted, seeing that classic swing, so long and smooth and quick, exposed, naked in its failure. Fisher threw the third time, Williams swung again, and there it was. The ball climbed on a diagonal line into the vast volume of air over center field. From my angle, behind third base, the ball seemed less an object in flight than the tip of a towering, motionless construct, like the Eiffel Tower or the Tappan Zee Bridge. It was in the books while it was still in the sky. Brandt ran back to the deepest corner of the outfield grass; the ball descended beyond his reach and struck in the crotch where the bullpen met the wall, bounced chunkily, and, as far as I could see, vanished.

Like a feather caught in a vortex, Williams ran around the square of bases at the center of our beseeching screaming. He ran as he always ran out home runs—hurriedly, unsmiling, head down, as if our praise were a storm of rain to get out of. He didn't tip his cap. Though we thumped, wept, and chanted, "We want Ted," for minutes after he hid in the dugout, he did not come back. Our noise for some seconds passed beyond excitement into a kind of immense open anguish, a wailing, a cry to be saved. But immortality is nontransferable. The papers said that the other players, and even the umpires on the field, begged him to come out and acknowledge us in some way, but he never had and did not now. Gods do not answer letters.

Every true story has an anticlimax. The men on the field refused to disappear, as would have seemed decent, in the smoke of Williams' miracle. Fisher continued to pitch, and escaped further harm. At the end of the inning, Higgins sent Williams out to his left-field position, then instantly replaced him with Carrol Hardy, so we had a long last look at Williams as he ran out there and then back, his uniform jogging, his eyes steadfast on the ground. It was nice, and we were grateful, but it left a funny taste.

One of the scholasticists behind me said, "Let's go. We've seen everything. I don't want to spoil it." This seemed a sound aesthetic decision. Williams' last word had been so exquisitely chosen, such a perfect fusion of expectation, intention, and execution, that already it felt a little unreal in my head, and I wanted to get out before the castle collapsed. But the game, though played by clumsy midgets under the feeble glow of the arc lights, began to tug at my attention, and I loitered in the runway until it was over. Williams' homer had, quite incidentally, made the score 4–3. In the bottom of the ninth inning, with one out, Marlin Coughtry, the second-base juggler, singled. Vic Wertz, pinch-hitting, doubled off the left-field wall, Coughtry advancing to third. Pumpsie Green walked to load the bases. Willie Tasby hit a double-play ball to the third baseman, but in making the pivot throw Billy Klaus, an ex-Red Sox infielder, reverted to form and threw the ball past the first baseman and into the Red Sox dugout. The Sox won, 5–4. On the car radio as I drove home I heard that Williams had decided not to accompany the team to New York. So he knew how to do even that, the hardest thing. Quit.

A FAMOUS WRITER of baseball fiction early in this century, Charles Van Loan had a message to tell with this one: Neither a borrower nor a lender be, for loan oft loses both itself and friend, and borrowing dulls the edge of the fast ball.

I O U

CHARLES E. VAN LOAN

BELIEVE ME or not, it wasn't the seventy-five fish that hurt. I have often been touched for that much money without bleeding internally, and if I have luck I expect to be touched for a lot more. I have had enough bees put on me to stock an apiary; one stinging more or less is nothing whatever in my young life, but I liked Dudley W. Fowler—liked him a whole lot; and it was finding out that Dudley wasn't real folks that hurt me. He was welcome to the money, but I hated to change my opinion of him. Did you ever feel that way about a fellow?

Then, again, I owed Dudley something; the town of Brownsville owed him something; and, though his method of collecting wasn't exactly what it should have been, we were disposed to let him get away with it, until—but that's the story.

Brownsville has always been baseball-crazy. We have never had a league of our own to cheer for; so we have adopted the whole bunch, majors and minors. Every time a World Series comes along there is a riot outside the office of the *Sentinel*, with arguments and fist fights, and everything that they have in New York and Chicago. We read the sporting papers, and we feel as much interest in the big fellows as if we lived in their towns and saw their games.

In the fall of 1912 we were pretty well stirred up over the approaching World Series between the Red Sox and the Giants. One afternoon late in September, when we were figuring what McGraw ought to do to win, Archie McNutt came rolling in from Pleasanton.

Pleasanton is the cool summer nest of the idle rich, north of here, in the mountains. It hasn't a daily paper or a Chamber of Commerce, but it has nine garages and two country clubs, and golf is about as far as Pleasanton goes in the sporting line. Archie McNutt is one of their leading citizens, on the links and elsewhere, and he hasn't been entirely spoiled by the money his father left him.

He listened to our conversation for a while, humped down behind the wheel of a long, narrow roadster, and then he said he didn't see how we could milk so much excitement off the end of a telegraph wire.

"I would rather," says he, "watch two scrub teams battling on a sandlot for a keg of beer than read the returns on the hottest World Series ever staged. . . . Why don't you organize a team of your own and have something to get excited about?"

"Oh, we got plenty of players," says Harley Freeman, "but they ain't any teams to play with, 'less we go outside the county."

"Is that so?" says Archie. "I'll get up a team and go against you."

"You forget we ain't got any golf clubs," says Old Man Sherwood. Archie overlooked the sarcasm.

"Tell you what let's do," says he: "Let's have a little World Series of our own, the first team winning four games to claim the championship of the county. Donate the gate receipts to charity."

"Hold on!" says I. "If Pleasanton wins, you can do anything you like with the gate receipts. If we win, the boys can split up the dough. They ain't squeamish about their amateur standings."

"Any way you like," says Archie. "All I

want is two weeks' time to get my men in shape."

They voted me the manager of the Brownsville team, with authority to go ahead and get one together. Jack Jamieson helped me a lot. He was in the American Association for two years before he decided to quit baseball and go into business. He was still a cracking good man behind the bat, though not so fast on his feet as he used to be. Jack looked over the volunteers for the different positions and picked the best of the talent that offered. We had outfielders galore, and infielders all over the place, but we seemed to be up against it for first-class pitching. Plenty of the Brownsville boys thought they could pitch, when all they had was a roundhouse curve or a fast straight ball. Jack tried out all the candidates before he made a report.

"I guess we'll have to take Charlie Nobles," says he. "He's got more than any of the others, which ain't saying a whole lot; but he may be able to put it over on a team of reformed golf players."

The first game of the championship series was played on our home grounds and was a painful surprise to Brownsville. Archie McNutt pulled a lot of rah-rah boys on us, including a young pitcher that would have been trying out with Detroit if his dad hadn't owned an automobile factory. This pitcher's name was Sassman; he was wrynecked and knock-kneed and left-handed, and he pitched baseball as hard as if he depended on it for his daily bread. We only got two runs off him, while the Pleasanton boys were walloping Charlie Nobles all over Recreation Park. The final score was eleven to two, which made us feel pretty sick.

That night Jack came over to my place—the De Luxe Billiard and Pool Parlors—and we held a council of war in the private office.

"Nothing to it!" says he. "Nobles ain't good enough for these college athletes. All he's got is a groover, and they laid for it and murdered it. If we don't pick up a real pitcher somewhere they'll take four straight from us."

Well, that wasn't any news to me; but where were we going to get this twirler? I didn't know; Jack didn't know—and just then there was a knock at the door and in walked Dudley W. Fowler. He was a tall, slim, good-looking chap in those days, not more than twenty-three or twenty-four, with the nerve of a burglar and a smile that warmed you in spite of yourself.

"Ah, gentlemen," says he, taking off his hat, "something tells me that I'm the man you're looking for."

"What told you we would be looking for anybody?" asks Jack, short and snappy.

"My friend," says Dudley, "it was the same thing that told me you've been some catcher in your time. I never laid eyes on you before this afternoon, but I know a real ballplayer when I see one. You loomed up in that company—believe me!"

"Well?" says Jack. "What of it?"

"If you had a pitcher to work with you," says Dudley, "you could beat these dudes from Pleasanton. A good curve ball would make suckers of 'em."

"Well?" says Jack.

"Oh, nothing," says Dudley, "only I've got a good curve ball—among other things. I hate to talk about myself," says he, reaching into his inside pocket, "but you might glance over these newspaper clippings. Fowler, that's me—Dudley W. Fowler. I could use a job in my business right now, and you could use a winning pitcher. How about it?"

"Sit down," says Jack, "till I look these over."

That was how Dudley W. Fowler came to Brownsville.

II

The newspaper clippings said that Dudley was a considerable pitcher, and they didn't give him any the best of it at that. Jack took him out to the park the first thing in the morning to see what he had in stock, and by eleven o'clock the old boy was back again, all lathered up with good news and enthusiasm.

"He's a wiz!" says Jack to me. "Got everything a pitcher ought to have—a grand curve ball, a swell fast one with a hop on it, and control till you can't rest. Darned if I can figure how he's managed to keep out of the big leagues with all that stuff. I'm going to cover a bunch of that Pleasanton money they were shoving under our noses yesterday—that's how good I think he is!"

The schedule called for two games a week—Tuesdays and Saturdays—alternating between the towns. The second game was played in Pleasanton, and the automobile crowd unbelted their idle bank rolls and bet us to a standstill, giving us odds of seven to five. That was because they saw poor old Nobles out there, pretending to warm up. I left Charlie on exhibition until Harley Freeman flashed me the signal that all our money was down;

and then Nobles came back to the bench and Dudley went out to unlimber a few. A chill came over the aristocrats as they watched the stranger warm up. They seemed to feel that we had taken a mean advantage of them. Archie, who was playing second base for his team, tried to start an argument.

"Of course," says he, "nothing was said about barring professionals, but we understood this was to be confined to the townspeople."

"Yes," says I; "and, of course, it ain't any crime to spring a crack college battery on us, is it? This knock-kneed pitcher of yours turned down some big-league offers. Want something soft?"

"But you had Nobles warming up."

"Well, what of it? Since when has a manager had to pitch a man just because he warms him up?"

"It's sharp practice," says Archie.

"But it's going to sharpen the competition a whole lot," says I. "This won't be any eleven-to-two slaughter—take it from me!"

It wasn't. Young Mr. Sassman straightened out his wry neck and pitched all the ball he knew how, which was a lot, but the team behind him was about as much help as a sore thumb. They fielded well enough, but they couldn't do a thing with Dudley. His curve ball had them all guessing; and when they thought they had solved it he switched to his fast one and kept the ball high up and too close for comfort. Early in the game old Jack got hold of the pill with the bases full, and the three runs he drove home were the only ones scored in the contest.

That night there was a celebration in Brownsville, with Dudley W. Fowler the guest of honor. Another youngster might have puffed up a bit under all the kind words and compliments, but he only grinned in a modest way and handed a lot of credit to Jack Jamieson. He said a man couldn't help but pitch winning ball to such a catcher; and naturally this made a big hit with our folks, and didn't hurt Jack's feelings any, either.

Late that night Dudley showed up at the poolroom and went into the private office. When I opened the door he was sitting at the table with his head in his hands.

"What's the matter?" says I. "Sick?"

"No," says he, looking up and sighing. "No. Just worried—that's all. Don't you care. It ain't any of your trouble."

"What's on your mind, son?"

"Nothing much," says he, and sighs again.

"You'd better tell me about it. Maybe I can help you."

"Thank you just the same. It's mighty fine of you, but—I'll get through somehow. I can ask my folks to wait a few days."

"Ask 'em to wait for what?"

He lit a cigarette and began to walk up and down the room.

"Well, you see," says he, "it's like this: My old man is in the hospital out in Denver, and he's got to have an operation. My sister wrote me about it last week, and I sent her all the dough I had—all I could spare, anyway—and I thought they could get along on that until I could pick up some more. It seems it wasn't enough. Now you've guaranteed me two hundred dollars if we win this series, and you've told me I won't lose anything even if we get beat; but we won't know for two weeks how we come out——"

"Don't let that worry you for a minute!" says I, reaching into my pocket. "I won quite a little chunk on the game today, and you're welcome to any part of it."

"Thank you just the same," says he, "but I'd rather not borrow. I have a kind of a dread of getting into debt. Maybe I can struggle through some other way—hock my watch, or something."

"Rats!" says I, pulling out my roll. "How much?"

"You're an awful good guy!" says Dudley. "Got a heart like an ox, and—well, if you insist, say seventy-five. It's a life-saver to me—that's what it is—and I'll slip it to you after the series is over."

"Then or any other time is all the same to me. You're as welcome as the flowers in spring."

And I wouldn't have said it if I hadn't meant it. He could have tacked a century onto that seventy-five just as well as not.

"I'll give you my I O U," says he, fishing out an envelope and a pencil.

"Oh, never mind that! Forget it!"

"I don't want to forget it," says he, writing on the back of the envelope. "There! 'I O U seventy-five dollars. Dudley W. Fowler. September, 1912.' That's just the same as a promissory note, ain't it?" He signed his name with a lot of curlicues and flourishes, and handed the envelope to me. "Keep that as a record," says he, pouching the seventy-five fish like a hungry pelican. "Gee, you don't know what a load that takes off my mind! There's only one thing tougher than being broke, and that's having to let people know about it. The folks here have treated me so well that I'd kind of hate to have them find out that I—I—" He stopped and looked at me.

"I ain't going to tell anybody," says I. "This is a private matter—between us two."

"You are a good guy!" says he, dropping his arm across my shoulders. "I guess I'm sensitive, because I've never had to do this before."

"When you've borrowed as much money as I have," I says, "you won't think any more of it than you do of taking a drink of water. . . . What did you say ailed your old man?"

To cut our own little World Series to a composite box score, Dudley pitched four games for us and won them all. Archie McNutt said he'd rather lose with a team of gentlemen than import any muckers, and he had his wish. Sassman stuck to the hitter end and took his trimmings like a little man, and Dudley became more and more of an idol in Brownsville.

The last game was played on our grounds; and that night Old Man Sherwood gave the boys a banquet at the Palace Hotel and allowed several of the fans to buy in at two dollars a plate. Old Man Sherwood runs the hotel; and, as he served the regular seventy-five cent dinner to the banqueters, he didn't lose anything by letting the players in free.

Jack Jamieson and I had a little confidential talk before we went over to the hotel. We had just finished figuring up the total gate receipts. They ran almost double what we had counted on.

"Let's see: We promised Fowler two hundred in case we won?" says Jack.

"That was the agreement—yes."

"And he won the series single-handed, you might say. What's the matter with showing our appreciation in the shape of a cash bonus? We've all won money on the side, betting on the games."

The proposition sounded good to me on account of my liking Dudley so well; so we put three hundred dollars in an envelope and took it over to the hotel—the two hundred we owed the boy and another hundred as a bonus. Jack was for having Old Man Sherwood present the dough after making a speech, but I vetoed the suggestion.

"Old Man Sherwood always gets balled up when he makes a speech," says I, "and rings in Gettysburg and the Battle of the Wilderness. Chances are he'd want to count the money out on the table before everybody, and make Dudley feel like a pauper. I'll pass him the envelope on the strict QT, and tell him there's a little something extra in it to show our appreciation."

The banquet, outside of the food, was a great success; and everybody made speeches. Even Jack Jamieson said a few words, to the effect that he had seen 'em come and he had seen 'em go, and that he had caught some pretty fair pitchers in his day, but never one like little old Dud, who was there a million, besides being the best of good fellers, and ought to be pitching for Mack or McGraw instead of wasting his time in the bushes.

We finally got Dudley on his feet; but he couldn't say much, except that he had done his best, and that wherever he went or whatever happened to him he should always remember Brownsville and the best crowd of real, true sports in the world—which, we took it, was us. When it was all over I took Dudley aside and slipped him the envelope.

"Here's what we agreed to give you," says I, "and a little present from the boys, on the side."

Now an ordinary roughneck ballplayer would have counted his dough then and there, to see how much that little present amounted to; but Dudley handled all money matters with delicacy and taste. He stuffed the envelope into his pocket without even looking at it, and kind of choked up.

"I'll bet you told 'em to do it," says he, putting his arm across my shoulders. "You are a good guy! You knew how much I needed it, didn't you?"

"Yes; but Jamieson didn't," says I, "and he was the one who suggested it."

Now if you'll believe me—and what's the use of your reading this little piece unless you do?—I never once thought of that I O U in my pocket; and if I had thought of it I wouldn't have fished it out for the world. It might have hurt his feelings—given him the idea that I was Johnny-on-the-spot—like a bill collector on Saturday night—on hand when I knew he had the coin, and taking no chances. I wouldn't choose him to think I was that kind of a man.

About noon the next day Old Man Sherwood came toddling into my place, all excited and breathless.

"He's gone!" says he.

"Gone? Who's gone?" says I.

"Why, young Fowler—Dudley."

"No!"

"Yes, I tell you: yes! I didn't disturb him for breakfast, knowin' he was up late last night; but at eleven o'clock I give him a bell or two. He didn't answer—and good reason why! He wasn't there. Bed hadn't been slept in nor nothin'! The station agent saw him hop onto the through Western Express at three this mornin'—"

"And you're worried about his bill?" says I.

"Hell, no!" says Old Man Sherwood. "I was goin' to make him a complimentary guest anyway, 'count of winnin' some money on his pitchin'. Been a long time since I took such a shine to a youngster. Doggone it, I liked him, Bill, and I'm sorry he didn't say good-bye—that's all."

"You've got nothing on me," says I. "He likely had his reasons for ducking out in a hurry. He'll write, or telegraph or something; see if he doesn't."

I got my letter the next day, mailed from the train. Dudley said he was sorry he had to leave in such a hurry, on account of starting west to see how his father was making it; and as for that little business matter he would take care of it as soon as convenient. The letter was signed: "Yours affectionately."

Well, that was all right. Seventy-five one way or the other wouldn't make or break me; the boy was welcome to it as long as he needed it. Jack Jamieson got a note from him too; and so did Harley Freeman, and Old Man Sherwood, and some of the others.

Evidently Dudley didn't find it convenient to take care of the little business matter, because he didn't write again. I supposed it was on account of his not being able to do much pitching in the wintertime, and let it go at that.

The weeks slipped into months and gradually we forgot him—out of sight, out of mind, like the saying goes. Whenever I opened up my pocketbook the I O U would remind me of him, and I'd wonder where he was and how he was making it. I had confidence in Dudley, and I didn't count that seventy-five as gone entirely. I expected to hear from him some day—when it was convenient.

We all got news of him the next spring—news that tore up the town of Brownsville like a forty-two-centimeter shell. We found it in the weekly sporting papers—a paragraph saying that the Orphans had picked up a promising recruit pitcher in the person of one Dudley W. Fowler, a semiprofessional star of the first magnitude. That was all it said, but it was enough to set us running round in circles and throwing our hats in the air.

We were just as proud of Dudley as if he had been born and raised in Brownsville, and it tickled us to think that, after all these years, we were going to have a real big-league representative—someone in whom we could feel a personal interest. We wouldn't have to take a back seat any more when the cigar drummers told us how well they knew Ty Cobb and Christy Mathewson. We could lay back and wait for an opening in the conversation, and then spring it, sort of casual-like:

"Speaking of pitchers, when Dud Fowler was on our team—"

Before we saw that paragraph in the paper we had never been able to crank up much interest in the Orphans, the general opinion being that they were just in there to round out an eight-club circuit and didn't amount to much, anyhow; but it was remarkable how sentiment changed overnight. We hadn't been able to see the Orphans as a pennant possibility, but now we couldn't see anything else; we knew that all they needed to put them in the running was one more good right-hander like Dudley. We forgot all about the Giants and the Cubs and the Pirates, and became Orphan fans through and through—we might have been a suburb of their home town, the way we carried on.

We subscribed to a lot of newspapers, so we could get full reports from their training camp, and not a word about Fowler escaped us. They were mostly good words too—they usually are before the season opens—and when the reporters spoke of him as a comer and praised his curve ball, we were as delighted as if they had said something complimentary about us.

I wrote Dudley a letter—a long one, telling him all the news of the gang, and how glad we were that he had made the grade and got in where he belonged; but he never answered it. It was mailed about the time the Orphans broke up their training camp and started north; so I figured it might not have been forwarded properly.

When the season opened we could hardly wait for Dudley to pitch his first game. Seeing that there was so much interest, the editor of the *Sentinel* arranged to get a telegraphic bulletin on the Orphan games, inning by inning, with the batteries; and the first time Dudley's name went up on the board the whole town closed up to watch the returns.

"Hey! Come on over to the *Sentinel* office. He's goin' to pitch!"

That was the word which rallied the Brownsville fans to a man. The Orphans were playing at the Polo Grounds, and Dudley was up against big Jeff Tesreau and the Giants; but that didn't make any difference to us. We stood there in the street and rooted for him while the ciphers kept going up, and when the Orphans scored three runs in the seventh inning I'll bet they could have heard us in Pleasanton.

The Giants got to Dudley for a run in the eighth, but that was all; and there was a hot time in Brownsville that night—believe me! We sent Dudley a telegram congratulating him and telling him to keep up the good work; and the *Sentinel* ordered a full account of the game from one of the New York papers and smeared it all over the front page under the heading: LOCAL BOY MAKES GOOD!

That was the beginning of Dudley's winning streak. He went right down the line, taking his regular turn in the box, and all teams looked alike to him. The wise Eastern critics said he was another Alexander, and the greatest discovery of the season; and every time he added a victory to his string there was a riot in Brownsville. You couldn't have told us that Dudley wasn't the greatest right-hander that ever lived—not without taking desperate chances.

It was after he won his ninth game that we began to talk about getting up a party to go over to Chicago and watch him hang it on the Cubs. I don't know who proposed it in the first place—the idea seemed to hit us all about the same time. We dug up the National League schedule and did some figuring on dates and things, and then Jack Jamieson took the floor.

"If he pitches in his regular turn they'll stick him in Monday to open the series," says he. "We could leave here Sunday night and get into Chicago in time for the game, visit round with Dudley afterward, and get back here Wednesday or Thursday. All in favor—"

The motion carried, with a whoop and a yell. The loudest whooper in the lot was Old Man Sherwood. He said the Palace Hotel could run itself while he was gone. There were nine of us in all—Jamieson, Harley, Freeman, Old Man Sherwood, Dutch Coffman, Frank Sperlock, Eddie McManus, Joe Parker, Marty Leach and me.

Some of the boys had to pretend they had important business in Chicago in order to square it with their wives; but the whole town knew better than that, and quite a mob turned up at the depot to see us off. Every man, woman and child wanted to send a message to Dudley, telling him they were pulling for him to get into the World Series and win it. We carried enough good wishes to make us all hump-shouldered.

When we got to Chicago there was just time to send our grips to a hotel Old Man Sherwood recommended as swell, but reasonable, and pile into a couple of taxicabs. Joe Parker, who won all the money in the poker game coming over, though a streetcar was plenty good enough; but the rest of us felt we might as well do the thing right while we were at it.

"We don't want Dudley to be ashamed of his friends," says Old Man Sherwood, "and we can Dutch-treat the ride, so's nobody will be hurt."

"No use in throwing money away," says Joe. "However, I'm with the gang. Let 'er roll!"

We reached the park just in time to see the beginning of the game, and there was such a crowd that we couldn't get anywhere near the visitors' bench. This was an awful disappointment, because we'd planned to be where Dudley could chat with us when he wasn't working. Instead of that we had to sit where we couldn't even see the players on the bench. The next disappointment came when the Orphans took the field behind a pitcher that we had never seen before—a big left-hander.

"Dudley's skipped his turn," says Jamieson; "but they'll surely pitch him to-morrow. We'll just have to wait—that's all."

Well, we made the best of it, and rooted our heads off for the Orphans. There were only nine of us, but what we lacked in numbers we tried to make up in noise and enthusiasm. The Chicago fans who sat near us got sore and bawled us out—especially when the Cubs began to score their runs; but we didn't quit. We yelled just as loud when we were four runs behind as we did when the score was tied. When the game was over, Jamieson fought his way down the aisle, hoping to get a chance to speak with Dudley; but he missed him.

"It's all right, though," says he when he came back to us. "It's all right. I found out what hotel they're stopping at, and we'll drop in there after dinner and spend the evening with Dudley—take him to a show, or something."

"Maybe he'll take us to a show," says Joe

Parker. "He ought to when we've come all this way just to see him."

We had dinner and slicked ourselves up a bit, and then started out to find Dudley. The clerk behind the desk said that he was in the dining room, and did we want to send in our cards?

"Let's not do that," says Old Man Sherwood. "Let's sit down outside the dining room and let him bump into us when he comes out. Surprise him—that's the stuff! Wait till he gets a flash at this bunch—he'll keel right over and yell!"

"Good idea!" says Jamieson. "We'll surprise him!"

Well, we got some chairs and lined up just outside the door, where anyone coming from the dining room would almost have to walk over us. Then everybody lit a cigar and waited. Pretty soon a crowd of young fellows came out, laughing and chatting; and the chattiest one in the bunch was Dudley, the bell cow of the herd!

He was just as slim and handsome as ever—maybe a little better dressed than when we had seen him last; but he was the same old boy, and as much at home in a five-dollar-a-day hotel as if he'd been born in one. He had the same old tricks too; we could see that. He was telling a funny story to a short, black-haired fellow that we found out afterwards was Potts, the outfielder, and his arm was laid along Potts's shoulders in a way that I remembered. It was all I could do to keep from jumping up and grabbing him!

We sat perfectly still and waited for him to see us and be surprised; but he sailed by the entire Brownsville delegation without knowing it was there—breezed along so close that we could have touched him, and went on out into the lobby, leaving us feeling like a lot of parlor ornaments.

"He never saw us!" says Old Man Sherwood. "Is the boy blind, or what?"

I couldn't wait any longer, and I was the first man to reach Dudley. He was standing by the street door, pulling on his gloves, and chatting with Potts. He looked at me when I came running up, with my hand out—just looked at me, that was all; and there wasn't any more light of welcome in his eye than you'll discover in the eye of a dried herring. That was what took all the tuck out of me—his perfectly blank, expressionless stare! It paralyzed my tongue too. I couldn't think of a thing to say but "Hello there!"

"Hello yourself!" says Dudley, giving me the up and down. "You've got the advantage of me, sir. What's the name, please?"

Well, sir, if he had hit me in the face it wouldn't have jarred me any more. While I was trying to get my wits to working and my mouth open, up came the rest of the boys.

"Howdy, Dud!" says Jamieson. "How's the ole boy?"

"Never better, thanks!" says Dudley, cool as an icicle. "But what's the idea of the mob scene? Haven't you got me mixed up with somebody else—or is this a joke?"

"Joke!" says Jamieson. "Don't you know me?"

"Joke!" says Old Man Sherwood. "When we came all the way from Brownsville just to see you? Joke?"

"Brownsville?" says Dudley, rubbing his chin. "Brownsville. . . . Oh, you must be mistaken. I never heard of the place in my life."

That was a knockout for fair; it landed on every man in our party.

"Never heard of it!" says Harley Freeman. "Say, didn't you pitch for our club last fall, and—"

Dudley shook his head.

"Not me," says he. "Must have been someone that looked like me."

"And you don't remember us?" About six of the boys spoke at once.

"How can I remember you when I never saw you before?" says he.

Then he turned to his new friend.

"I don't know what this is all about, Pottsey; but if we want to catch the first act of that show we'll have to be moving. These birds are playing hooky from their keeper; let's go before they get violent."

Before anybody could lift a finger, he was through the doorway and out on the street, with Potts after him. We stood and looked at each other, with our mouths open. I suppose there was a funny side to it, but it didn't appeal to us just then.

"Well, I'm damned!" says Old Man Sherwood. "Come on, boys! Let's be gettin' out of here. I got to have room to say what's in my mind!"

We made our escape from the place somehow and stood on the street corner, blinking at the electric lights. Some of the boys began to rave and tell what they'd do to Dudley if they ever met him in a dark alley, but all the talk was knocked clean out of my system. I was sick—downright sick. I'd wasted a lot of friendly feelings on a rat, and it was a shock to find out how much rat he was.

"Listen!" says Joe Parker when the conversation calmed down a bit. "I bet I know what ailed him. I kept kind of in the background, but I think he got a flash at me when he came out of the dining room. That's why he said he didn't know us."

"A flash at you? Why, what's he got against you, Joe?"

"Nothing," says Parker, taking out his pocketbook; "I've got something against him. A little matter of fifty bones. I guess he thought I'd come to collect it. . . . Here's his I O U. Want to see it?"

"Fifty dollars!" says Eddie McManus. "Huh! You're only a piker! I got one of them things in my pocket that calls for a hundred!"

"Oh, well," says Jamieson; "since we're all going to tell secrets, he got into me for a hundred and fifty."

"My soul!" says Old Man Sherwood, beginning to laugh. "And me thinking I was the only fool in the bunch! . . . Did he give you that hard-luck story 'bout his father bein' in the hospital at Syracuse?"

"It was Denver when he sung the song to me," says I.

"Appendicitis, wasn't it?" asks Dutch Coffman. "I paid for one of them operations myself. He put his arm round my neck and told me I was a good guy. I fell. Two hundred fish it cost me. Oh, what a bunch of suckers!"

I guess we would have stayed on that corner all night, comparing notes, if a policeman hadn't invited us to move on and not block the traffic. We went back to our hotel and held a council of war. Every man who had an I O U dug it up and spread it on the table. There were eight of 'em—he had somehow managed to overlook Frank Sperlock—eight of 'em, all dated and signed with curlicues and flourishes—Dudley W. Fowler. In all, they footed up to nine hundred and twenty-five dollars.

Seven of us had kept quiet on account of liking the boy and believing that he would make good some day. Joe Parker said that was his notion, too, but I'll always believe he kept his mouth shut because he thought he was the only one stung and didn't want to own up to it.

Dudley had what some women have got—the faculty of making each victim believe himself the only friend that really counted. Speaking for myself I just happened to have that I O U in my pocketbook; I wasn't on a collecting tour. Of course if he had offered to come across I wouldn't have stopped him, but I never would have broached the subject. I can't answer for the others.

"Now, then," says Jamieson, scooping the I O U's all up in a pile, "the question before the house is this: What are we going to do with this jackpot? What's the sense of the meeting?"

Joe Parker was for taking the evidence back to Dudley's hotel and raising a row.

"Maybe his boss will do something about it," says Joe.

"And we'd look like a lot of cheap sports," says Dutch Coffman. "Joe, you're in this plot on a short ante; so keep quiet. Personally I've kissed my two hundred good-bye already. It was only part of the dough I won on his games last fall; so I'm nothing out by knowing him. We're all in the same boat, and it's no use to squeal; but darned if I don't hate to let Dudley get away with the raw deal he handed us tonight! I'd like to go back at him somehow. Any suggestion for the good of the order?"

Well, there were plenty of 'em, but mostly leaning toward personal violence. That wouldn't do. We gabbed for an hour or more, and finally Jamieson said if we'd leave it to him he'd find a way to make Dudley regret his loss of memory.

"With the permission of the gang," says he, "I'll take possession of these I O U's. Understand me—you won't recover a nickel of 'em. You'll have to be satisfied with getting Dudley's angora. . . . No; I won't answer any questions, but we'd better reserve a front box at the ball park tomorrow."

"Seeing that we're turning the assets over to you," says Parker, always looking for something soft, "you might buy a drink."

"I'll do that little thing," says Jamieson "and I'll also give you a toast: Friend Dudley—here's hoping they pitch him tomorrow!"

Our hope came true. The box we rented for the occasion was over close to the Chicago bench, but this wasn't the reason we didn't cheer when the umpire announced that Fowler would pitch for the Orphans. We were a little bit worried about Jamieson. He had left the hotel immediately after breakfast and we hadn't seen him since. The Chicago fans didn't cheer the announcement, because they were nervous about this new phenomenon and his unbroken string of victories. We overheard some talk in the box next to us.

"Who? Fowler? Say, if this kid has got a goat John McGraw couldn't locate it! You know what that means. . . . Yep—cool as a cucumber! . . . Another Alexander, sure! . . . Impossible to rattle him."

I half suspected that something might happen before the game started; but I was wrong and there was no sign of Jamieson.

Dudley opened up on the Cubs with a lovely assortment of curves, and for two innings he had them eating out of his hand; they didn't get anything that looked like a hit.

"He'll make it ten straight! You listen to me!" says the man in the next box. "How about that control, hey? Steady as clockwork! Oh, he's a sweet pitcher!"

Dudley came to bat in the third inning and there was a faint ripple of applause in the stands—White Sox rooters, maybe, or visitors, like ourselves. Just as he stepped up to the pan and knocked the dirt off his spikes, an attendant in uniform ducked round the corner of the Chicago bench and started for the plate. He was carrying a package under his arm—something big and flat and square, done up in paper and tied with a red ribbon. The attendant handed the package to the umpire, pointed at Dudley, and ran back toward the stand.

All at once the Chicago infielders flocked to the plate, the rest of the Cub players boiled up out of the pit, and the Orphans left their bench and gathered round close.

"Hello!" says the man in the next box. "They're going to present Fowler with something. . . . Must have friends here today. Old-home-town stuff—what? Ballplayers are just like kids, ain't they? See 'em all trying to horn in on it!"

The umpire took off his mask and cap and made a little speech before he handed the package to Dudley, who didn't seem to know what to do with it. A few people began to cheer.

"Open it! Open it!"

One man yelled that, away up in the back of the stand; and right there I stopped breathing, for I knew the voice. It was Jamieson's. The crowd took it up:

"Open it! Open it!"

Dudley hesitated for a second; then he stripped off the paper and held the thing up in front of him. From where I sat it looked like a picture in a frame—but I knew it wasn't any lithograph that was under the glass. The other players crowded in close, with their heads together; there was a puzzled silence that lasted maybe a couple of seconds, but seemed longer—and then a whoop went up from the Chicago boys. They threw their caps in the air, and hugged one another, and laid down on the grass and rolled every which way, like lunatics. Even the sour old umpire had to smile.

Dudley couldn't see the joke at all. He slammed his present on the ground and would have jumped on it if one of the Cubs hadn't snatched it just in time and run with it to the grandstand, with Dudley after him. The Chicago player tossed it up into the crowd, where Dudley couldn't follow it; and then the fun began. About this time Jamieson dropped into the box, sweating a little, but otherwise calm and cool.

"I guess I'm a poor stage manager!" says he.

"For pity's sake!" says Dutch Coffman. "What is it? What did they hand to Dudley?"

"A Brownsville souvenir, under glass," says Jamieson. "Eight little I O U's in a frame, with the motto 'Should auld acquaintance be forgot?' I tipped some of the lads on the Chicago club that Dudley's present would be worth seeing, but I wasn't counting on letting the whole crowd in on the joke. They're getting it, though."

Yes; they were getting it. The Brownsville souvenir was traveling from row to row creating a riot as it went. I never saw people laugh so hard in my life. They nearly went into convulsions.

It must have been five minutes before the game was resumed, and Dudley had to stand there at the plate and wait. He took three wild swings at three bad ones and ran for shelter; but there wasn't any such thing as getting away from the advertising that the Brownsville souvenir was giving him. It was priming the crowd for his next appearance in the pitcher's box.

I don't really need to tell you the rest. You can guess that when Dudley walked out into the middle of the diamond a red-neck fan, with a voice like a foghorn, stood up and made a megaphone of his hands and asked him why he didn't pay his debts. You can guess that when Dudley began his graceful windup about a thousand people were struck with the same idea all at once, and started a sort of chant, taking the time of it from his motions—so:

"I! . . . Oh! . . . You!"

That was what found his goat and set it bleating and running in circles. You've seen a player change step to fool the fans when they were whistling the Rogues' March at him? Well, Dudley tried to hurry his windup to throw the chanters out of time, and succeeded in throwing away his control, instead. They I O U'd him into such a state of mind that he couldn't have thrown a baseball over a freight car, broadside on. He filled the bases, walked in one run, and then stuck a groover where Zimmerman could find it—and away went the old ball game.

The manager yanked him out of the box; and as he started for the bench, with his chin on his chest, about fifteen thousand people stood up and gave it to him all together:

"I! . . . Oh! . . . You! Oh, you! Oh, you! Oh-h-h, you!"

"That's his finish!" says the man in the next box. "Yes; you can kiss him good-bye right now. They've found out where he stables his goat, and this I O U stuff will be all over the league in no time. He'll never hear the last of it. . . . Lord, what a dog's trick! I wonder who pulled it on him?"

If the man bothers to read this yarn he will at least find out that there was provocation. He won't need to read it to find out that he was right about one thing: The fans and the players on the other clubs simply I O U'd Dudley out of the Big League—I O U'd him out of baseball.

It was coming to him, of course; but there are times when I feel ashamed of the part I had in it—times when I wish Jamieson hadn't been so hard on the boy. Dudley was no good, and all that; but—well, I'm just soft enough to be sorry.

"The Little Leaguers"

"Your husband may be a good engineer, but as an umpire I think he lacks something."

"Now watch how he turns slightly toward third and pauses to take his grip at the top—it's a curve."

"He wouldn't have dropped it if all those other boys hadn't been yelling at him."

"Was he safe or out?"

"Nice peg to second, Boyle... too bad he went to third."

"I got into the game—and we were only twelve runs ahead."

ASK PEOPLE about their most enduring odd memory of baseball, and it's flabbergasting how many of them say, "The pinch-hitting midget." There's a picture of him in the first *Fireside Book of Baseball*. Now, here, is the whole story, by the man responsible for it all.

From *Veeck—as in Wreck*

BILL VEECK *with* ED LINN

IN 1951, in a moment of madness, I became owner and operator of a collection of old rags and tags known to baseball historians as the St. Louis Browns.

The Browns, according to reputable anthropologists, rank in the annals of baseball a step or two ahead of Cro-Magnon man. One thing should be made clear. A typical *Brownie* was more than four feet tall. Except, of course, for Eddie Gaedel, who was three feet seven and weighed 65 pounds. Eddie gave the Browns their only distinction. He was, by golly, the best darn midget who ever played big-league ball. He was also the only one.

Eddie came to us in a moment of desperation. Not his desperation, ours. After a month or so in St. Louis, we were looking around desperately for a way to draw a few people into the ball park, it being perfectly clear by that time that the ball club wasn't going to do it unaided. The best bet seemed to be to call upon the resources of our radio sponsors, Falstaff Brewery. For although Falstaff only broadcast our games locally, they had distributors and dealers all over the state.

It happened that 1951 was the fiftieth anniversary of the American League, an event the league was exploiting with its usual burst of inspiration by sewing special emblems on the uniforms of all the players. It seemed to me that a birthday party was clearly called for. It seemed to me, further, that if I could throw a party to celebrate the birthdays of both the American League and Falstaff Brewery, the sponsors would be getting a nice little tie-in and we would have their distributors and dealers hustling tickets for us all over the state. Nobody at Falstaff's seemed to know exactly when their birthday was, but that was no great problem. If we couldn't prove it fell on the day we chose, neither could anyone prove that it didn't. The day we chose was a Sunday doubleheader against the last-place Detroit Tigers, a struggle which did not threaten to set the pulses of the city beating madly.

Rudie Schaffer, the Browns' business manager, and I met with the Falstaff people—Mr. Griesedieck, Sr., the head of the company, Bud and Joe Griesedieck and their various department heads—to romance our project. "In addition to the regular party, the acts and so on," I told Bud, "I'll do something for you that I have never done before. Something so original and spectacular that it will get you national publicity."

Naturally, they pressed me for details. Naturally, I had to tell them that much as I hated to hold out on them, my idea was so explosive I could not afford to take the slightest chance of a leak.

The Falstaff people, romantics all, went for it. They were so anxious to find out what I was going to do that they could hardly bear to wait out the two weeks. I was rather anxious to find out what I was going to do, too. The real reason I had not been willing to let them in on my top-secret plan was that I didn't have any plan.

What can I do, I asked myself, that is so spectacular that *no one* will be able to say he had seen it before? The answer was perfectly obvious. I would send a midget up to bat.

Actually, the idea of using a midget had been kicking around in my head all my life. I have frequently been accused of stealing the idea from a James Thurber short story, "You

Could Look It Up." Sheer libel. I didn't steal the idea from Thurber, I stole it from John J. McGraw.

McGraw had been a great friend of my father's in the days when McGraw was managing the New York Giants and my daddy was president of the Chicago Cubs. Once or twice every season he would come to the house, and one of my greatest thrills would be to sit quietly at the table after dinner and listen to them tell their lies. McGraw had a little hunchback he kept around the club as a sort of good-luck charm. His name, if I remember, was Eddie Morrow. Morrow wasn't a midget, you understand, he was a sort of gnome. By the time McGraw got to the stub of his last cigar, he would always swear to my father that one day before he retired he was going to send his gnome up to bat.

All kids are tickled by the incongruous. The picture of McGraw's gnome coming to bat had made such a vivid impression on me that it was there, ready for the plucking, when I needed it.

I put in a call to Marty Caine, the booking agent from whom I had hired all my acts when I was operating in Cleveland, and asked him to find me a midget who was somewhat athletic and game for anything. "And Marty," I said, "I want this to be a secret."

I never told Marty what I wanted him for. Only five other people knew. Mary Frances, my wife; Rudie Schaffer; Bob Fishel, our publicity man; Bill Durney, our traveling secretary; and, of course, Zack Taylor, our manager.

Marty Caine found Eddie Gaedel in Chicago and sent him down to be looked over. He was a nice little guy, in his mid-twenties. Like all midgets, he had sad little eyes, and like all midgets, he had a squeaky little voice that sounded as if it were on the wrong speed of a record player.

"Eddie," I said, "how would you like to be a big-league ballplayer?"

When he first heard what I wanted him to do, he was a little dubious. I had to give him a sales pitch. I said, "Eddie, you'll be the only midget in the history of the game. You'll be appearing before thousands of people. Your name will go into the record books for all time. You'll be famous, Eddie," I said. "Eddie," I said, "you'll be immortal."

Well, Eddie Gaedel had more than a little ham in him. The more I talked, the braver he became. By the time I was finished, little Eddie was ready to charge through a machine-gun nest to get to the plate.

I asked him how much he knew about baseball. "Well," he said, "I know you're supposed to hit the white ball with the bat. And then you run somewhere."

Obviously, he was well schooled in the fundamentals. "I'll show you what I want you to do," I told him.

I picked up a little toy bat and crouched over as far as I could, my front elbow resting on my front knee. The rules of the game say that the strike zone is between the batter's armpits and the top of his knees "when he assumes his natural stance." Since Gaedel would bat only once in his life, whatever stance he took was, by definition, his natural one.

When Eddie went into that crouch, his strike zone was just about visible to the naked eye. I picked up a ruler and measured it for posterity. It was 1½ inches. Marvelous.

Eddie practiced that crouch for a while, up and down, up and down, while I cheered him on lustily from the sidelines. After a while, he began to test the heft of the bat and glare out toward an imaginary pitcher. He sprang out of his crouch and took an awkward, lunging swing.

"No, no," I said. "You just stay in that crouch. All you have to do is stand there and take four balls. Then you'll trot down to first base and we'll send someone in to run for you."

His face collapsed. You could see his visions of glory leaking out of him. All at once, I remembered that the twist in the James Thurber story was that the midget got ambitious, swung at the 3–0 pitch and got thrown out at first base because it took him an hour and a half to run down the baseline.

"Eddie," I said gently, "I'm going to be up on the roof with a high-powered rifle watching every move you make. If you so much as look as if you're going to swing, I'm going to shoot you dead."

Eddie went back to Chicago with instructions to return on Saturday, August 18, the day before the game. In the meantime, there were details to be attended to. First of all, there was the question of a uniform. No problem. Bill DeWitt, Jr., the seven-year-old son of our vice-president, had a little Browns' uniform hanging in the locker room. Rudie stole it and sent it out to get the number 1/8 sewed on the back. Scorecards are traditionally printed up on the morning of the game, so listing him would be no problem at all.

Just for the heck of it, I took out a $1,000,-

000 insurance policy to protect us in case of sudden death, sudden growth or any other pernicious act of nature. Somehow no opportunity to tell anybody about that policy ever came up, no great loss since the whole thing cost me about a buck and a half.

We were hiring Eddie for one day at $100, the minimum AGVA scale for a midget act. Still, if he was going to play in an official game he had to be signed to a standard player's contract, with a salary set on an annual basis and a guaranteed 30-day payment upon termination. That was no real problem, either. We computed the salary on the basis of $100 a game and typed in an additional clause in which Eddie agreed to waive the 30-day notice.

I must admit that by the time Eddie came back to St. Louis we were playing the cloak-and-dagger stuff a bit strong. Eddie went directly to a hotel suite we had hired for him about ten blocks from the park. Instead of bringing the contract to his room, Bob Fishel set up a meeting on a street corner a block or two from the hotel. Bob drove up in his old Packard and Eddie slid into the front seat, scribbled his signature on two contracts and jumped back out. One of the contracts was mailed to league headquarters on Saturday night, which meant that it would not be delivered until Monday morning. The other contract was given to Zack Taylor, in case our promising rookie was challenged by the umpires. The morning of the game, I wired headquarters that we were putting player Edward Gaedel on our active list.

On Sunday morning, we smuggled Eddie up to the office for further instruction on the fine art of crouching. That was a little dangerous. I have always taken the doors off my office and encouraged people to walk right in to see me. We posted a lookout and from time to time either Mary Frances or Bob or Rudie would have to hustle Eddie out to the farm-system offices in the back. Always they'd come back with the same story. As soon as Eddie got out of my sight he'd turn tiger and start swinging his little bat. "He's going to foul it up," they all told me. "If you saw him back there you'd know he's going to swing."

"Don't worry," I'd tell them, worrying furiously. "I've got the situation well in hand."

Don't worry. . . . Just as I was leaving the office to circulate among the customers as they arrived at the park, Eddie asked me, "Bill . . . ? How tall was Wee Willie Keeler?"

Oh, boy. . . .

"Eddie," I said, "I've got your life insured for a million dollars. I've got a gun stashed up on the roof. But don't you let any of that bother you. You just crouch over like you've been doing and take four pitches, huh?"

As I was going out the door, I turned back one final time. "Wee Willie Keeler," I told him, "was six feet five."

Falstaff came through nobly. We had a paid attendance of better than 18,000, the biggest crowd to see the Browns at home in four years. Since our customers were also our guests for the Falstaff birthday party, we presented everybody with a can of beer, a slice of birthday cake and a box of ice cream as they entered the park. I also gave out one of Falstaff's own promotional gimmicks, salt-and-pepper shakers in the shape of a Falstaff bottle. The tie-in there was that we were giving the fans *midget* beer bottles as souvenirs of the day, a subtlety which managed to elude everybody completely.

The most surprising thing to me, as I moved through the crowd during the first game, was that nobody seemed to have paid the slightest attention to the rather unique scorecard listing:

1/8 Gaedel

Harry Mitauer of the *Globe-Democrat* did ask Bob Fishel about it up in the press box, but Roberto was able to shunt the question aside. (The next day, we had a hundred or so requests from collectors, so I suppose there are quite a few of the Gaedel scorecards still in existence around the country.)

Every baseball crowd, like every theater audience, has its own distinctive attitude and atmosphere. You can usually tell as they are coming into the park whether it is going to be a happy, responsive crowd or a dead and sullen one. With the Birthday Party and the gifts and the busfuls of people from the outlying towns, the crowd arrived in a gay and festive mood. Not even the loss of the first game could dampen their spirit.

We went all out in our between-games birthday celebration. We had a parade of old-fashioned cars circling the field. We had two men and two women, dressed in gay-nineties costumes, pedaling around the park on a bicycle-built-for-four. Troubadours roamed through the stands to entertain the customers. Our own band, featuring Satchel Paige on the drums, performed at home plate. Satch, who is good enough to be a professional, stopped the show cold.

In our own version of a three-ring circus, we had something going on at every base—a hand-balancing act at first base, a trampoline act on second and a team of jugglers at third. Max Patkin, our rubber-boned clown, pulled a woman out of the grandstand and did a wild jitterbug dance with her on the pitcher's mound.

Eddie Gaedel had remained up in the office during the game, under the care of big Bill Durney. Between games, Durney was to bring him down under the stands, in full uniform, and put him into a huge 7-foot birthday cake we had stashed away under the ramp. There was a hollowed-out section in the middle of the cake, complete with a board slab for Eddie to sit on. For we had a walk-on role written in for Eddie during the celebration; we were really getting our $100 worth out of him. As a matter of fact, the cake cost us a darn sight more than Eddie did.

As I hustled down the ramp, I could hear the crowd roaring at Patkin. Eddie could hear it too. And apparently the tremendous roar, magnified underground, frightened him. "Gee," I could hear him saying, "I don't feel so good." And then, after a second or two, "I don't think I'm going to do it."

Now, Bill Durney is six feet four and in those days he weighed 250 pounds. "Listen, Eddie," he said. "There are eighteen thousand people in this park and there's one I know I can lick. You. Dead or alive, you're going in there."

I arrived on the scene just as Bill was lifting him up to stuff him inside. Eddie was holding his bat in one hand and, at that stage of the proceedings, he was wearing little slippers turned up at the end like elf's shoes. Well, it is difficult enough, I suppose, for anybody to look calm and confident while he is being hung out like laundry. Nor do I imagine that anybody has ever managed to look like a raging tiger in elf's shoes. Taking all that into consideration, you could still see that Eddie was scared. He wanted out, "Bill," he said piteously, as he dangled there, "these shoes hurt my feet. I don't think I'll be able to go on."

We weren't about to let him duck out this late in the game. Durney dropped him in the cake, sat him down and covered the top over with tissue paper.

Up on the roof behind home plate we had a special box with a connecting bar and restaurant for the care and feeding of visiting dignitaries. By the time I got up there to join Bud Griesedieck and the rest of the Falstaff executive force, the cake had already been rolled out onto the infield grass. Along with the cake came Sir John Falstaff or, at any rate, a hefty actor dressed in Elizabethan clothes. *There* was a touch to warm the cockles and hops of the Falstaff crowd.

"Watch this," I chuckled.

Our announcer, Bernie Ebert, boomed, "Ladies and gentlemen, as a special birthday present to manager Zack Taylor, the management is presenting him with a brand-new Brownie."

Sir John tapped the cake with his gleaming cutlass and, right on cue, out through the paper popped Eddie Gaedel.

There was a smattering of applause from the stands and a light ripple of laughter.

In the Falstaff box, there was nothing but stunned silence.

"Holy smokes," Bud said, "this is what your big thing is? A little midget jumps out of a cake and he's wearing a baseball uniform and he's a bat boy or something?"

"Don't you understand?" I said. "He's a real live Brownie."

"You put funny shoes on a midget and he's a real live Brownie and that's going to get us national coverage?

Karl Vollmer, their advertising manager, was plainly disgusted. "Aw, this is lousy, Bill," he said. "Even the cake gimmick, you've used that before in Milwaukee and Cleveland. You haven't given us anything new at all."

I begged them not to be too unhappy. "Maybe it isn't the best gag in the world," I said, "but the rest of the show was good and everybody seems happy. It will be all right."

They were determined to be unhappy, though. The gloom in that box was so thick that our Falstaff could have come up and carved it into loaves with his cutlass. (That didn't seem like a very good idea at the moment, however, because Vollmer looked as if he was just about ready to grab the cutlass and cut my throat.) "This is the explosive thing you couldn't tell us about," Vollmer muttered. "A midget jumps out of a cake and, what do you know, he's a real live Brownie."

I did my best to look ashamed of myself.

In the second game, we started Frank Saucier in place of our regular center fielder, Jim Delsing. This is the only part of the gag I've ever felt bad about. Saucier was a great kid whom I had personally talked back into the game when I bought the Browns. Everything went wrong for Frank, and all he has to show for his great promise is that he was the only guy a midget ever batted for.

For as we came up for our half of the first inning, Eddie Gaedel emerged from the dugout waving three little bats. "For the Browns," said Bernie Ebert over the loudspeaker system, "number one-eighth, Eddie Gaedel, batting for Saucier."

Suddenly, the whole park came alive. Suddenly, my honored guests sat upright in their seats. Suddenly, the sun was shining. Eddie Hurley, the umpire behind the plate, took one look at Gaedel and started toward our bench. "Hey," he shouted out to Taylor, "what's going on here?"

Zack came out with a sheaf of papers. He showed Hurley Gaedel's contract. He showed him the telegram to headquarters, duly promulgated with a time stamp. He even showed him a copy of our active list to prove that we did have room to add another player.

Hurley returned to home plate, shooed away the photographers who had rushed out to take Eddie's picture and motioned the midget into the batter's box. The place went wild. Bobby Cain, the Detroit pitcher, and Bob Swift, their catcher, had been standing by peacefully for about 15 minutes, thinking unsolemn thoughts about that jerk Veeck and his gags. I will never forget the look of utter disbelief that came over Cain's face as he finally realized that this was for real.

Bob Swift rose to the occasion like a real trouper. If I had set out to use the opposing catcher to help build up the tension, I could not have improved one whit upon his performance. Bob, bless his heart, did just what I was hoping he would do. He went out to the mound to discuss the intricacies of pitching to a midget with Cain. And when he came back, he did something I had never even dreamed of. To complete the sheer incongruity of the scene—and make the newspaper pictures of the event more memorable—he got down on both knees to offer his pitcher a target.

By now, the whole park was rocking, and nowhere were there seven more delirious people than my guests in the rooftop box. Veeck the jerk had become Willie the wizard. The only unhappy person in that box was me, good old Willie the wizard. Gaedel, little ham the he was, had not gone into the crouch I had spent so many hours teaching him. He was standing straight up, his little bat held high, his feet spraddled wide in a fair approximation of Joe DiMaggio's classic style. While the Falstaff people were whacking me on the back and letting their joy flow unrestrained, I was thinking: *I should have brought that gun up here. I'll kill him if he swings. I'll kill him, I'll kill him.*

Fortunately, Cain started out by really trying to pitch to him. The first two deliveries came whizzing past Eddie's head before he had time to swing. By the third pitch, Cain was laughing so hard that he could barely throw. Ball three and ball four came floating up about three feet over Eddie's head.

Eddie trotted down to first base to the happy tune of snapping cameras. He waited for the runner, one foot holding to the bag like a pro, and he patted Delsing on the butt in good professional exhortation before he surrendered the base. He shook hands with our first-base coach and he waved to the cheering throng.

The St. Louis dugout was behind third base, which meant that Eddie had to cut completely across the infield. If it had been difficult to get him into the cake earlier, I was worried for a while that I would have to send Bill Durney out there again to carry him off the field. Eddie, after all, was a performer. In his small, unspectacular way he was a part of show business. He had dreamed all his life of his moment in the spotlight and now that it had come to him, he was not about to bow his head and leave quietly. He crossed that field one step at a time, stopping in between to wave his hat or bow from the waist or just to raise an acknowledging hand to the plaudits of the crowd. When he disappeared, at last, into the dugout he was the happiest little man you have ever seen.

If the thing had been done right, Delsing, running for Gaedel, would have scored and we would have won the game, 1–0. I was willing to settle for less than that. I was willing to win by one run, regardless of the final score, as long as that one run represented Eddie Gaedel. As it was, there being a limit to the amount of help you can expect from either the St. Louis Browns or fortune, Delsing got as far as third base with only one out and was then left stranded. We lost the game, 6–2.

Nothing remained but to wait for the expected blasts from league headquarters and, more particularly, from the deacons of the press, those old-timers who look upon baseball not as a game or a business but as a solemn ritual, almost a holy calling.

The press, for the most part, took the sane attitude that Gaedel had provided a bright moment in what could easily have been a deadly dull doubleheader between a seventh-

and an eighth-place ball club. Vincent X. Flaherty of Los Angeles pretty much summed up the general reaction when he wrote: "I do not advocate baseball burlesque. Such practices do not redound to the better interests of the game—but I claim it was the funniest thing that has happened to baseball in years."

It's fine to be appreciated for a day; I recommend it highly for the soul. It's better for the box office, though, to be attacked for a full week. I was counting on the deacons to turn Gaedel into a full week's story by attacking me for spitting in their cathedral. They didn't let me down, although I did feel the words "cheap and tawdry" and "travesty" and "mockery" were badly overworked. The spirit was willing, but I'm afraid the rhetoric was weak.

Dan Daniel, a well-known high priest from New York, wondered what "Ban Johnson and John J. McGraw are saying about it up there in Baseball's Valhalla," a good example of Dan's lean and graceful style. Non-baseball fans should understand that baseball men do not go to heaven or hell when they die; they go to Valhalla where they sit around a hot stove and talk over the good old days with Odin, Thor and the rest of that crowd. (I am assuming that the baseball people haven't driven the old Norse gods out to the suburbs. You know what guys like Johnson and McGraw do to real-estate values.)

To Joe Williams, Daniel's colleague on the New York *World-Telegram,* I was "that fellow Veeck out in St. Louis."

"It didn't matter that this made a mockery of the sport or that it exploited a freak of biology in a shameful, disgraceful way," Williams wrote. ". . . What he calls showmanship can more often be accurately identified as vulgarity."

I have never objected to being called vulgar. The word, as I never tire of pointing out to my tireless critics, comes from the Latin *vulgaris,* which means—students?—"the common people." (If you don't believe it, Joe, you could look it up.) I am so darn vulgar that I will probably never get into Valhalla, which is a shame because I would love to be able to let McGraw know how he helped that little boy who used to listen to him, enraptured, over the dinner table. From what I can remember of McGraw, he would roar with delight.

What that fellow Williams in New York didn't seem to realize—or did he?—was that it was he who was gratuitously and publicly calling Eddie Gaedel a freak. Eddie was a professional midget. He made his living by displaying himself, the only way we permit a midget to earn a living in our enlightened society. In more barbaric times, they were able to achieve a certain stature as court jesters. My use of him—*vulgaris* that I am—was the biggest thing that ever happened to him. In the week that followed, I got him bookings that earned him something between $5,000 and $10,000. I kept getting him bookings here and there for the rest of his life. Eddie hungered for another chance at the spotlight. Whenever he came to a town where I was operating he would phone and say, "OK, Boss, I'm ready."

I did use him for a couple of my gags. One of the last times was at Comiskey Park in Chicago, about a year before his death. Eddie and three other midgets, all dressed in regimental Martian clothing (gold helmets and shoes, coveralls, oxygen tanks), somehow dropped out of the heavens in a helicopter and landed directly behind second base. Quickly capturing our tiny second-base combination, Nellie Fox and Luis Aparicio, they made them honorary Martians and informed them—over the remarkably handy public-address system—that they had come down to aid them in their battle against the giant earthlings.

It was during this historic meeting that Eddie Gaedel uttered those immortal words, "I don't want to be taken to your leader. I've already met him."

The battle with league headquarters had begun before Eddie stepped into the batter's box. Will Harridge, the league president—for reasons best known to himself—had gone to his office that Sunday and had seen the report come over the Western Union teletype that I was trying to send a midget up to bat. While Hurley was still looking over the papers, our switchboard operator, Ada Ireland, sent word to me that Harridge was on the phone threatening to blow a fuse unless someone in authority came out to talk to him. I sent back word that we had all disappeared from the face of the earth.

A few minutes later, I was told that Will was trying to get me on the office teletype, which is in direct communication with headquarters. I told them to turn off the machine.

The next day, Harridge issued an executive order barring Gaedel from baseball. A new rule was promptly passed making it mandatory that all player contracts be filed with and *approved* by the president.

Naturally, I was bewildered and alarmed

and shocked. I was a few other things too: "I'm puzzled, baffled and grieved by Mr. Harridge's ruling," I announced. "Why, we're paying a lot of guys on the Browns' roster good money to get on base and even though they don't do it, nobody sympathizes with us. But when this little guy goes up to the plate and draws a walk on his only time at bat, they call it "conduct detrimental to baseball."

If baseball wanted to discriminate against the little people, I said, why didn't we have the courage to be honest about it, write a minimum height into the rules and submit ourselves to the terrible wrath of all right-thinking Americans? "I think," I said, "that further clarification is called for. Should the height of a player be three feet six inches, four feet six inches, six feet six inches, or nine feet six inches?" Now that midgets had been so arbitrarily barred, I asked, were we to assume that giants were also barred? I made dark references to the stature of Phil Rizzuto, who is not much over five feet tall, and I implied very strongly that I was going to demand an official ruling on whether he was a short ballplayer or a tall midget.

I hammered away at the phrase "little people," which had a solid political currency in those days. I had given Eddie Gaedel a speech on that theme too. "Everybody talks about protecting the little man these days," he was supposed to say, "and now that someone has finally taken a direct step to help the plight of the little man in baseball, Harridge has stepped in and ruined my career."

Political connotations, unfortunately, were lost on Eddie. When the time came for him to deliver his statement, he blew it. "Now that someone has finally taken a direct step to help us short guys," he said, "Harridge is ruining my baseball career." Ah well, you can't win them all.

In the end I had to agree, reluctantly, to bow to superior authority. "As much as it grieves me," I said, "I will have to go along with this odd ruling." I thought that was rather big of me, especially since I had only hired Gaedel for one day.

Something else happened, though, that I was not disposed to be so amiable about. The good deacons of the press had been wailing that unless Harridge acted immediately, the name of Eddie Gaedel would desecrate the record books for all time. Harridge dutifully decreed that Gaedel's appearance be stricken from all official records. This I wouldn't stand for. I had promised Eddie that he would live forever in the record books, which are cast in bronze, carved in marble and encased in cement. Immortality I had promised him, and immortality he would have. I reminded Harridge that Gaedel had a legal contract and had been permitted to bat in an official game presided over by the league's own umpires. If Gaedel hadn't batted, I pointed out, it would also mean that Bobby Cain hadn't thrown the pitches and that Swift hadn't caught them. It would mean that Delsing had come in to run for no one, and that Saucier had been deprived of a time at bat. It would mean, in short, that the continuity of baseball was no longer intact, and the integrity of its records had been compromised. If Desecration was the game they wanted to play, then I held a pretty strong hand myself.

Eddie crept back into the record books and remains there today. When he died, he got a front-page obituary in *The New York Times*, a recognition normally accorded only to statesmen, generals and Nobel Prize winners.

I did not recognize at the time that Gaedel's moment was my moment too. I knew it was a good gag. I knew it would delight the fans and outrage the stuffed shirts. I knew, in other words, that it would be a lot of fun. It never entered my mind, however, that it would be the single act with which I would become permanently identified. Even today, I cannot talk to anybody from St. Louis without being told that they were there the day the midget came to bat. If everybody was there who says he was there, we would have had a tidy gathering of 280,000.

I have done a few other things in baseball, you know. I've won pennants and finished dead last; I've set attendance records and been close to bankruptcy. At the age of fifteen, I was taking care of Ladies' Day passes at Wrigley Field. I owned my first ball club when I was twenty-eight. I have operated five clubs—three in the major leagues and two in the minors—and in three of the towns I won pennants and broke attendance records. Two of the three teams to beat the Yankees since I came to the American League in 1946 were my teams, the 1948 Cleveland Indians and the 1959 Chicago White Sox. The only other team, the 1954 Indians, was made up for the most part of my old players.

But no one has to tell me that if I returned to baseball tomorrow, won ten straight pennants and left all the old attendance records moldering in the dust, I would still be remembered, in the end, as the man who sent a midget up to bat. It is not the identification I would have chosen for myself when I came into baseball. My ambitions were grander than that. And yet I cannot deny that it is an accurate one. I have always found humor in the incongruous, I have always tried to entertain. And I have always found a stuffed shirt the most irresistible of all targets.

I'm Bill Veeck, the guy who sent a midget up to bat?

Fair enough.

JOHN GALLAGHER

Courtesy *Sport* Magazine ©

"Take the bum out!!"

Until his death in a railway accident late in 1891, Leonard Dana Washburn covered "Grandpa" Cap Anson's Chicago club for the old Chicago *Inter-Ocean,* and the passage of three-quarters of a century leaves him dimly remembered, if at all. On that account alone, we are most proud to add his name to the family of *Fireside Baseball* authors. Mr. Washburn's elaborate style was in the mode of the day; but what he did with it, as the following story suggests, stamped him one of the funniest baseball writers of all.

1891: Chicago 4, Pittsburgh 3

LEONARD DANA WASHBURN

You can write home that Grandpa won yesterday.

And say in the postccript that Willie Hutchinson did it. The sweet child stood out in the middle of the big diamond of pompadour grass and slammed balls down the path that looked like the biscuits of a bride. The day was dark, and when Mr. Hutchinson shook out the coils of his right arm, rubbed his left toe meditatively in the soil he loves so well, and let go, there was a blinding streak through the air like the tail of a skyrocket against a black sky. There would follow the ball a hopeless shriek, the shrill, whistling noise of a bat grappling with the wind, and a dull, stifled squash like a portly gentleman sitting down on a ripe tomato.

Then umpire McQuaid would call the attention of a person in a gray uniform to the fact that circumstances rendered it almost imperative for him to go away and give somebody else a chance.

There were ten of the visiting delegation who walked jauntily to the plate and argued with the cold, moist air. Mr. Fields lacerated the ethereal microbes three times out of four opportunities to get solid with the ball, and Brer Lewis Robinson Browning walked away from the plate with a pained expression twice in succession. The Gastown folks found the ball six times. Two of their runs were earned.

Mr. Staley, who pitches for the strangers, did not have speed enough to pass a streetcar going in the opposite direction. His balls wandered down toward the plate like a boy on his way to school. If our zealous and public-spirited townsmen did not baste them all over that voting precinct it was because they grew weary and faint waiting for them to arrive. Dahlen continued his star engagement with the bat, getting a single, a slashing double, and triple that missed being a four-timer only by the skin of its teeth.

Even with all this, it is probable that Pittsburgh would have won the game had it not been for a party named Miller, who played short for the wanderers. He covered about as much ground as a woodshed, and threw to first like a drunkard with a cork leg. By close attention to details Mr. Miller rolled up four errors, and three of them cost three runs.

The town boys won the game in the first and second innings. Ryan hit an easy one to Miller as soon as the procession started. Mr. Miller picked up the ball with great agility and hurled it with wonderful speed at an elderly gentleman on the top row of the bleachers. Then Reilly threw Cooney's effort so that Beckley could easily have landed it had he been eighteen feet tall. Carroll's two-bagger brought both Colts in.

In the second Wilmot removed the ball to the left-field fence. Mr. Browning threw to Miller, who at once fixed his eye on third base and threw the ball with unerring directness at president Hart, who was posing on the roof of the grandstand with a haughty smile. Wilmot scored. And in the seventh Willie Forget-Me-Not Hutchinson hit the ball a lick that brought tears to its eyes. Kittridge, who was just due, got a strong reverse English on the leather and started an artesian well in far-away left. Willie came right home.

Bierbauer's single and a measly throw by Kittridge gave a run to O'Neil's pets in the second. Beckley's beautiful triple and a sacrifice by Carroll fetched another, and in the ninth Reilly hit the ball a welt that caused it to back out over the north wall. That was all.

Grandpa Anson wasn't feeling real well, and said several saucy things to the umpire out loud. He was on first and Dahlen was on second when Carroll hit down to Bierbauer. That person choked the ball on the ground and thereby removed both the man Anson and the man Dahlen. The former claimed interference and tried to explain things to McQuaid in a voice that could have been heard at the stockyards. McQuaid pulled out his watch and began to study the figures, whereupon the big captain moved grandly to the bench, and the show went on.

As ONE of the Black Sox, Buck Weaver had his name erased from the record book (even though many felt he was innocent, as he himself claimed to the day of his death). Nothing, however, can erase the box score—or the shining memory—of his greatest day in baseball.

1917: Chicago White Sox 8, New York Giants 5

BUCK WEAVER
***as told to* HAL TOTTEN**

BACK IN THE WINTER of 1913–14, Charles Comiskey and John McGraw took a couple of ball teams around the world. I was on one of them and we were playin' for keeps—ridin' each other and there were plenty of hard feelin's.

Well, we hit Cairo, Egypt, and things got so bad we almost had a free-for-all right there. We got to ridin' Fred Merkle and Fred Snodgrass and callin' 'em boneheads, and the whole National League team got up in arms about it. Finally McGraw got in his two bits' worth —and that's the start of my story.

He started tellin' us off—and when McGraw told somebody off, they usually stayed told. But not us.

"Go-wan," I yelped at McGraw. "You got a powder-puff ball club. You're yellow. You ain't got the guts of a canary bird. I only hope we get you guys in a World Series. Then we'll show you what a real fightin' ball club is—you and your yellowbellies."

Now, remember—I'm just 28 years old. And here I am pullin' that kind of stuff on McGraw. Well, we ironed out that trouble. But none of us forgot about it. And you can bet McGraw didn't, either. So we go along and we get to the 1917 season. We win the pennant in the American League and the Giants win in the National. It looks like we're due for the big blowoff.

Well, we were ready for 'em. You know, before you go into a World Series, you scout the other club mighty careful—and I don't mean just how to pitch to 'em and how to play 'em either. You go over every man on the club and you figure which ones you can ride and which ones you can't. There's no use ridin' a guy if it only makes him play harder and better. So you want to know which ones to get "on" and which ones to lay off of.

We had our meetin' before the first game and we had everyone on that Giant team pegged. We knew just how to handle all of 'em. Then, just before we went out on the field, somebody had an idea. We knew they were expectin' a pretty rough ridin'. They probably were set for it and gunnin' for us. So why not give 'em a surprise—take 'em unawares? We agreed among ourselves not to say a word to any of 'em, no matter what happened or what they said.

The minute they came on the field, they started on us. They called us all the dirty so-and-so's and filthy such-and-suches you could think of. We never even looked at 'em. We didn't answer 'em, just looked the other way. Boy, then they gave it to us plenty.

"Thought you were a fightin' ball club," they'd holler. "Who're the yellowbellies now? Fightin' ball club? Hell!!!"

But still we didn't open our mouths. And

we win the ball game, 2 to 1, when Happy Felsch hit a home run in the fourth innin'. Well, it worked all right that day, so we did the same thing the next day. They gave it to us worse than ever then—they were mad and they tried to take it out on us. But we let 'em alone and we won that one easy, 7 to 2.

So we got to New York and on the train we figure to go on the same way down there. They weren't quite so noisy when we played that third game. But they showed us a big left-hander named Rube Benton and he could hit a 10-cent piece with a curve ball or a fast ball that day, that's how perfect he was. He shut us out, 2 to 0.

The next day they shut us out again, 5 to 0, with another southpaw, Ferdie Schupp, and they got chesty again. Called us a candy ball club and a lot of other things. Still kept our mouths shut.

But on the train that night we were wild. They had us on the ropes. We'd kept it in so long that we just had to get it out of us. So we decided that the next day we'd let loose. And that's the day I'm pickin as my greatest in baseball—October 13, 1917.

We went out to the ball park early, took the files and sharpened our spikes till they were like razors. We were goin' in there cuttin'. There was only one guy who didn't sharpen his spikes—that was Eddie Collins. Why? Well, he was a different type of ballplayer. He never went in for that sorta stuff because he figured they might come back at him and he'd get hurt playin' there in the infield. He was a great guy to look out for himself. If there was a tough gent comin' down to second, he'd yell for the shortstop to take the play.

When we went out on the field to take our hittin' practice, the whole Giant team was down the right-field line throwin' the ball around and warmin' up. We still didn't say anythin'. Dave Danforth, the old southpaw, was on the mound to pitch battin' practice, and I went up there first. I signed to Dave to give me one low and outside, and I reached out and smacked it on a line down among the Giant players. I wanted to knock a couple of 'em cold, and none of us yelled for 'em to look out.

They stopped warmin' up and turned around to look at me. Dave gave me another in the same place and I cracked that one down there too. Right away they started yellin' and wanted to know what was the big idea. Then I made my speech. I told 'em I was goin' to flatten a couple of 'em; that they thought they were a fightin' ball club; well, we'd show 'em a *real* fightin' team. I hit seven or eight line drives right down that line. But by the third one they were all off the field and sittin' down. And they stayed sittin' down until I got out of there.

Well, that started the ball rollin'. Every one of us gave it to 'em. Each of us had picked our man, and we gave him our very special attention. I had Art Fletcher, McGraw's scrappy shortstop, and I had him crazy.

We talked to 'em and they raged at us; we called 'em yellow and everything else we could think of. In the first inning Buck Herzog was forced at the plate and he tried to kick the ball out of Ray Schalk's hands with his spikes. He didn't. We went into every base with our spikes in the air—and we reminded 'em how sharp they were. When they'd tag us out, they'd grab the ball with both hands and slam it down on us. That was all right with us.

They got two runs in the first innin' but it only made us talk louder. We got one back in the third, but they got two more runs in the fourth and were leadin' us 4 to 1. We just got rougher. In the fifth innin' Felsch slid hard into first base and Holke and Herzog charged him and Heinie Zimmerman ran clear across the diamond and tried to jump on him. Then Fletcher made a rush at him, but Happy stood his ground and it looked like they were gonna tangle, but umpire Klem got between 'em and McGraw pulled Fletcher off.

In the sixth I was on first and Ray Schalk got a hit. I started for third and at second base Herzog and Fletcher were both in the way. I just crashed between 'em and went on to third. We figured on knocking 'em down first and then hollerin' to the umpires afterward. We hollered but they wouldn't let me score. I did a minute later anyway. They got another run in the seventh. But we put on a big rally in the seventh and scored three runs to tie it up. They folded up right there.

We won it in the eighth with three more runs and we had 'em crazy wild. Shauno Collins singled and McMullin sacrificed him along. Eddie Collins singled him home and on the hit-and-run, Jackson singled to right and Eddie went to third. Zim took the throw and tried to get Jackson at second and threw wild so Collins scored.

The boys on the bench were on Zim and he started for our dugout, but umpire Evans pulled him back. Felsch singled and scored Jackson. Hap went down to second and went in with his spikes in the air. Fletcher stepped out of his way but took the ball in both hands and smashed it down on Happy's stomach. Clarence Rowland, our manager, followed Fletcher all the way to first base and they had a helluva argument for four or five minutes until the umps broke it up. Rowland challenged Art—invited him to meet him under the stands after the game; but Art never did.

Well, that was all. We won the game 8 to 5. And the next day we knocked 'em off again 4 to 2 to win the Series. We showed 'em who was the fightin' ball club, and we showed 'em good.

And you wanta know somethin' I'll never forget? Remember what I told you about that argument in Cairo? Well, after the last out in the last game of the '17 Series, what happens but John McGraw comes tearin' across the field straight at me. He sticks out his hand and he says, "I wanta shake your hand, kid. You're the best, and I wanta take my hat off to you."

ORLAND BUSINO

Courtesy *The Saturday Evening Post* ©

"May we interrupt this program for a brief word from you?"

"CAN I throw harder than Joe Wood?" Walter Johnson said to an interviewer in 1912. "Listen, my friend, there's no man alive can throw harder than Smoky Joe Wood." All we need to go with that is for Mr. Wood to tell us, in this segment from *The Glory of Their Times*, that he broke in with the Bloomer Girls. ("So did Hornsby," Mr. Wood adds hastily.)

Not Far from Slumgullion Gulch

JOE WOOD

YOU KNOW, I often look back on it now . . . the Wild West . . . Buffalo Bill . . . cattle rustlers . . . outlaws . . . sheriff's posses. I see these western pictures on television, and sometimes it just hits me: I actually *lived* through all that in real life. Sort of hard to believe, isn't it?

At the turn of the century we lived in this little town of Ouray in the southwestern part of Colorado, not far from places with names like Lizard Head Pass and Slumgullion Gulch. And every day I'd see these big stagecoaches go by, drawn by six horses, two guards sitting up there with rifles, guarding the gold shipment coming down from the mines. Dad was a lawyer there—his law partner was later the attorney general of Colorado—and he was involved in some big cases for the Western Federation of Miners. During several of these cases they had to send in the state militia to guard him. Feelings ran high about unions in Colorado back in those days. He was a great trial lawyer. Hardly ever lost a case in front of a jury.

Later we moved to Ness City, Kansas, about 60 miles north of Dodge City, and that was rough country too. It was while we were living in Ness City that I first really started to play ball. That was in 1906, when I was only sixteen. I pitched for the town team—it was only amateur ball, you know, but that was the big thing in those days. We'd play all the surrounding Kansas towns, like High Point, Ransom, Ellis, Bazine, Wakeeney, Scott City—nearby places like that. The ball game between two rival towns was a big event back then, with both teams parading before the game and everything.

Anyway, I was Ness City's pitcher even though I was the youngest on the team by a good two or three years. Had a terrific fast ball with a hop on it even then. And I also played the infield when I didn't pitch.

A funny thing happened in September of 1906 that I'm not too keen about talking about, but I guess it wouldn't be exactly right to act like it never happened.

One day in September this Bloomer Girls team came to Ness City. In those days there were several Bloomer Girls teams that barnstormed around the county, like the House of David did twenty or thirty years later. The girls were advertised on posters around Ness City for weeks before they arrived, you know, and they finally came to town and played us, and we beat them.

Well, after the game the fellow who managed them asked me if I'd like to join and finish the tour with them. There were only three weeks left of the trip, and he offered me $20 if I'd play the infield with them during those last three weeks.

"Are you kidding?" I said. I thought the guy must have been off his rocker.

"Listen," he said, "you know as well as I do that all those Bloomer Girls aren't really girls. That third baseman's real name is Bill Compton, not Dolly Madison. And that pitcher, Lady Waddell, sure isn't Rube's sister. If anything, he's his brother!"

"Well, I figured as much," I said. "But those guys are wearing wigs. If you think I'm going to put a wig on, you're crazy."

"No need to," he says. "With your baby face you won't need one anyway."

So I asked Dad if I could go. He thought it was sort of unusual, but he didn't raise any objections to the idea. I guess it must have appealed to his sense of the absurd.

Fact is, there were four boys on the team: me, Lady Waddell, Dolly Madison, and one other, the catcher. The other five were girls. In case you're wondering how the situation was in the locker room, we didn't have clubhouses or locker rooms in those days. We dressed in our uniforms at the hotel and rode out to the ball park from there. I think everybody except maybe some of the farmer boys must have known some of us weren't actually girls, but the crowds turned out and had a lot of fun anyway. In case you're interested, by the way, the first team Rogers Hornsby ever played on was a Bloomer Girls team too. So I'm not really in such bad company.

It was the next year, 1907, that I *really* got started in organized ball, with Hutchinson in the Western Association. It all came about by accident. My brother Harley was going to the University of Kansas at the time, and he happened to tell a friend of his about me. This friend knew Belden Hill, who ran the Cedar Rapids club in the Three-I League, and as a result I was offered a contract with Cedar Rapids in January of 1907. Ninety dollars a month, that's what it called for. Before it came time to report to Cedar Rapids, however, Mr. Hill decided he didn't really need me after all, and he gave my contract to his friend Doc Andrews, who managed the Hutchinson club in the Western Association. He didn't sell me, he just *gave* me away.

I had a pretty good year there, won about 20 games and struck out over 200 men, and after the 1907 season was over I was sold to Kansas City in the American Association. I pitched there until the middle of the 1908 season, when John I. Taylor bought me for the Boston Red Sox, and I reported to the Red Sox that August.

Rube Marquard came up to the Giants from Indianapolis a month later. We'd pitched against each other many and many a time when he was with Indianapolis and I was with Kansas City, and we both went up to the big leagues at practically the same time. Neither one of us was nineteen years old yet: Rube turned nineteen on October 9 of that year and me, sixteen days later. Four years later we faced each other again in the 1912 World Series, and then again eight years after that in the 1920 World Series. By then both of us had been around a long time, but neither one of us had reached our thirty-first birthday.

Of course that Red Sox team I joined in 1908 turned out to become one of the best teams of all time. Tris Speaker had been on the club earlier that year but had been farmed out to Little Rock, where he hit .350 and led the league. He came back up a few weeks after I got there, and we started to room together, and we roomed together for fifteen years, first with the Red Sox and later with Cleveland. All the years I was in the American League my roommate was Tris Speaker.

There was nobody even close to that man as an outfielder, except maybe Harry Hooper. Speaker played a real shallow center field, and he had that terrific instinct—at the crack of the bat he'd be off with his back to the infield, and then he'd turn and glance over his shoulder at the last minute and catch the ball so easy it looked like there was nothing to it, nothing at all. Nobody else was even in the same *league* with him.

Harry Hooper joined the Red Sox the next year. He was the closest I ever saw to Speaker as a fielder. It's a real shame Harry was on the same club as Spoke, having to play all those years in his shadow. Just like Gehrig with Ruth, or Crawford with Cobb.

I won 11 games for the Red Sox in 1909, 12 in 1910, and then 23 (including a no-hitter) in 1911 and 34 in 1912. That was my greatest season, 1912: 34 wins, 16 in a row, 3 more in the World Series, and, of course, that big game I pitched against Walter Johnson on September 6, 1912.

It was on a Friday. My regular pitching turn was scheduled to come on Saturday, and they moved it up a day so that Walter and I could face each other. Walter had already won 16 in a row, and his streak had ended. I had won 13 in a row, and they challenged our manager, Jake Stahl, to pitch me against Walter, so Walter could stop my streak himself. Jake agreed, and to match us against each other he moved me up in the rotation from Saturday to Friday.

The newspapers publicized us like prizefighters: giving statistics comparing our height, weight, biceps, triceps, arm span, and what not. The champion, Walter Johnson, versus the challenger, Joe Wood. That was the only game I ever remember in Fenway Park, or anywhere else for that matter, where the fans were sitting practically along the first-base and third-base lines. Instead of sitting back where the bench usually is, we were sitting on chairs right up against the foul lines, and the fans were right behind us. The overflow had been packed between the grandstand and the foul lines, as well as out in the outfield behind ropes. Fenway Park must have contained twice as many people as its seating capacity that day. I never saw so many people in one place in my life. In fact the fans were put on the field an hour before the game started, and it was so crowded down there I hardly had room to warm up.

Well, I won, 1–0, but don't let that fool you. In my opinion the greatest pitcher who ever lived was Walter Johnson. If he'd ever had a good ball club behind him, what records he would have set!

You know, I got an even bigger thrill out of winning three games in the World Series that fall. Especially the first game, when we beat the Giants, 4–3. In the last of the ninth they got two men on with only one out, and I started to get a little nervous. Only one run ahead and two Giants in scoring position. A sacrifice fly would have tied it, and a hit would have beaten us. But I struck out both Art Fletcher and Otis Crandall, and we won it. They say that was the first time Crandall ever struck out at the Polo Grounds. I fanned him with a fast ball over the outside corner. I doubt if he ever saw it, even though he swung at it. The count was three and two and that pitch was one of the fastest balls I ever threw in my life.

So there I was after the 1912 season—including the World Series I'd won 37 games and lost only 6, struck out 279 men in days when the boys didn't strike out much, and I'd beaten Walter Johnson and Christy Mathewson one after the other. And do you know how old I was? Well, I was twenty-two years old, that's all. The brightest future lay ahead of me that anybody could imagine in their wildest dreams.

And do you know something else? That was *it*. That was it, right then and there. My arm went bad on me the next year, and all my dreams came tumbling down around my ears like a damn house of cards.

I was fine that winter of 1912. After the Series we went back to Boston and got a reception that would make your head spin. I rode through the city in the same car with manager Jake Stahl and Mayor John F. Fitzgerald. That was Honey Fitz, President Kennedy's grandfather. He was the mayor of Boston then.

Honey Fitz had gone back and forth on the train with us between Boston and New York so as not to miss a single game of the World Series. The Boston Red Sox had a contingent of fans called the Royal Rooters, and their theme song was something called "Tessie." Old Honey Fitz used to sing "Tessie" louder than anybody.

Then it happened. In the spring of 1913 I went to field a ground ball on wet grass, and I slipped and fell on my thumb. Broke it. The thumb on my pitching hand. It was in a cast for two or three weeks. I don't know whether I tried to pitch too soon after that, or whether maybe something happened to my shoulder at the same time. But whatever it was, I never pitched again without a terrific amount of pain in my right shoulder. Never again.

I expected to have such a great year in 1913. Well, I did manage to win 11 games, with only 5 losses, and I struck out an average of 10 men a game. But it wasn't the same. The old zip was gone from that fast ball. It didn't hop any more, like it used to. The season after that I won 9 and lost 3, and in 1915 I won 14 and lost 5. But my arm was getting worse and worse. The pain was getting almost unbearable. After each game I pitched, I'd have to lay off for a couple of weeks before I could even lift my arm up, let alone throw. Still, in 1915, I led the league with an earned-run average of 1.49.

In the winter of 1915 I was desperate. I must have gone to hundreds of doctors over the previous three years, and nobody seemed able to help me. Nowadays a shot of cortisone would probably do the job in a flash, but that was over fifty years ago, you know. Hell, they didn't even know about insulin back then, not to mention cortisone.

Finally somebody told me about a chiropractor in New York, so every week that winter of 1915–16 I took the train into New York, and this fellow worked on my back and my arm. All very hush-hush—an unmarked office behind locked doors—because in those days I don't believe it was legal for a chiropractor to practice.

After each treatment this chiropractor wanted me to throw as long and as hard as I possibly could. He said it would hurt, but that's what he wanted me to do. So after he was through working on me, I'd go up to Columbia University, where Andy Coakley was the baseball coach, and I'd go into a corner of the gym and throw a baseball as hard as I could. I'd do that until I just wasn't able to stand the pain any more. And I do mean pain. After about an hour I couldn't lift my arm as high as my belt. Had to use my left hand to put my right into my coat pocket. And if I'd go to a movie in the evening, I couldn't get my right arm up on the armrest.

So in 1916 I didn't play at all. I retired. I stayed on the farm here in Pennsylvania, fed the chickens, and just thought and thought about the whole situation. Only twenty-six years old and all washed up. A has-been. I put up a trapeze in the attic, and I'd hang on that for hours to stretch my arm out. Maybe that would help—who could say? But it didn't.

I stayed on the farm all through the 1916 season. That fall, though, I began to get restless. Well, that's putting it mildly. What it was, I was starting to gnaw on the woodwork, I was getting so frustrated. Maybe I could come back. So what if I couldn't pitch any more. Damn it, in 1912 I'd hit .290 in addition to winning 34 games. I could hit, and I could run, and I could field, and if I couldn't pitch, why couldn't I do something else? Doggone it, I was a *ballplayer*, not just a pitcher.

I phoned my best friend, Tris Speaker, and told him I wanted to try again. Spoke had been traded from the Red Sox to Cleveland just before the 1916 season started. Tris said he'd see what he could do. Meanwhile the Red Sox had given me permission to make any deal for myself I wanted, provided it was satisfactory with them. So on February 24, 1917, I was sold to the Indians for $15,000, and once again I went to spring training, this time with the Cleveland Indians, all of twenty-seven years old and a relic from the distant past.

I'd hear fathers saying to their kids, "See that guy over there? That's Smoky Joe Wood, used to be a great pitcher long ago."

Lee Fohl was managing Cleveland at the time, and he encouraged me every way he could. And for my part I tried to show him that I could do more than pitch. I played in the infield during fielding practice, I shagged flies in the outfield, I was ready to pinch-run, to pinch-hit—I'd have carried the water bucket if they had water boys in baseball. The hell with my pride. I wasn't the Invincible Joe Wood any more. I was just another ballplayer who wanted a job and wanted it bad.

And it paid off. My arm never did come back, but the next year, 1918, they got short of players because of the war, and I was given a shot at an outfield job. Well, I *made* it. I hit .296 that season, and for *five* years I played in the outfield for Cleveland. In 1921 I hit .366. Could have played there longer, too, but I was satisfied. I figure I'd proved something to myself. So in 1923 when Yale offered me a position as baseball coach at the same salary as I was getting from Cleveland, I took it. Coached there at Yale for twenty years, from 1923 to 1942.

My biggest thrill came one day in 1918, shortly after they gave me a chance in the outfield. That day we beat the Yankees, 3–2, in a game that lasted 19 innings. It was at the Polo Grounds, the same ball park where six years before I'd won two World Series games as a pitcher for Boston. But now, as an outfielder for Cleveland, I hit two home runs, and the second one came in the 19th inning and broke up the ball game.

That was one of the biggest days of my life. May 24, 1918. The season was pretty young yet, and I hadn't been in the outfield very long. It was up to me to show Lee Fohl I could do the job. But from that day on he knew I could do it, and so did I. And the worst was finally over.

LIKE TO HEAR about a perfect game? You've already listened to a man who broadcast one (Vince Scully, on page 398). In the piece directly following this one, you'll read a fine writer's description of one (Dick Young, on page 498). Right now, let's listen to a great old-timer—who pitched one.

1904: Boston 3, Athletics 0

CY YOUNG
as told to FRANCIS J. POWERS

A PITCHER's got to be good and he's got to be lucky to get a no-hit game. But to get a perfect game, no run, no hit, no man reaching first base, he's got to have everything his way. There's been only a handful of perfect games pitched in the big leagues since 1880.

I certainly had my share of luck in the 23 years I pitched in the two big leagues because I threw three no-hitters and one of them was perfect. You look at the records and you'll find that Larry Corcoran, who pitched for the Chicago Nationals "away back when," was the only other big leaguer ever to get three no-hitters and none of them was perfect.

So it's no job for me to pick out my greatest day in baseball. It was May 5, 1904, when I was pitching for the Boston Red Sox and beat the Philadelphia Athletics without a run, hit or man reaching first. I'll be seventy-eight next month, but of all the 879 games I pitched in the big leagues that one stands clearest in my mind.

The American League was pretty young then, just four seasons old, but it had a lot of good players and good teams. I was with St. Louis in the National when Ban Johnson organized the American League and I was one of the many players who jumped to the new circuit.

Jimmy Collins, whom I regard as the greatest of all third basemen, was the first manager of the Boston team, and in 1903 we won the pennant and beat Pittsburgh in the first modern World Series.

Before I get into the details of my greatest day, I'd like to tell something about our Red Sox of those days. We had a great team. Besides Collins at third we had Freddie Parent at short, Hobe Ferris at second and Candy La Chance on first. You find some real old-timer and he'll tell you how great those fellows were.

In the outfield were Buck Freeman, who was the Babe Ruth of that time, Patsy Dougherty, who later played with the White Sox, and Chick Stahl. Bill Dineen was one of our other pitchers and he'd licked the Pirates three games in the World Series the fall before.

Every great pitcher usually has a great catcher, like Mathewson had Roger Bresnahan and Miner Brown had Johnny Kling. Well, in my time I had two. First, Chief Zimmer, when I was with Cleveland in the National League, and then Lou Criger, who caught me at Boston and handled my perfect game.

As I said, my greatest game was against the Athletics, who were building up to win the 1905 pennant, and Rube Waddell was their pitcher. And I'd like to say that beating Rube anytime was a big job. I never saw many who were better pitchers.

I was real fast in those days, but what very few batters knew was that I had two curves.

One of them sailed in there as hard as my fast ball and broke in reverse. It was a narrow curve that broke away from the batter and went in just like a fast ball. And the other was a wide break. I never said much about them until after I was through with the game.

There was a big crowd for those times out that day. Maybe 10,000, I guess, for Waddell always was a big attraction.

I don't think I ever had more stuff and I fanned eight, getting Davis and Monte Cross, Philly shortstop, twice. But the boys gave me some great support and when I tell you about it, you'll understand why I say a pitcher's got to be awfully lucky to get a perfect game.

The closest the Athletics came to a hit was in the third when Monte Cross hit a pop fly that was dropping just back of the infield between first and second. Freeman came tearing in from right like a deer and barely caught the ball.

But Ollie Pickering, who played center field for Mr. Mack, gave me two bad scares. Once he hit a fly back of second that Chick Stahl caught around his knees after a long run from center. The other time Ollie hit a slow roller to short and Parent just got him by a step.

Patsy Dougherty helped me out in the seventh when he crashed into the left-field fence to get Danny Hoffman's long foul; and I recall that Criger almost went into the Boston bench to get a foul by Davis.

Most of the other batters were pretty easy, but all told there were 10 flies hit, six to the outfield. The infielders had seven assists and I had two, and 18 of the put-outs were divided evenly between Criger and La Chance.

Well, sir, when I had two out in the ninth, and it was Waddell's time to bat, some of the fans began to yell for Connie Mack to send up a pinch hitter. They wanted me to finish what looked like a perfect game against a stronger batter.

But Mr. Mack let Rube take his turn. Rube took a couple of strikes and then hit a fly that Stahl caught going away from the infield.

You can realize how perfect we all were that day when I tell you the game only took one hour and 23 minutes.

We got three runs off Waddell and when the game was finished it looked like all the fans came down on the field and tried to shake my hand. One gray-haired fellow jumped the fence back of third and shoved a bill into my hand. It was $5.

The game was a sensation at the time. It was the first perfect game in twenty-four years, or since 1880, when both John M. Ward and Lee Richmond did the trick. It also was the second no-hitter ever pitched in the American League. Jimmy Callahan of the White Sox pitched the first against Detroit in 1902 but somehow a batter got to first base.

During my twenty-three years in the big leagues I pitched 472 games in the National League and won 291, and then I went into the American League and won 220 there. So all told I worked 879 games and won 511 and far as I can see these modern pitchers aren't gonna catch me.

By the way, you might be interested to know that in my last big-league game I was beaten 1–0 by a kid named Grover Cleveland Alexander.

1964: Philadelphia Phillies 6, New York Mets 0

DICK YOUNG

This was Father's Day, 1964, at Shea Stadium, and the little girl sat there behind home plate and listened to people all around her saying that Jim Bunning was perfect, which she knew all the while, because that was her daddy they were talking about, and to her he was perfect long before he cut down 27 straight Mets yesterday.

Aside from Barbara Bunning, 12 and pert, and Mrs. Mary Bunning, blond and beautiful, 32,026 fans sat in on the momentous event—and wound up cheering against their Mets in this 6–0 ball game. They wanted to be a part of history, for this was a time to remember in two respects. It was:

- The first perfect game in modern NL annals.
- The first time in baseball's modern era that a man had pitched no-hitters in both leagues.

Bunning, as a member of the Tigers in 1958, fired a no-hitter against the Red Sox. On that day, he recalls, he hit a batter and walked two. This time, nobody reached base, and only two carried Bunning to three balls. The count went full on Ron Hunt in the fourth, and on Hawk Taylor in the eighth. Hunt fanned swinging, Taylor was called out on strikes.

Bunning needed one piece of fielding brilliance to achieve perfection—and got it. It was midway through the game, one out in the fifth, when Jesse Gonder, a south-swinger, ripped a low liner to the right of the second baseman. Tony Taylor left his feet in a headlong dive. The ball banged into his glove and out, and dribbled to the ground at his knees. Taylor reached frantically, picked it up and came up throwing to nail Gonder by two steps.

"It was a great play," said Bunning appreciatively.

Said Antonio Taylor, Cuban turned Philadelphian, "I deedn't know I save no-hitter. I deedn't know he pitch no-hitter till eighth inning."

Bunning knew it in the fifth. "You always become aware of it around that time," he said. He grinned a silly little grin. He had been grinning and babbling foolishly all day, he admitted. It was the intense heat. "I do that," he admitted, "to take my mind off how hot it is. It keeps me loose."

"He was really silly," said Gus Triandos, who caught the perfect game. "He was jabbering like a magpie. On the bench, before the ninth, he said, 'I'd like to borrow Koufax' hummer for the last inning.' Then he's out there with two hitters to go, and he calls me out and says I should tell him a joke or something, just to give him a breather. I couldn't think of any. I just laughed at him."

Triandos had been the other man in the winter deal that sent Bunning from Detroit to Philly for outfielder Don Demeter and Jack Hamilton, a pitcher. Triandos recalled that he had caught a no-hitter before this: the one knuckleballer Hoyt Wilhelm threw at the Yankees when they were with Baltimore in 1958.

Somebody asked Triandos if this one had been easier to catch.

"Are you kidding?" he howled. "Did you ever try to catch a knuckler?"

"Hey," yelled a voice from across the noisy Philly clubhouse. "The National League is real easy, isn't it?"

That was Johnny Callison, and he was grinning. He had been an American Leaguer, with

Chicago, early in his career, and now he has been blossoming into stardom. Johnny's homer opened the sixth inning, when the Phils scored four times off Tracy Stallard and blew open the game. They had nibbled Tracy for a run in each of the first two frames, and in the sixth Bunning blasted a two-run double off the straining fingertips of center fielder Jim Hickman.

Relative to Callison's facetious remark about the NL, a newsman tried to get Bunning to say this game had been much easier than his no-hitter against the Red Sox—the inference, obviously, being that this was against the Mets.

Bunning wasn't buying the belittlement of the competition. "Of course Boston had a better-hitting club," he said, "but this team has some good hitters, too. Look at yesterday. They got 16 hits."

Jim said he thought the Mets' fans were "tremendous," the way they cheered him at the end. They were on their feet for the final pitches to Johnny Stephenson, the pinch-hitter who was to become K-victim No. 10 as Bunning wound up with a flourish. He had whiffed pincher George Altman for the second out in the ninth, and now young Stephenson, the rookie, stood between Bunning and fame.

Was he glad to see a kid like that up there?

"You're not glad to see anybody up there at a time like that," said Bunning, a bit perturbed at the innuendo. "They're all tough. I figured if I got three curves over to him, I'd get him."

"Three curves!" said Stephenson later. "I got five curves." Two of them had missed as the count went to 2 and 2, and now the 32,000 people were on their feet, necks craning. The silence was momentarily stifling.

Stephenson was trying to outguess Bunning on the next pitch. "I figure he had thrown me four straight curves, and might try to get the fast ball past me."

Bunning fired. Stephenson swung. The ball hooked downward, under his bat.

"Can you beat that?" said the rookie. "I'm looking for a fast ball, and he throws me a change-up curve."

The people roared at the final out, and as Bunning's mates ran onto the field to mob him, and pound him from the infield to the dugout, the New Breeds stood and clapped and finally chanted, "We want Bunning . . . we want Bunning."

After a couple of minutes he made his reappearance to do a TV show with Ralph Kiner near home plate. Bunning tipped his hat warmly to the cheering crowd, then tossed the cap to the ground for the interview.

Kiner, just before chatting with Bunning, shook the hand of Ed Sudol off camera, and congratulated him on umpiring the perfect game.

"I knew it was a no-hitter," Sudol said to Kiner, "but I didn't realize it was perfect. Do you mean I umpired a perfect game?"

The old ballplayer in Kiner couldn't resist saying, "No, you didn't, but it was."

There had been one controversial call—the full count pitch to Hawk Taylor in the eighth. It was a breaking ball, and Taylor thought it broke outside. He took a step toward first, heard "Strike three!" and opened his mouth to protest. Realizing the ball had been dropped by the catcher, Taylor figured it was time to run rather than talk. He broke for first, and was tossed out.

"It was definitely outside," Taylor insisted. "Timmy Harkness was sitting in the stands behind the plate, and he says the ball was outside."

Barbara Bunning was sitting behind the plate, too. She says the pitch was right down the middle.

Asked if he received any Father's Day presents, Bunning said, "I haven't been home yet. I suppose I will." . . . Mrs. Bunning and Barbara came to see the game, and the World's Fair. They thought the Fair was great, but the game was better.

ARCHIE ZAMLOCH retired from baseball in 1910—but was still going strong when he joined forces with a later hitting great, Lefty O'Doul, to produce the handbook on batting from which the following extracts are here reproduced.

From *Where Are Baseball's .400 Hitters of the Dead Ball Era?*

ARCHER W. ZAMLOCH, SR., *and* FRANK "LEFTY" O'DOUL

IN HITTING, it is necessary to have good form, and as in other sports, swinging a bat correctly means having smoothness, rhythm, timing and balance. Unquestionably, there are some athletes in all sports who have these qualities without the need of being taught. There simply are some men who are better coordinated than others, whose reflexes work faster, who have a better sense of timing. This does not mean that hitting cannot be taught, or that hitters cannot acquire the smoothness of a man swinging an ax easily in a full arc at a tree.

Good form in hitting requires certain essentials. The most important single factor, I have come to believe from my observations of great hitters, including Joe DiMaggio, Babe Ruth, Tris Speaker, Ty Cobb, Harry Heilmann, Ted Williams and others is this: KEEP YOUR HEAD STILL!

If you keep the head still, you will take the first step toward acquiring smoothness, rhythm and the timing you want. If he moves his head, he automatically shifts his body. A hitter who keeps his head still—and by that I mean does not move it forward toward the pitcher during the swing, or up or down—will naturally have better results. He will not stride too far. He will keep his back foot anchored securely to the ground. His hips will move out of the way so that the bat can come around. He will not dip his hips or his body so that the ball will slide over his bat and cause a pop-up. He will hit the ball out in front and he will hit it hard and full. Getting out in front really means hitting the ball well out in front of you. (Before the ball crosses the plate.) Another way of saying it is "The body is behind the ball and the bat." The whole swing is a spinning action.

Here is my formula for the mechanics of hitting. Keep the head in one position, get a comfortable, well-balanced erect stance. Hit against the braced front leg and be sure you hit the ball in front of your body where you can see it, at least a foot ahead of your body on the big part of the bat. Swing at arm's length to get a full arc. Your front arm will guide the bat and the bent back arm when it straightens with the uncocking of the wrists will provide the power. The swing is all done in one motion. You can't be thinking of all these things when you are at the plate, so it takes practice to put them together.

There is more than form to hitting. Good hitters must guard the plate. You must be close enough to cover the plate with your bat. Good hitters don't swing at bad pitches, balls over their head, or too wide or too low. They make the pitcher come into the strike zone, and that's the way you want to stand, so that your bat covers the vital strike zone.

The good hitter too will always look for the fast ball. If he's ready to hit the fast ball, he can adjust his timing for the slower curve and change of pace. But if he's looking for the curve, the fast ball will be thrown by him.

Many players today use a long, lightweight bat, but I think a bat 34 inches, weighing 35 to 36 ounces, is better suited to most hitters. It is the form and not the length of the bat which will bring results.